For Reference

Not to be taken from this room

SOMETHING ABOUT THE MUSIC

Guide to Contemporary Repertory

SOMETHING ABOUT THE MUSIC
GUIDE TO CONTEMPORARY REPERTORY

•

SOMETHING ABOUT THE MUSIC **1**
Interviews with Seventeen American Experimental Composers
by
GEOFF SMITH AND NICOLA WALKER

SOMETHING ABOUT THE MUSIC **2**
Anthology of Critical Opinions
edited by
THOMAS P. LEWIS

SOMETHING ABOUT THE MUSIC **3**
Landmarks of Twentieth-Century Music
by
NICK ROSSI

SOMETHING ABOUT THE MUSIC **4**
Some Performer's-Eye Views
(in preparation)

SOMETHING ABOUT THE MUSIC

Guide to Contemporary Repertory

2

ANTHOLOGY OF CRITICAL OPINIONS

Edited by

THOMAS P. LEWIS

Ref.
MT
90
S63
1990

PRO/AM MUSIC RESOURCES, INC.
White Plains, New York

KAHN & AVERILL
London

COPYRIGHT © 1990 BY PRO/AM MUSIC RESOURCES, INC.

All rights reserved under International and Pan-American Copyright Conventions. Printed in the United States of America.

Portions of this volume were previously published in the following **periodicals**: *Atlanta Journal, American Music, The American Music Teacher* (Music Teachers National Association), *American Record Guide, ASCAP in Action, Aptos (CA) Sunday Morning News, Associated Press, Austin American-Statesman, Baltimore (Evening) Sun, The Boston Globe, The Catholic World, Chicago Tribune, Chorus!, Clavier, Colorado Springs Gazette Telegraph, Dallas Morning News, Dallas Times Herald, The Double Reed, Fanfare: The Magazine for Serious Record Collectors, Glasgow Herald, Harrison [NY] Women's News, Hartford Times, High Fidelity, Inharmoniques, Jazziz, The Journal of Band Research, The Kansas City Star, The Kenyon Review, Lansing [MI] State Journal, Los Angeles Times, Main Line [PA] Times, Minneapolis Star and Tribune, Music and Letters, Music Journal, Musical America, The Musical Quarterly, The National Observer, The New Records, New York Daily News, New York Journal-American, The New York Times, The New Yorker, Newsweek, Notes* (Music Library Association), *Omaha World-Herald, Opera, Opera News, Opus, Ovation, Perspectives of New Music, Philadelphia, The (Philadelphia) Bulletin, Philadelphia Inquirer, Philadelphia Penn, Post-Courier, The Piano Quarterly, Providence Evening Bulletin, Rhythm, Ridgefield [CT] Press, Saint Louis Globe-Democrat, Saint Louis Post-Dispatch, Saint Paul Pioneer Press and Dispatch, San Antonio Express, The San Diego Union, San Francisco Chronicle, San Francisco Examiner, Santa Barbara News Press, Saturday Review, The Sentinel, The Star-Ledger, Stereo Review, Symphony, Tempo: A Quarterly Review of Modern Music, Time, The Village Voice, The Washington Post, The Washington Star and News, The Washington Times, Watsonville [CA] Register-Pajaronian, Westchester [County NY] Artsnews, Westchester [County NY] Newspapers, Winnipeg Free Press.* Other materials have been adapted from liner notes for **recordings** issued by the following: Arabesque Records, Cambridge Records, Chandos Records, Columbia Records, Composers Recordings Inc., Crystal Records, Danacord Records, Desto Records, Elektra Records, Grenadilla Records, Hyperion Records, Laurel Records, Leonarda Records, Louisville Records, Lyrita Recorded Editions, Musical Heritage Society, New World Records, Nonesuch Records, Orion Records, Owl Records, Poseidon Society, RCA Records. Brief selections have been made from program notes copyrighted by the following **orchestras**: Chicago Symphony Orchestra, The New York Philharmonic. Excerpts have also been made from the following **published books and pamphlets**: George Balanchine and Francis

Mason, *Balanchine's Complete Stories of the Great Ballets* (Doubleday & Company), Gerald Bordman, *American Musical Theatre* (Oxford University Press); Martin Cooper, ed., *The New Oxford History of Music: The Modern Age, 1890-1960* (Oxford University Press); John Eaton, *Involvement with Music: New Music Since 1950* (Harper & Row); Simon Emmerson, ed., *The Language of Electroacoustic Music*; Cole Gagne and Tracy Caras, *Soundpieces: Interviews with American Composers* (The Scarecrow Press); Don Gillespie, ed., *George Crumb: Profile of a Composer* (C. F. Peters); Don Gillespie, ed., *Roger Reynolds: Profile of a Composer* (C. F. Peters); S. L. Grigoriev, *The Diaghilev Ballet, 1909-1929*, transl. by Vera Bowen (Constable & Co. Ltd.); David Hummel, *The Collector's Guide to the American Musical Theatre* (Scarecrow Press); Diane Peacock Jezic, *Women Composers* (The Feminist Press); Abe Laufe, *Broadway's Greatest Musicals* (Funk & Wagnalls); Carol Lucha-Burns, *Musical Notes* (Greenwood Press); Richard Chigley Lynch, *Musicals! A Directory of Musical Properties Available for Production* (American Library Association); Denis Miller, *Perle on Perle* (League of Composers/Music Associates of America); Ethan Mordden, *A Guide to Orchestral Music* (Oxford University Press); Andrew Porter, *Music of Three More Seasons, 1977-1980* (Alfred A. Knopf); Andrew Porter, *Music of Three Seasons, 1974-1977* (Farrar Straus Giroux); Stanley Sadie, ed., *The New Grove Dictionary of American Music* (Grove Dictionaries); Stanley Sadie, ed., *The New Grove Dictionary of Music and Musicians* (Grove Dictionaries); Flora Rheta Schreiber and Vincent Persichetti, *William Schuman* (G. Schirmer); Robert Simpson, ed., *The Symphony* (Penguin Books); Virgil Thomson, *A Virgil Thomson Reader* (Houghton Mifflin). **The editor and publishers of Pro/Am Music Resources, Inc. acknowledge these authors and source publications with thanks.** Research for this volume was carried out in part at the New York Public Library at Lincoln Center, the Library of the State University of New York at Purchase, and the White Plains Public Library—to whose staffs, in particular, the editor expresses his sincere appreciation.

The title "Something About the Music" was inspired by the Gale Research Company's long-established series *Something About the Author*.

THOMAS P. LEWIS is also the editor of *Musicology in Practice: Collected Essays by Denis Stevens, The Pro/Am Book of Music and Mythology, The Pro/Am Guide to U.S. Books About Music,* and *A Source Guide to the Music of Percy Grainger*. These and other projects have benefitted from a 1979 Harper & Row Cass Canfield Sabbatical Award and $10,000 grant, for which the Editor expresses his deep appreciation.

FIRST EDITION

Published in the United States of American 1990 by
PRO/AM MUSIC RESOURCES, INC.
63 Prospect Street, White Plains, New York 10606
ISBN 0-912483-66-0 (cloth)
ISBN 0-912483-54-7 (paper)

Published in Great Britain 1990 by
KAHN & AVERILL
9 Harrington Road, London SW7 3ES
ISBN 1-871082-25-0 (cloth)
ISBN 1-871082-24-2 (paper)

Back cover photo: From the ballet *Frankie and Johnny* by Jerome Moross, 1938 Chicago Federal Theatre Production, featuring Ruth Page, Bentley Stone. Photo credit: Candid Illustrators, Chicago IL. Courtesy Ruth Page Foundation, Chicago IL.

For

Nick and Mary Clarke

partners in the adventure of publishing

CONTENTS

PREFACE & ACKNOWLEDGEMENTS / xix

John Adams / 1
Nixon in China (opera) 2
¶*Chairman Dances from "Nixon in China"* 3

William Albright / 6
Five Chromatic Dances for Piano 7

David Amram / 19
American Dance Suite for Chamber Orchestra 20
Concerto for Violin and Orchestra 22
Shakespearean Concerto for Chamber Orchestra 23
Songs of the Soul (symphony) for Orchestra 24
The Trail of Beauty for Mezzo-Soprano, Oboe
   and Orchestra 25
Twelfth Night (opera) 29

Dominick Argento / 31
Te Deum 31

Leslie Bassett / 33
Echoes from an Invisible World for Orchestra 33
Preludes for Piano 34
Sextet for Piano and Strings 34
Variations for Orchestra 35

Arnold Bax / 38
Spring Fire (symphony) for Orchestra 39
Symphony 1 42
Symphony 2 45
Symphony 3 48
Symphony 4 49
Symphony 5 54
Symphony 6 56
Symphony 7 58
¶*Symphonies 1-7 — A Footnote* 62

Jeremy Beck / 65
Ballade for Piano and Orchestra 65
Quartet 2 for Strings 66
Scherzo for Clarinet, Violin and Cello 67
Sonata for Cello and Piano 67

John Becker / 69
Symphony 3 (*Symphonia brevis*) for Orchestra 69

Niels Viggo Bentzon / 72
Sonata 18 for Piano 72
Sonata 19 for Piano 72

Contents : viii :

[Niels Viggo Bentzon — continued]
   Sonata 20 for Piano 72

Ernest Bloch / 75
   Quartet 1 for Strings 75
   Quartet 2 for Strings 80
   Quartet 3 for Strings 85
   Quartet 4 for Strings 88
   Quartet 5 for Strings 90

Karl-Birger Blomdahl / 93
   Symphony 3 95

William Bolcom / 97
   Twelve New Etudes for Piano 102
   Songs of Innocence and of Experience for Solo Voices,
      Chorus and Orchestra 106

Henry Brant / 111
   An American Requiem for Wind Symphony Orchestra 111
   Western Springs: A Spatial Assembly for 2 Orchestras,
      2 Choruses, and 2 Jazz Combos 112

Havergal Brian / 117
   Symphony 3 117
   Symphony 10 124

Thomas Briccetti / 115
   Sonata for Flute and Piano *115*

Howard Brubeck / 126
   California Suite for Orchestra 126
   Dialogues for Jazz Combo and Orchestra 126
   Overture to "The Devil's Disciple" for Orchestra . . . 130

Chandler Carter / 132
   Night Scenes for Speaker, Flute, Clarinet,
      Two Percussionists, Piano and Celesta 132
   Prayers of the People for Speaker, Alto, Tenor,
      Chorus and Orchestra 132
   Symphony for Medium Voice and Orchestra 132
   Variations for 2 Flutes, Oboe, English Horn,
      2 B^b Clarinets, 2 Horns and 2 Bassoons 133

Chick Corea / 134
   Concerto for Piano and Concerto 134
   Inside Out 135

John Corigliano / 139
   Concerto for Clarinet and Orchestra 139
   Pied Piper Fantasy (Concerto) for Flute and Orchestra 141

George Crumb / 144
   Variazioni for Orchestra 158

John Eaton / 160
   Danton and Robespierre (opera) 160

Donald Erb / 172
The Hawk (concertino) for Alto Saxophone,
   Brass, Percussion, and Saxophone Ensemble ...172
The Seventh Trumpet for Orchestra 173
Sonata for Clarinet and Percussion 173
Trio for Violin, Keyboards, and Percussion 174

Ross Lee Finney / 176
Landscapes Remembered for Orchestra 178
Quartet for Oboe, Cello, Percussion and Piano 179
Skating on the Sheyenne for Symphonic Band 179
Spherical Madrigals for Chorus 180
Two Studies for Saxophones (1 player) and Piano ..180
Two Acts for Three Players for Clarinet,
   Percussion and Piano 181

Nicolas Flagello / 182
Capriccio for Cello and Orchestra 183
Contemplazioni di Michelangelo for Soprano and
   Orchestra 183
Sonata for Piano 184
Symphony 1 184
Symphony 2 (*Symphony of the Winds* for Wind Orchestra)184
Te Deum for All Mankind for Chorus and Orchestra .185

Miriam Gideon / 186
Creature to Creature for Voice, Flute and Harp 187
The Resounding Lyre for Tenor and Instruments ...187
Sonnets from Shakespeare for Baritone,
   Trumpet and Strings 188
Spirit Above the Dust for Mezzo-Soprano and
   Instruments 188
Wing'd Hour for Tenor, Flute, Oboe, Violin,
   Cello and Vibraphone 189

Philip Glass / 191
Einstein on the Beach (opera) 194

Mark N. Grant / 199
Echoes of a Lost Serenade for Flute, Guitar and Harp .200
Epiphanies: A Childhood Album for 10 Winds 200
Overture to "Chautauqua" 200

Hans Werner Henze / 202
Orpheus Behind the Wire for Chorus 204

Alan Hovhaness / 206
Alleluia and Fugue for String Orchestra 208
Anahid (Fantasy) for String Orchestra 208
And God Created Whales for Orchestra
   and (Pre-Recorded) Whales 208
Avak the Healer for Soprano, Trumpet & Strings ...208
Celestial Fantasy for Strings 208

[Alan Hovhaness — continued]

Concerto 1 (Arevakal) for Orchestra 208
Concerto 7 for Orchestra 209
Concerto 8 for Orchestra 209
Elibris (Dawn God of Urardu) (concerto)
   for Flute and Strings 209
Floating World (Ukiyo) for Orchestra 209
Fra Angelico for Orchestra 209
Khaldis (concerto) for Piano, Four Trumpets [or
   any multiple thereof], and Percussion 209
Lousadzak (The Coming of Light) (concerto)
   for Piano and Orchestra 209
Magnificat for Soprano, Alto, Tenor, Baritone,
   Chorus and Orchestra 210
Symphony 2 (Mysterious Mountain) 211
Symphony 4 for Wind Symphony Orchestra 211
Symphony 6 (Celestial Gate) for Small Orchestra . . . 211
Symphony 7 (Nanga Parvat) for Wind Symphony
   Orchestra 211
Symphony 9 (Saint Varatan) 211
Symphony 25 (Odysseus Sympony) 212
Talin (concerto) for Viola (Clarinet) and Strings . . . 212
Upon Enchanted Ground for Flute, Cello, Harp
   and Tantam 212

Karel Husa / 220

Apotheosis of This Earth for Wind Ensemble
   (or Orchestra with Chorus) 220
Concerto for Wind Ensemble 224
Music for Prague, 1968 226
Quartet 3 for Strings 227
Two Sonnets from Michelangelo for Orchestra 228

Kamran Ince / 229

Cross Scintillations for Piano Four-Hands 230
Ebullient Shadows for Orchestra 230
Infrared for Orchestra 231
My Friend Mozart for Piano 233
Waves of Talya for Six Players 234

Ben Johnston / 235

Journeys for Contralto, Chorus and Orchestra 236
Quartet 2 for Strings 236
Quartet 3 for Strings 236
Quartet 4 (Amazing Grace) for Strings 236
Sonnets of Desolation for Chorus 236

Wilfred Josephs / 247

Concerto for Brass 247
Concerto 1 for Piano and Orchestra 248
Doubles for Two Pianos, Four Hands 249

Contents

    Requiem for Bass-Baritone, Chorus, String
       Quintet and Orchestra 250
Gail Kubik / 254
    Magic, Magic, Magic for Solo Voices, Chorus
       and Piano (or Orchestra) 258
    Symphony Concertante 258
Fred Lerdahl / 260
    Fantasy Etudes for Flute, Clarinet, Violin, Cello,
       Percussion and Piano 260
    Quartet 1 for Strings 260
    Quartet 2 for Strings 263
Andrew Lloyd Webber / 265
    Jesus Christ Superstar (rock opera) 265
    Requiem 268
Witold Lutoslawski / 271
    Novelette for Orchestra 271
    Symphony 3 272
Tod Machover / 276
    Bug-Mudra for 2 Guitars, Percussion
       and Conductor 284
    VALIS (opera) 286
John Madden / 291
    The Chime Child for Chorus 291
Miklós Maros / 292
    Symphony 1 292
Philip P. Martorella / 293
    Please Come Inside (song) for Solo Voice (or Chorus)
       and Piano 293
    Sonata 2 for Viola (or Clarinet) and Piano 293
    Starlight Transmissions for Piano 293
William Mayer / 295
    A Death in the Family (opera) 295
    Enter Ariel (6 songs) for Soprano, Clarinet and Piano 298
    Inner and Outer Strings for String Quartet and
       String Orchestra 296
    Octagon for Piano and Orchestra (or 2 Pianos) 296
    Passage (7 songs) for Mezzo-Soprano, Flute and Harp 298
Gian Carlo Menotti / 301
    Concerto in A Minor for Violin and Orchestra 301
    The Marriage (opera) 301
Federico Mompou / 305
    Cançons Becquerianas for Voice and Piano 305
Jerome Moross / 306
    Concerto for Flute with String Quartet 306
    Frankie and Johnny (ballet) 307
    Sonata for Piano Duet and String Quartet 306

Andrzej Panufnik / 311
Autumn Music for Orchestra 313
Symphony 1 (*Sinfonia rustica*) 313
Symphony 2 (*Sinfonia elegiaca*) 313
Symphony 3 (*Sinfonia sacra*) 313
Symphony 4 (*Sinfonia concertante*) 314
Symphony 5 (*Sinfonia di Sfere*) 314
Symphony 6 (*Sinfonia mistica*) 314
Symphony 7 (*Metasinfonia*) for Organ,
   Timpani and Strings 314
Symphony 8 (*Sinfonia votiva*) 314

Stephen Paulus / 325
Concerto for Violin and Orchestra 326
The Postman Always Rings Twice (opera) 327
So Hallow'd Is the Time (Christmas cantata) 329
Symphony in Three Movements (*Soliloquy*)
   for Orchestra 331
The Village Singer (opera) 334

Krzysztof Penderecki / 338
Concerto for Violin and Orchestra 338

George Perle / 341
Ballade for Piano 363
Concertino for Piano, Winds and Timpani 363
Six Etudes for Piano 367
Six New Etudes for Piano 367
Quintets 1-4 for Winds 369
Songs of Praise and Lamentation for Solo Voices,
   Chorus and Orchestra 372
A Short Symphony 373

Dana Perna / 375
Two Early Ayres for Woodwind Quintet 375
Deux Berceuses for Flute and Piano (or Orchestra) . 375
Three Conversations Between Two Flutists 375
Fantasy-Sonata for Unaccompanied Flute 375
Nonet (*In Memoriam Charles T. Griffes*) for Winds . . 375
Two Preludes for Wind Ensemble 375

Vincent Persichetti / 377
Concerto for Piano, Four Hands 379
Dryden Liturgical Suite for Organ 381
Parable for Solo Trombone 382
Reflective Keyboard Studies for Piano 382
Serenade 4 for Violin and Piano 382
Serenade 7 for Piano 383
Sonatas 1-12 for Piano 383
Three Toccatinas for Piano 392

Tobias Picker / 393

    Octet for Oboe, Bass Clarinet, Horn, Violin,
      Cello, Double Bass, Harp and Vibraphone/
      Marimba 393
    Rhapsody for Violin and Piano 394

Máximo Diego Pujo / 395
    Cinco [5] Preludios for Solo Guitar 395

Alfred Reed / 396
    A Festival Prelude for Symphonic Band 396
    The Garden of Prosperpine (symphonic pastorale)
      for Wind Band .396
    Symphony 1 for Symphonic Band 397
    Symphony 2 for Symphonic Band 397

Jay Reise / 402
    Rasputin (opera) .402
    Symphony 2 411

Silvestre Revueltas / 414
    La noche de los mayas for Orchestra 414
    Sensemayá for Orchestra 418

Roger Reynolds / 420
    Quick Are the Mouths of Earth for Chamber Ensemble 421
    "...the serpent-snapping eye" for Trumpet, Percussion,
      Piano and 4-Channel Computer-Synthesized Tape 423
    Transfigured Wind 2 (concerto) for Flute, Orchestra
      and 4-Channel Computer-Processed Tape 424
    Whispers Out of Time for Violin, Viola, Cello,
      Double Bass and String Orchestra 427

Vittorio Rieti / 430
    Le Bal (ballet) 435
    Barabau (ballet) 435
    Native Dancers (ballet) 435
    Dodici Preludi for Piano 439
    Second Avenue Watzes for 2 pianos 440
    La Sonnambula [The Night Shadow] (ballet) 435

Ned Rorem / 441
    Three Choruses for Christmas 445
    Eagles for Orchestra 441
    Serenade on Five English Poems for Mezzo-Soprano,
      Violin, Viola and Piano 444
    String Symphony for String Orchestra 441
    Sunday Morning for Orchestra 441

Arnold Rosner / 450
    The Chronicle of Nine (opera) 451
    Quartet 4 for Strings 453
    Requiem 453
    Sonata 2 for Cello and Piano 453
    Sonata for Horn and Piano 453

[Arnold Rosner — continued]
Symphony 5 455

Christopher Rouse / 456
Gorgon for Orchestra 456
Phantasmata for Orchestra 458
Symphony 1 459

Miklós Rózsa / 462
Quartet 1 for Strings 462
Quartet 2 for Strings 462
Rhapsody for Cello and Piano 462
Sonata for Piano 463
Toccata capricciosa for Cello Solo 463

Edmund Rubbra / 464
Symphony 2 465
Symphony 5 468
Symphony 6 469
Symphony 8 469
Symphony 10 473
The Symphonies of Edmund Rubbra: A Perspective . . . 474

Harald Saeverud / 482
Symphony 5 (Quasi una fantasia), ... 482
Symphony 6 (Sinfonia Dolorosa) 483
Symphony 7 (Psalm) 483
Symphony 9 484

Alfred Schnittke / 486
Concerto 3 for Violin and Chamber Orchestra 488
Concerto Grosso for Two Violins, Strings, Cembalo, and Prepared Piano 488
In Memoriam... for Orchestra 490
Quartet 2 for Strings 492

Ruth Schonthal / 493
The Canticles of Hieronymus for Piano 493
Music for Horn and Chamber Orchestra (or Piano) . . . 495
Princess Maleen (fairytale love story for children) . . 497
Quartet 1 for Strings 499
Totengesänge for Soprano and Piano 501
Variations in Search of a Theme for Piano 502

William Schuman / 503
Three Colloquies for Horn and Orchestra 503
Concerto for Violin and Orchestra 505
The Mighty Casey (opera) 505
Quartet 4 for Strings 509
A Question of Taste (opera) 506
Symphony 3 509
Symphony 6 509

Joseph Schwantner / 518

New Morning for the World: "Daybreak of Freedom"
    for Speaker and Orchestra 518
Toward Light for Orchestra 519
Veiled Autumn (Kindertodeslied) for Piano 520

Robert Simpson / 521
Quartet 7 for Strings 522
Quartet 8 for Strings 522
Quartet 9 for Strings 526
Quartet 10 (For Peace) for Strings 528
Quartet 11 for Strings 528

Stanislaw Skrowaczewski / 530
Concerto for English Horn and Orchestra 530
Concerto for Orchestra 531
Music at Night for Orchestra 531
Symphony for Strings 533
Trio for Clarinet, Bassoon and Piano 534

Stephen Sondheim / 535
Anyone Can Whistle (musical play) 535
Company (musical play) 536
Follies (musical play) 538
The Frogs (musical comedy) 541
*A Funny Thing Happened on the Way
    to the Forum* (musical comedy) 542
Into the Woods (musical play) 543
A Little Night Music (musical show) 544
Marry Me a Little (musical show) 545
Merrily We Roll Along (musical play) 546
Pacific Overtures (musical play) 546
Saturday Night (musical show) 548
Side by Side by Sondheim (musical revue) 548
Sunday in the Park with George (musical show) . . .549
Sweeney Todd, the Demon Barber of Fleet Street
    (musical play) .550

Augusta Read Thomas / 552
Black Moon (Cantata 2) for Chamber Orchestra . . .552
echos for Soprano, Mezzo-Soprano and Chamber
    Orchestra 552
Haiku for Violin, Cello and Chamber Orchestra . . .554
Two Pieces for Orchestra 555
Requiem for Children's Chorus and Youth Symphony 555
Vigil for Cello and Chamber Orchestra 555
Wind Dance for Large Orchestra 555

Virgil Thomson / 557
Ballet and Film Scores Transcribed for Piano:
    *The Plough That Broke the Plains, Filling Station,
    Lord Byron on the Continent, Louisiana Story* 557

Michael Tippett / 558
- *Concerto* for Double String Orchestra 558
- *The Mask of Time* (oratorio) 558
- *Quartets 1-3* for Strings 564
- *Sonata 4* for Piano 568

Eduard Tubin / 571
- *Symphony 1* 571
- *Symphony 2 (Legendary)* 571
- *Symphony 3* 571
- *Symphony 4 (Sinfonia lirica)* 571
- *Symphony 5* 571
- *Symphony 6* 571
- *Symphony 7* 571
- *Symphony 8* 571
- *Symphony 9* 571
- *Symphony 10* 571

George Walker / 576
- *Address* for Orchestra 576
- *Concerto* for Trombone and Orchestra 577
- *Lyric* for Strings 577
- *Prelude and Caprice* for Piano 577
- *Sonata 4* for Piano 577
- *Spatials* for Piano 577
- *Variations on a Kentucky Folk Songs* for Piano 577

Dan Welcher / 580
- *Concerto* for Flute and Orchestra 581
- *Dance Variations* for Piano 583
- *Della's Gift* (opera) 584
- *Prairie Light: Three Texas Watercolors of Georgia O'Keeffe* for Orchestra 584
- *Quartet 1* for Strings 585
- *Sonatina* for Piano 585
- *The Visions of Merlin* (tone poem) for Orchestra . . . 585

Alec Wilder / 587
- *Sonata* for Clarinet and Piano 587
- *Suite 1 (Effie Suite)* for Tuba and Piano 587

Ellen Taaffe Zwilich / 589
- *Concerto* for Flute and Orchestra 592
- *Concerto Grosso 1985* for Orchestra 592
- *Double Quartet* for Strings 595
- *Sonata in Three Movements* for Violin and Piano . . . 595
- *Symphony 1 (Three Movements for Orchestra)* 596
- *Symphony 2 (Cello Symphony)* 599

INDEX OF COMPOSITIONS / 603

DIRECTORY OF SELECTED ARTS INSTITUTIONS, LICENSING AGENTS, MUSIC PUBLISHERS AND SUPPLIERS, NATIONAL MUSIC CENTERS AND RECORDING COMPANIES / 613

INDEX OF ANNOTATORS / 618

ILLUSTRATIONS

1. William Bolcom / Joan Morris note paper design / 110
2. Carnegie Hall backstage after performance of *Dialogues* (Brubeck) / 128
3. Rehearsal at Carnegie Hall (Brubeck, *Dialogues*) / 128
4. Carnegie Hall program — *Dialogues* (Brubeck) / 129
5. Chick Corea Elektric Band / 135
6. Score portion from *Makrokosmos* Vol. II (Crumb) / 145
7. Score portion from *Creature to Creature* (Gideon) / 188
8. Score portion from *My Friend Mozart* (Ince) / 232
9. Score portion from *String Quartet 2* (Johnston) / 238
10. Score portion from *String Quartet 3* (Johnston) / 239
11-12. Score portions from *String Quartet 4* (Johnston) / 240
13. Score portion from *Fantasy Etudes* (Lerdahl) / 261
14. Tod Machover with EXOS Dexterous Hand Master Glove / 285
15. Score portion from *Inner and Outer Strings* (Mayer) / 297
16. Scene from *Frankie and Johnny* (Moross) / 308
17. Formal organization of *Autumn Music* (Panufnik) / 315
18. Scene from *Rasputin* (Reise) / 407
19. Roger Reynolds, Harvey Sollberger / 429
20. Igor Stravinsky, Vittorio Rieti / 433
21. Ruth Schonthal — Bonn / 494
22. Ruth Schonthal — near Frankfurt / 495
23. Program for *Princess Maleen* (Schonthal) / 496
24. Score portion from *String Quartet 1* (Schonthal) / 500
25. Score portion from *Trio* (Skrowaczewski) / 532
26. Program for *Wind Dance* (Thomas) / 554
27. "Peanuts" cartoon: Ellen Taaffe Zwilich / 590
28. Score portion from *Concerto Grosso 1985* (Zwilich) / 593

Preface & Acknowledgements

I

Pro/Am Music's SOMETHING ABOUT THE MUSIC series has a three-fold purpose:

1) to provide some specific examples of the incredible richness and diversity of contemporary music;

2) to make some specific performance recommendations— with information on location of scores, availability of recordings, and an overview of the nature and dimensions of each work cited;

3) to suggest something of the attitudes and points of view of musicians *towards* this music—and also, parenthetically, with respect to music generally, at various times in its history.

The first three titles in this ongoing series include *Volume 1*, by Geoff Smith and Nicola Walker—consisting of interviews with 17 American experimental composers, with notes on selected works; *Volume 2*—the present volume, which highlights music by an additional 78 composers throughout the world, most of whom continue to be active today;[1] and *Volume 3*, by Nick Rossi—which centers on approximately 50 (for the most part currently neglected) masterworks of the past 70 years or so. A **fourth volume** also in preparation treats contemporary music from the points of view of some of its performers. While these four initial volumes are by no means exhaustive—and for the most part are meant to introduce musicians and other readers to lesser-known music in a variety of genres, rather than to go over ground that has been covered by other publications—it is hoped that this presentation will, indeed, acquaint or reacquaint present-day lovers of music with the enormously pleasurable, interesting, often provocative and diverse abundance of music that artists of varying ages and aesthetic orientations are providing today, or have done in the recent past. Which of these will, in centuries to come, be regarded as the indispensable giants of music

---

1   Statistical breakdown, by country of birth—U.S. (49 composers), England (8), Poland (4), Germany (2), Hungary (2), Argentina, Canada, Czechoslovakia, Denmark, Egypt, Estonia, German Volga Republic, Italy, Mexico, Norway, Spain, Sweden, Switzerland—1 each.

history is an issue to be decided and re-decided as one generation gives way to another; meanwhile, it is the opinion of the authors and editors of the present volumes that we live in an age of considerable musical vitality.

II

Principal sources for the materials presented in this second volume are—individual composer statements, many of which were prepared especially for this book; excerpts from published reviews and notices, including program notes for concerts and recordings; and selections from more extended critical essays and monographs. Sources for each entry are identified following the quotations. A summary list of the original publishers and other sources is given on the copyright page (above), in addition to which an alphabetical list of commentatorss—keyed to the works they describe—appears at the end of the book.

III

To some the cup remains—at least—half empty; to others, at the very least half full...

Media commentator Martin Bookspan—who has become familiar to many radio and television listeners as the voice of the New York Philharmonic—has written, "The more audiences hear of new music, the more they will want. It's all a matter of exposure. And exposure today is largely a matter of recording."[2]

To this one might reply that, nevertheless, generally speaking, even such recordings remain modest sellers at best and—alas—most are rarely (if ever) played on classical or other radio music stations.

William Bolcom—a valued composer who with and without his wife, the singer Joan Morris, is a genuinely popular performer as well—expresses a largely "down" point of view, in the March 1990 issue of *Musical America*. "We are, it seems," he writes,

> currently witnessing a crumbling of the façade of the serious music scene in the United States. The most recent Harris Poll cites a general attendance loss at arts events of 12 percent since 1984, including 9 percent at classical music concerts and 23 percent (!) at opera and musical theater events.... The serious music publishing industry is almost defunct... It is well known that, as home taping grows apace, sales of

---

[2] Quoted by Stephen Sinclair, "Recording American Composers", in *The Cultural Post* VIII/2; reprinted in the *AMC [American Music Center] Newsletter*, Spring 1983.

records and cassettes are suffering in direct proportion.... It is nearly impossible to make a living exclusively as a serious composer.

Without denying either the genuineness or the seriousness of the issues which composer/pianist Bolcom brings our attention to, nevertheless it does seem possible to make a reply, of sorts:

1) What does one mean by the or a "serious" music scene—if rock and other popular forms continue to attract large audiences? On the one hand, are audiences for music of this kind less than serious? On the other—personal preferences aside—it seems thoroughly improper to deny that popular idioms generally, which must also include works by jazz artists, and by popular theater composers such as Andrew Lloyd Webber and Stephen Sondheim, are at least "serious". Perhaps, indeed, "classical art" composers ought to join forces with—learn from—the opposition, in some way?[3]

2) While a decline of attendance at opera and musical theater events may be regretted, nevertheless, *(a)* one wonders if this is really an isolated phenomenon—in other words, are people "going out" at all, these days? For that matter, can they afford to? Even the movies—which continue to be *very* popular "arts events", after all—are expensive, while a somewhat more rarified night at the opera for two in New York can easily cost more than two hundred dollars! *(b)* It seems possible that audience declines in one medium are—at least partly—compensated for by audience gains in some other. For example, one guesses that this year's televised Metropolitan Opera Ring Cycle must have excited audiences very much—and possibly even *instructed* many of us with respect to just what is "going on" in the land of Wotan. Indeed—not without considerable financial and other commitment, and risk—public television in particular has championed the *serious* performing arts on a scale which may be unrivalled since the introduction of the long playing record.

3) It is also possible that relative stagnation in one part of the classical repertory is—at least partly—compensated for by a degree of health in some other part. For example, see the remarks by composer Alfred Reed, below, in which he observes that large numbers of school and other bands appear to be flourishing throughout the country, and, along with this, a thriving band repertory.

---

[3] For example, many rock concerts are as much communal as they are musical events. Thus, either "classical art" music ought not to seek to compete on these particular grounds, in the first place; or, ought to work for greater "mass excitement" too, if you will—as e.g. the symphonies of Tchaikovsky and Brahms and Beethoven, and the finest passions and oratorios of Bach and Handel, inevitably do.

Preface & Acknowledgements : xxii :

4) The problems of *music publishers* may be very serious—especially given the "networking" capacities of library and other customers, and the widespread use of copying devices. Still, *(a)* the increasing practicality of home or personal computer-generated scores—including, apparently, complicated orchestral scores—ought to make it possible to distribute (and, indeed, to compose) more music than ever before; *(b)*, the music industry is very likely undergoing changes some of which may relate to *general* social and economic factors and conditions, and some of which may not be all bad.[4] Indeed the music publishing industry would appear to share many distribution and other problems—and challenges—with a changing *publishing* industry (book, magazine, other), overall.

5) Finally—though one deeply regrets the financial hardships endured by composers—I think it would be naive to suppose that the situation has ever been much different, historically. At about the time of Eden, apparently, men and women were taught that *the arts ought to be free to consumers*—its is their birthright—although it is all right to be paid for the means of reproduction, such as musical instruments, batons, typewriters, computers, printing presses, recording equipment, vinyl, paper, and carton stuffing for shipping UPS. As a corollary it was apparently to be understood that under *no* circumstance were ordinary painters, composers, writers, choreographers, etc. to be paid something for their work. Liquor products, yes—the writing of songs and symphonies that elevate the human soul, never.

The easiest way to avoid having to pay such people is to wait until they are dead.

* * *

I do not mean to belittle Bolcom's call of alarm, in any way. I mean only to set legitimate complaints such as these in something of a broader socio-historical and finally *teleological* perspective....

Bolcom, a responsible artist, also has some interesting positive recommendations:

> How do you get people to pay real attention to music again?[5] A possible answer: people become interested in activities in which they have participated even reasonably

---

[4] For one of many interim reports on the music publishing industry, see e.g. Steve Rauch, "Music Publishing Today", in *The American Music Teacher*, October 1990.

[5] This assumes that "real" attention is not being paid to music at the present time—and/or that "real" attention *was* paid to music before (but not now). Both of these assumptions are highly questionable. See above. (Ed.)

well. (In my case, I was terrible at all sports and thus have little interest in them, but I did show aptitude in music and consequently am devoted to it in all its aspects.) In a society wherein fewer and fewer people are playing instruments, except toward professional aspirations, identification with art music is going to become more and more tenuous for most people....[6]

[We ought to] work toward a synthesis of our musical culture.... Let us look at the world of American song, for example. By their superior achievement, songwriters and composers as diverse as Irving Berlin, Jimmie Rodgers, Stevie Wonder, Cole Porter, Samuel Barber, Bob Dylan, and Charles Ives — and so many other men and women — have contributed to an American prosody, a flexible and vigorous style of setting words and music together, that points toward the dissolution of commercial boundaries. A singer conversant in a broad range of these styles, as well as in traditional serious music, will tend toward greater universality of expression, as well as a better, more understandable diction....

Still, we are left with the specter of the nonparticipating musical public....

I propose a *serious* amateur culture. If music schools could combine the training of professionals with that of serious amateurs without the condescension to the latter so often found today, they could perform a valuable public service, aside from making life more enjoyable for all concerned....

Couldn't we inspire [amateur players] to become participating musicians, excellent ones, who [only] happen to do something else for a living?...

Our music schools should still offer serious degree programs; I do not wish for a return to the collegiate amateurism of the turn of the century. But if those same schools could reach out to the community and broaden the musical education of young and older Americans....

Such an ideal certainly seems worth striving for. If technology (car radios and the like) has taken music out of the hands of amateur two- and four-hand piano players — all of whom studied with Liszt — perhaps a reordering of educational priorities generally might help to put it back into them... so to speak. Still, there do remain those who — like myself — cannot, and never will, play, or sing, or dance.[7]

---

6 And yet — do rock concert enthusiasts inevitably play the drums, or sing? (Ed.)
7 For additional remarks by William Bolcom — in a 10/90 letter generously sent to the Editor for this publication — see Bolcom composer entry, below.

IV
A MODEST PROPOSAL

Satirist Jonathan Swift, in his famous "Modest Proposal" (1729), suggested that a reasonable cure for overpopulation would be to murder newborn infants.[8] In a similar vein one might propose, as an encouragement to playing and enjoying "classical" art music, extermination of rock stars, universal compulsory opera attendance, and a Commission on Public Musical Morality *(PMM/Com)*, which, however, goes against America's belief in democracy.

I have what I believe is a more workable plan, which I submit now in all sobriety:

As a part of every public concert, include at least one work — of any duration — by a (reasonably) living composer.

Really — it is quite as simple as that!

A number of things will necessarily ensue:

1. Audiences will gradually come to recognize — and, in at least that sense, participate in — music of their own time. Schubert's *Symphony 9* (or 7 or whatever) in C Major is one of the most bewildering pieces of music that I have ever heard, and I bless the invention of cupboards or whatever it was in which his manuscript came to be found after its creator's untimely death. But even Schubert must give way, sometimes, to the rhythms of *West Side Story* — in which a listener of today hears some of the sounds and voices of his or her own contemporaries, which are very different indeed from those of 1820s Vienna.

2. Performers will learn by doing. The job of tackling "new" music ought to become progressively easier — and also, I should think, more rewarding.

3. Composers will begin to make a *little* — albeit *very* little, perhaps — money for that which they do — from awkward things such as permissions and so on, and perhaps even royalties from the sale of at least one copy of the score, from which cheap unreadable copies are subsequently made. At a concert I attended not too long ago, in the main auditorium of the State University of New York at Purchase's fine performing arts center, an all-Rampal program consisted entirely of works by Mozart, Poulenc, Prokofiev, and a few other not completely unfamiliar eminences long deceased. At this concert, all of the following groups and individuals are likely to have

---

8   More precisely, *A Modest Proposal for Preventing the Children of Poor People from being a Burthen to Their Parents or Country* recommended that starving Irish sell their own infants as food, and thus secure a modest, inoffensive livelihood.

achieved at least some financial reward for their contributions to a generally pleasant evening: Rampal himself of course, his supporting artists, the managers of the performing arts center, the organization which had sponsored the event, the people who handed out the programs, and the custodial staff. Also, a cash bar in the lobby did what appeared to be a fair business during the intermission.

Only *one* class, or group of individuals, managed to be exluded — the persons who wrote the music. Mozart, Poulenc and Prokofiev did not — so far as I could tell — receive a penny, or a groschen or franc or rouble. I should think they must have been equally indifferent to whatever enhancements of their respective reputations coincidentally chanced to accrue.

In fact — on behalf of this most *precious* commodity in all of music — people who — at the very least — ought to be considered on *something* approaching the level of their interpreters — I mean, of course, *composers* — I am quite puzzled, and dismayed!! Surely composers make *some* small contribution to the delights of a musical evening (or afternoon, or parade or what have you)?

4. *Music itself* must surely benefit, as each composer, having the odds of public performance shifted — at least a little — in his or her direction, must surely learn, as well, from the experience of *hearing it done* — from experiencing some public reaction to one's otherwise terribly private dreams and constructions.... Mustn't composers go mad, who so rarely hear their sounds taken up from off the paper, and done up in public? Have we still no pity for poor Schubert (again), whose *C-Major Symphony* sounds had to remain, for the most part, stuck in his head? Beethoven's deafness was nature-ordained; must other composers be made to suffer that same unpleasant fate, by public resolution?

5. Perhaps music publishers, too, will not do so badly. Instructions as to how to *read* the new scores will, of course, bring vast riches to the revivified Simrocks of our time, in their own right. Indeed, as the frequency of such performances increases, mustn't *some* revenues from sales and rentals develop? Let us not forget that many of the great orchestras and opera and dance companies, together with string quartet organizations and popular flutists and fiddlers, already have trunkfulls of Mozart! Of Crumb and Hovhaness, of Bloch and Tubin and Schnittke and Zwilich, of George Lloyd (whose lovely *Symphony Nr. 7* I have omitted from the present volume), I assume they have not.

By way of enforcement, there must also be a *penalty*, however, for any violation of this single, very simple cardinal rule, which is so easy to remember. After years of contemplation and study, I will urge the following:

Preface & Acknowledgements : xxvi :

Persons failing to include at least SOME music by composers known to be more or less alive—in EACH and EVERY one of their public performances—are to be CONDEMNED to a minimum of twenty hours community service in the tent, cave, or hovel of some composer of their choice—there to witness, first hand, the AWFUL DISTRESS of those whom they have so sorrowfully neglected, as they go about doing the at least useful tasks of sweeping off the back porch, washing up broken crockery, feeding the baby, mending the toy piano saved from Christmas long ago on which the composer's last SONATA was penned with discarded bits of charcoal etc.

V

Imagine a culture in which *no* book can be published unless the author has been dead for at least thirty-five years; in which *no* television program is allowed to air until long after its writers are comfortably dead; in which *no* movies can be produced by living directors or screenwriters; in which *no* journalism can be tolerated until the reporters are dead... also, rock performers *are not to be permitted to play their own music on stage until after they are dead.*

VI
ON CHOOSING WORKS FOR THE PRESENT VOLUME

Generally speaking I sought for variety of all kinds. I regret that so few popular songs of the present day have been included—plus any number of other omissions—but, I hope that such deficiencies may be corrected—at least in part—in volumes to come.

Generally speaking I have taken someone's having some keen enthusiasm for a given work as my principal criterion for including it. Tastes vary, to be sure.

More than 330 works have been selected for the present anthology. Usually less well known pieces have been chosen over those which may be familiar already to most performers and listeners. Thus highly regarded composers such as Crumb and Penderecki may be represented by just a few (perhaps relatively infrequently performed) compositions, while other, less familiar names may be represented by (numerically) a larger showing. On the whole, balances have been sought—not within the entry for any given composer—but with respect to the repertory overall. Thus an attempt has been made to achieve variety with respect to genres, musical styles and aesthetics, and even the ages of the various composers.

Omission from the present volume in no way implies a slight either to a given composer, or to any particular work. Undoubtedly, some of the selections will—to some readers and performers—seem

: xxvii : *Preface & Acknowledgements*

very odd. As the narrator of *Slaughterhouse Five* once said — so it goes. One does what one can!

It is the editor's hope that readers will not want to dwell on what may have been omitted (for whatever reason), but will welcome the attention given to works which *have* been included. As a point of general information, *volume 1* in this series includes works by Anderson, Ashley, Behman, Branca, Cage, Chatham, Corner, Fast Forward, Fulkerson, Garland, Knowles, Lucier, Niblock, Oliveros, Yoko Ono, Wolff, and Young. *Volume 3* revisits individual compositions by Antheil, Arnold, Babbitt, Barber, Bartók, Benjamin, Berg, Berio, Bland, Bo, Boulez, Britten, Bussotti, Cage, Castelnuovo-Tedesco, Chávez, Copland, Cotton, Cowell, Davis, Dunner, Durville, Ferneyhough, Gan-Ru, Gershwin, Ginastera, Glass, Hanson, Harris, Henze, Hindemith, Horne, Ives, Koskinen, Lim, Lloyd, Machover, Martinu, Mathias, Maxwell Davies, Messiaen, Milhaud, Mìra Fornés, Moore, Penderecki, Piston, Prokofiev, Rorem, Satie, Schoenberg, Schuller, Shostakovich, Staudte, Still, Stockhausen, Stravinsky, Subotnik, Takemitsu, Thomson, Tippett, Varèse, Vaughan Williams, Victorio, Villa-Lobos, Walton, Webern, Weir, Wuorinen, and Zwilich. Some composers figure in more than one volume — but, not with the same compositions.

Although I think it is important to maintain high standards (or else one will probably lose the very audiences for which one is striving), this particular volume is not an excercise in judging or rating anything. Although, personally, I believe that every work included here *is* of an unususally high caliber, I would prefer to leave issues of "good" and "not so good" etc to others.[9]

The compositions which are described here are taken note of in a spirit of cheerful adventure... indeed, in the hope of having good fun with the very "business" of music making (and listening), which, while serious enough, need not be painful.

---

[9] The complaint is sometimes heard, "where are the Bachs and Mozarts of today?" However, it seems to me as pointless to lament an absence of twentieth-century Bachs and Handels as it is to lament an absence of eighteenth-century Strausses, Sibeliuses, Kerns, Shostakoviches and Brittens. If it is true that artists of genius are rare enough in *any* age, it is also true (I should think) that artists appear in every age who express the particular genius — and sounds and flavor — *of* their time. What a challenge, then — and, perhaps, responsibility — for contemporary critics and performers to seek them out.

VII
ACKNOWLEDGEMENTS

Special thanks to so many of the composers represented here, for their interest and support in many ways.[10]

Acknowledgement with equal gratitude is tendered to the many publications in which various materials originally appeared — all of which are identified throughout the text. A complete list of published sources is given on the reverse title page, at the head of this volume.

I am particularly indebted to the cooperation and participation of Don Gillespie (C. F. Peters), George Sturm (Music Associates of America), Corey Field (European American), Richard Kapp (Philharmonia Virtuosi), and Eero Richmond (American Music Center).

Maurice Hinson — a friend to all musicians and students, and especially to contemporary composers — has offered his counsel and encouragement, and continues to inspire with his own, tireless example.

Critics Kyle Gann and Frank Brancaleone are two of the many who prepared materials especially for this volume.

Walter Simmons has done much to educate us all with respect to new music by many composers. He writes frequently for an outstanding publication, *Fanfare: The Magazine for Serious Record Collectors*, edited by Joel Flegler.

Closer to home I wish to thank personal friends such as Mark Grant and Dana Perna (who, in addition to being represented as composers, have contributed to several of the entries on others), Paul Kirby, and Stewart Manville. Karen Baker — co-conspirator in so many happy enterprises of life — has been a constant source of wisdom and encouragement.

---

10 William Schuman, unable to make a personal contribution, has nevertheless written the Editor "I certainly wish you every success in publishing material about American [and other] composers." This kind of response — which shows an openness, and genuine commitment to music itself — has been typical.

JOHN ADAMS

B. 1947, Worcester MA. *Educ:* Harvard Univ, Dartmouth Coll. *Taught at:* San Francisco Cons. Clarinettist; composer-in-residence Marlboro Fest, San Francisco SO; dir, New Music Ens. Guggenheim Fellow. *Works incl.: American Standard, Available Light, Grand Pianola Music* (2 s/2 pnos/small orch), *Harmonielehre* (orch), *Harmonium* (chor/orch), *Light Over Water, Onyx* (tape), *Phygian Gates* (pno), *Shaker Loops* (string septet or orch).

A note on the composer: "The minimalists, as Reich, Adams, Glass, and others quickly came to be known, have turned out to be quite as diverse as the twelve-tone composers, the Viennese Classicists, the German Romantics, or any other such group. Their common ground is easy to define—repetition, steady pulse, and consonant harmony. After that come the distinctions, and that is where it gets interesting. Distinctions of intention and distinctions of ability: how imaginatively does a composer use a restricted harmonic vocabulary, how refined is his or her ear for instrumental color, how sure the sense of how to assemble the elements of a piece (literally of 'composition'), how precise the knowledge of when to do more of the same, when to move to something new, when to return, how certain the feeling for tension and release?....

"Adams's first orchestral work, completed in 1980 and called *Common Tones in Simple Time*, is a pure and beautiful essay in what one might call extreme or truly minimal minimalism, without melody, and with all other elements such as color, rhythm, and harmony treated with extraordinary delicacy. His music is like [Steve] Reich's in the sense that Mozart's is like Haydn's, but it is also as different from it as Mozart's is from Haydn's. And only a year after the completion of *Common Tones in Simple Time*, as he was putting the finishing touches on the grandly laid out *Harmonium*, Adams referred to himself as a 'minimalist bored with minimalism'. Expressively, and thus of necessity technically as well, *Harmonium* does indeed go far beyond the bounds of 'clasical' minimalism, as for that matter had *Shaker Loops* for string septet (1978, with a string orchestra version made in 1983), and as in their various ways have the major works since then—the exhuberant and parodistic *Grand Pianola Music* (1982), the searching, often anguished *Harmonielehre* (1985), and now *Nixon in China*.

"Adams believes in the rich possibilities of his chosen musical language. He likes to quote the assertion by the composer Fred Lerdahl that 'the best music utilizes the full potential of our cognitive resources' (Lerdahl cites Indian raga, Japanese koto, jazz, and most Western art music as good examples, Balinese gamelan and rock as musics that fail in this respect). More, Adams, who really is one of those composers who love music, not just their own music, and whose knowledge is encyclopedic, believes in his harmonic style as a human necessity and is willing to risk taking the controversial position of maintaining that our response to tonal harmony is not so much cultural as genetic. 'Something tremendously powerful was lost when composers moved away from tonal harmony and regular pulses,' he has said. 'Among other things the audience was lost.'...[1]

"Adams's music enters the ear easily, but it is not simple, certainly not simple-minded, and never predictable. At no point, were the music suddenly to stop, could you foresee with certainty what comes next, even when the sense of pattern seems at its clearest. An example: for the first 159 measures of *Nixon in China* the violins, violas, and keyboards in the orchestra play rising scales; moreover, for the first thirty of those measures the scales are the same, aeolian (the white keys on the piano from A to A) and always rising through one octave. But to these scales, woodwinds and slower scales (about one-seventh the speed of the others), bass instruments contribute a series of pedals on A, F, and C, trombones add a little four-note sputter from time to time, and every now and again the whole is punctuated by a high 'ding'. You never know when the bass is going to change, how tightly the slower scales will be lapped, when the trombone sputters or the 'dings' will appear. The scales come to outline new harmonies, the bass line adds C-sharp and then B-flat to its repertory, the scales stop part-way to double back upon themselves or move beyond the compass of a single octave, the pattern of eight notes to the bar is broken by sixes, fives, sevens, fours. Eventually, when the chorus comes in, the scales recede to become background and accompaniment." — Michael Steinberg, from program notes for Elektra/Nonesuch recording of *Nixon in China* (1987).

Nixon in China (opera) (1987). *Lib.:* Alice Goodman. 145m *Recs.:* Elektra/Nonesuch 79177 (Stereo LP; also as CD 9 79177-4): 9 solo voices, chorus, Orchestra of St. Luke's, Edo de Waart, cond.; Elektra/Nonesuch (CD) 79193 (also as Stereo LP and cassette): selections from complete recording (Act I Scene 2; Act II Scene 1 [excerpt]; Act II Scene 2 [excerpt]).
1 t, 2 b, 1 b-bar, 2 s, 3 m-s; chorus

---

[1] The question of contrasts between the nature and the appeal of tonal and of non-tonal music is a fundamental theme in twentieth-century music history, on which the present volume often touches. (Ed.)

Orch: 2 (2 picc)-2 (1 E hn)-3 (2 b cl)-0-4 sax; 0-3-3-0; 1 perc, 2 pnos, synthesizer; strings: 4-3-4-2

¶*The Chairman Dances from "Nixon in China" for Orchestra* (1985). *Rec.*: Elektra/Nonesuch LP 79144 (digital, also as cassette 79144-4 SR): San Francisco SO, Edo de Waart, cond. *Pub.*: Associated Music Publishers.

"To some, *Nixon in China* seems like a preposterous topic for an opera. Our disgraced former President, wearing a business suit and pontificating onstage? Pat Nixon, resplendent in dowdy dresses and sensible shoes? Chairman Mao, singing his philosophical aphorisms? Is this what opera is all about?

"Not only is this what opera is all about, this is what opera has always been about. Opera has traditionally dealt with epic historical events and mythic characters;[2] its task has been to shrink such such matter to manageable size without sacrificing its grandiosity. Yet in our century, opera has lost touch with contemporary life. Our opera houses are museums, parading the same fossilized relics year after year. And the few composers who bother to write opera are reluctant to tackle contemporary issues, even though, as John Adams has said, 'we hardly need another opera on a Shakespeare play or a Greek myth.'

"It was director Peter Sellars who saw the operatic potential in Richard Nixon's 1972 visit to China and who convinced Adams and librettist Alice Goodman that it merited serious consideration. Goodman, quite rightly, refused to treat the topic as a parody, aiming instead for a 'heroic opera' in which 'every character is as eloquent as possible.' Set primarily in rhymed couplets, the libretto is that rarity in operatic literature: a work of poetry that can be read with pleasure as a self-contained entity.

"Goodman's libretto has been much maligned, for the most part unfairly. By turns chatty, humorous, and profound, it preserves the essential humanity of its characters while allowing them to loom as icons for clashing cultures and philosophies. The second scene of Act I, marking the historic meeting between Nixon and Mao Tse-tung, is astonishingly realistic, blending awkward small talk, poetic metaphors, and cross-cultural misunderstandings. And Act III closes the opera on a wrenchingly poignant note: the principal characters spend a sleepless night reminiscing about their past, consumed by nostalgia and self-doubt. United by human foibles, smaller than the myths they represent, they yearn for confirmation of their life's

---

[2] Well... not always. For every *Turandot*, at least one *Bohème*; for every *Idomeneo*, at least one *Così fan tutte*? (Ed.)

work. 'I have grown old and done no more work than a child,' says Premiere Chou En-lai. 'How much of what we did was good?'

"Unfortunately, Dr. Henry Kissinger does not take part in this self-examination. In fact, in creating the role of Kissinger, Goodman all too quickly jettisoned her proclaimed heroic stance, stooping instead to vicious parody. Such a buffo portrayal of Kissinger has a coarsening effect on the scenes in which he appears, lowering the opera from the realm of myth to the level of caricature.

"Perhaps the role of Kissinger should be seen as a metaphor for the clashes in tone that permeate the entire libretto. Occasionally there are jarring juxtapositions of trivial small talk and high-flown rhetoric. And there is a striking dichotomy between the essentially straightforward chronological narrative of Act I and the surreal, non-narrative structure of Acts II and III.

"Yet these are not fatal flaws, principally because opera, after all, is poetry to be sung. And Adams' music is magnificent, never faltering in either craft or inspiration during the opera's two-and-a-half hours. Rarely has a composer made such an auspicious operatic debut; certainly neither Verdi nor Wagner had much reason to be proud of his initial effort.[3] With Adams already at work on a second theatrical project—dealing with events in the Middle East—we are confronted with the full-blown emergence of a major American opera composer.

"Those who have followed Adams' musical development know that he has always possessed an intuitive theatrical gift. Despite his debt to minimalism, Adams' music is dramatic rather than static, building to huge climaxes, imbued with a neo-Romantic expressive force. Adams maximizes the potency of events on the stage by means of carefully paced modulations, vivid orchestration, and rhythmic drive.

"None of these elements would be sufficient, of course, if Adams lacked a genuine melodic sense. Fortunately, he displays a real flair for vocal writing, creating sweeping melodies that for the most part avoid slipping into bald, dry... declamation. And it is a particular pleasure to witness his skill with the English language, for he devises settings that remain sensitive, yet not subservient, to the rhythms of speech.

"Because he possesses such melodic flexibility, Adams can create characterizations on the basis of vocal style. He differentiates so skillfully between melodic types that even in ensembles his characters

---

[3] Fighting words! To each his own view! Meanwhile, one shares the writer's enthusiasm for the topic at hand. (Ed.)

retain their dramatic integrity. This Mozartian polyphony of characterization is particularly apparent in Act I, Scene 2, and in Act III: Nixon is nervous, choppy, but earnest; Mao is more sustained but obviously fatigued; Chou is fluid and stunningly poetic.

"When the characters turn to their solo arias, the cleverness of Adams' stylistic synthesis finally becomes apparent. Instead of abandoning the pulsating rhythms and repeated arpeggios of minimalism, he has merely moved them into the background. By assigning the orchestral accompaniment the task of preserving minimalism's rhythmic impetus, he has freed the vocal lines from melodic repetition and allowed them to soar. And soar they do: in Nixon's breathless, humorous Act I aria, delivered just after the 'Spirit of '76' has landed in Peking; in Chou's noble lyricism during the banquet scene of Act II; in Pat's wide-eyed, unpretentious response to her private tour; and in the strident, doctrinaire coloratura aria of Madame Mao (Chiang Ch'Ing) that closes the Act II ballet.

"Filled with references to the dance-band music of both Nixon's and Mao's youth, Adams' score seems quintessentially American. In the best postmodernist spirit, Adams mingles American vernacularisms with historical allusions that range from Wagner to Schoenberg. Yet *Nixon in China* remains a brilliantly unified score, in no small part because of the intensely committed performance it receives [in the present Nonesuch recording]....

"*Nixon* is a delight for the eye as well as the ear. What a pleasure it is when commerce and art, merchandising and the creative spirit, unite behind a project so worthy of their mutual efforts." — K. Robert Schwarz, in *Musical America*.

WILLIAM ALBRIGHT

B. 1944, Gary IN. *Educ.:* Juilliard Prep Dept, Univ of MI, Paris Conservatoire. *Taught at:* Univ of MI. Organist, pianist. *Awards & grants:* Fulbright, Guggenheim fellowshps; Koussevitzky Fndn, Amer Acad of Arts and Letters awards; Queen Marie-José Prize. Composer-in-residence American Acad (Rome). *Works incl:* choral works (*A Song to David*), *Frescos* (ww qt), *The Magic City* (opera), organ (*De spiritum, The King of Instruments* [with narrator], *Organbooks* (3), *Pneuma*), piano (*The Dream Rags, Grand Sonata in Rag, Pianoàgogo*), *Seven Deadly Sins* (7 players & opt narrator), *Shadows* (gtr), sonatas (a sax), *Stipendium peccati, Take That* (4 drums).

Composer statement: Artists other than musicians alone may smile at — and, perhaps, nod their agreement with — this composer's articulate assessment of his own craft and motivations:

"Being asked to describe one's own music is a little like being asked by a dinner guest 'What's in this sausage'. Sometimes it's better not to know.

"But — public figure that I am — I am forced frequently to speak about my music, and I have thus come up with a few notions of its content. Part of what it is about is the expression of one or more of four qualities: aggression, sensuality, humor and spirituality. Any individual piece may reflect one of these expressions as a primary concern; others may be more balanced among two, three or four.

"Although some may think that the expression of aggressive tendencies in my music is a way of acting out — albeit in a socially acceptable fashion — my own psychopathic tendencies, I prefer to think of it as a way of exploring an individual approach to rhythmic vitality. Strongly pulsed, somewhat violent, rhythms are a characteristic of much of my music. More deeply considered, however, the music has a strong *structural* base in the counterpoint of many approaches to the notion of 'sound in time': pulsed, metronomic, metric rhythm is contrasted with organic, freely-flowing, conversational rhythm. In addition, the symmetrical (divisive) rhythmic organization of Western dance music (the basis of Western instrumental music) is enlivened by an awareness of the (additive) syncopated music organization of much non-Western music and jazz.

"Sensuality and its expression brings my music close to the most important way we, as humans, communicate. When I finally grew up (in my mid-thirties) I discovered how to express this fundamental human need. *Five Chromatic Dances*, here described, represents this well.

"Humor is a profound aspect of my mode of expression as a human being. Avoidance of this important characteristic of existence seems to me myopic and neurotic. Even my most 'serious', private music contains some small elements of this ennobling state. I also am proud of my music that is profoundly silly.

"Spirituality is in some ways the most complex of all four expressions. Although I've written some music for established spirituality (i.e., religion), I feel the need to express a wider concern of humans for grasping the unknown, the super-human. In this effort, I have found the resources of the organ and electronic music — with their 'artificial' assists of motorized blower and A.C. current — to be ideal. Vast time and dynamic spaces can be explored by these *media*, and the sense of wonder that I attempt is extremely important to me.

"Lastly, I'd like to propose a music of generosity; a music open to all kinds of styles and experience. In a sense, I would agree with the post-modernist architect Robert Venturi that 'I prefer messy diversity to boring unity'." — William Albright, 10/21/90.

Five Chromatic Dances for Piano (1976). 30m Comm. by Thomas Warburton. *Rec.:* Composers Recordings Inc. (Stereo LP) CRI SD 449: Thomas Warburton. *Pub.:* Henmar Press (C. F. Peters).
1. *Procession and Rounds*. 2. *Masquerade*. 3. *Fantasy-mazurka*. 4. *Hoedown*. 5. *The Farewell*.

FIVE CHROMATIC DANCES — ESSAYS AND REVIEWS I: "William Albright's half-hour long *Five Chromatic Dances* is without question one of the most significant compositions for solo piano written in the past twenty years. The five movements, carefully arranged, are each placed in a context which allows for maximum dramatic effect.

"The opening movement, *Procession and Rounds*, cleverly defines the field of action (i.e., the piano keyboard). The movement is in two vastly different sections which define, among other things, the instrument's outermost ranges (low — high), possible tempi (slow — fast), potential modes of motion (steady — erratic), and dramatic magnitude (phlegmatic — hysterical).

"The second movement, *Masquerade*, is primarily light and playful. However, self-interruption plays an important role, and though it is done rather humorously in this movement it alludes nonetheless to a more serious kind of 'two-musics' schizophrenia which plays an important part in the dramatic content of later movements.

"The third movement, *Fantasy-mazurka*, is a gloriously beautiful Chopin reincarnation. Albright suggests in a footnote to the movement that 'the notation should serve primarily as a guide to the desired improvisatory, ruminating effect.' There is a contrasting, rhythmically precise middle section in which, once more, two ideas are fused; the section is labelled: 'in two perspectives'.

"The next movement, *Hoedown,* is obstreperously boisterous at just the moment when the piece needs such a wild outburst. Again there is a contrasting middle section—a seductive *habanera*—but the overall effect of the movement is that of barely controlled fury. As a result, the final movement, *The Farewell,* seems even more peaceful, more resigned and elegiac than it could have been in another setting. It is a masterfully conceived movement. The simplest possible melody is heard at the extremes of the keyboard. It is interrupted ('two musics' again), repeated, interrupted once more, and then developed into a long, transcendent peroration accompanied by a flowing series of vibrating tremolos. Inevitably, it appears alone again one final time, fading slowly away to bring the entire composition to a close.

"The word 'chromatic' in the title calls the listener's attention to an important conceptual aspect of Albright's compositional endeavor. Throughout this large work he alludes to many differing chromatic styles, some of which originate in the music of centuries prior to our own. That he is able to do this, combining styles of different vintage, maintaining at the same time a sense of compositional unity, and that he is able to convey so powerful and personal a message with such confidence—these achievements mark his arrival as one of this country's most important composers."—David Burge, in *Notes* (Music Library Association), 6/81.

FIVE CHROMATIC DANCES—ESSAYS AND REVIEWS II: "While each of the [five] movements is distinct and complete, the whole forms a continuous cycle with the *Procession* of the first movement functioning as introduction and *The Farewell* of the last acting as conclusion.

"The work is conceived in the grand romantic piano tradition. Sustained, subtly shifting tremolandos of the last movement remind one of Beethoven's use of the same effect, perhaps, as in the middle movement of the 'Ghost' Trio. In the *Masquerade,* one remembers the etudes and preludes by Debussy, and the *Tempo di habanera* in *Hoedown* makes a veiled reference to Debussy's *Soirée dans Grenade.* The intense and colorful harmonies, especially in the first and third movements, suggest the music of Messiaen. One is reminded of Chopin in the *Fantasy-Mazurka,* especially in the improvisatory opening and the eloquent lyricism of the closing. Despite an allusion to Chopin's *Mazurka* in A Minor, Op. 17, Nr. 4, at the conclusion of the third movement, it is as through Albright were coming to the cadence on his own rather than simply quoting.

"The music exploits oppositions, either contrast in mood, opposition of registers, or shifting of inflections. Albright portrays the contrasts in mood with evocative tempo indications. In the first movement, the opening *molto misterioso* of the *Procession* yields to the 'delirious, obsessive' *Rounds*. In the fourth, a 'joyous, ecstatic' opening dance is abandoned for *Tempo di habanera*, 'with a mysterious spirit'. Likewise, in the second movement a 'Dance-like *delicato*' interrupts the opening *Scherzando*; 'assertive, brassy'. While the Dionysian spirit ultimately prevails in the first and fourth movements, a more Apollonian cast pervades the closing of the second and third movements and the whole of the fifth movement. Thus, the *misterioso* that opens the *Procession* returns at last for the 'mystically ringing' close of the final moments.

"As a counterpoint to the contrasts in mood, the music opposes the various regions in the compass of the piano. For example, the *Procession* begins in the lowest register while the *Rounds* are heard in the very highest. Indeed, the lowest A acts as a pedal in much of the former, while the highest C is a sinister herald in the latter. At the climax of the *Masquerade*, there is a brilliant sweep from the top to the bottom of the keyboard and the resulting 'static, hushed' denouement lies in the middle. In *The Farewell*, the whole of the piano is embraced in that the tremolando acts as a peaceful accompaniment to the counterpoint of two lines played (bell-like) deep in the bass and high in the treble. The eerie quality of the central section in the *Fantasy-Mazurka* is derived from the *fortissimo* cries in the upper register, which disturb the incessant ticking in the middle register, ultimately disappearing. Albright ends the work with a question, a stark melody played simultaneously at extremes of the piano compass.

"The first pitches of the *Procession* — B, C, and B-flat — establish the tonal framework of the cycle. The B finds its significance as the initial pedal tone for the lyric portion of the *Fantasy-Mazurka* and as a dominant to the E-oriented *Hoedown*. C becomes the center for the opening of *Masquerade* in addition to furnishing the high notes of the *Rounds*, and B-flat is then the dominant to the E-flat of the opening of the *Fantasy-Mazurka*. Through B-flat, the 'tonal fundamental' descends to A early in the *Procession* and ultimately to G-sharp in the *Mazurka*. With B as the axis, whether explicit or implicit throughout the work, the ending of *The Farewell* is left at a distance on the two satellites, B-flat and C, finally coming to rest on C.

"Underylying the cycle of moods, registers, and tones is a transformation of musical substance that leads from the beginning to the middle and away from the middle to the end. The steadiness of the *Procession* returns in the middle section of the *Fantasy-Mazurka*. The rhapsodic, recitative-like music of the *Rounds* softens somewhat in the *Masquerade,* and ultimately becomes the lyric, freely-flowing melody of the *Mazurka*. On the other side, tremolos, which are ornamental in the melody of the *Mazurka,* turn into demonic fiddle passages in the *Hoedown* but end ultimately as the serene tremolando of *The Farewell.*" — Thomas Warburton, from program notes for the Composers Recordings Inc CRI SD-449 release.

Movement	Sections	Tonal frame
Procession and Rounds	Molto misterioso	A/B^b/B
	Delirious, obsessive	$F^\#$
Masquerade	Scherzando; assertive, brassy/ Dance-like[4]	C $F^\#$
Fantasy-Mazurka	Improvisatory, tender	E^b-D^b
	Chimerical, inscrutable	B-E
	In two perspectives (even, mechanical)	D^b/B
	Piu lento, molto rubato	B^b-A-$G^\#$
Hoedown	Joyous, ecstatic; Dizzily fast	E-B
	Tempo di habanera	B-D^b
	Joyous, ecstatic	E-B
The Farewell	Hollow, mystically ringing/ Tender, pure	B
	Hushed and liquid	D^b
	As at beginning	C

FIVE CHROMATIC DANCES — ESSAYS AND REVIEWS III: "To appreciate William Albright's *Five Chromatic Dances* (1976), one need only listen to a good recording or play through the score. But that appreciation deepens even more as one becomes aware of the rich context of these pieces by examining their relationship to other pieces and styles of music.

"The dance-suite tradition dates back to the Renaissance and is familiar to many through the suites of Froberger and Bach. Because of their evocative character, one may easily imagine choreography for the *Five Chromatic Dances,* but they do belong to a tradition of stylized dances that are not meant to be danced. In fact, while they incorporate strong rhythms whose pulse is an important part of the effect, the almost total absence of regular notated meter in these *Dances* indicates their connection with a wealth of twentieth-century rhythmic ideas: the additive rhythms of Stravinsky (compare the

---

[4] / = Ideas or elements in alternation.

music after the double bar on page 26, 'menacing but boisterous; strongly rhythmic', with *'Les Augures Printaniers'* of *Le Sacre du Printemps*); the syncopated drive of hard bop (compare the last two-and-one-quarter systems of page 33, 'with jazz-like abandon... swing it!', with Lennie Tristano's piano style); and the mechanical angularity of the Futurists, and their recent heirs, the minimalists (compare the music of pages 20-21, 'Eerie, in two perspectives... even mechanical', and its irregularly-spaced interruptions with Antheil's *Ballet mécanique* [1925] or Steve Reich's *Four Organs* [1970]). The slowly changing patterns of pages 39-44, 'gently undulating... with great peace', present a way of shaping musical time that makes it interesting to compare this final dance, *The Farewell*, with the timelessness of Mahler's setting of *'Ewig'* in the final song of *Das Lied von der Erde*, which bears the same name.

"The incorporation of such a wide variety of ways of shaping time within a single artistic statement places substantial demands on the composer's skill in shaping formal structures. Furthermore, the twentieth century presents a special problem with regard to form: with the abandonment of thematic repetition in Debussy's *Jeux*, and with approaches that vary so radically from Webern's miniatures to Stockhausen's 'moment form' and the experiments of John Cage, it has become increasingly difficult for composers to make decisions in an age that values novelty for its own sake. In such an age, the unselfconscious unity of these *Dances* is refreshing. This unity derives from a formal coherence based on a variety of kinds and levels of repetitions or associations in a way that emphasizes their historical context.

"One rather simple formal repetition that is, however, far-reaching in its effect can be found in the final movement. *The Farewell* is cast in a simple ABA form.[5] The A sections of this movement combine the highest and lowest registers of the piano, framing the B section both temporally and registrally. This usage underscores the important function of extreme register throughout the dances. The first

---

5   When the A section returns, it sounds a step lower. The *Rounds* also conclude with a statement that is modified and lowered a step.

movement begins with a *Procession* that exploits the lower registers, ends with the lowest notes on the instrument, and is followed by *Rounds* that begin with the highest note on the piano. As the middle movements focus primarily on the middle registers of the piano,[6] the first and last movements frame the work in the same registral and temporal ways that the A sections of *The Farewell* frame that movement. The union of extreme registers in the final movement creates something of a conclusive synthesis. In their exploitation of the full range of the piano, the *Five Chromatic Dances* echo a tradition that begins with Chopin and Liszt and includes Ravel's *Jeux d'eau* and *Gaspard de la nuit*.

"While some of Albright's colorful uses of the timbral resources of the piano find expression in the relationships of specific pitches, some of them emphasize timbres whose specific pitches are of secondary significance.[7] The rumble of the lowest register derives some of its character from the inharmonicity of those strings, and the special echo effect in *The Farewell* (*sffz pp*, second system, page 38) derives some of its character from the resonance of an undamped piano to its highest note—a resonance that makes the attack of a note more important than its pitch. The instruction of page 10, 'damp string by hand', makes the release of a note more important than its pitch.[8] This conception of timbre and pitch finds resonance in the perfor-

---

6   Just as extreme registers do not vanish entirely in the B section of *The Farewell*, they also play a role in the middle movements. In addition to punctuating important formal divisions (e.g., at the end of page 12 and begining of page 13, at the beginning of the *Fantasy*, and at the end of *Hoedown*), the extreme registers are also used to connect larger sections of the work (e.g., Albright points out a descending line that spans the third movement and connects it to the fourth; E^b1, first note; D^b1, last measure page 15; C1, beginning of last line page 16; B0, first note page 17; B^b0, beginning of second line page 22; A1, near end of last line page 22 [descending seconds have become ascending sevenths—the piano can only go so low]; $G^\#2$, end of *Mazurka*; G3, beginning of *Hoedown*).
7   Note in this regard Schoenberg's remark in his *Harmonielehre* of 1911: 'a note is perceived by its color, one of whose dimensions is pitch. Color, then, is the great realm, pitch one of its provinces.'
8   The care given to the releases of notes can also be seen on the second system of page 3 where the individual successive releases of the different voices of a single simultaneity are expressly indicated.

mance directions of pages 26 and 34, 'L.H. ad lib!, a rhythmic noise with a contour'. Twentieth-century piano writing is apparent in the depress-silently-and-hold-with-sostenuto-pedal technique of pages 9, 12, and 13 (cf. Schoenberg, Bartók); in the rapidly repeated notes of *Hoedown* (cf. Ravel); and in the echo effects of pages 8, 10, 17, and 38 (cf. Crumb, Messiaen).[9]

" 'Interrupting' (e.g., pages 6, 11, 30, 38) and 'parenthetically' (e.g., page 36), together with the 'two perspectives' of pages 20-21 that interrupt each other, suggest that the 'discontinuity' Edward Cone associates with Stravinsky's style is also an element of Albright's style.[10] This discontinuity may be related to shifting relationships between figure and ground (see page 2, 'bring out soprano a little bit... grad. recede soprano below texture') that mirror the concern with figure and ground in some of M. C. Escher's prints.[11]

"Some of the repetitions that unify the *Five Chromatic Dances* are of a subtler nature. Certain small sets of pitches appear in various guises throughout the piece. One of these,

(and its inversion, retrograde, retrograde-inversion, and transpositions) is prominent at the beginning and ending of the *Procession* as well as at the conclusion of the theme that begins and ends *The Farewell*, thus framing the first and last movements and therefore the whole piece. The sinewy chromaticism of this pattern recalls the melodic writing of Bartók.

"Because we tend to hear all steps (whether whole-steps or half-steps) as equivalent (i.e., qualitatively different from leaps) and generally do not expect adjacent half-steps, the third note of this set always fills an unanticipated space, creating the impression of two juxtaposed ways of filling tonal space with steps. In this sense, pas-

---

9   Albright sees his pianistic special effects as reflecting a French tradition that includes Berio and especially Boulez's *Third Piano Sonata*.
10 Cone, 'Stravinsky: The Progress of a Method', in *Perspectives of New Music* 1 (1962), pp. 18-26. However, this should not be viewed as entirely unique to Stravinsky's style. See e.g. Jonathan Kramer, 'Multiple and Non-linear Time in Beethoven's Op. 135', in *Perspectives of New Music* 11 (1973), pp. 122-45.
11 Albright notes the influence of cinematographic technique, suggesting that intercut, flashback, focus, and fade allow the expression of surreal and altered time concepts. He points out how unusual the achievement of Charles Ives was in a kind of 'fast cutting' that predates the advent of such techniques in motion pictures, and says of the presentation of multiple time frames in *The Unanswered Question* 'nothing like that had happened in Western music until that time... Ives could only have drawn these things from Dream'. Audiences familiar with Albright's music may note his own fascination with the world of dreams.

sages of juxtaposed white-note and black-note scales (page 5, second measure; page 31, small noteheads) tend to sound like an extension of the treatment of this small set. Another extension of this idea can be found in the alternation of tonally distantly related triads in the *Masquerade* whose resultant soprano often produces the three-note pattern described above.

"Similar juxtapositions can be found in the works of other twentieth-century composers. In the opening measures of Debussy's *Feux d'artifice* scale fragments are juxtaposed. Later in the same piece (see the example in Watkins' study, page 114), different transpositions of the three-note pattern (as simultaneity) described above are juxtaposed. Also in the same piece, tritone-related triads are juxtaposed. One may recall also the F#/C opposition of Ravel's *Jeux* that is reflected in Stravinsky's famous *Petrushka* chord. This kind of opposition exists in much of Stravinsky—cf. the juxtaposed ways of steps filling a tritone in *Firebird*

—and Bartók (cf. the opposition of black-note and white-note patterns in 'Boating' from *Mikrokosmos* Book 5).

"Another important set repeated throughout *Five Chromatic Dances*... [appears on page 22,] where it descends by half-step in the left hand (cf. Ravel's *Le Gibet*, Berg's *Warm die Lüfte*, and Debussy's *Pour la danseuse aux crotales* [1915], where this half-step descent occurs above a circle of fifths bass). Whereas page 19 quotes both right and left hands of Chopin's *Mazurka* Op. 17 Nr.4, page 22 quotes the right hand, substituting the pattern described above for Chopin's 6/3 and 7/3 chords.[12] This pattern is a favorite of modern jazz pianists.[13] The *habanera* of *Hoedown* (pages 29-31) not only features this set prominently, but recalls Debussy's *Puerto del vino* and *Soirée dans Grenade*, both of which also feature this set.

"While these repetitions and associations are interesting, perhaps the most artistically compelling are Albright's transformations (e.g., the opening sonority of *Hoedown*—familiar as the sound of a violin's open strings, a country dancer's call to order, but also familiar from Berg's *Concerto for Violin*—is transformed into the B section of *The Farewell*, which periodically comes to rest on chords also composed

---

12 Chopin's *Prelude* in E minor, which also uses a left hand of descending 6/3 and 7/3 chords, features a melodic unfolding of this important set.
13 According to the composer, the music of page 22 was the first part of the *Dances* to be composed and was meant to sound like improvised jazz: 'Manhattan at 3 AM'. The connection of this music to the Chopin *Mazurka* set the compositional process in motion.

of two dyads of perfect fourths or fifths). However, a detailed discussion of these should, perhaps, await another paper." — Steve Larson, from an essay forwarded to the Editor by the composer. Mr. Larson adds: "The romanticism of twentieth-century composers such as Barber, Bloch, Britten, Prokofiev, Rachmaninoff, Shostakovich, Vaughan Williams and Zemlinsky suggests that, while the neo-romanticism of Albright's Chopin quotation (like Rochberg's use of quotation) represents a return-to-the-past, obviously in so doing it also continues an established twentieth-century tradition. The idea prevalent in many quarters that 'art-music' has abandoned tonality would seem to suggest that artists such as Charlie Parker, Thelonius Monk, Clifford Brown, Chick Corea, Bill Evans, Dave McKenna, etc. have not created 'art music', then — an assumption that will not go unchallenged as, like Albright, more composers look to modern jazz as a fertile field for exploration."

FIVE CHROMATIC DANCES — ESSAYS AND REVIEWS IV: "Pianists are exceedingly fortunate that composers have continued to write major works for the instrument. In the not too distant past there was talk of the death of the piano, the tradition of Romantic soloist/matinee idol no longer *au courant* with the Webernites, the Cagians, or the threat of thermonuclear war. And, if truth be told, considering the number of pianists who could play anything later than Debussy, who would blame the composers if they never wrote another note of piano music? Nevertheless, beginning in the early 1970s a number of substantial, meaningful works for solo piano, starting, perhaps, with George Crumb's *Makrokosmos* series (inspired by Debussy and Bartók), came into being to the possible salvation of the continuation of the piano repertoire. The American repertoire, in particular, has been enhanced recently with new pieces from such diverse composers as Elliott Carter (his 1981 *Night Fantasies* is already twice recorded!) and John Adams (who proves that minimalism can produce twenty-minute works, as with *Phrygian Gates*).

"William Albright should be well known to followers of the American music scene: he is active as a composer, as an organist of immense virtuosity, and as a revivalist of the classic rag, Harlem stride, and boogie-woogie styles of popular piano playing. His *Five Chromatic Dances*, dating from 1976, were composed on a commission from Thomas Warburton, who superbly performs them on [the] CRI recording. This is without a doubt a major work, and no pianist interested in the twentieth century should be without the recording.

"Influences from the past abound, but the work is in no way derivative. The opening dance, *Procession and Rounds*, begins with a steady eighth-note movement in the bass register, an otherworldly plainchant wandering chromatically about but going nowhere. Lines emerge only to fall back into the murky texture. Sudden sforzando chords leap out and foreshadow the second half of the movement—the *Rounds* section is played entirely in the treble range and is best described by quoting Albright's marking in the score: 'delirious, obsessive, and crazy... drunken.'

"In his excellent liner notes Warburton suggests that the second dance, *Masquerade*, is reminiscent of the etudes and preludes of Debussy. There is also a nursery rhyme quality to the movement, serving the framework of the entire composition as a good-natured scherzo. The writing is marvelously pianistic, full of pedal effects and sensitive 'fades' of articulation and texture, which Warburton performs with great panache.

"Both the third and fourth dances are in ABA form and are probably the most readily approachable by the average listener. The *Fantasy-Mazurka* begins as an improvisation; slowly the left hand develops a chord progression similar to some of Chopin's more chromatically involved harmonic schemes. The right hand continues its improvisatory and highly expressive melody. Interrupting this reverie without warning is the middle section, marked 'Eerie, in two perspectives'; its harmonic language is closest to Messiaen at his most apocalyptic. The opening material returns, and ever so slowly the right hand also becomes Chopinesque. The movement ends with an extremely effective and painfully beautiful near quotation of the *Mazurka*, Op. 17, Nr. 4. The *Hoedown* is a raucous celebration of virtuosity marked 'joyous and ecstatic; dizzily fast'. It takes its inspiration from country fiddling, and if anyone can dance as fast as Warburton plays it, we should all line up to see it! The surprise here is the middle section, marked *Tempo di habanera*. Such are Albright's powers of compositional assimilation that the juxtaposition works— perhaps he free-associates alliteratively.

"The final movement, *The Farewell*, contains some of the most beautiful writing for the piano in *any* work of this century. Opening with a melody played by both hands six octaves apart, it is marked 'hollow, mystically ringing'. Gradually a hushed tremolando emerges, similar in feeling to those in the late piano works of Beethoven. Low bass tones punctuate the texture and grow in intensity, recalling the opening of the *Procession*. As gradually as it came, the tremolando recedes, and the work ends with the widely spaced melody fragmented into only two notes, dissolving into nothing.

"At [thirty] minutes the work approaches the proportions of an Ives sonata and is similarly all-inclusive. For all that, this reviewer is most reminded of the Schumann of *Kreisleriana* and the *Humoreske*. In these works, as in the Albright, the spirit of the dance has transcended the physical and has become an all-pervasive essence. Quotations and self-references appear like characters in a play, and above all there is the fantastic imagination that dares to capture in sound the inexpressible. Let us hope the *Five Chromatic Dances* receive all the attention they deserve." — Robert Weirich, in *American Music*, Winter 1985.

FIVE CHROMATIC DANCES — ESSAYS AND REVIEWS V: "With William Bolcom (his friend and fellow faculty member at the University of Michigan) William Albright has been in the forefront of the recent tendency among American composers to combine the past and the present, the classical and the popular, into a stew wherein the elements remain distinct from, but not contradictory to, one another. The coincident or consecutive occurrence of a ragtime bass, operatic melody, country-and-western lilt, and electronic accompaniment seems in this erudite and often witty historicism to be demonstrating the validity — and even the interrelatedness — of all types of music. Substance, composers like Albright insist, is a composer's gift, not a genre's given; there are many, many musics all around us, so we should try to become broadly informed — and broadly discerning.

"That is the polemical message of Albright's pluralism, and, as you might intuit,[14] it puts an extra burden on his own composition: as rich in reference as his pieces are, they must be musically substantial, not just clever displays of musicological virtuosity....

"[In his 1966 composition *Pianogogo*] the supposedly conflicting styles do not just follow on one another's heels, they modify one another into a coherent pianistic essay — and the piece is very much concerned with pianism — that is as droll as it is unsettling. The musicological references are yet slyer in the *Five Chromatic Dances*, written a decade later. In fact, despite all the allusions claimed in the liner notes, one might simply describe the [thirty] minute work as a late exploration of chromaticism. All the models, from Beethoven to Messiaen, are considered, but none are aped, and even the allusions that must be admitted must be sought. If the *Dances* are not quodlibets, then, are they merely show-off pieces by a gifted musicologist? They are not just that: they are 'show-off' pieces by a gifted *composer*, one informed enough to fit himself squarely within an extensive tradition and expand it. Perhaps Albright does not extend the actual range of chromatic possibilities on the piano (after a century and a half of chromatic experiment that range could probably be extended

---

14 It is also — along with the tonality/atonality issue — a leading theme in 20th century musical aesthetics, and of the present volume. (Ed.)

only with electronic enhancement), but he does contribute a distinctive, gorgeous, and electrifying piece to the repertoire.

"The *Dances* sound to this amateur keyboardist like a fun challenge to the performer, too. They demand some virtuosity and an almost theatrical sensitivity to dynamics, but with anyone on speaking terms with the piano music of Debussy, Liszt, or Ives, such demands should not be hard to meet." — Peter Frank, in *Fanfare: The Magazine for Serious Record Collectors*, 9-10/82.

DAVID AMRAM

B. 1930, Philadelphia PA. *Educ.:* Oberlin Cons, George Washington Univ, Manhattan Schl of Music. Honorary Doct Laws, Moravian College, Muhlenberg College, Univ Hartford. Composed for theater, TV, film, jazz bands; performer (incl Cafe Bohemia, National SO, Manhattan Woodwind Quintet), conductor (incl approx 17 orchestras each year). 1st composer-in-residence NY Philharmonic. *Autobiography: Vibrations. Works incl.:* cantatas (*Let Us Remember, A Year in Our Land*), chamber works (strng qt, vln sonata, trio [sax/hn/bsn]), concertos (bsn, hn, sax [*Ode to Lord Buckley*], vc, ww/brass/jazz qnts [*Triple Concerto*]), film scores (*The Manchurian Candidate, Splendor in the Grass, The Young Savages*), incidental music (incl 25 NY Shakespeare Festival prods), jazz pieces, *King Lear Variations* (wnds/perc), operas (*The Final Ingredient*).

Composer statement: "Music, to me, represents the pure expression of sounds rooted in nature, the histories of peoples around the world as reflected in their unique ways of expressing themselves and of course the relatively brief few hundred years of Western notated and recently recorded music that tend to obliterate the thousands of years of music that have come before. The magnificent European tradition that I was brought up in is a part of a whole.

"The Native Americans, or Indians as improperly named by Columbus, who was lost, say that to them, the European version of history is HIS STORY. Since the peer culture determines what is history, and what is great art, we still suffer in the U.S. from the vestigial remains of what was once near terminal Austro-Hungarian Empire-itus.

"Having grow up loving Brahms, Schubert, Beethoven and Mozart, it took knowing Charlie Parker, Duke Ellington, Thelonius Monk, Dizzy Gillespie, Tito Puento, Pete Seeger and countless folk, jazz, Latin American, American Indian and Middle Eastern performers and on-the-spot composers to make me understand *why* their music was so moving. It all came from the same place. A love and reverence for roots and tradition, a reverent and superb choice of notes, a knowledge of the ancestral drum that beats in every human heart-beat even before birth, and a desire to communicate uplifting spiritual statements in sound, often in spite of everything, are the components of all great musics of the world.

"In English classes, I was always taught, 'Write what you know from your own experience.' I have applied that rule to my composing, conducting and performing. My compositions are extensions and often idealized portraits in sound that reflect the blessings I have received from a life around the world from the jungles of Central America and Brazil to the mountains of the Khyber Pass, from the synagogues on the Lower East Side of New York City to jam sessions with Thelonius Monk and Sonny Rollins, from playing the Brahms Horn Trio in Germany to conducting major symphony orchestras around the world and from playing on Native American reservations and folk festivals with Cajun and Irish traditional musicians. All of the experiences influence my composition. Sometimes unconsciously, sometimes specifically. The five pieces I have commented on [below] reflect this direction. Being a composer-conductor-performer is an honor, a blessing and a responsibility. It means sharing, respect for others and passing on what you learn from the masters."

American Dance Suite for Chamber Orchestra (1986). 15m Comm.by Richard and Audrey Kauders. *Prem.:* Omaha S Chamber O, Bruce Hangen, cond. *Publ.:* C. F. Peters (study score; parts also available on rental).
1. *Cheyenne.* 2. *Blues.* 3. *Cajun.*

"I decided to make this work a dance suite as a result of working with Jacques d'Ambroise, the dancer, choreographer and founder of the National Dance Institute in New York.

"Mr. d'Ambroise wanted some of my [other] music for a dance he was to create. After watching the excitement of seeing my composition choreographed (Mary Tyler Moore tap-danced in one section!), I decided I would write a piece celebrating American dance forms, as a concert piece that could create a ballet in the listener's mind, and perhaps someday be danced to.

"The first movement, *Cheyenne,* uses some traditional melodies of the Cheyenne people. An introductory fanfare is followed by a traditional Cheyenne melody taught to me by Hyemeyohsts Storm, the author of *Seven Arrows*. This social dance melody is developed and followed by a traditional Cheyenne hand-game song, 'Nu-usm nonotz'. After further development of both of these melodies, sometimes played together, we hear a setting of a Cheyenne war dance which highlights the unusual rhythms and structure of this highly sophisticated ancient music. After a brief return of the beginning fanfare, the horns introduce the final traditional dance melody, a fast war dance, followed by fragments of the earlier melodies and ending with the drum and rattle.

"The second movement, *Blues,* is a tribute to the contribution of jazz to the enrichment of our century, as music to dance to and music of great emotional depth.

"This music uses only the strings, and the melancholy theme and development celebrate the tranquil and spiritual aspects of a style of music that has influenced all music and listeners around the world. Rather than a rendering of traditional blues it is a tribute to some of the masters like Charlie Parker, Thelonius Monk, Dizzy Gillespie, Lionel Hampton, Gerry Mulligan, Charlie Mingus and Oscar Pettiford – all of whom I have known and performed with earlier in my life.

"The final movement, *Cajun*, celebrates another indigenous form of American music that came to us via the Celtic people who lived in Brittany, came to Canada three hundred years ago as French-Speaking Acadians (Cajun is a corruption of the word Acadian), and arrived in the U.S. settling in Louisiana. There their Celtic-French-Canadian music was influenced by the music of Native American and Afro-American cultures developing into the unique Cajun culture of today.

"The lively melody, 'The Fox Hunt', is a slip-jig played first by the piccolo and accompanied by traditional Celtic rhythms and contemporary Cajun percussion instruments including the spoons. After several statements with varying orchestration, a second melody of my own, a Cajun waltz (inspired by eating Crawfish Etoufe while performing in Port Arthur, Texas and New Orleans) is introduced. The waltz uses the triangle, bongos and washboard, instruments common to contemporary Cajun music called 'Zydeco' which I have performed with several Cajun ensembles at folk festivals. After the clarinet completes the waltz, the strings and different choirs of the orchestra join in.

" 'The Fox Hunt' is restated and then is joined by the waltz and finally a re-statement of the Cheyenne social song and fanfare from the first movement, to bring the composition to a conclusion." – David Amram.

"[At the premiere] Amram brought a Cheyenne flute [on stage] to play the round dance motif from the first movement of the suite and a penny whistle to play a few bars of the Irish jig from the third movement. Because of the history of the American Indian culture in the Omaha area, Amram said he chose Cheyenne music for the first movement.... For the second movement, he tries to produce the mood of slow dancing to the blues. He does this, he explained, not by using traditional blues rhythms and harmonies, but with his own dissonant, uneasy, and poignant harmonies.

"The lusty, ebullient third movement starts out with a nine-count slip jig called the 'Irish Fox Hunt'. He then introduces some Cajun folk music – [juxtaposes] these two melodic themes contrapuntally—and then brings back the Cheyenne theme for the final *tour de force.*" —Kyle MacMillan, *Omaha World-Herald.*

Concerto for Violin and Orchestra (1981). 25m *Comm.* by Ford Foundation. *Prem.:* Charles Castleman (vln), St. Louis SO, Leonard Slatkin, cond. *Publ.:* C. F. Peters (piano reduction; orchestra score & parts also available on rental).
1. Allegro moderato. 2. *Blues* (Andante espressivo). 3. *Celtic Rondo* (Allegro con brio).

"The first movement is written in the traditional sonata form, using the violin as leader and commentator to the various choirs of the orchestra. It serves as a prelude or overture to the melancholy and nostalgic second movement, which is based on the indestructible 12-bar blues pattern which has endured this century in so many different forms. The violin, through the work of such artists as Stuff Smith, Joe Venuti, Ray Nance and Stéphanie Grappelli, has become a voice in jazz as well as the many folk forms we associate with the Prince of the orchestral family. I have tried to use it in a context of my own experience in jazz, much the ways Brahms and Bartók used the folkloric music they grew up with and loved in their compositions.

"The quiet ending of the second movement leads to the sprightly entrance of the spoons and *bodrahn* for the Celtic Rondo. After the theme is stated and restated, about halfway through this final movement there begins a musical depiction of a fox hunt, using all the traditional Irish songs about foxes I could find. Having played numerous folkloric festivals in both Canada and the United States in which Irish slip jigs, reels, airs and songs were performed, I know first-hand how this music survives on this continent today. All of the traditional tunes I used are identified in the score: first there is a fragment of 'Johnny, I hardly knew ye', then we hear 'Ellen O'Grady', 'Paddy's Resource', 'The Bridge of Athlone', 'The Hunt', 'The Wearing of the Green', 'Off to the Hunt' and 'Hunting the Hare'. Then there is a musical representation of the hunters shooting. Since I'm an animal-lover, I have them miss the fox, and we can hear the howling of the hounds in the distance, signaling that their prey got away. Then the solo violin and harp (an instrument with especially strong Irish associations) introduce the last of the traditional melodies, the beautiful 'When the Foxes Sleep'. None of the folk material is heard again; the original theme of the rondo is then restated, and with it the work concludes." —David Amram.

"There aren't many good, audience-pleasing works for violin and orchestra, [but] David Amram has contributed one with his *Violin Concerto*....

"Probably the Amram concerto isn't very difficult to learn and play—it's built for the most part on diatonic themes, and the quota of left-hand pizzicatos, harmonics and double-stops is dealt with briefly in a first-movement cadenza.

"It certainly isn't difficult music to hear. It's an unpretentious piece [with] a Gershwinesque blues rhapsody in the second movement. The finale is made of jolly Irish tunes—things like jigs and reels. The whole work lasts about 25 minutes but seems shorter.

"Amram shows a keen sense of timing and proportion in his music. He knows when to build and relax excitement, when to take breath, how to change pace and keep the listener's ear, as in a good conversation." —Frank Peters, *St. Louis Post-Dispatch*.

Shakespearean Concerto for Chamber Orchestra (1959). 22m
Recs.: Flying Fish Records (Amram, Genovese, Nadien, Serbagi), Washington Classical Series (Serbagi, Roseman, Barrows, Cowan).
Publ.: C. F. Peters (study score; parts also available on rental).
0-1-0-0; 2-0-0-0; strings (featured vla)
1. Allegro moderato. 2. Andante con moto. 3. Allegro giocoso.

"David Amram's *Shakespearean Concerto* in a *concerto grosso* style was drawn from music he had written for *Twelfth Night*, one of twenty-five scores he had composed for Joseph Papp's New York Shakespeare Festival productions from 1956-1967. [For David Amram's opera on this theme, with libretto adapted from the play by Joseph Papp, see below]. The second movement uses the melody of Feste's song found near the end of the play. The music, like the man, demonstrates intelligence, a quick wit, ready humor and a pleasant mixture of craft and charm, ready and eager to reach into popular sources for material.

"In a May, 1962 article in *Horizon*, critic Alan Rich wrote, 'If he [Amram] had to settle for a description of his style, he would probably call it "Hebraic-Elizabethan-American".'

"The concerto is readily accessible. The scoring is lucid and the piece sounds and the score looks deceptively simple, a product of an easy craft. The simplicity and directness of expression grow out of the composer's musical instinct and his ability to say what he means clearly and (enviably) easily, in comprehensible musical terms. There is no program for this piece. The first movement is built on material reminiscent of folk tunes with syncopated rhythms and contrasting lyrical interludes. It is in sonata form with a pastoral theme introduced in the development, and an abbreviated recapitulation that includes a reminiscence of the pastoral theme at the end.

"The *Andante con moto* is a tender, lyrical expression in which the solo viola is first given the song melody. The middle section uses techniques of melodic imitation and rhythmic augmentation of the song melody in the bass in building to the climax. There is a short backwards glance at the song melody at the close. A recurring cadential figure, made up of a broken descending triad, figures prominently in this movement as had one of three descending tones (alla 'Three Blind Mice') in the first movement.

"The *Allegro giocoso* is a Rondo in ABACA scheme. It is an irreverent, puckish, musical thumb-to-the-nose statement with jazzlike passages — a kind of urbane romp. At one point, the upper string players are instructed to tap their fingers on their instruments, like so many fingersnaps while the beat goes on below in the guise of a walking bass. At the conclusion, one quick statement of the first movement's opening motive precedes the final salute." — Francis Brancaleone, based on his 5/90 review for the Gannett Westchester (NY) Newspapers.

"Amram's *Shakespearean Concerto* is thoroughly contemporary in feeling, well put together and admirably scored, blending a solo oboe and two horns in a cleverly constructed and sensitive amalgam of instruments." — Max de Schauensee, *Philadelphia Penn*.

Songs of the Soul (symphony) for Orchestra (1987). *Prem.:* Jewish Arts Festival O of Long Island. *Publ.:* C. F. Peters (perform materials available on rental).
1. *Incantation*. 2. *Song Without Words*. 3. *Dance of Joy*.

"[At its 1989 Spoleto Festival performance] the work sounded to me like a genuine winner. The first moments echo the sounds of the Shofar, then proceed into all sorts of colorful oriental melodic material drawn from exotic regions of Jewish history: Ethiopia, the Mid and Far Easts, Spain and Portugal. The slow second section is gorgeous. The final *Dance of Joy* is a brilliant *freilach*, a traditional dance bursting with drums and high spirits. [This music] has all the ingredients needed for a big popular success." — Robert Jones, *Post-Courier*.

"*Songs of the Soul* is dedicated 'to the unsung heroes of traditional music who have kept the flame alive, and my father, who taught me to respect the heritage of all people.'
"The piece has three diverse movements... with a common thread of Middle Eastern musical origins. The first movement is based on a Passover chant of Ethiopian Jews, the second on cantoral singing and the third on Eastern European Klezmer music and Sephardic melodies.

"It's a fitting mix for Amram, whose father is part Sephardic, or of Spanish Jewish ancestry, and whose mother was Ashkenazic, or of Central and Eastern European Jewish ancestry. Add to that combination Feasterville, Pa., where Amram, destined to be known as 'the Renaissance man of American music', grew up on a farm, and an integrated neighborhood in Washington, where he was [first] exposed to jazz....

"On still another part of the musical spectrum, [the composer] has cultivated an expertise in ethnomusicology, learning and recording native music from Kenya to Pakistan, and Panama to Egypt. He plays the Guatemalan turtle flute, Mexican dog flute, Irish tin whistle, and a Sri Lankan temple horn fashioned of a seashell and brass.

"Whether it's Appalachian or African, Amram says, ethnic music has a resilient flavor, surving time and distance. None has been more of a survivor than Jewish music. 'Somehow in thousands of years of wandering, the Jewish people have been able to maintain an alphabet, a language, a religion, and also a certain feeling about music. Like most traditional music, it shows the beautiful humanistic and spiritual part of us as a people.' " —Geoff Walden, *Westchester Newspapers*.

The Trail of Beauty for Mezzo-Soprano, Oboe and Orchestra (1977). 30m *Comm. & prem. by:* Rose Taylor (ms), John de Lancie (ob), Philadelphia O, Eugene Ormandy, cond. *Other perf.:* Winnipeg (Canada) SO. *Publ.:* C. F. Peters (vocal score; parts also available on rental).
orch: 1 picc-2-4 (1 E^b cl, 2 bcl)-2-1 cbsn; 4-2-3-1; 6 timp, large perc section (incl native American insts), harp; strings
1. *Prologue and Navajo Prayer*. 2. *Thanks to the Earth Where Men Dwell* (*text:* from the Iroquois Constitution). 3. *Song of the Sky Loom* (*t.:* from a song of the Tewa Pueblo people). 4. *Every Part of This Soil Is Sacred* (*t.:* from Chief Seattle's Speech to Governor Stevens) — *Epilogue*.

"It has been a pleasure to conduct this significant contribution to *truly* American music. The music and text derive directly from the American Indian *ethos*, and bring us an imperishable image of the eternal dreams of the people who walked this land centuries ago. Amram, through his particular genius, and his hard work at digging at the sources, has built a marvelous musical tapestry, full of wonderful sounds and colors.

"The work is also a tribute to Marcel Tabuteau [to whom it is dedicated], for many years our solo oboe, and the predecessor and teacher of John de Lancie, our equally talented first oboe, who is playing the premiere." — Eugene Ormandy.

"Mr. Amram has laid out *The Trail of Beauty* in four sections, which symbolize, he advises, the 'four signs' or 'four directions' which are cited frequently in Indian lore. He has used several authentic Indian melodies (each carefully identified in the score) in the material for the oboe and orchestra, but not in any of the music for the singer, all of which is original.

"The prologue opens with a brief but evocative oboe solo, following which the mezzo enters (her first two syllables sung before the orchestra joins in), singing a text drawn from a Navajo prayer, which sets the tone of simplicity and dignity which is to prevail throughout the work.

"The second section, whose words are taken from the Iroquois Constitution, opens dramatically, with bass drum and tom-tom, joined by sleigh bells and other small percussion instruments; winds, horns, trumpets and finally the entire brass section build swiftly to a grand proclamation, then allow the mezzo to enter without accompaniment; the oboe makes his first entry under the last word of the first line of text, and then segments of the orchestra return. Following the line 'To the medicinal herbs and the trees' is an instrumental interlude based on a Santee Sioux Rabbit Dance, the first authentic Indian theme used in the work and one which recurs in the fourth section.

"The third section is a brief slow movement identified as a passacaglia on the traditional Laguna Pueblo melody *'Aiya Gaitani Yoni'*. The text sung by the mezzo is that of the 'Song of the Sky Loom', from the lore of the Tewa Pueblos. The movement opens with an extended oboe solo, then continues as a duet for voice and oboe until its midpoint, when muted violins, harp and triangle are the first orchestral instruments heard; the final lines are again for voice and oboe alone.

"Section four is the longest part of the work, comprising a setting of lines from the Dwamish Chief Seattle's speech to Governor Isaac Stevens of Washington Territory in 1854 and an Epilogue in which the opening material is heard again. The main part of this section, 'Every Part of This Soil Is Sacred', opens with four cellos playing a melody of Cheyenne origin which, according to Mr. Amram, is sung today by Indians of various tribes throughout the U.S. and Canada and might be regarded as 'a rallying song of strength and unity'. The other instruments enter gradually, the oboe's first appearance coming in the second line of the sung text. The Rabbit Dance from the second movement is heard briefly between sung portions, and under the mezzo's line 'Because it is rich with the blood of our ancestors' the bass drum beats a rhythm marked 'Like a heart-beat'.

"At the point at which the settlers are told to expect the ghosts of the Indians to return, there is an extended orchestral interlude in which various themes are brought in: the first is the 'Song of Geronimo' (noted as having been sung to Natalie Curtis by Chief Geronimo in 1903), set for oboe and strings; next, with the oboe at rest, comes a 'Song of Sitting Bull' (from the music of the Teton Sioux people), followed in turn by *Tawi' Kuruka'*, a Pawnee song of the Bear Society. The 'Geronimo' and opening Cheyenne themes are recalled, and then muted horns and trombones introduce *Tapko Daaguya'*, a Kiowa song of the antelope ceremony. The interlude ends imposingly with a Sioux Honor Song, introduced by the oboe with only the bass drum for accompaniment at first, building to a climax and subsiding for the return of the mezzo; when her song is sung, the final comment is made by the oboe alone, leading to the Epilogue which, as noted above, is a reprise of material from the work's opening section." — Richard Freed, for The Philadelphia Orchestra.

"Amram's style is intensely lyrical, long-lined and rooted in tonality. The unusual combination of oboe and voice is a constant that flows through the varied orchestra sounds, the authentic Indian music and the composed native idiom.

"Technically, the writing for oboe is straightforward. Amram's style is lyrical and flatters the inherent singing quality of the instrument. The virtuosity required is the skill of song, of expression and of finding balances with the voice and the text." — Daniel Webster, *Philadelphia Inquirer*.

"David Amram had an interesting idea when he decided to base his new composition on 'poetry, prayers and speeches of native American peoples' and to use motifs from Indian music liberally in his composition.

" 'Haunting' is the word for the music [of the opening section], and even more for the long passage in the final movement which uses Chief Seattle's words to express the Red Man's relation to the land, with an admonition to the white usurper: 'The very dust on which you now stand... / At night when the streets of your cities and villages are silent / They will throng with the returning hosts / That once filled and still love this beautiful land.'

"[This is] superbly crafted, thoughtful, evocative music." — Joseph McLellan, *The Washington Post*.

"The music... has a dignity and a serenity that somehow extends beyond the formal elements of music. Amram has treated his source with great reverence and dignity. To this he has added some lovely, lyrical melodies for soprano and his great skill as an orchestrator." — Neil Harris, *Winnipeg Free Press*.

* * * * * * * * * * * * * * * *

A PRIMER FOR YOUNG MUSICIANS

Among David Amram's manifold musical activities, he regularly conducts young people's concerts. His advice for aspiring musicians:

- Don't be afraid to practice.
- Be patient. Figure that as long as you're inhaling and exhaling you have plenty of time to improve.
- Any time you're in any other country, the most important way to be a good student of music and life is to learn how to say please and thank you.
- Assume that you will always be overqualified. Whether you're playing as a soloist with a symphony orchestra, at a wedding, in a bar, for a football game, at a jam session, or singing around a campfire, remind yourself you're always in Carnegie Hall.
- Keep an open mind and an open heart for all music and musicians that give the feeling of being sincere and dedicated.
- Respect every musician you perform with and every person who comes to listen to you.
- No computer or synthesizer can ever be programmed to know how to have a good time and share a sense of love and beauty with others.
- Never forget that music is a joyous, harmonious, healing celebration of life that embraces the sense of family and shared humanity.

—*Westchester [County NY] Sunday Newspapers*, 9/6/87.

Twelfth Night (opera) (1968). 150m *Lib.*: William Shakespeare play, adapted by Joseph Papp. *Prem.*: Lake George (NY) Opera Festival. *Pub.*: C. F. Peters (perform material on rental).
chamber orch: 1-1-1-1; 2-1-1-0; timp, perc (2 players); strings
In 2 acts.

"*Twelfth Night* may be one of the few half-commissioned operas in history: it was begun for Joseph Papp's Shakespeare series in Central Park (Papp worked with Amram in condensing the text, which otherwise sticks close to the original), and it was intended for the 400th anniversary year. But money ran out and the uncompleted score went into a drawer. The Lake George company heard about it when making its own Shakespeare plans, and commissioned the remainder of the work—I was told most of Act II....

"Amram has risen deftly to the bait of Shakespeare's wit, and created a workable and happy comic opera—a sure hit, in fact, if the first-night reaction is any measure....

"The writing in Act I is lean, linear, and faintly Elizabethan, the kind of thing Amram does beautifully, with instrumental sketches that may be obvious but are no less successful—contrabassoon antics for Sir Toby, stuffy, four-square business for Malvolio, a captivating minuet for Sir Andrew and Sir Toby, and so on. The comic characters, in short, are well provided for; the ladies are scarcely less so, for they are continually accompanied by lovely combinations of woodwinds."—Shirley Fleming, *High Fidelity/Musical America*, 10/68.

"It teems with melodic life. Its orchestra treatment has the amiable quality of sounding more modern than it is (plenty of clever percussive effects), and its total impression is of an opera meant above all to be enjoyed."—Herbert Kupferberg, *The National Observer*.

"The very opening bars of *Twelfth Night* are the outline of the melody which Feste sings at the very end of the play. This setting of 'The wind and the rain' and additional motifs, instrumental groupings and tonal relationships for each of the characters provide the musical basis for the opera. With the single exception of Feste's singing of 'Sigh no more, ladies', the libretto remains faithful to the words of Shakespeare.

"Because of the exclusion of some of the characters and the condensation of many of the speeches for musical purposes, the opera is not an attempt to musicalize Shakespeare but rather to use his magic as the focal point of the dramatic implications and the humor and bittersweet relationship among the protagonists of the drama."—David Amram.

"Amram shows remarkable skill in ensemble writing, thematic development and musical characterization. Moreover, throughout the score, [he] lets the singers' vocal lines—and most importantly, their words—be heard to optimum effect. He also show a sure hand in orchestration." —Bill Zakariasen, *New York Daily News*, 6/30/86.

"The score fuses unabashedly lyrical means with tart instrumental colors. It proposes songs clothed in mock-antique fittings, and it turns out to be an opera with such conventional things as arias, love duets and big, act-ending ensembles.

"It also has a couple of moments of sonorities so craftily realized that listeners take for granted what is in the air. In the second act, the Duke is singing while two other men sing wordless counterpoint. That creates an atmosphere of extraordinary richness which tends to magnify the impact of the sung words and the melodic line supporting them.

"The viola song at the end—a neo-Shakespearean pun—may be the most golden moment in the score.... The orchestral writing turns to gentleness and consonance as the work reaches its close." —Daniel Webster, *Philadelphia Inquirer*.

"Mr. Amram employs a flexible tonality in *Twelfth Night*, shifting between elegant recollections of Renaissance modality and his own lyric brand of contemporary style. What's most impressive about the score is the smoothness with which he leaves one approach to take up another. Feste's ballades don't stick out as sore thumbs even though they hark back to a bygone musical age. Mr. Amram has somehow managed to make them compatible with the arias and declamation of the other characters in the play.

"No less noteworthy is his ability to strike a balance between full-scale arias and straightforward dramatic delivery, between solos, duets, trios, and all sorts of other ensembles. The music shifts from comic to serious to even passionate seamlessly. You never hear the gears changing.

"Finally, and perhaps most importantly, *Twelfth Night* is beautiful, plain and simple. And that's something a critic can't explain, and perhaps shouldn't even try to." —Michael Caruso, *Main Line Times*.

DOMINICK ARGENTO

B. 1927, York PA. *Educ.:* Peabody Cons, Eastman Schl of Music. *Taught at:* Univ of MN. Co-fndr Hilltop Opera Co (Baltimore), Center Opera Co (later Minnesota Opera). *Awards & grants:* 1975 Pulitzer Prize, Fullbright grant, Guggenheim Fellow, Honorary degrees York (PA) Coll, Valparaiso (IN) Univ; member, Inst of Amer Acad and Inst of Arts & Ltrs. *Works incl.:* chamber music, choral pieces, incid. music (*Oresteia, St. Joan, Volpone*), operas (*The Boor, Casanova's Homecoming, Christopher Sly, Miss Havisham's Fire, Postcard from Morocco, The Voyage of Edgar Allan Poe, A Water Bird Talk*), orchestral (*The Mask of Night, A Ring of Time*), *The Resurrection of Don Juan* (ballet), solo vce & insts (*From the Diary of Virginia Woolf*).

Te Deum for Chorus and Orchestra (c.1988). 40m *Comm. & prem.:* Buffalo Schola Cantorum, Buffalo PO, Thomas Swan, cond.
In six sections.

"As a 50th birthday present to itself, the Buffalo [NY] Schola Cantorum, the region's most venerable choral organization, commissioned Dominick Argento to write a major choral/orchestral work. He responded with a setting of the *Te Deum*, but with secular Middle English poems that he felt reinforced the meaning of the Latin liturgical text interspersed in each of the work's six major sections....

"Argento has produced a truly gorgeous work of about 40 minutes' duration, couched in a wholly comfortable but fresh tonal idiom. Its scoring produces a bright, positive timbre, with expert and satisfying use of the instrumental choirs against the voices, and with imaginatively selective insertion of crucial solos by horn and various woodwinds. On top of this, there is a frequent garnish of tinkling metallophones giving the textures an ethereal, gossamer quality. Expressively, the *Te Deum* strikes a fine balance between majestic sonorities and the earthier, jauntier rhythms that propel some of the English-text sections.

"The changes from Latin to English are generally accomplished with a marked alteration in musical character. Since some of the sections return to Latin at the end, there are, effectively, 14 clearly defined subsections within the six larger divisions. For all its undeniable beauty, these relatively rapid transformations give the work, when viewed dispassionately, a somewhat fragmented structural contour rather than a strong sense of longer line.

"The third section is especially appealing — a setting of '*Patrem immensae majestatis*' in simple, heart-tugging, American open-plains sonorities, succeeded by the Middle English 'when nothing was but God alone' in a rocking, mocking rhythm that alternately speeds, slows, plods, and gallops. The movement progresses harmonically in a circle of fifths, giving a continually more uplifting spirit to the music, concluding with the chorus pianissimo against a whispered flute—a lovely denouement. With performances already planned in three other cities, Argento's *Te Deum* seems a likely and worthy addition to the roster of major 20th-century choral works." —Herman Trotter, in *Musical America*, 9/88.

LESLIE BASSETT

B. 1923, Hanford CA. *Educ.:*Fresno State College, Univ MI, École Normale de Musique (Paris). *Taught at:* Univ MI. *Awards & grants:* Guggenheim Fellowships, Naumburg Recording Award, NEA, Natl Council on the Arts & Humanities, Amer Acad/Inst Arts & Letters, MI Council for the Arts, Sudler Wind Band Competition. Member Amer Acad/Inst of Arts & Letters, American Composers Alliance. *Works incl.: Colloquy* (orch), *Music* (sax/pno), *Nonet* (4 winds/4 brass/pno), string quartets.

Echoes from an Invisible World for Orchestra (1976). 18m *Commissioned & prem. by:* Philadelphia O, Eugene Ormandy, cond. *Other perfs.*Boston SO, New York PO, Cleveland O, Chicago SO, Los Angeles SO. *Rec.:* CRI Records (Stereo LP) SD 429:Baltimore SO, Sergiu Comissiona, cond. *Pub.:* C. F. Peters.
In 3 movements.

Commissioned by the Philadelphia Orchestra with funds from the National Endowment of the Arts for the U.S. Bicentennial of 1976, this work has had more than 60 performances by major orchestras to date (1988). It represented the U.S. at the Tel Aviv World Music Days of 1980. "The title comes from a description of music given by Giuseppe Mazzini, compatriot and close friend of Garibaldi, who spoke of music as the echo from an invisible world. The score was begun in California and completed at the Rockefeller Foundation's Center in Bellagio on Lake Como." — Leslie Bassett.

"Each of its three movements rises from quietude, creates an air of color, then subsides into the mist.... Bassett is an orchestral virtuoso. His expanded percussion group produced subtle shimmers and gourd-rattling. The strings were used in clusters of sound that were designed to glow. He piled brass voices in ascending pyramids, chose the English horn to sing a particularly resonant line in the middle section. The whole work is made from such attractive sounds and alterations of those sounds that it beguiles and soothes listeners and asks some poetic response." — Daniel Webster, *Philadelphia Inquirer*.

"Likely to survive the attrition of time and the caprices of fashion is [Basssett's] fastidiously made *poema*, inspired by a description of music by the Italian author and patriot, Giuseppe Mazzini. [The work is] lucid and euphonious... [demanding] absolute surety and subtlety of execution." —Roger Dettmer, in *Fanfare: The Magazine for Serious Record Collectors,* 3-4/81.

Preludes for Piano Solo (1984). 18m *Prem.:* Benning Dexter. *Pub.:* C. F. Peters.
1. *Flourish.* 2. *Toccata.* 3. *Processional.* 4.*Declamation.* 5. *Peal.* 6. *Aria.* 7. *Clangor.*

"*Preludes* were composed for Benning Dexter, pianist colleague at the University of Michigan, who gave the premiere performance in 1985. The piece is, in part, a transformation of passages from a work that had been begun for carillon but was never completed, never performed. Evidence of carillon technique can readily be found in the *Preludes,* and a fair share of the actual notes and gestures from the earlier source have made it into the piano music. Bell-like associations serve to enhance the color and variety of the pianism, yet the *Preludes* are beyond a doubt piano music." —Leslie Bassett.

Sextet for Piano and Strings (1972). 20m Comm. by Koussevitsky Fndn/Library of Congress. *Prem.:* Juilliard Quartet, John Graham (vla), William Masselos (pno). *Rec.:* Composers Recordings Inc. (Stereo LP) CRI SD 323: Concord String Quartet (Mark Sokol, Andrew Jennings, vlns, John Kochanowski, vla, Norman Fischer, vc), John Graham (vla), Gil Kalish (pno). *Pub.:* C. F. Peters.
In 4 movements.

"Leslie Bassett has spent much of his adult musical life at the Unviersity of Michigan, where he is chairman of the composition department. Since his *Variations for Orchestra* won the Pulitzer Prize in 1966, he has enjoyed a wide and ever-widening reputation as a composer of refinement and originality. He writes:
" 'The *Sextet* came into being as the result of several considerations. Nine years had passed since my last chamber music for strings, the *Third Quartet* written in Rome, and I wanted to work again with an ensemble capable of high intensity and poignancy. The piano was added for its incisive quality and extended low register and the extra viola to improve the balance between the strings and piano and to add warmth. I strove to make the work structurally clear, to project many moods, and to call upon a rich variety of instrumental colors. The music alternates between clearly metrical passages, which predominate, and unmetered areas in which metrics gradually move out of phase or disappear entirely. Metrical passages, often closely-knit rhythmically, usually place the piano and strings in dialogue. The first two movements are restless and fast, though quite different in mood and content. Both rise to climactic points, then end quietly.

The third movement is slow, the fourth assertive and driving. Much of the musical material emerges from three consecutive major thirds on D^b, D, and E^b above middle C, played against a pedal E in the same octave. These closely-grouped notes generate in turn many lines and sounds which have strong influence on all major areas of the music.' " — from liner notes for Composers Recordings Inc. Stereo LP CRI SD 323.

"The *Sextet* is wonderful imaginative craft at work in interesting material. The last movement is full of excitingly scuffy music." — Richard Dyer, *Boston Globe*.

"A tense and remarkably homophonic work." — Joan Reinthaler, in *The Washington Post*.

Variations for Orchestra (1962-63. 25m Winner, 1966 Pulitzer Prize in Music. U.S. representative at the UNESCO International Rostrum for Composers in Paris, 1966. *Prem.:* RAI (Radio O of Rome), Ferrucio Scaglia, cond. *Perf.:* Philadelphia O, Eugene Ormandy, cond. *Rec.:* Composers Recordings Inc. (Stereo LP) CRI SD 203: Radio Zurich SO, Jonathan Sternberg, cond. *Pub.:* C. F. Peters.

"The *Variations for Orchestra* was the last work composed during my two years as recipient of the Prix de Rome at the American Academy in Rome, 1961-63. Begun in late November of 1962 and completed the following May 1st, the *Variations* took shape with the sounds of the Radio Orchestra of Rome (RAI) in my ears. I attended most of the concerts of this excellent ensemble; and knowing that it would be giving the premiere of the work, I realized that I could ask for things that would be beyond the capabilities of lesser orchestras. I wanted to write a large, powerful, single-movement work that would place the listener in the midst of a form he could perceive and yet at the same time involve him in the gradual unfolding of a thematic-motivic web that would require his most thoughtful attention.

"The *Variations* are not based on a theme. The opening motivic introduction consists of four small areas or phrases, each of which is more memorable as color or mood than as theme, and each of which serves in some respect as the source of two variations. The first variation, for example, grows from the short repeated notes that appear early in the introduction; the second from a quintuplet figure and other minutiae from the second phrase; the third from a short but soaring clarinet line in the third phrase, etc. Naturally each of the variations exposes a significant amount of material that is not directly drawn from the introduction, but which I believed would be able to project and complete the sections. The last four variations take up some aspects of the introduction that may have been overlooked or minimized in the four earlier sections. Some of the variations are attached to those that follow or precede them, others are not. A sizeable conclusion, opening rather like the beginning, completes the work, after revealing once again several of the motivic elements in climactic context.

"The musical material of the *Variations* came about by very personal means. I was fascinated by orchestral texture, and conceived each section from a textural point of view long before pitches were considered. At the opening, for example, the double-basses are divided four ways, resulting in a quiet, low-pitched blur of sound that would convey the inmpression of introduction, of expectation, of upbeat. Likewise I strove to maintain what might be called a backdrop of basically unimportant sounds (colors, really; soft percussion, muted figures, harmonics, etc.) that would continue the expectant quality of the introduction into many of the variations that followed, giving the entire form a thrust toward the conclusion. One 12-note series (drawn from a set of pieces for women's choir that I had just completed) appears occasionally and certainly had some influence upon the musical language; but this work is quite removed from serial process. There is an unobtrusive tonal organization, non-functional in the usual sense, yet meant to increase the significance of two or three pitches.

"I consider the *Variations* to be one of the most deeply motivated musical statements I have made. Many of the technical considerations faced at the time of composition have by now, two years later (1965), been largely forgotten or confused with those present in more recent works; but I remember that I found the process of more or less continuous statement, yet statement with developmental or reflective overtones, to be very exciting. The variation process, free from many of the customary melodic considerations and obligations, seemed to me to given new depth to melody, even though at the same time it made melody far less memorable." — Leslie Bassett, from liner notes for Composers Recordings Inc. Stereo LP CRI SD 203.

Elsewhere, the composer adds: "The music is [meant to be] clear in form and readily perceived by the audience. It is music intended for professional orchestras or good community symphonies, varied and effective in mood and color."

"Bassett's composition [is] a work of genuine substance... a kaleidoscopic web of shifting instrumental sounds [which is] quite engrossing." — Robert Douguay, *Hartford Times*.

"The [Philadelphia] Orchestra played the American pre-miere... a piece from this decade and very much of these times. The difference between the *Variations* and much of the serial and pointillist music that has appeared since the death of Anton Webern is that Bassett has something distinct to say and surpassing skill in saying it. His big orchestra, augmented by celeste, piano, vibraphone, was used to stir up shimmering colors and points of sound. The variations are not on a melody but on moments of sound and those moments grow from germ to brilliant flowering. The instruments were balanced as finely as one finds in chamber music with massed effects sparingly and effectively used." —Daniel Webster, *Philadelphia Inquirer*.

ARNOLD BAX

> **SPECIAL FEATURE**
>
> The symphonies of Arnold Bax may no longer be regarded as "contemporary" with respect to dating, precisely, however they are clearly of a 20th century style and — many would argue — deserve a firmer place in surveys of "modern" music. So let us pause to reconsider major works by a let-us-not-forget British composer — of, in fact, *not* so very long ago. (Ed.)

B. 1883, London; *d.* 1953, Cork, Ireland. *Educ.:* Royal Acad of Music. *Works incl.:* chamber music, concertos (cello, pno, vln), *Symphonic Variations* (pno/orch), tone poems *(Christmas Eve in the Mountains, The Garden of Fand, In the Faery Hills, Mediterranean, November Woods, Nympholept, Summer Music, Tintagel)*, vocal music.

"Through the 1930s, Bax was an honored presence in concert halls on both sides of the Atlantic. Among his admirers were Rachmaninoff and Vaughan Williams; among his podium champions, Henry Wood, Hamilton Harty, and Serge Koussevitzky. But in the wake of World War II his unashamedly heroic-romantic music was judged irrelevant, and it quickly disappeared from concert programs. Realizing all too well how out of step he was with the times, the hitherto prolific Bax found his creative energies quickly dissipating.

"There it might have ended, but Bax now seems in the middle of fully a second post-mortem revival. His music is still a rarity in the concert hall, even in his native England, but on recordings it's taken on a life comparable to the heydays of the 30s. The biggest contributors to the new Baxian wave are England's Chandos Records and the Scottish conductor Bryden Thomson, who have just completed [1989] a new survey of all seven of the composer's symphonies,[15] plus nearly all the tone poems and concertos. The Chan-

---

15 In fact, there are eight symphonies, including *Spring Fire* (1913). The latter appears on a Chandos disc performed by Vernon Hadley and the Royal PO (see below). A major study of the composer by the author of many of the notes for this entry has also been published recently — *Bax: A Composer and His Times* by Lewis Foreman (Scolar Press, 1984). (Ed.)

dos project had a notable, if less comprehensive, precursor in a series of Bax recordings done by the Lyrita label back in the 1960s and 70s....

"Bax had, in a sense, two styles. One, mainly early, was Scriabinesque—impressionistic, highly colored and sometimes a little overheated. It was a natural voice for a composer who as an adolescent had fallen under the spell of Yeats's early poetry and the rest of the Celtic Twilight world of fairies and sprites. But he found inspiration, too, in the real world of rugged seascapes, notably those of western Ireland and Scotland; much about his music seems windswept and wave-washed.

"If hazy, Scriabinesque atmosphere dominates Bax's tone poems, there's more than a little of the sea's ruggedness, even violence, in the seven symphonies that were products of his maturity. (He was nearly 40 before penning the First.) The experience of the early tone poems tells in the opulent orchestrations, but the symphonies' content is sterner stuff; nowhere will you find a closer musical equivalent to Yeats's 'terrible beauty'....

"Conventional wisdom among some British critics holds that the last four lack the coherence of the first three. But there's a certain distillation process, too: the later symphonies open themselves to a directness of utterance—to boldly memorable tunes, even—that's rare earlier on. The *Sixth*'s opening imprints itself immediately on the memory, and the *Seventh* has some rollicking ideas hardly less arresting; [while] the *Fourth* is the most uncomplicatedly cheerful of the lot." —Scott Cantrell, in *The New York Times*, 7/7/89.

Spring Fire (symphony) for Orchestra (1913). *Rec.:* Chandos Records (Stereo LP) ABRD 1180: Royal PO, Vernon Hadley, cond. 1. *In the Forest Before Dawn* (3m)—2. *Daybreak and Sunrise* (5m). 3. *Full Day* (7m). 4. *Woodland Love (Romance)* (8m). 5. *Maenads* (8m).

"The British composer Arnold Bax came to maturity at the time Richard Strauss, Debussy and Sibelius were first appreciated by London music lovers. Although Bax was enchanted by these composers their influence was soon absorbed into a highly personal musical language which he developed during the decade before the First World War. Bax's reputation largely rests on his orchestral music, and immediately after that conflict he was launched into British musical life with a succession of colorful and evocative scores, yet many of the vivid orchestral works which he wrote during his development have remained unheard for years—indeed, Bax never heard *Spring Fire!* Now that we know these earlier orchestral scores we can appreciate that the high point of his creativity started much earlier than any previous commentators (including the composer himself) have given him credit for.

"At the climax of his early maturity his development was stimulated by a then fashionable paganism under the all-pervading influences of Diaghilev's *Ballets Russes* and [its] composers. In this mood Bax became particularly keen on certain poems by Swinburne, writing the tone-poem *Nympholept* to evoke a 'perilous pagan enchantment haunting the midsummer forest.' The evocative first chorus in Swinburne's poem *Atalanta in Calydon*, then only recently set chorally by Bantock, stimulated Bax's imagination, and he conceived *Spring Fire*, which was written during 1913. It was probably his most unlucky score. The first performane at the 1914 Norwich Festival was cancelled owing to the outbreak of the First World War. In 1916 it was announced for inclusion in a Royal Philharmonic Society concert conducted by Sir Thomas Beecham but at the last minute cancelled owing to its difficulty. In 1919 Bax's friend Balfour Gardiner again had it on a list of works to be performed that year but was unable to bring it to performance. It remained unperformed for the remainder of Bax's life, and in 1964 the present writer was loaned what was believed to be the only manuscript score, which he returned to Chappell & Co. the night before their catastrophic fire in which it was destroyed. Later another score was discovered, but for several years the work was believed lost and unplayable.

"Bax regarded *Spring Fire* 'as a kind of freely-worked symphony.' The surviving manuscript score numbers the movements I to V, though in the fair copy score destroyed in 1964 Bax had run the first two together and numbered them I to IV.

"The first section is headed 'In the Forest Before Dawn'. In this section, Bax wished 'to suggest the uncertain and pensive hour immediately before daybreak in the woodlands. It has been raining. The branches drip softly, and a damp delicate fragrance rises from the earth.' The second section, 'Daybreak and Sunrise', follows without a break. Bax continued: 'The rippling and dripping sounds cease suddenly, and there is a strange hush. Then — very remotely — wind instruments begin to sound short, capricious figures, as though the beautiful and quaint denizens of antique woods were awakening from their winter sleep, and were still calling to one another through the brakes and long distances of rainy leaves.

"'The light spreads rapidly, and soon the whole forest is astir. The nymphs stretch their languid arms in the copses, and fauns and satyrs, and bizarre half-human shapes skip with mad antics down the deep glades. The sun rises on a glittering and dazzling earth.'

"The crescendo that ends the first two parts leads straight into the *Allegro vivace* of the third, 'Full Day'. For the first time a specific quotation from Swinburne heads the score:

> Come with bows bent and emptying of quivers,
> Maiden Most Perfect, lady of light,
> With a noise of wind and many rivers,
> With a clamour of waters, and with might.

Part Four, *Woodland Love*, now follows and is called 'Romance' by the composer. The music is marked '*Molto Moderato* (Half the Time of the Preceding)'.

> For winter rains and ruins are over.
> And all the season of snows and sins,
> The days dividing lover and lover,
> The light that loses, the night that wins.
>
> And time remembered is grief forgotten,
> And frosts are slain and flowers begotten
> And in green underwood and cover
> Blossom by blossom the Spring begins.

This is one of young Bax's favorite moods and the music opens with a melody marked 'Romantic and Glowing'. Shortly the marking 'drowsily' appears and it thus continues as the clarinet and oboe have solos before harps and piano fill out the texture. The movement ends with a characteristic Baxian sound: woodwind and then trumpets and horns weave a gentle fabric of orchestral color over low string chords and rippling harp arpeggios and it 'finally almost dies away in some strange harmony as though the forest-lovers had become drugged with their own ecstatic dream.'

"Bax calls the fifth movement 'Maenads'. The lovers are rudely awakened, their self-absorption 'suddenly dissipated by the approach of a turbulent rout of satyrs and maenads.'

> And Pan by noon and Bacchus by night,
> Fleeter of foot than the fleet-foot kids
> Follows with laughing and fills with delight
> The maenad and the bassarid.

'The dryads, maenads, and bassarids fly dancing and screaming through the woods, pursued relentlessly by Bacchus and Pan and their hordes of goat-footed and ivy-crowned revellers. Gradually elements from earlier parts of the composition become mingled into the thematic weft of this musical daphnephoria. It is as though the whole of nature participated in the careless and restless riot of youth and sunlight.'" —Lewis Foreman, from liner notes for Chandos Records LP ABRD 1180.

Symphony 1 in E Flat for Orchestra (1921-22). Rec: Lyrita Recorded Edition (Stereo LP) SRCS 53 (also as Musical Heritage Society Stereo LP MHS 1586): London PO, Myer Fredmen, cond.; Chandos Records (Stereo LP) ABRD 1192 (also as CD CHAN 8480, cassette ABTD 1192): Ulster O, Bryden Thomson, cond.
1. Allegro moderato e feroce. 2. Lento solenne. 3. Allegro maestoso — Allegro vivace ma non troppo Presto.

"In an autobiographical radio talk in 1949, Bax referred to 'the ivory tower of my youth.' Certainly, his life up to the time of the Great War does not appear to have been overshadowed by any really shattering events. His was a serene and optimistic young manhood: at the beginning of 1914 he must have seen a golden future, his music was growing in success, his writings (under the pseudonym Dermot O'Byrne) almost equally so, he had a wide circle of talented friends, particularly in Ireland and was three years married with a young family.

"By the end of the Great War all this appears to have been soured: quite what it was that removed Bax from his 'ivory tower' is difficult to say. Perhaps just a cumulation of events against the backcloth of the War.

"Probably the real change in Bax's outlook on life came with the Easter Rising of 1916. Most of his literary confreres were involved, and as he wrote in *Farewell My Youth* (his short autobiography) after 1914 he was 'never again to see one of my Dublin friends in the land of Ireland. The golden age was passed.'

"At the end of the autobiography he describes how, cycling near Dublin, he had something of a premonition of the terrible events to come:

> As I stood there, panting for breath, a sombre cloud shrouded the sun, a sudden chill air came from the east, and I shivered. Reluctantly, I discovered that the magic of the day was gone. The wind grew colder and something warned me to delay there no longer. Soberly I rode down the long seaward hill back to town. What was amiss? Had I a premonition of the world tragedy looming over the horizon of a near future? Or did I sense the imminence of a more personal sorrow?

"The execution of friends in Ireland caused an emotional reaction, and 'with painful intensity of emotion just after the rebellion' he wrote *A Dublin Ballad,* a small collection of poems that make his involvement immediately obvious:

> For what last music did your thought await
> That rainy morning in the barrack yard,
> Fronting those narrow cylinders of fate
> While the slow seconds pulsed on dull and hard?
>
> Tonight the four great guardian surges throb
> Like funeral drums along bewildered strands,
> And through their crashing scum the cold winds sob,
> Flinging pale screaming wreaths to stars and sands.

"In the *First Symphony,* the slow [second] movement in particular seems to reflect some of the moods echoed in these poems. This movement is an emotionally charged elegy of quite unexpected power, and towards the end the music seems to suggest the mourner sinking down in numbed despair:

> They are stripped bare of all desire,
> Save to sink down on some green slope
> And snap the chains of nerve and hope,
> And numb the wounds of soul and sense
> In these old hills' indifference.

"Thus the emotional events of the closing years of the War—the War itself, the Irish rising, the death of his father, the break-up of his marriage, even the Russian Revolution—must have emphasised the feeling of irrevocable change. It is impossible to ignore the influence all this must have had on the fiery music of the *First Symphony,* written during the first half of 1921 and orchestrated during 1922. Any artist, and especially an emotional and mysical, introverted figure like Bax, a man of wide culture and sensitivity, must be influenced by [his] times and [his] personal experience of them. The experiences of the period 1916-18 undoubtedly had a shattering effect on the art of that sensitive musician, Arnold Bax.

"Bax had learned his mastery of the orchestra in a long series of tone poems written between 1905 and 1917, but his interest in sonata form grew out of his sonatas, for piano and violin and piano. The *Piano Quintet* (1914-15) and the *Symphonic Variations* (1916-18) are evidence that he was needing a larger canvas on which to work. In 1921 he started writing a *Third Piano Sonata,* but it was pointed out to him by Harriet Cohen and other friends that this was indeed a symphony. The first movement was orchestrated from the sonata, but the original slow movement was unsatisfactory viewed in orchestral terms, and so Bax conceived the present movement and added the 'scherzo-finale' uniting the last two movements of the conventional symphony into what was to become his own characteristic form, the final march-passage foreshadowing the epilogues of later works.

"The first movement is a more-or-less conventional sonata form, with an aggressive first subject group marked *Allegro moderato e feroce* and a typical slow tune for second subject. However, the composer's grip on his material relaxes very little during this movement, and it is fully satisfying. Bax summed it up in a program note written for an American performance in 1924:

> The fierce, almost defiant character of the first two themes colors the music of this introductory section, and seems to suggest some conflict. [In the development section] the music seems to express in still more emphatic fashion the idea of strife.

"The slow movement is marked *Lento solenne,* and is quite unlike anything else in all Bax. A searingly powerful elegy, of remarkable instrumental resource, and considerable emotional impact. Bax wrote:

> Here the mood is both mystic and elegiac. At the outset two clashing tonalities are sounded faintly... with an accompanying rhythm from side drum (played with snares loosened, as at a military funeral). Then 'cellos and basses give out a lamenting phrase; the principle subject follows, announced by muted trombones and tuba, with a continuation, a dirge-like phrase for trombones, over a rhythm in lower strings.

This movement is remarkable for the reminiscence of bugle calls in almost all its themes, and the power the composer creates with his solemnly marching trombone chords.

"The last movement is much brighter in mood. After a ten bar introduction, in which echoes of Bax's pastiche-Russian music in his *The Truth About the Russian Dancers* is heard, the music whirls away with quite unexpected lightness. The work ends with a kind of triumphal march derived from the idea that opened the whole work, and the end comes with a last big climax.

"Early in his life Bax was quite open about his sources of inspiration and the programmatic nature of his music, but as he grew older he increasingly insisted that what he wrote was 'pure' music. In another program note on the *First Symphony* he tried to reject any programmatic connection, as he mentioned in his 1948 broadcast:

> I wrote that the harsh and stormy music was an example of pure music, unassociated with contemporary events. Whereupon a New York critic upbraided me as 'the quibbling Bax' and added 'of course this music from beginning to end represents the reaction of the composer's mind to the Great War.' These are deep matters, and I must admit that scarcely ever in later years have I been tempted to seek again the ivory tower of my youth, even if I could find my way there.

"It will be noted that even here he side-steps the issue at the last minute. It seems inconceivable that this is not a product of that same creative drive that made him write:

> And when the devil's made us wise
> Each in his own peculiar hell,
> With desert hearts and drunken eyes
> We're free to sentimentalize
> By corners where the martyrs fell."

—Lewis Foreman, from liner notes for Musical Heritage Society LP MHS 1586.

Symphony 2 for Orchestra (1924-26). (37m) Rec: Lyrita Recorded Edition (Stereo LP) SRCS 54 (also as Musical Heritage Society Stereo LP MHS 1632): London PO, Myer Fredmen, cond.; Chandos Records (Stereo LP) ABRD 1203 (also as CD CHAN 8493, cassette ABTD 1203): London PO, Bryden Thomson, cond.
1. Molto moderato—Allegro moderato. 2. Andante. 3. Poco largamente—Allegro feroce.

"Arnold Bax... received the Royal Philharmonic Society's Gold Medal in 1931, was knighted in 1937 and in 1941, was appointed Master of the King's Musick, an appointment he held until his death in Ireland—in Cork—in 1953. The composer of seven symphonies and over fifty other major orchestral works and much other music besides, he has tended to be judged on a very small part of his total output. The first two symphonies are probably his most important works, and their almost total neglect for forty years has meant that a proper assessment could not be made.

"Bax was at his artistic peak—'on fire creatively' as he himself put it—for a comparatively short time, and even as early as the late 'twenties his overpowering *need* to write music was beginning to fade.

"The *Second Symphony* is one of Bax's very best works. It was written between 1924 and 1926. However, it did not achieve its first performance until December 1929, and that in America: indeed, it is interesting to note that three of the seven symphonies were first played in the United States, the *Second,* the *Fourth* and the *Seventh.*

"This *Second Symphony* depicts — at least in its outer movements — like *Egdon Heath* 'a landscape singularly colossal in its swarthy monotony,' although unlike haggard Egdon, Bax's vision is peopled with human figures, warm but fleeting, who flit across the bleak landscape. The temperature may be low, but considerable emotional forces are unleashed: as Bax remarked in a letter 'I put a great deal of time and emotion into the writing.' 'It should be very broad indeed, with a kind of oppressive catastrophic mood.'

"The first movement is in almost direct line from the tone poems, and contrasts with the opening movement of the *First Symphony,* which had been in a more traditional sonata form as was in keeping with its origin as a piano sonata. The mood in this movement is that of *November Woods* in which an emotional crisis was depicted in terms of stormy nature, and is even more convincingly argued.

"The symphony opens with a long introduction of some sixty bars, in the first ten of which appear four ideas that reappear throughout the work, notably in the outer movements. The introduction paints a scene as Bax has described, heavy with impending catastrophe, the tension being heightened by a chromatically rising bass figure.

"The eventual commencement of the *Allegro moderato* of the movement brings no relief. The music is passionate and tempestuous, and apart from two short slow interludes maintains a continuous driving energy that is most convincing.

"The opening of the second movement, *Andante,* is again reminiscent of Holst, but Bax quickly signs his name with the horn call in the second and third bars. The music makes its effect by almost entirely lyrical means, and is built about three interrelated climaxes, the first of which — a high string passage in running semi-quavers over a slow moving bass — is the emotional heart of the whole work; an affirmation of confidence in life in the face of adversity. The movement finally ends quietly, the composer only just missing the repose for which he had been searching ever since the outset of the *First Symphony.*

"The psychological interrelation of the first three symphonies of Bax has often been remarked upon, but is worth restating. The demon that possessed Bax in the *First Symphony* is really only presented in that work; having relieved himself of his burden in its stating, Bax expiates it in this *Second Symphony,* which can be regarded as a chart of his spiritual and emotional wanderings in the mid 'twenties. Thus in the *Third Symphony,* written in 1928 and 1929 after the composer had discovered what was to become his artistic retreat at Morar in Scotland, he attempted a stylistic and emotional synthesis, finding repose in the serene *Epilogue*.

"It has been suggested that this work might be viewed as 'one vast love-song', and certainly in the slow [*Andante*] movement at least the music would seem to support such a view — a passionate and finally exultant outpouring. Much earlier in one of his Irish poems published under the pseudonymn of Dermot O'Byrne he had written:

> ...a few poor songs of mine have crept
> Within the doorway of a woman' heart,
> And whilst they whispered there her eyes have oft
>   times wept
> Because her beauty made proud flames to dart
> Through one man's inmost sanctuary of dreams, and he
> In her warm tears found immortality.

"The last movement of the symphony is the most 'oppressive' and 'catastrophic' of the three. After a ten bar introduction *(Poco largamente)* the music erupts with a fury *(Allegro feroce)* that will surprise those who have only previously known Bax in his tone poems and chamber music: a hollow marching symptomatic of the prevailing mood. However the surprise of the whole work is the literal quotation of some twelve bars from the opening passage of the first movement, an event unparalleled in any other of the composer's scores.

"This movement in particular demonstrates Bax's orchestral brilliance and resource in a vivid way. The parallel with early Stravinsky and Ravel is particularly noticeable here. The use of piano, celesta and glockenspiel, as well as two harps add to the composer's palette a brilliance that tends to be missing from the more Nordic and ruminative later scores. In addition the low piano notes and the organ add an almost pagan power: one wonders if Bax is still thinking of the shattering events of the previous decade:

> Long strips of sky torn shred by shred
> To bind the cerecloths for souls dead,
> Mad souls that loved this tragic land
> Better than God could understand.

"The penultimate 59 bars are in fact an epilogue — more formed than in the *First Symphony* — although not marked as such. We can witness here Bax tentatively exploring the use of the three-movement-plus-epologue form that is such a feature of the later symphonies. The music finally fades *niente:* the desolation that Bax paints at the close will not be more fully realised in music for another twenty years and the last movement of Vaughan Williams' *Sixth Symphony*. And yet, there is some slight consolation, and peace will be achieved in the next essay in symphonic form:

> And now that time is grey with falling leaves
> And the long twilight hurries into night,
> Amid my country's ruined harvest-sheaves
> I sing my memories through the fainting light."

> —Lewis Foreman, from liner notes for Musical Heritage Society LP MHS 1632.

Symphony 3 for Orchestra (1928-29). *Recs.:* English recording, cond. by John Barbirolli; RCA Gold Seal Records (Mono LP) GL 42247: London SO, Edward Downes, cond.; Chandos Records (Stereo LP) ABRD 1165 (also as CD CHAN 8454, cassette ABTD 1165): London PO, Bryden Thomson, cond.
1. Lento moderato (21m). 2. Lento (13m). 3. Moderato (16m).

"After the *Second Symphony* [Bax] appears to have experienced a stylistic composer's block, and was consciously trying to develop his style. He achieved this in his *Third Symphony*. In the thirties this became the most popular of his symphonies. Conceived during the Autumn of 1928 and completed in February 1929, it was Bax's first music to be written at Morar, in Inverness-shire. Earlier works had been written in Donegal, but for the next ten years it was to Morar he went to get much of his music onto paper. Bax established himself at the Station Hotel, Morar, and 'there, sometimes in polar conditions, in a dingy unheated room, working in an overcoat, he proceeded to set out the sketch he had previously written with constant recourse to the keyboard' at his Hampstead lodgings.

"When it was written, the issue of programmatic music was a contentious one—and even composers who had quite self-evidently responded to non-musical stimuli were disinclined to admit it. Clearly the curious form of many of Bax's major works, but particularly the symphonies, is indicative of there being something behind the music, a fact commented on by critics in the 1930s. Bax never explained himself, and our only clue in the *Third Symphony* is a brief quotation from Nietzsche with which he prefaced the short score, but suppressed from the published full score:

> My wisdom became pregnant on lonely mountains;
> upon barren stones she brought forth her young.

"A few pointers to one or two idiosyncratic features are all that is necessary for the newcomer to the music. The first movement, consisting of alternately slow and fast music, is dominated by a compelling central brooding slow meditation, which occupies nearly half the movement. The crowning anvil stroke and what the viola player Bernard Shore called 'one of the greatest climaxes in modern music' are moments which once heard remain in the mind. The ensuing slow movement's horn and trumpet calls are wonderfully evocative, and at one point we hear sea music reminiscent of his earlier tone poem *Tintagel.* The Finale encapsulates the roles of scherzo and finale, and is concluded with a long magically quiet Epilogue, itself almost [possessing] the stature of a separate movement. The uttterly individual sounds that Bax conjures up in the middle section of this Epilogue are clearly the musical realisation of some mystical aural experience. He described just such an occasion in his autobiography: 'I suddenly became aware that I was listening to strange sounds, the like of which I had never heard before. They can only be described as a kind of mingling of rippling water and tiny bells tinkled.'" —Lewis Foreman, from liner notes for Chandos Records LP ABRD 1165.

Symphony 4 for Orchestra (1930-31). *Rec:* Chandos Records Ltd (Stereo LP) ABRD 1091 (also as CD CHAN 8312, cassette ABTD 1091): Ulster O, Bryden Thomson, cond.
1. Allegro moderato (17m). 2. Lento moderato (14m). 3. Allegro— Tempo di marcia trionfale (11m).

> I think that in the lives of all men there must be fleeting moments invested by the imagination from some intangible cause with a vast and awe-inspiring significance out of all proportion to the actual event.... For in such an instant the veil of enchantment that was woven about our memories in the cave of birth is lifted, only to fall again, alas! before our vision has time to become accustomed to the light that broods upon eternal things.... On very rare occasions its happens, perchance, to some men to be able to seize for a fraction of a second the hem of the departing dream, and between the clouds of its twilight hair to catch a half-glimpse of those fateful eyes before they fade again into the folded shadows of the ages.

"Thus wrote the 29-year-old composer, in his short story called 'The Lifting of the Veil'. It encapsulates his experience of momentary states of ecstatic vision which underly his greatest music. Bax was an intuitive artist who (in his own words) did not 'possess a gift' but was 'possessed by it as by a demon.'

"Bax came from an affluent middle-class family. Born in Streatham in South London, his most formative years were spent in the family home which stood in extensive grounds near Hampstead Heath in North London. He never had to take a paid position, and always had a private income.

"In 1902, while a student at the Royal Academy of Music, he happened to read W. B. Yeats' long narrative poem 'The Wandering of Usheen' and afterwards confessed that 'in a moment the Celt within me stood revealed.' He soon went to Ireland in such a state of spiritual excitement that his existence 'was at first utterly unrelated to material actualities.' Most of his time was spent in the far West, and in particular at the Donegal coastal village of Glencolumcille, a place to which for thirty years he was frequently to return, and where many of his works were written.

"His financial independence did allow Bax to travel widely, and in his twenties it was not only Ireland he visited; at least two extended visits were made to the German city of Dresden, and later he pursued a Ukrainian girl to Moscow, St. Petersburg and the Ukraine — incidentally taking in *Prince Igor* and the Russian Imperial Ballet on the way.

"Bax's earliest attempts at composition were piano pieces, obviously modelled on Chopin and Schumann. Later it was Tchaikovsky and Wagner, and still later Richard Strauss who contributed elements to his developing student technique. Then came Ireland, and he attempted to write 'Irishly, using figures of a definite Celtic curve.' Later still he looked to Debussy, Ravel and the orchestral apparatus of those composers who wrote for Diaghilev, in particular the early ballets of Stravinsky, which had so far-reachign an influence on the orchestral styles of the British composers of Bax's generation. In Bax's hands these many elements became totally absorbed to form a highly personal and instantly recognisable voice.

"In 1902 Bax wrote a *String Quartet* in A major, which was notable for being cast in three movements, Bax noting on the score that the third movement was 'intended to serve both as Scherzo and Finale.' Thus so early in his career he had already embraced the form in which the symphonies would later be cast. The following year he wrote another quartet — in E major — the slow movement of which, prefaced by a quotation from Yeats, was orchestrated as his first orchestral tone poem with the title *Cathaleen-ni-Hoolihan*.

"While in Dresden Bax completed, though never orchestrated, a massive Germanic symphony. The following year came another extended quasi-symphonic score, a *String Quintet* in G, which by virtue of its rich textures and extended working suggests a symphony for strings rather than a chamber work. During this time Bax had been rather half-heartedly tinkering with an opera, but although he wrote a five act drama under the title *Déirdre*, very little music was written, and much of what was finally appeared in orchestral dress in the trilogy of tone poems he called *Eire* — individually entitled *Into the Twilight*, *In the Faery Hills* and *Roscatha*.

"Although it is persuasive to try to see here characteristic elements of the middle and closing movements of Bax's later symphonies, really we have to look to *Roscatha's* immediate successor, the extended choral and orchestral setting of a pastoral scene from Shelley's *Prometheus Unbound*, to which he gave the title *Enchanted Summer*, to see a first convincing pre-echo of Bax's later approach to the symphony. In three sections but playing continuously, *Enchanted Summer* not only demonstrate's Bax's early command of the impressionistic orchestra but also contains an intriguing foretaste both of the opening of the tone poem *Tintagel* and the climax of the *Sixth Symphony*.

"Bax's most successful works during the Great War were orchestral tone poems, including the sequence of scores by which he is usually remembered — *The Garden of Fand* (1913, orch. 1916), *Summer Music* (1917, orch. 1921), *Tintagel* (1917, orch. 1919) and *November Woods* (1917). These all had autobiographical overtones, as did the massive three movement *Piano Quintet* (1914-15) — really a symphony manqué — and the extended *Symphonic Variations* (1916-18) for piano and orchestra.

"When it came, Bax did not actually conceive his *First Symphony* (1921-22) as an orchestral work at all, but as a piano sonata. Almsot immediately he orchestrated the outer movements, and wrote a new slow one conceived in orchestral terms. Within two years he was at work on a *Second Symphony*, though it was not completed until March 1926; the *Third* followed in 1928-29. Yet he was not really thought of as a symphonist in the minds of his British audience until the 1930s. The *Second* and *Third* symphonies were both first heard in London in 1930, the year he was working on two further works on a similar scale, the *Winter Legends* for piano and orchestra (completed 3 April 1930) and the *Fourth Symphony* (completed in full score by February 1931). Three further symphonies followed in 1932, 1934 and 1939, but by the Second World War Bax had said almost all he had to say....

* * *

"The *Fourth Symphony* was written in the Autumn and Winter of 1930. It is dedicated to Paul Corder, the composer son of Bax's composition teacher at the RAM, Frederick Corder, and one of Bax's companions in Dresden in spacious Edwardian days. (The dedication was probably a 'thank you' for the work that Corder and Marjorie McTavish, music teacher and mutual friend, did on the score, clarifying and simplifying Bax's notation.) It was first performed in Los Angeles conducted by Basil Cameron in March 1932, and in London conducted by (Sir) Malcolm Sargent in December 1932. Published in 1932, it was later Bax's first orchestral work to appear in miniature score, in 1934.

"Like *Tintagel* more than a dozen years before, this symphony marks the initial high point of a love affair, which again finds subconscious expression through the imagery of Atlantic breakers.[16] The sea may be heard in many of Bax's scores—he even admitted to its appearance in the *Sonata for Two Pianos*—and it forms a constant background to many of his Irish short stories written over the pseudonym of 'Dermot O'Byrne'. For example this evocation from the story called 'Ancient Dominions':

> From the depths arose the narcotic whispering of the tide, to some souls the most moving music that ever awakened the nostalgia for beauty unrevealed or lost on the wind.... At the edge of the sea the drowsy waves broke in a long thin crest of foam, rising and subsiding rhythmically with the beat of the tide, and a little beyond this the weltering turmoil of the bar glared under the moon. The white gleam of it was so sharp that it seemed at any moment about to burst into some intenser expression than was possible to light alone, as if it must break into some trumpet tone shrilling above the heavy crash of the surf. Further out the Atlantic dreamed impenetrably, an enormous grey allurement, tender and terrible.

Bax first stayed in Morar on the West Coast of Scotland in the Winter of 1928. Returning in 1930 he subsequently went there every year in the wintertime using it as a retreat where he could work uninterrupted. Mary Gleaves, his companion for the last 25 years of his life, accompanied him on these sojourns, which ended in 1940. In the quiet of Morar Bax brought to their finished form works he had started elsewhere, and the first substantial score to be written thus was the *Fourth Symphony*. Part of the first movement was worked out

---

16 In 1917 [the composer and the pianist Harriet Cohen] spent over six weeks together at Tintagel, in North Cornwall. In October Bax wrote his tone-poem *Tintagel*, which ostensibly evokes the ruined castle and the Atlantic, with overtones of the historical associations of the place. Clearly he was also celebrating his own passion in surging sea-music of memorable brilliance and vigor, as he had already done in the earlier ocean-evocation *The Garden of Fand*.

at his Irish refuge of Glencolumcille, but the seascapes that he essays in this music are mainly to do with the natural grandeur of the coast and islands of the Western Highlands in late Autumn and Winter, like Glencolumcille still a place 'lorded by the Atlantic.'

"Throughout the 1930s the critic Ernest Newman made no secret of the fact that although he liked and admired Bax's music, 'the connection of the ideas sometimes evaded me. As with all music of this type, we are conscious of something having gone on in the composer's mind that would be clearer to us for a little verbal explanation.' As he became older Bax was increasingly unwilling to essay other than purely musical explanations of his works. Yet in his letters he made clear what motivated his art, writing to Arthur Benjamin 'the only music that can last is that which is the outcome of one's emotional reactions to the ultimate realities of Life, Love and Death.' To Mary Gleaves he wrote of 'ordinary life and all the grimness which most of my music deals with.'

"In fact, the *Fourth Symphony* is a hedonistic and triumphant interlude between the more serious autobiographical works that frame it. For this reason it demands the best possible recorded sound, brilliant playing, and, in the outer movements an organ that makes its presence felt to underline the most exultant moments of this pagan celebration....

"The first movement launches straight into the opening theme which stamps out its *allegro mdoerato* over an E^b pedal colored by the organ's 16 ft. stop, which unambiguously underlines the key and at the same time gives a sense of some deep stirring or undertow in this vigorous evocation of the autumn sea at flood tide on a breezy, sunny day. Quickly a second idea appears, consisting of upward rushing semiquavers that fall back and then rush up again, still evoking the incoming sea. A pendant theme follows rising on a 'Scotch snap' only to fall back again. It will be elaborated later into a long *allegretto semplice* tune. Finally the first subject group is completed with an idea in running semi-quavers and a dotted motif that is repeated round the orchestra with strongly rhythmic decoration, and if this is still sea-music we experience a passing autumn squall with material from the opening ideas again in evidence.

"The long *cantabile espressivo* tune that now follows is first played by solo oboe accompanied by just four clarinets. Quickly a second tune appears on flutes accompanied — a typical Baxian touch this — by cor anglais [English horn], harp, and four solo celli playing soft chords. These two slow tunes constitute the second subject group of the first movement and are subject to lyrical working in the strings and the wind. Also worth watching out for are typical evocative but enigmatic slow interludes, as if the composer while revelling in the physical impact of his autumn ocean has sensed that the 'veil of enchantment' might have been about to lift, only for the mood to elude him as the sea renews its physical presence with crashing waves.

"In the slow movement [*Lento moderato*], even more than in the first, Bax writes sea music reminiscent in its technique of earlier scores in this vein. Perhaps most surprisingly is the ghost of Bax's 'dreamy and passionate' piano solo, *A Romance*. The principal falling motif of that piece appears throughout the music. Three bars before cue 21, towards the end, Bax suddenly introduces an extended quotation from it, starting at the fourth bar of page 6 of the published score. This orchestral realisation continues for 26 bars.

"The opening of the last movement [*Allegro — Tempo di marcia trionfale*] has a greater impact even than the first with its fortissimo muted trumpets trilling in triads, and slashing string chords. The music already has the hint of a great pagan march about it. A quiet interlude intervenes, and it is interesting to note how Bax can allow his brilliant musical tapestry to subside onto just one instrument — or in one place flute and harp. A climax ensues, and then after a further interlude Bax launches his triumphal march, which in a dozen pages of pagan splendor, with the organ underscoring the mood, brings this happy and invigorating work to a resounding close." —Lewis Foreman, from liner notes for Chandos Records LP ABRD 1091.

Symphony 5 in C Sharp Minor for Orchestra (1931-32). (40m)
 Recs.: Lyrita Record Edition (Stereo LP) SRCS 58 (also as Musical Heritage Society Stereo LP MHS 1652): London PO, Raymond Leppard, cond.; Chandos Records Ltd (Stereo LP) ABRD 1356 (also as CD CHAN 8669, cassette ABTD 1356): London PO, Bryden Thomson, cond.
1. Poco lento — Più mosso — Allegro con fuco. 2. Poco lento. 3. Poco moderato — Allegro — Epilogue.

"The seven symphonies of Arnold Bax belong to the years between the two world wars; the first was begun in 1921 and the last finished in time for the New York Fair of 1939. Many critics have seen Bax as a primarily rhapsodic composer whose inspiration is more suited to the symphonic poem than to the symphony. However, the very breadth of the symphonic canvas offered scope to his imagination that the symphonic poem could not wholly encompass. Bax was in his late thirties when he began his *First Symphony* and had many of his finest works, such as *The Garden of Fand* and *Tintagel*, behind him. Indeed, the First World War saw Bax at the height of his powers and the *First Symphony*, though it originally began life as a piano sonata, showed no mean grasp of the symphonic canvas as well as a genuine mastery of the orchestra. Small wonder that it should have created so favorable an impression as it did when it was given under Albert Coates in 1922 and later at the Prague ISCM Festival of 1924. Admittedly its debt to Russian music is as strongly felt as anything in his pre-war music: the pregnant opening motive recalls the kind of symphonic gesture one encounters in, say, the *Second Symphony* of Borodin, and the first movement has a certain compactness and cohesion that he did not develop in the later symphonies. Rather he followed the brooding and evocative Celtic element that one finds in the slow movement. The *Second Symphony* (1924-25) has this wildness of imagination and vividness and opulence of color that serves to establish instantly an atmosphere that is as compelling as it is wholly individual. The opening of the symphony offers a parallel with the beginning of the *Second Sonata* and though there are many ideas in this symphony that are conceived directly in terms of the orchestra, Bax's imagination was not idiosyncratically orchestral in the way that, say, Berlioz's or Sibelius's was. Likewise his piano writing bears traces of orchestral habits of mind even though he was a natural (and indeed formidable) pianist. The *Third Symphony* (1929) is more inward-looking than its predecessor though its sense of mystery is no less potent. It is the best known (or rather the least neglected) of the seven and for this very reason some Baxians have been unable to resist the temptation to underrate it. However, it is in many respects more characteristic in its range and variety of mood as well as its musical and imaginative resource than is the *Fifth*. The *Fourth*, which dates from 1931, is by general consent the least impressive of the cycle; it is the most self-indulgent and the least concentrated.[17]

"The *Fifth Symphony* was begun the following year and bears a dedication to Sibelius: it received its first performance in January 1934 under the baton of Sir Thomas Beecham. Much of the thematic substance of the symphony derives from its opening figure whose melody on clarinets in thirds is built on a repeated five-note rhythm with the accent usually on the fourth note. The idea is taken up by the strings and throughout the movement one is never very far from the contours found here. Nor do we move away from the initial key center for some time. Another feature of the themes of all three movements is that they move within a more restricted compass than is usually the case with the Bax symphonies though many of the usual landmarks are nonetheless discernible — ostinato figures, epilogue

---

17 Which, of course, is not to dismiss the *Fourth Symphony*. Among its many features are the lighter moods and the sea evocations mentioned by Lewis Foreman, above, including suggestions of "a rough sea at flood-tide on a sunny day" (composer, of the first movement). (Ed.)

complete with ground bass and the familiar three movement pattern. But the *Fifth* shows him checking the purely lyrical impulse to which he could give such generous vein in favor of a greater degree of motivic integration. Perhaps the example of his dedicatee prompted him in this direction even though Sibelius's mastery of organic thinking sprang from different sources. After the opening motive has established itself, the tempo quicks (the Più mosso three bars before figure 5) but the first contrasting figure comes soon afterwards (four bars after figure 7) when the strings outline one of those characteristic ideas of Bax's dominated by its opening syncopated rhythm. A short quicker section in quavers, first on strings then on woodwind, lead into a more lyrical idea (the first three notes of the scale of E minor turning back in chromatic step towards the tonic). This has been anticipated in the cellos and double-basses a little earlier on and is in its turn a preparation for a lyrical second theme. So far the music has remained pretty firmly in the environs of E minor, the tonic, and even the main lyrical idea (a bar after figure 19) is in the tonic major. This, then, is the melodic substance of the movement which Bax handles with his accustomed skill. The course of the movement is not difficult to follow and it ends with a return to the material of the opening.

"The second movement *[Poco lento]* has the same dark atmosphere and brooding intensity of Celtic legend that one encounters in the first three symphonies and its main theme (on violas, cellos and double-basses four bars before figure 2) is also related to the basic idea of the work. Its appeal is simple but powerful and much of the subsequent material of this rhapsodic movement can be seen to relate to it either in its rhythmic shape or melodic contour. After a brief eight-bar introduction, the finale begins energetically (it almost recalls the Holst of *Uranus*) and maintains its momentum apart from a slow interlude (figure 27) until the final epilogue whose slow ostinato anticipates the opening of the *Sixth Symphony*." —Robert Layton, from liner notes for Musical Heritage Society LP MHS 1652.

Symphony 6 for Orchestra (1934). *Recs:* Lyrita Record Edition (Stereo LP) SRCS 35 (also as Musical Heritage Society Stereo LP MHS 1198): New Philharmonia O, Norman Del Mar, cond.; Chandos Records (Stereo LP) ABRD 1278 (also as CD CHAN 8586, cassette ABTD 1278): London PO, Bryden Thomson, cond.
1. Moderato—Allegro con fuoco (10m). 2. Lento, molto espressivo (11m). 3. Introduction—Scherzo and Trio—Epilogue (18m).

"Conflict lies at the heart of Arnold Bax's seven symphonies. His rather self-indulgent youthful music had shown itself capable of tragedy in such things as *November Woods* (1917), the *Piano Quintet*

(1915), and the *Second Piano Sonata* (1919), but the *First Symphony* (1921-22) reflected a psychic upheaval that must have shaken him to the foundations. He has denied that it was the first world war, and we take his word for it that there was no *conscious* influence; but the Easter Rising was another matter. Padraig Pearse was Bax's dearly loved friend, and his execution rocked Bax on his heels; like Yeats in his "Easter 1916" he anticipated trouble, but not quite this. Purely musical considerations also play a part in the troubled atmosphere of the symphonies. Great and subtle beauty, bleak austerity, and sheer violence existed side by side in his musical nature, and they never learned to lie easily together. Symphonic form proved an ideal battle ground for these aspects, motivated both by the struggle of a richly imaginative mind with a logical form, and by his deep psychic conflict. The synthesis is unique and powerful.

"His *First Symphony* is a short, grim outburst, his *Second* broods over its implications with occasional eruptive violence, peace comes fitfully to the *Third*. This conflict is devastating—the sound of it is like great winged things tearing each other in their flight, and it is obvious that Bax was deeply impressed by the Demon's Chorus from his much admired Elgar's *The Dream of Gerontius*. The *Fourth Symphony* suspends the conflict for a moment in its boisterous good humor, the legendary *Fifth* brings to the fore, in its finale, a kind of theme that Bax himself called 'liturgical', which is heard to triumph over a dance of pagan abandon. The seeds of further conflict are thus sown. The calm, serene *Seventh* forms a kind of Epilogue (a typical Bax device) to the whole sequence; but in between the *Sixth* bursts in fury.

"The *Sixth Symphony* was written in 1934, mainly in Morar, Inverness-shire, and performed for the first time at a Royal Philharmonic Society concert on November 21, 1935, under Sir Hamilton Harty. Those who know (and love) the northwest coast of Soctland will find the *Sixth Symphony* one of music's most uncanny psychic equivalents; this music is redolent of that wild beauty. It is not out of the question that Bax, like Walton in his *First* and Vaugham Williams in his *Fourth*, was troubled by a sense of the coming passing of worlds. The Introduction to the first movement opens with a grinding ground-bass that is to be heard on and off throughout the movement, topped by a barking brass phrase. This ostinato is speeded up to form the bass of a first subject of wailing urgency that enters with the *Allegro con fuoco*, after the *Moderato* has ended with a brief, grim pause that is one of the rhetorical strokes of the symphony. The second subject is unmistakable; in complete contrast it is a hesitant, poignantly beautiful tune for three flutes against the magical intoning of the four horns. That is the thematic matter of the movement;

the argument is the naked opposition of shy beauty and violence. It is a taut, urgent movement, with a stormy, truncated recapitulation.

"The slow movement *[Lento, molto espessivo]*, after six bars of oppressively scored introductory matter, during which the main theme is hinted at, exposes a haunted tune that is so typical of Bax that it might serve as the exemplar of this kind of Bax tune. It drifts through the troubled dream of the slow movement, sometimes fragmentarily, with the effect of Dante's happiness remembered in sorrow. There is another theme, with a Scottish snap, that is heard first on the trumpet, and which seems full of the spirit of place. There is a brooding, sullen climax, which ends in a strange episode. The first tune is heard in full against complex, gloomy brass writing; then a somber beating begins in the drums, and a derivative is passed in review, with the brass punctuating threatingly. The music fades out with a last, sad hint of the first tune.

"The Introduction to the finale begins with the first subject of the last movement as a clarinet solo, and goes on to a quiet but dramatic appearance of a liturgical theme. This in *Lento moderato* tempo that gradually accelerates to a fierce six-eight *Scherzo,* with the first subject leading in the bassoons. The mood is equivocal, the dynamics explosive. The trio starts abruptly, and is of quiet simplicity; its subject bears kinship with the lyrical themes of both preceding movements. As it ends the Scherzo resumes stormily. From now on a climax is built up that is the apex, not only of this symphony, but of the whole sequence of six; when it comes it is of terrible violence. It is heralded by the first subject in trombones and tuba, and then in full brass; but the last terrific uproar consists of the liturgical theme crowned with screaming woodwind. The tempest sinks to silence, with all the implications of tragedy. Instead, the Epilogue shines with a last assertion of imperishable beauty. Against magical scoring the horns intone the two subjects, united in peace. The last word is with the liturgical theme, accompanied only by a pedal in the double basses. Soft chords, and silence. Perhaps it was the solution, whatever it was; Bax's *Seventh* and last is untroubled by the conflict that had raged from the opening notes of the *First*. Perhaps its resolution gave us Bax's finest symphony." — Peter J. Pirie, from liner notes for Musical Heritage Society LP MHS 1198.

Symphony 7 for Orchestra (1938-39). *Recs.:* Lyrita Record Edition (Stereo LP) (also as Musical Heritage Society Stereo LP MHS 3618): London PO, Raymond Leppard, cond.; Chandos Records (Stereo LP) ABRD 1317 (also as CD CHAN 8628, cassette ABTD 1317): London PO, Bryden Thomson, cond.
1. Allegro (16m). 2. Lento — Più mosso *(In Legendary Mood)* (14m). 3. Allegro — Theme and Variations — Epilogue (15m).

"Bax's career was slow to develop, but as he came from a rich middle-class family he was under no pressure to earn his own living, and so he was able to travel and to follow his musical and other interests as the fancy took him. Thus he became something of a musical nomad, living unostentatiously though comfortably, and never remaining in the same place for more than a few months. After his marriage in 1911 he lived in London and later in Dublin, and during the Great War he had several addresses in the Thames Valley, but after the break-up of his marriage in 1918 he rented a small flat in Fellowes Road, Hamstead where he based his activities until the Second War intervened, when he took a room at a pub — The White Horse — in Storrington, and was based there for more than twelve years. It is strange that this man from a propertied family never actually lived in a house that he, himself, owned.

"In the period up to the Great War Bax developed a mastery of the orchestra that few of his British contemporaries could match, exhibiting a definite style of his own, yet not one that lovers of his later music would necessarily recognise — indeed, the quasi-symphony, *Spring Fire*, an exact contemporary of *Daphnis and Chloe*, opens in a remarkably similar way to parts of Ravel's score, yet neither [composer] had heard the other.

"During the Great War Bax was not a combatant owing to a heart complaint that troubled him all his life and ultimately caused his death [in October 1953, shortly before his 70th birthday]. However, he tried to enlist on several occasions and finally had to content himself with being a special constable. As a result he was able to devote most of his energies during the conflict to writing music, and thus at the end of the War had a large portfolio of compositions to place before the public which irrevocably established his position on the British musical scene as a new and 'modern' composer with something to say.However, Bax has yet to be performed with any regularity in the United States. (Ed.)

"There then followed during the two inter-War decades a series of seven symphonies which consolidated Bax's stature and eventually resulted [in his receiving numerous honors in his own country during the thirties and forties].

"[However] as the thirties progressed to their ultimate disaster, Bax found it increasingly difficult to compose, and became dissatisfied with what he was writing. At the end of his Coronation march *London Pageant* he wrote 'finished, thank God!' and the *Violin Concerto* which he also wrote in Coronation year — 1937 — was held back and not performed until November 1943.

"It was in this mood that he came to the *Seventh Syphony*. The devil that had pursued him through the earlier symphonies had been finally laid to rest in the Epilogue of the *Sixth*. The *Seventh* is technically the most secure of Bax's symphonies, and at the same time the most relaxed. The summation of the two main streams of his creative life—the symphonic poem and the symphony—at least as far as orchestral music is concerned.

"After he had completed the orchestration of the *Violin Concerto* in March 1938 Bax went straight on to compose this symphony. The short score of the first movement was completed on June 18 and the whole work was in short score by October. He then took the train to the wild west coast of Scotland, following the Mallaig line to Morar where he stayed, orchestrated the score, and soaked in his favorite scenery, with superb seascapes across to the islands of Rhum, Eigg and Muck. The orchestral score was finally completed during January 1939. The symphony was commissioned for the New York World Fair, where it received its first performance in June 1939 under Sir Adrian Boult. As a commissioned work he had to dedicate it to 'The People of America', but it is probable that Bax was at work on it before he received the commission, and his original intention is visible on the manuscript where Basil Cameron's name has been crossed through.

"The first movement is a seascape.... The symphony opens with a magnificent long opening paragraph of 60 bars, followed by a general pause. A pianissimo pedal A flat is established by tympani and divisi bass: a very soft gong roll provides a moment's coloration before the first theme is stated by the clarinets. It is a Sibelian sounding theme from the same source as that at the beginning of the opening movement of Bax's *Fifth Symphony*. The theme is four bars long, though Bax extends it by holding the final chord over a further bar, and it is then repeated in a higher register, the violas joining in, before a second falling motif on violas, celli, muted trombones and bassoons lead to a passionate restatement of the opening idea on the violins. The way the falling motif is itself dressed orchestrally and the coloration given to the ever-present pedal backcloth by flutes, clarinets, muted trumpets, and harp, is a fine demonstration of Bax's orchestral technique. Eventually the movement is fast, and though in Bax's usual symphonic manner there are slow interludes, they do not impede the flow or the impact of the climaxes. Rather are they colorful memories that occasionally intrude into an aging man's physical enjoyment of the waves smashing onto the shore, of the Northern light and the wild coastling with the dim purple shades of the islands out to sea. The momentum is maintained as the opening idea is transformed into a long Baxian tune, in the strings, only to be outdone by another long slow tune which first appears on oboe and celli. Having stated his material Bax proceeds to weave a varied tapestry from it, more tone poem than symphony, but fully convincing none the less. Eventually the long slow tune reappears at a passionate climax (between cues 39 and 42), the music quietens, and a strange closing sequence develops in which ghostly versions of the opening woodwind idea and the passionate theme reappear before the movement ends in a mood of quiet regretfulness with muted brass chords, still over a tympani pedal on A flat.

"The slow movement *[Lento—Più mosso]* is a clear ternary design, and is thus reminiscent, in shape at any rate, of the earlier symphonic poems. The opening alternates three ideas in a variety of instrumental colors, after which follows the more literary central section, marked *In Legendary Mood*. Finally the music of the opening returns and the music ends on a note of Autumnal musing. This movement has been something of a problem to early interpreters. The difficulties all relate to tempi and internal balance of the orchestral sound, and of the six conductors who have ever attempted this work, in the slow movement at least, Raymond Leppard succeeds in a way that none of his predecessors did.

"The third movement *[Allegro—Theme and Variations—Epilogue]* opens with a 32-bar ceremonial prelude, which alternates common time with 3/2, thus giving it a rhythmic flexibility and just removing it from the arena of the ceremonial march, though its effect is to remind us that soon afterwards Bax's music was to include film scores and music for state occasions. Having created a sense of occasion the opening quietens over a two-bar tympani roll and then the celli and bassi quietly state the theme, which is then taken up by the higher strings. The theme is then repeated in various different sections of the orchestra, and indeed throughout the movement the theme is varied but little, other than in tempo and rhythmic accentuation. So the effect is rather that of a passacaglia than of a theme-and-variations proper. Occasionally the music of the prelude reappears, but this is not surprising because the rising phrase at the very beginning of the theme comes from the rising tail of the opening fanfare.

"Including the variation that continues from the statement of the theme there are seven variations altogether, the last of which is the Epilogue. The use of the Epilogue as part of the structure of a symphony is something that was only developed to any extent by British composers, and although Vaughan Williams' *London Symphony* was probably the first major example, the technique was brought to a high state of perfection by Bax, in whose hands it became a major characteristic of his symphonic writing. Previous symphonic

Epilogues had attempted either an emotional resolution (in the *Third* and *Sixth Symphonies* and *Winter Legends*) or a triumphal one (in the *Fourth* and *Fifth Symphonies*). The Epilogue to the *Seventh Symphony* is a long one, in which the mood of hushed acceptance is curiously compelling and final, as if Bax is saying farewell not only to this work but also to his whole cycle of symphonies, and indeed to serious composition and his loved wild places where he had orchestrated all his major works from the *Third Symphony* onward. Shortly afterwards he was to write his autobiography *Farewell, My Youth*, a farewell which he said musically in this epilogue. His dream of fair women and of a land of the Sunset in the Far West had both turned sour, and he finally has to admit, as he had written many years before:

> 'Tis dark upon the mountains of the heart
> And all the lights have dropped from out the skies
> I know not whither the world's old glory flies
> Nor of its gleaming paths nor where they start
> I wake alone and desolate days begin
> And angry sea-winds drive the Autumn in."

— Lewis Foreman, from liner notes for Musical Heritage Society LP MHS 3618.

¶*Symphonies 1-7: A Footnote.*

"Among the definitions of 'romantic' given by the Oxford Dictionary are the following: 'preferring grandeur or picturesqueness or passion or irregular beauty to finish and proportion; subordinating whole to parts or form to matter.' Bax described himself as a 'brazen romantic'; and he added — 'by which I mean that my music is the expression of emotional states: I have no interest whatever in sound for its own sake or in any modernist "isms" or factions.' In his autobiography, *Farewell, My Youth,* he describes his first conscious apprehensions of beauty — a vision of the beauty of the natural world: 'It was the hour of sunset, and as we stood there, an unimaginable glory of flame developed in the west so that all the wooded heights seemed on fire.' Soon after came the sense of sorrow for the mutability of all things: the regret that a particular day of beauty was passed beyond recall wrung his heart so cruelly, he tells us, that he wept bitterly. 'This tenderness of pain, half cruel, half sweet, is surely an essential quality of the never clearly defined "romantic mood".'

"There we have the key to Bax's world of imagination. The combination of pantheism and mysticism often finds expression in pages of haunting beauty, such as the Epilogue of the *Third Symphony*. Although there is no specific 'program' for any of the seven symphonies, their feeling, their range of moods is similar to the best of the earlier orchestral works—the tone-poems with definite pictorial and associative titles, such as *In the Færy Hills*, *The Garden of Fand* and *Tintagel*. The first movement of the *First Symphony*, in fact, had originally been written as a tone-poem; only later did its symphonic character become apparent....[18]

"What justifies the name 'symphony' for [Bax] is the fact that different kinds of moods and emotions are vividly brought into contrast and conflict, finally to be resolved in a manner that is personal and also formally satisfying. Basically the language is Wagnerian, with strong Russian influences, from Tchaikovsky to Rimsky-Korsakov and even early Stravinsky. Debussy's colorful world, also, is of great importance. Added to this is the 'Celtic wonderland' influence, expressing itself in harmonic arabesques of sound, exhuberance of invention, richness of texture, imagination tending to run riot. The copious and easy flow of ideas in the symphonies has often resulted in music that is episodic in character rather than logically developing. Fluency has frequently taken the place of intense and sustained musical thinking. The result is like an instinctive drama of the emotions rather than a logically sustained argument; but the experience is nevertheless compelling and genuinely sym-

---

18 Raising the question, what *is* a symphony (or tone-poem). Is the four-movement *Manfred* of Tchaikovsky *(a)* in retrospect, a more or less "conventional" romantic symphony, *(b)* a sequence of four thematically and otherwise related symphonic poems, or *(c)* a symphony in four symphonic poem-like movements? Does the sequence of four *Lemminkäinen* poems by Sibelius constitute a symphonic evening, or program; i.e., do they collectively make up a symphony? Contrarily, are the *"Kullervo" Symphony* of Sibelius, *"Pastorale"* of Beethoven, *Symphonie fantastique* and *Roméo et Juliette* of Berlioz, and *Symphony No. 3* of Mahler not symphonies at all? If these are all symphonies, then why is *Ein Heldenleben* not? I should think that the *Symphony 13* of Shostokovich, powerful as it is, is probably not a symphony, and that Brahms' *Tragic Overture* probably is one (can be heard either as the first and only surviving movement of an unfinished symphony, or, as a completed symphony in one movement—*No. 2a in D minor*, 1880-81, along the lines of Schubert's *"Unfinished" Symphony* in B minor!). On balance—and giving only one opinion, of course—I should take a "symphonic" structure to be one which *(a)* is of an essentially orchestral character, and *(b)* transmits a sense of ample scale, weight, substance, consequence or importance—applicable, of course, not only to the *"Eroica"* of Beethoven, but also to the less grandiose *Classical Symphony* of Prokofiev, and also to hundreds of classical models (including "lighter" works by Johann Christian Bach, Sammartini, Boccherini, Haydn, Mozart). A true symphony probably *(c)* proposes that a journey of some importance has been undertaken—if only with regard to details of form—in the direction of a destination of some consequence; and, from possibly distant or ambiguous beginnings. Probably such a journey has also been completed—triumphantly, as in the *Fifth Symphonies* of Beethoven and Bruckner, or, more thoughtfully, and sadly, as in Tchaikovsky's *Sixth*. Finally a symphony ought *(d)* to *move* (regardless of tempo)—thus, almost everything written by Rachmaninoff may be essentially "symphonic"! (For some additional thoughts on this topic, see John Clark interview with William Schuman—Schuman entry— below.) (Ed.)

phonic. A tremendous — almost primeval — musical impulse informs these works. The moods range from ferocious defiance to calm resignation, from the feeling of impending disaster to the haunting sense of sadness and regret for things passed beyond recall. The symphonies are often dismissed as amorphous by those who imagine that Bax consists only of Celtic mistiness and 'atmosphere'. In fact they have considerable strength and frequent astringence; and formally the thematic material is presented with consistency and purpose. There is always great flexibility, but the resulting design is both disciplined and highly original. Most often the basis is sonata form. Indeed, the composer has said that the symphonies deviate little from the lines laid down by the classical composers of the past. The orchestration is a striking and very individual aspect of these works. Although Bax (like Ravel) preferred to compose at the piano (so as to be in direct contact with the material of sound) this did not alter the fact that the orchestral texture was a vital part of the original conception (as the composer's sketches abundantly show)....

"Bax is at present out of fashion and neglected. But he found symphonic expression through instinctive musical values, and great artistic sensitivity, formal and technical mastery, and a keen intelligence. A challenge of this sort cannot be indefinitely ignored. With other Romantic works regularly filling such a large proportion of our concert programs, it is particularly regrettable that Bax's *Third Symphony*, for example, should now be heard so rarely; for here the communication between composer and audience is as clear and vivid as in a symphony of Tchaikovsky." — David Cox, in Robert Simpson, ed., *The Symphony* II (Penguin Books, 1967).

JEREMY BECK

B. 1960, Painesville OH. *Educ.:* Yale Univ, Duke Univ, Mannes Coll of Music. *Taught at:* Mannes Coll of Music. *Awards & grants:* Mary Duke Biddle Fellowship, 3 Natl Fed Music Club Awards, Meet the Composer grants, New Dramatists Composer/Librettist Workshop Grant. *Works incl.: The Battle of Lexington* (wind ens), *Divertimento* (vln/rec/hpsd), *Four for Four* (fl qt), inc. music Shakespeare plays, *Once a Year on Christmas Eve* (children's opera), *Sinclair Listens* (orch), sonatas (ob, vln).

Composer statement: "Now is a very exciting time to be a composer. The orthodoxy of the avant-garde is breaking down and young composers (like myself) have found fresh energy in tonality. This is partly due to what I call the inversion of influence. For hundreds of years, the harmonic and structural ideas of Western 'art' music have crept into popular music over a period of time fifty years or so after they were originally introduced. (For example, the influence of 19th-century European opera and operetta on Broadway composers such as Jerome Kern or Richard Rodgers.) The inversion of this influence in our time stems from the fact that composers of my generation have grown up with rock music and all its sub-categories pervasively around them. To be a teenager in the United States in the 1970s and not to have had this influence, one would have had to grow up in a cave. Now, in the last decades of the 20th-century, we hear critics and listeners alike asking 'is rock dead?' or is it now 'a mere formula of chords and theatrics?' Are these not the same questions posed in regard to much of 'art' music today and of the last twenty years? It is my view that the future of both classical 'art' music and rock music lies in a natural integration of aspects of the two. Many attempts in the past at such an integration (by some so-called 'art-rock' bands and certain minimalist composers) have been simplistic pastiches. A true integration can only occur through a natural synthesis by a composer equally at home in the two traditions. My approach is to take theoretical and structural concepts developed by certain composers of this century (Berg, Carter, Bartók) and apply them to the new tonal music I hear—tonality which is functional, but not in an 18th- and 19th-century sense. It is a tonality derived from a gravitational tendency and the emotional drive found in the best and most powerful of rock music."

Ballade for Piano and Orchestra (1987). 10m *Comm. & prem.:* Deborah Jamini (pno), New York Chamber Players, Yves Abel, cond.

Ms.: score, parts & recording at American Music Center; score & parts also available on rental, The Ashmere Music Group.
1-0-1 B^b cl-1; 0-1 B^b tpt-1-0; perc; strings

"The *Ballade* for piano and orchestra, although in one continuous movement, contains both slow and fast musical sections which are pretty clearly defined within the larger scheme. The music throughout is really more of a duet for piano and orchestra than being for a soloist with accompaniment. The first slow section begins modally in B^b and attempts to rise harmonically. It gets to C, but then slips back to the modal area of B. In tandem with this tonal insecurity, the main melodic material focuses on a teetering back and forth between the major and minor third of the local tonic area.

"The fast music interrupts the ascent of modal areas and returns the music to B^b. The main figure here in the piano is based on an expansion of intervals from B^b, sometimes symmetrical, sometimes not. This is developed, taken through a variety of modalities, but inevitably brought back to B^b until the climax of the section: the return of the slow music, now in D. Seemingly, the opening attempts at a model ascent have returned, successfully, but the second statement of the opening material appears in A^b. This section then cadences in B^b, apparently ending the piece, only to have the fast music interrupt once again, this time in a superimposed minor modal area over the 'final' tonic major chord. This return of the fast music functions as a coda and, ultimately, brings the piece home to rest in B^b." — Jeremy Beck.

Quartet 2 for Strings (1990). 17m *Prem.:* Ciompi String Quartet. *Ms.:* score & recording at American Music Center; score & parts also available for purchase, The Ashmere Music Group.
1. Adagio–Allegro – Preciso–Adagio. 2. Animato.

"The structure of Movement 1 is based on the integration of the first two traditional movements of a string quartet: the first movement being in Sonata form and the second being an Adagio of some sort. Here, I begin with the slow music (in A–B–A form) which, after building to its own climax, moves on to the fast music. The structure of this music is pretty clearly sonata form with two contrasting themes preceded by an introduction. The first theme of the fast music is a syncopated version of the B section from the slow music. In the spirit of the form, the recapitulation acts more as a dip in the tension of the development which ultimately builds to the climax of the entire movement: the return of the Adagio. The form here is then A-B-codetta with the movement ending quietly and slightly ambiguously. The lack of complete closure allows the same material to be taken up in Movement 2 in a series of continuing variations where the traditional Scherzo (third movement) and Rondo (fourth movement) forms are synthesized.

"Harmonically, the opening gesture in the viola (a major seventh, E-D$^{\#}$) defines the tonal centers of the first movement and one of the main harmonic relationships between the first two integrated movements (Sonata and Adagio). The opening Adagio has a tonal centricity of E^b/D$^{\#}$. The Allegro which follows focuses on E. When the Adagio returns (to E^b/D$^{\#}$), the viola's major seventh has been structurally achieved at this climax. This harmonic relationship is then re-enforced at the climactic close of Movement 2 (also the true close of the *Quartet*)." — Jeremy Beck.

Scherzo for B^b Clarinet, Violin and Cello (1990). 4m *Prem.:* Greg Thymius (cl), Lee Chin Siow (vln), Susannah Chapman (vc). *Ms.:* score & recording at American Music Center; score & parts also available for purchase, The Ashmere Music Group.

"I am not interested in creating music which merely surprises, amuses, condescends or is obscurely intellectual. I *am* interested in exploring new tonal relationships using harmonic materials which are essentially diatonic and/or modal, but which have little or no relationship to the functional harmonic practices of the past. I seek to develop these relationships through the application of certain serial techniques usually only found in the music of atonal or 12-tone composers. Such a synthesis of tonal materials with serial techniques allows what appear to be familiar materials and gestures to be organized in new and subtle relationships within carefully defined tonal centers. In keeping with this exploration, I choose to compose in forms which are, at least superficially, familiar. For instance, the *Trio* section of my *Scherzo* for clarinet, violin and cello is not new material, but a variation of the opening motive: creating the 'required' contrast. Also, the return of the opening material is only the return of its *character*, not the literal music. Putting this discussion aside, the music I write is ultimately meant to be emotionally expressive; all the foregoing is in the service of this aim." — Jeremy Beck.

Sonata for Cello and Piano (1989). 16m *Prem.:* Fred Raimi (vc), Jane Hawkins (pno). *Ms.:* score, parts & recording at American Music Center; score & parts also available for purchase, The Ashmere Music Group.
1. Animato. 2. Grave. 3. Allegro giocoso.

"The opening harmonic progression of my *Sonata* for cello and piano presents the harmonic structure and inter-relationships of all three movements. The tonal center of the first movement is A^b and a pattern of underlying major thirds unfolds from this center. The movement cadences in an E major area. The second movement is in C minor, feigns a cadence in A^b (recalling the opening key) and then resolves to C minor again. The last movement (a rondo), as a tonal companion to the first, begins in E major (the cadence of the first) and ends with the final statement of the movement's opening material in A^b, returning to the tonality of the entire piece. Although I do not use functional harmony in the classical sense, I am interested in exploring new functional hierarchies. These often arise out of a particular type of voice-leading or the psychological sense that certain 'hard' dissonances 'need' to 'resolve' to certain 'soft' dissonances." —Jeremy Beck.

JOHN BECKER

B. 1886, Henderson KY; d. 1961, Wilmette IL. *Educ.*: Wisconsin Cons. *Taught at:* Notre Dame Univ; College of St. Thomas, St. Paul; Barat College of the Sacred Heart; Chicago Musical College. Edit. bd, *New Music Quarterly*. *Works incl.*: choral pieces, concertos (hn, pno), *Soundpieces* (var insts), stage works, 7 symphonies.

Symphony 3 (Symphonia brevis) for Orchestra (1929; 1933-37).
Prem.: Minneapolis SO, John Becker, cond. *Perf.:* New York P, Leonard Bernstein, cond. *Rec.:* Louisville First Editions Records (LP) LS-721. *Pub.:* C. F. Peters.
3-3-2-4; 4-4-3-1; timp, xyl, pno; strings
1. *A Scherzo in the spirit of Mockery* (5m). 2. *Memories of War — Sorrow — Struggle — A Protest!* (12m)

"This is the first publication of a major symphonic work of this mightily neglected composer. Becker was an avant-gardist particularly active during the thirties and one of the very few in the midwest who allied himself with the luminaries Cowell, Ives, Riegger, and Ruggles, all of whom he knew personally and who in turn held him in high regard.

"Becker is a unique stylist. His artistict stance was a retreat to a quite distant past from which vantage point he projected into the future as far as his vision would take him. From the wealth of language available to the composer on that timescape, Becker selected his vocabulary very carefully, restricting himself to essentials: pristine images of melody, empirical dissonant harmony, a decided rhythmic sense, a clear form. He was not alone in trying to find order out of the musical chaos of his time; but with Becker the solution was an elemental music, economical, direct, and sentient with humanitarian overtones. He meant to be understood, to have us know his meaning above all, and in the process to have us, perhaps, also appreciate his rhetoric.

"External forces (best left to a historical study) worked to keep Becker out of American concert life. The third symphony was one of the very few works to break through the wall of obscurity which built up around [him]. It was composed in 1919 and subjected to orchestral revision between 1933 and 1937....

"The symphony 'was written with an outraged spirit. It was not intended to be beautiful in the sentimental sense.' Becker's short title-page inscription further protests against war, starvation, hypocrisy, 'intolerance, prejudice, pretense, and sham.'

"The first movement, marked 'A Scherzo in the spirit of Mockery', is in ABA form (fast, slow, fast) with the second occurrence of A an exact repeat of the first, plus a coda. Precisely repeated motives, phrases, and entire sections are characteristic of Becker. Even within A, formal repeats are called for; and B is actually a 14-measure theme twice stated, the second statement being only a different orchestration which builds to a greater climax than the first. The A section is largely *tutti* orchestra. Its effect is loudly dramatic, motoric, precipitous and biting. The slow, expansive theme of B is a typical Becker creation. Separately considered, the melody, as well as the countermelody, is scalar, freely chromatic, with hints of tonality — not unusual phenomena in atonal or polytonal writing. The chordal bass accompaniment is in even, metrical beats and is made up of three superimposed fifths whose note selection is in willful opposition, for the sake of dissonance, to those employed in the other parts. Combined, the three levels of sound are intrinsically extremely dissonant but as they are orchestrated by Becker, they are in such a perspective that the dissonance somehow is less dissonant and the lyricism is intensified, Thus, the ear, although attacked by complex sounds, is able to capture the essential ideas with surprising ease.

"The second movement (*larghetto*; 'Memories of War — Sorrow — Struggle — A Protest!') is somber, dirge-like, and noble, rising to three great climaxes. The climaxes act as dividing points, for each results from a different working out of basic thematic material. The piano is often used: as a color mix, a reinforcement of textural density and volume, as a figurative line. Becker uses no 'irrational' melodic rhythms, a trait common to many of his works. Notes receive fairly even mathematical time divisions which make for disarmingly simple-looking scores. However, forward movement and variety are achieved through tempo changes — some quite subtle ('a trifle faster', 'a trifle slower', 'lingeringly'), and metrical changes (5/2, 7/4, and the half-beat meter 4-1/2 / 2).

"It goes without saying that the harmonic structure is extremely dissonant. But Becker is a strong lyricist and an inventor of simple, clear motivic ideas. Harmonic complexity is often merely the rhetorical mode for delivering concise, easily assimilable melodic and rhythmic ideas limned by a novel orchestral technique.

"There is little in the entire movement not derived from the first twelve measures wherein are four thematic units of two measures each. (Two measure units, in fact, abound throughout the movement.) The themes may be identified this way: mm. 1-2, T1; mm. 5-6, T2; mm.8-9, T3, a slight alteration of which is used for the second measure of T4, at rehearsal letter A (mm. 11-12). The working out of these themes is mostly in rhythmic dimunution in linear combinations. Themes 1 and 4 occur most frequently. The former provides the grave mood of the opening section in the shape of 10 slow half-notes in 5/2 meter, scored for piano, clarinet and bassoon. This is an arresting theme whenever it occurs in its original form. But Becker often subordinates this theme as an inner or upper melodic figuration in eighth notes. It is further transformed into sixteenth notes at the sardonic and brittle climax six bars before rehearsal letter D (piano and xylophone). Theme 4 is likewise given extensive treatment in dimunution (four bars after E) and also carries the movement to its powerful close.

"This work is an important example of American avant-garde symphonic thought of the 1920 and 30s. It should be in the repertory of our professional orchestras. Furthermore, it is well within the technical abilities of the college-level orchestra. The preface [to C.F. Peters' published score] by Don Gillespie cites seventeen sources for this authoritative edition and testifies to the extreme care with which he has rendered the score." — Christopher Pavlakis, in *Notes* (Music Library Association), 3/77.

NIELS VIGGO BENTZON

B.1919, Copenhagen, Denmark. *Educ.:* Royal Danish Cons. *Taught at:* Royal Danish Cons. *Works incl.:* ballets, concertos (cl, fl, ob, perc, pno, strings, vc, vln), operas, piano pieces, quartets, 15 symphonies, vocal pieces.

A note on the composer: "Bentzon is among the most prolific composers of the 20th century, and from the mid-1960s he has been composing even more abundantly than before. His talent was recognized early in his career, and as a result a large quantity of his enormous output has been published and recorded. In the post-Nielsen era of Danish music he ranks as one of the best-known and most extensively performed composers." — William H. Reynolds, in *The New Grove Dictionary of Music and Musicians* (1980).

Sonata 18 (Op. 459) for Piano (1983). 15m *Rec:* Danacord Daco 225: composer.
1. Moderato. 2. Allegro. 3. Adagio. 4. Moderato. 5. Allegro.
Sonata 19 (Op. 460) for Piano (1984). 15m *Rec:* Danacord Daco 225: composer.
1. Moderato. 2. Allegro. 3. Allegretto. 4. Moderato.
Sonata 20 (Op. 461) for Piano (1984). 12m *Rec:* Danacord Daco 225: composer.
1. Allegro. 2. Allegretto. 3. Adagio.

"In the past few years record collectors have had the opportunity to get to know some of the major symphonic works by Niels Viggo Bentzon, that extraordinary and prolific Danish composer. This year has been made memorable by the appearance of his *Fourth Symphony*, his landmark in metamorphosis technique. And now 1985 has been made even more memorable by the appearance of [the composer's own recording] of his latest piano sonatas. For it is Bentzon's piano music, possibly above all, that marks him as a truly important composer of our day....

"Bentzon's piano *oeuvre* deserves to be mentioned in the same breath with the eminent 20th-century giants of piano literature, and not just because of sheer weight of numbers. (And those numbers are staggering. He has, to date, at least 20 sonatas, six other programmatic but unnumbered sonatas, two sonatas for two pianos, five separate sets of 24 preludes and fugues, and dozens and dozens of other pieces for everything from one to 12 pianos!)

"So what makes Bentzon's piano music so exceptional, you rightly ask. Granted there is an indebtedness to Hindemith in Bentzon's contrapuntal intensity, but everything else is Bentzon's own. His music is old and new at the same time—tonal but highly chromatic in a lucidly intricate manner. The piano language is virtuosic, consummately logical in its development, colorful and subtly shaded, and most of all thematically spontaneous and imaginative. The man writes for the piano as naturally as you and I write letters to loved ones.

"The five-movement *18th Sonata* is the finest work on [the Danacord Daco disc, which is distributed in the U.S. by Qualiton]. It begins uniquely as if it were church music. A slow hymnlike theme, comprising the whole first movement, is put through various harmonic alterations above a wandering, soft bass ostinato. Then in the fourth movement the theme returns with the roles reversed: the hymn theme is in the bass and the treble offers up the soft ostinato. Very effective. The second and fifth movements are *allegros* that quick-step with the pulse (though not the melodic contours) of Prokofiev. The middle movement is an *adagio* built out of the contrast of chording and filigree.

" The four-movement *19th Sonata* is of a far different temperament. It has slow outer movements that frame the inner marchlike and lyrical movements. The melodic material of the first movement is reworked into a grand presentation of musical thought in the final movement—profound but not heavy, significant and not at all pretentious.

"The *20th Sonata* is in three movements — more rhythmically acute that the other sonatas and with an uncharacteristic open-ended conclusion. The opening *allegro* spins out tremolo passages that are integral to the forward thrust of the material. The second movement weaves an incessant ostinato line supporting a rather diffuse melodic web. The final *adagio* has a somberness and intensity interrupted only briefly by a few tremolo passages. The engimatic ending comes shortly after a quick reprise, in slow motion, of earlier ostinato lines. All good sonatas, and in the case of No. 18, superior music." − Stephen W. Ellis, in *Fanfare: The Magazine for Serious Record Collectors*, 9-10/85.

"My 18th, 19th and 20th piano sonatas were all composed during 1983 and 1984. In terms of economy of material and concentration of form, the three sonatas comprise a whole—none of them plays for more than sixteen minutes. *Nr. 18* – opus 459 – falls in five parts, of which the first corresponds musiclly with the fourth, and the second with the fifth. The sonata opens with a hymnic theme supported by a gliding, ostinato bass development. In the fourth movement the rôles are changed.; the treble takes over the gliding movement while the bass presents the hymn theme. The two *allegro* sections are characterized by my so-called *secco* piano style, which can be traced all the way back to my first sonatas from the 1940s. The middle section of this sonata is an *adagio* with a *cantabile* melody of a lyrical-vegetative mood.

"*Sonata nr. 19* — opus 460 — is equally concentrated of form and content. The sonata's two outer movements are slow and of related thematic material, where the last movement can be said to dramatize the ideas presented in the first. The *allegro* section, movement nr. 2, is abrupt and direct in its musical effects. It is succeeded by a lyrical *intermezzo* whose cadences lead into the more open and direct musical expression of the last movement.

"*Sonata nr. 20*, opus 461, falls in three parts. Tempo-wise the sonata is gradually scaled down through the three movements, the conclusion lying in the *adagio* of the last movement. The first movement, *Allegro*, makes use of a characteristic tremolo technique which here becomes an integral part of the steadily advancing musical pulse. The second movement is a lopsided *sarabande* — it seems to stumble over itself, all the while preparing the tempo for the final *Adagio*. Towards the conclusion, this last movement develops into a violent progression that is only resolved in a coda of repeated notes. The final chord poses a question, or rather puts an exclamation mark that requires no answer." — Niels Viggo Bentzon, from program notes for Danacord Records DACO 225 recording.

ERNEST BLOCH

> **SPECIAL FEATURE**
>
> The five string quartets of ERNEST BLOCH may be well known to many musicians and concert-goers (indeed, some would include them on a list of the outstanding works of all time in the string quartet literature), however, it seems safe to assume that for most of the rest of us they remain unheard and—therefore—"worthy, perhaps, but unknown", at best. As in the case of ARNOLD BAX (see above) it may seem stretching a point to include Bloch, himself, in the present sampling of "contemporary" composers; still, his *Fifth Quartet* is dated 1956... surely closer to our "own time" than, say, the quitar and string quartets and quintets of Boccherini, or the violin and other concertos of Vivaldi, which, I believe, *are* played with some frequency? To be sure it is too late for the composer himself to enjoy material or other benefit from performances of his music—but, shall we deprive ourselves of the pleasure of playing and listening to it, only because of this unhappy fact? (Ed.)

B. 1880, Geneva (Switzerland); *d*. 1959, Portland OR. *Educ*.: Hoch Cons, Frankfurt. *Taught at*: Mannes Schl of Music; Univ CA, Berkeley. Dir., Inst of Music, Cleveland; dir., San Francisco Cons. *Works incl*.: chamber works, concertos (2 *Concerti grossi*, pno, vln), *Helvetia* (sym poem), *Israel Symphony*, *Macbeth* (opera), *Sacred Service*, *Schelomo* (vc, orch), sonatas (vln), symphonies (incl. *Sinfonia breve*).

Quartet 1 in B Minor for Strings (1919). Ded. to Flonzaley Quartet. *Recs*: Columbia (6 12" 78 rpm discs) M-393: Stuyvesant Quartet; London Records LLA-23: Griller Quartet; Arabesque (3 Digital Stereo LPs) 6511-13: Portland String Quartet (Stephen Kecskemethy, Ronald Lantz, vlns, Julia Adams, vla, Paul Ross, vc); Laurel Records (Stereo LP) LR-120: Pro Arte Quartet (Norman Paulu, Martha Blum, vlns, Richard Blum, vla, Parry Karp, vc).
1. Andante moderato (13m). 2. Allegro frenetico (12m). 3. Andante molto moderato *(Pastorale)* (12m). 4. *Finale* (Vivace allegro con fuoco) (15m).

"This work marks the end of what has been called Bloch's 'Jewish Cycle' and indicates the transition between his life in Europe and his beginnings in America. Having begun the *Quartet* in Geneva, while completing the Finale after his arrival in New York, he wrote a letter to Alfred Ponchon of the Flonzaley Quartet with indications concerning performance of the work [of which the following are excerpts]:

> Mon cher Alfred:
> I am in the process of annotating the quartet. As I am not sure I have time to transfer these notes to the parts, and as I am eager to finish the work, I must make Machiavellian calculations. I would have liked, as is my custom, to write the musical indications. One keeps the other notes to one's self. But I am obliged to proceed otherwise. Forgive this 'soul exposure'. Also since I won't see you I will give you some indication which also could be useful so that you will know exactly what I wanted, what I experienced—I dare not say 'what I realized' as this is not for me to say.
> Part I—*LAMENTO*. Decidedly of JEWISH inspiration—mixture of bitterness violence and of pain.... This old bruised race whose sufferings throughout the centuries cannot be measured.... Recall those poor old fellows which you have certainly met in the streets, on the roads (around Geneva), with their long beards, sad, desperate and dirty... and who still have some hope (what hope?).... There is all of that in my Lamento. Later a very Jewish theme of faith and ardour (which is found in others of my Jewish works), and then harsh and raucous, and more Hebraic especially the viola part to which I could almost give words. In fact all that I am telling you here will seem idiotic to you. It is in the music you will feel it. If it is not, you must have pity on me.... This first part is perhaps the most difficult for interpretation because of its freedom—my perpetual variations of nuances and movement—fluctuations which must naturally merge into some unity.
> Part II—I am almost certain that this *Allegro Frenetico* will make you grind your teeth at first, regardless of your familiarity with modern music. My view of humanity is not too kindly. It is a horrible grimace, a witch's stew with no small part of bile. Here is continuity of tempi—it goes without stopping. (If it is Jewish, it's in spite of myself this time. I gave it no thought.)
> In the Trio of this movement *(scherzo)* I was inspired by reminiscences of the painter Gauguin. There is some Tahiti in here, distant Pacific isles at any rate, especially in that or-

namental passage where the four instruments, leaving their role for an instant, become almost exotic; here sonority alone and polyrhythm is required.... I don't doubt that you will find the manner in which to render the color I intend, that I imagine... souvenirs of colonial expositions, in default of world travel experiences which have been beyond my means to date. (But after all I may have failed utterly.) *Je me suis 'fichu dedans' jusqu'au cou*. Hell is paved with the best intentions... you will find abuses *frenetico, feroce, furioso* in this *scherzo*....

Part III — *PASTORALE*. I have already written to you about this. It was composed almost entirely in open air, in the woods, the mountains. (I owe it to myself!) Let me explain. For ten years, I have been taking notes for a great symphony, *On the Mountains*. Life has not been kind to me; I've had to hold back, to wait. I was too bitter to write this work of peace and calm. So at times, rarely, I have poured a part of it in some shorter works. The *Pastorale* is one of them, though there is nothing 'pastoral' in the usual sense of the word, you'll see. It is rather a 'reverie' in the solitude of nature. I hope that my music will speak better than what I wrote.

The theme of the *Lamento* comes back later, full and serene, almost with affection. The theme following the viola could be the land. For me, it smells of smoked lard, the milking shed.... Here is a strange thing, this theme came I know not why. I can't help it. It belonged as well as the next theme, to a hunting scene in a project dating ten years ago for a lyric drama 'in Prehistoric epoch' (Lacustre)... a sort of savage lullaby. I explain all this because I find no other explanation myself....

I am sending you I. II. III — the score and parts by post. Best wishes from
  E.B.
    (The *FINALE* I hope to send next week)

"*FINALE — VIVACE ALLEGRO CON FUOCO*. There is no record of Bloch's sending more information on this movement to Ponchon, but a brief statement about this was published later:

> The *FINALE* is rhapsodic in style and intended to emphasize the subtle bond of character which without a set program links together the four movements of the Quartet.

"A better description of the *Finale* is found in David Hall's summary for the premiere recording by the Stuyvesant Quartet:

> It is the summing up, beginning with an introduction that recalls thematic materials from the three preceding move-

ments. The thematic materials of the main part of the movement bespeak conflict and lamentation, leavened by an occasional ray of hope. The development of these themes serves to intensify the element of conflict and to almost burst the bonds of the chamber music medium. The outcome is signaled in the funeral epilogue and a recall of the Quartet's initial motif together with the Swiss themes from the third movement. The end is the peace that come with resignation.

—Suzanne Bloch, from liner notes for Arabesque Digital Stereo LP recording 6511-13.

"Bloch was often at great pains to clarify [his intentions for works of his hebraic or 'Jewish Cycle', such as *Schelomo*, the first quartet, *Israel Symphony*, and *Baal Shem*]: 'I do not propose or desire to attempt a reconstruction of the music of the Jews... or to base my work on melodies more or less authentic. I am not an archaeologist. I believe that the most important thing is to write good and sincere music — my music. It is rather the Hebrew spirit that interests me, the complex, ardent, agitated soul that vibrates for me in the bible.' And later: 'To what extent it is Jewish, to what extent it is just Ernest Bloch, of that I know nothing. The future alone will decide.'

"His philosophy can be traced back to his apprenticeship with Knorr in Leipzig. He acknowledged that Knorr taught him to think independently and develop his own musical personality. It is interesting to look at Knorr's other pupils, for among them were Cyril Scott, Hans Pfitzner and Ernst Toch. When you add Bloch's name to this list, a more disparate group is hard to imagine! Bloch obviously continued this attitude in his own extensive teachings, for among his students are Roger Sessions, Bernard Rogers and Quincy Porter.

"The string quartet of 1916 was Bloch's first published chamber music, and he was 36 when he wrote it. It is the musical bridge of his emigration to the United States, for the first three movements were written in Switzerland and the last on his arrival in New York. He credits Alfred Pochon, of the famous Flonzaley Quartet, with encouraging him to finish what were rough drafts which obviously impressed Pochon when they were shown to him on a visit to Switzerland. The circumstances of its compositon, as well as the work itself, were to remain very special to Bloch: 'this quartet was composed at a period of double crisis; the crisis of the world, and the crisis of my own life, the expatriation from my native country, Switzerland. It certainly shows the traces of both — without being an 'autobiograph', as one has written, it embodies in a certain sense my *Weltanschauung* at the age of 36.... No work of mine, since that time, can be compared to it in this respect.'

"Bloch wrote his own notes for the first recording of the work on 78's (Stuyvesant Quartet) and in them was at pains to correct the view that the work is rhapsodic, as it is often described:

> The whole quartet falls into the regular "classical" form. It may appear very free at times, melodically, modally, rhythmically, but it certainly is neither "rhapsodical" nor freer, for instance, than the first movement of *Eroica* or of the *String Quartet in F, Op. 59*, with their stupendous liberties of invention and development of material.

"The quartet is in four movements, beginning with an anguishing *Andante moderato*. After a probing entrance, the cyclic or motto theme (to occur throughout the work, excepting the second movement) is stated in a mournful descending phrase from the first violin and answered by the cello. This asserts itself and leads to a quotation from *Schelomo* (just written) which is freely treated. A bridge, *Tranquillo*, is followed by the second subject. The development of the motto and two themes is an intensely troubled and searching one that leaves a strong feeling of discontent as the movement closes.

"The second movement, *Allegro frenetico*, is the most striking of the quartet. A ferocious outburst of considerable disturbance is augmented by irregular rhythms and string writing devised to magnify the sound of the four instruments (an arrangement for full string orchestra of this quartet would be a fresh addition to the repertoire). This is contrasted by a middle section of complete change of mood. Bloch describes this calm episode:

> It has been inspired by a distant recollection of Gaugin,
> whose paintings had deeply impressed me a few years before.

This reference would have to have come from the composer. The tumult resumes leading to a coda prefaced by 'faint memories of Tahiti' and a brutal *Presto* ending.

"The third movement, *Andante molto moderato*, is a pastorale. This movement of respite opens with the evocation of another world: 'nature, contemplation and dreams, far away from men's struggles.' This mood passes on to the Swiss pastorale which in turn changes to a kind of naive folksong which Bloch termed 'prehistoric lullaby' — a visionary dream which is interrupted and returns the listener to the opening of the movement.

"The fourth movement, *Vivace*, structurally is a sonata with introduction and extensive coda. It opens re-invoking the pastorale, but it is quickly borken up by the return of the motto in tense accents, followed by quotations from the second and third movements. The movement proper begins propelling three themes of varied character through individual developments of great invention, eloquence and energy. The struggles of the first movement return and cover a range of expression from utter desolation to slim rays of hope, here and there. The coda, or epilogue, is funereal music interrupted by recollections of previous motives, and the quartet ends with a feeling of resigned acceptance.

"Bloch was to write four more string quartets with a surprising 30 years separating the first from the second (1946). These two quartets are his greatest achievements in chamber music." — John Erling, from liner notes for Laurel Records LP LR-120.

Quartet 2 for Strings (1946). Ded. to Alex Cohen. N.Y. Music Critics Circle Award, 1947. *Perf.:* Griller Quartet. *Recs:* London Records LLA-23: Griller Quartet; Arabesque (3 Digital Stereo LPs) 6511-13: Portland String Quartet; Laurel Records (Stereo LP) LR-126: Pro Arte Quartet.
1. Moderato (7m). 2. Presto (Scherzo) (8m). 3. Andante (8m). 4. Allegro molto (14m).

"After 1941 there is a marked attenuation of a specifically 'Jewish' quality to [Bloch's] compositions (with the obvious exception of the 1951 *Suite Hebraic*), or at least that element is given much more subjective treatment in his music. There is no radical change in his style during this period except for this one element—the rhapsodic expression, rhythmic drive and dramatic temperament are still there, but everything is more tightly conceived. The *Second Quartet* is a prime example of this: it strongly resembles the *First Quartet* in architecture but at little more than half the length.

"Bloch began work on it in 1940, but the Second World War had a crushing effect on him, and he did not complete it until 1946 (only the *Suite Symphonique* was published during the war). In a letter to his daughter he wrote: 'It will be very dry, not easy to listen to and I doubt it will be liked.' He was to be dumbfounded by Ernest Newman's review of the Griller Quartet's premiere of it in England in 1946. Newman wrote: 'In my opinion, it is the finest work of our time in this genre, one that is worthy to stand beside the last quartets of Beethoven.' (!)

"The first movement, *Moderato,* begins in the violin with a motto theme of a mysterious searching nature and, like so many of Bloch's works, this motto permeates the entire quartet giving it more than just a thematic unity. One by one the other strings join in, and it is developed in an atmosphere of Blochian uncertainty. This is soon broken by the appearance of a second theme in the viola and cello, again of mysterious stamp. The interplay reaches a pause, and the first violin returns with the motto, developing it, *cantabile,* over an excited accompaniment. A recapitulation, followed by the re-appearance of the second theme, *pianissimo,* fades out with the motto again in the first violin.

"The second movement, *Presto,* is really a scherzo with an initial theme, highly syncopated, of a stabbing, jagged character that gives off sparks. The rhythm changes after a vigorous working of the opening, and the viola introduces a strongly accentuated theme; and all instruments return to the coruscant opening. The trio is the odd-man-out in this quartet. It is an inverted canon, with Bloch's favorite interval, the tritone, serving as the theme. This theme uses all twelve notes of the chromatic scale—technically dodecaphonic, although Bloch never uses it in any formal or Schoenbergian sense at all. It is just there, like the microtones in the *First Piano Quintet*. It may have been a nod to what was happening around him in the musical world and his disdain for it. (Interestingly, a few years before, Bartók made a similar twelve-tone inclusion in the first movement of his great *Violin Concerto,* but after quoting it gave it an unmistakable orchestral raspberry!) The scherzo returns in a new guise of rhythmic and melodious changes, and after a brief reprise of the trio it ends with energetic finality.

"The third movement, *Andante,* compared to the two movements it separates, is a soothing nocturne. However, its quietude is underlaid with a feeling of uncertainty that, although ill-defined, gives one the sense that it has portents of something else to come. Its two themes are soon joined with the ever recurrent opening motto and all is woven into a continuous and melodious polyphony.

"The last movement, *Allegro molto,* is the heart of the work—all before is a preparation for a magnificent *passacaglia* and *fugue.* Very few compositons in the literature reserve the climax and center of gravity for the last movement, but this is one of them. The subject is derived from the motto, here played with more speed, leading to a climactic *fortissimo,* and after a pause, the *passacaglia* and *fugue* begin. The theme is stated in octaves by all four instruments, played with majestic ardor. The *passacaglia* theme passes through the strings, and at the midpoint of the development the music broadens, with the motto introduced as counterpoint in the first violin. The primary tempo resumes, more rhythmically, and this passage is the introduction to the *fugue.* The *fugue* subject is given to both violins playing in unison—the viola soon joins with a counter-theme and both are given a vigorous treatment in fugal counterpoint. Memories of previous material pass in a review of the entire quartet—leading to a closing epilogue with a whispered recall of the opening motto in the first violin.

"Bloch once said of the *First Quartet* that 'it represents me completely, as I felt, at least in 1916.' Surely this quartet must have served the same purpose for him in 1946. After the exhilarating last movement, one can almost see Newman rising from his seat to rush out and write his review."—John Erling, from liner notes for Laurel Records Stereo LP LR-126.

"On July 24, 1940, his sixtieth birthday, my father wrote to me telling me how, after a long phase of being 'crushed and overwhelmed by the nightmare of recent news,' he was regaining his 'equilibrium' with studies of Beethoven's *Eroica* in preparation for the course he was to give at the University of California at Berkeley. He had been making comparative studies of Beethoven's sketches and this must have influenced his later compositions.

> This first part has been finished—40 pages! I had started the second, an enormous task, but passionately interesting... one redoes, backwards, all the work of Beethoven and one follows his mind and his heart—one goes into ecstasies over his superb technique and the infallible logic that guides him. I have discovered (after 45 years of study) a thousand details that had escaped me up to now... it is a whole world and the step between the second Symphony and this one is the greatest a composer has ever taken! The orchestration, too, is a miracle of sobriety, invention, imagination, and mastery. From the standpoint of rhythm it is incomparable! Frequently there are seven or eight sketches for a passage or even more. (Nottebohm does not give them all.) I have copied all of them in different colors of ink above the final version.... This comparative study is extraordinary, a lesson every hour, in each measure! You can sometimes see in it, after the most unbelievable groping, the development of all of Beethoven's thinking.
>
> I had also begun, I believe I told you, a new quartet. [He said it was very dry and doubted it would be liked.] I had to interrupt it when I could no longer live in music during the disasters in Europe—the collapse of all those values which constituted my life, our lives. But the first part *(lento)* is finished, and I believe it is something completely new. There is no thematic development, no tonal restrictions, no repetition of motifs—and still the story unfolds with absolute logic and organic continuity. Why? I don't know. I do not know any literary work that even comes close to it. If I can succeed in writing the whole quartet in this way, it will be extraordinary, a complete regeneration of my style—(though it's pure Bloch).

"He finished [his Beethoven studies] — with time to spare! He gave his courses at Berkeley and completed a large orchestral work, *Suite Symphonique;* at the same time, he was working on the *Quartet*. He later said: 'This Quartet is only 38 minutes and the score occupies comparatively few pages; but you should see the preliminary sketches.'

"MODERATO. Of the *Quartet's* four movements, this first (as Bloch had written in 1940) is completely free both thematiclly and tonally. It is both cohesive and direct, while being vague and atmospheric. The opening theme, played by a solo violin, recurs throughout the work, appearing as a final 'thought' at the end of the first, third, and last movements. One becomes aware of the importance of the descending minor third introduced in the movement by a theme simultaneously played on the viola and cello. Even though this movement is different from the others, one cannot visualize another introduction to what follows.

"PRESTO (SCHERZO). This movement, in sharp contrast to the first, begins with the four instruments introducing the *Quartet'* five-note main theme. These notes will be heard in all three sections, transformed into all possible shapes and expressions. The melodic, harmonic, and rhythmic structures and treatments in this movement are extremely complex, defying short analysis. Other themes come and go but are subservient to the strength of the main theme. It remains in constant motion with the only respite being in the middle (trio) section, where the theme is dispersed among the four instruments. It is a rather short break, though, and the motif, omitting the fifth note, returns, played by the two violins. This omission gives the theme a more aggressive character. The music reaches its climax through an *ostinato* pattern in the cello and gradually dies down to a *pianissimo* halt. Starting again, it leads to the initial five-note theme repeatedly moving upward by a minor third, step by step. Finally, the lower instruments play the complete theme in triplets. The violin follows with the regular theme as the music reaches a *fortissimo*. There follows one beat of silence *(largamente),* and the movement concludes with all four isntruments playing the theme.

"ANDANTE. This slow movement is closer to the *Pastorale* of the first *Quartet*. All of Bloch's slow movements express a feeling of peace — contrasted at times with moments of conflict and tension — but the movements always end serenely. The viola plaintively plays the five-note main theme in a slow tempo, with a quiet rhythmical accompaniment. Then the cello and, finally, the second violin join in to set a lyrical mood. The opening theme is repeated twice, and later another theme on the introductory violin is echoed by the viola. The second violin plays the opening theme before repeating the newly introduced theme. The first violin follows playing the major theme's first four notes, and is echoed by the second violin. After reaching the climax, the movement returns to a *tempo calmo,* where the violin, again, plays the new theme. The second violin repeats the main theme echoed by the first violin. The movement ends softly, like a whisper—the violin reiterating the opening theme, *con sordino.*

"ALLEGRO MOLTO. It has been said that this movement is so rich and full of material that it could pass for a complete quartet in itself. The introduction leads into a *passacaglia* based on the major theme with fifteen variations. A *fugue* on the same motif follows, and the movement concludes with an epilogue, in which the *Quartet's* opening theme is rendered during the final measures.

"Ernest Newman's comments and brief description of this movement are appropriate in rounding off this *Quartet:*

> Technically it is of exceptional interest; from an embryo in the second of the four movements (the *Presto-Scherzo*) there comes into being an entity which from that point onward moulds the whole Quartet from the inside into a single organic substance, differently accentuated or rhythmed. As the work goes on, it assumes one personality after another till it expands in the *finale* into, first of all, the theme for a powerful *passacaglia,* then, re-rhythmed yet again, into the subject of a mighty *fugue.* The whole work is rounded off in unexpected but inevitable rightness with a serene reminiscence in the final bars of a tiny *melisma* with which the first movement had opened....
>
> All this, however, is not just dazzle-book craftsmanship for craftsmanship's sake. It is the organic result, not the motivating cause of the musical thinking, which is unique in modern chamber music for its alternation of subtle contemplative beauty and torrential power.
>
> —Suzanne Bloch, from liner notes for Arabesque Digital Stereo LP recording 6511-13.

"In his brilliant essay, 'Ferrucio Busoni: Historia Abscondita' (in *Fanfare*, VII:3), Adrian Corleonis describes Busoni's concept of 'unity of key', through which he circumvented the *cul de sac* of an over-systematized notion of tonal relationships that permeated the Austro-Germanic musical mentality like a religious obsession. Busoni's 'unity of key' was an alternative to the theoretical strait-jacket that soon led to serialism, which was embraced as scripture by those compelled to substitute one dogma for another. But, as Corleonis admits, Busoni was one of many composers during this period who had the courage and independence of mind to explore the opportunity for a new tonal freedom. Scriabin, Sibelius, Nielsen, Vaughan Williams, and many others—in addition to the obvious example of Debussy—all found their own individual ways around the tonality 'problem', exposing exciting possibilities rather than extinguishing them.[19]

"Ernest Bloch arrived on the scene at a time when the innovations of Debussy and Strauss (it is fashionable today to minimize the radical side of Strauss) were in the air. Drawing from them and from his own turbulently emotional Jewish temperament, he forged a highly articulate language in which the perennial polar balance between Dionysian abandon and Apollonian control achieved an unprecedented expressive tension. Bloch, perhaps less intellectually sophisticated than a Busoni, but musically cosmopolitan by instint, plunged into the theoretical maelstrom without inhibition and seized the new tonal freedom with bold confidence, relying only on his own artistry and craftsmanship. It is in this, the development of a true musical 'expressionism', that Bloch's greatest aesthetic contribution lies.

"The *Quartet No. 2* (1946) is the finest of Bloch's five essays in the medium, joining the *Violin Sonata No. 1* (1920) and the *Piano Quintet No. 1* (1923) as his most important chamber music. In comparision with the two earlier works, however, the quartet reveals a higher level of compositional maturity. The previous tendency toward rhetorical extravagance is now distilled into tighter, more concentrated structural designs, with no sacrifice of emotional intensity. The work begins with a mysterious contemplation for unaccompanied violin, unstable both rhythmically and tonally. As this soliloquy is gradually answered contrapuntally by the remaining voices, a mood is set for the exploration of an unknown spiritual territory—a mood, I might add, that reminds me strikingly of Vaughan Williams' *Flos Campi*, although I may be alone in this perhaps strange association. By the time the last movement, a brilliant passacaglia and fugue, has reached its culmination, the forces of aberration and the forces of rationalism have achieved a partial reconciliation."—Walter Simmons, in *Fanfare: The Magazine for Serious Record Collectors*, 5-6/84.

Quartet 3 for Strings (1951). *Prem.:* Griller Quartet. *Recs:* London Records LLA-23: Griller Quartet; Vox Records SVBX-5109: New World Quartet; Arabesque (3 Digital Stereo LPs) 6511-13: Portland String Quartet. Ded. to the Griller Quartet. N.Y. Music Critics Circle Award, 1954.

---

19 On this central issue of tonality/alternative structuring in 20th-century music, see also George Perle interview below and other views and responses. The debate or "problem" continues to be explored. (Ed.)

1. Allegro deciso (4m). 2. Adagio non troppo (6m). 3. Allegro molto moderato (7m). 4. Allegro (8m).

"Bloch was seventy-two years old when he composed this *Quartet*. It was first performed in 1953 by the Griller String Quartet and received unanimous praise from both the public and the press. When Bloch was interviewed, he expressed amazement 'that it made such an impression. It is shorter and less dramatic than what I have done so far. In some ways it is more intellectual.' In response to the suggestion that this music was more subdued in its dissonances, he said: 'It is quite natural that a man of 72 does not react and feel as he did at 20, 30, 40, and 50.... In spite of that there is some biting irony in the *Scherzo* of this Quartet.' When asked if he thought this was his best *Quartet*, he replied: 'Do you prefer turkey or duck? If they're well done, each has its personality.'

"The *Third Quartet's* 'personality' centers around a series of falling fifths that permeate the entire work. Of these, two pairs form the first four notes of a twelve (semi)-tone row in the fourth movement. This marks the first time Bloch used such means of procedure.

"ALLEGRO DECISO. The first movement begins with a long, sharply trilled note by all four instruments, as if warning the listener of what is to come. Then, still in unison, pairs of descending fifths are played in a strong, rhythmical beat followed by relentless passages in triplets. A short, dotted quarter note with a sixteenth note above is then followed, in Bloch's typical style, by a return to the lower note. In just one page of the score one discovers three differing elements introduced in the movement. The falling fifths moving steadily (at times ascending in inversion) lead to a gentler passage. This continues to a *crescendo* utilizing a lyrical melody. The gentle mood, however, does not break down until the climax—a return to the opening trills in *fortissimo* with the descending fifths changed rhythmically. After an unexpected *subito piano*, marching toward the conclusion, a mixture of elements from the first part is heard—contrasts in nuance, falling octaves, running eighth notes, *pizzicati*—all *crescendo* to a sudden stop. Softly and slowly the earlier triplet pattern is heard, with harmonics in the background. Then, like a bolt from the skies, falling octaves drop to the movement's close.

"ADAGIO. This is one of Bloch's most beautiful slow movements. As always, it expresses the serenity that he longed for during the turmoil of his life. The opening is played by the solo viola—a long held note—then is ornamented with a delicate pattern of chromatic half-steps. Meditation-like, it continues with the other voices joining in playing eloquent themes. In this context, the falling fifths have a totally different meaning. The movement flows along, reaching its height in a gradual, expressive curve, returning to the meditative quality of the opening, and finally ending with a peaceful epilogue.

"Of this movement, a New York critic wrote: 'When this Quartet is recorded, I shall play this *Adagio* till I know every phrase by heart. It should be good to live with that music in you.'

"ALLEGRO MOLTO MODERATO. In some of Bloch's recently discovered notes, he details the problem of interpretation of this movement:

> This *Scherzo* combines over 12 different motives.... I hope, however, that this does not interfere with the great unity of the piece. It is quite regular, A_B_A, though not rigidly symmetrical...
> About the exact speed, as you know, the essential is to give the impression of that speed and, as is often the case, a very little slower tempo may fulfill better that aim, in allowing to preserve the clarity, to confer the proper accents and render more sensibile the rhythmical divisions.

"This movement, beginning with an energetic ternary pulse, is at times like a dance with a sardonic twist (which, by the way, is often found in Bloch's *Scherzi*). The music's continuous beat is peppered with abrupt short fragments. The falling fifths are much less evident, but when they do come, such as in the cello part, they have a percussive effect. After a jagged *pizzicato* passage, a cheerful but rather vulgar theme occurs, identified as 'grotesque' in Bloch's notes.

"The middle (B) section's contrasting, mysterious sonorities are effefctive with their thin harmonies accompanying the viola and cello. The music seems more like an interlude—until the delicate chromatic pattern from the *Adagio* is heard. This leads into the heralding of the future theme of the *Finale*, accompanied by triplets bringing the recapitulation of the first section's material, which includes the 'grotesque' melody. At the end a flurry of rapid scale passages brings the movement to a close.

"FINALE—ALLEGRO. Bloch wrote the following on this movement:

> The essential motif of the *Finale* has a somewhat related parentage with the start of the first movement. (Descending fifths also found in II and III.) But the whole motif is based on the twelve semi-tones of the scale...! Please, do not mention it to anybody.... I wonder how many critics or musicologists will ever notice it?... Only, contrarily to Mr. Schoenberg, it is not harmonized arbitrarily, mechanically... and, this apparently atonal motif becomes gradually almost outrageously tonal, as you will see.

"In this movement, the twelve-tone row is introduced in its entirety by the two lower instruments. It is then followed by a diffused section in which the instruments seem to hesitate—unsure about playing this theme. With contrasting nuances, the music slows down. This is the introduction to the real entrance of the theme—transformed rhythmically. It is a long, complex part of the movement, based on a theme incorporating motives from the other movements which are interwoven and transformed. To some it sounds almost like a *passacaglia*. This substantial part of the *Finale* brings about a *Fugue*, of which Bloch wrote:

> I hesitated very much... to treat it as a *Fugue*, on account of the *Finale* of the Second Quartet; but it is so completely different and seems so obvious, that I could not resist. It is again, quite regularly constructed on the initial twelve Tone-Row, but you will see how they become more and more tonal, and so acquiring their full musical significance.
> [Bloch then indicates that at no. 57 (25 measures after the *Fugue's* start)] the theme is inverted in the Cello part, and from no. 65 (forty measures before the end) the triumph of Tonality, Order, Organization from an apparently inorganic start!
> May Humanity follow such a course!"

— Suzanne Bloch, from liner notes for Arabesque Digital Stereo LP recording 6511-13.

***Quartet 4* for Strings (1953).** *Recs:* London Records LLA-23: Griller Quartet; Arabesque (3 Digital Stereo LPs) 6511-13: Portland String Quartet. Ded. to Ernest Chapman.
1. Tranquillo—Allegro energico—Tranquillo (8m). 2. Andante (7m). 3. Presto—Moderato—Presto (5m). 4. Calmo—Allegro deciso—Calmo (9m).

"This *Quartet* differs from the others in its general shape. The first and last movements are similar in their treatment of thematic material mainly based on a motive of a pair of falling tritones that intertwine constantly. Both also possess the same mood patterns in the same order: calm—fast—calm—fast—calm. The two middle movements are in vivid contrast, both harmonically and melodically.

"Olin Downes, music critic of *The New York Times*, in his review of the first American performance of this work, wrote:

> The moods are introspective and range from those of a chip of the furious Bloch of old, to the mystical communion of his

latest years. There is indeed a curious combination of the old earthiness and gusto, and the later inwardness and serenity that seems to have evolved within this passionate artist with the passing of the decades.

"*TRANQUILLO—ALLEGRO ENERGICO—TRANQUILLO.* In the opening section of the first movement, the viola introduces the first theme. The first violin then repeats and prolongs it in a descending line. Such descending thematic passages are used constantly throughout the movement. The *Allegro energico* that follows is as rhythmic as the preceding section is diffuse, having short ascending motives entwined with various forms of the basic material. The return to the *Calmo* section brings back the *Allegro* in which the descending motives are supported by ascending lines in the cello. The ascending and descending motion is characteristic throughout this movement, culminating in a final *moderato*. In the downward passages, falling thirds are used, moving to an *epilogue* that could almost be a dirge... fading away.

"*ANDANTE.* The beginning of this movement contrasts greatly, both harmonically and melodically, [with] the previous movement. It is more modal in character, almost like an old song, having a definite beginning and end. In the midst of this comes a gentler passage which turns out to be the 'furious' opening of the *First Quartet's Scherzo*, now transformed. More motives like this occur, but as the music evolves, a transition possessing harmonic complexities becomes apparent, even though the thematic material is in the same vein. As the *tempi* fluctuate subtly, a string of rather atonal notes played by the violin rises unexpectedly in a graceful curve descending to one of the simple themes heard earlier, finally fading to a whisper. A more mysterious mood follows; the background played on the *ponticello* accompanies the return of the curved line heard earlier. There follows a progression leading to the great climax, a *fortississimo*. By some miracle, all returns back to the gentle opening theme from the *First Quartet*, and a peaceful ending.

"*PRESTO—MODERATO—PRESTO.* This is a masterly constructed piece in which, in the midst of descending and ascending *pizzicato* intervals and running passages of bowed eighth notes, one hears a not too pretty theme. This is typical of Bloch's sardonic musical humor found in most of his *Scherzi*. But what enters after a short break is a rather childish theme of six measures divided into three sections based on a primitive *pentatonic* tune (supposedly Eskimo) found by Bloch in 1911 during research for lectures on esthetics in Geneva. He used to sing this melody, with unintelligible words, to his children. Though in the quartet he is completely true to the phrasing, rhythm, and melodic configuration, he transformed it atonally. He uses it constantly and freely, progressing to a *crescendo* and a sudden break.

"In the *Moderato* section, the tune is heard *sul ponticello,* both more slowly and with less good humor, almost in a complaining tone. This tune, used so often in this movement, could be very monotonous if it weren't treated so inventively. Sometimes only the first three notes are repeated on different pitches, giving the section a sense of progression. As it moves, the *ostinato* skips of a tritone and the chromatic steps in the bass lead back to the *Presto.*

"*CALMO—ALLEGRO DECISO—CALMO.* The first section of this movement is more of an introduction, beginning with the viola playing descending tritones, taken up by the cello, continuing down to its lower register. A few beats later, the first section of the primitive tune of the *Scherzi* returns played by the cello followed by the violin. This leads to the *Allegro Deciso,* amusingly introduced by a tone row which is of central importance to the rest of the movement. It is introduced gradually, a few notes added each time as it progresses to its highest note, finally descending without interruption. At this point the violin softly plays the first section of the primitive theme; the viola continues it to the close of this section. A long progression leading to the *Andante* uses fragments of the tone row together with material from preceding movements. It slows down with the introduction of the themes from the second movement, changing the color of the movement once again. In the transition to the final section, the row is heard in retrograde, in inversion, and in imitation with fragments scattered among all parts until the original row is heard again with mellow harmonies. A few notes of the primitive theme are played by the second violin and viola as the music reaches the final chords."—Suzanne Bloch, from liner notes for Arabesque Digital Stereo LP recording 6511-13.

Quartet 5 for Strings (1956). *Recs:* Concert Disc 225: Fine Arts Quartet; Arabesque (3 Digital Stereo LPs) 6511-13: Portland String Quartet. Ded. to Suzanne Bloch-Smith.
1. Grave— 2. Calmo (18m). 3. Presto—4. Allegro deciso (14m).

"Bloch's last *Quartet* was composed when his health had deteriorated greatly, although there was no sign of the cancer that was to take his life three years later. In fact, he wrote ten works in those final three years, ending with music for unaccompanied strings, while retired and settled in a big house facing the Pacific. With strong choral textures and in spite of thematic material still in chromatic rows, this entire work is fairly tonal. In these respects the *Quartet* differs from the last three.

"GRAVE—ALLEGRO—GRAVE. This movement's tonal center seems to be C minor. Its rich harmonic texture, retrospective mood, and Blochian syncopated rhythmic pulse underlie the eloquent material which brings us to the *Allegro*. The fluctuation of *tempi* reverts to *calmo* and back in a fugal passae, then dissolving to triplets and returning to the original *Calmo*. This movement contains seven different thematic motives, all atonal. Yet despite this, the dissonant ending centers around C minor.

"CALMO. This movement begins without a break from the first. Through also a slow section, it is characterized by Bloch's syncopated rhythm that is part of the opening theme of the first movement. This will recur throughout this section. Its tonal center is A flat major.

"Lyrical themes are heard above, a reminder of Bloch's other works, with *tempo* fluctuations. This leads to a 'false' return of the *Calmo*, now in C major, progressing with greater intensity, then returning to the opening section. The first violin then rises in an *arpeggiated* line based on an augmented A flat triad, ending on a final A flat major cadence.

"PRESTO. The *scherzo* leads cheerfully to the trio utilizing short rhythmic fragments and previously heard atonal material above the jagged texture. Bloch, using a guitar-like accompaniment in the cello and viola, brings to the fore one of his more sardonic and slightly vulgar themes.

"ALLEGRO DECISO. This movement begins with strong chords, like a final statement, rather unusual for a Bloch quartet. Thematic material from the other movements is reintroduced, blended in a rich tapestry based on ascending and descending intervals and rhythmic patterns heard before.

"I was visiting my parents during the writing of this *Quartet* and was shocked to see the changes in my father. Once quite a formidable character, he was now frail and gentle. He was most concerned about the ending of this work, having been dissatisfied with what he had written so far. Finally, I went with him up to his studio, a large, bare, cold room above the garage. There he showed me several endings he had sketched. One of them seemed to me to be very effective and I pointed it out as the best. He shook his head mildly and said, 'No, it is not organic to the rest of the music... I want everything to fall into place.' A few days later, he became quite happy, having found what he wanted. We went upstairs where he played the ending for me. He had written phrases that became shorter and shorter, finally coming to a rest. Then there appears a fragment of a phrase, another short rest, all finally concluding with an anguished chord and a final silence. I realized that all had fallen into place.

"Three years later I arrived at the hospital where my father had been in a coma. I stood at his hospital bed and suddenly the nurse said, 'Now.' There I saw and heard the end of this, his last *Quartet:* the short phrases, the rests, the anguished expression on his face, and then the end. Everything had trully fallen into place." — Suzanne Bloch, from liner notes for Arabesque Digital Stereo LP recording 6511-13.

KARL-BIRGER BLOMDAHL

B. 1916, Växjö (Sweden); d. 1968, Kungsängen (nr. Stockholm). *Taught at:* Royal College of Music (Stockholm). Music Dir., Swedish Radio. *Works incl.:* concertos (pno, vla, vln), dance scores, operas *(Aniara, Herr von Hancken),* symphonies, trios.

"A few months before he passed away in June 1968, Karl-Birger Blomdahl attended Stockholm Opera's hundredth performance of *Aniara.* That was nine years after the world premiere, probably a record for a serious modern music drama on one and the same stage.

"Even before Blomdahl and the poet Erik Lindegren had completed their opera at the end of the 1950s, *Aniara* — the tragic futuristic vision of a spaceship which gets off course with all its passengers and is doomed to circle the heavens for all eternity — had been the cultural property of educated Swedes, at that time as an epic poem by Harry Martinson. But no music drama has succeeded in surviving merely by virtue of the topicality of its subject matter and the literary qualities of its text. The decisive factors are the expressive power of the idiom, its individuality, and dramatic effectiveness; in the case of *Aniara,* a dance called the 'Yurg', at first intoxicated with life, later increasingly hot-headed and desperate (a great dance scene); the electronic accompaniment for Mima; and the intense drama, simultaneously parodistic of the Jubilee-celebration with its sudden ominous oscillations between the military discipline of hymns for the chorus and the religious ecstasy of the Poetess's vocalise, in the high soprano register.

"*Aniara* made Blomdahl a popular figure, as did his charming and completely relaxed appearances on a number of radio and TV programs, many of them with a non-doctrinaire pedagogical content....

"Having received a very thorough musical education from Hinding Rosenberg during the years around 1940, Blomdahl began composing in a style influenced by Hindemith. At the end of the 1940s, he made exhaustive studies of Bartók, Stravinsky, and the Viennese school. It was on this platform that he took his stand, when, in 1950, he composed the work which made him known, his third symphony, *Facetter.* Blomdhal's characteristic traits as a composer are here fully developed. Especially noticeable are the rhythmic definition, the architectural, effectively calculated increases in intensity with their almost orgiastic climaxes, the long-spun, vegetative lyrical moods and the acrid, often ponderous coloring. Many of these traits are also found in the choreographic suite *Sisyfos* (1954) — with, however, the addition here of various impressionistic techniques, such as are encountered in Stravinsky's early ballets.[20]

"Between *Facetter* and *Sisyfos*, Blomdahl wrote another of his most important works: *I speglarnas sal [In the Hall of Mirrors]*, 1952, for narrator, soloists, choir, and orchestra. As his point of departure he took Erik Lindegren's collection of poems *Mannen utan väg [The Man Without a Path]*, 'exploded sonnets' in an idiom inspired by surrealism. Their philosophy is pessimistic. Memories from the war years flame up, as our thoughts revolve round the evil and anxiety inherent in human nature. By composing *Mannen utan väg*, Blomdahl became a poet of his time. 'Explosion' became a musical technique, too: in pointillistic writing for both voices and instruments, in episodes for speaking chorus, in chilly, glassy-clear orchestral effects. [Other works reflecting Blomdahl's engagement in contemporary problems included his choral work *Anabase* (1956) and the opera buffa *Herr von Hancken* (1964), something of a black *Falstaff*]....

"Between two extremes—deep involvement in contemporary problems on the one hand, and [a] tendency toward absolute, concertante music on the other [e.g. the frequently performed *Chamber Concerto* for piano, woodwinds and percussion, 1953]—one can place one of Blomdahl's last and most individual works: *Forma ferritonans* for orchestra (1961). Here, the composer lets a sound—or rather a cluster—grow out of the depths towards a tremendous climax, only to break up into small particles, which in their turn coalesce toward the end into an evocative waltz. The music is inspired by the industrial processes in one of the big Swedish steelworks.

"*Altisonans* (1966)—Blomdahl's last completed work—is a vision of space in pictures and electronic sounds, the material being taken from the song of two worlds: nightingale and blackbird songs are woven together with the music of space itself, from traveling satellites. *Altisonans* means 'that which sounds out of space'....

"Karl-Birger Blomdahl's last public appearance was a speech he made at a student gathering in which he called himself a 'traditionalist'. What he meant will be apparent from the following lines:

> Every science, of whatever kind it may be, is a single huge collage, the collected experience of the human race within various fields. Never forget that the extreme advances toward the future get their power and sense from the total

---

20 Critic Benjamin Pernick writes: "Jazz-tinged Stravinsky neo-classicism is appended to Bartók in the eight-movement suite from the ballet *Sisyphus*. The final movement *(Dance of Life)* has a strong *Sensemayá*-like ritualistic quality"—a reference to the Revueltas work, described later in this volume. (Ed.)

experience of the human race through the centuries, individual and collective. You young people are spearheads, and I wish you sharpness and striking power. They are necessary in our chaotic epoch, threatened as it is with destruction. They are necessary, too, if we are to break through the ramparts, the great walls, to find new ways and open breathing points for fresh, live-giving winds, providing oxygen for a circulation which would otherwise stagnate." — Bo Wallner, in *Perspective of New Music*, Spring-Summer 1969.

Symphony 3 (Facetter [Facets]) for Orchestra (1950). 20m Recs.: Swedish Discofil (Mono LP): orch. cond. by Sixten Ehrling; Caprice (Stereo LP) CAP 1251 (also as CD CAP 21365): Stockholm PO, Sixten Ehrling, cond.
In one movement.

"In Karl-Birger Blomdahl's *Third Symphony* we have the most coherent and significant symphonic statement to come out of Scandinavia during the immediate postwar years. Rosenberg's most brilliant pupil, Blomdahl — whose exciting career was cut off in 1968 at the untimely age of 52 — at first leaned in the direction of Hindemith's measured neoclassicism with an occasional dash of the Shostakovich 'grand manner' populism (cf. the major works of the 1940s — the *Second Symphony*, the *Concerto Grosso*, the violin concerto). But this once-somewhat-notorious symphony signaled a whole departure generated by Blomdahl's preoccupation with the Vienna School as well as the implications of Stravinsky's rhythmic innovations, all pointing towards the milestones of the 1950s — the piano concerto, the ballets *Sysiphos*, *Minotaurus*, the oratorio *In the Hall of Mirrors* — culminating in the internationally celebrated 'space-opera' *Aniara*.

"Pointedly subtitled 'Facets', the *Third Symphony* offers a prismatic and kaleidoscopic series of mutually reflecting perspectives on the 12-note motif announced forlornly but menacingly by the solo flute at the very start, which seems to give birth to itself out of a contemplative desolation into which the work ultimately recedes at its close. But between these two respective points of genesis and demise, the thematic materials undergo a varied and dramatic sequence of transformations which correspond loosely to the four movements of a traditional symphony. Throughout this long architectonic arch, Blomdahl succeeds in maintaining and exploiting the tension between his expressionistic impulses and his constructivist rigors to create an organically integrated and dynamically forward-moving formal scheme. With its combined lyrical and motoric elements thus played off against each other within a naturally evolving framework, Blomdahl's characteristic and contradictory tendencies towards neurotic hysteria and Dionysian apocalypse become part of a controlled psychological progression which can be interpreted in either a subjective or a historical context or both. In either case, there's no doubting we are experiencing a genuine response to the first shocks of the post-atomic age of individual despair and potential worldwide cataclysm.... It is a pleasure to welcome [the] first stereo recording of the most important Swedish symphony composed between the older generation of [Hilding] Rosenberg and [Gösta] Nystroem and the spectacular outpouring of the [Allan] Pettersson canon." — Paul Snook, in *Fanfare: The Magazine for Serious Record Collectors*, 3-4/83.

"Top recommendation [for the Caprice recording conducted by Sixten Ehrling].... Blomdahl's *Third Symphony* blends Bartókian (the *Concerto for Orchestra*, the last three quartets) timbres with Bergian harmonies. Structured as five linked blocks, it boasts a huge percussion crescendo rivaling those in the Mahler Second or *Wozzeck*." — Benjamin Pernick, in *Fanfare: The Magazine for Serious Record Collectors*, 1-2/90.

WILLIAM BOLCOM

B. 1938, Seattle WA. *Educ.:* Univ of WA (Seattle), Mills College, Paris Conservatoire, Stanford Univ. *Taught at:* Univ of WA, Queens & Brooklyn Colls (CUNY), NY Schl of the Arts, Yale Drama Schl, Univ of MI. *Awards & grants incl.:* Composer-in-residence, NYU Theatre Arts Programme, Cabrillo Festival CA; Kurt Weill compsn award; Marc Blitzstein award; Guggenheim (2), Koussevitzsky, Rockefeller Fndn, NEA grants. Frequently concertizes as a pianist, often with his wife the singer Joan Morris. *Works incl.:* concertos (cl, pno, vln), *Décalage* (vc/pno), *Dream Music* (var insts), *Frescoes* (2 pnos), operas (*Dynamite Tonight, Greatshot*), piano solo (*3 Dance Portraits, Fantasy-Sonata, Garden of Eden, 10 Monsterpieces, Romantic Pieces*), 10 strng qts, *Sessions* (var insts), 5 symphonies, vocal (*Cabaret Songs, 3 Donald Hall Songs, 3 Irish Songs, Open House*).

Composer statement: As a composer, teacher, and performer with a great deal of on-stage concert experience, William Bolcom is in an excellent position to observe and interpret various aspects of writing, publishing and playing contemporary music. In the following letter to the Editor he responds in part to the latter's remarks concerning his 3/90 *Musical America* article (for which see page *xviii*, above), and touches on other topics, as well. A fuller version of the composer's original article can be found in the Fall, 1988 issue of the University of Michigan's *Michigan Quarterly Review*.

"To answer your question on page *xix* of your Preface and Acknowledgements: 'What does one mean by the *serious* music scene — if rock and other popular forms attract large audiences?' This is, I assure you, not my own original term; in fact I hate it, as it implies that everyone not in it is not serious — popism, I suppose; it's almost racist. No, the term has a long history in the music business and is used by publisher, record company, concert agency, and opera house alike; 'serious' refers to Bach, Beethoven, Brahms, the whole canon built around the opera, concert, and symphony institutions, modern music written for such forces. The real reason, in fact, why new music written for orchestra or concert or opera has not made an inroad with the general public is that people do not go to concerts in the percentage (nor to movies or theater or galleries) that they once did in the big cities exclusively (movies made it out to the hinterlands but not the others nearly so much), but watch TV mostly; so how are they supposed to tell Tower from Torke, Albright from Amram, if they haven't heard the concert or happened to listen to the piece on some college station or [New York's] WNYC or the like (which already means a committed listener to Art)?

"Your other question: 'shouldn't "classical, serious" composers learn from the "opposition",' is one my whole life has addressed. I feel claustrophobic about the limitation in audience and impact in the world my music perforce has because I write for the orchestra. I also rankle at the fact that the orchestra has not evolved to include the technological extensions and the incorporation of new instruments and instrumentalists on a constant basis, as it did in the past until the First World War (with the exception of the percussion section). This freezes it in time; the modern symphony orchestra is a Collegium Musicum designed for Tchaikovsky through Mahler as the central repertory. In my *Songs of Innocence and of Experience* I expanded the orchestra to include: saxophones, many diverse percussion instruments, electrified violins, electric piano, guitar and bass; and hired people experienced in the styles of these instruments as they have developed. In Stuttgart it was funny to see the lifestyle collision of the opera-orchestra middle-aged portly German players and the young, badly-dressed louts brought in for the sax, electric guitar and electric bass parts! We put up a partition-board between the rockers and the strings, who couldn't restrain their vinegar-faces when the youngsters played. But it's just this kind of collision that delights me.

"Blake said, 'Damn braces! Bless relaxes', which can be read two ways, both true, if you gerundify every other word each time. It is one of the central koans of my life. The schism between pop and serious, or vernacular and aristocratic (just as bad) music, is so deep that neither side benefits from the other. Both industries are distinct; one is for profit, the other resolutely 'non-profit', and their mutual dislike is always under the surface. Those like me who chafe at having to be in one camp or the other exclusively know how each side of the chasm has suffered. So I damn the brace that holds me from most of the audience; I deplore the sinking level of education most people here suffer under, and I realize that this limits the possible subtlety of musical language one could use if the desire is immediate consumption (which should be possible to any artist when the idea behind a work calls for this immediacy). Also, I bless the relax of watertight concepts in new music; I am delighted to see young composers frankly acknowledge and embrace their rock heritage (if such be the case), rather than try to suppress or deny it, as they did 15 years ago.[21] In the end, the only people who will transform our outmoded musical institutions (and that INCLUDES the dog-eat-dog hard-nosed criminal superstructure of the pop business in all its forms; Steely Dan once said about the pop-record business executives, 'Some of these guys ought to be washing cars') will be the creative artists themselves, who will demand changes according to their strong and irresistible vision, whatever that may become.

"I have often been berated for not being 'original'. I am said to possess no style of my own. In that I have not patented a type of interval treatment or poured the same stylistic brown sauce on all of my pieces, I plead guilty. But I do have faith in my total style; I am in love with the many genres of music and have learned that it is important to respect the genre you are contributing to if you want its expressive potential in your music. My use of it transforms the style into 'something of mine', and there a careful musicological reading will find similar chicken-tracks musically in everything I've done. A similar case is the *oeuvre* of Kurt Weill; no matter whether for German, French, or English, or American audiences, he respected the style of each; it is now, 40 years after his death, that we can begin to appreciate the similarities as well as the differences in each of his works in various styles (including the early Busoniesque avantgarde period). We now recognize any Picasso for a Picasso. I seem to belong to this genre (if not necessarily the quality — that is a matter of opinion), of the kind of inclusive artist that strives, as Blake did, for Exactitude.

"My other reason for using so many genres of music is that I am fascinated with their interrelationships. At first shocking, a juxtaposition makes better sense with repeated hearings — if it is the right juxtaposition; not all will bear fruit. Over time I have learned to make juxtapositions smoother if I like; in some way this depends on sensing that your recipient, the audience, has come to agree, because then the musical language is expanded, more can be expressed. (But some juxtapositions should keep their shock value; I still feel a shiver when the B-flat section of the last movement of Beethoven's

---

21 In this context see also composer statement by Jeremy Beck, above — in addition to commentaries and music by John Adams, William Albright, Howard Brubeck, Chick Corea, Philip Glass, Tod Machover, and many others. Indeed, along with the tonal-atonal music issue, that of the merits of "eclecticism" — including pronouncements on the relative vitalities of so-called "popular" and "classical" idioms — appears to be a central theme or issue of 20th-century musical aesthetics generally. (Ed.)

Ninth comes on, and not all of that is pleasant, but I'm glad it's there.)" — William Bolcom, 10/17/90.

FROM AN INTERVIEW WITH MARK WAIT IN *THE PIANO QUARTERLY* NR. 142 (1988).

"MARK WAIT: You have one of the most fascinating *sets* of careers that I know of. You have had an extensive recording and performing career, both as soloist and with Joan Morris. You're also, and I suppose primarily, a composer.

"BOLCOM: Well, I think of myself primarily as a composer, but I also say that I'm a *musician* first and foremost. And I think that means that it's all the same in the end. One day you're paid to do something, and the next day you're not, but you do it anyway.

"I think the person who taught me most that there wasn't any big division between these things was the great Eubie Blake.

"The difference between improvising, or working out something kind of nice and light at the piano, and composing is that in composing you can encapsulate time. A composed piece may be short, but you may have agonized over four or five notes for a long time. It's like having cognac instead of raw wine. You've had time and the distillation process is at work.

"But there's no real line between improvising and composing, or between composing and performing. Eubie taught me that. He would work out an arrangement. (He didn't like to play a piece if he hadn't worked out an arrangement.) He though an arrangement was a kind of halfway step—somebody else's piece, and you had to put your own kind of fix on it.

"In the past there were other guys who did that, too. It was expected. When a great clavecinist came in and did a piece by some other great clavecinist, he was expected to put his own wrinkle on it. And if the composer was in the audience and the performer *didn't* add his two cents, the composer probably thought, 'You're doing it wrong. I wanted to hear *your* part of it.' I'm sure that was true. And it's just as true today with the jazz players. They *expect* it: 'What's *your* fix on that?' And in a living tradition, that's what happens. Unfortunately, we don't seem to have that attitude in our schools now. We've soaked them in formaldehyde, and it's too bad....

"WAIT: Now let me ask you about your second set of *Etudes* [for piano solo].

"BOLCOM: They're different from the first set, which was composed around 1965. The first ones were really very much in the Boulez tradition, which I was very much involved with then. But various things here and there have taken more prominence in my life since then, and now there's even a kind of mad Rag Infernale in the second set. The new etudes are much more tonal. I think the first group were much more difficult technically. They were written when I was a mad monster pianist.

"WAIT: I have heard the first set performed. They're brilliant.

"BOLCOM: It's a good set. It's okay. But they were written when I was able to do the West Coast premiere of Stockhausen's *Kontrapunkte*. I had those kind of chops in those days.

"WAIT: Are they published?

"BOLCOM: Not yet. All twelve are finished, and the set will be published this summer [1988]. The intention was to write pieces that represent the apotheosis of the whole idea of etudes."

SOME ADDITIONAL NOTES ON THE COMPOSER: "While composing some madrigals 20 years ago, William Bolcom stumbled onto an odd coincidence: 'I discovered that the funeral hymn "Abide with Me" and the wedding march from *Lohengrin* fit in perfect Irving Berlin counterpoint—a funeral-marriage, Love with Death.' This is not a discovery that would impress most composers, but Bolcom is not like most composers. So when the Philadelphia Orchestra performed his powerful new *Fifth Symphony* last week [Jan 1990], the second movement featured, along with intimations of both *Tannhauser* and Tommy Dorsey, that bizarre wedding of Wagner and 'Abide with Me.'

" 'If you mix popular and classical forms, it brings life to both genres,' says Bolcom. 'By making them touch, something fresh, new and organic grows. I like the traditional and the newest culture coexisting in the same piece. The classical masters had that possibility—Haydn is full of pop tunes—and I want it too.'

"Bolcom demonstrated his eclecticism spectacularly in his 1984 setting of all 46 poems in William Blake's *Songs of Innocence and of Experience*, a three-hour extravaganza that called for a rock band as well as a concert orchestra, plus three different choirs and nine soloists. The songs ranged from a haunting quasi-Renaissance madrigal to a smashing reggae finale....

" 'I am an omnivore,' [Bolcom] says. He fed on the Beatles, for example, and what have been called the 'song jewelers': Gershwin, Kern, Berlin. 'I liked this music. It satisfied something.' He also discovered ragtime and helped spearhead its revival in the 1970s with a nonchalantly elegant recording of rags by Joplin, Lamb, Scott and himself. More important he began accompanying mezzo-soprano Joan Morris around the country in dear old ditties like 'Will You Love Me in December as You Do in May?' They married in 1975, and still give nearly 50 concerts a year. 'Performing this stuff with Joan had an enormous influence on my music,' Bolcom says.

"Eclecticism of this kind is not, of course, Bolcom's invention. Louis Moreau Gottschalk, the Civil War-era virtuoso, wrote symphonies as well as show pieces. Charles Ives, whom Bolcom greatly admires, embedded folk songs in his massive orchestral works. Gershwin composed both opera and musical comedies, and in later years Kurt Weill, Virgil Thomson and Leonard Bernstein, among others, have distinguished themselves as musical magpies. Some think, in fact, that eclecticism is what is now fashionable in this unideological age, and that is partly what accounts for Bolcom's recent success."—Otto Friedrich (with reporting by Nancy Newman), in *Time*, 1/29/90.

Twelve New Etudes for Piano (1986). 38m Ded. to Paul Jacobs, John Musto & Marc-André Hamelin. Winner, 1988 Pulitzer Prize. *Rec.*: New World Records Stereo LP NW 354 (also as CD NW 354-2): Mark-André Hamelin. *Pub.*: E. B. Marks (Hal Leonard).

"This is the second of two volumes of twelve *Etudes*, the first of which was composed between 1959 and 1966 (and recorded by the composer)....

"These are etudes in synthesis as well as in pianism. Bolcom's wide-ranging sensibilities and compositional technique give him access to an extraordinary assortment of imagery. His delight in juxtaposing stylistic opposites tempts him to tickle one idiom in the ribs with another. The result is a kaleidoscope of vignettes imprinted by Bolcom's uniquely laconic ear.

"In the preface to the score, Bolcom writes: 'I now embark on a stylistic and harmonic synthesis no longer involved with any local style—that of a fusion of tonality *into* non-centered sound (often miscalled 'atonal'), as a planet in space draws gravity toward itself. Within this spatial (yet tonal) universe one can attempt to calibrate one's distance from a strong tonal center with greater accuracy.' He goes on to explain that the tension between stylistic evolution and stylistic conservatism 'produces a potential richness of musical energy that for my part I find enormously fecund and exciting. With the growth of skill in the management of this tension, it becomes possible to arrive at a musical speech that is at once coherent and comprehensible *and* in constant expansion.' Of particular interest is the fact that, as Bolcom is an accomplished pianist, the quality and intensity of the pianist's physical address to performance is a fundamental factor in his compositional process. It gives his music an authenticity that effectively anchors the sophistication of his thought.

"The composer provides the following descriptions in the score [movement titles are italicized—Ed.]:

Book 1
  1. *Fast, furious*, headlong, but controlled. Sweeping gestures of hands, forearms, the body. Freedom of movement. 14 Oct. 1977. [1m]
  2. *Récitatif.* Recitative style, rubato; finger-changes for smoothness' sake; smooth passage of line between hands. 2 May 1977. [3m]
  3. *Mirrors* Very light, rhythmic. Leaps, distorted mirrors, lateral stretches between fingers. 6 Dec. 1977. [2m]
Book 2
  4. *Scène d'opéra.* A steady, rhythmic ostinato versus varied irrational rhythms. 25 Aug. 1980, revised 25 Nov. 1982. [3m]
  5. *Butterflies, hummingbirds.* The lateral tremolo. Mercurial changes in color, attacks and rhythm. 31 Apr. 1980, revised 31 Aug. 1986. [2m]
  6. *Nocturne.* Absolute contrast in dynamics and tone. 1 Apr. 1981 [4m]
Book 3
  7. *Premonitions.* 'Free-falls' into piano keys; size of tone without banging. Inside-piano plucking. 29 Sep. 1982. [3m]
  8. *Rag infernal (Syncopes apocalyptiques.* Lateral hand-jumps and stretches. Use of practically *no* pedal. 17 Nov. 1982. [2m]
  9. *Invention.* Controlled legato lines with minimal pedal. Clear delinieation of voices. 28 Apr. 1983. [3m]
Book 4
  10. *Vers le silence.* Use of the pedals. Wide leaps and dynamic contrast. Trills. 1983–28 August 1986. [6m]
  11. *Hi-jinks.* Lively, with a strange and ghostly humor. Dynamic contrast (in the piano section least naturally apt). 1983–29 Aug. 1986. [2m]
  12. *Hymne à l'amour.* Contrast of timbres, mostly by means of pedal. Orchestral sonorities. 1983–2 Sept. 1986. [7m]"

—Austin Clarkson, from program notes for New World recording NW 354.

"These etudes reflect a remarkable variety of compositional and pianistic techniques. They range from about one to seven minutes in length and they include a writing style that is tonal as well as atonal. They feature some blues harmonies, hand and forearm clusters, tremolos, plucked strings, chains of trills, wide leaps, ostinatos, rapid changes of dynamics and registers, free as well as very strict rhythms, notation on as many as five staves, and complicated use of all three pedals, as well as some stretches of fast notes with no pedal at all.

"The two most technically difficult of the etudes are probably Nos. 5 and 8. The former, titled *Butterflies, Hummingbirds*, requires sudden changes of color, attack and rhythm at a rapid tempo; the latter, titled *Rag Infernal*, features an extremely taxing left-hand part, with wide leaps played very fast at *ppp* without pedal. More modest requirements, technically and maybe musically, are found in the bluesy No. 2, '*Récitatif*', and the hypnotic Nos. 4 and 6, '*Scène d'opéra*' and *Nocturne*. The entire work is worth the attention of serious pianists, to whom the recording on New World Records by Marc-André Hamelin is highly recommended." — Charles Timbrell, in *The American Music Teacher* (Music Teachers National Association), 10-11/89.

"The piano etude is a child of the early nineteenth-century, and the most well-known etudes for piano continue to be those of Chopin and Liszt. However, remarkable sets of etudes have been written by many early twentieth-century composers, among them Stravinsky, Bartók, Scriabin, and Debussy, and in more recent times by George Perle, John Corigliano, and György Ligeti. William Bolcom can now be added to this list. His *Twelve New Etudes for Piano* is a substantial addition to the etude repertoire.

"This is the second set of etudes written by Bolcom; the first, *Twelve Etudes for Piano* (Bryn Mawr: Merion, 1971), was composed between 1959 and 1966 and recorded by the composer on Advance FGR-14S. The *Twelve New Etudes*, begun in 1977, were originally intended for Paul Jacobs. Upon Jacob's unfortunate death in 1983, Bolcom ceased working on the set but decided to complete it after pianists John Musto and Marc-André Hamelin each played some of the etudes in 1986. He has dedicated the work to all three pianists.

"The best etudes have always been written by composer-pianists who have an extensive knowledge of the instrument, and these are no exception. While Bolcom considers himself primarily a composer, he has also had an extensive career as a performer, both as soloist, recording works of Gershwin, Joplin, Milhaud, and Bolcom, and in collaboration with his wife, Joan Morris, in numerous recordings of American popular song. Bolcom's tremendous facility at the keyboard shows through in these etudes, which, although presenting great technical challenges, lie well for the instrument.

"As a composer Bolcolm has attempted to break down the distinctions between serious and popular music, writing in styles ranging from atonal to ragtime to cabaret. Unlike the first set of etudes, which are in the Boulez-Stockhausen tradition and are more stylistically unified, these *Twelve New Etudes* reflect the changes in Bolcom's compositional thinking that occurred over a period of ten years, from 1977 to 1986. Thus one finds such diverse styles as the Webern-like imagery of the third etude (1977) and the madcap rag of the eighth (1982).

"The etudes are grouped in four books of three, with each etude addressing a particular problem stated at the beginning of the piece. Unlike etudes of the nineteenth and early twentieth centuries, which addressed such technical matters as double thirds, double sixths, octaves, trills, and so forth, these etudes are more often concerned with such musical matters as color, legato, timbre, and mood. For example, the sixth focuses on 'absolute contrast of dynamics and tone', the eleventh on 'ghostly humor'. Titles are equally divided between French and English, and like those in the first set, these etudes can be played singly, in groups, or as a complete set.

"For the most part arranged chronologically, the etudes reflect not only Bolcom's myriad compositional sensibilities but also his sense of humor. The second etude, for example, begins as a recitative with numerous V-I cadences; it is followed by a Satie-like waltz marked 'Shyly', with the Satie quote: 'C'est mon coeur qui se balance ainsi [It is my heart that swings this way]'.

"These etudes require first-rate pianism. While technically they are somewhat less difficult than the first set, they still pose significant problems. But for the pianist who possesses the fingers to master the technical difficulties and the imagination to master the musical ones, these *Twelve New Etudes* will prove to be rewarding indeed." — Lois Svard, in *Notes* (Music Library Association), 12/89.

"The *New Etudes*, in the tradition of the genre, require a combination of muscularity and musicality. They are composed in a language that brings together elements of tonality and dense chromaticism, and several are blatantly picturesque. The fourth, for instance — called '*Scène d'opéra*' — has a steady, repeating bass line that suggests the underpinning of an operatic scene, while the treble line skitters wildly above it. In the fifth, *Butterflies*, the musical portrayal of the graceful fluttering insect is perfect.

"Others are more abstract, but each of the dozen, whether rumbling and ostentatiously virtuosic, or more introspective, make daunting demands on the pianist's agility and sense of color. In Mar-André Hamelin's beautifully etched, transparent renderings [in the New World Records release], even the least programmatic of the pieces leave distinct and almost visual impressions." — Allan Kozinn, in *The New York Times*, 7/31/88.

"In his [unpublished] preface to the score Bolcom makes a point of separating himself from his earlier *Twelve Etudes* (1959-66). 'I now embark on a stylistic and harmonic synthesis no longer involved with any local style—that of a fusion of tonality into non-centered sound (often miscalled "atonal")'....

"Perhaps the most vivid of the *Twelve New Etudes* is *Etude 5 (Butterflies, hummingbirds*. The lateral tremolo...'). At the same time the cycle boldly juxtaposes one etude with another, exemplifying Bolcom's tendency, to use the apt phrase of annotator Austin Clarkson, 'to tickle one idiom in the ribs with another.' Every conceivable kind of articulation and attack is required, including tone clusters and plucking inside the piano. By the same token, Bolcom can be characteristically mercurial in his mood swings. Cases in point are *Etudes 7 and 8*: '*Premonitions* (senza tempo) with its free falls into piano keys; size of tone without banging. Inside-piano plucking'; there is, I might add, a concluding fragmentary quotation of the *'Tuba mirum'* text from the *'Dies Irae'*, exclusively for the guidance of the performer.[22] All of this is directly followed by *Rag Infernal (syncopes apocalyptiques)*, to be played 'as fast as practicable.' It involves 'lateral hand-jumps and stretches. Use of practically no pedal.' Even more striking is the juxtaposition of the 'slow, even, implacable' ending of *Etude 10* ('*Vers le silence'*) with its prolongations of sound, extremes of register, and a [verbal] quotation of *'Rex tremendae'* directly followed by *Etude 11* (*Hi-jinks*). Marc-André Hamelin [in the New World recording] gives a performance that is unlikely to be surpassed for some time."—Joshua Berrett, in *American Music,* Summer 1989.

Songs of Innocence and of Experience (A Musical Illumination of the [46] William Blake Poems for Solo Voices, Chorus and Orchestra (1956-81). 160m *Prem.:* Stuttgart (West Germany) orchestra, soloists and chorus, Dennis Russell Davies, cond. *Other perfs.:* Univ of MI orchestra, soloists and chorus, Gustav Meier, cond.; Chicago IL perf.; Sara Arneson, Joan Morris, David Caldwell, college & prof choruses (dir Harry Saltzman), children of the Cathedral Choristers (dir Donald Barnum), Brooklyn PO, Lukas Foss, cond. *Score* available from E. B. Marks Music (Hal Leonard).
Voices: s, m-s, contr, boy s, t, bar, b, country, rock, folk singers (5-10 soloists); mixed, madrigal & children's choruses
Orchestra: 3-3-3-3; 2 sax-6-5-5-3; 6-7 perc, org, pno, hp, elec & acoust gtrs, b gtr; 2 elec vlns, strings
In nine sections and three larger divisions—the latter corresponding to poems of youth (innocence), maturity, and old age (experience).

Full-length song cycle encompassing musical styles from romantic to modern, from country to rock, utilizing more than 200 vocalists

---

22 In written, not musical form.

and instrumentalists. "My explorations in all sorts of music from America's past have been to learn the roots of our musical language, so that I can build from them." —William Bolcom.

"Bolcom's piece is a masterwork, twenty years in the making, by a musician so versatile that his reputation as a serious composer probably has suffered. Bolcom, who teaches at the University of Michigan, is known best to audiences and record buffs as the talented pianist half of the song team he has formed with his wife, Joan Morris. But he deserves recognition on his own.

"In the 1950s, at the Paris Conservatory, Bolcom's shoo-in first prize at the composition competition was knocked down to second when the finale of his string quartet broke into 'Rockin' My Soul in the Bosom of Abraham'. In a world that praised purity of style—and especially the purity of the international atonal style—Bolcom's habit of putting a whole world of music into his pieces was confounding. Tonal, atonal, rock, reggae, cowboy, *coloratura*, art song, cabaret—Bolcom's style today is still a conversation among styles threaded together with a rigorous intellect, a virtuoso ear and a punster's instincts. But now the time is right....

"In Bolcom's hands, the [Blake poems of the *Songs of Innocence* and *Songs of Experience*] waltz, sway, swagger and rock; they sob, dream, shiver, panic, and smile with pure joy. The work uses every imaginable combination of performers, from an old-fashioned *a capella* chorus to a cowboy singer and a few guitars. The music ranges with astounding virtuosity and imagination. [In this work the composer's] craft is absolutely secure.

"Bolcom wrote the first Blake setting at the age of seventeen—a slithering, swollen waltz in B-flat minor for 'The Sick Rose' that is being destroyed by a worm. Among the last tunes was 'The Fly', another halting waltz. In between, Bolcom wandered to bizarre, distant and sumptuously coloristic regions. The logic of each setting seems impeccable, and the transition from one to the other often brilliantly arresting. To round an anxious atonal corner and land smack in the middle of an exhuberant rock song is half the fun in listening to this work." —Nancy Malitz, in *Ovation*, 8/84.

"William Bolcom's setting of Blake's *Songs of Innocence* and *Songs of Experience* is not an opera, though I can imagine a scenario for it. But surely [the opera-going public] should take note of a theater piece that takes three hours to play and employs orchestra, large chorus, small chorus, madrigal group, children's chorus and nine soloists—especially if it is a work of such grand power and significant intent. Even after allowing for the fact that these are among the most emotion-laden poems in our language—and 'songs', to boot, with rhythms that dance into music if you merely speak them well—I think Bolcom's accomplishment here is the most important contribution to the literature of the large-scale since Samuel Barber's *Vanessa* a generation ago.

"There are 46 poems, plus a vocalise of the chorus as animal (human animal, but animal), and the styles range from Webern to country, from Walton to Broadway, from late Debussy to early rock. 'Eclectic' is the obvious description, which has not been avoided; to my taste, the word 'pragmatic' is better. Especially in the bitter ninth and last 'part', which explores the varieties of expressionism, Bolcom has bridged a chasm of two centuries, and cultural divisions even broader, to heighten Blake's terror and despair at what God has permitted. But the work is also full of pleasures—the choral shout and electric-violin *obbligato* in 'The Echoing Green', the achingly high *tessitura* of the soprano above the chromatic strings in 'Cradle Song', the rhythmic exactitude of folk-song voice over a clarinet at the top of its register in 'The Divine Image', the evocations of Richard Strauss in 'Night', the Schoenberg references of wood block and bull fiddle and muted trumpet in 'The Little Boy Lost', the *a capella* intricacy of 'The Little Girl Lost' (used—Blake left an option—in the *Experience* rather than the *Innocence* section of the cycle.)"—Martin Mayer, in *Opera*, 4/87.

"Subtitled 'A musical illumination of the poems of William Blake', [this] cantata could also stand as illumination of the breadth of Bolcom's musical outlook....

"Written and engraved by Blake between 1789 and 1794, the complete set of 46 poems embodies the panorama of world experience, from simple joys to man-inflicted cruelty as seen through a child's eyes. Poet and composer alike draw on a glowing lyric vocabulary. Sweet, fragile tunes—an enchanting setting of 'The Shepherd' for one, with a folk singer onstage and a bucolic band off in the distance—stand beside horrific, large-scale outbursts as Blake and Bolcom recoil at the underside of the human condition. Near the end of the cycle, the poet visits London where 'the youthful harlot's curse blasts the newborn infant's tear'. Bolcom lights his shaky steps with the glare of screaming synthesizers in 'apocalyptic rock tempo'. For the most famous of the poems, every schoolboy's pet 'Tiger', Bolcom has framed Blake's 'fearful symmetry' in the menacing tone of men's voices hurling out a growling speech-song over the roar of percussion....

"At the end of *Songs*, Blake, brooding, finds that 'Cruelty has a human heart'. Here, Bolcom seems to compose against the mood;

over a steady reggae beat, one by one the singers take up the poem, and the music swells to an exultant climax. 'Somebody once reproached me for always having happy endings to my music,' says Bolcom. 'But after reading books like *Fate of the Earth* I became obsessed with saying something positive, to celebrate whatever ilfe there still is.' With American music still not completely triumphant in its struggle for recognition, Bolcom's big new score is reason to celebrate." —Alan Rich, in *Newsweek*, 1/19/87.

"Bolcom composes music that audiences can like and critics can respect. His Blake cantata... is for huge, Mahlerian forces designed to play convincingly nearly every idiom this country has known. There are knotty yet always passionately expressive sections that recall the more conventionally modernist classical music he wrote in his student days. There are soulful Appalachian folk tunes and, as the climax to the entire score, a surging reggae anthem dedicated to the memory of the late Bob Marley....

"[Bolcom's music] is music that speaks to Americans through American idioms, making a ringing affirmation out of the eclecticism that affects all the arts today, and robs lesser artists of focus. Right now, Bolcom is the most convincing and successful practitioner of an omnivorous style that unites the classical and popular traditions into a communicative, accessible music stiffened by the backbone of originality. It's a school that Charles Ives inspired and that has also been practiced—in different ways and with different emphases—by such other American composers as Kurt Weill, Virgil Thomson, Leonard Bernstein, Lukas Foss, George Rochberg (whose critical writings Bolcom edited), David Del Tredici, Peter Shickele and John Adams." —John Rockwell, in *The New York Times Magazine*, 8/16/87.

"Bolcom's reputation has been that of a consummate miniaturist.... How does such a miniaturist build a musical structure that won't be blasted off the stage by the poet? The admittedly obvious lesson here is that, if enough finely wrought miniatures can be cemented together according to a valid larger pattern, a mighty mosaic wall can result." —Leighton Kerner, in *The Village Voice*, 2/3/87.

"Bolcom has been a notable song composer, and he obviously feels these texts deeply. His response is to treat each poem individually, both in terms of the orchestration of the setting and in terms of the musical style employed.... The choices he makes for each individual Blake setting strike one as apt, and often involve only a fraction of the performing forces. What this approach accomplishes is not the fragmentation of the whole into parts, but a sort of continuous mosaic in which each song becomes an end in itself yet by its very jewel-like beauty leads the audience onwards to the next. Since Bolcom's compositional technique is assured, and one song melds immediately into the next (there are a few short orchestral interludes), a sense of momentum is kept up through the span of each section (separated by two intermissions).

"But what underlies the cycle, and gives it the particular flavor that prevents its becoming a storehouse of reminiscences of other musics, is that Bolcom has subsumed into his own writing the varieties of American music. In this, I can only compare his compositional procedure with the poetry, not of Blake, but of Walt Whitman. The work is a teeming world, a world which makes of the English poet Blake a particularly American product. It is an amazing incidence of illumination and transformation." — Patrick J. Smith, in *Musical America*, 10/84.

William Bolcom / Joan Morris note paper design

HENRY BRANT

B. 1913, Montreal (Canada). *Educ.:* Inst of Musical Art, Juilliard Schl of Music. *Taught at:* Columbia Univ, Juilliard Schl, Bennington College. Guggenheim Fellowship. *Works incl.:* concertos (jazz cl, sax, vln), *Crossroads* (4 vlns), orchestral pieces *(Encephalograms, Labyrinth, On the Nature of Things, Whoopee in D major)*, symphonies in B^b, F, vocal pieces.

An American Requiem for Wind Symphony Orchestra (with Optional Soprano Voice)(1973). 15m *Prem.:* American Wind SO, Robert Austin Boudreau, cond. *Pub.:* Henmar (distr. C. F. Peters—score; performance materials on rental).
In three sections.

"Henry Brant studied with George Antheil, Aaron Copland, and Wallingford Riegger. Typical of his style is a multi-level concept applied to space (players located throughout a performance space including the audience), materials (different groups often exploring different materials simultaneously), and even styles (materials developed with intrinsically contrasting stylistic techniques). Exemplary of this approach is Brant's *Grand Universal Circus*, a large three movement (acts) work completed in 1956 utilizing diverse forces spread throughout a concert hall involving polyrhythmic, polymetric and polyphonic concepts.

"Performance notes [for *An American Requiem*] are lengthy, primarily defining spatial location of six different widely separated instrumental groups and four separated single players including an optional voice (soprano on biblical texts from Isaiah and Habakkuk). The primary group of the ensemble is a group of sixteen woodwinds sitting on the stage in a semicircle with their backs to the audience (the conductor faces the group and the audience at centerstage). The horn, trumpet, and trombone sections contrast the individual parts of the woodwinds with unison rhythmic materials and are situated out in the hall. The fifth section is made of various bells (including 'pipe-chimes', the construction of which are described by the composer loosely as three sets of seven pipes each set, a half inch or so different in diameter, with different pitches obtained by two or three inch length differential). Two tubas join the brass in homorhythmic unison with single parts for pipe organ, voice, church bells (recorded on tape if necessary) and timpani. The instrumental writing is genuinely idiomatic but also very difficult. The separation of performers is absolutely necessary to the piece (including spatial figurations of one group entering 'fractionally later than others by reason of timelag in the hall').

"*An American Requiem* is a long (15') three section work with a steady tempo throughout (quarter note = 69). The first section opens with the formative material of the work: a nine note horizontal motive of a half-step cluster bordered on each end by whole steps. Each note of this line is paralled homorhythmically by eight other instruments forming a mirror of the horizontal material (i.e. a vertical cluster bordered on each end by whole steps). This kind of consistency of vocabulary between melodic and harmonic content is continued throughout the work. Contrasting this dissonant idea in the winds is a static organ part of triadic content (c minor, B^b minor, etc.) which is characteristic of both the first and third sections. The quasi-pitched pipe-chimes add a surrealistic touch to the multi-leveled music.

"This opening section (by far the longest of the three) is in three large periods with the first a kind of introduction (static and expository in nature), the second a rich counterpoint (spatial as well as notes) with sections in parallel motion as subjects, and the third exploring waves of sound slowly evolving and devolving with as many as twenty different lines at a time. The optional vocal solo separates this section from the second as well as the second from the third. The second main section develops the polyphony of the first with contrasting sectional flutters in the brass, trills in the percussion and the carillon in hemiola with the rest of the ensemble. The third main section returns to the organ triads and variations of the initial expository material.

"This brief analysis barely touches the intricasies of this extraordinary work. Brant has carried the Ives polysonic traditions to significant musical ends. One would hope that many live performances by our increasing numbers of professional wind ensembles will ensue.... Brant continues to be one of America's most underrated composers and his slow production of very complex works will not change that soon. His amazing virtuoso mind seems unconvinced that rating is of any consequence (thank god!)."—David Cope, in *Notes* (Music Library Association), 12/81.

Western Springs: A Spatial Assembly for 2 Orchestras, 2 Choruses and 2 Jazz Combos (1984). *Comm. & rec.:* Composers Recordings Inc CRI SD 512: La Jolla Civic/University SO, David Chase & Amy Snyder (choral conds), Thomas Nee & Henry Brant (orch conds).

"Since the composition of *Antiphony 1* (1953), Henry Brant has explored timbre and space because 'spatial amalgams of highly contrasted musical events, freely associated yet controlled, present opportunities for representing in the concert hall, musical equivalents of the incessant bombardment of social and environmental catastrophes which bedevil daily existence' (liner notes for *Henry Brant—Music 1970*, Desto DC-7108, 1970). He generally places several ensembles each possessing a unique musical identity and language, in various locations in a performing space, where, together and in shifting combinations, they engulf the listener in a sometimes euphonious, sometimes cacophonous blend of contrasting styles, tempi, and timbres. Clarity is achieved through spatial separation.[23]

"The text [for *Western Springs*], prepared by the composer, describes the locations, flow charts, and so on of hot springs in the United States. In live performance the [two] orchestras are situated on opposite sides at the front of the hall, while the [two] mixed choruses, each paired with a small combo, are located at the back.

"The work is divided into two parts, each consisting of many smaller sections, which often alternate between the orchestras and the choruses and combos. For the orchestra there is much austere and well-wrought contrapuntal writing, as well as meditative, lyrical passages that reveal the influence of Ives and Riegger. The choruses speak, shout, and sing the text, and electronic effects emanate from both the orchestras and choruses. In addition, there are improvised passages, suggestions of the big band era, and colorful use of bells and timpani. The mélange of vivid contrasts is unified by thematic ties in the orchestral passages and by a work song rendered canonically by the choruses frequently throughout the work....

"*Western Springs* is one of several compositions scored for extremely large forces (it requires more than 200 musicians), employing an ever-wider range of musical styles. This may discourage performances, but the La Jolla Civic/University Symphony and Chorus and the assisting jazz musicians have shown here in their fine and enthusiastic performance that *Western Springs* might find a place in the repertories of college ensembles. [The recording performs] a great service to those interested in current developments in

---

23 A more recent work, *Prisons of the Mind*, premiered by the Dallas SO at the Morton H. Meyerson Symphony Center in Dallas in April 1990, is also a "spatial symphony" which, in the words of *Musical America* reviewer Olin Chism, "utilized practically every nook and cranny of the center's architecturally complicated auditorium.... [It involved] some 314 musicians and eight conductors, supplemented by two high school concert bands and two Caribbean steel-drum ensembles.... Musicians were on stage, in balconies and boxes, on the choral terrace, perched precariously on the facade of the hall's pipe organ, and secreted inside large reverberation chambers high above the audience.... These ensembles made a mighty noise." (Ed.)

American music." — Emily Good, in *Notes* (Music Library Association), Summer 1987.

THOMAS BRICCETTI

B. 1936, Mt. Kisco NY. *Educ.:* Eastman Schl of Music. *Grants & awards incl.:* ASCAP grants, Ford Fndn fellowships, NEA commissions (3). Mus dir St. Petersburg (FL) SO, Florida Sun Coast Opera Co, Ft Wayne (IN) PO, Omaha SO, Orchestra Sinfonia di Umbria (Perugia, Italy), Orchestra Stabile di Bergama (Italy); assoc cond Indianapolis SO; guest cond Cleveland O, Oslo PO, Baltimore SO, O de la Suisse Romande, Brno P, Louisville O, Detroit SO, NY P, Prague P, Danish State Radio O. *Works incl.:* 2 *Caprices* (tpt/chamb orch), choral (5 *Love Poems, The Definitive Journey*), concerto (vln), *Divertimento* (wind nonet), *Eurydice* (1-act opera), *The Fates* (fl/hp), *Nocturne* (vln/pno), orchestral (*The Fountain of Youth, Illusions*), 3 *Songs* (high vce/chamb orch), *Symphony 1, The Visions of Kamm* (sym wind ens).

Sonata for Flute and Piano, Op 14 (1960). 15m *Prem:* Ørnulf Gulbransen (fl), Thomas Briccetti (pno). *Other perfs.:* James Politis (fl); Harold Jones (fl), Francis Brancaleone (pno). *Pub.:* McGinnis and Marx.
1. Moderato. 2. Andante cantabile. 3. Prestissimo.

"The premiere performance took place in Oslo, Norway in 1960 with the celebrated Norwegian flutist Ørnulf Gulbransen and the composer at the piano. It was subsequently recorded at the studios of the NRK (Norwegian Broadcasting) and broadcast many times in the following years.

"The *Flute Sonata* appears in the repertoire lists of the American Flute Club and has enjoyed numerous performances throughout the country and in Europe. Its American premiere took place in 1963 in a concert sponsored by the Philadelphia Flute Club, with James Politis (then principal flutist of the Metropolitan Opera Orchestra) as soloist. During the 1991 season the *Sonata* will be performed numerous times throughout Italy by the Duo Angela Patricia Jones and Donna Stoering on the national concert series sponsored by Gioventù Musicale Italiana.

"The work is in the traditional three movement form, and its musical language, although quite personal, takes root in the great romantic and impressionistic piano literature. It is a virtuoso piece for both flute and piano, quite taxing in public performance." – Thomas Briccetti.

"I found the Briccetti *Sonata* well written for the flute. It exploits the flute's many possibilities. It was gratifying to play a sonata as strong as the Prokofiev sonata." — Harold Jones, flutist, 10/90.

"Briccetti's *Sonata* is a complex duo sonata that requires considerable technique and musical maturity from both instrumentalists. Briccetti speaks with an original, post-Romantic voice that ranges from tenderly lyrical to bitterly acerbic, and unleashes feelings of power that threaten to break out of control. It compels a deep emotional response." — Francis Brancaleone, pianist, music critic Gannett Westchester Newspapers, 10/90.

HAVERGAL BRIAN

> **SPECIAL FEATURE**
>
> HAVERGAL BRIAN, a distinguished British composer of earlier this century, nevertheless wrote some of his most important works in later years... in very "contemporary" times after all, since the dates of his last ten symphonies are 1965–1968. His music is keenly appreciated by Brian specialists, of course; in no small part due to their efforts, it is also gaining respect among more general audiences. (Ed.)

B. 1876, Dresden, Staffordshire (England); *d.* 1972, Shoreham-by-Sea, Sussex (England). *Works incl.:* concertos (orch, vc, vln), operas (*Agamemnon, The Cenci, The Tigers, Turandot*), 32 symphonies.

Symphony 3 in C# Minor for Orchestra (1932). *Prem. at a public concert* (1987): SO of Composers Platform, West Midlands, Paul Venn, cond. *Rec.:* BBC studio recording (1974): New Philharmonia O, Ronald Stevenson, David Wilde (pnos), Stanley Pope, cond.; Hyperion (CD) 66334 (also as Cassette KA-66334; distr. Harmonia Mundi): BBC SO, Andrew Ball, Julian Jacobson (pnos), Lionel Friend, cond. 4[4 picc]-4[2 E hn]-E^b cl-4 A cl[2 b cl]-4-c bsn;8-4-4-2; 6 timp (2 players), perc (b drum, side drum, t drum, cymbals, tamb, cast, triangle, gong, xyl, glock), celesta, 2 harps, 2 pnos, organ *ad lib.*; strings
1. Andante moderato e sempre sostenuto e marcato (14m) 2. Lento sempre marcato e rubato (14m). 3. Allegro vivace (8m). 4. Lento solenne (13m).

"Brian's first four symphonies are all scores of outsize ambition and large-scaled expressive scope. And they are all works of his musical maturity: [especially insofar as the last seven symphonies were written after the age of 90,] Brian is more of a contemporary 20th century symphonist than the year of his birth, 1876, would suggest. All of the first four symphonies are an English composer's effort to build on central European symphonic traditions. Brian attempts a Mahlerian comprehensiveness in combination with the formal logic and conciseness of Sibelius, though in these early symphonies the Mahler-like maximalist is to the forefront. Yet the sound of the music recalls neither Mahler nor Sibelius. Nor is it relatable, even by a long stretch, to Elgar or Strauss, both much admired by Brian. The Brian sound, indeed, recalls no other composer, and the music seems to exist in a bizarre, free-ranging imaginative world of its own.

"Brian certainly did not make things easy for himself. The *Gothic Symphony* outdoes both Mahler's *Eighth* and Schoenberg's *Gurrelieder* in its orchestral and choral requirements, while the purely instrumental *Third* makes use of a more normal but still very large complement: 120 players in the Hyperion recording, including a battalion of percussion, organ, and two pianos. No doubt this prodigious orchestration was part of the reason the composer never heard the symphony performed.

"I have always found the *Third* one of the tougher Brian nuts to crack. It extends sight-lines into past traditions yet forges into the future with an array of experimental techniques and complex contrapuntal textures rivalling Schoenberg's *Pelleas and Melisande* and the Ives *Fourth*. The resultant perspective of the new seen over the backdrop of the old is vertiginous. Only a composer of Brian's intractable originality could hold so much together. Malcolm MacDonald,[24] who is beyond doubt the foremost authority on Brian's symphonic music, thinks the *Third* one of Brian's greatest scores. It could be argued that later symphonies find a more incisive form, an even more distinctive melodic substance. There is, I think, some truth in this; but none have the world-spanning trajectory of the first four.

"The immense first movement, with its slow obsessive march rhythms, contrasting lyrical episodes, and wildly proliferating textural fantasy, presents the greatest interpretive difficulties. Brian's inexhaustible orchestral inventiveness crops up in two passages near the beginning of the movement. The first occurs between the statement of the lyrical first and second subjects, a march episode with instruments gathering in the heights and depths of the orchestra, moving with ungainly steps in a raucously exhuberant processional. Then, after the second subject, comes an extraordinary phantasmal event, a Brianesque happening of high weirdness and staggering orchestral virtuosity. These two pages (almost as strange to look at in score as to hear) with their multiple dynamics, rhythmic cross-hatchings and strings divided into ten parts, recall the athematic universal sounds in Ives's *Fourth* and *"Holidays"* Symphonies. There follow some fantastically scored pages: solo passages for many instruments, exotic percussion effects, and near the end an extended cadenza for

---

[24] The editor of *Tempo* quarterly review, whose many books include *John Foulds and His Music: An Introduction* and *Ronald Stevenson: A Biography* — both published in the United States by Pro/Am Music Resources, Inc. (Ed.)

the duo pianos and two timpanists. This is not always easy on the ear. Brian creates some ruggedly primal sounds. After this heroic vision, the slow movement seems at first a pastoral contrast with an extended rhapsodic episode for solo violin. Soon, however, clouds gather on the horizon and the music enters into an alien soundscape with towering storms forming in the orchestra and soon blotting out any pastoral associations. The music twice rises to darkly radiant climaxes, only to dissolve into a haunting and beautifully mysterious passage which is cut off by the entry of the heavy-brass descending with ponderous balefulness into the depths. It is this kind of unfettered imaginative flight that gives some of Brian's critics pause. During the 1930s this baroque phantasmagoria, so removed from the symphonies of Elgar, Vaughan Williams or Bax, must have seemed almost monstrous.[25]

"Then, by way of complete surprise and contrast, Brian gives us in the scherzo a joyful, boisterous movement replete with leaping brass fanfares, cartwheeling woodwinds and, in the trio, what sounds like an anglicized Viennese waltz. This is one of Brian's most approachable and appealing pieces, a jubilant interlude setting off the weighty complexity of the rest of the symphony. The finale, beginning in Brian's favorite heroic-elegiac vein, progresses in slow-moving tidal polyphony with echoing fanfare passages, through episodes of stormy grandeur before reaching, in the final bars, a climax of overpowering orchestral sonority.

"As often in Brian symphonies, this ending presents fundamental problems, both psychological and interpretive, for performers and listeners. Does it represent total victory or an explosion of frustration? Is it less a confirmation than a confrontation? Brian's music is edged with powerful oppositions, sometimes almost a siege of contraries. The music seems to be struggling for unity and cohesion against counterforces trying to blow it apart. This effect — along with the strange atmospherics — can be disorienting, and no doubt in part accounts for the reservations of some critics. We do not need to read his biographies to know that Brian was a most unusual man: every bar of his music proclaims it. The 32 symphonies[26] are works of tumultuous ferment traveling along the edge of a cryptic abyss, Brian attempting to impose order on some vast, night-shaded primal world. The *Third* is, to a certain extent, a problem symphony, immensely powerful and variegated but withal, curiousy enigmatic, leaving fascinating questions in its wake. [Meanwhile] the final bars are

---

25 To my ears (in 1989) while still "rugged", the work hardly seems so "monstrous", but familiar, rather, and in its own special way quite beautiful. (Ed.)
26 One (the first) is presumed lost, and so the "official" count is 32. (Ed.)

not merely roof-raising but house-annihilating." — Richard E. Tiedman, in *American Record Guide*, 11-12/89.

"Brian's composing was not, as is often thought, a mere old man's hobby, but a sustained life work extending over more than three-quarters of a century. His concentration (in the end almost exclusive) on symphonic form was a characteristic of the latter half of this exctaordinarily long creative career. The lost *Fantastic Symphony* was just one work from a respectably large body of music produced before World War I, and he did not finally take up the deepest challenges of the genre until he was well past forty.

"The *Gothic [Symphony No. 1]* emerged between 1919 and 1927. His next creative task was the orchestration of his opera *The Tigers*, sketched before that symphony, and after this was completed nearly a year elapsed before a *Second Symphony* began to take shape. No. 2, for orchestra alone, was far more orthodox in scale and structure, though still a very substantial piece by any other standards. The full score was completed on 6 April 1931, and only six days later Brian began to sketch its mighty successor.

"It seems that No. 3 was not begun as a symphony. On 25 May 1931, two days after the first movement was completed in outline, Brian wrote to Sir Granville Bantock that he had 'resolved the Concerto into a Symphony.' This is the only such reference, but it surely means that the *Third* was initially conceived as a concerto for piano, or rather, perhaps, the two pianos that loom so large and diversely in the final score. We should also note that this first movement uses the instruments far more extensively than the other three, which were still unwritten at the time of the letter. The pianos only appear in the latter half of the *Lento* second movement, parts of the *Finale*, and not at all in the *Scherzo* (the movements were composed in that order).

"On 21 June he began the second movement and completed its short score on 1 July, despite the 'many hindrances' complained about just over a week later in a letter to Bantock which goes on: 'I like the second movement now — it is bigger than such as I played to you from the first movement.' Composition of the work gathered pace: the *Finale* was completed on 16 July after four days' work, and the *Scherzo* despatched in a final two-day blaze of exuberant creativity celebrated in a further letter to 'Dear Gran' on the 20th: 'I finished the sketch of my new Symphony last night. As I heard the slow movement in a very slow 3 — I had to evolve a 2/4 Scherzo which sounds as though it had been written in Vienna... It will take a long time to decipher and write out my sketches...'

"The 'long time' stretched to 28 May 1932 when the full score was finally completed. This was hardly surprising, given the full-time writing and editing commitments at the magazine *Musical Opinion* which Brian had been fulfilling since his appointment as Assistant Editor in June 1927, not to mention the sheer size of the *Symphony* and its orchestration.

"While the *Third Symphony* has its fair share of dissonance, march rhythms, angular string writing, hard-edged percussion-topped scoring and abruptly cut off climaxes — more than enough to proclaim its kinship with later Brian — other features equally hark back to moods in his earlier music; of pastoral innocence, Elgarian nobility and sheer unbuttoned fairground riotousness. Withall it remains his most expansive, objective, heroic and lyrical symphony — all characteristics in keeping with the connotations, both aspiring and celestial, of the enigmatic word 'Altarus', the apparent title which Brian wrote on the score and then partially erased. In more than its number, as well as the disposition and relative dimensions of its movements, is this work Brian's 'Eroica' (without claiming further comparability with the greatest of all Third symphonies).

"*First movement: Andante moderato e sempre sostenuo e marcato*. A trenchant twenty-four bar introduction, growing out of an extraordinarily portentous unison C sharp octave on the pianos and doublebasses, with *mp* gong stroke leads to a long-breathed but curiously dour first subject melody, initially played by solo clarinet and divided strings *Più lento e espressivo*. After a linking passage dominated by the first piano, the first subject is repeated with fuller scoring and proceeds via a sudden percussion-driven *Allegro moderato* to the B minor second subject complex, *Poco più lento*. This, one of the longest and most haunting melodies in Brian's output, passes from multi-divided strings to winds, pianos and glockenspiel, then all these together. An episode of fantastic, *pointilliste* flickerings, then stalking trombone chords, lead to a full restatement of the second subject, inreasingly overlain by dissonant figuration that all but obliterates the melody. This grinds to a typically precipitous Brianic impasse beyond which flute and clarinet in octaves, haunted by a *staccato* piano figure, uncertainly survey the landscape. *Espressivo* strings find a sense of direction, tension picks up, and the music crescendos into an *Allegro con brio*. Formally, an extremely expansive exposition has now precipitated a kind of development section which, from wholly new material including a 'Broad-Massive *Sempre Dolente*' melody, leads — via pounding piano octaves derived from the introduction — to real contrapuntal development of the first subject. A *Più allegro e con brio* link dominated by pianos, side drum and xylophone at length brings a recapitulation crashing in. Sonata-style designs are rare in Brian, and more rarely yet does he treat us to the luxury of full-scale melodic repeitions, but here first and second subjects pass in full resplendent train (but with plenty of internal development still going on!), the latter born aloft first by woodwind and brass choirs haloed in glistening cascades of piano octaves, then strings, *con molto espressione,* and lastly the full forces, driving to a peak of ecstatic, Romantic fervor. This collapses into a *molto marcato* preparation by bassoons, horn and lower strings for a new and extended visitation by the rising piano octaves, four times repeated, and separated by prolonged tattoos from both timpanists. In a mood heavy with foreboding and frustrated energy, the movement's massive coda is released — a ponderous, lurching march 'as heavy as possible to the close.'

"Second movement: *Lento sempre marcato e rubato.* The first movement is not only the longest but also the most structurally complex and disturbed in the symphony. Despite its coda's unresolved tension, however, some profound psychological conflict does seem to have been eased at the passing of the movement, for the remainder of the work exists at a far more essentially serene level. The *Lento* unfolds from hesitant, but premonitory fragments of figures into a lengthy exposition of melodic ideas, one of the most distinctive first heard on a solo flute and then violin (one of several places where the textures thin out to allow one instrument to carry the music forward with a single melodic line). With very little of either the agonized disjunction or the heady fervor of the first movement, the second alternates between Alpine grandeur and pastoral calm, with at its center a long, pivotal violin solo uncoiling against shifting melodic fragments on woodwind, horns, harp and strings, gradually exhaling all tension to a *sostenuto molto* meditative quiescence, resting at last on an E. A solo timpanum repeats the E and the music moves into life again with a statement on first violins and violas of the flute/violin tune, this with almost Vaughan Williams-like candor. From now on the movement ascends through a series of glasical vistas — every department of the huge orchestra used to the utmost dramatic and coloristic effect — to mountainous climaxes of truly Brucknerian grandeur during which the pianos, silent for most of the movement, reappear. They descend with the heavy brass through a series of giant chordal steps and, left almost by themselves at the last, usher in a beautiful, long-drawn pastoral coda. An oboe muses over familiar melodic ideas against *pp* lower strings, its song finally passing to a flute which sinks to rest beneath quiet brass chords.

"Third movement: *Allegro vivace.* Brian continues with what we might well expect from many a Classical or Romantic composer, but certainly not him — a regular (almost!) *Scherzo-and-Trio:* first a brilliant fast march enclosing a *Grazioso e dolce* central section initially on flute and string quartet, then a Trio that's even more of a surprise — a lilting waltz melody sounding as if it had strayed from the world of Viennese operetta. Nevertheless, for all its first innocence, the Trio's development proceeds with leaps and textures and trills that speak more with the accent of Richard than Johann, and when Brian brings back the march not as a literal repeat but more heavily and dissonantly scored with full wind and brass employed for the first time in this movement, it comes as no real surprise to find him cleverly drawing back step by step into the symphony's central progress, in preparation for the *Finale*.

"*Fourth movement: Lento solenne.* Brian does not often let us into the workshops of his mind and spirit, but another letter to Bantock gives a valuable insight into the composer's perception of the impetus behind the *Third Symphony*' elegiac *Finale*. After recounting his 'keen interest in a German Professor at Heidelberg University — Friedrich Gundolf... A great fellow — who has pursued Goethe and Shakespeare all his life,' Brian goes on: 'When I was working at the Finale of my new Symphony — it deviated (like its predecessor...) into an elegiac or Funeral poem. I couldn't escape it — it had to be. After I had finished my Symphony — I rushed up to town — bought a *Berliner Tageblatt*, put it in my bag — but didnt *(sic)* even look at it until Monday night this week... I was astonished to find that I had written the finale at the time of Gundolf's death — and actually completed it about the time of his funeral in Heidelberg. It may be a coincidence — but it is a curious and sad one.' Note the 'had to be' and 'may be'.

"Requiem for Friedrich Gundolf or not, the *Finale's* progress from the long opening bass clarinet theme through episodes magically remote, starkly violent, and consolatory, to the overwhelming conclusion seems in retrospect inevitable. The rich polyphonic growth of the first theme thickens and darkens before a *Poco largamente* climax (with pianos reappearing for the first time since the second movement) gives way to off-stage trumpet and horn fanfares. A slow timpani crescendo precipitates the irruption of jagged development (some of the first movement's tensions here reasserting themselves) which in turn eventually quietens and leads to the second main theme. The tension gradually rises again, piano tone increasingly irradiates the orchestral texture, and the movement proceeds towards its conclusion in great unhurried waves — Brucknerian parallels again becoming apparent — in which both main themes are developed and extended. Finally, the organ adds its voice for the first time, trombones and tubas shoulder the whole edifice beneath a veritable aviary of trills from woodwind and strings, and the climax of this massive *Symphony*—a four-bar *Lento assai* 'Epilogue' (no Baxian leave-taking this!)—explodes in a crushing affirmation of power."—David J. Brown, from liner notes for Hyperion KA66334 cassette.

Symphony 10 in C Minor for Orchestra (1954). 47m *Prem.*: Philharmonia O, Stanley Pope, cond. (BBC broadcast). *Rec.*: Unicorn 2027 (distr. Harmonia Mundi; orig. Unicorn RHS 313): Leicestershire Schools O, James Loughran, cond. Autograph full score British Museum. *Pub.*: Musica Viva (facsimile study-score).
In one movement (four principal sections: *Adagio e solenne/Adagio—Allegro con fuoco—Lento espressivo*—March finale with coda).
Triple woodwinds; 4-4-3-euphonium-1; timp, 2 harps, glocken, xyl, triangle, cymbals, b drum, 5 side drums, thunder & wind machines; strings

"Thanks to the recording companies,[27] Havergal Brian is no longer an endangered composer. It is now possible to hear a survey of the symphonies ranging from 1, the colossal *Gothic* (1919-1927), to the complex and tumultous 16 (1960) and the sprightly and cryptic 31 (1968). Over the last 17 years, 11 symphonies have been recorded. This provides a representative selection, but such is the manifold diversity of these works, each as distinctive as a fingerprint, that only when all 32 are available will our selection be truly comprehensive. So there is a long way to go.

"After completing his giant 4-hour cantata *Prometheus Unbound* in 1944, Brian only began composing again in 1948. The seven symphonies written between then and 1957 give us a stretch of his most accessible music. Some of Brian's later symphonies, with their dense congeries of ideas, riotous motivic play, and unrelenting contrapuntal texture, can be daunting for even the agile-eared listener. But in Nos. 6 through 12, while these elements are certainly present, they are made more approachable by a graphic imagery that anchors the music in the course of Brian's typical on-rushing and volatile forms.

"Brian's *Tenth*, completed just after his 78th birthday in 1954, is particularly rich in these pictorial qualities. It begins with magnificent march music, harsh and strident, instinct with heroic strivings. This initial march rhythm is a binding force that is almost constantly present in the dramatic progression of the symphony. It gives

---

[27] And to the many champions of his music, such as the presen reviewer, Lewis Foreman, Paul Rapoport, Robert Simpson, Harold Truscott, David J. Brown and Malcolm MacDonald—author of the definitive three-volume study of the complete symphonies. I do think it is too bad that more of the recordings couldn't have been made when the composer was alive, and thus in a somewhat more advantageous situation to appreciate them! (Ed.)

the music a journeying character amidst multitudinous landscapes. Brian makes use of sonata logic if not the actual form. The symphony is continuous, but the outline of four distinct movements can be discerned. The end of the 'first movement' provides an experience pervasive in Brian's symphonies. It is as if the music's fabric is breaking up: rifts appear, portals open, and the listener is plunged with a giddy shift of perspective into strangeness, chaos—even nothingness. In the *Tenth*, it reveals a mystical stasis, luminous and ethereal, as if evoking starry immensities.

"In Brian's music, with its quick interplay of forces, a counter-terrain is always near. Out of mystery, with the greatest possible contrast, springs the symphony's scherzo. It is unmistakable storm music, a howling gale swept forward by a raucously propellent percussion array augmented by wind and thunder machines. This is Brian at his most vividly virtuosic.

"Again, in starkest contrast, comes a lyrical slow movement. In its tender yet stalwart masculinity the extended lyric solo for violin is almost a signature theme for the composer—an utterly Brianesque melodic invention. It reaches a rapturous climax for full orchestra, making way for the symphony's 'finale', a return to march music at once stark, exultant and fiercely triumphant. The savage march suddenly breaks off, seemingly adrift. And here, as at the close of the *Seventh Symphony*, there strikes a phenomenon outside the experience of the music: an enigmatic quiet brass chord over deep palpitations from the bass drum. The solo violin returns over tremolo strings, hoveringly, as if in rapt contemplation. And then to a quietly burgeoning radiance in the orchestra, it merges and melds into the softly glowing light as a slow-turning transformation of the opening march ends the symphony in mysteriously transcending calm.

"I have described the *Tenth* in some detail because it seems to me one of Brian's greatest scores. The symphony is now over 36 years old. In that time it has been performed in public only once. Conductors are not by and large a curious lot."—Richard E. Tiedman, in *American Record Guide*, 7-8/90.

HOWARD BRUBECK

B. 1916, Concord CA. *Educ.:* San Francisco State Coll. *Taught at:* Mills College, San Diego State Coll, Palomar College (Dean, Humanities Div). *Works incl.:* choral works, orchestral (*Brandenburg Gate, Elizabethan Suite, The Gardens of Versailles, Latin American Suite, Symphonic Movement on a Theme of Robert Kurka*), piano pieces, quintet (ww).

California Suite for Orchestra (1942). *Prem.:* San Francisco SO, Howard Brubeck, cond. *Pub.:* Derry Music Co.
2 (pic)-2-2-2; 4-2-2-1; timp, 2 perc; strings
In four movements.

"Its ideas were suggested by things Californian. [The first movement or overture stems from] suburban life as I knew it in the period between the wars; the second (*Night Song*) by a pastoral scene; the third (*Barn Dance*) by a former Western institution. The finale involves a hymn suggested by the ruggedness of the Kit Carson Spur country and a processional of the pioneers who braved that territory." — Howard Brubeck.

"Mr. Brubeck will go down in history as the only composer who has ever written a piece of music about California without mission bells and the lowing kine tinkling o'er the lea." — Alfred Frankenstein.

Dialogues for Jazz Combo and Orchestra (1956; rev. 1959). 23m *Prem.:* San Diego SO, Howard Brubeck, cond. (orig. 3-movement vers.); Dave Brubeck Quartet (Dave Brubeck, pno, Paul Desmond, a sax, Joe Morello, drums, Eugene Wright, bs), New York P, Leonard Bernstein, cond. (rev 4-movement vers.). *Recs.:* Columbia CS 8257: , Dave Brubeck Quartet, New York P, Leonard Bernstein, cond. *Pub.:* Derry Music Co.
1. Allegro (7m). 2. Andante (*Ballad*) (5m). 3. Adagio (*Ballad*) (5m). 4. Allegro (*Blues*) (6m).

From a letter to the Editor: "The president of the San Diego Symphony on whose Board I served became obsessed in 1955 with the idea that Dave [Brubeck, the composer's brother (Ed.)] should be scheduled to play the *Rhapsody in Blue* with the orchestra, then conducted by Robert Shaw. When I explained that Dave was essentially a jazz musician and confined himself to on-the-spot improvisations based on traditional popular tunes she responded by saying that I should write some tunes on which he could improvise with the orchestra. I thought of Bach and prayed to Him with apologies to both. The idea of this kind of work had been in my consciousness for some time. The opportunity appealed. Dave accepted the challenge and Bob [Shaw] kindly invited me to conduct the first performance in July, 1956. After much revision the four movements as they now stand were given their first performance by the New York Philharmonic in 1959, except for the brass section variation in the second movement which was added for the 1960 recording session.... [The work] led to many arrangements I made for jazz improvisors and orchestra which are still used by Dave."

Additional notes by the composer: "In this work an attempt is made to construct a score giving the orchestra an important part to play which adheres strictly to written notes, while the particular combination, or 'combo', of jazz instruments is free to improvise on the material of the movement.

"The work is to a large degree a theme and variations technique. The forms are mainly jazz forms. There is some variance from jazz structure but this has been handled in a manner which permits the jazz musician to work as he normally works, in the realm of harmonic, melodic and rhythmic variations on a set basic pattern. As a matter of fact jazz is full of rules and restrictions to the extent that one may find irony in the definition of jazz as 'the language of protest'. Whatever it protests is accomplished with a set of rules that would make Fux thrill with delight. These rules may have yet to find their way into a theory book, but exist they certainly do, with very definite restrictions on melodic, rhythmic and harmonic usage.

"The first movement is new. It replaces two earlier attempts which were performed but withdrawn from performance for a multitude of reasons. Mainly they did not solve the problem of integration of the orchestra and combo. In this movement the orchestra dominates the scene for approximately one and one-half minutes during which the main idea is stated with 'comments' by the combo. In the second section a 32-bar (AABA) 'chorus' is presented by the orchestra and combo; the material is derived from the opening idea. This is followed by six additional improvisation sections in which the orchestra and combo perform together but with emphasis shifting in importance between the two groups. The movement is concluded by a 16-bar coda in which the orchestra plays a simple figure derived from the original idea in a notated ritard against a steady unritarded solo played (improvised) by the combo drummer.

"The second movement is based on a 16-bar chorus first stated by the combo pianist solo. The nature of the orchestra part is essential-

Carnegie Hall backstage, after first New York Philharmonic performance of *Dialogues* for Jazz Combo and Orchestra: Howard Brubeck, Leonard Bernstein, Dave Brubeck *(left to right). Columbia Records photo.*

Rehearsal at Carnegie Hall: Howard Brubeck, Gregory Millar leaning on stage; Dave Brubeck Quartet, Leonard Bernstein, New York Philharmonic on stage. *Columbia Records photo.*

One Hundred Eighteenth Season

New York Philharmonic

Leonard Bernstein, MUSIC DIRECTOR   **1959 - 1960**
Carnegie Hall

6064th, 6065th, 6066th Concerts

Thursday Evening, December 10, 1959, at 8:30 ("Preview")
Friday Afternoon, December 11, 1959, at 2:15
Saturday Evening, December 12, 1959, at 8:30

LEONARD BERNSTEIN, Conductor

ARTHUR GOLD and ROBERT FIZDALE, Duo-Pianists
WILLIAM LINCER, Violist
DAVE BRUBECK QUARTET

Fourth program in a series devoted to "The Concerto"

BACH   Brandenburg Concerto No. 4, G major,
for Two Flutes, Violin, and Strings
     Allegro
     Andante
     Presto
     JOHN WUMMER (Flute)
     ROBERT MORRIS (Flute)
     JOHN CORIGLIANO (Violin)

MOZART   Concerto for Two Pianos and Orchestra,
E-flat major, K. 365
     Allegro
     Andante
     Rondo: Allegro   ARTHUR GOLD and ROBERT FIZDALE

INTERMISSION

STARER   Concerto for Viola, Strings, and Percussion
(First performances in the United States)
     Andante mosso   Lento
     Presto leggiero   Molto allegro
                       WILLIAM LINCER

H. BRUBECK   Dialogues for Jazz Combo and Orchestra
(First performances in New York)
     Allegro   Adagio — Ballad
     Andante — Ballad   Allegro — Blues
     DAVE BRUBECK QUARTET
     DAVE BRUBECK (Piano)   JOE MORELLO (Drums)
     PAUL DESMOND (Alto Saxophone)   EUGENE WRIGHT (Bass)

Messrs. Gold and Fizdale play the Baldwin Piano

Steinway Piano   Columbia Records

Please note: Next "Odd" Thursday and Friday Concerts December 31 and January 1.
Next Saturday Series "C" Concert January 9.

First New York performance; note also U.S. premiere of Robert Starer *Viola Concerto*, and appearance of composer John Corigliano's father (the orchestra's concertmaster) as soloist in the Bach.

ly accompanimental until the final variations during which it introduces new melodic material against the harmonic background of the original theme treated canonically. This leads to restatement of the original theme by the orchestra with combo accompaniment.

"The third movement also uses a 16-bar theme. The first statement of it by the combo saxophone over string accompaniment is preceded by an orchestral solo section in which the melodic ideas of the 16-bar theme are stated in greater freedom by the English horn with cello accompaniment.

"The last movement replaces two earlier movements.... After a short introductory section in which the orchestra states motives to be used later, with some interjecting from the combo drummer, the movement settles down on 'the Blues'. The 12-bar pattern of the blues is maintained by the combo. The orchestra plays in a 16-bar pattern against this. After two sections in which the woodwinds first, followed by the brasses, play with the combo, the orchestra has a blues section in a related key. The combo joins with the orchestra in a return to the original key and a coda section which features the dexterity of the combo drummer.

"It should be noted that the work is so constructed that the combo would be free to add solo improvisations to be decided upon in advance by themselves and the conductor. However, only the fact of their use would be decided in advance; the nature of the improvisation and its duration can be left to the imagination of performer and sensitive conductor who would be expected to cue the orchestra back in after the final bar of an improvisational section."—Howard Brubeck, in The New York Philharmonic Program Notes, 12/10-3/59.[28]

"I found the work as engrossing as any contemporary composition I have recently come across, and even the staid dowagers at the Friday afternoon performances [of the New York Philharmonic premiere] were moved to shouts of spontaneous joy. [*Dialogues* is] jazz, all right; it [also] shows a masterly command of symphonic orchestration.... It is enchanting in its lyricism... and it contains a great deal that is of intellectual interest."—Winthrop Sergeant, in *The New Yorker*.

Overture to "The Devil's Disciple" for Orchestra (1952). *Prem.:* San Diego SO. 10m *Pub.:* Derry Music Co.
2 (pic)-2 (Eng hn)-2-2; 4-2-3-0; timp, 2 perc, pno; strings

---

[28] Portions also reprinted as liner notes for Columbia recording *Bernstein Plays Brubeck Plays Bernstein*, reissued as Stereo LP CS 8257.

"This is not an overture in the French or Italian forms, nor does it follow the sonata allegro form of the nineteenth century concert overture. It is an overture in the sense that it makes an appeal to the play. It is neither a chronicle of the events of Shaw's play nor a record of its characters, but rather reflects a response to the play's ideas." — Howard Brubeck.

CHANDLER CARTER

B. 1962, Sanford NC. *Educ.:* Univ of NC, Boston Univ, City Univ of NY Graduate Ctr. *Works incl.:* choral music, *From the Prophecy of Isaiah* (t/orch), piano etudes, string quartet.

Night Scenes for Speaker, Flute, Clarinet, Two Percussionists, Piano and Celesta (1985). *Text:* Lou Lipsitz. 15m *Score:* Carter Chandler, 160 West 56th Street, New York NY 10019.
1. Prologue: *The Night.* 2. Scenes: *Evening and Nighttime Blues.* 3. Epilogue: *Sunday Night in the City.*

"By combining the three poems of *Night Scenes* I attempted to evoke and ultimately address some of the dehumanizing aspects of modern America which the separate texts describe. The images of anxiety and isolation in *The Night* find both amusing and disturbing manifestations in *Evening and Nighttime Blues.* I chose *Sunday Night in the City* as an epilogue because of Mr. Lipsitz's remarkable conclusion, in which he steps out from behind his symbolic, even surreal world of images and events and confesses his faith in modern man's innermost spirit." — Chandler Carter.

Prayers of the People for Speaker, Alto, Tenor, Chorus (12 Singers) and Orchestra (1986). *Texts:* Episcopal Book of Common Prayer; Edna St. Vincent Millay, *We have gone too far;* William Butler Yeats, *The Second Coming.* 25m *Score:* Carter Chandler, 160 West 56th Street, New York NY 10019.
2 (pic)-2 (E hn)-2-2' 4-2-3-1; timp, 3 perc, pno, cel, harp; strings

"In composing *Prayers of the People,* I wanted to address some of the hypocrisies inherent in organized religion. To that end, I juxtapose the liturgy of the church (or at least *a* church) with poetry of two of the church's and modern society's most vehement and impassioned critics (Millay and Yeats, respectively). I do not presume to resolve the two sets of texts. I merely explore the liturgy again, this time using a speaking chorus, in the hope of evoking a more honest, thoughtful reading." — Chandler Carter.

Symphony for Medium Voice and Orchestra (1987-88). 25m *Score:* Carter Chandler, 160 West 56th Street, New York NY 10019.
3 (pic)-2 (E hn)-2 b cl-2 cbn; 4-2-3-1; timp, 3 perc, pno, celesta, harp; strings
Prologue: *The Eagle* (text: Alfred Lord Tennyson). I. *Ode to a Nightingale* (text: John Keats). II. *To a Waterfowl* (text: William Cullen Bryant).

III. *The Dalliance of the Eagles* (*text:* Walt Whitman). IV. *The Wild Swans at Coole* (*text:* William Butler Yeats).

"I originally composed this symphony as a song cycle for voice and piano entitled *Flight*. However the breadth of the poetry, especially that of Keats' *Ode to a Nightingale*, demanded a broader means of expression. The common theme of the poems justifies grouping them in this manner. However, due to the striking differences in style and aesthetic between the five poets, the musical response to these various texts covers a relatively large expressive spectrum. Each movement would be described as tonal, yet the degree of dissonance varies widely between and within movements. Oddly enough, the most consonant movement, that set to Yeats' *The Wild Swans at Coole*, communicates the most ambiguous and oblique message." — Chandler Carter.

Variations for 2 Flutes, English Horn, Two E^b Clarinets, 2 Horns and 2 Bassoons (1988). 10m *Prem.:* Holzbläser, Dana Perna, cond. *Score:* Carter Chandler, 160 West 56th Street, New York NY 10019.

"I never actually state a theme to this set of variations. The two principal motives that are subsequently varied appear in the first measure of the introduction, yet I would not consider them a theme as such. The variations present themselves in a peculiar fashion, making enigmatic, even disruptive appearances in other sections, only to disappear again. I tried not only to evoke several different emotional states through the various guises of the motives, but also to create a second level of musical and emotional development by juxtaposing these attitudes and their corresponding musical manifestations." — Chandler Carter.

CHICK COREA

B. 1942, Chelsea MA. Perf. with Willie Bobo, Cal Tjader, Herbie Mann, Mongo Santamarie, Stan Getz, Blue Mitchell, Saraha Vaughan, Gary Burton, Miles Davis, others. Dir., Return to Forever, Chick Corea Akoustic Band, Chick Corea Elektric Band, others. *Awards & grants incl.:* 4 "Composer of the Year" *(Down Beat)*, 10 "Best Electric Piano" *(Downbeat)*, 9 "Best Jazz (or other) Keyboardist" *(Keyboard)*, 18 Grammy Award nominations, 9 Grammy Awards. *Recordings:* more than 60 for Atlantic, Blue Note, CBS, Deutsche Grammophon, ECM, Elektra Musician, Groove Merchant, GRP, Phillips, Pickwick Intl, Polydor, Solid State, Teldec, Vortex/Atlantic, Warner Bros, others.

Composer statement (about music and the *Concerto* for Piano and Orchestra): "ABOUT MUSIC: Music and the Arts in general have always been the last frontier on Earth for the joy of the freedom of expression and communication. And, in my mind, an art form isn't necessarily confined to the concert stage or museum as life itself can be lived as an art form.

"Music is many things to me. It's the luxury and freedom of total creation; and, at the same time, it's a much needed antidote to life in a troubled world.

"ABOUT MY *CONCERTO* FOR PIANO AND ORCHESTRA: The form of the concerto is the same as the one Mozart used with 3 movements, and orchestrated simply using a chamber orchestra of 40 players.

"There were two experiences that contributed to my decision to write the concerto. One was my first experience performing the music of Mozart which was helped and inspired by Friedrich Gulda, Nicolas Harnoncourt, and the Concertgebau of Amsterdam. The other was a trip to Portland, Oregon that I made along with fellow Scientologists and members of other religions in an effort to help maintain freedom of religion in the United States which, at that time, was being attacked through the court system of the state of Oregon. I then decided to dedicate the concerto to the Crusade for Religious Freedom since I saw how this freedom is one and the same as the freedom we cherish as artists to think and create."—Chick Corea, 22/9/90.

A note on Chick Corea and the *Concerto* for Piano and Orchestra: "Chick and I collaborated once before, when we recorded Mozart's 'Eliva Madigan' Andante (C major piano concerto) and Beethoven's *Für Elise* for the *Greatest Hits of 1790* album for Columbia. I

Chick Corea Elektric Band: Frank Gambale, Dave Weckl, Chick Corea, Eric Marienthal, John Patitucci *(left to right).*

orchestrated *Für Elise*—originally a solo piano work—around his playing.

"We premiered the *Concerto* for Piano and Orchestra in 1987, with the Philharmonia Virtuosi and the composer at the piano. It is in three movements—a completely written piece that leaves room to negotiate. It looks to historically legitimate or classical forms, but the melodic and rhythmic material is basically jazz rooted. It was great fun to do."—Richard Kapp, conductor, 10/13/90.

Inside Out for Five-Piece Band (1990). *Rec.:* GRP Records GR-9601: Chick Corea Elektric Band (Frank Gambale, gtr, Dave Weckl, drums, Eric Marienthal, sax, John Patitucci, bass, Chick Corea, pno).

"The Elektric Band debut LP was a free-form showcase [*The Chick Corea Elektric Band*, GRP A-1026 (1986)]. The second LP, *Light Years* [GR-1036 (1987)] was more comemrcial, but no less tantalizing. With the third LP [*Eye of the Beholder*, GR-1053 (1988)], Corea and his band delivered moodier, contemporary music with a twist. The *Eye of the Beholder* was a monumental achievement that straggled the line between a smooth middle-of-the-road style and a hardened progressive style.

"Somehow this master craftsman manages to come up with a different signature for each new LP while keeping its context relevant to its predecessors. With *Inside Out*, Corea has done it again, and threatens to turn the jazz world upside-down.

"The players on this [fourth] LP have been with Corea since the second. Bassist John Patitucci and drummer Dave Weckl, who also join Corea in the Akoustic Band, guitarist Frank Gambale and saxophonist Eric Marienthal comprise the five-piece band, and each player's personality has become an established part of the group's music. It's as if five distinct voices are singing in harmony, performing the most adventurous, challenging music Corea has ever written.

"Amazingly, Corea wrote the music for *Inside Out* in two weeks, and the band spent four days rehearsing and four more recording. This gives a spontaneous, vibrant feel to the LP.

"The title track starts with an accessible groove that draws the listener in. From there, the musical montages artfully gain speed and agility until 45 minutes later, when the final notes of the brilliant *Tales of Daring* toll musical triumph.

"An underlying vitality plays throughout every track. Corea has put a lot of stock in the musicians he has decided to record with, and so has steered clear of allowing this LP to become a Chick Corea project featuring faceless players. The emphasis is on the band, not Corea. At every turn, someone in the group steps out on his own while the other players guide the music along on its intended course. There are even a few instances when the band reverts to a three-piece shade of Akoustic Band style, as in the closing swing beat of *Kicker*.

"Corea and Marienthal speak together softly in *Child's Play*, a beautiful interplay of harmony and melody between piano and saxophone. The song is helped immensely by the MIDI grand piano, an instrument Corea uses dominantly on this LP. The piano hammers interrupt a light ray, which in turn triggers a MIDI switch that instantly accompanies the piano with the sound of full-string orchestration. The instrument, first used on *Eye of the Beholder*, allows Corea to remain behind the piano and achieve a fuller keyboard effect.

"Without a doubt, the biggest achievement of *Inside Out* is the closing *Tales of Daring*.

"The song is broken up into four chapters, with the first laying the groundwork for the three that follow. The song uses moody togetherness on its opening passages, leading to 'Chapter 2', when the players take turns showing off. Patitucci in particular shines with wild six-string bass-playing.

" 'Chapter 3' may be the most explicit, most exciting forum Corea has ever written. It's a fast cat-and-mouse game between Corea's piano and Weckl's drums, which builds until the rest of the band joins in and leads the song to its concluding chapter, when the first three chapters are synopsized and expanded.

" 'Chapter 4' concludes with a grandiose bang, leading to what sounds like wooden chimes blowing in the wind, then a fade into silence." — Todd Caudle, Colorado Springs *Gazette Telegraph*, 2/3/90.

"This album may well mark the coming of age for this incarnation of Chick's band, much the same way *The Romantic Warrior* [CBS PC-34076 (1976)] was a benchmark in the 70s. For awhile, the nucleus of the group was clearly Corea, John Patitucci, and Dave Weckl, with Eric Marienthal and Frank Bambal seeming to exist somewhere on the periphery, even as talented as each is individually. With *Inside Out*, the group has congealed into a balanced quintet, with Chick's compositions catering to the strengths and character of each familiar voice.

"As complex as the material is, Corea actually wrote the entire album during a concentrated two-week span, plus a mere four days of rehearsal and four days of recording to complete the disc. The rhythmic complexity in the writing is numbing at times, as Chick's tunes often are, certainly not for faint-of-heart sight-readers. Each band member rises admirably to the occasion, while contributing staggering virtuosity as well.

"Of the album's three multi-part adventures, *Tale of Daring* is the centerpiece. It is an intrepid exploration into the darker realms, most apparent during the opening of 'Chapter 1' and during Chick's solo interlude in 'Chapter 3' which showcases his sublime use of dissonance. The collective trading and overlapping of frenetic phrasing during 'Chapter 4' culminates the entire effort with a vitalizing zing." — Gene Ferriter, in *Rhythm*, 5/90.

" 'With this record, I tried to see what was the strength of the [Elektric Band] quintet and push toward it,' says Chick Corea of his latest project, *Inside Out* on GRP. 'Everybody plays brilliantly. I mean, the guys really bit into this one. They're all reading maniacs and they make the music their own very, very quickly. They can look at a part I've written out and they start to mold it and interpret it almost immediately until it becomes their own. That's what really gives the quintet a niche of its own....

" 'It's a big plus to enjoy the musicians I'm writing for, to enjoy how they play. Now I hear their sound clearly in my mind when I'm composing, which was the point I had hoped I'd eventually reach with this band. That was the original plan in forming a band that stayed together. I had a desire to get one group of musicians who wanted to do the same thing long enough to let it grow into a kind of familiarity. I think that's where we're at with the band now.'

"While the title cut provides an easy, accessible entrance into the album, tunes like *Make a Wish*, which unleashes Gambale's formidable sweep-picking chops, and *Stretch It*, which showcases Patitucci's fluid sax-like phrasing on six-string electric bass, push the band to exciting heights, technically and musically. But the real meat of this latest Elektric Bamd offering is a highly orchestrated four-part suite, *Tale of Daring*, a tour de force which builds to grandiose peaks in the spirit of Return to Forever's swan song, *Romantic Warrior*.[29] Following a cinematic overture, Marienthal blows strong alto sax statements followed by a bravado bass solo by Patitucci. The third part of this opus features a playful exchange between Corea and Weckl, which leads up to a monstrous guitar solo by Gambale. And on the frightening fourth part, the band trades fours like in the heyday of fusion.

"For the entire project, Corea remained behind the acoustic grand, which in this case was a Yamaha MIDI grand that simultaneously triggered various synth colors and textures. His entire performance was recorded directly into a Synclavier digital synthesizer which allowed him then to go back and systematically alter the synth voicings to get the proper sounds to enhance the mood of each song. As he put it, 'having the MIDI grand piano makes it so I can realize these orchestration ideas without losing my central point of performance, which is from the piano. So I was actually able to redo the orchestrations after the fact, which gave me a little more flexibility as an arranger.' " — Bill Milkowski, in *Jazzis*, 4-5/90.

---

29   Among Return to Forever albums have been *Return to Forever*, ECM 811 978-2 (1972); *Light as a Feather*, Polydor 827 148-2 (1973); *Hymn of the Seventh Galaxy*, Polydor 825 336-4 (1973); *Where Have I Known You Before*, Polydor 825 206-2 (1974); *No Mystery*, Polydor 827 149-2 (1975); *The Romantic Warrior*, CBS PC 34076 (1976); *Musicmagic* — with some changes in personnel, CBS PC 34682 (1977); and *The Best of Return to Forever*, CBS JC 36359 (1980). (Ed.)

JOHN CORIGLIANO

B. 1938, New York NY. *Educ.*: Columbia Univ, Manhattan Schl of Music. *Taught at:* Natl Cathedral College of Church Musicians (DC), Lehman Coll. Music dir. Morris Theatre (NJ), pres. Music for the Theatre. Composer-in-residence, Chicago SO. *Works incl.*: choral (*A Black November Turkey, Dylan Thomas Trilogy*), concertos (ob, pno), film scores (*Altered States, Revolution*), *The Ghosts of Versailles* (opera in progress), *Kaleidoscope* (2 pnos), orchestral works (*Elegy, Promenade Overture, Summer Fanfare, Symphony 1, Three Hallucinations*), *Poem in October* (tenor/fl/ob/cl/string qt/hpsd), sonata (vln).[30]

Composer statement: "It has been fashionable of late for the artist to be misunderstood. I think it is the job of the composer to reach out to his audiences with every means at his disposal... Communication of his most important ideas should be the primary goal." — from a composer brochure issued by G. Schirmer, Inc.

Concerto for Clarinet and Orchestra (1977). 29m *Comm. & prem.:* Stanley Drucker (cl), New York PO, Leonard Bernstein, cond. *Recs:* New World Records (Stereo LP) NW 309 (also released as *dbx*-encoded vers, *dbx* SS 3033): Stanley Drucker (cl), New York PO, Zubin Mehta, cond.; RCA Records 7762-1-RC: Richard Stoltzman (cl), London SO, Lawrence Leighton Smith, cond. *Pub.:* G. Schirmer (Music Sales) (study score; cl/pno reduction; performance materials on rental)
1. *Cadenzas.* 2. *Elegy.* 3. *Antiphonal Toccata*
1 pic-3-3 (E hn)-2, b cl-cbn; 6-4-3-1; timp, 3 perc, harp, pno; strings (14-14-12-12-at least 6 cb)

"The more I hear of John Corigliano's music the more strongly I concur with Aaron Copland's evaluation quoted in Philip Ramey's notes [to the RCA recording]. Corigliano is 'the real thing, one of the most talented composers on the scene today'. Attendance at the recent world premier of his *First Symphony*, dedicated to the memory of several friends who had died of AIDS (and recorded in concert by Erato), was further confirmation that this composer has a lot to say and that he says it powerfully and eloquently, with an individuality

---

30 Viewers of PBS-TV's long-running *Great Performances* series may recall the arresting title music which is played against clouds sweeping dramatically across an intensely blue sky. The music is by John Corigliano. (Ed.)

that is often lacking in [other] 20th Century American music. The *Clarinet Concerto* was composed in the summer and fall of 1977 on commission from Leonard Bernstein and the New York Philharmonic, who gave its first performance in December of that year. The first movement, 'Cadenzas', has a disturbing, almost otherworldly quality to it, while the second, 'Elegy', is a touching, truly haunting memorial to his father, John Corigliano, Sr., for 23 years the distinguished concertmaster of the Philharmonic. The finale, 'Antiphonal Toccata', represents the composer's attempt to lighten the *Concerto*'s mood and is rhythmically alive and filled with imaginative ideas."
—Allen Linkowski, in *American Record Guide*, 7-8/90.

"Mr. Corigliano's *Clarinet Concerto* might just make the perfect vehicle for bringing young rock- and jazz-oriented listeners into the concert hall; for while it is indeed a sophisticated work with a complex formal structure and a harmonic base that takes in everything from major/minor tonality to clusters and 12-tone rows, it also aims for a purely visceral appeal. The orchestration, which uses every last player in the [New York] Philharmonic, calls for lots of percussion, long sections of melodic string and wind writing, and antiphonal choirs of brass and wind players stationed in the balconies around the hall. The solo clarinet part is as virtuosic as anything in the instrument's literature, yet it has many lyrical passages too, particularly in the second movement, 'Elegy', which contains a dialogue between the clarinet and a solo violin. Parts of the work are rather theatrical—a quality Mr. Corigliano says was inspired by Leonard Bernstein, who conducted the premiere of the *Concerto*.

"Many of these same qualities can be found in other works by [John] Corigliano as well. His *Oboe Concerto* (1975) is equally as picturesque, beginning with a fantasy that plays upon the oboe's role in the orchestra's tuning ritual and ending with a rhythmically insistent Moorish dance. The *Piano Concerto* (1968) shares with its woodwind counterparts a wide array of timbres and a decidedly lyrical bent. And all these aspects are mirrored yet again in the composer's chamber music and vocal works." —Allan Kozinn, in *The New York Times*, 4/27/80.

"It was for Stanley Drucker, the [New York] Philharmonic's superb principal clarinetist, that Corigliano composed his wildly imaginative *Clarinet Concerto*, as part of the series of concerted works for the orchestra's principal players commissioned by Francis Goelet. But, as the composer himself has pointed out, the work was really created for the entire orchestra—a 'concerto for orchestra'—giving every section and many individual players virtuoso opportunities.

"Corigliano literally grew up with the Philharmonic. His late father was its concertmaster for twenty-three years; he himself had some lessons from Drucker and worked with Leonard Bernstein and the orchestra for a time as a member of the production team for the televised Young People's Concerts. The première of the concerto in December 1977, with Bernstein conducting, was one of the most exciting events yet presented in Avery Fisher Hall, its special impact generated by the incredible difficulty of the solo part and Drucker's magnificent playing, by the sheer exhuberance of much of the score, and by the broadly felt 'family references' to the Philharmonic.

"In the first movement, headed 'Cadenzas', Drucker identifies himself [in the recorded performance] as the master for whom the part was created. The second, 'Elegy', is a memorial to Corigliano Sr. in which the solo violin has an extended dialogue with clarinet. The last, 'Antiphonal Toccata', quotes Giovanni Gabrieli's *Sonata Pian' e Forte* and not only has antiphonal effects produced by the orchestra on stage but has several brass players distributed around the hall, extending the range of musical effects and at the same time in a sense extending the Philharmonic's musical 'family', drawing the audience into it by scattering musicians in the boxes and aisles. While the unique excitement of the première would probably be impossible to duplicate under any conditions, the full aural impact is most successfully recaptured in [New World's] absolutely magnificent recording." — Richard Freed, in *Stereo Review*, 5/81.

"[Corigliano's] concerto actually sounds quite similar to his score for the film *Altered States*, with its chaotic, brilliantly colored frenzy. Containing everything from Gabrieli fragments and antiphonal effects achieved by special seating to 12-tone rows blazing in giant fireballs of sound, the *Concerto* whips up a tremendous amount of activity, which, in a stunning performance like [Mehta's with Stanley Drucker and the New York Philharmonic], is enormously effective. Despite a subdued, somber, slow movement, the work is so concentrated with 'events' that the listener's attention never flags." — Walter Simmons, in *Fanfare: The Magazine for Serious Record Collectors*, 5-6/81.

Pied Piper Fantasy (Concerto) for Flute and Orchestra (1981).
35m *Comm. & prem.:* James Galway (fl), Los Angeles PO, Myung-Whun Chung, cond. *Other perfs.:* James Galway (fl), Baltimore SO, David Zinman, cond.; James Galway (fl), Chicago SO, Jarvi, cond. *Rec.:* RCA Records 6602-2-RC: James Galway (fl), Eastman Philharmonia, David Effron, cond. *Pub.:* G. Schirmer (Music Sales)(performance materials on rental)

solo: fl (tin whistle or pic) — 2 (opt 3rd fl, pic)-3-3 (E^b cl, b cl)-3 (cbn); 4-3-3-1; timp, 4 perc (incl vib, glock, xyl), hp (opt 2), pno, celesta; strings (min 14-12-10-8-6); children's group (9-18 fl, 2 perc)

"Among its many accomplishments, the Baltimore Symphony Orchestra does rat imitations as well as any musical ensemble I have heard. It's also pretty good on tightfisted medieval German burghers and quite convincing when it portrays a sunrise or sunset.

"All of the above were among the orchestra's assignments when it played the Washington [D.C.] premiere of John Corigliano's *Pied Piper Fantasy*. Corigliano's gift for musical description matches his gift for melody, and in portraying the Piper's battles (first against the rats, then against the citizens who refuse to pay him), the composer demands virtuoso orchestra playing.

"He also has a sense of theater. The score specifies that the soloist should be costumed in a cape, and in the final movement, when the Piper shifts from flute to tin whistle, a group of children playing flutes and drums marches into the concert hall, gathers around the Piper and marches out into the lobby with him, the sound fading into the distance while the house lights go down and the orchestral sound is reduced to a whisper. The work is well recorded on RCA, but a live performance is quite a different experience. So is the record when heard after you have seen a live performance.

"Musically, Corigliano is a complete master of his material and the score compensates in color for what it lacks in profundity. The composer, a romantic at heart, seems to enjoy using nontonal material to portray the bad guys and bad moments in his story." — Joseph McLellan, in *The Washington Post*, 4/15/89.

"Three qualities that distinguish many of Mr. Corigliano's works are offered in spades here, all bound together so intextricably that it is difficult to know which to mention first.

"One is an unabashed theatricality. Mr. Corgigliano has tinkered with the story to allow for several cathartic confrontations between the flutist-Piper and the orchestra, which alternately represents the defiant rats and Hamelin's officious burghers. In the end, he has the soloist switch from flute to pennywhistle, and supplies a small army of young flutists and drummers who follow the Piper up an aisle and out of the hall.

"At the service of this theatrical flair are the composer's brilliance as an orchestrator, which lets him paint his battles with a panoramic vividness — and his unbounded eclecticism. In the murky opening section, which depicts the depth of night, he paints in a cluster-laden, hazy atonality. This dissolves into a fully diatonic sunrise, against which the Piper plays his melodic signature theme.

"As the work unfolds, Mr. Corigliano uses controlled cacophony (percussion, oboe squeaks, martellato bow-strokes and sweeping glissandos) to represent the rats; a blend of Baroque chorale style and Shostakovich-like parodistic bombast to represent the burghers; patches of open, Vaughan Williams-like sonority, to suggest moments of peace; and a Renaissance *saltarello* as a march for the Piper and his band of children.

"[At the Washington performance] Mr. Galway sailed easily through the fleet solo lines of his battle music, and endowed his songlike Piper's theme with his trademark warmth and color. He didn't seem to feel particularly silly wearing the red and yellow Piper's cape that hung awkwardly over his tuxedo, or bounding up the aisle with his pennywhistle and youthful entourage. The orchestra played its multiple roles with equal panache, and the audience loved it." — Allan Kozinn, in *The New York Times*, 4/4/89.

"The solo writing ranges from the most sustained lyrical flights to a dizzying array of rapid staccato runs, flutter-tonguing and other contemporary techniques, set against an orchestral canvas rich in color-effects. But it's one of the remarkable things about this music that how it's put together seems much less important than the fact that everything works." — John von Rhein, in the *Chicago Tribune*, 4/21/89.

GEORGE CRUMB

B. 1929, Charleston WV. *Educ.:* Mason College of Music, Univ of IL, Univ of MI, Berkshire Music Ctr, Hochschule für Musik (Berlin). *Taught at:* Univ of CO, Univ of PA Schl of Music. Rockefeller, Guggenheim, Coolidge Fnd grants; winner, 1967 Natl Inst Arts/Letters Award, 1968 Pulitzer Prize. *Works incl.: Ancient Voices of Children* (voices/insts), *Black Angels* (elect stng qt), *Echoes of Time and the River* (orch), *Eleven Echoes of Autumn, 1965* (vln/fl/cl/pno),*Lux Aeterna* (s/insts), *Madrigals* (s/insts), *Makrokosmos* (pno[s]), *Night Music* (var ensembles), *Night of the Four Moons* (s/fl/banjo/elect vc/perc), *Quest* (gtr/sax/hp/db/2 perc), *Songs, Drones and Refrains of Death* (bar/insts), *Vox Balaenae* (elec fl/elec vc/ampl pno)..

Composer statement (a conversation between George Crumb and composer Mark Grant[31]):

"MARK GRANT: Assuming that a promising new talent comes to you for advice or guidance, what might you have to say to him or her with respect to career expectations... pursuing a career in music.

"GEORGE CRUMB (presently a member of the music department faculty at the University of Pennsylvania, Philadelphia): Well, it's a difficult question, because it is a difficult field to be in. The rewards are not so large, especially when you're starting out. Eventually things will improve a little as you keep working and get older and get more performances and so forth—but, it's not an easy field to be in.

"I recommend to my students here at Penn that they develop whatever versatilities they have... if they are able to conduct or perform, or have organizational skills of any kind in music, cultivate these aspects, too.

"MG: In your case it seems to me that a lot of people have the perception that you formulated a mature style somewhat late (though you were still a pretty young man)—I think there was a feeling that you were not seeking performances of your early compositions, that the works that came after the *Five Pieces for Piano* in the early 60s, and the pieces that you did in the late 60s and the 70s, were the ones that people tended to associate with your creative genie... but, in fact, you were at it long before that.

---

31 This conversation was recorded especially for this volume on 9/6/90. An entry on music by Mark Grant appears below. (Ed.)

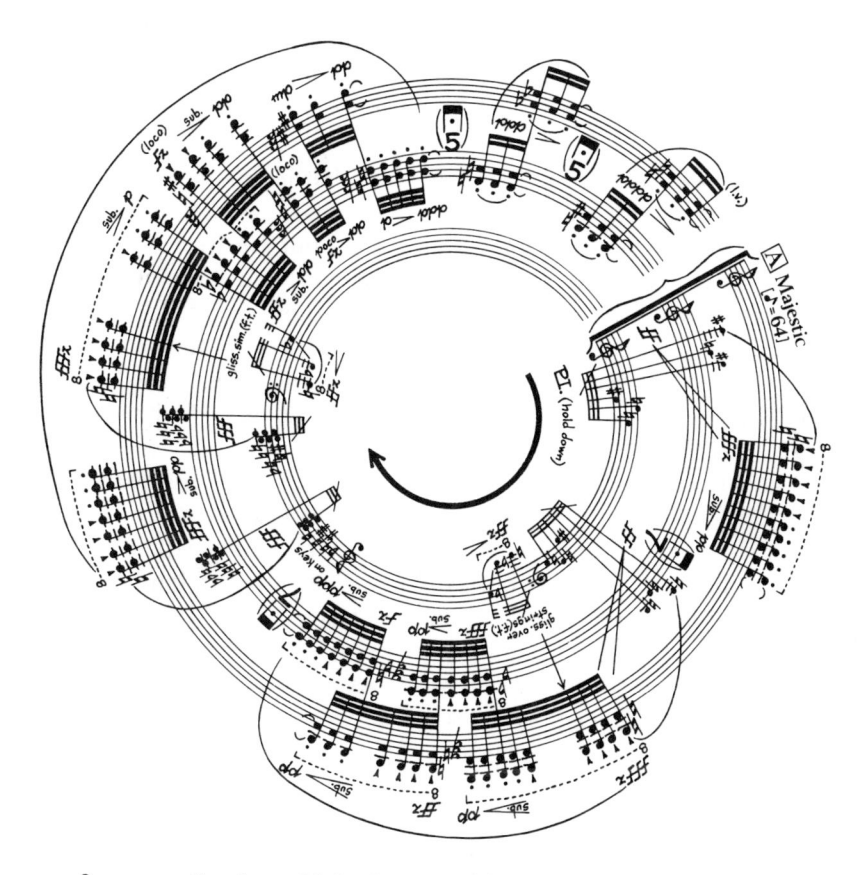

Score portion from *Makrokosmos*, Vol. II. Reprinted from Don Gillespie, ed. *George Crumb: Profile of a Composer* (C. F. Peters, 1986).

"GC: It's true... I sort of found my own way when I was in my thirties. I don't think that's exceptional nowadays. I think the evolution of personal style seems to come much later in our century. It seems there are no Mozarts or Schuberts or Mendelssohns or even Beethovens who were into their own music in their twenties — their early twenties — or before. I don't know what accounts for this.

"MG: Is it the proliferation of so many different styles — there is so much more input around us that we have to assimilate before we can put our finger on our own — or is it that there are no giants [with that kind of talent]? I find this hard to believe because I see prodigiously talented young men and women — very gifted people who do things with amazing facility in their twenties.

"GC: Well, I think you're right. There is so much that we have to work through before we can find ourselves — the influences are so diverse and immense... in number, in all directions... historically...

there are more composers writing now... we know more about all the ethnic musics in the world—that's one thing. But it also may be true that we have yet to produce composers of the kind you're talking about, which occurs very rarely in our history. There are only a handful of them.

"MG: One of the things about your work that amazes me—I'm fascinated by your own calligraphy and notation—not just its intricacy and control of so many parameters and detail, but the sheer care, and the labor involved—you must have certain drafting instruments that most composers don't have to be able to draw those circles. You must either have a compass or a way of circularizing a staff roller.

"GC: Those are exceptional—those symbolic notations I used—in fact I did have a compass, which draftsmen would use, which would roll a single line in ink.

"MG: Your scores are quite beautiful to look at visually. They seem to embody such a lot of creative intensity.

"GC: I guess I did get into that. I think of certain other earlier composers whose music is very beautiful to look at—it has a kind of artistic sense. I'm thinking of Chopin, or Debussy—even Mozart's has a real character to it.

"MG: I studied with a composer who was also a painter—I was also reminded a little of some of the scores of Stravinsky when he used all those different colored pencils.

"GC: Yes.

"MG: It's almost like putting a watch together—you can see the differentiation of strands of this with strands of that—you can retrace his steps and look at what he was doing.

"GC: Yes, there's a tradition of that. Alban Berg's *Wozzeck* is multi-colored, too—that's in the Library of Congress. For example, the on-stage music is in one color, and so forth. That's an old tradition in music.

"MG: Do you ever work at the piano, or did you at some time in the past?

"GC: Yes, both—if I'm writing for piano or a work that involves a prominent part for the piano, I'll tend to sit at the piano, otherwise at my desk... or sometimes back and forth. I'm not tied to either.

"MG: Because much of your music is so much an expression of a surreal world or some kind of esoteric landscape that it would seem to me that it would not be composed at the piano. That is just my reaction. On the other hand your works for the keyboard, the *Makrokosmos* for example, are so pianistic in their way—the blend is quite wonderful—the feeling for piano, and also a kind of removed secret world...

"Turning to another question, what differentiates this kind of [concert or art] music from more popular forms?

"GC: One thing of course is that much of the popular music is written I guess for commercial reasons—to have an immediate appeal and make money. I don't think that's in the forefront for some of us, it's not the thing we're thinking about in doing our music. The idea is that the music might possibly have a little power to carry to another time.

"MG: Yes.

"GC: There are no guarantees for that, either!

"MG: How do you manage the back-and-forth between doing your own composing and teaching and various other responsibilities that are not immediately related to one's work.... I ask this because you've been so productive.

"GC: I don't feel a tension between the two. I rather enjoy the teaching and it is kind of a welcome relief from the other.... it complements the other [composing], it enables you to be a little in touch with what young people are thinking. Also, if you're talking about certain very basic things to your students, then you think about them yourself again and again. Of course when I started I had to teach to earn my daily bread, you see. But I enjoy it. And it's not a strenuous schedule now.

"MG: Do you have a feeling about some of the directions that have gotten a lot of attention and publicity in the last five or ten years, e.g. minimalism and the schools of Philip Glass and John Adams (though they are very different from each other)—or some of the other younger composers that are out there?

"GC: In regard to minimalism, I guess I can find very few points of contact in terms of my own interests. But I guess I would say, who knows, perhaps they're right—only time determines what music is strong enough to survive. We can't know at this point because we have no perspective.

"MG: Is there some time in years at which you think there is a deciding point? I mean, like a hundred years? Because people in the serial or Second Viennese schools are always saying it took Bach a hundred years, or a hundred and fifty years.

"GC: No [laughing]—I think even ten years already tells us something.

"MG: Even ten years?

"MG: Oh, yes, I think so. Twenty years, maybe. I don't think it took Bach that long. I think his music had enormous impact during his lifetime... I think this is exaggerated, this explanation by the twelve-tone composers—I mean, many of them. The ones that have constructed this mythology. I'm not sure it's accurate.

"MG: You mean you think it's sour grapes?

"MG: Oh well I don't know what it is! But they talk about certain of Beethoven's works being so slow in being appreciated, but I think it wasn't so. Maybe the *Grosse Fuge*—but, my goodness, that's only one piece. For Pete's sake! The same too with all the others. If they want to talk about that maybe they should restrict themselves to the 20th century. Because the most bold works they want to think of— most of them were quickly assimilated into the literature. Chopin, Moussorgsky, Wagner, so much of the late Beethoven or the most chromatic Mozart things, whatever you can name were quickly [taken in].

"MG: What are some of the past or current developments in music that interest or appeal to you the most—not just as a composer, perhaps, but also as a listener?

"GC: Traditional music?

"MG: Yes, concert music.

"GC: Well... all of it. I think being a composer means your ears are open to all the music in the world and certainly all of our western traditional music. I love it all, and it all seems important to me. I think music is all one piece—I've never understood separating it out—it's all connected in my mind.

"MG: The school of Cage might say that you should start at day one...

"GC: No, that's psychologically an impossibility. Even he [laughing] got a lot from Eastern music and so forth.

"MG: Are there any current, maybe younger composers whom you find especially interesting? any Americans?

"GC: Oh there's a lot—I would not want to mention particular names because I would leave out somebody. I think there are so many who are doing interesting things. Yes, I think something may just come out of all this, I'm very hopeful. There are always young composers who are finding new ways. I don't know where it's all going, of course!

"MG: One other thing I might ask—coming back to the beginning—what do you say to a young composer who can't get any performances, and the audience for this music seems limited compared to the greater public and the greater society around us who listen to other kinds of popular music? It is daunting to build a career of any kind, to get performances... You're swimming upstream so much of the time, you're competing unfairly with other creative people, too, when I think you really ought to be competing just with yourself. But there's only so much foundation grant money to go around, or whatever... it's a tough situation.

"GC: Well, it is hard. In a way though there's a lot more available than there was when I was younger—more grants, awards, prizes, contests. Of course I think there are also many more younger composers—in any case, it's not easy. Maybe there's no reason why it should be easy... I don't think it ever was. If a person has something to say I imagine it'll be said, even if the performances are deferred, or you get maybe a bad performance instead of a good performance. I guess if there's real quality in music people fall over themselves to play it—in time at least. They might not recognize it for a while. It may be such a highly personal style, or something so very original that it takes a while for people to get on to it. It may seem outré or too fantastic or something. I think the scene is really hopeful. There are so many more young musicians now who are able to play this stuff—that *has* changed.

"MG: Yes. So you feel hopeful about your own students?

"GC: About young people in general. People have to keep working and mature and find a personal voice. There's no way you can teach that. That's a conceptual thing, a part of the psyche or central nervous system or something, one has no control over that. You teach more external things. But if it's there I think it'll develop. [Smiling.]"

MUSIC: DOES IT HAVE A FUTURE? (ARTICLE)

Editor's note: The word "eclectic" has been used frequently in describing contemporary art music—sometimes derogatorily, as if to imply that a particular composer has no special voice of his or her own; sometimes neutrally—acknowledging that such a composer is, at the very least, musically sophisticated; and sometimes a great deal more positively, perhaps on the premise that reference e.g. to times and cultures not one's own (including references to folk idioms) is—itself—an important part of the "message" of the music of our age. Indeed there *is* something modern, I should think, about Shostakovich's quotations from Rossini's *Overture to "William Tell"*, for example, in the first movement of his last symphony. Although interpretations will vary, to my ears this inclusion by a Russian survivor of Stalin and the 900-day siege of Leningrad of supremely *echt* Italian romantic opera music—which, moreover, has the effect in the U.S. at least of appearing to set the Swiss fighter against tyranny on the Lone Ranger's horse, Silver—is a deliciously quirky message of global brotherhood which seems quite suited to our time.[32]

George Crumb—among the most honored of modern composers, who *does*, indeed, have a voice distinctly his own—explores this important theme of a diversified musical culture in the following article:

"MUSIC: DOES IT HAVE A FUTURE?[33] The question 'What will the music of the future be like?' frequently arises in discussions with composers and with audiences. I suspect that some ulterior meaning is usually implied—either a sense of doubt that music will ever again be as vigorous and impressive as it was in some past 'golden age', or conversely, the hope that the undeniably frenetic activity of the present presages some future 'golden age', as glorious and as rich in achievement as any of the past! Even the most timid attempt at prophecy must be based on a close appraisal of earlier developments and present trends. The future will be the child of the past and the present, even if a rebellious child.

"The retrospective glance is a relatively easy gesture for us to make. If we look at music history closely, it is not difficult to isolate certain elements of great potency which were to nourish the art of music for decades, if not centuries. The dynamic concept of sonata-structure is a striking example of an idea that bewitched composers for two centuries, at least through Béla Bartók. Sonata-structure was, of course, intimately connected with the evolution of functional tonality, and tonality itself, independently, represents another germinal concept of great potency.

"What, then, are the significant and characteristic tendencies and impulses in contemporary music which might conceivably project into the future? I am certain that most composers today would consider today's music to be rich, not to say confusing, in its enormous diversity of styles, technical procedures, and systems of esthetics.

---

32 It can also be difficult to *detect* one style from another. For example, much of the "popular" song repertory of America's finest "Tin Pan Alley" composers—including Irving Berlin, George Gershwin, Jerome Kern, Cole Porter and Richard Rodgers—are coming now to be regarded—rightly, I should think—as classic American "art songs". Personally, I might select Kern's *Show Boat* and Gershwin's *Porgy and Bess* as possibly the two most outstanding musical works produced by American composers in any genre to date... Meanwhile, if both of these are genuinely "operatic", must the term "opera", itself, be redefined?

33 Orig. publ. in *The Kenyon Review*, Summer, 1980; rev. vers. in Don Gillespie, ed., *George Crumb: Profile of a Composer* (C. F. Peters, 1986).

Perhaps an attempt to isolate the unique aspects of our music will give us some perspective on our future prospects.

"One very important aspect of our contemporary musical culture—some might say the supremely important aspect—is its extension in the historical and geographical sense to a degree unknown in the past. To consider firstly the extension through time: in a real sense, virtually all music history and literature is now at our fingertips through both live performances and excellent recordings, whereas earlier compsoers knew the musics of only one or two generations before their own time. The consequences of this enlarged awareness of our own heritage are readily evident in many of our recent composers. For example, the influence of medieval music on the British composer Peter Maxwell Davies comes to mind. For many such composers, the sound of medieval music—at times harsh and raw, at times fragile and hauntingly sweet—would more closely approximate the contemporary ideal than would, say, the sound of a Brahms or of a Richard Strauss. I have observed, too, that the people of the many countries that I have visited are showing an ever increasing interest in the classical and traditional music of their own cultures. Perhaps we have come to think of ourselves as philosophically contemporaneous with all earlier cultures. And it is probable that today there are more people who see culture evolving spirally rather than linearly. Within the concentric circles of the spiral, the points of contact and the points of departure in music can be more readily found.

"The geographical extension means, of course, that the total musical culture of Planet Earth is 'coming together', as it were. An American or European composer, for example, now has access to the music of various Asian, African, and South American cultures. Numerous recordings of non-Western music are readily available, and live performances by touring groups can be heard even in our smaller cities. Such influences would, of course, be felt on different levels: only a few Western composers would have a sophisticated technical knowledge of the Indian *Raga*, for example; but, in general, the sounds, textures, and gestures of this music would be well known. This awareness of music in its largest sense—as a worldwide phenomenon—will inevitably have enormous consequences for the music of the future.

Unquestionably, our contemporary world of music is far richer, in a sense, than earlier periods, due to the historical and geographical extensions of culture to which I have referred. As a standard for comparison, it is revealing to take a representative European composer of the nineteenth century and define his 'cultural horizons'. I think a good choice is the French composer Hector Berlioz, since his music was regarded as avant-garde by his contemporaries. If we first consider the historical dimension, I think we should have to agree that Berlioz's contact with any music written before the Viennese Classical period was minimal. Beethoven was avowedly a very powerful influence on his development, [but] I doubt that Berlioz had any real understanding of Baroque style or technique, judging from the curiously inept handling of the *fugato* style in several of his works. Berlioz spoke of Palestrina in disparaging terms. In regard to his contact with non-Western music, we know that he visited London in 1851 in connection with the Great Exhibition held there. While in London, Berlioz heard some Chinese and Indian music in authentic performance, and this most progressive and modernistic composer of the time could make no sense at all of what he heard. His description of Chinese music:

> I shall not attempt to describe these wildcat howls, these death-rattles, these turkey cluckings, in the midst of which, despite my closest attention, I was able to make out only four distinct notes.[35]

His description of Indian music is even less flattering!

"Perhaps the true cross-fertilization process between musical cultures did not begin until after World War II, although one can trace the first premonitions in Mussorgsky and especially in Debussy toward the end of the nineteenth century. This represented a relatively high degree of sophistication, indeed, when compared with Mozart and Beethoven, for whom exotic music meant the cymbal and bass drum borrowed from the Turkish Janissary music!

"Apart from these broader cultural influences which contribute to the shaping of our contemporary musical psyche, we also have to take into account the rather bewildering legacy of the earlier twentieth-century composers in the matter of compositional technique and procedure. Although we must be impressed by the enormous accruement of new elements of vocabulary in the areas of pitch, rhythm, timbre, and so forth, I sense at the same time the loss of a majestic unifying principle in much of our recent music. Not only is the question of tonality still unresolved but we have not yet evolved anything comparable to the sure instinct for form which occurs routinely in the best traditional music. Instead, each new work seems to require a special solution, valid only in terms of itself. There is, to be sure, a sense of adventure and challenge in articulating our conceptions, despite the fact that we can take so little for granted; and

---

35 Hector Berlioz, *Evenings with the Orchestra*, transl. and ed. Jacques Barzun (Alfred A. Knopf, 1956), pp. 249-50.

perhaps we tend to underestimate the struggle-element in the case of earlier composers. Nonetheless, I sense that it will be the task of the future to somehow synthesize the sheer diversity of our present resources into a more organic and well-organized procedure.

"Perhaps we might now review some of the specific technical accoutrements of our present music and speculate on their potential for future development. The advent of electronically synthesized sound after World War II has unquestionably had enormous influence on music in general. Although I have never been directly involved in electronic music, I am keenly aware that our sense for sound-characteristics, articulation, texture, and dynamics has been radically revised and very much affects the way in which we write for instruments. And since I have always been interested in the extension of the possiblities of instrumental idiom, I can only regard the influence of electronics as beneficial. I recently participated in a discussion with Mario Davidovsky, who, in my opinion, is the most elegant of all the electronic composers whose music I know. Davidovsky's view is that the early electronic composers had a truly messianic feeling concerning the promise of this new medium. In those euphoric days of intense experimentation, some composers felt that electronic music, because of its seemingly unlimited possibilities, would eventually replace conventional music. Davidovsky now regards the medium simply as a unique and important language at the disposal of any composer who wants to make use of it, and as a valuable teaching tool for the ear. In any case, it is obvious that the electronic medium in itself solves none of the composer's major problems, which have to do with creating a viable style, inventing distinguished thematic material, and articulating form.

"The development of new instrumental and vocal idioms has been one of the remarkable phenomena of recent music. There undoubtedly have been many contributing factors: the influence of folk instrument techniques; the influence of jazz, and, later, rock techniques; the liberation of percussion instruments (a development for which Bartók is especially important); and finally, the advent of an ever-increasing number of young instrumentalists and singers who specialize in the performance of contemporary music, and who themselves are interested in probing the idiomatic resources of their instruments. The development of the idiom, of course, has been an ongoing process over the centuries; in fact, it is incumbent upon each age to 'reinvent' instruments as styles and modes of expression change.

"An example of this process can be seen in the evolution of the piano idiom. In the hands of Beethoven the expressive range of the instrument was progressively enlarged. The gradual expansion of the piano in terms of range, sustaining power, and brilliance and the introduction of the *una corda* pedal effect were fully exploited in the enormous body of literature which Beethoven conceived for the instrument. It must have seemed to many of Beethoven's contemporaries that nothing more remained to be done. And yet, shortly after Beethoven's death in 1827, Chopin published the *Etudes*, Opus 10. This astonishing new style, based essentially on the simple device of allowing widely spaced figuration to continue vibrating by means of the depressed damper pedal, opened up a whole new approach to the instrument. Important new breakthroughs in piano idiom were then achieved by Debussy around the turn of the century and by Bartók a few years later. And in our own day, the concept of piano idiom has been enormously enlarged once again by the technique of producing sound through direct contact with strings. I think it can truly be said that the potential resources of instruments can never be exhausted: the next generation will always find new ways!

"The revolutionary treatment of vocal idiom in the new music has been an interesting development. The traditional *bel canto* ideal has been very much enlarged by the influence of popular styles of singing and also by non-Western types of vocal timbre. In conjunction with this development, the traditional voice-piano medium seems to have given way to a new genre, consisting of voice and a varied instrumental chamber ensemble. A curious phenomenon is that the soprano voice type seems to clearly dominate; the other voice types have been more or less neglected by recent composers, and as a consequence, I suppose, we seem to have very few excellent singers, other than sopranos, who specialize in the new music.[36] Other significant tendencies in the area of vocal composition are the relative neglect of the choral medium and the failure, thus far, to create a new type of large-scale music theater. In respect to opera, it strikes me that Alban Berg really tied together all the strands of the tradition in his *Wozzeck* and *Lulu*, and I feel that nothing of comparable significance has been done since. In any case, the task of finding fresh approaches to opera and to choral music will be inherited by the future.

"Perhaps of all the most basic elements of music, rhythm most directly affects our central nervous system. Although in our analysis of music we have inherited a definite bias in favor of pitch, rather than rhythm, as being primary, I suspect that we are simply unable

---

36   Or, possibly, it is the other way round? A possible explanation of the predominance of new music for soprano and instruments was, simply, the participation of artists such as Bethany Beardslee and the late Jan De Gaetani, marvelous singers who made themselves available *to* the composers of new works for voice. How reluctant some composers are, indeed, to undertake work which they have been heartily assured, beforehand, that no one wants (ever) to perform! (Ed.)

to cope with rhythmic phenomena in verbal terms. It might be argued that the largest aspect of rhythm is pulse, and it is interesting to observe that, whereas the nineteenth century tended to rank composers on the quality of their slow movements — since it was assumed that slow music was more difficult to write — the situation at the present time has been completely reversed. The problem now seems to be the composition of convincing fast music, or more exactly, how to give our music a sense of propulsion without clinging too slavishly to past procedures, for example the Bartókian type of kinetic rhythm. Complexity in itself, of course, will not provide rhythmic thrust; and it is true that harmonic rhythm has to operate in conjunction with actual rhythm in order to effect a sense of propulsion.

"Three composers — two traditional and one contemporary — especially interest me with regard to their imaginative handling of rhythm and might possibly have some bearing on our current approach to rhythmic structure. The first is Beethoven, whose sense of rhythmic control was absolutely uncanny. Of all compsoers, he was the master of the widest possible range of tempos, from *prestissimo* to *molto adagio*. The Beethoven *adagio*, particularly, of the third style period, offers a format which might be further explored in contemporary terms: within the context of an extremely slow pulse, a sense of much faster movement is achieved by tiny subdivisions of the beat. Such a device offers contrast and yet gives a sense of organic unity. Another composer whose rhythmic sensitivity impresses me is Chopin. I am thinking primarily of certain of the nocturnes, in which he achieves a sense of 'suspended time' (as in much new music), but also provides a feeling of growth and progression through time. And lastly, I would mention [Olivier] Messiaen with regard to his use of the 'additive rhythmic principle', which, in his *Technique of My Musical Language,* he associates with Hindu music. I feel that this principle could become increasingly important in the further development of our rhythmical language.

"When we come to a discussion of the role of pitch in new music, we enter an arena of widely conflicting opinions. In general, I feel that the more rationalistic approaches to pitch-organization, including specifically serial technique, have given way, largely, to a more intuitive approach. There seems to be a growing feeling that we must somehow evolve a new kind of tonality.[37] Probably the ideal solution, anticipated, it seems to me, by Bartók, is to combine the possibilities of our chromatic language — which is so rich and expressive in its own right — with a sense of strong tonal focus.

---

37 See essay by George Perle, below. (Ed.)

"An interesting practice in music since the atonal period of the Viennese composers has been the widespread use of a few tiny pitch cells. One such cell, which pervades the music of Anton Webern and Bartók, is the combined major-minor third: C–E–E-flat; another such universally used cell is the perfect fourth flanked by tritones: C–F-sharp–B–F; another is the chromatic cluster: C–C-sharp–D. These three cells, in various permutations, together with a few other basic types, are astonishingly prevalent in contemporary music of whatever style.

"There has been considerable experimentation in the field of microtones in recent years, but to Western ears at least, a *structural* use of microtones is frustratingly difficult to hear. Microtones seem to be most frequently used in a *coloristic* manner, for example in 'bending' pitches. It would be very difficult to predict what role any microtonal system might play in a work composed in the twenty-fifth century, but since music must somehow relate to our central nervous system, which has evolved over countless eons, a widespread use would seem problematical.

"I have already alluded to the problem of form in new music, arising primarily from the erosion of so many traditional forms which depended on functional tonality. Of course the simpler, more primitive forms remain to us, and the variation principle is always available. Two basic types of form, both of which were known to earlier music, seem to have a peculiar attraction for recent composers. These two types are diametric opposites. One is the 'non-repetitive' principle, which implies a progression along a straight line without ever referring back to itself. The other could be called the 'minimal' type, which usually consists of a repetition *ad infinitum* of one idea, whether it be a rhythmic motif, a chord, or a melodic succession of pitches. Curiously, both types are represented in Arnold Schoenberg's music: the 'non-repetitive' in several works, and the 'minimal' in the *'Sommermorgen an einem See (Farben)'* from the *Five Pieces for Orchestra*. Of course, both types could more correctly be termed formal procedures rather than conventionally articulated formal structures like the sonata-structure or the rondo-structure. In any case, these aforementioned two types do not easily lend themselves to large-scale structure; their overextension would most likely produce fatigue and monotony. And so, perhaps we must again reevaluate the more traditional principle of repetition-with-contrast, which served the earlier composers so well.

"Perhaps many of the perplexing problems of the new music could be put into a new light if we were to reintroduce the ancient idea of music being a reflection of nature. Although technical discussions are interesting to composers, I suspect that the truly magical and spiritual powers of music arise from deeper levels of our psyche. I am certain that every composer, from his formative years as a child, has acquired a 'natural acoustic' which remains in his ear for life. The fact that I was born and grew up in an Appalachian river valley meant that my ear was attuned to a peculiar echoing acoustic; I feel that this acoustic was 'structured into' my hearing, so to speak, and thus became the basic acoustic of my music. I should imagine that the ocean shore or endless plains would produce an altogether different 'inherited' acoustic. In a broader sense, the rhythms of nature, large and small — the sounds of wind and water, the sounds of birds and insects — must inevitably find their analogues in music. After all, the singing of the humpback whale is already a highly developed 'artistic' product: one hears phrase-structure, climax and anticlimax, and even a sense of large-scale musical form!

"I am optimistic about the future of music. I frequently hear our present period described as uncertain, confused, chaotic. The two decades from 1950 to 1970 have been described as 'the rise and fall of the musical avant-garde', the implication being that nothing at all worthwhile was accomplished during those years. I have even heard the extremely pessimistic idea expressed by some composers that *Comoedia finita est'* — all possible combinations have by now been exhausted and music has finally reached a dead end. My own feeling is that music can never cease evolving; it will continually reinvent the world in its own terms. Perhaps two million years ago the creatures of a planet in some remote galaxy faced a musical crisis similar to that which we earthly composers face today. Is it possible that those creatures have existed for two million years without *new* music? I doubt it."

Selected comments by the composer: "I am often haunted by the thought that all of the many musics of the world are coming together to form *one* music. *Lux aeterna* was conceived in the spirit of this idea...."[38]

"I have always considered music to be a very strange substance, a substance endowed with magical properties. Music is tangible, almost palpable, and yet unreal, illusive. Music is analyzable only on the most mechanistic level; the important elements — the spiritual impulse, the psychological curve, the metaphysical implications — are understandable only in terms of the music itself. I feel intuitively that

---

38   Gillespie, ed., *op. cit.*, p. 5.

music must have been the primeval cell from which language, science, and religion originated....[39]

"Music might be defined as a system of proportions in the service of a spiritual impulse."[40]

Variazioni for Orchestra (1959). 25m *Prem.:* Cincinnati O, Max Rudolf, cond. *Rec.:* Louisville (Stereo LP) LS 774: Louisville O, David Gilbert, cond. *Pub.:* C. F. Peters
3-3-4-3; 4-3-3-1; perc (5), hp, cel, mand; strings
In eight connected movements.

"*Variazioni* comes at the beginning of a period that represents Crumb's decisive turn toward his mature style. It still carries over the strong influence of Bartók from the composer's youth, in addition to a 'touch of Schoenberg and Berg, and a pinch of Dallapiccola'.

"The work is scored for large orchestra with harp, mandolin, and a considerably enlarged percussion section. The composer has exploited the possibilities of using smaller orchestras within the larger framework in order to achieve maximum contrast in color and texture. The full weight of the orchestra is felt in only three of the eight movements which constitute *Variazioni*.

"In formal structure, as Crumb explains, *Variazioni* does not strictly follow the conventional pattern of theme, variations, and coda. It adds another dimension in the form of 'fantasy-pieces', which serve as digressions. All the variations are derived from the original theme but the 'Fantasia' sections are independent of any formal association with it. The eight parts are performed without pause.

"After a short introduction of five bars, the theme (based on a twelve-tone series) is presented in a very delicate scoring. Variation 1, a *pezzo antifonale* (antiphonal piece), is scored for strings alone. Variation 2 is a toccata of great intensity, which is followed by the first *Fantasia*, entitled *notturno* (nocturne). The next section, Variation 3, is a scherzo. Then comes the *Trio estatico*, Variation 4, which is the centerpiece of the entire structure and quotes the original theme in full. Variation 5, *Da capo: Burlesca*, is followed by a second *Fantasia*, a *Cadenza*, in which percussion is prominent, and which features mandolin and harp in soloistic passages. The seventh section, Variation 6, is an *Ostinato*. The eighth and final part, *Fantasia— Variazione: Elegia e coda: Tema*, rounds out the work by combining all the entities—theme, variation and fantasy—and employing all the

---

[39] Oliver Daniel, "George Crumb" (Broadcast Music Inc., 1975), in Gillespie, ed., *ibid.*, p. 20.
[40] Gillespie, ed., *ibid.*, p. 77.

instruments of the orchestra." — Don Gillespie, in Gillespie, ed., *George Crumb: Profile of a Composer*, 1986.

"How times have changed for George Crumb. The 1959 *Variazioni*, his first work for orchestra, had to wait six years — until May 8, 1965, in Cincinnati, under Rudolf — for its premiere. Today [1981], of course, Crumb is one of the handful of U.S. composers whose works can be guaranteed performances almost before the ink is dry.

"The *Variazioni* are embryonic Crumb: though carrying undeniable influences of Bartók (especially *The Miraculous Mandarin*), Berg, and Schoenberg, the music has frequent chamber-music transparency, sections of exotic instrumentation, and the use of free-form interludes in formal development, all prime features of the mature Crumb, post-1962. Structurally the work comprises an Introduction, followed by a Theme with six Variations and three interspersed Fantasias. The Introduction is built on a double signature pattern, derived from Crumb's own name and the name of a friend. The Theme uses a 12-tone row non-serially, with an A-A-B-A-B-Coda sequence. The Variations are, in turn, *Antiphonal Piece, Toccata, Scherzo, Trio Estatico, Burlesca,* and *Ostinato*. The three interrupting Fantasias are exotically prepared (for their day), with microtonal intervals, harmonics, novel performing techniques, and a dominant trio scored for mandolin, celeste, and harp. This is a rich, superb work." — Stephen W. Ellis, in *Fanfare: The Magazine for Serious Record Collectors*, 11-12/81.

JOHN EATON

B. 1935, Bryn Mawr PA. *Educ.:* Princeton Univ. *Taught at:* Indiana Univ. Artistic dir. IU Center of Electronic and Computer Music. Composer-in-residence Indiana Univ, Amer Acad (Rome). *Awards & grants:* 3 Prix de Rome, 2 Guggenheim grants; comm. Fromm Fndn, Koussesvitzky Fndn, Natl Endowmnt for the Arts, North German Radio, Young Audiences of America, Public Broadcasting Corp. *Author of: Involvement with Music: New Music Since 1950. Works incl.:* operas *(The Cry of Clytemnestra, Herakles [Hercules], Myshkin, The Tempest),* Trio (vln/vc/pno), voice & instruments *(Blind Man's Cry, Holy Sonnets of John Donne).*

Composer statement: "Composers and performers are generally closer than they have been for years. There is a larger audience for new music than ever in recent memory as well. In fact, considering that in past centuries only a tiny percentage of the population was ever involved in formal music, composers today address perhaps the largest and most varied audience in musical history. With mass communication, new pieces by leading composers often address a worldwide audience.

"It has never been as exciting to be a composer as today. With the discovery and now consolidation of a host of new materials, with the warm human relationship with performers, with the possibility of reaching people on many different levels throughout the world, it is a joy to be involved in new music." — John Eaton, *Involvement with Music: New Music Since 1950* (Harper & Row, 1976).

Danton and Robespierre (opera). *Lib.:* Patrick Creagh. 120m *Prem. & rec.:* Composers Recordings Inc (3 Stereo LPs) IUS 421: Indiana Univ Opera Theater Production, Thomas Baldner, cond. *Pub.:* Malcolm Music (Shawnee Press).
6 male, 7 female, chorus, orch (in orig. prod., chorus of 250 with orch. of 120)
4-4-6-6; 4-4-4-2; 3 harps, 2 pianos, electronic instrs; strings (suggested 82); onstage brass band
Act I. Scene 1: Late August, 1792. Two-level stage — crowd scene along the way to Paris (lower level), threatened by advance of Prussian, Austrian, and French emigrée troops; meeting of the Assembly (upper level). Conspirators plan to break into the prisons and slaughter more than 1100 inmates. Robespierre drops his arm like a guillotine blade, signalling the beginning of the massacre. Scene 2: A room in Danton's house. Camille Desmoulins tells Danton of the

massacre going on in the prisons. Scene 3: Upper stage, Danton rallies the crowd; lower level, Robespierre becomes hysterical. Act II. Scene 1: The streets of Paris a year or so later; the reign of Terror has begun. Scene 2: Danton and his new wife Louise in the country. Scene 3: Paris, Danton accused by the Assembly. Act III. Scene 1: At a dinner arranged to try to reconcile Robespierre and Danton. Danton pleads for a united front, breaks down in tears. Scene 2: Camille's sister Lucille sings a lament for France. Scene 3: Beginning of the plot against Danton; Robespierre, St. Just and Couthon sign an act of indictment against Danton and Camille. Scene 4: Danton defends himself at the Revolutionary Tribunal. Scene 5: Dark stage; Louise and Lucille recount the betrayal of Danton—followed by cold light of dawn; Danton, Camille and others led to the guillotine. Scene 6: Danton's death brings the height of the Terror; Robespierre almost maniacal. Entrescene: in complete darkness, whisperings begin, growing into a confused babble of voices—this is the conspiracy to bring down Robespierre. Scene 7: the Full Assembly. All the delegates except St. Just and Couthon hurl their accusations against Robespierre. Robespierre shoots himself, but the bullet is deflected and only hits his jaw. He, St. Just and Couthon are taken to the guillotine. The crowd rushes in, bawling insults and singing "Death to the tyrant!" Robespierre gives an unearthly cry as his head is pushed down. The guillotine falls.

Notes by the composer: "BACKGROUND OF THE OPERA. The French Revolution is generally considered the beginning of modern history. It contained nearly ever trait of modern societies in embryo and was one of those moments in which the human soul's every tendency—toward nobility or degradation, toward lofty idealism or the basest corruption, toward intense love and fierce hate—was writ large: the very stuff of opera!

"In its most extreme period—from the 1791 citizens' army repulsion of the invasion staged by the massed forces of the counter-revolutionaires and the armies of the countries which sought to destroy the infant republic, to the abrupt end in 1794 of the Reign of Terror, which (often overlooked in the macabre shade of the guillotine) was one of mankind's earliest attempts to form a rational society based on political, social, and economic liberty and equality—in this most extreme period, two extraordinary leaders were pitted against each other: Danton, the saviour of the Republic, and Robespierre, the would-be architect of the new society.

"Danton was first and foremost a humanist; Robespierre, an idealist. Danton, a realist in terms of ends who was willing to give each person the freedom to pursue his own happiness as long as it did not impinge on others' ability to do likewise, loved and was loved by people. Robespierre, an idealist in terms of ends, but often a complete realist in what means he used to achieve his ends, loved *The People* and wanted to impose his dreams on them, by brute force if necessary.

"In Robespierre's defense, it must be said that some extreme measures were indeed necessary if this inchoate mass, which had suffered such intoelrable cruelties under decadent aristocrats for years, was to be transformed into his ideal citizenry by measures such as right to work laws, graduated taxes, universal education and a United Nations. Both leaders had their share of 'truth and right' — in fact, they desperately needed each other: Robespierre was guillotined only 113 days after the death of Danton.

"Perhaps their separate visions are common with those of other pairs in other revolutions: Trotsky (Danton) and Lenin (Robespierre) — with St. Just, the 'Apostle of Blood', who, like Stalin, loved only *The Revolution* — Castro and Che Guevara, Chou En Lai and Mao Tse Tung. Certainly in writing *Danton and Robespierre* I did not feel that I was creating a morality play or a remote historical piece but rather that I was addressing our own time in terms people of today would understand only too well.

"THE MUSIC. For years I have been fascinated by and devoted to the development of a richer yet simpler music based on notes (pitches) other than those found on the piano keyboard. The possibilities of expressing psychological nuance and dramatic movement are enormously expanded by singing and playing notes that lie between the white and black keys. This should not be thought of as theoretical or artificial — on the contrary, every performer of folk and vernacular music in the world (including jazz, bluegrass, and other musics of our own culture) use such subtle inflections and nuances constantly and naturally.

"How does one use these microtonal materials within the musical mechanism of our own Western formal (classic) music? My solution is to divide the woodwinds, brasses, and pianos into A and B groups: the A group is tuned normally; the B, a quarter-tone lower — approximately one-half the distance between neighboring notes on a piano keyboard. These pitches are not rigidly fixed, however. From the quarter-tone positions players on woodwind and brass instruments can adjust their notes slightly, while singers and players on stringed instruments need only fix the position of the accurate quarter tones as a compass point to chart their journey into the rejuvenating regions of microtonal melody. The tuning of the three harps divides the distance between neighboring piano notes into three parts: one sounds normally, the second a sixth of a tone higher, the third a sixth of a tone lower.

"The electronic instrument, on the other hand, is tuned in 'just intonation'—that is, all the pitches are put in harmonic relation to one note. In that system, some keys are wonderfully true, but others become increasingly sour. I use this peculiarity to express the particular revolutionary vision of Robespierre. It is pure at the outset of the organ prelude, but the further it moves away from the basic key and into remote keys, and by analogy, the more deeply involved Robespierre becomes with specific human and social problems, the more the music becomes impure or inhuman sounding.

"The prelude recurs several times (in the music accompanying the September Massacres, in Robespierre's Hymn which begins Act III Scene 3, and in the scene accompanying the height of the terror following the guillotining of Danton), and reflects in microcosm the process of moving from the absolute purity of the basic key to the greatly out of tune final chords (a dissonance which is augmented later by techniques of electronic music).

"In Robespierre's 'Mad Scene', Act III Scene 6, the prelude, played electronically, forms the basis of the musical and dramatic movement. Robespierre begins singing with the harmony of the prelude, but goes more and more out of tune with it, like a man losing control of his mind and soul. On top of this, the orchestra reiterates the music associated with killing throughout the opera, and also accompanies the September Massacres and the references to the executions of the Reign of Terror. The three strands coexist and develop with varying degrees of independence.

"I hope the listener [to the original cast recording] will follow the libretto in order to see the interaction of music and drama and will tolerate the occasional stage noises, movement from one mike toward another (or even sometimes the singing off mike) while trying as much as possible to imagine 250 people on a large and extravagantly lighted stage."—from liner notes for CRI Stereo LP recording IUS 421.

"*Danton and Robespierre* is a large, exciting, adventurous, and vividly theatrical piece, one that James Levine and John Dexter should now acquire for the Met or Mr. [Julius] Rudel for the [New York] City Opera. Contemporary works of such virtue are not common. It would be sad if this one were to disappear after just three performances of the admirable Bloomington [Indiana University] production.... In *Danton and Robespierre*, Eaton's varied concerns—dramatic music, vocal writing, electronic instruments played live, and microtonal enrichment of the thirteen notes making up the octave of Western music—are brought together in masterly fashion.

"Eaton and his librettist, the Irish poet Patrick Creagh, thought at first of writing an opera in three acts which would deal with three pairs of contrasted revolutionaries: Danton and Robespierre, Trotsky and Lenin, and Che and Castro. That was just an idea, and one that they quickly realized would be unmanageable unless the real historical conflicts—of temperament and character as well as of political methods—were simplified and schematized to an extent that would make them both false to history and uninteresting as drama. So they decided to confine themselves to Danton and Robespierre, and deal with them fully. Eaton summarizes the subject matter as 'the conflict between Danton, an idealist who sought just means to achieve realistic ends, and Robespierre, a realist for whom any means were justified to reach idealistic ends.' He has written an urgent and topical opera. It had its inception during the student unrest of the late sixties; it reached the stage during days when 'realists' in Italy were seeking to inaugurate a Reign of Terror; and all that its words and music say has bearing on what men are thinking and doing in a world most of whose nations are again seeking, at different speeds and in different ways, to achieve freedom, equality, and brotherhood in Socialist societies.[41] *Danton and Robespierre* is an opera about idealism, about compromise, about kindness and love, about human weaknesses, and about the hideous strength of cold-blooded righteousness.

"There is a passage in *The Prelude* which never fails to shock me—when Wordsworth, walking 'over the smooth Sands of Leven's ample Aestuary', learns by chance from a passerby that Robespierre is dead, and exults in the news with fierce, uncharacteristic vindictiveness"

> O Friend! few happier moments have been mine
> Through my whole life than that when first I heard
> That his foul Tribe of Moloch was o'erthrown,
> And their chief Regent levell'd with the dust....
> Great was my glee of spirit, great my joy
> In vengeance...

And although that glee is succeeded by calmer thoughts of 'how... the mighty renovation would proceed,' Wordsworth on his stroll is still moved by 'uneasy bursts of exultation.'

---

41   These words written by *New Yorker* music critic Andrew Porter in 1978 have particular reverberations, of course, with respect to events in central Europe at the end of 1989 and during the early months of 1990. (Ed.)

"Most people, I imagine, have mixed feelings about the French Revolution. Wordsworth and Beethoven, born in 1770, both charted the years of enthusiasm when 'Bliss was it in that dawn to be alive, But to be young was very heaven,' and the disillusion that followed when, in the poet's words, 'The sun that rose in splendour... put his function and his glory off,' or, in the composer's words, Napoleon showed himself 'nothing more than an ordinary human being,' prepared to 'trample on all the rights of man and... become a tyrant.' Art enables us to apprehend the Revolution through many different eyes. Georg Büchner's play about one episode of it, Dantons Tod [Danton's Death], has had a large influence on Danton and Robespierre. Büchner was born in the last year of the First Empire. In 1834, he published a fiery pamphlet, The Hessian Messenger, which begins 'Freedom for the huts! War on the palaces!' The next year, he wrote Dantons Tod. On one level, his drama seems like an attempt to rewrite Hamlet in a political setting. It casts itself readily with a Hamlet company: Hamlet as Danton, Claudius as Robespierre, Ophelia as Lucille Desmoulins, Laertes as Camille Desmoulins, Horatio as Lacroix, Polonius as Saint-Just, and the gravediggers, scarce altered, as tumbrel drivers and executioners. But Büchner intended more than a literary exercise. In a letter about the play, he wrote:

> The dramatic poet is in my eyes nothing but a writer of history.... His greatest task is to come as close as possible to history as it actually happened. His book must be neither more nor less moral than history itself.... The poet is not a teacher of morality: he creates figures, he brings past times to life, and the public should learn from that, as well as from the study and observation of history, what is going on around them.

"Eaton and Creagh do not set out to be teachers of morality, either. They present but do not preach. It is a strength of their opera. To Büchner they owe the general construction in short, kaleidoscopic scenes; the way the Paris crowd episodes are handled, and some of their detail; and the vivid portrayal of Robespierre in strange, visionary monologues. (In both play and opera, Robespierre comes close to being the tragic hero of the action.) Some of the parallels may derive from a common source: both Büchner and Creagh allow Robespierre to speak in words that he actually spoke, and Danton's famous speech to the Assembly on September 2, 1792 ('*Il nous faut de l'audace, encore de l'audace, toujours de l'audace*'), alluded to in the play, is delivered in the first-act finale of the opera. The play covers the last months of Danton's life. The opera starts a little earlier, on the eve of the September Massacres, in 1792, and ends with Robespierre's execution, in July 1794, sixteen weeks after Danton's. We lose the delightful grisette Marion, one of Büchner's most memorable figures (she is reborn as Jenny in Brecht and Weill's *Mahagonny*); we gain Gabrielle, Danton's first wife. In general, Eaton and Creagh's Danton is more uxorious, more domestic, less carefree than Büchner's. He is also less witty, and does not go to the scaffold with a jest on his lips.

"There has, of course, already been a very successful opera on *Dantons Tod* — Gottfried von Einem's, performed first at the Salzburg Festival in 1947 and then widely for several years throughout Germany. Little of its music remains in my mind — only the impression of a strong play provided with an apt and skillful continuous musical accompaniment.[42] But while Büchner's *Dantons Tod* is indeed a strong play, Creagh's *Danton and Robespierre* is a better *dramma per musica*. I must not give the impression that the libretto is simply *Dantons Tod* remodeled. Although the debts to Büchner are plain, the historical incidents chosen and adapted for musical treatment, and the invented episodes — their shaping and their sequence — have been worked out anew, to form a scheme in which the musical developments are part of the dramatic enactment. There are three acts. The first shows Danton as patriot and orator. The second contrasts Robespierre's Reign of Terror with Danton's brief country retirement, and ends with his return to the Assembly, to speak moderation. The third opens with a final, vain attempt at reconciliation between Danton and Robespierre, and then moves swiftly to the double tragedy. Public scenes alternate with private episodes: on the one hand, arias, duets, and ensembles involving, in different combinations, Danton, Gabrielle, Louise (his second wife), Lucille, and Camille; on the other hand, Robespierre alone with his single-minded obsession.

"The form of the opera and the powerful Bloomington staging, directed by Hans Busch, designed by Max Röthlisberger, and lit by Allen R. White, can hardly be discussed separately. The composer's and librettist's visions — a single figure onstage, musing, and then, an instant later, an assembled crowd of hundreds; pitch darkness, and then, sounding through it, from every corner of the auditorium, a menacing whisper and a soft drumming that grow louder and louder until, with a sudden flash, the full Assembly in session is

---

42 Some listeners would think more and some less of von Einem's work. It only distresses me that music of a certain quality should come to be dismissed at all, since the "horde" of seriously conceived music is still relatively small, and thus all of it is to be cherished. Here it must be admitted that music in general continues to have an extraordinary champion in Andrew Porter — whatever his objections to a work may be, he always seems to *care*. (Ed.)

revealed, and, below it, the threatening crowd — were carried out to thrilling effect. On the large, deep stage of the Bloomington Musical Arts Center (a stage second only to the Met's, it is claimed), Mr. Röthlisberger had constructed a large, deep, exciting set, one that could contain within it a variety of other scenes — some small, some large, some shallow, some deep — in a way that quite avoided the monotony of unit sets such as the Met *Prophète, Aida,* and *Rigoletto* are played in. About five hundred students were used in the show — but that figure includes backstage workers and also the Singing Hoosiers, who appeared only in film sequences, marching against the Prussian invaders. In round figures, there were about two hundred people on the stage and a hundred in the pit.

"A large orchestra is required.... Half the winds and one of the pianos are tuned a quarter-tone below regular pitch. One of the harps is tuned at regular pitch, one a sixth-tone higher, one a sixth-tone lower. The strings and the singers — including the chorus — are called on to pitch in quarter-tones. (That is to say, between the notes C and D they must be able to sound not just the single note C-sharp/D-flat but the three distinct notes C-semisharp, C-sharp/D-flat, and D-semiflat.) My ear, corrupted by years of listening to singers whose natural vibrato often covers a quarter-tone or more, and to string and woodwind players with wide vibrato, was not fine enough, I confess, to discern how accurately the music was stated. (An old Beecham story seems relevant here: Leon Goossens sounds a rich oboe A as the orchestra's tuning note, and Sir Thomas remarks, 'Gentlemen, take your pick.') Except in steady and expressed solo lines, it was hard to take conscious cognizance of the quarter-tones. One tended to 'read' them as the nearest regular note, slightly 'bent' for the purpose of expression in much the way that a singer singing traditional music will on occasion deliberately (or unconsciously) for the purpose of expression 'bend' a note and pitch it a shade sharp or a shade flat. It may be that this is the way Eaton means us to hear them. So far as I can make out, he uses the quarter-tones not in any abstruse harmonic system but as an enrichment of expressive possibilities. Harmonies are 'clean' or 'dirty', pure or tainted, uncompromising or generously accommodating. A chord struck by the three harps quivers uneasily; on a single harp, it is precisely defined. In any event, the microtones cause no difficulty to the ordinary listener. At the start of the opera, there are opposed street cries from vendors of fish and loaves. The fishwife sings at regular pitches, accompanied by horns conventionally tuned; the baker's wife sings a quarter-tone 'off', accompanied by clarinets similarly 'off'; the bitonality, the opposition, takes on keener and readily apprehended edge. Microtones are also used to striking effect in the brief instrumental prelude. In just intonation, pure in the key of C major, an electronic organ plays a simple chorale that begins in C major and modulates, step by step, until it reaches F-sharp major, the furthest possible key — and in doing so the instrument becomes at first slightly, and at last excrutiatingly, out of tune. It is a simple but effective symbol of an ideal — represented by an 'ideal' tuning — that will fit one set of circumstances but becomes increasingly inapplicable to others. The chorale is associated with Robespierre. There is a moving passage in Act III where he sings it (to the words 'O God, O great Creator, Look down on what we do') accompanied by strings — four solo cellos. And they, of course, as string players do, make constant microtonal adjustments, impossible on a keyboard instrument, which keep the harmonies perfectly in tune, all the way from C to F-sharp. There is a terrifying episode later in the act, after the death of Danton, where Robespierre tries to repeat his prayer and it goes horribly out of tune.

"For all the intricacies of Eaton's score, it is direct and readily comprehensible. No more than Alban Berg is he afraid of big, straightforward, traditional theatre strokes: ostinatos, sudden outbursts, unisons, firm tonal anchors against which to measure degrees of dissonance and tension. His writing for the chorus is adventurous and exciting. His writing for the orchestra is varied and very colorful. Moreover, and perhaps most important of all, *Danton* is a mellifluous opera, composed with a command of lyrical vocal gestures that reveal character and are also good to sing. Without that quality, an opera does not live.

"[All in all,] this is... a remarkable work." — Andrew Porter, in *The New Yorker*, 5/22/78.[43]

"From the very outset of *Danton and Robespierre*, one has to admire composer John Eaton. It took courage, not to mention self-confidence, to deal with political stresses of the late eighteenth century in the musical idioms of the late twentieth on a scale so grand that the comparison that leaps to mind is Meyerbeer. And though opera still thrives on nostalgic references, both subtle and not so subtle, few composers can indulge themselves to this extent and come through unscathed, accused of neither gimmickery nor cliché.

"Only the most cynical listener would even think of leveling such accusations at *Danton*; Eaton's work stubbornly refuses to stoop to shoddiness, and his superb manipulation of tension and impeccable sense of theatrical timing show the sure hand of genius. I say 'stubbornly' because there are touchy moments: the old tremolo trick

---

43   Reprinted in *Music of Three More Seasons, 1977-1980* (Alfred A. Knopf, 1981).

to the line 'their souls tremble like drops of water'; a glissando of disillusionment with the realization that 'these are the forged letters, this is the false witness.' But—and this is a big but—when the souls tremble, their fear is reflected to chilling effect in the shaking of the women's voices; and the revealing glissando comes from the high strings that had, just seconds before, been writing those letters: they are the voices of the subversives as well as the voices of doom.

"Patrick Creagh's libretto takes up the tale late in August 1792, when the young French Republic was threatened by Prussian invaders, and follows the resistance up to 1794, when both the heroic Danton and 'The Incorruptible' Robespierre lost their heads. The words are not as eminently successful as the music. Creagh occasionally takes the short way out, and his sense of perspective sometimes seems vague: is he posing in the eighteenth century, or looking back from the twentieth; is he or isn't he pretending to be French (the Gallic names sound strange in the otherwise American speech); is he consciously pitting the women's sensitivities against the men's cruder determinations, or is this a passing coincidence?... But the whole of the work is greater than the sum of its parts, as any successful opera should be. I, for one, couldn't care less about either Danton or Robespierre, yet despite the libretto's problems, I came out caring a lot about this theater piece and hoping that it will have a long and happy life on the world's stages.

"The score is an ever imaginative, sometimes startling combination of elements, beginning with the out-of-kilter organ that ushers in Act I, Scene 1, and continuing in that scene with an ensemble of deftly characterized street folks who quickly epitomize the rabble and masses the French leaders (one hesitates to say heroes) had to rouse. If these and other folksy scenes are reminiscent of Benjamin Britten, this is to the credit of both composers, since realism and individuality reign. And the Britten similarity does not persist. Eaton's constantly colorful musical language uses a raft of devices, both avant-garde and retrospective, for instruments and voices alike. His methods of fitting words to music are as precise, as rhythmically astute, and as creative as any that have surfaced in the last fifty years. The music is a vibrant commentary on the text, and the instruments take on lives and personalities of their own.

"*Danton* takes practically the population of Paris to perform; nine principal singers, more than two dozen minor characters, a mixed ensemble serving as Citizens and Rabble, a large chorus for the Crowd and the Volunteers, and a male chorus of political Delegates. Like Eaton's subsequent opera, *The Cry of Clytemnestra* (smaller, but no less ambitious in scope), *Danton* was first produced by the Indian University Opera Theater in Bloomington. The provinces, you say.

Well, Bloomington may not yet have Bloomingdale's, Soho, or Noho, but this is no product of the hinterlands in operatic terms. CRI's recording was taken from the original university presentation, and it is superb in every respect. Only applause between the acts (and at the end of the delicate love duet for Danton and his second wife, Louise) betrays that it was not taped entirely under closely monitored studio conditions. Balances seem perfect, and conductor Thomas Baldner lets all the colors and comments come through. While the live-performance circumstances surely gave the realization an extra bit of zest, the exigencies of the stage were never allowed to get in the way of purely technical accomplishment.

"Eaton has written his principal vocal lines for virtuosos, men and women with dramatic force and flexibility, and with ranges of more than two octaves. The Hoosier cast never cringes at these assignments. The large orchestra's parts are equally difficult, and here the achievements of the Indiana forces are even more impressive." — Karen Monson, in *High Fidelity*, 7/80.

"Eaton uses all of today's resources, including serial techniques, microtones, and electronics. One of the first performers of live electronic music, [he] has blended these resources plus conventional instruments into a coherent conglomeration. Unlike many composers of electronic music, Eaton is active in opera and uses electronics in them. *Danton and Robespierre* is his fourth opera. *Myshkin*, his television opera based on Dostoyevsky's *The Idiot*, uses electronics extensively. It was broadcast over PBS about four years ago. Turnabout once had a recording of Eaton's *Concert Piece* for Syn-Ket and Orchestra (the Syn-Ket is a portable electronic synthesizer). Two discs of mostly electronic music were once on domestic Decca, and CRI 296 has three works, including *Blind Man's Cry* for soprano and synthesizer ensemble.

"*Danton and Robespierre* is of epic scale... comparable to Mahler's *Eighth* or Schoenberg's *Gurrelieder*. In addition, the Indiana University production was multi-media, and I've heard reports that its visual aspects were quite extraordinary. Structurally the three-act opera is conventional, with arias, duets, ensembles, and big crowd scenes. More important, it is good drama. The integration of music, text, and action is excellent.... Ultimately the revolutionary mob itself becomes a principal character. Musically and dramatically the opera is a study of how events can grow beyond the control of those who shaped them and eventually pull them down in their undertow.

"Eaton's score is eclectic. Yes, there is extensive use of microtones and electronics, and yes, it does sound modern. But — it is *not* wildly avant-garde and there is no wildly leaping disjunct vocal writing. *Danton and Robespierre* is an eminently singable opera. The orchestration is colorful and the choral writing outstanding. There are also lyrical parrts, most notably in the music given to Louise, Lucille, and Gabrielle. The electronic instrument and microtonal material are used largely to 'express psychological nuance and dramatic movement.' The opera's prelude, for example, is first played on the electronic organ. It recurs in the September Massacres, Robespierre's Hymn (Act III, Scene 3), the chaos following Danton's execution, and in Robespierre's 'mad scene' (Act III, Scene 6). As Robespierre's involvement deepens and his mind and soul crumble, the prelude becomes increasingly distorted and dissonant. In his mad scene Robespierre starts singing with the harmony of the prelude, going increasingly out of tune as the scene progresses. Simultaneously the orchestra is replaying music which accompanied killing in earlier scenes. To achieve the eerie sounds and effects made possible by microtonality, Eaton divided the winds, brass, and pianos into two groups: one group tuned normally, the other a quarter-tone lower. Singers and brass were directed to center pitch on quarter tones.

"[The CRI recording of this work] is a most important release, unreservedly recommended." — Ben Pernick, in *Fanfare: The Magazine for Serious Record Collectors*, 7-8/80.

Donald Erb

B. 1927, Youngstown OH. *Educ.:* Kent State Univ, Cleveland Inst of Music, Indiana Univ. *Taught at:* Cleveland Inst of Music, Southern Methodist Univ, Univ of Melbourne, Indiana Univ, Bowling Green State Univ, Case Inst of Techn. Composer-in-residence Cleveland Inst, Case Western Reserve Univ, Dallas SO; Guggenheim Fellowship, grants Ford Fndn, Rockefeller Fndn, Natl Council on the Arts. Chairman, NEA composer-librettist panel; pres., American Music Ctr. *Works incl.:* choral (*Fallout, Kyrie*), concertos (cbn, cl, kybds, perc, tbn, tpt, vc), *Hexagon* (6 insts), orchestral pieces (*Christmas Music, Symphony of Overtures*), *Phantasma* (fl/ob/hpsd/db), quartets.

The Hawk (concertino) for Alto Saxophone, Brass, Percussion, and Saxophone Ensemble. *Pub.:* Highgate Press (distr. Galaxy).

"Donald Erb, an outspoken champion of contemporary music, is usually associated with 'classical' genres. *The Hawk* illustrates one more facet of his diverse capabilities, and utlizes the experiences gained in years of arranging for dance bands in his youth. Scored for the typical stage band of five saxophones, four trumpets, four trombones, and rhythm (piano, electric bass, and 'jazz set drummer'), it also calls for electric piano, electric organ, and two percussionists playing harmonicas, vibes, timpani, tam tam, slide whistle, gallon jug, cymbal, crystal goblet, marimba, glockenspiel, and chimes. Inspiration for the work came from an event early in the composer's life: 'Somewhere around 1940 I heard Coleman Hawkins playing *Body and Soul*. It was one of the formative moments of my life. "The Hawk" is certainly one of the greatest jazz musicians America has ever produced, and this piece, lovingly named after him, is my way of acknowledging a considerable artistic debt.'

"Erb has molded chance elements, tone clusters, multiphonics in the saxophones (with fingerings clearly marked for those who may not be familiar with this technique), and jazz and blues improvisations with traditional notation to produce a work of strong intensity and overwhelming effect. Highly demanding of all the instruments, the first alto sax part in particular is a brilliant display of technical skill, complete with extended cadenza. The opening movement begins slowly and softly, and builds to a fortissimo climax before leading directly into the second. Beginning once again very softly, the second movement builds in intensity towards a fast hard-driving climax on the 'highest note possible', with a descending glissando and closing section diminishing to *niente*. The published score contains clear explanations for any symbols that may not be familiar to the performers." —Raoul F. Camus, in *Notes* (Music Library Association), 9/83.

The Seventh Trumpet for Orchestra (1969).

"Two of the most successful works to appear [around] 1970 in the orchestral and chamber music fields were *The Seventh Trumpet* by Donald Erb and *The Ancient Voices of Children* by George Crumb. Both [composers] are Americans who participated in the search for new materials in the 1960s. Both are excellent musicians who are unsystematically and intuitively consolidating highly personal styles from the new materials.

"Erb came into formal music from the laboratory of jazz. He explored new instrumental colors with Bertram Turetsky and others. Although Erb's early music was serial, he soon moved toward the other side of the spectrum. He invented and employed all kinds of aleatoric devices and notations in a very precise and concise way, using them only when they were the most efficient, logical, and musical way to produce particular sonorities or movement of sonorities.

"*The Seventh Trumpet* begins with a single instrument trill. It is unmeasured and accelerates. Other instruments that have the same device are cued in by the conductor. Incredible coloristic devices are employed as the piece unfolds. Players are asked to whistle and speak. They also play their instruments in untraditional ways and use toy instruments. Erb is particularly inventive in handling percussion: a large bottle partially filled with water is bent as it is constantly tapped to give an 'electronic filtering'. But, nevertheless, all these devices and colors are drawn to a personal vision of great strength and magnitude, a mystical vision of the apocalypse." —John Eaton, in *Involvement with Music: New Music Since 1950* (Harper & Row, 1976).

Sonata for Clarinet and Percussion (1979). *Prem.:* Boston Musica Viva (William Wrzesien, cl, Dean Anderson, perc). *Pub.:* Merion (Theodore Presser).

"Donald Erb is well-known for his craft in instrumentation, a skill acquired through a long practice of working closely with professional performers. The *Sonata for Clarinet and Percussion*... continues a series of fine chamber music works, often featuring percussion with other instruments.

"The composer uses the newest extended instrumental techniques pushing his performers to the extreme limits of their technical abilities. But at no moment in the piece is this predilection for advanced virtuosity indulged in at the expense of optimum conditions for instrumental balance. The idiomatic sound qualities of the instruments seem to be the primary concern of the composer at all times. The piece... requires a percussionist prepared to display the utmost virtuosity in multiple keyboard playing, bowing techniques on the vibraphone, and jazz trap set techniques. The clarinettist has to be very efficient in extended high range and in multiphonics. Although the piece is technically demanding, the musical intentions are clear so that the performer can grasp them immediately and set precise goals; this in turn will help in solving the technical problems and in articulating the piece properly.

"The piece is in four related parts separated by cadential points. Jazz influences are manifested in free flowing beautiful melodic shapes, and, in the fourth part, in the use of the drum set in typical jazz idiom. (The choice of the combination of clarinet and percussion is itself reminiscent of traditional New Orleans music.) The harmonic contour, based on a series of perfect fifths, is slowly built up by the sustaining power of two harmonicas (in C and in D) in the second part and an organ (recorded or live) in the third. The hollow quality of successive parallel perfect fifths simultaneously heard in the clarinet and the vibraphone or marimba is a particularly seductive feature of the piece.

"Erb's sonata is a beautiful contribution to a fast expanding repertoire for clarinet and percussion. It is full of life and fun, and will please the numerous groups of this combination that have recently sprung up everywhere: clarinettists and percussionists get along well together." —Jean-Charles François, in *Notes* (Music Library Association), 12/82.

Trio for Violin, Keyboards, and Percussion (1977). *Rec.:* Crystal Records (Stereo LP) S505: Ronald Gorevic (vln), James Primosch (keybds), Charles Wilkinson (perc).
In five movements.

"The extroverted Mr. Erb. When he composes, listeners are always in for a rollicking time. His trio for violin, keyboards (piano, electric piano, electric organ, and celesta), and percussion is a five-movement piece that, as Erb says, represents his 'usual approach to composition. It is a result of my own perception of sound rather than any esthetic.' Erb's 'perception' is timbral effects of wide variety, which are established right from the work's onset. The second movement does a maniacal number on the overture to *The Marriage of Figaro*. (Mozart is Erb's favorite composer.) The slow third movement is the core of the piece—a sonorous stew that simmers and reverberates. The fourth movement recalls Erb's 'barroom' days, as he puts it, and has virtuoso cadenzas for each player. If the movement's frequent violin glissandi are meant to be bawdy, the piano poundings the release of inhibitions and the hell-bent percussion the frenzy of youth, then I guess I see the connection. The final movement is two short minutes of contemplative coda, with soft acoustics from keyboards and percussion. Erb's musical bravura isn't to everyone's taste, even to people who like modern music, but I have always found his works a good kick and constantly listenable. (His percussion concerto is one of the very best of the genre. Erb has a concerto for keyboards and orchestra, premiered in Akron in 1981, and wouldn't I like to hear that!)"—Stephen W. Ellis, in *Fanfare: The Magazine for Serious Record Collectors*, 11-12/82.

ROSS LEE FINNEY

B. b. 1906, Wells MN. *Educ.:* Univ of MN, Carleton College, Harvard Univ. *Taught at:* Smith College, Mt. Holyoke College, Hartt Schl of Music, Amherst College, Univ of MI. Member Phi Beta Kappa, AMS, Natl Ins Arts/Letters. *Awards & grants:* Guggenheim Fellowships (2), Pulitzer travelling fellowship, Brandeis Gold Medal, Rome Prize, Collidge & Koussevitzky Fndns. Composer-in-residence, Univ of MI. *Author of: The Game of Harmony, Making Music. Works incl.:* choral, concertos (a sax, perc, pno, strings, vln, vc), operas (*Computer Marriage, Weep Torn Land*), piano pieces, 8 qts (strngs), qt & qnts (pno, strngs), 4 symphonies, trio (pno/ vln/vc).

Composer statement: (in letters to the Editor) "[Here are some of the notes you request...] One of my blocks is that I never keep (or read if I can avoid it) critical reviews of my works. My wife collects them, and there are some ten big scrap books in the attic (which will go to the New York Public Library), but, here are a few words...

"Over my life-time, which almost spans a century, music has had different meanings. When I was a child in North Dakota, both performing and composing music was an all-absorbing game. I played the cello and was in great demand to play in both our family orchestra and the community orchestra. My great ambition was to play and compose better than anyone else. Even when we moved to Minneapolis and I went to high school and finally to the University, my ability to perform was competitive. Only gradually did I come to realize that music was a profession as well as a game; that a great artistic world opened up only after hard work.

"Composing music had always been related to performing. Even when I began studying and analysing music at the University, it never entered my head that theory led to composing as improvisation did; quite the other way around, composing led to theories that might improve but surely complicate the musical ideas that came to mind.

"After I worked my way through college (teaching cello) and to Europe to study with Nadia Boulanger (playing in a jazz orchestra), I came into contact with an extremely talented group of composers who talked constantly of being an *American composer*. New ideas about music began to develop in my mind. A composer had to be not only a master of his craft but also uniquely himself, and he had to reflect in his music who he was.

"This view of music dominated my thinking for many years until after my involvement in World War II. I came to feel the need of a more expressive musical vocabulary. The over-emphasis on nationalism and the rapid changes in the electronic media made me feel that the triadic tradition was inadequate. I felt that tonal structure depended on a polarity that included the total pitch resources available.

"Interest in serialization had been stimulated by my studies with Alban Berg in the 30s, but it never led to an acceptance of an orthodox twelve-tone technic. My interest in electronic music lead to the re-examining of instrumental technics, but never to a desire to compose computer music. Music remains for me a language for expressing my individual feelings and convictions.

"Perhaps it was inevitable that in the mid-sixties I found memory playing an important role in my music, a role that became more and more important as I got older—such works as *Landcapes Remembered* (1971), *Variations on a Memory* (1975), and *Narrative in Retrospect* (1984).

"I don't feel that my music has changed fundamentally over the years. I was delighted when Martha Braden made a recording (CRI CD 560) of four of my piano works (*Fantasy*, 1939, *Piano Sonata Nr. 3 in E*, 1942, *Sonata quasi una Fantasia*, 1961, and *Narrative in Retrospect*, 1984) that reflect the way I have thought about music over the years."

Additional note on the composer: "After 1947, when he was awarded a second Guggenheim Fellowship, Finney composed much chamber music and was particularly concerned with problems of structure. His concept of the tensions of opposing musical forces, which he calls 'complementarity', his preference for strong rhythmic motivation, his concern with variation, and his fascination with time (as a philosophical as well as a musical phenomenon) were factors in forging this style....

"[After moving to the University of Michigan in 1949, as composer-in-residence,] Finney became more involved with serial technique. The *String Quartet 6* (1950) uses three 12-tone series; the *Fantasy in Two Movements* (1958) uses one, with one permutation. In 1959 he began to serialize nonpitch elements, deriving changes in tempo and the proportions of formal divisions from the pitch series in such works as the *Concerto for Percussion* (1965). Most characteristic of Finney's technique is the use of a structured series, particularly with balancing or mirror-image hexachords. These hexachords are generative and are fulfilled both in interaction and compression— 'the greatest compression of the hexachord' Finney calls a 'source set', a term first used in the *Fantasy in Two Movements*.

"Finney used serial materials in elaborate forms, through juxtapositions of sections of driving impulse and floating sonorities, and this led him to a further exploration: of memory as a musical phenomenon, transcending simple nostalgia and the fashionable quotation of materials from other times and places. For Finney memory is a process, a flowing of complete and incomplete elements, of unexpected lucidity and frustrating indefinition, a process related to variation; Finney finds that variation is not the repeating but the reexperiencing of the theme. His further experiments with the concept of memory culminated in the choral and orchestral trilogy *Earthrise: Still are New Worlds* (1962), *The Martyr's Elegy* 1967), and *Earthrise* (1978), works that are not only time-centered but also space-centered, bordering on the mystical." — Edith Boroff, in *The New Grove Dictionary of American Music* (1986).

Landscapes Remembered for Orchestra (1971). 14m *Pub.*: Henmar (distr. C. F. Peters — score; perform. materials on rental).
1 (picc, alto)-0-1-0; 0-1-1-0; perc (1), pno, hp; strings

"This work is based on nostalgic memories and uses folk songs that I sing with the guitar. In composing it I came to realize that many of these songs were based on symmetrical hexachords that used all twelve notes of the scale, and could be quoted within the fabric of the work." — Ross Lee Finney.

"[In my music I don't usually] quote many things. [But] from my childhood on, I have always sung folk songs with guitar. My family sang all the time. I still, every now and then, get up with my guitar and sing a song. For instance, you know *Landscapes Remembered*; well, so much of it is based on

O bury me not on the lone prairie.

To me, the openness of that, the intervallic quality, is very American. The jump of the octave.

In Scarlet Town, where I was born,
There was a young maid dwelling,
Made all the boys come runnin' round
For love of Barbrie Ellen.

Look at the way that melody catapults over long intervals. So I usually quote things that are genuinely in my background. There's no fake here; I don't get out books on folk songs. There are a lot of folk songs that I don't sing. For instance, I have never sung Negro spirituals because I think I'd sing them badly, and I value them too highly to desecrate them with my Welsh voice....

"I'm terribly interested in memory, and quotation has to do with it. What is the basis of memory? Why does one remember something, and what does memory do to continuity? This interests me. [There is one aspect of memory in variation form,] but there's another aspect, and this comes out in *Landscapes Remembered*. Do you remember that that piece starts with a vibraphone chord? The vibraphone chord is F-G-A-B^b-C-D; that is one of the most basic hexachords that you can have in the twelve-tone technique. Its counterpart, the other six notes, is B-C$^\#$-D$^\#$-E-F$^\#$-G. So there is a parallel, a symmetrical hexachord, where you get the twelve notes that way. Now, there's been all this talk about how twelve-tone techniques of this century were suddenly discovered; but what is that hexachord? It's B^b, F, C, G, D, A; it's the circle of fifths. Just how long has the circle of fifths been around? Also, as a natural result of that hexachord—F-G-A-B^b-C-D—you have a pentatonic scale. In other words, if you were to take F-G-B^b-C-D, what melodies belong to that?

Nearer my God to Thee...

So suddenly, in the hexachordal theory that has dominated my music, I find all kinds of roots back into my memory. I don't find that it's restrictive.

"Of course, there are lots more theoretical ways that I could talk about it. For instance, Milton Babbitt talkes about 'source sets'. As I understand it, they are groups of notes that you find reiterated on different levels. I call it an associative structure—again, memory. In other words, you remember a certain note organization, and this comes out in many different places and on many different levels. As I said, I find this very much related to memory, and I find that this is something that can be utilized in terms of even my own personal, human memory."—From an interview with Cole Gagne and Tracy Caras, in Gagne & Caras, *Soundpieces: Interviews with American Composers* (The Scarecrow Press, 1982).

Quartet for Oboe, Cello, Percussion and Piano (1979). 15m
Pub.: Henmar (distr. C. F. Peters—score & parts).

"This work is not based on memories of anything—it is a chamber work which features the diversity and virtuosity of the broken consort."—Ross Lee Finney.

Skating on the Sheyenne for Symphonic Band (1977). 12m *Pub.:*
Henmar (distr. Peters—score; performance materials on rental).
1. *Figure Eights*. 2. *Northern Lights*. 3. *Crack the Whip*.

"The twelve-minute work is scored for symphonic band, including alto flute, English horn, contrabass clarinet, contrabassoon, and a wide variety of percussion instruments, and is in three contrasting movements. The first, *Figure Eights*, is based upon a two-bar rhythmic motif, the second being the retrograde of the first, evoking the image of a skater on the frozen North Dakota river creating smooth symmetrical patterns on the ice. A brief waltz section brings memories of olden times, but chance elements and shifting meters bring one back forcefully to the present. The second movement, *Northern Lights*, captures the splendor of the aurora borealis in a soft slowly changing tonescape featuring the alto flute, celesta, and soprano woodwinds. The third movement, *Crack the Whip*, is a joyous escape to childhood pleasures, complete with cascading scales in the woodwinds, glissandi in the trombones, and shifting rhythms delightfully tossing one to and fro, and ending in a furious climax. The work is an impressive addition to the repertoire of original works for band." — Raoul F. Camus, in *Notes* (Music Library Association), 9/83.

Spherical Madrigals for Chorus (1947). *Texts:* English poets from Marjorie Hope Nicolson collection *The Breaking of the Circle*. 15m *Rec.:* GSS-111: Gregg Smith Singers. *Pub.:* Henmar (distr. C. F. Peters).
1. Love is a circle. 2. When again all these rare perfections meet. 3. All-circling point. 4. His body was an orb. 5. On a round ball. 6. Nor do I doubt. 7. See how the arched Earth.

"The seven songs all contain circular symbolism. Musically, too, Finney concentrates on this circular theme by employing the circle of fifths. According to the composer, *Spherical Madrigals* was strongly influenced by his love of singing madrigals, especially those by Monteverdi." — Gregg Smith, from GSS-111 recording program notes.

Two Studies for Saxophones (1 Player) and Piano (1981). 10m Pub.: C. F. Peters (ed. Laura Hunter).

"This two-movement work is for the undergraduate and graduate saxophonist who knows a good and willing pianist. The piece requires the saxophonist to switch (as in a pit orchestra) back and forth on soprano saxophone and alto saxophone. The pianist is required to strum strings and to be technically proficient. Musically, the work is worth the required preparation. A fine recital, seminar and theory class performance selection." — Susan Hegberg, in *The American Music Teacher* (Music Teachers National Association), 9-10/87.

Two Acts for Three Players for Clarinet, Percussion and Piano (1970). 16m *Pub.:* Henmar (distr. C. F. Peters—score & parts).
Act I. Scene 1—*Sweet and Low*. Scene 2—*The Plot Thickens. Intermezzo.*
Act II. Scene 1—*Romance*. Scene 2—*The Chase.*

"This work is based on my memory of the early 'flicks', and the performance should be visual as well as musical. It is a show, and the music is based (as so much of my music is) on symmetrical hexechords."—Ross Lee Finney.

NICOLAS FLAGELLO

B. 1928, New York NY. *Educ.:* Manhattan Schl of Music, Accademia di S. Cecilia (Rome). *Taught at:* Curtis Inst of Music, Manhattan Schl of Music. *Awards:* Fulbright Fellowship. Cond. Chicago Lyric Opera (1961), New York City Opera (1967), Rome SO. *Works incl.:* band, choral, concertos (flute, piano, sax qt, string orch, vln), harp pieces, *Lautrec* (suite for orch), operas (incl. children's opera *The Piper of Hamelin*), piano pieces, songs for voice & piano.

Composer statement: "My entire life has been immersed in the European musical heritage that has surrounded me since birth. My father was an accomplished musician, and even performed professionally on the oboe both in Italy and in the United States. My mother had originally been trained as a mezzo soprano. Her father, Domenico Casiello, was one of the last students of Verdi and became a leading conductor and composer in Naples.

"I began taking piano lessons from an aunt—also a conservatory graduate—when I was 3-1/2 years old. By the time I was eight I was ready to study theory and composition, as well as the violin. My younger brother Ezio, today a well-known operatic bass baritone, also shared this varied and intensive musical preparation.

"I loved this tradition that surrounded me; thus music has always been for me the most natural means of expression. Early encounters with Rachmaninoff, Strauss, Sibelius, Toscanini and others, and my long apprenticeship with Vittorio Giannini, intensified my feeling of attachment to this great heritage. In addition, the fact that I spent much of my childhood and adolescence in Europe meant that I have never felt like an 'American' musician, with the isolation from the well-springs of tradition that that implies. As a composer, I have never desired or needed to reject or rebel against this heritage. To the contrary, I am proud to make my personal contribution to it, and am not afraid to submit my work alongside that of my predecessors. As unfashionable as such a creed may appear today, I compose to express myself, in a language that is natural and contemporary to me and comprehensible, I believe, to my audience. I have tried to fulfill Mozart's dictum that the greatest task for a composer is to challenge the most sophisticated musician while still entertaining the most modest listener."

From *The New Grove Dictionary of Music and Musicians:* "Flagello's music might be said to represent a fusion of an Italianate lyrical-dramatic with a German metaphysical approach, tempered by an American concision of structure. The major works are marked by brooding despair and violent agitation, which find release in massive climaxes of shattering impact. Despite its emotional effusiveness, the music is closely argued and remarkable skilful and imaginative in its handling of subtle instrumental colors. Flagello's later compositions are highly chromatic and dissonant, while retaining the earlier propensity for heartfelt melody and harmonic richness, and showing a clear anchoring in tonality at structural peaks." —Walter G. Simmons.

Capriccio for Cello and Orchestra (1962). 16m *Rec.:* Serenus (Stereo LP) SRS 12003: George Koutzen (vc), Orchestra Sinfonica di Roma, Nicolas Flagello, cond. *Pub.:* Boston Music Co. (or c/o VPF Music, 78 North Route 303, Congers NY 10920).
cello solo; 2-2-2-2; 2-2-1-0; perc., celesta, harp; strings.

The *Capriccio*'s title refers to its free, rhapsodic form, tightly organized around a single motif. This is a dark, brooding work of almost unrelieved gloom, building to a climax of incredible intensity and force; the work is harmonically dissonant and recitative-like in phraseology, within a post-romantic stylistic syntax. "[The work displays a] keen sense of form.... the cello writing is beautifully arranged. The orchestration is expert." —*American Record Guide*. "A work of great gravity, with an unerring unity of mood, structure, and style." —*Fanfare: The Magazine for Serious Record Collectors*.

Contemplazioni di Michelangelo for Soprano and Orchestra (1964). 21m *Text:* Michelangelo. *Prem.:* Donna Jeffrey (s), orch. cond. by Nicolas Flagello. *Rec.:* Serenus (Stereo LP) 12005: Nancy Tatum (s), O Sinfonica di Roma, Nicolas Flagello, cond. *Pub.:* Boston Music Co. (or c/o VPF Music, 78 North Route 303, Congers NY 10920).
soprano solo; 2-2-2-2; 2-2-1-0; perc., harp, celesta; strings
1. *Come puo esser?* [How can it be I am no longer I?] (4m) 2. *Ben doverrieno* [For all this anguish and for all this sighing...]. (8m) 3.*Ben fu* [Preparing for your eyes the brightest ray...]. (3m) 4. *Di più cose* [My eyes are grieved by all the things they knew...]. (6m)

The cycle consists of contrasting settings of four sonnets by Michelangelo, in post-romantic operatic vein. "Flagello is an enormously talented composer for voice... superb orchestral accompaniments as well. If this is not great music, we will gladly turn in our typewriter and quit." —*The New Records*. "[The *Contemplazioni di Michelangelo* is] a towering song cycle of truly operatic grandeur." —*Fanfare: The Magazine for Serious Record Collectors*. "Flagello has created inspired pages, with a grand spirit, solid formal structure, and an elaborate and interesting harmonic fabric." — *El Comercio* (Peru).

Sonata for Piano (1962). *Rec.:* Serenus (Stereo LP) SRS 12002: Elizabeth Marshall. *Pub.:* Boston Music Co. (or c/o VPF Music, 78 North Route 303, Congers NY 10920).
1. Andante con moto e rubato. (6m) 2. Rubato quasi recitativo. (5m) 3. Allegro vivace quanto possibile. (5m)

A difficult but idiomatic sonata, an outgrowth of the major piano works of the late 19th century. The first movement is alternately somber and tempestuous; the second a gloomy *barcarolle*; the third is a frenetic *moto perpetuo*. "[Here is an] apotheosis of super-charged pianistic grandiloquence." — *Fanfare: The Magazine for Serious Record Collectors*. "[Flagello's Piano Sonata] produced a concentrated, galvanized energy, that did not overlook recognizable thematic development amidst quantities of dissonance." — *Providence [RI] Evening Bulletin*.

Symphony 1 for Orchestra (1968). 34m *Prem.:* Manhattan O, Nicolas Flagello, cond. *Pub.:* Theodore Presser.
3-3-3-3; 4-3-3-1; perc., piano, celesta, harp; strings
1. Allegro molto. 2. Andante lento. 3. Scherzo—Allegretto brusco. 4. *Ciaconna.*

A powerful and intense composition, extremely dark, pessimistic, and violent in tone and mood. The work is harmonically dissonant and rhythmically irregular, but all within the expressive conventions of the post-romantic style. It follows traditional formal models with reverence and discipline. —"A really notable addition to the literature. The work is beautifully expressive, doesn't meander, and is brilliantly orchestrated to boot." —*Music Journal*.

Symphony 2 (Symphony of the Winds) for Wind Orchestra (1970). *Rec.:* Cornell University (Stereo LP) CUWE-23, c/o Wind Ensemble, Lincoln Hall, Cornell Univ, Ithaca NY 14853: Cornell Univ Wind Ens, Marice Stith, cond.

"*Symphony of the Winds* continues to support the conviction [that Flagello is] one of the most powerful and distinctive compositional personalities on the scene today. This is an impressively compact work of striking psychological tone, in which hauntingly affecting mental states are crystallized through a meticulous musical syntax. Neither in sonority nor in spirit does this symphony resemble ordinary 'band music', yet it displays a wiry solidity that distinguishes it from the neo-romantic lushness of Flagello's orchestral music. The subtitle 'Symphony of the Winds' has an enigmatic double meaning, as the composer has appended metaphorical rubrics to each movement: 'Torrid winds of veiled portents'; 'Dark winds of lonely contemplation'; 'Winds of re-birth and vitality'. Flagello's music generally displays a gloomy expressiveness whose personal intimacy is uncommon in this emotionally inhibited age, and the 1970 symphony is no exception. But its apparent effusiveness is tightly controlled by a masterful sense of structure and coherence, so that Flagello's handling of purely traditional techniques results in a powerful, provocative, and individual statement of broad appeal." — Walter G. Simmons, in *Fanfare: The Magazine for Serious Record Collectors*, 11-12/79.

Te Deum for All Mankind for Chorus and Orchestra (1967).
12m *Text*: Whittier, Latin. *Prem.*: All-NYC Chorus and Orchestra, B. Chancy, cond., 1969. *Pub.*: Carl Fischer.
SATB; 3-2-3-2; 4-3-3-1; perc., harp, organ (opt.); band (opt.); strings

"This 12-minute ode to brotherhood (combining Whittier's poem *Laus Deo* with Latin liturgy) works well as a festival finale. The choral parts are dissonant and contrapuntal, though the work has been performed by youthful ensembles. Very expressive, with much emotional variety; builds to a convincingly triumphant conclusion." — Walter G. Simmons.

MIRIAM GIDEON

B. 1906, Greeley CO. *Educ.:* Boston Univ, New York Univ, Dalcroze Schl, Columbia Univ. *Taught at:* Brooklyn College, City College NY, Jewish Theological Seminary, Manhattan Schl of Music. Member Amer Acad/Inst Arts and Letters. *Works incl.:* choral, *Fortunato* (opera), voice/insts (incl. *The Condemned Playground, Nocturnes, Questions on Nature, Rhymes from the Hill, Songs of Youth and Madness*).

Composer statement (from a letter to the Editor): "I am honored to be included in your distinguished collection of contemporary composers.... As for what I might say about composing, since it is my priority—except for people... and love... which are, of course, part of the whole business—I can tell you that I have been composing since the age of eleven, when I gave up striving to be a world-renowned concert pianist for the joy of composing piano pieces of a spectacular banality that even I assessed correctly at that time. The fact that I emerged from those depths to a point where I now like what I compose is a tribute to the all-embracing power of music, which recognizes the true and beautiful, and remains eternally in their spell."

"The music of Miriam Gideon shows a striking balance between construction and communicativeness, with both elements being immediately perceived by the attentive listener. While she would not be considered a prolific composer, she has over 50 titles to her credit, fairly evenly distributed in the earlier years among instrumental, orchestral, and vocal music. As early as 1957, she had already established herself as a serious voice among serious musicians, as evidenced by an article of George Perle's in which he wrote: 'To her the inherent ambiguity of pitch-functions in the contemporary tone-material means that one must be more careful than ever, and this sense of the significance of every note pervades her work. A melodic or harmonic idea will recur with one or more individual elements inflected by a semitone, a shade of difference that may or may not have a large structural meaning but that imbues her music with a kind of personal, reflective quality, almost as though the composer's search for the ideal formulation of her thought had become part of the composition itself.'

"In later years, her attraction to text settings has come to the fore and she has been particularly drawn to composing for voice with small instrumental ensembles. In this category are *The Condemned Playground* (1963; with words by Horace, Milton, Spokes, Akiya, Baudelaire, Millay), *Questions on Nature* (1964; Adelard of Bath),

Spiritual Madrigals (1965; Ewen, Suezkint von Trimperg, Heine), *Rhymes from the Hill* (1968; Morgenstern), *Nocturnes* (1976; Shelley, Untermeyer, Sherman), *Songs of Youth and Madness* (1977; Hölderlin), and *The Resounding Lyre* (1979; a reworking of the *Spiritual Madrigals*). She will often opt for 'dual settings', i.e., first composing music for an English text and then setting the words in the original language (as in Milton's translation of Horace's Latin). In composing music for a long passage from Baudelaire's *Flowers of Evil*, only a one-line refrain appears in French, the rest being in English to make more immediately understandable 'the magical interaction of the sinister and the beautiful.' Or, as in the whimsical verses of Christian Morgenstern, the words are left entirely in the original language. And yet again, as in a poem about Hiroshima, she had the original English poetry translated into Japanese. 'It's just the fascination of getting the same *idea* in two different languages and finding the right clothing to drape on the same skeleton, at the same time resolving this diversity into an integrated whole.'...

"She was only 19 when she graduated from college [Boston University] and moved back to New York. Composing steadily, she found that she was particularly drawn to musical setting of words and around then [c.1924] wrote what she now regards as her first piece. Her heritage—a humanistic father whose field was language [he had been a professor of philosophy and modern languages at Colorado State Teachers College] and a mother who read poetry to her two girls and instilled a permanent love for this art form—began to make itself felt, and she set out to develop connecting links between words, ideas, emotions, and music which have been the hall mark of her creativity ever since." —George Sturm.

Creature to Creature for Voice, Flute and Harp (1985). *Text:* Nancy Cardozo. Comm. Jubal Trio. *Pub.:* Mobart Music (distr. Jerona Music—score & performance material).
1. *The Fly.* 2. *Spider.* 3. *Snake.* 4. *Firefly.* 5. *Hoot-Owl.* 6. *Interlude.* 7. *L'-Envoi [Cricket].*

"The six poems that I have set are drawn from a longer cycle—*Creature to Creature: An Animalculary*—by Nancy Cardozo. I have tried to capture the sly wit and tenderness of each of these miniatures and their varying moods by a minimum of 'effects', letting each flying or crawling creature speak as directly as possible through the instruments and voice." —Miriam Gideon.

The Resounding Lyre for High Voice (Tenor) and Instruments (Flute, Oboe, Bassoon, Trumpet, Violin, Viola, Cello) (1979). *Rec.:* Composer Recordings Inc. (Stereo LP) CRI SD 493: Constantine Cassolas (t), Speculum Musicae, Robert Black, cond. *Pub.*: Mobart Music (distr. Jerona Music—score & parts).

Sonnets from Shakespeare for Baritone, Trumpet and Strings (1950). 16m *Rec.*: Composers Recordings Inc. (Stereo LP) CRI SD 527: William Sharp (bar), PRISM O, Robert Black, cond. *Pub.*: Mobart Music.
    1. *Music to Hear [Sonnet 8]*. 2. *Devouring Time [Sonnet 19]*. 3. *Ritornelle 1*. 4. *Full Many a Glorious Morning [Sonnet 23]*. 5. *Ritornelle 2*. 6. *No Longer Mourn for Me [Sonnet 71]*. 7. *No, Time, Thou Shalt Not Boast That I Do Change [Sonnet 123]*. 8. *Ritornelle 3*.

Spirit Above the Dust for Mezzo-Soprano and Instruments (1981). *Texts:* Anne Bradstreet, Archibald MacLeish, Norman Rosten. Comm. by Elizabeth Sprague Coolidge Fndn. *Rec.*: Composer Recordings Inc. (Stereo LP) CRI SD 493: Elaine Bonazzi (ms), Contemporary Chamber Ens, Arthur Weisberg, cond. *Pub.*: C. F. Peters.

Wing'd Hour for Tenor, Flute, Oboe, Violin, Cello and Vibraphone (1983). *Texts:* Dante Gabriel Rossetti, Christina Rosetti, Walter De La Mare. 9m *Rec.:* Composers Recordings Inc. (Stereo LP) CRI SD 527: Constantine Cassolas (t), PRISM O, Robert Black, cond. *Pub.:* C. F. Peters.
1. *Prelude.* 2. *Silent Noon.* 3. *My Heart Is Like a Singing Bird.* 4. *Interlude.* 5. *Autumn.*

"For Miriam Gideon words and music are almost inseparable. As she told Tim Page of the *New York Times* (October 19, 1986): 'Looking back, I have to say that my early pieces show little innate talent.... But I was already addicted to poetry, and when I came across a poem that genuinely moved me when I was about 18, something in me was ready to latch onto it, and I realized that something had come into being that had not been there before. From that point on, whether I was working with words or not, I was a composer.'

"Through the years Gideon has retained her fondness for setting poetry to music, and the largest body of her works is formed by choral work, songs, and the more than fifteen song cycles for solo voice and chamber ensemble for which she is best known. Although a number of the latter are already available on disc, *Sonnets from Shakespeare* and the more recent *Wing'd Hour*—released by CRI as Gideon celebrated her eightieth birthday—deserve wider circulation and are welcome additions to the Gideon discography.

"In *Sonnets from Shakespeare* one is struck by the immediacy of the musical settings of the poetry. The five sonnets, each set distinctively, convey widely contrasting moods; these settings are separated by three instrumental 'ritornelles', which also serve to unify the cycle musically. Gideon's delicate and lyrical melodic writing, placed above a translucently scored atonal underpinning, also imparts an intimacy and beauty to the work.

"*Wing'd Hour,* composed in memory of a close friend, is a cycle setting of three poems by Dante Gabriel Rossetti, Christina Rossetti, and Walter De La Mare. As in the earlier work, Gideon has used instrumental interludes as a cohesive element, but here the harmonic language is more dissonant and the melodic writing more angular. The coloristic possibilities provided by the chamber ensemble are fully explored, and, while the texture is often thicker than in *Sonnets,* here, too, the music is a fitting complement to the words."—Emily Good, in *American Music,* Winter 1988.

Of a performance of *Sonnets from Shakespeare:* "Strings and a single sweet trumpet blended with uncanny subtlety under the bard's musical metaphors to create an inspired effect."—Carter Harman, in *The New York Times,* 1951.

"Three of the sonnets I have set are concerned with the idea of Time: *Devouring Time, No longer mourn for me,* and *No, Time, thou shalt not boast.* These stormy verses alternate with the serene *Music to hear* and *Full many a glorious morning.* The cycle opens with voice alone, soon joined by the strings. Instrumental ritornelles are used as separations between the songs, and as a recall of moods and thematic ideas. The strings maintain a strong profile throughout, while the trumpet threads its way, and comments, almost like a second human voice.

"*Wing'd Hour* was composed in 1983 in memory of a dear friend, who, with his wife, read and loved poetry. The poems chosen were among their favorites, and constitute a kind of cycle: the awakening of love, love's fulfillment, and death and loss. In *Silent Noon*, after palpitating figures in winds and strings, the vibraphone announces the tentative start of the drama which is to follow, becoming more outspoken and joyous in *My heart is like a singing bird*. All instruments are whittled down and laconic in the brief but ominous *Interlude*, and become poignant with loneliness in *Autumn*." — Miriam Gideon, from program notes for Composers Recordings Inc. CRI CD-527 release.

"Gideon, who has composed in all forms, has recently [c.1984] been focusing on vocal chamber music. *Spirit Above the Dust* is a setting of seven poems by three American poets — Anne Bradstreet, Archibald MacLeish, and Norman Rosten — which offer various interpretations of life in America. The harmonic language is agreeably atonal, and the melodic lines are exceptional in their ability to turn intervallically disjunct materials into beautifully formed phrases that create a sense of conjunctness and order. Her setting of Rosten's 'Black Boy' is particularly lovely, and the subtle inclusion of folklike material impressively complements the poet's 'searing indictment of a lynching'....

"*The Resounding Lyre* offers a useful contrast. The work, a setting of three German poems from the 13th century to the present, [displays the composer's] bold, sure hand. Miriam Gideon has been composing for many years; this critic is among her fans, and I think that you too will be moved by her gifts. These include a taste in texts that reflect high personal and social concerns, and a musical vocabulary over which she enjoys every manner of mastery." — David Sachs, in *Fanfare: The Magazine for Serious Record Collectors,* 7-8/84.

Philip Glass

B. 1937, Baltimore MD. *Educ.:* Peabody Cons, Univ of Chicago, Juilliard Schl. Fulbright scholarship, Ford & Rockefeller Fndn grants. Dir. Philip Glass Ens. *Works incl.:* film scores (*Chappaqua, Mishima*), incid. music, *Music in Fifths, Music in 12 Parts,* operas (*Akhnaten, The Juniper Tree, The Photographer, Satyagraha*), *Two Pages*.

Notes by the composer (1) — FROM AN INTERVIEW WITH COLE GAGNE AND TRACY CARAS (c. 1982):

"GAGNE/CARAS: In writing about your music, critics have employed several terms: 'hypnotic', 'minimalist', 'trance', 'solid state'. Do all these terms help clarify what you're doing, or do you think they tend to be misleading?

"PHILIP GLASS: I think they're almost all misleading, although lately I've come to dislike 'minimalist' less than I dislike other descriptions. Insofar as 'minimalist music' refers to a specific historical period, let's say from 1965 to 1975, the term is meaningful. But it's rarely meant in a limited way.

"When people talk about 'hypnotic states' or 'trance states', or 'druggy states' or 'religious states', what they're really saying, in a rather clumsy way, is that the music shares a non-ordinariness with certain other experiences. But you can't say that everyone who doesn't speak English speaks the same language.

"For me, what sets the music apart is the fact that it's non-narrative; and because it is non-narrative, we don't hear it within the usual time frame of most musical experiences. As I look at most other music, I see that it takes ordinary time, day-to-day time — what I call colloquial time — as a model for its own musical time. So you have story symphonies and story concertos — even the modernist tradition continues that to a large extent. There's still almost a compulsion with composers to deal with themes and the treatment of themes. The theme becomes the focus of the listener's attention, and then what happens to the theme happens to the listener via a certain psychological trick of identification. This obviously happens in the great concertos of the nineteenth century, with the tortuous journey of the violin and so forth, with happy endings and sad endings. It's almost on the level of 'major keys are the happy keys, and minor keys are the sad keys'; unfortunately, a lot of people experience music in such a simplistic way.[44]

"When music doesn't deal with subjects and treatments, as in my music, which is often a process where the musical material and its evolution becomes part and parcel of the structure of the music, then you don't have the psychological access to the music that I [have] described elsewhere. That's why we don't hear the music as narrative or as a model of colloquial time. What we're hearing then is music in another time system. Now, we have a lot of other experiences in our lives that take place in non-colloquial time systems. Some of them happen to be drug experiences; some are religious experience; some are nature experiences. There are a wide variety of them, and even within those experiences there are a wide variety of them. They're not at all the same; what they share in common is that they're non-ordinary experiences. So when people say to me that music is druggy or trancey or this or that, I think they're confused; they're confusing a variety of experiences that share in common their difference from ordinary life, but which have vast differences between them. On the simplest level: This is music that, at least for me, requires a state of attentiveness, or provokes one; whereas, clearly there are drugged and hypnotic states that are various states of sleep. I mean, to use a term like 'trance music' — I remember as a boy in Baltimore seeing people going to sleep during the symphony concerts. So apparently anything can put you to sleep. I couldn't have been more than seven or eight, and I remember that I was shocked to see people snoring away during a performance of Beethoven's *Ninth Symphony*; I couldn't believe that they were doing that. And of course, they're snoring away to this day. So, sometimes when I'm playing a concert and I see people nodding off, I don't feel so bad;

---

44   Although the composer seems to be saying only that some audiences take in music in a "simplistic" way — which, I suppose, is undebatable — I think it ought to be stressed that neither so-called "narrative" music nor emotional associations with major and minor keys are — themselves — necessarily simplistic or simplistic by nature. For one thing the term "narrative" implies, not merely story-telling in a literary sense, but an *ordering* of some kind, in which context both Beethoven and Stravinsky, for example, however differently, can be said to have employed "narrative" structures. For another "emotional associations" of *any* kind are surely enormously complex, eventually... insofar as they do indeed reflect and color, and help to create, an entire "world" for each individual, as Binswanger, Laing, Sartre, Heidegger, and so many other writers of our century have clearly shown. (Ed.)

it's a great tradition!" — Philip Glass, in Cole Gagne and Tracy Caras, *Soundpieces: Interviews with American Composers* (The Scarecrow Press, 1982).

Notes by the composer (2) — FROM A GLASS/THOMSON/SANDOW PANEL DISCUSSION (1989):

"GREGORY SANDOW: So, Philip, who are the conductors beside Dennis [Russell Davies] who are making their careers playing your music?

"PHILIP GLASS: Not a lot. First of all, as far as the symphony orchestras are concerned, I write really for opera orchestras. Most of my orchestra music is opera music. One of the reasons for that is because I don't care to write a piece that only gets played once or twice.[45]

"I just had a violin concerto premiered a couple of weeks ago [1989] in New York. Afterwards I was talking to someone — he was actually from the theater world — and he said, 'How many performances will they give of your violin concerto?' And I said, 'Well, of course, they'll only do one.' And he said, 'Well, what a waste of time — they've rehearsed it and they'll only do it once.' I explained that in the theater we often do ten, twenty, or thirty performances, which for a composer is very interesting, but the difficulty in the concert stage is that you get one performance or two. Perhaps they'll do a Saturday night and a Sunday matinée, and that's it. So I never cared to spend much time writing symphonic music because you just don't get many performances.

"Another reason is no one ever asked me to do it. I get asked to write operas, but I don't get asked to write symphonies. But I would have to struggle with the idea of devoting that much time and effort. In theater terms, a symphonic work is a fairly short work. But even so, you know I think there's another fact, too, about this — I do think that theater composers and symphonic composers or concert composers are very different kinds of people. I think there's a very good reason why Brahms did not write a lot of operas and Verdi didn't write a lot of symphonies. I think that they are what we call a *métier*, and that if your *métier* is working in the theater you are inclined to do that, and that you begin to lose the habit of thinking in terms of the concert stage in that way. When people ask me what kind of music I write, I get around the whole business by saying I am a

---

45   See also comments by Alfred Reed and William Schuman, elsewhere in this volume. However, while many composers do seem to be unusually fortunate with respect to frequency of commissions (the names of John Corigliano and Ellen Taaffe Zwilich coming to mind too, for example), perhaps this also is misleading in that, probably, *most* of the art productions of *most* artists in all the various media have *not* been so favored. In sum: people create for different reasons. (Ed.)

theater composer, which is how I experience the work. When I played here in Lawrence, Kansas, almost all the work I did was work transcribed from the theater for concert hall.

"So, to tell the truth, I don't waste my time very much with worrying about working for orchestras for that reason. You get very little commitment, there's very little money, you get very few performances, and it's all in all a headache from my point of view. Whereas in the theater a work can be done in the first two years of its life easily fifty times...." — from J. Bunker Clark, transcr. & ed., "The Composer and Performer and Other Matters: A Panel Discussion with Virgil Thomson and Philip Glass, Moderated by Gregory Sandow", in *American Music*, Summer 1989.

Einstein on the Beach (opera). *Lyr.*: Philip Glass. Co-conceived & dir. by Robert Wilson. Approx. 5 hrs *Perfs.*: New York (Metropolitan Opera), Avignon, Venice, Belgrade, Paris, Brussels, Hamburg, Rotterdam, Amsterdam. Rec.: Tomato TOM-4-2901 (4 Stereo LPs; reissued as CBS Masterworks M4 38875 [LP vers] and as M4K 38875 [CD vers]): The Philip Glass Ens, Michael Riesman, cond.
Company of 21 who sing, act and dance (incl. singer/solo violinist as Einstein); 3 saxophones (alternating with flute, clarinet), 2 electric organs, with amplification controlled by sound engineer
In 4 acts

"The Metropolitan Opera's commitment to contemporary music is probably slighter than that of any other major house.[46] It was not always so. During Gatti-Casazza's twenty-seven seasons, he kept the New York public abreast of what was being composed elsewhere, producing significant operas from Germany and Italy while they were still new, and he introduced some fifteen new American pieces, often starrily cast. It is true that none of the latter have lasted; the wastage rate in new operas is high. *Mona*, *The King's Henchman*, *Peter Ibbetson*, *The Emperor Jones*, and *Merry Mount* are titles remembered; who but a historian can name the composers of *Shanewis*, *Cleopatra's Night*, and *In the Pasha's Garden*? The premières of *La Fanciulla del West* (1910) and *Il trittico* (1918) — and, to a lesser extent, of Humperdinck's *Königskinder* (1910) and Giordano's *Madame Sans-Gêne* (1915) — have secured for the Met a modest place in the history of operatic creation, but it is a long time since the eyes of the world were turned on

---

[46] If the observation bears repeating, it must be admitted that the Metropolitan Opera does make a huge contribution to American cultural life, and also that even within its essentially conservative limits it continues to flourish only in spite of severe financial and other hurdles. Perhaps one ought to (1) express one's appreciation for what the Met does well, and (2) continue to encourage the institution to pursue more adventuresome paths... (Ed.)

it to discover the outcome of a commission from a leading composer—something like a new score from Sessions, Henze, Tippett, or Berio. Since the move to Lincoln Center, only two new operas have been baptized by the company—Barber's *Antony and Cleopatra* (1966) and Marvin David Levy's *Mourning Becomes Electra* (1967). If James Levine and John Dexter have placed some exciting commissions for future seasons—if, say, Carter, Crumb, Druckman, or Bolcom is even now working on a Metropolitan opera—the public has still to learn of it. Even local premières of works whose merit has been tested elsewhere have become few. None of Thomson's operas have been taken up by the Met, although his *Lord Byron* was written for it, and his *Mother of Us All* could surely have been a Bicentennial hit. The reasons for doing Massenet's *Esclarmonde*$FPresumably as a vehicle for Joan Sutherland. (Ed.) rather than Session's *Montezuma*, for doing Meyerbeer's *Le Prophète* rather than Bernd Alois Zimmermann's *Die Soldaten* or Henze's *We Come to the River*, are obvious. But one of those reasons—that the public stays away from contemporary operas—was challenged last month when two performances of Philip Glass's *Einstein on the Beach* were both sold out. And yet the most adventurous intendant in the world might think twice before billing *Einstein*. It is a four-act opera that lasts for nearly five hours without an intermission. It has no plot in any conventional sense. The 'libretto' consists for the most part of numerals sung or spoken (counting out the rhythmic patterns of the score) and sol-fa syllables (do, re, mi, etc., naming the notes sung). The music is in essence a series of extended *moto perpetuos*, each of them lasting longer than Ravel's *Bolero*.

"*Einstein on the Beach* was not part of the regular season but was presented on two Sunday evenings by the Byrd Hoffman Foundation in cooperation with the Met. It lends itself to guest appearances, being a self-contained 'two-truck show' (scenery and sound equipment pack into two forty-foot containers) that has already toured widely in Europe. *Einstein* opened in Avignon last July, and visited Venice for the Biennnale, Belgrade for the International Theater Festival, Paris for the Autumn Festival, Brussels, Hamburg, Rotterdam, and Amsterdam. Since it arrived at the Met prepared and complete, it was a practical as well as an exciting addition to the fare in a theater whose resident troupe is unaccustomed to tackling contemporary scores. The orchestra is the Philip Glass Ensemble (five instrumentalists and a sound engineer), plus a singer and a solo violinist who takes the role of Einstein. A versatile company of twenty-one sings, acts, and dances; one of the leading singers joins the ensemble to play, with effortless mastery, a long organ cadenza that is the music for a scene in the last act.

"*Einstein* is described as an opera 'by Robert Wilson—Philip Glass'. The two planned the work together, plotted the time it was to occupy and determined its large structure. Music and lyrics are credited to Glass, direction and décor to Wilson. There are three basic images: a train, a courtroom that dissolves into a prison, and a field of dancers with a spaceship in the sky above them. If these are called A, B, and C, then Act I consists of A and B, Act II of C and A, and Act III of B and C. Act IV presents developments of all three images: the train has become a building; from the prison only the bed remains (a rectangle of light, it moves on an empty stage); the spaceship is no longer a model overhead but a large cellular structure filled with people. Five episodes for the couple on the stage and varied musical forces form prologue, entr'actes, and epilogue. At first, these seem to function like the intermezzi that were played between the acts of an *opera seria*, or the *kyogen* interludes between the plays of a nô cycle, but they carry so much musical (and, at the last, emotional) weight that they can be regarded as the main matter of the opera, and the acts themselves as extended intermezzi or developments. Although *Einstein* has been generally treated as if it were a work by Wilson with incidental music by Glass, it is very different—in tone, structure, pace, and appearance—from Wilson's earlier pieces. To describe it as a characteristic Glass score with scenic accompaniment by Wilson (and choreographic accompaniment by Andrew deGroat) would be nearer the mark but still not quite accurate. It is a *Gesamtkunstwerk* in which Wilson's romantic profusion, allusiveness, and collage techniques are tempered by Glass's sharp-focus insistence on pure structure....

"*Einstein* is precisely organized, tautly patterned, economical in its forces, and austere in its décor. Instead of the rich colors and textures and the visual elaboration of [Wilson's] *Deafman Glance*, there are simple, largely geometrical scenes in a muted color range. If pressed, I suppose I could concoct some sort of scenario that emerged during the presentation. The images cohere. In the first scene, a child throws paper airplanes from a high platform; in the last, a toy rocket ship zooms up into space. Einstein fiddles while a drop curtain behind him spells out statistics on destruction caused by a nuclear explosion. A man involved in ceaseless mathematical calculation is a recurrent symbol. The images of motion also invoke ideas of relativity. ('Does Oxford stop at this train?' asked the professor of physics, embarking at Paddington.) But what *Einstein* was 'about' for me was much what Glass's *Music with Changing Parts* is about: the effect of rhythmic patterns and short melodic motifs endlessly repeated but slowly altering; of bright, insistent timbres whose colors gradually shift as one instrument, then another cuts into or drops from the texture; of simple harmonic progressions rooted in laws of acoustics (one of the main themes of *Einstein* is a IV-V-I sequence) underpinning *moto-perpetuo* activity. In his *Music in Twelve Parts*, Glass asked for 'another mode of listening—one in which neither memory nor anticipation (the usual psychological devices of programmatic music, whether Baroque, Classical, Romantic, or Modernistic) has a place in sustaining the texture, quality, or reality of the musical experience.' A listener to his music usually reaches a point, quite early on, of rebellion at the needle-stuck-in-the-groove quality, but a minute or two later he realizes that the needle has not stuck: something has happened. Once that point is passed, Glass's music—or so I find—becomes easy to listen to for hours on end. The mind may wander now and again, but it wanders within a new sound world that the composer has created. The simple harmonic foundations induce a feeling of security. Lively incident soon recaptures one's full attention. A listener's memory, it should be added, does play a part in *Einstein*, since there are recurrent themes, picked up in one scene from another and sometimes reflecting, sometimes in counterpoint to, the recurrent visual imagery. Another source of listener's rebellion, however, may be the sheer loudness of the music. *Einstein* is scored for two electric organs and three saxophones, alternating with flute or clarinet, all heavily amplified, as are the voices. Twice, during the first performance, I felt that at sustained climaxes the level of noise emerging from the tall banks of loudspeakers on either side of the proscenium arch was not merely painful but probably perilous, too. For the second performance, I found a seat not directly in the line of sonic crossfire.

"In common, Wilson and Glass require a suspension of the usual time scale observed in Western theaters and concert halls. In this— but in this alone—their works are akin to the nô cycles that last from dawn to dusk, and *kathakali* cycles that last from dusk to dawn. In an age when Erik Satie's *Vexations*, a few bars for solo piano, *très lent*, played over and over again for twenty-four hours, can find performances, when Stockhausen begins his *Piano Piece IX* with the same chord sounded 227 times and builds his *Stimmung* on one chord sustained for seventy-five minutes,[47] audiences are readier than their fathers were to sit and savor slow-shifting, chronic experiences— hypnotized by repetition, stimulated by the observance of tiny changes, not bored. *Einstein* is busier, more active, than those pieces. Glass's score may be incantatory, but it is not lulling.

"Wilson and Glass also share an ability to obtain dedicated, amazingly accomplished, unflagging performances from the artists they

---

47 But is it music! (Ed.)

work with. Instrumentalists, actors, and singers had *Einstein* by heart. How, without the aid of rosaries, they knew when to repeat and when to move on I cannot guess." — Andrew Porter, in *The New Yorker*, 12/13/76. Reprinted in *Music of Three Seasons, 1974-1977* (Farrar Straus Giroux, 1978).

"It had been a while since I'd listened to the whole of *Einstein,* and the experience [of hearing it again on the CBS Masterworks reissue] confirms my opinion that it is a work destined to endure when the hoopla fades. Some of the dance sections still seem to border on the interminable, and as Johnson said of *Paradise Lost* no one ever wished them longer than they are. The highlights of the work for me are the opening, a sort of post-relativity Gregorian chant, with numbers in place of sacred texts, and the various settings of absurdist parodies, often spoken out of sync by two voices in opposite speakers. I wonder if the influence is Glenn Gould's 'contrapuntal radio' or the odd conversational decorum of the !Kung bushmen of Botswana, according to which 'often two or three people will hold forth at once in a single conversation, giving the listener a choice of channels to tune in on' (see Richard B. Lee's article in *Hunters and Gatherers Today*, ed. M.G. Bicchieri, New York: Holt, Rinehart and Winston, 1972).

"Since *Einstein,* Glass has taken off in several different directions... but *Einstein* [has] remained the seminal work." — Edward Strickland, in *Fanfare: The Magazine for Serious Record Collectors,* 11-12/84.

MARK N. GRANT

B.1952, New York NY. *Educ.:* Univ of Rochester, Pomona College, Mannes Schl, Juilliard Schl. Reviewer (*Opera, Ovation*), consultant on archival piano films (Juilliard Schl, PBS TV), ed. *Remembering Franz Liszt*. Works incl.: *Elegy Appassionato* (vln, pno), piano works (*Phantasmagoric Nocturne*), *Waltz Metamorphosis* (3 gtrs).

Composer statement: "Though I continue to write music for various instrumental combinations, my primary drives as a composer are increasingly directed to the creation of works for the musical theater to my own original texts. The medium of the musical theater affords me a single canvas on which I can blend my literary, dramatic, and musical energies: a fusion which, I increasingly find, is what I am fundamentally 'about' creatively. Also, purely on the musical level, the theater seems to release my most potent and abundant composing energies. My first theater work, *Chautauqua*, has been in progress for several years. It is an intricately plotted, dramatically complex piece which intermixes elements of the legitimate theater, the opera, and the musical comedy. The dramaturgy makes no concessions to the conventions of opera-libretto compression—the script is a fully developed play—yet there is an opera-like profusion of music throughout: arias, songs, ensembles, interludes, and, somewhat unusually, underscoring of spoken dialogue, which necessitates special sound design. Still, the style of the piece is musical theater and not opera, because it is neither through-sung nor through-composed, if 'through' means end-to-end and non-stop.

"I think a composer finds his only and true agenda by tapping his deepest currents of emotional excitement, blowing on them furiously, and then figuring them forth in his music. One can only be, and finally must be, oneself. I have to feel a complete expressive involvement in every note I write and I try to endow every bar with a uniform intensity of attention and presence. More than once people have remarked on the 'intensity' of my music.

"My muse is not susceptible to the cajoleries of 'systems'. For me, composing systems, formulae, and the *objets trouvés* of the various *au courant* musical jargons can be meaningful only if they coincide with what one is, not with what one manipulates oneself to be. I personally gravitate to a language of postmodern neo-romanticism, expressed in a vocabulary of tonality/quasi-tonality at times smooth, at times spiky—but words cannot summon up a composer's 'sound'."

Echoes of a Lost Serenade for Flute, Guitar and Harp (1984). 15m *Prem.*: Clarissa Coffey (fl), Dorothy Bastian (gtr), Deborah Hoffman (hp). *Pub.*: Bardic Edition.

"*Echoes of a Lost Serenade* is intended to convey, emotionally, two programs: that of a lover's serenade unrequited, turned bittersweet, and even sour; and that of an elegy for the loss of traditional romantic sentiment in much of today's music. Throughout the piece, sweet *cantabile* episodes alternate with bite, spice and skewed focus, as if the three picturesque romantic serenaders were turning, in the twinkle of an eye, into Picasso's cubist *Three Musicians* and then right back again. The flowing serenade gradually gathers tension, reaches a climax about midway through, and then collapses into near silence, with the individual players taking their turns uttering anguished and ghostly phrases punctuated by enigmatic pauses. Finally the opening lyric material reappears, but now broken down into echoic reminiscences and painful *cri de coeur*-like recitatives, until at the very end there is a last wistful summoning up of the lyric material." — Mark Grant.

Epiphanies: A Childhood Album for 10 Winds (1987). 18m *Prem.*: Dana Perna, Holzbläser Ensemble. *Pub.*: Bardic Edition.
2(picc)-1-e.hn-2-2; 2-0-0-0
1. *Intimations of Memory*. 2. *The Children's Hour* — Scherzo. 3. *Pastoral*. 4. *Epilogue*.

"The title *Epiphanies* denotes not the religious sense of divine revelation but rather the poetical sense of the word, of a revelation of the essence of the character of a thing, a mood, or the spirit of a place or moment, a usage first applied by the writer James Joyce to short paragraph-long sections of prose he would write in which he attempted to distill the whole compass of a much larger story. In this work the composer is mentally turning the leaves of a photo album of his childhood, gazing back wistfully on childhood images and moments from the matured point of view of an adult, and attempting to distill some of his innermost thoughts about these images into musical moods." — Mark Grant.

Overture to "Chautauqua" (1987). 5m [From a "music theater opera" in 3 acts and 17 scenes (in progress). *Lib.*: composer, based on his original story. *Prem. (excerpts):* Fashion Institute of Technology, New York City. Videotape of FIT production on deposit with Theater on Film and Tape Collection, Rodgers & Hammerstein Archive, Lincoln Center, New York.] Ms. available at American Music Center.

More than 100 characters, featuring 18-30 actors and singers, most of whom perform multiple roles. Required singers: 2s, 1 mez, 1a, 2t, 1b-bar, 1 low b, 3 light male "Broadway" voices.
3(pic)-2-3(b.cl.)-2(hcklphn *ad lib.*); 2-2-2-1; timp, 2 perc, harp, piano, synthesizer; strings. Also piano 4-hands version.
[Act 1: An office on Wall Street, 1925 (and flashbacks to c.1905). Act 2: A radio station, etc., c.1920; return to 1925. Act 3: A courtroom, etc.; a Boston boardinghouse, years later.]

"*Chautauqua* is one attempt to pick up the lost thread of the 'Broadway opera' tradition once heralded by *Porgy and Bess, Candide,* and the works of Weill and Blitzstein, and stretch it further. It is a disinherited tradition, lately abandoned to the Europop musical on the one hand,[48] and on the other to such non-linear music-theater styles as performance art, mixed-media collaboration, dance theater, and neo-dadaism—styles which I feel no affinity with, and sometimes even find anti-theater in their eschewal of narrative suspense, emotional catharsis, and other fundamental theatrical values.

"The Chautauqua was a carnival-like variety show of turn-of-the-century America, whose trademark was a peculiar brand of high-pressure positive thinkers whose fast-patter speeches painted pictures of an impossibly optimistic tomorrow. Set against this background—also involving other episodes from and impressions of American life—*Chautauqua* traces the rise and fall of Willie Warmflash, a sensational child prodigy destroyed by the very forces that seemed to augur his success and happiness. Fully staged, *Chautauqua* puts a kaleidoscopic, carnival-like America on stage; the piece may also be performed with smaller forces, using two pianos and synthesizer.

"The *Overture* includes themes from Charmian's 'Four-Leaf Clover' Aria and the Chautauqua calliope waltz."—Mark N. Grant.

---

48 E.g. Lloyd Webber, *Les Misérables, Chess.* (Ed.)

HANS WERNER HENZE

B. 1926, Gütersloh, Westphalia (Germany). *Educ.:* Braunschweig Schl of Music, Kirchenmusikalisches Institut (Heidelberg). Comp.-in-residence, Tanglewood MA. *Works incl.:* ballets (*Anrufung Apolls, Labyrinth, Tancredi*), cantatas & oratorios (*Das Ende einer Welt, Das Floss der Medusa*), concertos (db, ob/hp/strngs, pno, vln), operas (*Boulevard Solitude, Der junge Lord, Der Prinz von Homburg*), 5 string quartets, 7 symphonies.

"Mr. Henze, who is 62 years old [1988], wears the badge of an activist on the political left. In 1953, out of a continuing revulsion over the Nazi legacy, he left his native Germany and settled in Italy. In 1969 he wrote a requiem for Ché Guevara. Its Hamburg premiere ended abruptly when the police invaded the hall and arrested student agitators and the librettist, Ernest Schnabel. The sequel to that scandal was Mr. Henze's *Essay on Pigs,* a declamatory work that proclaimed the 'necessity to revolt' against unacceptable conditions.

"It was also during the 1960s that Mr. Henze wrote an article defining the role of 'the secluded artist, the outlaw', who bypasses 'the successful consumer middle class' and dedicates himself to 'individuals and minorities' of his own persuasion. The aim of such a composer, Mr. Henze said, must be 'provocation'.

"In person, Mr. Henze is anything but a hot-eyed radical. With pages from his opera-in-progress spread on a work table... he is solicitous about a visitor's comfort, chooses his English words with the care of a schoolmaster and even looks a bit like a cherub. He says his main political activity these days consists of attending city council meetings and discussing festival budgets with politicians....

"[With regard to] his creative struggles, Mr. Henze says he has reached a new plateau in his work. And his decision to go to Italy—he now lives in the town of Marino, in the hills south of Rome—stems from his rejection of not only Nazi Germany but also the postwar European avant-garde that centered on composers like Pierre Boulez and Karlheinz Stockhausen and the annual festival at Darmstadt, Germany.

" 'I went to live in southern Italy to build up my own life, develop my own school of thought, and to write the sort of music that I wanted to write without being influenced or discouraged by my colleagues who wrote different music,' says the composer. 'I live very well in the country and I write my music, and I'm beginning to pull together the experiences of my life to come to an essence and to a kind of harmony. And this is happening quite naturally. It has something to do with aging, I suppose, and also with success, I suppose. When time passes and events get more distant, you are also better able to judge them with that distance.'

"Mr. Henze's view of art as an outlaw activity goes back to his boyhood in Germany, where he learned to love music while attending chamber music performances in a partly Jewish home. He remembers thinking of Dvorak's *'New World' Symphony* as 'the proud voice of Czechoslovakia with a message of survival and triumph against the ruling fascist power'. To this day he feels uneasy on returning to his homeland, although he likes the musical atmosphere in Munich, where this spring he directed a month-long festival devoted to music theater pieces by composers under the age of 40.

"It's hard, he says, for an artist not to throw himself into political struggles in Europe, where the parliamentary system involves the public closely with the government. Thus, during the student uprisings of the late 1960s, when for the first time Mr. Henze saw young Germans rebel, he felt compelled to become 'part of that.' The experience led him to begin reading, 'very late in my life,' philosophy and other theoretical writings in addition to the novels and poetry he had loved since his youth....

"Is there a contradiction in [his] writing music of sometimes daunting complexity while espousing populist, socialist and revolutionary causes? If so, it doesn't trouble Mr. Henze. Contradictions, he says, 'are very important' as 'part of the dialectics of existence.' Furthermore, he has devoted himself increasingly in recent years to work with amateurs, children's opera, conducting and educational approaches to making music—especially contemporary music—attractive to people.

"The evolution of Mr. Henze's musical and political thought over the last two decades is mirrored in the *Sixth* and *Seventh Symphonies*. The densely scored *Sixth*, which received a Tanglewood performance during Mr. Henze's residency [there] in 1983, contains quotations from revolutionary songs and has a tone of anger, if not rebellion. He composed the work in 1969 for the National Symphony Orchestra of Cuba while he was living in Cuba for a year.

"The *Seventh*, which Seiji Ozawa will conduct [at Tanglewood] with the Boston Symphony Orchestra, was completed in 1984 for the Berlin Philharmonic. In a note on the symphony, Mr. Henze calls it the most 'philharmonical,' or purely orchestral, of his seven. The music, he writes, offers 'my own interpretation of our conflict-ridden times,' but can best be understood as arising from the traditional German symphonic style and 'our classical canon of beauty.'

"Mr. Henze refuses to discuss the specific concerns in the *Seventh*, on grounds that knowledge of them 'would spoil it' for everyone.

On other other hand, he says, neither he nor the rest of society can ignore the greenhouse effect, the Chernobyl nuclear explosion and other manmade threats to existence. If some of that anxiety is reflected in the *Seventh Symphony*, he says, 'people can identify without quite knowing what it is that makes this identification.'...

"Mr. Henze sees composition today in a kind of golden age. He particularly admires the work of two of his 1983 Tanglewood students, David Lang and Michael Torke of the United States; he says Britain is bursting with talent, including Oliver Knussen, the Tanglewood faculty member who invited him back as composer in residence.

" 'I think the new generation of composers, luckily enough, is taking all the freedom of expression necessary to detach themselves from the models and to find a proper personal way of expression, regardless of a betrayal of a cause or not,' he says. 'You know, in my days, if you allowed a major or minor chord, you would have had it—you would have been executed in front of the Darmstadt music hall. Well, I think that has changed a lot.' " —Andrew L. Pincus, in *The New York Times*, 7/31/88.

Orpheus Behind the Wire for Chorus (SSSAAATTTBBB)(1981-83). *Text:* Edward Bond, Germ. transl. by the composer. *Pub.:* Schott (European American).

"A major new choral work by Hans Werner Henze, *Orpheus Behind the Wire* is a setting in English with German translation of a cycle of five poems by the British playwright Edward Bond whose previous collaboration with Henze included the opera *We Come to the River*. Bond has deftly and very movingly interlaced themes from the Orpheus legend with references to unnamed barbarisms of our time. Orpheus and Eurydice have become political prisoners who view each other for the last time 'over a frozen wave of wire, perhaps their ashes mingled...' Following the death of Eurydice, Orpheus is pictured as an old man ruminating on his career as singer: 'first [my music] was wild... later all sounds came from the tips of my fingers,' and now 'I sing with the earth *a capella*.' In Bond's final lines a theme emerges: the music of Orpheus is music of triumph and freedom.

"Henze's inspired musical setting equals the intensity and beauty of the poetry. Scored for mixed chorus *a capella* divided into twelve parts, the extreme difficulty of the work is somewhat mitigated by the composer's careful regard for voice leading and his use of referential triadic harmonies at strategic moments. An array of interesting choral textures includes a soft sustained cluster in lower voices supporting a declamatory passage for women's voices in four-part harmony; the occasional use of *sprechtstimme* and shouts at climactic moments; and, in one passage, the piling up of four independent ostinato units, each in three parts and each working within its own tonal center. One movement (No. 3, 'You who survived') contrasts a solo tenor (or tenor section) with the full chorus. Melismatic wailings of the tenor represent Bond's 'poet' who dies by his own hand. As background to the tenor's poignant vocal lines, the chorus responds in dialogue in subdued tone, answering and repeating his words. Another interesting passage occurs in the fourth movement ('It has changed'). The elderly Orpheus, with a vision of hope, observes 'But there is still music, first it was wild...' For these words Henze creates a jubilant passage of dancing melismas in all six voice parts. The entire movement is for men's voices, which balances nicely with the second movement for women's voices." — William B. Wells, in *Notes* (Music Library Association), 6/86.

ALAN HOVHANESS

B. 1911, Somerville MA. *Educ.:* NE Cons of Music, Tanglewood. *Taught at:* Boston Cons. *Awards:* Fulbright, Guggenheim, Rockefeller grants, Endicott Prize. *Works incl.:* choral, concertos (tpt, orch, vln), *The Holy City* (orch), *Mountains and Rivers Without End* (10 insts), piano, operas, quartets, 60 symphonies.

Composer statement: "I try to create melodies imitating the soul of nature, trees, mountains, rain, wind. Nature is the home of religion, death and resurrection."

Some twenty years ago, an astonishing 1,080 performances of Hovhaness works were reported by Broadcast Music, Inc. for a single year... In the opinion of many critics and other listeners, the music of Alan Hovhaness deserves a continued place in the music programs of today.
Excerpts from biographical notes published by C.F. Peters Corporation, 1967: "The first strong influences on young Hovhaness were the study of astronomy and the music of the Armenian composer-priest Gomidas Vartabed. Also, long walks among the hills of New Hampshire brought about curious meditative moods in the young composer, accompanied by strong sensations of being both in a New England countryside and at the same time in some oriental country such as China or India, with mountains becoming giant melodies...."
"In 1933 he won the Samuel Endicott Prize for a symphony in three movements which was performed by the New England Conservatory Orchestra conducted by Wallace Goodrich. This early symphony is no longer in existence. [Movements 1 and 3 of Hovhaness' officially designated *Symphony 1*, Op. 17/2, were composed in 1936 and performed for the first time in England with the BBC Symphony conducted by Leslie Heward—May 16, 1939.]
"Hovhaness [performed as an] organist in an Armenian church in Watertown, Massachusetts, where his original style of improvising in ancient modes during services attracted music lovers from distant cities. [He] studied the old Armenian notations collected by Father Hagop Makjian. Because of the discipline and inspiration of this study, [he] composed many books of new melodies, and developed his own long melodic line, creating giant melodies in both slow and fast tempi. An outstanding example of this is his *Symphony 8, Arjuna*, which he composed early in 1947. This symphony remained unperformed until February 1960, when it received its world premiere in

Madras, India, after which it was performed in Japan, Korea, Germany, France, Hawaii, and over CBC Vancouver.

"Reviewing a Hovhaness Carnegie Hall concert in the New York *Herald Tribune* in 1947, Virgil Thomson wrote of Hovhaness's music: 'It's expressive function is predominantly religious, ceremonial, incantatory, its spiritual content of the purest.... The high quality of the music, the purity of its inspiration, is evidenced in the extreme beauty of the melodic material, which is original material, not collected folklore, and in the perfect sweetness of taste it leaves in the mouth. There is no vulgarity in it, nothing meretricious, silly, easy or of low intent. It brings delight to the ear, and pleasure to the thought. For all its auditory complexity — for ornateness is of the essence — it is utterly simple in feeling, pure in spirit and high-minded. Among all our American contributions to musical art, which are many, it is one of the most curious and original, without leaning at any point on ignorance, idiosyncrasy or personalized charm.'"

"The oriental melisma inheres in Mr. Hovhaness' melodic line. But he writes also in counterpoint that is not academic and that is based upon other scale forms than our major and minor. His utterance is by turns mystical, fiery, prophetic, and always of a lofty character." — Olin Downes. (c.1951)

"His music is designed to create and maintain an ecstatic peace, to define a period of tranquility and motionless joy. He achieves this suspended quality partly by feeling the fifth — or dominant, rather than the root or tonic note as the point of rest and arrival. (This interval-of-the-fifth feeling is peculiar to much Asiatic music, but it was characteristic of European music too in its earlier stages until the time of Perotin in the eleventh century.) Chiefly, the state is evoked by the rhythmic texture, the layers of pulsating, non-climactic sound that 'unroll before the eye' — as Virgil Thomson once described it. The Hovhaness wallpaper texture achieves a surface of equalized tension rather as an Arab grille, a Persian wall panel, or a painting by Klee or Miro." — Peggy Glanville-Hicks (1950).

"A key to the art of Hovhaness may be turned in digesting his statement concerning one of his works: 'My *Symphony No. 4* probably has spiritual influences of the composers Yegmalion, Gomidas Vartabed, and Handel.' The absurd billing of the well-known Westerner with the two completely mysterious Easterners — as if all three enjoyed a comparable vogue—is typical Hovhaness: naive, solipsisitic, eclectic, and involved with 'spiritual influences' of all sorts.[49]

"Hovhaness is not a primitive (a natural talent, unrefined by technical training), though he at times sounds like it. On the contrary, he has built on his education with exhaustive research into the musical styles of the East (he himself is half-Armenian). Moreover, he is one of the most industrious of composers. But his intention, frequently, is to intricate a kind of primitivism through a mystical, hallucinatory, cultist sound—an acid rock of symphony. Many buffs of serious music cannot relate to Hovhaness; a lot of people who don't regularly encounter Beethoven or Mahler find Hovhaness just the thing.[50] His is one of the most distinctive signatures in the book of composers; if you're intrigued, try *Mysterious Mountain [Symphony No. 2]*, or sample *"And God Created Great Whales"* for humpback whale solo (on tape) and orchestra."—Ethan Mordden, *A Guide to Orchestral Music* (Oxford University Press, 1980).

Alleluia and Fugue for String Orchestra, Op. 40b (1940). 10m *Rec.:* MGM (LP) E-3504; *Crystal Records (CD) 810: Philharmonia O, David Amos, cond. Pub.:* Broude Brothers.

Anahid (Fantasy) for Flute, English Horn, Trumpet, Timpani, Percussion and Strings, Op. 57/1 (1944). 14m *Rec.:* MGM (LP) E-3504; Crystal Records (CD) 810: Philharmonia O, David Amos, cond. *Pub.:* C. F. Peters.

And God Created Great Whales for Orchestra and (Pre-Recorded) Whales, Op. 229/1 (1970). 12m *Perf.:* New York PO, André Kostelanetz, cond. *Rec.:* Columbia (Mono LP) M-34537: New York PO, André Kostelanetz, cond.; Crystal Records (CD) 810: Philharmonia O, David Amos, cond. *Pub.:* C.F. Peters.
3(picc)-2-2-2; 4-3-3-1; timp, 4 perc, hp; strings

Avak the Healer for Soprano, Trumpet & Strings, Op. 65 (1945-46). 20m *Pub.:* Peer-Southern Organization.

Celestial Fantasy for Strings, Op. 44 (1944). 7m *Pub.:* Broude Brothers.

Concerto 1 (Arevakal)(Season of the Sun) for Orchestra, Op. 88 (1951). *Rec.:* Mercury (LP) MG 50078. *Pub.:* Associated Music Publishers.
2-2-2-2; 2-2-0-0; timp, perc; strings

---

49 On the other hand, Hovhaness could simply mean what he says!—that among those who influenced his fourth symphony are Yegmalion, Vartabed, and Handel. (Ed.)

50 Lest this seem overly condescending to the composer (which I expect is not the author's intention), I will add a third category— those who encounter Beethoven and Mahler regularly, and also like Hovhaness. (Ed.)

Concerto 7 for Orchestra, Op. 116 (1953). 20m *Comm. & rec.:* Louisville (Mono LP) LOU-5454: The Louisville O, Robert Whitney, cond. *Pub.:* Associated Music Publishers.
2-2-2-2; 4-2-3-1; timp, perc, hp, celesta; strings
"1. Allegretto. The exposition is a canzona for flutes ending with oboe and horns. A development in strings and brass in canon culminates in a hymn for brass. The recapitulation is a new canzona for clarinets, bassoons and oboe. 2. Allegro *(Jhala-Scherzo)*. IJhala is a term borrowed from Hindustani classical music. Porcelain water cups are played by a stick. The figuration derived from this style is called *Jhala*. The instrument called *Jhala-Tarranga* means 'waves of water'. 3. Double Fugue — Epilogue *(Hymn to Louisville)*. An introduction leads to the exposition of the first subject in the horns. The lively second subject in strings is developed and combined with the first subject. Canons in woodwinds lead to a free hymnlike variation. A rapid canon in strings accompanies a brilliant canon variation in brass. A final lively canon in strings and woodwinds becomes the accompaniment to a final bell-like canon in brass. The work concludes with a brief epilogue entitled *Hymn to Louisville*." — Alan Hovhaness, from liner notes for Louisville LP LOU-5454.

Concerto 8 for Orchestra, Op 117 (1957). 20m *Recs.:* Poseidon Society (also CD as Crystal Records 810): Philharmonia O, David Amos, cond. *Pub.:* C. F. Peters.
2-2-2-2; 2-2-1-0; timp, perc, hp; strings

Elibris (Dawn God of Urardu) (concerto) for Flute and Strings, Op. 50 (1944). 10m *Rec:* Crystal Records (CD) 810: Philharmonia O, David Amos, cond. *Pub.:* Peer-Southern Organization.

Floating World (Ukiyo) for Orchestra, Op. 209 (1964). 12m *Pub.:* C. F. Peters.
3-3-2-2; 4-3-3-1; timp, 3 perc, hp, celesta *(ad lib.* 4-7 perc, 2 hp); strings

Fra Angelico for Orchestra, Op. 220 (1967). 17m *Rec.:* Poseidon Society (LP) 1002 (reissued as Crystal Records CD 804): Royal PO, Alan Hovhaness, cond. *Pub.:* C. F. Peters.
3-3-3-3; 4-3-2-1; timp, 4 perc, 2 hp, celesta; strings

Khaldis (concerto) for Piano, Four Trumpets [or any multiple thereof], and Percussion, Op. 91 (1951). 18m *Rec.:* Poseidon Society (LP) 1011 (distr. Crystal Records): Martin Berkofsky (pno), William Rohdin, Dan Cahn, Francis Bonny, Patrick Dougherty (tpts), Neal Boyar (perc). *Pub.:* Robert King.

Lousadzak (The Coming of Light) (concerto) for Piano and Orchestra, Op. 48 (1944). 15m MIRecs.: Dial: Maro Ajemian (pno), orch. cond. by composer; MGM (LP; reissued by Heliodor): Maro Ajemian (pno), orch. cond. by Carlos Surinach; Musicmasters (CD) MMCD 60204: Keith Jarrett (pno), American Composers O, Dennis Russell Davies, cond. *Pub.:* Peer-Southern Organization.

Magnificat for Soprano, Alto, Tenor, Baritone, Chorus & Orchestra, Op. 157 (1958). *Text:* Engl. adaptation by Hugh Ross. 28m
Rec.: Poseidon Society (LP) 1018 (distr. Crystal Records): Audrey Nossaman (s), Elizabeth Johnson (a), Thomas East (t), Richard Dales (bar), Univ of Louisville Choir, The Louisville O, Robert Whitney, cond. *Pub.:* C. F. Peters.
0-2-0-0; 2-2-1-0; perc, hp; strings
¶Also vers. for soprano, alto, tenor, chorus & organ (or piano).
"No. 1. The music opens with a *Celestial Fanfare*, an introduction beginning with a murmuring passage in the basses which rises to a climax and recedes. Trombone, horn and trumpet sound a long melodic line of religious mood. No. 2. *Magnificat [My soul doth magnify the Lord]* is for chorus. The organum for all voices leads to a brief fugato, ending again in an organum. No. 3. *Et exsultavit [And my spirit hath rejoiced in God my Saviour]* is a tenor solo accompanied by murmuring pizzicato passages in the violas. Nos. 4 and 5. *Quia respexit [For he hath regarded the low estate of his handmaiden: for behold all generations shalol call me blessed]* is a soprano solo leading to a women's chorus in three parts *(omnes generationes)*. The chorus is accompanied by rhythmless murmuring in the lower strings and harp. No. 6. *Quia fecit mihi magna [For he that is mighty hath done to me great things]* is for bass solo and chorus, accompanied by free rhythm in the basses. A wild and stormy rhythmless passage in the strings rises to a thunderous climax and recedes to a pianissimo. No. 7. *Et misericordia [And his mercy is on them that fear him]* for soprano solo. Violas and cellos hold a four-note cluster throughout. The oboes play a rapid melody which is taken up by the soprano voice. No. 8. *Fecit potentiam [He hath shewed strength with his arm]* for alto voice. A solemn trombone solo sounds the prelude and postlude. No. 9. *Esurientes implevit bonis [He hath filled the hungry with good things]* for tenor solo and men's chorus. A free-rhythm passage in the strings from fortissimo to pianissimo leads to the held A in the men's chorus. In Byzantine style the tenor sings a florid melody over the held A. No. 10. *Suscepit Israel [He hath holpen his servant Israel]*, for four-part women's chorus. Oboe, string and harp accompany the voices. No. 11. *Sicut locutus est [As he spake to our fathers]*. Bass solo and chorus. An introduction for oboes and horns leads to a passage in the strings. The chorus enters, every voice chanting in its own time, like the superstitious murmuring of a great crowd, rising like a wave of sound and receding again into the distance. A similar passage in the lower strings becomes the background to a bass solo. Later oboes and horns lead to a rhythmless passage in the violins. Again the murmuring chorus rises to a fortissimo climax in free rhythm and diminishes to pianissimo. No. 12. *Gloria patri [Glory be to the Father and to the Son]*. An introduction for trombone solo accompanied by murmuring basses leads to a

rhythmless climax in the strings. 'Gloria' is sounded by the sopranos and then the entire chorus. A heroic melody in the style of a noble galliard is sounded by first and second trumpets and is taken up later by the chorus. The music builds to a final climax. I have tried to suggest the mystery, inspiration and mysticism of early Christianity in this work." — Alan Hovhaness.

Symphony 2 (Mysterious Mountain) for Orchestra, Op. 132 (1955). 17m *Prem.*: orch. cond. by Leopold Stokowski. *Recs.*: RCA (LP; CD reissue as RCA 5733-2-RC): Chicago SO, Fritz Reiner, cond.; Musicmasters (CD) MMCD 60204: American Composers O, Dennis Russell Davies, cond. *Pub.*: Associated Music Publishers.
3-3-3-3; 5-3-3-1; timp, hp, celesta; strings

Symphony 4 for Wind Symphony Orchestra, Op. 165 (1959). 21m *Pub.*: C. F. Peters.
3-6 fl, 2-6 ob, 1-2 eh, 2-6 cl, b cl, 2-6 bsn, cbsn; 4-6 hn, 2-6 tpt, 4-6 tbn, tba; 4 perc, hp
1. Andante (Hymn and fugue). 2. Allegro (Dance — trio — dance). 3. Andante espressivo (Hymn and fugue).

Symphony 6 (Celestial Gate) for Small Orchestra, Op. 173 (1959). 20m *Pub.*: C. F. Peters.
1-1-1-1; 1-1-0-0; timp, chime, hp; strings
In one movement.

Symphony 7 (Nanga Parvat) for Wind Symphony Orchestra, Op. 178 (1959). 14m *Pub.*: C. F. Peters.
3-6 fl, 2-6 ob, eh, 2-6 cl, 2-6 bsn; 4-6 hn, 2-6 tpt, 3-6 tbn, tba; 4 perc, hp
1. Con ferocità. 2. March. 3. *Sunset*.

Symphony 9 (Saint Vartan) for Orchestra, Op. 180 (1949-50). 44m *Recs:* MGM; Poseidon Society (LP) 1013 (distr. Crystal Records): John Wilbraham (tpt), Alan Hovhaness (pno), National PO, Alan Hovhaness, cond. *Pub.*: Peer-Southern Organization.
0-0-0-0-a sax; 1-4-1-0; timp, perc, pno; strings
Part I: 1. *Yerk* (song) for trombone, percussion & strings. 2. *Tapor* (processional canon) for 3 trumpets & percussion. 3. *Aria* for horn & strings. 4. *Aria* for trumpet & strings. 5. *Aria* for horn & strings. 6. *Bar* (dance canon) for timpani, percussion & violins. 7. *Tapor* (processional) for trumpet, vibraphone & strings. 8. *Bar* (dance canon) for timpani, percussion & violins. 9. *Bar* (dance canon) for timpani, percussion & violins. 10. *Estampie* for timpani & strings. 11. *Bar* (dance canon) for strings. 12. *Bar* (dance canon) for timpani, vibraphone & strings. 13. *Aria* for trumpet & strings. 14. *Lament (Death of Vartan)* for trombone & piano. 15. *Estampie* (double canon) for 4 trumpets, timpani, percussion & strings.
Part II: 16. *Yerk* (song, *To Sensual Love*) for alto saxophone, timpani & strings. 18. *Estampie* for timpani & strings. 19. *Bar* (dance canon) for timpani, vibraphone & strings. 20. *Aria* for trumpet & strings. 21. *Bar*

(dance canon) for timpani & strings. 22. *Bar* (dance canon) for timpani, percussion & strings. 23. *Bar* (dance canon) for timpani & strings. 24. *Finale* (estampie, double canon) for 4 trumpets, timpani, percussion & strings.

Symphony 25 (Odysseus Symphony) for Orchestra, Op. 275 (1973). 36m *Rec.:* Poseidon Society (Stereo LP) 1014: Polyphonia O of London, Alan Hovhaness, cond.
1(piccolo)-1-1-0; 1-1-1-1; timpani, perc; strings

Talin (concerto) for Viola (Clarinet) and Strings, Op. 93/1 (1951-52). *Recs.:* MGM Records: Emmanuel Vardi (vla), orch. cond. by Izler Solomon; Recital (CD) CD-508 (distr. by Allegro; also Peters International PLE 071): Lawrence Sobol (cl), Orchestra da Camera di Roma, Nicolas Flagello, cond. *Pub.:* Associated Music Publishers (vla & strings).

Upon Enchanted Ground for Flute, Cello, Harp & Tantam, Op. 90/1 (1951). 4m *Pub.:* C. F. Peters.

Although critic Walter Simmons has not been without reservations concerning the music of Alan Hovhaness, he has remained an ever curious and supportive listener to new performances and recordings. His commentaries—here abridged from the 1-2/80 and 11-12/89 issues of *Fanfare: The Magazine for Serious Record Collectors*—offer valuable insight regarding important stylistic characteristics of this enormously prolific and gifted American composer:

"From each stage of Hovhaness' evolution, key works stand out as embodying a genuinely transcendental sort of spirituality, expressed with great subtlety and sensitivity. From the 1940s there is the fiery primordial, yet visionary Armenian splendor of works like *Lousadzak, Khaldis,* and *Anahid;* and there are those evocations of early-Christian ecclesiastical ecstasy, such as *Alleluia and Fugue, Avak the Healer,* and the *Celestial Fantasy.*

"During the 1950s, these two threads were woven together, and combined with influences from India and Japan, in a profusion of highly varied, original, and fully convincing compositions, from the exquisite delicacy of a miniature masterpiece like *Upon Enchanted Ground* to the substantial, almost symphonic impact of works like the *Concertos Nos. 7 and 8 for Orchestra, Talin,* and the *Symphony No. 2, 'Mysterious Mountain',* and *Symphony No. 6, 'Celestial Gate'.*

"During the 1960s, what had hitherto been a relatively minor element in Hovhaness' music—quasi-aleatoric waves of buzzing sound that rose in giant crescendos and then receded—began to assume central importance. This technique was often combined with a kind of slow, angular, canonic melodic style with sliding pitches, derived from ancient Korean music, giving birth to works that, at their best, as in *Floating World-Ukiyo* and *Fra Angelico*, evoke a spirit of wild, menacing chaotic power and frenzy, or timeless cosmic serenity.

"In the 1970s, another stage in Hovhaness' evolution began to emerge, as he appeared to embrace certain harmonic and melodic materials that had previously seemed inimical to the diatonic purity of the Hovhaness idiom: he introduced a large dose of chromaticism into his polyphony, and elevated the half-diminished-seventh chord to primary harmonic stature. Along with these harmonic innovations appeared a marked simplification of texture and, most of all, a distinct retardation of rhythmic motion....

"[Notes on additional compositions:]
"*Concertos for Orchestra:* The *Concerto No. 8* for orchestra [is] the final installment in a genre that drew Hovhaness's attention during the 1950s. These *Concertos*, which are in no way virtuoso showpieces in the Bartók manner, are among the most consistently successful works in the composer's enormous canon. Best known are the *Concerto No. 1, 'Arevakal'*, which *Concerto No. 8* resembles in style, and the uncharacteristically symphonic *Concerto No. 7*. Similar to others in the series, the *Concerto No. 8* alternates between solemn incantations that draw upon the Armenian cantorial style and uplifting polyphonic hymns featuring diatonic counterpoint enhanced by frequent use of reverent suspensions. An Armenian-style march and a very uncharacteristic, Satie-like but charming 'pastoral dance' provide contrast. Solo trombone fulfills the cantorial role, while imaginative instrumental touches enhance the sonorous aspects. The *Concerto No. 8* is the sort of work that attracted so many followers to Hovhaness a couple of decades ago.

"*Anahid* [is] a brilliantly exotic fantasy for chamber orchestra in undiluted Armenian style. Listeners... will be stunned by the blazing splendor, subtle delicacy, and wild ferocity found in this work from the mid-1940s, when the composer's explorations into his Armenian heritage were still fresh and new. It is wonderful to have this work available again, now in a modern recording.

"*Alleluia and Fugue:* another work from the 1940s. This was the piece through which I was first introduced to Hovhaness's music. I was captivated by its rich parallel triads in organum style, by its haunting modal melody with primitive imitative counterpoint, accompanied by open fifths, and by the vigorous Handelian fugue that followed.... I found this unfamiliar language (I hadn't yet heard Vaughan Williams' *Tallis Fantasia*) to be a revelation from the very first note. Its apparent independence from time or place and its awe-inspiring sense of pure spirituality held out the promise of a magical gateway into hitherto unimagined expressive realms—a promise that was fulfilled by my subsequent immersion in twentieth-century music. I have since learned that Hovhaness's music has played a similar role in the musical lives of other young people, and this is a role to which it is well suited.

"*Elibris:* dating from 1944—the same year as *Anahid*—[this] ten-minute 'concerto' for flute and strings consists of a slow, incantational section, followed by a dance-like finale, both in Armenian style, with clear thematic affinities to such other works as *Lousadzak* and the *St. Vartan Symphony*.

"*And God Created Great Whales:* The biggest surprise on the [Crystal Records CD] is *And God Created Great Whales*, dating from a time (1970) when Hovhaness had been concentrating on Japanese and Korean sources of musical inspiration. This was also the time when whales—and, particularly, the discovery that they created 'music'—sound patterns with distinct, definable shapes—were very much in the news.... In the new recording the work, which combines prerecorded whale 'songs' with themes found in prior works by the composer, [has a] remarkably powerful [effect].

"*Symphony 2 (Mysterious Mountain)* is Hovhaness's best-known composition and the one through which he has won most of his admirers. Its great popularity may be attributed to two factors: One is the... splendid 1958 performance and recording [by Fritz Reiner and the Chicago Symphony Orchestra], which, if I am not mistaken, has never been out of the catalog. The other chief explanation involves the music itself: its smooth, euphonious treatment of the symphony orchestra, as well as its pervasively serene spirit, disturbed only by the tempestuous second subject of a double fugue comprising the central section of the work, which eventually reaches a majestic climax. It is a very easy work for the most timid listener to enjoy—nor is this to its discredit.

"It is worth nothing that although *Mysterious Mountain* is cataloged as No. 2 in a series of symphonies now numbering well beyond sixty, it is not an early work. Rather, it belongs to Hovhaness's third style period, when much of his music was characterized by the consolidation of both early Christian and Armenian features within a full symphonic context. It was during that period (early 1950s through early 1960s) that he began to identify his prodigious flow of orchestral works as 'symphonies', although, in truth, few of them have ever approximated the structural characteristics generally associated with the term.

"*Lousadzak* [is] a work of stunning originality and unflagging inspiration—in short, one of Hovhaness's unqualified masterpieces. The name *Lousadzak*, an Armenian neologism meaning 'dawn of light', was originally appended as a subtitle to *Concerto for Piano and*

String Orchestra, although the work has at least as little relationship to the concerto tradition as *Mysterious Mountain* has to the symphonic tradition. It was written in 1944, during the composer's intensive exploration of his Armenian heritage as a means of discovering his own creative and spiritual identity.... Stripping away the fundamental tonal-harmonic syntax of western music altogether, Hovhaness attempted to create a uniquely personal language based on the instrumental styles and vocal melos of Armenian music, while retaining western instrumental resources as a practical medium. Thus, in the one-movement *Lousadzak*, the pianist has no virtuoso passage-work—not even a chord to play—only melismatic, arabesque-like filigree in the manner of middle-eastern dulcimer music, supported by simple modal polyphony in the strings. Yet the overall shape of the piece—a slow, gradual rise from the somber, mysterious depths that culminates in an ecstatic, rhythmically exhilarating primal dance—evokes the notion of 'dawn of light' in the most abstract, cosmic sense.

"Hovhaness's *Talin* was originally composed in 1952 as a work for viola and strings and was recorded a few years later by Emmanuel Vardi, with a string orchestra conducted by Izler Solomon. [This version], as performed with incisive, burning intensity by violist Vardi, emerged as one of Hovhaness's most consistently inspired works, with an alternation in its outer movements between solemn Armenian melisma in liturgical style and rich Renaissance polyphony evoking a sense of passionate reverence. [The work has also been performed in a version for clarinet and strings.]"

Other comments:

"The real mystery of the *Mysterious Mountain* [Symphony 2, Op. 132] is that it should be so simply, sweetly, innocently lovely in an age that has tried so terribly hard to avoid these impressions in music." —Hubert Roussel.

"*Symphony No. 2* [is] a work of impenetrable transcendence. The mountain of the title is mysterious not only in the composer's ambiguously evocative sounds, but in its lack of programmatic identity: what mountain where? Hovhaness does not tell. 'Mountains are symbols,' he states, 'of man's attempt to know God.... To some, the Mysterious Mountain may be the phantom peak, unmeasured, thought to be higher that Everest, as seen from great distances by fliers from Tibet. To some it may be the solitary mountain, the tower of strength over a countryside—Fujiyama, Ararat, Monadnock, Shasta, or Grand Teton.' Everyone hears something different here— but everyone hears *something*. This is provocative music, one of the few symphonic compositions of recent years likely to become a popular favorite. There are three movements, two lyrical and introspective spaces surrounding a double fugue. Majestic in its immobile contemplation, the first movement casts a wonderful spell, amplified by the second movement with its churchly chorale of strings. Midway through the second movement, a second theme breaks in in fast tempo—now the fugue is really rolling—and what might be termed the 'mountain' theme dominates the texture to splendid effect. The third movement returns us to earth in a solemn chant of muted brasses under a dancing violin line. This gives way to the music of the first movement, even more compelling on its second hearing, hovering weightlessly, an enigma in the form of a hymn."—Ethan Mordden, *A Guide to Orchestral Music* (Oxford University Press, 1980).

"*Symphony No. 4* for Wind Symphony Orchestra. The characteristic Hovhanessian Oriental myustery opens the first movement, which the composer calls a 'hymn and fugue'. Timeless, spaceless sounds interspersed with brass chorales; then the fugue, energetic and mellifluously Baroque. The marimba, an African xylophone, launches the second movement, a chain of dances. Here especially Hovhaness exploits his penchant for the Eastern timbre (tone color). A real xylophone replaces the marimba, succeeded by timpani, glockenspiel, vibraphone, harp: a percussionist suite. The third movement offers another hymn and fugue, rising to a grand ceremony of sound in brass, chimes, and gong."—Ethan Mordden, *A Guide to Orchestral Music* (Oxford University Press, 1980).

"*Symphony No. 7 (Nanga Parvat)* for Wind Symphony Orchestra. Nanga Parvat ('Without Trees') is one of the world's more remote mountains, snowbound in Kashmir. For this salute to its forbidding majesty, Hovhaness composed a symphony for wind instruments (that is, wood and brasses) and percussion in his habitual three movements. The first, *Con ferocità* (ferociously), uses incessant drum rhythms to suggest the barbaric power of the Himalayas. The second movement, 'March', depicts (in the composer's words) 'wild improvised marches in raucous woodwinds and false brass unisons,' with Hovhaness' typical use of repetitive melody in unvarying accompanimental textures.[51] The third movement, 'Sunset', closes the short work with a solemn native pageant. An odd echo of Christian

---

[51] Rather famously, the "hypnotic" effect of the composer's melodic and harmonic repetitions or near-repetitions prefigured aspects of later "minimalist" techniques and effects. (Ed.)

worship peeks through the otherwise Eastern gauze; at the end, Hovhaness likens his high woodwind tone clusters (groups of adjacent notes played together) to 'shafts of light through craggy peaks'." — Ethan Mordden, *A Guide to Orchestral Music* (Oxford University Press, 1980).

"The *Saint Vartan Symphony* [No. 9, Op. 180] looms as one of Hovhaness's true masterpieces... a highly colored, intensely emotional work teeming with extra-ordinary invention and originality... rising with the inevitability of Greek drama toward a searing climactic finale. Its form is unique; it is a symphony in mosaic, a huge and vital hymn of praise — now contemplative, again surgingly, almost violently joyful. And, always, it seems music which spirals upward to heaven, unconcerned in its course with worldly things." — Edward Cole.

"One of Alan Hovhaness's most striking works — in a large catalog well laden with striking works — is his *Saint Vartan SYmphony*. It is in twenty-four short movements, divided into two main sections. Saint Vartan, an Armenian warrior-saint, dates from around the 5th century. This work is charged with emotion and tension, is marvelously contrasted, and moves along with logic and determination. It is always beautiful in melodic line and harmonic idiom.... [Here] is a very beautiful work which should enjoy a greater popularity, [by] one of our top talents today; [it] is possibly his masterpiece." — Enos F. Shupp, Jr., in *The New Records*, 11/73.

Symphony No. 25 (Odysseus Symphony). Being unmistakeably in an Hovhaness idiom, this symphony includes features and effects found in other works — melting brass solos; a momentum which appears somehow to *increase* (deepen), and so compound a given rhythmic pulse; playful filips from a single string or other instrument; and passages, simply, of thoroughly relaxed (and relaxing) peace and quiet. Yet, as the smaller sections blend to form a single, longish work, all these and other inventions seem ever fresh — especially when one happens upon this piece for the first time. Typically, the "journeyings" of this Odysseus seem not quite of this earth, nor is it even a particular journey so much as a reaching toward something (or someone) attainable, perhaps, only through sound. (Ed.)

"Since I was nine years old I have had a tremendous love for Homer's *Odyssey*, which I read in the Palmer prose translation. This work opened great vistas to me, as I had always experienced from earliest childhood the sensation of traveling great distances out into the universe or through strange mountainous countries on what seemed like bridges of gossamer threads. The visions of the blind bard seemed to pull me into a journey through time as well as space and to bring me into realms of distant ages.

"*Odysseus Symphony* is a spiritual journey to the distant beloved. In canonic passages for violins Penelope weaves her magic web which she unweaves every night to project over vast distances and communicate with Odysseus in his wanderings over oceans of world storms. Love music forms a bridge of sound over which the lost and tempest-tossed Odysseus returns to Penelope. A triumphal homecoming is followed by a spiritual homecoming." — Alan Hovhaness.

"*Concerto No. 8* for Orchestra (1953). Calmly contrapuntal, immediately appealing yet rich in texture, profound but not in the least intimidating, it seems to have issued from a consciousness wholly untouched by 20th Century *angst*. This can be either a credit or a debit, depending on your point of view (or your mood). In a work of this length (about 20 minutes) I find Hovhaness absolutely convincing. Likewise the brief *Alleluia and Fugue* for strings (1942), another rich, radiant piece, which, if I am not mistaken, shows the influence of such [Henry] Cowell works as the *Hymn and Fuguing Tunes* and perhaps even of Vaughan Williams." — in *American Record Guide*, 1-2/90.

"Because of his ability to produce beautiful sounds from whatever combination of instruments he is working with (right up to full orchestra) and [because of] the unabashedly melodic character of his work, his music possesses instant appeal....

"That Mr. Hovhaness is capable of tightening his [sometimes] simplistic compositional methods into a coherent and powerful musical statement is proven by *Fra Angelico*, Op. 220, a beautiful symphonic poem. Significantly, the composer's program notes for this work refer to the great monk who 'painted in the Eastern spirit.' " — Paul Turok, in *The New York Times*, 8/14/88.

"[*Magnificat*, Op. 157,] is a beautiful, inspired work, full of haunting melody, mystical harmonic effects, and strong religious feeling. It is music that reaches the listener almost immediately, communicating some of the mysticism surrounding religion and particularly early Christianity. A timeless quality pervades it for Hovhaness blends antiquarian and contemporary sounds ingeniously. Perhaps this very fluidity is the secret of its fascination." — Miles Kastendieck, New York *Journal-American*, 1964.

"[Let me] draw attention to Crystal Records' worthwhile project [of distributing eighteen discs of Hovhaness' music originally available from Poseidon. These releases include] the *Magnificat* (the loveliest ever written) and..... a newer recording of the *'Saint Vartan'* *Symphony* [No. 9], a masterwork [originally recorded by MGM, as well as] old friends like the *'Khaldis' Concerto*. What [this set of LP recordings] has done is, in effect, to disprove the often-maintained idiocy that Hovhaness' music is all of a kind, or piece — a platitude akin to saying that all members of another race look alike. They don't. It isn't." — John Ditsky, in *Fanfare: The Magazine for Serious Record Collectors*, 1-2/83.

KAREL HUSA

B. 1921, Prague (Czechoslovakia). *Educ.:* Prague Cons, Acad Musical Arts (Prague), Ecole Normale de Musique (Paris), Conservatoire National (Paris). *Taught at:* Cornell Univ. *Awards:* Pulitzer Prize, Lili Boulanger Prize, Bilthoven Festival, Guggenheim Fellowship, 2 Orpheus Awards (Kappa Kappa Psi). *Works incl.:* band (incl. *Al Fresco*), chamber, choral, concertos (brass qnt/strings, orch, perc, tpt/winds), *Fantasies* (orch), *Fresque* (orch), *Mosaiques* (orch), piano, symphonies, *The Trojan Women* (ballet).

Composer statement (to the Editor): "[I think the enclosed notes on *Apotheosis* and other works] should all be self-explanatory.... Please feel free to choose. Thank you for including me in your book, I feel honored!"[52]

Apotheosis of This Earth for Wind Ensemble (1970; rev. 1973 for Orchestra with Chorus). 26m *Comm. & prem.:* Univ of Mich Schl Band and O Assn., Karel Husa, cond. *Other perfs.:* Bowling Green State Univ S Band, Karel Husa, cond.; Cornell Univ Glee Club and Chorus, Cornell SO, Karel Husa, cond.; Univ Buffalo S Band; Eastman Wind Ens, Frederick Fennell, cond.; Atlanta SO and Chorus, Robert Shaw, cond.; Cornell Glee Club and Chorus, Syracuse SO, Karel Husa, cond. *Pub.:* Associated Music Publishers. Orch vers: pic-3-3-E hn-b cl-2-c bsn; 4-4-4-1; timp, 6 perc; strings
1. *Apotheosis.* 2. *Tragedy of Destruction.* 3. *Postscript.*

"Karel Husa is not only one of our most important composers — he is also one of the finest conductors in the business today....

"*Apotheosis* is written in the tonal language made familiar by such composers as Ligeti and Penderecki, but it speaks directly from the heart to the heart. It is a work of terrifying intensity, a prolonged scream of anguish occasioned by 'man's brutal possession and misuse of nature's beauty' and the ultimate total destruction of 'this beautiful earth' that seems inevitable unless we change our ways.

"Within the short space of less than 30 minutes, Husa shapes a vast sound picture of our planet, first as a point of light in the universe, then as a growing organism, and finally, as catastrophe and death. The basic material from which this frightening tone poem is constructed is astonishingly simple — long, bleak, bare, non-vibrato horizontal lines; increasingly complex percussion (the piece calls for

---

52 Lest the composer — a true gentleman — seem self-serving, it should be added that some of the following commentaries have been supplied by the Editor. (Ed.)

six percussionists); unremitting dissonance contrasted with unions; agonizing slow crescendos.

"Despite its technical difficulties, *Apotheosis* has been a smash hit on the band circuit, with more than 300 performances since its 1971 world premiere. In its orchestral garb, it could become equally popular." — Irving Lowens, *Washington Star and News*, 4/26/73.

"The chorus is used as a wordless vocal complement to the orchestra — sometimes cooing, hissing, howling, clapping hands, stamping feet. Among the instrumentalists are six very busy percussionists, and the marvelous din depicting the *Tragedy of Destruction* is real gut excitement. In the concluding *Postscript* individual members of the chorus utter the words 'this... beautiful... earth'. *Apotheosis* has everything — power, passion, mysticism, even peace and ecology." — Richard Freed, *High Fidelity/Musical America*, 7/73.

"There are times when an artist feels the need to express in his work an idea concerning the present state of world affairs. I must say that I was never concerned with such ideas in my music until the summer of 1968 when I wrote the *Music for Prague, 1968*. Although I have previously composed pieces with titles expressing their character or mood, most of my works have no programmatic elements. While this is evident with respect to my *Quartets, Concertos, Symphony* and *Sonata*, it also applies to my *Apotheosis of This Earth*. This work has no detailed 'program' of any kind, but it does attempt to express musically the present alarming and tragic situation of mankind on this planet. Here is the complete 'Note' to the score:

> The composition of *Apotheosis of This Earth* was motivated by the desperate state of mankind and by its immense problems, as seen in everyday killings, war, hunger, the extermination of fauna, huge forest fires and the critical contamination of the entire environment.
> Man's brutal possession and misuse of nature's beauty — if continued at today's reckless speed — can only lead to catastrophe. The composer hopes that the destruction of this beautiful earth can be stopped, so that the tragedy of destruction — musically projected here in the second movement — and the desolation of its aftermath (the 'postscript' of the third movement) can exist only as fantasy, never to become a reality.

"In the first movement, *Apotheosis*, the Earth first appears as a point of light in the universe. Our memory and imagination approach it in perhaps the same way as it appeared to the astronauts returning from the moon. The Earth grows larger and larger, and we can even remember some of its tragic moments (as struck by the xylophone near the end of the movement).

"The second movement, *Tragedy of Destruction*, deals with the actual brutalities of man against nature, leading to the destruction of our planet, perhaps by radioactive explosion. The Earth dies as a savagely, mortally wounded creature.

"The last movement is a *Postscript*, full of the realization that so little is left to be said: The Earth has been pulverized into the universe, the voices scattered into space. Toward the end, these voices — at first computer-like and mechanical — unite into the words 'this beautiful Earth,' simply said, warm and filled with regret... and one of so many questions comes to our minds: 'Why have we let it happen?'...

"It has been gratifying to me to hear excellent performances of this composition since [the premiere]. It is always more or less a step into the unknown when one writes a piece, using devices which have not been explored previously. I did not know how many of the young players in bands would know how to finger some of the quartertones, but I found out that either they experimented with some 'false' fingerings, or produced them with lips, or they knew either Bartolozzi's book[53] or other charts on fingerings of these quartertones. I also am amazed at the quality of young performers one finds in colleges, universities and even in high schools today; their technical abilities as well as quick understanding and realizing of musical ideas is most comforting to know. I did not expect when I wrote this work that so many ensembles would be able to perform it so well. The only problem — and the one I did not expect — is the narration of the syllables and broken words leading to the phrase 'This beautiful Earth' in the last movement. I realize now that a player who is uninhibited with his instrument, is able to put warmth, gentleness, tragedy, despair [into his playing] when he produces the tone, is shy to say a word or two on stage! In all the performances I have conducted or heard, the spoken word is *never loud enough* for the first four times (m. 12-13; m. 23-24; m. 36-38 and m. 42-44) when the syllables and broken words are recited. On the other hand, the whole sentence as said in m. 57 is usually strong enough (sometimes even too loud). For the last time (m. 63-64) it is preferable to have one person in the front of the ensemble to say the phrase simply, but with sincere emotion.

"Among other suggestions, I should like to point out important lines: starting m. 23 in the first movement, the alto clarinet plays note

---

53 Bruno Bartolozzi, *New Sounds for Woodwind* (Oxford University Press).

g, bassoon in the next m. 24 has *f sharp* and in the same measure on the last beat bass clarinet plays *quarter-tone higher d;* all these three notes should be smooth, but distinctly heard as important melodic line, which continues with the same three instruments and added baritone saxophone until m. 43. Composers before 1900 would have written this whole melody for one instrument only and might have doubled it with one or more other instruments. Another line that should come out is in horns with tenor saxophone starting m. 53; later, also the saxophones, alto, bass clarinets, bassoons and string bass, and in m. 68 trumpets, horns and trombones. In m. 80 the flutter-tonguing of the muted trombones together with marimba tremolo must be audible and come stronger and stronger (and always heard), leading into the muted, flutter-tongued trumpets until m. 108.

"It is important that tension increases progressively from the first measure of the *Apotheosis* without 'falling down' until m. 134. Here the xylophone will beat the thirty-second notes as strong and loud as possible, but not faster than indicated (quarter note approximately 60) yet freely. Sometimes I heard them played so fast that they resemble more to tremolos. In the second movement, the low and pedal notes of all instruments must be constantly loud and powerful. In the score I am suggesting two, three or even four string basses. I often feel that in the music for bands and wind ensembles one string bass is not enough to give a strong bass line. In the *Apotheosis of This Earth* several of them are necessary in order to obtain the powerful effect. Other composers, such as Stravinsky in his *Concerto for Piano and Winds* and Dahl in his *Saxophone Concerto* already specify four string basses in their scores. In m. 75-82 the trumpet entrances should be very much accented and strong. Starting m. 82, the *fugato* has to come out phrase by phrase from all entering instruments. Aleatory passage in m. 120-121 is notated approximately in seconds, but this timing will depend on the strength, power or speed of the movement and it is up to the conductor to feel at that moment, *when* the crescendo has reached its maximum in these measures and whether prolonging these measures would weaken the effect. The same is valid for all the free passages in this work. In m. 129-131 the Glockenspiel, Vibraphone, Xylophone and Bel Lyra must sound as 'alarming' as possible (fff) and the indicated *crescendi* and *decrescendi* should be respected. The bass drum and large gong mallets must be used; particularly, the sound of the gong must be low and long. To give an idea for these terrifying percussion sounds I remember pictures I have seen in movies of the sun during the eclipse; incredible explosions in orange and red color occurred on the sun's surface. The bass drum and large gong's 'explosion' sounds culminate in m. 140

with crash cymbals and suspended cymbal. At the end of this movement the percussion will slow down progressively, freely (according to the approximate notation) and all instruments will get softer in the last two measures, but not more than a *mezzo-forte*. There should be not much pause after this movement (on the other hand about 15-20 seconds should space the first movement from the second). The entrances of the clarinets should be heard, although only gently; they should sound as a 'pulse' or 'wave' somewhere in the space; the same effect is in clarinets m. 14-16 and horns m. 16-19. The entrance of the medium tom-tom in m. 24 should come out as a continuation of the spoken sounds; the stick used should not be too hard (medium) and the tom-toms should not be small ones. The rhythm of the spoken syllables as well as of the tom-tom must be precise, as written, in sextuplets. These sounds are to remind us of some computerlike beeps scattered in the universe. Important also is the sound of the xylophone in m. 55; it should be a gentle sound (not hard sticks), precise and in the octave as written, not one octave higher as sometimes I have heard it played. And speaking about the xylophone, I would like to add a word about the ending of this work. The 'signal' sounds in the last five measures will be played softer and softer, into a virtual disappearing, but no *ritardando* should be made within the group of these signal notes. It will be up to the conductor to decide how many repetitions of the last measure are to be done. I have conducted three, but at times also four, five, six, even seven, depending on the impact of the performance and quietness of the public.

"I have composed the *Apotheosis of This Earth* on the shore of beautiful Lake Cayuga [NY] extending from my window on three corners from north to south via east. With constantly changing skies and colors of the lake, accompanied by aleatory sounds of waves, birds, and movements of insects and animals, it never seems to me possible that man could one day achieve involuntarily the destruction of this planet. However, the once clear water is getting dirtier, and dead fish, beer cans, and algae bloom are appearing in greater quantities on the shore... And how about all the other things in the world? The biologists are saying that, if we do not start to do something about it now, we are heading into lack of oxygen around this planet due to the pollution of seas. This is not pessimism or lack of faith, this is simply a fact and voice of warning. I am not a biologist and can only warn with music. Why not?" — Karel Husa, in *The Journal of Band Research*, Spring 1973.

Concerto for Large Wind Ensemble (1982) 22m Comm. by Mich State Univ Alumni Band; ded. to Mich State Univ Bands (Stanley De

Rusha, dir.). Winner, Sudler Interntl Wind Band Competition; Medal of the Sousa Order of Merit. *Prem.:* Michigan State Univ Wind S, Karel Husa, cond. *Other perf.:* U.S. Marine Band, Col. John R. Bourgeois, cond. *Pub.:* Associated Music Publishers (score & parts on rental).

2 picc (fl), 4 fl, 3 ob (1 Engl hn), cls in E^b, 9 cl in B^b (in 3 groups), a cl in E^b, b cl in B^b, cb cl in B^b, 2 bsn, c bsn, 2 a sax in E^b, 1 t sax, 1 bar sax in E^b, 1 b sax in B^b, 4 hn in F, 8 tpt in B^b, 4 trb, 2 bar, 2 tuba, timp (5 drums), perc (4 players).

1. *Drum Ceremony and Fanfare.* 2. *Elegy.* 3. *Perpetual Motion.*

"The *Concerto for Wind Ensemble* is meant to be a display of virtuoso passages, given to solo instruments as well as to the groups that make up the ensemble. In the *Fanfare* of the first movement, the brass section is 'concertizing' in the groups of four brass quintets (2 trumpets, horn, trombone and tuba or barytone), spread from left to right in back; the saxophonists (S, A, T, B) are placed in front of the brass quintets, and finally the woodwinds occupy the front of the stage, with percussion on the left and right sides. These groups, like the brass quintets, play in the *concertante* manner, especially in the first and last movements. At the same time, each movement will contain individual solo passages, such as the tympani in the beginning (*Drum Ceremony*), the long flute soli and later English horn and other low woodwinds in the *Elegy*, and then numerous instruments in the third movement, the *Perpetual Motion*.

"The composition of the *Concerto* was prompted by the excellency of wind and percussion players today and by the incredible growth of wind ensembles, orchestras, bands in the last twenty-five years.[54] The work is intended for their enjoyment." —Karel Husa.

"Husa's piece is a powerful study of wind instruments, exploring new and creative ways of blending these sounds together... Traditionally, sections of instruments are grouped homogeneously (sections of trombones, trumpets, horns and so on), but in this concerto they were organized in four groups of brass quintets, spread out in the last row of the wind ensemble. Because of this unique grouping, the spectacular and thrilling music echoed across the stage and created a stereophonic effect. Listening to this concerto was a stimulating musical experience.... The solo instruments always came through without being covered by other instrumentation. The sounds were unique and the total outcome was thrilling. [Husa's]

---

54 See also commentary by composer Alfred Reed, below. (Ed.)

concerto is destined to become a classic." — Ken Glickman, *Lansing State Journal*, 12/5/82.

"Mr. Husa's three-movement concerto is a major contribution to the wind ensemble literature. The opening section, *Drum Roll and Fanfare*, makes considerable demands on the five percussionists with their extensive battery, while the following *Elegy* features solos by flute and other winds. Mr. Husa's music is rife with brief tunes and melodic figures treated in moderately modern harmonies. The exciting rhythmic drive makes this music seem faster than it is." — F. Warren O'Reilly, *The Washington Times*, 4/19/82.

Music for Prague, 1968 for Orchestra (1968-69). Orig. vers. for band. 20m *Prem.*: Ithaca College Concert Band. *Recs.*: Golden Crest (LP): Univ of MI Sym Band, Karel Husa, cond.; Louisville (LP): The Louisville O, Jorge Mester, cond.; ERRL/Belwin-Mills (LP): Univ of TX Sym Band, Moody, cond. *Pub.*: Associated Music Publishers. 3-3-3-3; 4-4-3-1; timp, perc, harp, pno; strings (also band vers.)

"Though based in the United States, Husa has made frequent trips to [Europe], conducting and recording with many European orchestras. Profoundly affected by the events of August, 1968, he was moved by the tragic outcome of the Russian invasion into Czechoslovakia to compose *Music for Prague, 1968*.

"The work makes use of a 15th-century Czech war chorale, 'Ye Warriors of God and His Law', poignant writing for the percussion section, and ringing bells that are reminiscent of 'The City of Hundreds of Towers'. This major twentieth-century piece for orchestra (or band) has enjoyed some 7,000 performances since its premiere.

" '[This is] music of searing intensity.... After a quiet introduction and a vigorous fanfare in the brass, the strings sing out a great anguishing song which depicts the tragedy in Prague's history. A ghostly interlude for percussion instruments alone leads to an energetic, driving toccata which, together with a mighty chorale played by the entire orchestra in unison, ends the work. It is rare for such forceful contemporary works to elicit repeated curtain calls [from our local audiences], but this one did. (*Atlanta Journal*, January 17, 1975).' " — James G. Roy, Jr.

"Husa's dream of returning to a free Czechoslovakia finally became a reality in February of this year [1990] when he was invited to conduct the State Symphony Orchestra in his *Music for Prague, 1968* on a program with other Czech composers whose works also had been banned during the Communist era.... [In part] a tribute to the democratic movement led by President Václav Havel, [the program] was planned as the First Festival Concert of the newly founded Association of Czech Composers and Artists. Husa describes his reactions to conducting in Prague again after so many years: 'If I would think about all that has happened to me and to my country since 1946,[55] I'm afraid it would have been too moving. I had to just conduct.'

"Husa composed *Music for Prague, 1968* after the 'Dubcek Spring' when Czechoslovakia tried to enact some measure of self-determination but was brutally invaded by the Soviet Union. At the time Soviet tanks were rolling into Czechoslovakia quelling the democratic movement, Husa was in his summer cottage in Cayuga Lake, New York, searching for an idea for a commission by Ithaca College for a work for wind ensemble. Filled with outrage and grief at the news he heard on his transistor radio, he began to compose *Music for Prague, 1968* and finished it in a record-breaking six or seven weeks....

"*Music for Prague, 1968* is a 20-minute work in four movements set against a military rattle of snare drum and featuring a solo piccolo symbolizing Prague's delicate and brief moment of freedom. Woven into the work are the first four bars of a 15th-century Hussite war chorale, 'Ye Warriors of God and His Laws', a melody that has stood for resistance and hope for hundreds of years and has been used by many Czech composers, including Dvorák and Smetana. The tolling of bells is heard throughout the composition, since Prague is known for its cathedrals and bell towers. The work is a dramatic tone poem with a demanding maze of shifting tempos, textures, and mood changes. *Music for Prague* is the first of three 'manifestos', considered the most powerful and significant of Husa's compositions. (The other two manifestos are *The Apotheosis of This Earth*, composed in 1970, and the ballet *The Trojan Women*, 1981.) However, the composer thinks of these works as universal rather than specifically political." — Vivian Perlis, in *Musical America*, 9/90.

Quartet 3 for Strings (1969). 19m Commissioned by the Fine Arts Quartet. Winner, 1969 Pulitzer Prize. *Rec.:* Everest (LP): Fine Arts Quartet. *Pub.:* Associated Music Publishers.
In four movements.

"The *Third String Quartet* employs unusual techniques: bows bouncing on the strings at a rate controlled by the weight of the bow, playing behind the bridge, unusual tremolos, and plucking the strings

---

55 When he left the Conservatory and Academy of Music in Prague—first to Paris, where he studied composition with Nadia Boulanger, Arthur Honegger and others, and then, in 1954, to the United States, to teach at Cornell University.

with the nails instead of with the finger. All of these effects are so well integrated into the fabric of the music that they seem logical extensions of a cohesive musical idea.

" 'In my previous two quartets,' Husa has said, 'I did not preoccupy myself with new sonorities as in the new *Quartet No. 3*. Also, the new composition spotlights the several instruments in rather free forms: the viola in the first movement; cello in the second; the two violins in the third.... I feel that I have been able to find some unusual paths for bow and finger.'

" 'To say it exploits the full color range of four-stringed instruments is to do [the piece] scant justice. It is a work that creates its own logic, tending in each movement to move from complexity to simplicity, as if arguments were being resolved. After the third of the four movements the audience were unable to restrain themselves and burst into applause (Malcolm Rayment, *Glasgow Herald*, August 17, 1971).'

" '[The *Third String Quartet* is] the product of an ingeniously sophisticated musical mind.... of a master craftsman and a musician of singularly individual imagination (Elliott W. Galkin, *Baltimore Sun*, January 11, 1969).' " —James G. Roy, Jr.

Two Sonnets from Michelangelo for Orchestra (1971). 16m *Rec.:* Louisville (LP): The Louisville O, Jorge Mester, cond. *Pub.:* Associated Music Publishers.
3-3-3-2; 4-3-3-1; timp, perc, harp; strings
1. *The night [La notte]*. 2. *To God [A Dio]*.

" A somber and majestic tone poem revealing the composer's mastery of orchestral color. After hearing the *Two Sonnets*, Henry Fogel observed in the *Syracuse New Times* (January 20, 1974) that Husa is 'perhaps one of the finest composers anywhere... who, while making use of devices developed in recent years, still writes music that cuts across all lines and special tastes and simply appeals because it is good music.'

"The wide appeal of Karel Husa's music is attested to by the proliferation of his broadcasts, by festivals of his works in colleges and universities, and by performances of his music in a spectrum ranging from the great symphony orchestras to high-school bands. Elliot Galkin in his *Baltimore Sun* article (quoted above) called Husa 'one of the most interestingly human — and humane — musical minds in this country's recent history.'" —James G. Roy, Jr.

KAMRAN INCE

B.1960, Glendive MT. *Educ.:* Oberlin Cons, Eastman Schl of Music. *Awards:* Prix de Rome, Guggenheim Fellowship, BMI and ASCAP Awards, Rose Prize–Brooklyn PO, MacDowell and Yaddo Fellowships, Lili Boulanger Memorial Prize (1988). *Works incl: Concerto* (pno/orch), *Deep Flight* (orch), piano pieces *(The Blue Journey).*

Composer statement: "I was born in America, but grew up in Turkey where I received my primary education in music.... As a composer I feel very fortunate to be living in the 1980s. No longer are composers bogged down in the so-called 'schools'. No more are we trying to do something absolutely new to shock and in consequence to get attention. Every radical avenue has been explored, it is all behind us. Now the excitement begins....

"It is how you can synthesize all the past together with how you can synthesize aspects of today's modern cultures that starts the process of creating a signature. Since we are no longer following certain predetermined paths, it is thus more valuable if we come up with distinctive voices—those voices are the results of a much wider freedom. Rather than reactions to the avenues of various 'schools', reactions to today's distinct signatures resulting from a synthethis will determine the future of music.

"What I try to accomplish in my music is to create a sense of drama, in which the listener breathes with the music, becomes a part of it, and [as Andrew Porter wrote] is forced to take sides. One way in which I do this is to present every idea in its most pure, concentrated, simple, striking and effective form. A big aid to the drama is the psychological effects caused by how you play with the listener's memory. What determines form for me is time, which in turn is actually memory. It is how you play with the expectations, let downs, satisfactions created by our memory that creates the form. Therefore the most important aspect of form in my music is when and how I present certain vibrant (regardless of character) pivotal sections, when I do bring these sections back, what do I add to them when I bring them back, and when and how I free the music away from them.

"The synthesis that creates my music contains effects of minimalism, primitive (tribal) sounding multi-tonality and atonality, new romanticism, noise, rock, jazz, pop, imitation and synthesis of various nature, urban and industrial sounds."

Cross Scintillations for Piano Four-Hands (1986). 12m *Prem.:* Ian Gaukroger, Sylvia Wang (Purcell Room, London, 1986). *Perf.:* Earplay Ensemble (1987), Eastman Musica Nova Ensemble (1988). *Pub.:* European American. Commissioned by Ian Gaukroger & Sylvia Wang; ded. to the memory of Charles Ives.
1. Sonorous, with sparks. 2. Sparks on fire. 3. Flashing reverberations. 4. Crazy beams. 5. Distant reflections. 6. Resonant transformations. 7. Sonorous echoes. 8. Spattering beams. 9. Beyond Scintillations. 10. Sonorous, final sparks.

"When I was composing *Cross Scintillations*, my thoughts were not directed to the traditional four hand pieces (with four hands divided into accompaniment and primary hands), but rather to the creation of a piece for a super piano, played by a pianist with four hands. Since there are no pianists with four hands, this work must be played by two pianists. Having four hands at my disposal, I wanted to form a rich sound pallet with many colors. This meant playing normally as well as inside the piano. Effects that are achieved inside the piano include plucking strings with fingernails and the metal part of a pencil, dampening strings, etc. In addition, the sostenuto pedal is used throughout, and the players are asked to sing and hum towards the end. All the above effects create an orchestra of sounds emanating from the piano and the pianists.

"*Cross Scintillations* has qualities similar to my orchestral work *Infrared Only* [below], where sections of contrasting styles are repeatedly made to collide. As the piece is dedicated to the memory of Charles Ives, the different sections of this work too are sharply contrasted: song-like sections are followed by atonal sounding sections; pointallistic-serial sounding violent sections are followed by delicate-tonal sections; primitive sounding multi-tonal sections are followed by twisted rock chords; rock chords are suddenly turned into a soft accompaniment for a hymn, etc." — Kamran Ince.

Ebullient Shadows for Orchestra (1986-87). 14m *Prem.:* Minnesota O, Leonard Slatkin, cond., 1987. *Pub.:* European American.
picc-3-3-2 B^b cl-b cl-3-c.bsn; 4-3-3-1; timpani, 3 perc, harp, piano; strings

"When the Minnesota Orchestra asked me to write a work inspired by the romantic music/literature of the 19th century, I felt the idea was great, as my music already employed various 'new-romantic' sounds and effects. I knew I wanted to write an orchestra piece in the 19th century tradition with grand gestres, bold contrasts and vibrant changes of moods. One thing I needed to do was to look at those 'new-romantic' sounds and effects with a magnifying glass.

"The main inspiration behind *Ebullient Shadows* is the passion and sensitivity of the early 19th century romantic literature, primarily Goethe. In this literature every thought is felt in the deepest possible way, with the greatest consequences. The facts and agonies of life are strongly felt: love exists with pain; happiness exists with doubt; despair exists with hope, etc. In parallel to that, *Ebullient Shadows* presents every idea in its strongest and deepest form. These ideas coexist with their opposites: grand passages are followed by very intimate ones; mysterious passages are followed by assuring ones; loud sounds exist with very soft sounds, etc.

"Despite the inspirations of the 19th century, what gave me the idea for the opening (a very mysterious start followed by an instant explosion of grand proportions) is quite futuristic—imagine being in a space ship, turning around a dark planet and suddenly being in front of a planet you have never seen before, with incredible vibrant colors.

"In *Ebullient Shadows* I wanted to create an emotional *tour de force* during which the listener is a part of every measure of the music. What accompanied *Ebullient Shadows* during the premiere given by the Minnesota Orchestra and Leonard Slatkin that summer evening was the worst thunderstorm Minneapolis had for years—perhaps it was appropriate...."—Kamran Ince.

Infrared for Orchestra (1985-86). 20m *Prem.:* Worcester (MA) SO (movt 1); New York Youth S (movt 2), David Allan Miller, cond. *Perf.:* Baltimore SO, David Zinman, cond., 1989 (movt 1). *Pub.:* European American.
picc-2-2-2-b cl-2-c.bsn; 4-3-3-1; timpani, 3 perc, harp; strings
1. *Before Infrared.* 2. *Infrared Only.*

"*Infrared Only* was commissioned by the New York Youth Symphony. The initial idea came to me as I was driving at night from Rochester to New York City. The activities of night, which I could not see but only imagine, made me become fascinated with infrared—a light which enables us to see in the dark. This light represented and evoked a new world of high speed and action for me... The action is partially accomplished by the psychological differences created by sections of contrasting styles repeatedly being collided head on. Other levels of action are to be found within sections—some of them are static, others very aggressive. Listener's ear, which remembers and relates stylistically similar sections, creates different levels of hierarchy. These different levels of hierarchical movement and constant action create a sound that is continuously fresh and full of excitement.

KAMRAN INCE

"After writing and hearing *Infrared Only*, I thought it would be great to counter it with a piece of opposite qualities—calm, slowly developing, more sensitive, and having an ironic, emotional quality. My goal was to write a work that could also be performed individually, as well as with *Infrared Only*. The result was *Before Infrared*, which was finished in July, 1986. This work was first read by the St. Louis Symphony Orchestra and Leonard Slatkin, and later performed by the Worcester (MA) Symphony Orchestra and more recently by the Baltimore Symphony Orchestra with David Zinman in January, 1989.

My Friend Mozart

Kamran Ince

Reprinted from *Changes Faces: New Piano Works by Robert Beaser, Kamran Ince, Stephen Paulus, Tobias Picker, Christopher Rouse, Joseph Schwanter and Alvin Singleton,* with introductions by Maurice Hinson (European American Music Corp. / Helicon Music Corp.).

"*Before Infrared* depicts the journey to a very distant land of Infrared. The shape of the piece is that of a large arch, with the sides of the arch being very slow and quiet (almost motionless) and the middle section being extremely fast and loud. The beginning depicts the location before the voyage and the ensuing preparations. The fast-middle section is the voyage itself and the various locations traveled along the way to the final destination (Infrared). After reaching the final destination, the flow of musical ideas is suddenly obscured and the music returns once again to a very slow and quiet section, remembering and dreaming where it has come from. The work ends with peaceful vibrations of cymbals slowly blending in with the silence.

"The two movements can be performed together, or as separate works. Both were written to achieve maximum effects from the orchestra while requiring minimal technical difficulty." — Kamran Ince.

"*Infrared Only* is a strong, striking composition... a succinct, tautly shaped score, which covers a good deal of ground in ten minutes. If I describe the piece as suggesting Varèse imposed on Mahler, that may seem an odd combination. But *Infrared Only* is an odd — and fascinating — composition. The Varèse sounds are not the sustained 'solid objects' of *Octandre* but similar noises hammered out in repeated chords. There is something here of Bernd Alois Zimmermann's way of bringing extremes into a confrontation where pretenses and politeness are dropped, and naked declarations embarrassing to a gentle-minded listener force him to consider and take sides. I resisted the work initially, but about halfway through was won. In further hearings it has continued to fascinate me.... Kamran Ince is a name to watch for." — Andrew Porter, *The New Yorker*.

My Friend Mozart for Piano (c.1987). *Publ.:* Helicon Music / European American (score).

"*My Friend Mozart* was written in Rome, Italy, on a rainy day in mid-October. I had been reading a lot about Mozart those days, and was very affected by his endless struggle to exist. He was struggling to exist in order to write the incredible works that we listen to today with such ease. I have always felt that Mozart is my friend: somehow, I can always communicate with him. This piece is a celebration of a friendship with Mozart and an expression of my emotional response to his life-long fight to survive." — Kamran Ince.

Performance notes by Maurice Hinson: "This atmospheric piece is based on contrasting textures that produce contrasting sections. The opening section A (measures 1-11) provides a rocking left-hand figuration under a syncopated right-hand melody. Accelerandos and ritards are integrally worked into this section and throughout the piece. Section B (measures 12-23) features repeated chords between the hands that gradually accelerate while getting louder. Measures 24-27 are reminiscent of section A. Section B returns at measures 28-40 at a higher pitch level.

"Measures 41-57, section C, exploits octotonic usage with accents over a gradually descending line. The closing section, measures 58 to the end, contains references to the opening A section, plus short choral-style passages. The free, mildly dissonant, tonal usage centers around E minor and is basically triadic.

"Even though this piece is short, Ince displays excellent motivic development, balance, and overall shaping of lines. Much pedal use provides color throughout, and an elegiac mood hovers over most of the piece. The title is thought-provoking—maybe referring to the triadic harmony and melodic style. Who knows, perhaps Mozart would have composed in this style if he were living today."

Waves of Talya for Six Players (1988). 16m *Prem.*: Terra Australis Ensemble (North American New Music Festival, Buffalo NY, 1989) *Pub.*: European American. Commissioned by Koussevitzky Foundation, ded. to the memory of Serge and Natalie Koussevitzky.
flute/piccolo, B^b clarinet, piano, percussion, violin, cello

"One of the composers I admire the most is Brahms. The driving force behind his music for me is anger and passion, to a degree I can not find in any other composer. The main inspiration for my chamber music is also anger and passion. When I write for chamber groups, I find those two feelings the most irresistible ones, and *Waves of Talya* is a good example of what can result.

"Talya is the old name of Antalya, the beautiful Mediterranean port city of Southern Turkey. As a child I went there on vacations, and was always fascinated by its powerful waves, and the sound effects of the pebbles moving with the tides created after the crashing of the waves. The inspiration behind many of the sections of *Waves of Talya* are those waves of Antalya, their shapes, movements, and their sounds.

"*Waves of Talya* could be described as being in three continuous movements. The first and last are dominated by the endless poundings and after-effects of the waves. This endless energy of the waves calms down in the second movement, where the sea becomes very gentle and motionless. The peaceful calmness of the second movement is suddenly broken by the arrival of the third movement, again containing the endless energy of poundless waves and their after-effects."—Kamran Ince.

BEN JOHNSTON

B. 1926, Macon GA. *Educ.:* College of William and Mary, Cincinnati Cons of Music, Univ of CA, Mills College. *Taught at:* Univ of IL. Guggenheim Fellowship. *Works incl: Calamity Jane to Her Daughter* (s/small ens), Carmilla (opera), chamber music (*Diversion, Duo* [2 vlns], *Lament, 12 Partials*), choral works (*Mass, On Love*), dance scores (*Gambit*), *Night* (cantata), piano works (*Aubade, Celebration, Etude, Satires, Sonata*).

Composer statement: "When I was eleven years old a friend of my parents took me to a lecture at Wesleyan Conservatory in Macon, Georgia. An acoustician was speaking of the debt owed to the German acoustician Hermann von Helmholtz by the school of impressionist composers. He focused upon Claude Debussy, at that time a favorite of mine. Demonstrating with a monochord and giving the Greek tradition of tuning, he showed that the combination of awakened scientific interest and radical rejection of academic musical traditions produced a new conception of harmony.

"I never forgot that lecture and many years later as a freshman student at the College of William and Mary, I elected to do my English term paper on the physics of music. That was when I actually read Helmholtz and later writers on the same subject. World War Two intervened followed by about two years self-exile as a dance-band pianist, after which I returned to William and Mary and completed my degree. It was in my first year of graduate study, at Cincinnati Conservatory of Music, that a musicologist brought Harry Partch's *Genesis of a Music* to my attention. I was fascinated and wrote to him care of University of Wisconsin Press. The letter was forwarded to Partch in Gualala, California, and we began a correspondence which led eventually to my going to California to work as an apprentice in his studio. I was with him for about six months learning his way of making music and helping him record some of his works. When his health compelled him to close the studio and move to the Bay Area, I enrolled at Mills College to study with Darius Milhaud. This led in less than a year to my taking a position teaching at the University of Illinois where I remained for almost thirty-five years.

"It was almost ten years before I was able to devote myself to music in just intonation, the natural outcome of working with Partch. I had to establish real credibility as a composer before performers could be induced to attempt the tuning tasks I wanted to set them. It was only after I had received a Guggenheim Fellowship in composition that this option opened for me.

"At first my works reconciled serial composition with just tuning but demanded no higher overtone relations than triadic music. After about ten years of this I moved to include higher partial relations bit by bit, and at the same time radically simplified the surface impression which my music presented to a listener. Microtones were a by-product of the tuning, not a primary goal, but I became known as a microtonal composer. My first interest has always been in the acoustical purity of intervals and the resulting structures. This was always the basis of my work.

"I believe that unless the very substructure of music is itself a symbol of what one wishes to convey in composing music, the effectiveness of the music as art is seriously compromised. To wish to clarify the complex by precise and uncompromising accuracy in relationships says something about one's attitude to human life in general."

Journeys for Contralto, Chorus and Orchestra (1987). *Texts:* folksong, Carl Sandburg. *Prem.:* Karen Brunson (contr), Springfield (IL) SO, Kenneth Keisler, cond. *Pub.:* Smith Publications.

Quartet 2 for Strings (1964). *Prem.:* Composers Quartet. *Pub.:* Smith Publications.
In 3 movements.

Quartet 3 for Strings (1967). *Prem.:* Concord Quartet. *Pub.:* Smith Publications.
In one movement.

Quartet 4 (Amazing Grace) for Strings (1973). 10m *Comm. & prem.:* Fine Arts Quartet (Leonard Sorkin, Abram Loft, vlns, Bernard Zaslav, vla, George Sopkin, vc). *Recs.:* Gasparo (Stereo LP) GS-205: Fine Arts Quartet; Electra/Nonesuch (LP & CD): Cronos Quartet. *Pub.:* Smith Publications.

Sonnets of Desolation for Chorus (SSAATTBB) (1980). *Text:* G. M. Hopkins. *Comm., ded. & prem.:* New Swingle Singers. *Pub.:* Smith Publications.

NOTES ON STRING QUARTETS 3 AND 4: "Ben Johnston studied with Milhaud, as well as with John Cage and Harry Partch. His *String Quartet No. 4* could be subtitled 'Variations on "Amazing Grace"'. The familiar American hymn-tune is first stated in more or less parallel organum over a gentle countermelody. The variations run a gamut of musics, including a gamelan and a hint of the blues. Because of its familiar materials and procedures, as well as its brevity, the work will have great appeal to a wide variety of audiences. If performed with the composer's *Third String Quartet*, the combined work, with an obligatory silence of 60 to 120 seconds intervening, is entitled *Crossings*." — Mary Wallace Davidson, in *American Music*, Summer 1983.

NOTES ON SELECTED WORKS BY BEN JOHNSTON:[56] "Ben Johnston is a Southern composer, with roots in 12-tone music, who became one of the early proteges of just-intonation instrument builder Harry Partch. As such, Johnston's music represents a remarkable attempt to fuse 12-tone writing and even strict serialism with just intonation, additionally complicated by the subtle coloring of Southern hymnody ever in the background. These heterogenous influences have led to a wide variety of music, and to a plethora of innovative composing methods designed to fuse unrelated ideas into a viable, very personal language.

"In his early string quartets, for example, Johnston created *rows of pitch areas*, within which each pitch could take on a different tuning dependent on context; an idea reminiscent of (though it never sounds like) the *ragas* of Indian music. His *Second* and *Third String Quartets* (1964 and '67 respectively) use a 53-pitch-per-octave scale drawn from justly-tuned perfect fifths and major thirds, that is, ratios of 3:2 and 5:4. The *Second Quartet's* dissonant opening movement is a structuralist tour-de-force. Each of its 54 measures begins on the next higher pitch than its predecessor, returning to the opening C at measure 54. The movement is also an arch form, built from 5/8 and 8/8 measures which give a sense of expanding and contracting rhythm. Movement 2, hymnlike despite its careful pitch structuring, emphasizes consonant intervals, and is marked by a melodic motive descending and ascending through thirds and fifths. The third movement is an exact palindrome, most active in the middle, built on a 31-note row. It is rare among Johnston's works in that its microtones take the form of brief pitch bendings and glissandos.

"*Quartet Nr, 3* is in one mercurial movement. Subtleties of tuning are emphasized by relegating pitch class to different registers in a Webernesque manner. For instance, within the first few measures several Cs an octave above middle C are heard, notated variously as C, D^{bb-}, $B^{\#}$, C+, and C-. Within one pitch class, the pitch wavers with each occurrence, and the subtle effect is very audible if one is attuned to it. This atonal yet often consonant movement is intended to be followed, after a one- to two-minute pause, by *Quartet Nr. 4*, the pair to be jointly entitled *Crossings*. The *Fourth Quartet*, perhaps Johnston's most popular work, is a theme and variations on the hymn 'Amazing Grace'. Between them the two quartets mark a juncture in Johnston's work at which the patterning of overtones veers in a more intuitive direction.

---

56 Prepared for this publication by critic Kyle Gann. Mr. Gann is the author of the forthcoming, authoritative book *The Music of Ben Johnston* (Excelsior Music Publishing Company). —Ed.

Measures 1-18 showing enneagram structure of the second movement of *String Quartet Nr, 2*. Copyright © 1985 by Smith Publications.

"*Sonnets of Desolation* (1980) was Johnston's first work to venture as far as the 13th overtone, and it defines a new choral idiom of remarkably sweet consonance and fluidly shifting harmonic colors. Based on four Gerard Manley Hopkins sonnets about spiritual crisis, the piece moves between tonal centers with a sensitivity that makes even complex overtone harmonies chorally feasible (if still exacting). 'I wake and feel the fell of dark, not day' intones its poem in brooding recitative over hummed open fifths, while 'That nature is a Heraclitean fire' achieves a unique (for chorus) calliope effect with its sliding phrases of 7 and 5 beats over a hocketing scat-singing accompaniment. Johnston follows the rhythm of Hopkins's texts gracefully in one of the loveliest, smoothest choral works since Schoenberg.

Quartet No. 3

Microtonal version of C in *String Quartet Nr. 3*. Copyright © 1985 by Smith Publications.

"Traces of Southern harmony rarely appear in Johnston's work as explicitly as in his 1987 choral and orchestral piece *Journeys*. Like the *Fourth String Quartet*, *Journeys* is based on a well-known song, the 'Mountaineer Love Song' sometimes known as 'He's Gone Away'. The orchestral introduction is a stirring essay in modal counterpoint, made more vibrant by the pure-overtone consonance of its tuning. The first part's closing chorus — 'I'm going away for to stay a little while, but I'm coming back, if I go ten thousand miles' — is in perfect, flowing Southern choral style. Part 2 is a setting of section 13 from Carl Sandburg's *The People, Yes*, with an extended contralto solo and all pitches drawn from overtones of either C or E. One listens almost in vain, though, for the tuning to sound peculiar; deeply-felt and intensely consonant, *Journeys* contains not a measure that sounds dry or cerebral." — Kyle Gann, 10/90.

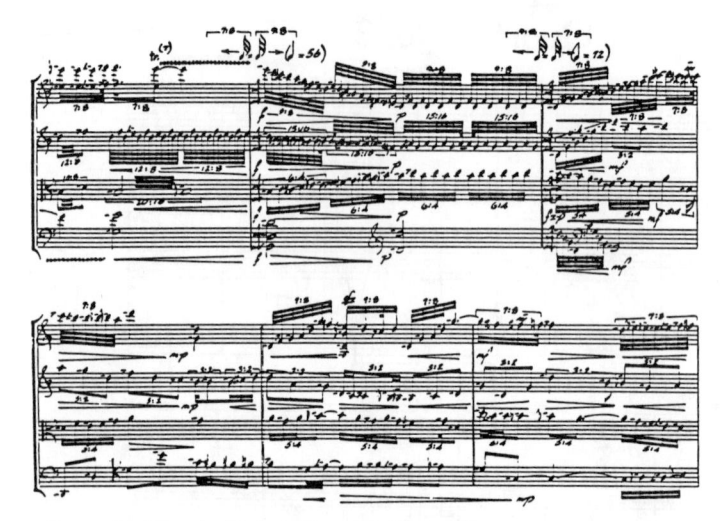

Complexities in *String Quartet Nr. 4,* first system on page 15 of the score. Copyright © 1985 by Smith Publications.

Nested 3/2 rhythmic relationships in the second variation of *String Quartet Nr. 4.* Copyright © 1985 by Smith Publications.

NOTES ON "PROPORTIONALITY" AND JOHNSTON'S *FOURTH QUARTET*:
"Ben Johnston's *Fourth String Quartet*... makes use, as do his other recent compositions, of the concept of proportionality, theoretical aspects of which Johnston himself has outlined in this journal....[57]

"The essence of proportionality is that the relationships between the elements of a system are determined by comparing the values (frequency, duration, etc.) of the elements themselves to each other as ratios, and not by reference to any equally segmented linear scale or measurement. Using pitch organization to illustrate, the major third in equal temperament can be envisioned as encompassing four equal units of a linear scale; but the proportion 5:4 is a phenomenon sovereign of the ever present possibility of subdivision. This phenomenon may be tuned, when heard aurally, without reference to any other phenomena by the elimination of beats (the pulsations to which we are so accustomed in the tone quality of the piano).

"The recognition of the concept of proportionality in reference to pitch means that the creation of any equal tempered scale (no matter how many tones per octave) is not possible, because intervals from an octave down to the most miniscule microtone subdivide proportionally into unequal segments. Moreover, as soon as only three tones are present in a system it may be necessary to shift slightly the pitch levels of these tones in the event that they are successively considered to be most directly proportional to more than one member of the system.

"The *Fourth Quartet*... utilizes proportionality so comprehensively in structuring various parameters of the compositional fabric that in comparison to earlier examples of its use Johnston would appear to have made significant applicational expansions of the principle; the quartet most fully exemplifies his theories. An integral part of the increased importance of proportionality is that the form of the work is a theme and [9] variations modeled on a Beethovenian ideal, and the extraordinary compass of the events contained within this structure is a provocative demonstration of the dynamic vitality of the proportional concept itself. Furthermore, the astonishing diversity of the textures coalesced in the course of these variations enables one to view with increased understanding Johnston's other recent compositions, including some works which at first glance might appear to be contradictions of the microtonal intricacies to be found in his well-known *Second String Quartet* (1964).

---

57 *Perspectives of New Music* See in particular 'Scalar Order as a Compositional Device', PNM vol II No. 2 (1964), pp.56-76; also 'Proportionality and Expanded Musical Pitch Relations', PNM vol V No. 1 (1966), pp.112-20.

"A false impression of stylistic contrareity in his production could result from mistakenly believing that Johnston's principal desire has been to divide the octave into increasingly smaller segments or to add microtonal extensions to the equal tempered twelve-tone system. Such an assumption would miss Johnston's intention entirely for his primary concern is to use systems that are proportionally (and also acoustically) logical, *whether such systems contain few or many elements*. In fact, the vast gamut of possible systems encompassed by the concept of proportionality has been of very great interest to Johnston, and he has desired the possibility of creating simple textures using but a few proportional divisions of the octave as much as the possibility of creating more complex textures using a great number of proportional divisions of the octave.

"The number of tones which will make up a proportional system is related to two factors: the amount of chromaticism employed and the number and size of the prime generative integers utilized in forming proportions.[58] By controlling these two variables a composer can have access to a spectrum of pitch systems of immeasurable dimensions; too large, in fact, ever to be completely explored.

"Utilization of a portion of this spectrum in the creation of highly diverse textures is a procedure which has already proven fruitful for Johnston. The *Second String Quartet*, though using no prime generative integers larger than five, is pervasively chromatic, and includes complex passages containing as many as 53 tones per octave. In his *Mass* (1972), Johnston expands the intervallic system by including the prime generative integer seven, but limits chromaticism by composing with 'diatonic' modal scales, thereby creating much less overall complexity than in the *Second String Quartet*. A theoretical approach somewhat similar to that of the *Mass* was used in writng music for the off-Broadway production, *Carmilla* (1970); however, at the time of its staging no electronic instrument was available which would provide for the incorporation of appropriate microtonal

---

[58] A prime integer cannot be divided by an integer except itself or 1: examples are 2, 3, 5, 7, 11, etc. Prime integers can generate an infinite number of integers which are their multiples; thus the prime integers 2, 3, and 5 could generate 4, 6, 9, 10, 12, 15, 16, 18,... [infinity]. In a proportional musical system the number of generations involved is directly related to the amount of chromaticism employed.

tunings.[59] *Third String Quartet* (1967) is a serial composition using 53 divisions of the octave, and in one elaborate passage the starting pitch of each successive row moves up one degree in a 53 tone microtonal scale. The *Fourth Quartet* explores the potential of fluctuating proportional complexity; it uses as few as five proportional divisions of the octave and as many as twenty-two.

"A notable change in Johnston's recent work is a shift from serial to centric applications of his proportional concepts.[60] The partially serial *Second String Quartet* and the wholly serial *Third String Quartet* represent the application of proportionality to a compositional technique Johnston was actively employing at the time he began to utilize proportional intervals. The centric organization of *Carmilla* and the *Mass* was partially suggested by the hypothesized musical naivete of the prospective audiences for these works, and the accessibility of their exterior is calculated, though with different intentions for each work. The unpretentious elegance of the *Mass* is a genuine expression of Johnston's religious optimism, whereas the ingratiating tunefulness of *Carmilla* is a seduction loaded with irony.

"The seriality or centricity of these particular works would seem to be the result of *ad hoc* considerations; however, one problematic aspect of employing serial methodology in combination with proportional intervals may have become evident to the reader—the saturated chromaticism implicit in the serial method produces a very large number of tones per octave even when using simple proportional intervals. If serial procedures are employed with ratios containing integers up to and including five, 53 or more tones per octave will probably be required. If this is the case, imagine the number of tones per octave that might be generated in a serial compositon utilizing ratios containing the larger integers of seven, eleven, and

---

59 Johnston recently gained access to a *Scalatron*, an electronic instrument manufactured by the Motorola Company, which, while not easily providing for the comma correction one might often desire, does allow the convenient formation of an extremely large number of fixed scale forms in various precise tunings.

60 The use of the term 'centric' is a deliberate avoidance of the word 'tonal', which has in general become too closely associated with functional triadic harmony to be used in other contexts without creating misconceptions. The term centric is intended to imply systems with definite pitch hierarchies, of which functional harmony is but one example.

thirteen.[61] If one accepts the premise that in almost every instance that a new relationship is incorporated into a composition many new pitches will be required to fulfill instances of that function *exactly*, then the total number of relationships designated is a consideration of some importance.[62]

"Some form of centric organization, by limiting to a certain extent the total number of intervallic functions required, can serve to moderate the total number of pitch classes which will be produced by the introduction of larger prime generative integers into the ratios used in the compositional process. As Johnston is beginning to introduce larger such integers into the systems of his recent compositions, desiring to explore relationships generated by these integers, a turn away from the pervading chromaticism of serialism may partially represent a judicious avoidance of hyper-microtonalism at this particular stage of his work. Probably more important is Johnston's growing experience with proportionality as an organizational technique, which, being ultimately hierarchical, simply functions most effectively for him in tree-structure morphology, rather than serial or indeterminate morphology.

"The *Fourth Quartet*, with all its variety and complexity, is centric throughout. It is perhaps more dependent upon proportional organization for its internal coherence than any of Johnston's previous compositions. The difference in compositional method between the serial *Third Quartet* and the centric *Fourth Quartet* makes the prefatory note to the *Fourth* of especial interest: this instruction states that the *Third Quartet* may be played before the *Fourth*, separated by a long silence, to create a two-movement entity. This pairing is another indication of the catholicity of Johnston's recent use of proportionality, and demonstrates that in his view the undeniable stylistic contrast which separates these two quartets is not as significant as a primal conception of order which unites them.

"Though not so titled by Johnston, the one-movement *Fourth Quartet* is in theme and variations form: the theme is the traditional American hymn, 'Amazing Grace'. The use of a hymn so replete with extramusical religious and nationalistic associations invites com-

---

61 Johnston is very much interested in the potentialities of these higher integers, and is presently helping to develop a computer program which would systematically explore them.

62 In equal temperament a finite number of pitches (such as twelve) is able to represent more intervals than are actually present because one's mind habitually assumes that the interval heard is an out of tune version of a simpler (in tune) interval (proportion) appropriate to the context. Thus on hearing C to G on the piano, our usual assumption is that the interval intended was a perfect fifth, 3:2, which in actuality is not the interval that the instrument produced. Nonetheless, despite this sanity-preserving graciousness, the ear *can* hear the difference by comparison.

parison with Ives and others who have incorporated indigenous religious, folk, and patriotic melodies into their work. A connection with Ives seems particularly apt in that the texture of this quartet appears simultaneously to stem from the hymn and to transcend it — this transcendental atmosphere ultimately transforming our perception of the hymn itself and making distinction among the original substance, the transformation, and the transformed imagery difficult. This fusion of borrowed material and seemingly heterogeneous compositional technique into a total conception of unified effect similarly imports to many of the works of Ives a remarkable aura of idiosyncratic profundity....

"Viewing the quartet as a whole, the controlled and fluctuating complexity of the work's proportional system can be seen as being central to the dynamic arch formed by the overall structure. Gradual changes in the number and size of the prime generative integers, coupled with rhythmic mirrorings of pitch proportions, enable Johnston to create an extremely wide ranging set of variations which are all part of the same conceptual system.

"The rhythmic innovations of the quartet are perhaps its most striking technical aspect. While the 'metric modulations' of Eliott Carter and the serialization of rhythm by a number of composers are both related in some way to Johnston's procedures, correlation of pitch and rhythmic structures is achieved in this work in several strikingly original ways. And as a concept, the level on which pitch and rhythmic organization is correlated is probably more akin to the patterning methods of late Medieval and early Renaissance composers than to any contemporary influence.

"This quartet as a whole presents interesting contrasts between innovative and traditional ideas. The form of the work, a theme and variations based on a simple and well-known melody, seems somewhat anachronistic, while the technique of using fluctuating proportional complexity is so novel as to be almost unprecedented. The rhythmic manipulations of the quartet are even more remarkably innovative, but the pitch organization is ultimately much more traditional than that of the majority of works of the last two decades [c.1955-75]. As a performance medium the string quartet is basically treated quite conservatively, yet the demands made upon the players' performing skills are forbidding precisely because of their very uniqueness.

"This complex blend of old and new in a unique and fascinating combination is an intriguing aspect of Johnston's music, and perhaps because of this alloy when one hears even the most unconventional passages in his compositions there is a notable lack of a sense of esotericism. Whatever the reason, his music seems to function in a way the ear is prone to comprehend.

"Johnston's attitude toward the past is quite different from that of his mentor in the development of proportional pitch systems, Harry Partch. Partch, the sequestered pioneer of a monodic style based upon proportional tunings, was one of the most unique composers this country has produced. The singularity of his musical speech and the fact that most of his music is written for instruments of his own design and making has prevented any wide dissemination of his work, but the challenge of his ideas remains a haunting one. Johnston's quotation in Variation V must be regarded as an homage to Partch, both the man and the composer, with whom Johnston worked for a time. Yet the contrasts between Partch and Johnston are dramatic: Partch's writings reveal a genuine revolutionary whose attitude toward most of the traditions of Western music was one of disdain or indifference, whereas Johnston has a deep respect and even love for a very wide range of Western music from the avant-garde to the Middle Ages.

"This rather fundamental difference in orientation toward the past sets apart their creative efforts: where Partch attempted almost singlehanded to create a unique body of music, in opposition to most of the recorded history of Western music, Johnston is seeking to revitalize certain aspects of a heritage for which he has much esteem, but which he feels is at present being restricted by obeisance to a tuning compromise which we (or at least he) can no longer afford to make." — Randall Shinn, from "Ben Johnston's *Fourth String Quartet*", in *Perspectives of New Music*, Spring-Summer 1977.

WILFRED JOSEPHS

B. 1927, Newcastle-upon-Tyne (England). *Educ.*: Guildhall Schl of Music. Leverhulme Scholarship, Internatl Composing Competition (Milan); composer-in-residence, Univ of WI, Roosevelt Univ. *Works incl.*: ballet (*Equus, La Répétition de Phèdre*), choral works (*Tenebrae*), concertos (brass bnd, cl, db, ob, orch, pno, 4 pnos, vc, vla, vln), operas (*Alice in Wonderland, Rebecca, Through the Looking Glass*), overtures, *Papageno Variations* (ww sextet), 4 string quartets, sonatas (db, cl, fl, pno, vc, vln), 10 symphonies. Music of Wilfred Josephs available from Orpheus Publications.

A note on the composer: "Josephs now ranks as one of our most fertile and imaginative composers. Nearly everyone in [Britain] has heard his work at some time or other on account of his readiness to write incidental music for radio and television, but few are familiar with his output for the concert-hall of over 130 opus numbers. Joseph's music parallels in many ways that of Malcolm Arnold and Gordon Jacob in scale, style, and scope, but his natural eclecticism covers a formidable range of ground and [there] are many guises of his musical persona." — Bret Johnson, in *Tempo: A Quarterly Review of Modern Music*, Nr. 148, 3/84.

Concerto for Brass, Op. 88 (1974). 14m *Ded. & prem.*: National Youth Brass Band, Geoffrey Brand, cond. *Rec.*: Trax Classique TRXCD 114: London Collegiate Brass, James Stobart, cond.
1 s E^b cornet, 9 B^b cornets (4 solo), 1 flugelhorn, 3 E^b horns (1 solo), 3 B^b baritones, 4 trombones, 1 b trombone, euphonium, 2 E^b bass tubas, 2 B^b bass tubas, 4 percussion

"A highly virtuosic piece, requiring tremendous technique and musicianship. Subtitled 'in variation form', the work has 25 continuous variations, the basic form being:

> Variation 1
> Theme
> Variations 2-24
> Finale (Variation 25)

"Structurally, the *Concerto* bears a striking resemblance to Rachmaninoff's *Rhapsody on a Theme by Paganini*. (Many of Josephs' finest compositions make use of an organically-developed variation-form.)

"The work begins with commanding cornets (variation 1). The theme marked *leggiero e delicato* is then picked out in a slow tempo by tiny staccato semiquavers. Variations 2-5 treat the material as a passacaglia. A new theme on solo horn is introduced, growing into a full-blown march. The opening phrase returns in variations 12 and 13, as the mood grows more serious in character. A lightly scored 'Intermezzo' (variation 19) leads to the beautiful variation 20 (*poco adagio*), with a theme for solo horn over quiet trombone chords. Growing out of a jolly tune announced by the flugelhorn and first bass, variation 21 serves as a trio. As the excitement builds, a climax is reached at variation 24, as all of the themes combine in a march which even Sousa might have been proud of. The Finale (variation 25) briefly alludes to variation 3; the theme is restated before a succession of reminiscences bring this exhilarating piece to its resplendent finish." — Dana Perna.

Concerto 1 for Piano and Orchestra, Op. 48 (1965). 27m *Prem.*: Yonty Solomon (pno), Royal PO, Charles Groves, cond.
Orch: 2-2 (1 Engl hn)-2 (1 b cl)-2 (1 cbsn); 4-3-3-0; timp, perc, harp; strings

"Although Wilfred Josephs wryly notes that he has begun about 20 concerti since his student days, he once admitted that:

> For a period of about seven years, the piano was [an] anathema to me. I found it uninteresting and unresponsive. My feelings changed when I was commissioned to compose my *Piano Sonata No. 2* and gradually the urge to write a concerto began to set the creative juices flowing.

"He was encouraged by his parents-in law, Henrietta and Samuel Wisbey, who also commissioned the *Concerto 1* begun in January 1965 and completed 20 October of the same year. The work was premiered in London 5 March 1967, as a part of the Camden Festival, under the direction of Sir Charles Groves; since then Josephs has composed many works for the piano — including a second concerto.
"The composer continues:

> During that period, my work was usually built on a single theme heralded at the outset. This concerto utilizes two such themes which provide all the melodic material by a process of continuous variation (a legacy of my one-time interest in the 12-note system). It is also quite tonal in parts. An element of struggle as well as the opposing element of 'playing together' have become so much a part of the piano concerto that I needed two sets of ideas, or themes, on which to work.

The first movement begins slowly on low strings announcing the first subject. Before the second subject, the tempo quickens with a fanfare-like episode (in the piano part) based on the sound of a wood pigeon (I believe) which took lease in our garden for the entire summer of 1965 and was dubbed 'the piano concerto bird'. The second subject arrives on the piano, the orchestra sustaining the harmonies. Thenceforward, the whole work develops from these two themes.

The second movement begins very slowly and develops into a fast scherzo with a slow ending, making it a ternary A-B-A form. The final movement is a Passacaglia which appears at first to be very slow, but, this is an illusion. The movement is in 3/4 time, marked 'vivo' with the metronome marking of ♩ = 180. While the passacaglia theme in the lower instruments is generally written in dotted halves, the running figures occuring above must be executed virtually as fast as possible."

— Dana Perna.

Doubles for Two Pianos, Four Hands (1970-73). 25m *Rec.:* Novello (Stereo LP) NVL 104 (also tape, NVLC 104; CD, NVLCD 104)/Harmonia Mundi: Heidi Hendrickx, Levente Kende.

"Subtitled *Twice 22 Doubles on Two Themes by Two Composers for Two Pianos*. The themes were taken from Mozart's A minor Rondo for piano, K. 511 of 1787, and Rameau's *'La Poule'* ('The Hen') from *Nouvelles suites de pieces de clavencin* of 1728. Since 'doubles' is an old-fashioned term for variations, this particular work is full of *double-entendres*.

"The two themes are presented independently. As the work unfolds, each theme begins to take on the character of the other (as can be heard in the 'pecking' quality of one of its variations). While the composition overall has many passages which are quite humorous and witty, there is nothing glib about *Doubles*. Many of the variations flow quite directly and simply into the ones that follow. Since Josephs' conception is so logical, no notes are wasted in its nearly half-hour playing time. By the end of the work a number of other composers and/or original themes have also passed in review. On this point Joseph acknowledges the influence of his English contemporary, Robin Holloway:

I'd got to know Holloway's Schumann pieces just when I was working on *Doubles*, so, when a tune wanted to turn into 'Over the Sea to Skye', or the *Hammerklavier* or Debussy's 'Golliwog's Cakewalk', I didn't stop—I just let it

happen."
—Dana Perna.

"The English composer Wilfred Josephs is one of those facile and versatile eclectics who can toss of a melodic TV theme for *Masterpiece Theatre* just after completing a knotty, extravagant post-serial score like the *Fourth Symphony* of 1967-1970 or this astonishingly original work for two pianos entitled—appropriately enough and allowing for every manner of punning paranomasia on the concepts of enfoldings and mirrorings—*Doubles* or, to give it its full and humorously fulsome name—*Twice 22 Doubles on Two Themes by Two Composers for Two Pianos*.

"This remarkable piece is quite simply the best new work for two pianos this listener has encountered in ages, ranking right up there with the contemporary classics of Bartók, Stravinsky, Hindemith, and Persichetti sonatas as well as the numerous lighter pieces by Milhaud, starting with *Scaramouche*. What Josephs has done in this 1970-1973 effort is to take two rather distinct and stodgy well-known themes from the Baroque-Classical era (Mozart's A-Minor *Rondo* and Rameau's '*La Poule*') and used them as the scaffolding from which to hang a tremendously allusive, perversely ironic, and exhilaratingly complex series of continuous variations of exceptional ingenuity. In fact, almost the whole history of Western art-music from Perotinus to Satie seems to be encapsulated in this sometimes kinky, always kinetic work, as the two themes are intertwined, undermined, deconstructed, and reintegrated into a musical kaleidoscope of enormous diversity of mood and strength of facture. At one particularly delicious point—after an eruption of dissonant obstreperousness—the music takes a deep breath and teasingly shifts into a 3/4 berceuse rhythm *à la 'gymnopedie'* which gradually works itself up into a paroxysm of *La Valse*-like ferocity. But repeated hearings will reveal—to each individual pair of ears—new facets of this hugely various and inventive conception—a quodlibet which seemingly has something in it for everyone.... *Doubles* is a work to seek out and reckon with."—Paul A. Snook, in *Fanfare: The Magazine for Serious Record Collectors*, 3-4/90.

Requiem for Bass-Baritone, Chorus, String Quintet and Orchestra, Op. 39 (1963).
60m *Prem.:* La Scala, Nino Sanzogno, cond. *Other perf.:* Chicago SO. *Rec:* Unicorn-Kanchana DKP 9032: Robert Dawe (bar), Adelaide String Quartet, Adelaide Chorus, Adelaide SO, David Measham, cond. *Pub.:* Weinberger.
Orch: 2 picc-2 Eng hn-2 b cl-2; 4-2-3-0; 4 perc, harp; strings (incl solo qnt of 2 vlns, vla, 2 vcs)

Part I. 1. *Requiescant* (string qt). 2. *Yitgadal* (chorus, orch). 3. *Yehey Sh'mey Raba* (double chorus, orch). Part II. 4. *Yitbarach* (b-bar, orch). 5. *Lacrimosa* (string qnt). Part III. 6. *Yehee Shem* (b-bar, double chorus, orch). 7. *De Profundis* (orch). 8. *Ezru Meyim* (b-bar, double chorus, orch). Part IV. 9. *Monumentum* (string qnt). 10. *Ohseh Shalom* (b-bar, chorus, orch).

"Wilfred Josephs' *Requiem*, Op. 39, won the First International Competition for Symphonic Composition of the City of Milan and La Scala in December, 1963. This award helped unequivocally to establish Dr. Josephs as a composer of international repute. Two years later, on 28/29 October 1965, the *Requiem* received its world premiere at La Scala, which was followed by numerous other performances and a recording. In 1972 — when this piece lasting nearly an hour was presented three times by the Chicago Symphony Orchestra — Carlo Maria Giulini dubbed it 'the most important work by a living composer'.

"These successes transformed Josephs' life and career since, until then, he had earned his living entirely through the practice of dentistry. The *Requiem* represents the composer at a crucial stage in his stylistic development, too. The teaching of Max Deutsch, with whom he had studied in Paris (1958), had helped the young composer to assimilate the lessons of the Second Viennese School. He had come to a realization that, with Schoenberg's 'emancipation of the dissonance' long achieved, there was no further need to exclude tonal structures from music as if the latter were only potential sources of a kind of musical infection! Although the formal organization of his *Requiem* is, in fact, based on techniques which stem from the 12-tone method, they are no longer narrowly 12-tone in character.

"The arrest and trial of Adolf Eichmann in the late 1950s reawakened Josephs' grief and horror at the sufferings of Jews during the Second World War. In 1961, between February and June, he composed a string quintet titled *Requiescant*, in memory of those who had perished. He later conceived the idea of incorporating this three-movement piece in a choral work which would be a setting of the Kaddish traditionally recited by Jewish mourners as a part of the liturgy. At the same time, the choice of text was not meant to restrict the work solely as a memorial to the Jewish dead — for the theme of the work is universal.

"There is only one fast movement in the *Requiem*, 'Yehey Sh'mey Raba' (Nr. 3). This also has more loud music than any of the other movements. In general, just as the dynamics of the *Requiem* are prevailingly quiet, so are its tempi. In addition to the six vocal numbers and three *Requiescant* movements for string quintet, there is one purely orchestral movement, Nr. 7, entitled *'De Profundis'*.

"Bernard Jacobson observes (1986):

> If the restraint of this *Requiem's* grief is as noteworthy as its eloquence, the explanation perhaps lies in a particular characteristic of the Kaddish text: nowhere does it mention death or the dead. It is a funeral prayer concerned only with life and with the glorification of God, an apparent paradox especially apt for the many-layered expressive powers of music.
> — Dana Perna.

"The music has an unusual emotional character and structural design: this is partly due to the fact that it is really two works welded together, incorporating as it does the earlier (1961) *Quintet in Three Movements for Strings* (opus 32), [into the] *Requiescant pro Defunctis Iudaeis*. There can be no doubt that the *Requiem* is the most personal musical statement Josephs has yet made, and that it is a work of the greatest integrity and sincerity. The composer eschews all trace of outward pomp, contrivance, and artifice unless it is germane to the spiritual message of the music and text. Rarely have I heard music of such inwardness; and yet the still, small voice of calm is perceived at its heart despite the overwhelming weight of lamentation and grief which the austere coloration and prevalent leanness of texture bring to bear. The result is a Jewish liturgical work; all the more of an enigma to Gentile ears, not only unused to Hebrew, but also the the Jewish attitude toward death, as expressed in the dignified obeisance of the Kaddish text. Yet the work does not have a strong traditional 'Jewish' feel about it in the way of, for example, Bloch's music: a pining for the homeland — no, this sparseness, especially in the quintet sections, is closer to the Hebraic style of Schoenberg. The other essential element is an 'Englishness' notably close to that of Holst, whose *Ode to Death* is echoed in the cool woodwind choirs which frequently complement the voices. So here we have a piece which commands attention on several different levels, despite its prevailing introspection, and it was no doubt these characteristics which commended the work to such notables as Ghedini and Guilini and led to its 1965 premiere at La Scala.

"The opening *Yitgadal* section is germinal, but at the intensely slow pace which characterizes the whole piece. The one sudden burst of sound, *'U-ve-chayeh dee chol yisrael'*, recedes as fast as it appeared and it is *Yehey Sh'mey Raba* ('Let his name be blessed') which is the most (and really only) outwardly dramatic movement, a tightly-held ostinato for chorus and orchestra, creating an incantatory effect. The only section for bass, baritone, and orchestra, *Yitbarach*, is the most mystical and remote; whereas the overpowering 'Amen' in *Yehee Shem* is just one of the many startling *sforzandi* which crop up when least expected. There is one short movement for orchestra alone, *De Profundis*, a slow procession. *Ezri Meyim*, the eighth movement, has some unusual dynamics, especially for chorus, with diminuendi on high notes and other unorthodox musical emphases on the words. The string quintet's three movements are evenly spaced, and the work's final movement, *Ohseh Shalom*, is whispered in an undertone by the chorus until the sudden blast of 'Kol Yisrael' and a final *sforzando* for full orchestra before the music fades into silence." — Bret Johnson, in *Tempo: A Quarterly Review of Modern Music*, Nr. 153, 6/85.

Gail Kubik

B. 1914, Coffeyville OK; d. 1984, Los Angeles CA. *Educ.:* Eastman Schl, Harvard Univ. *Taught at:* Scripps College, Claremont Grad Schl, Teachers College. Staff composer, NBC. *Works incl.:* choral works, film scores (*documentaries, Gerald MacBoing Boing*), *Mirror for the Sky* (opera), 3 symphonies.

Composer remarks (from a 1979 radio interview): "The fact is we live in a century in which nothing is settled, in which mankind is intellectually, emotionally, spiritually unsure of itself. There is no hard core to 20th-century life which says that there is something bigger than I am — I'm not commenting on religious faith, because of course the churches still exist... but, there is no certitude. We have the existentialist philosophy: its lesson is, we're here, and I suppose the only reason to give credence to the idea of the dignity of man is that somehow he will make the best of it, and that if you don't cut your throat that in itself may be a reason of some kind for saying that life is worthwhile! Now, what does this do for the arts? In the arts, vast numbers of people have lost their innocence, they no longer believe that going to a concert is akin almost to a religious experience...

"INTERVIEWER: Recently, your cartoon film *Gerald McBoing Boing* had a BBC audience of about 90,000 people....

"KUBIK: Until a composer has made contact with that great mass audience he almost certainly doesn't have any identify because he can't make any impact on 20th century society.... including truck drivers... the *cognoscenti*... the jet set...

"I can assure you that music has changed more in thirty years than in the past three hundred.

"Now we are living in a fragmented society where everybody is doing his own thing and I'm not exaggerating when I say there are almost as many schools of contemporary composition as there are practitioners. Still one could say there is the conservative group — the group that says life has a continuity... that we did not burst into the world as though it were year one and music had not been invented.

"You try to stretch the language, as Proust does, as Joyce does... without abandoning the language.

"The background music industry has brought into being a race of composers who treat music as a tailor treats cloth." — from an interview with Mark Grant.

ARTICLE: ON BEING A PROFESSIONAL MUSICIAN IN AMERICA. "Despite considerable artistic and commercial success, Gail Kubik wasn't widely known outside of academic and film circles. But his friend, composer Harold Shapero, says that Kubik will be remembered as 'one of the last real American composers.'

"Kubik had been something of a *Wunderkind*. Born in Oklahoma in 1914, he was a violin prodigy who toured the Midwest with his two brothers and mother as the Kubik Ensemble.

"He entered the Eastman School of Music on scholarship at 15 and later went on to study with Walter Piston at Harvard and Nadia Boulanger in Paris. His *Second Violin Concerto* won first prize in the Heifetz Competition—sponsored by Heifetz himself—in 1940, and that same year, at age 26, Kubik was hired as a staff composer by NBC Radio to compose and arrange music for the NBC Symphony Orchestra.

"In the late 1940s and early 1950s Kubik, still in his 30s, was a hot property. Working for hire for the media, he wrote what he called functional music: sound tracks for film documentaries (*Memphis Belle* for the Air Force in World War II), Hollywood movies (*The Desperate Hours* with Humphrey Bogart and Frederic March), animated cartoons (*Gerald McBoing-Boing,* which won an Oscar in 1951), radio (the 'Great Plays' on NBC radio in the 40s) and television (Walter Cronkite CBS specials).

"Later, he would cannibalize and rework his own material from these scores into symphonic works for the concert hall. Even his Pulitzer Prize-winning *Symphonie Concertante* (1952) [below] was developed out of motifs originally written for the 1949 Hollywood film *C-Man* with John Carradine.

" 'Your functional music, for a serious composer, ends up constituting a notebook for all sorts of ideas for a big abstract piece,' he once said.

"As a result of this double composing strategy, a few odd strokes of luck, and business acumen as a real estate landlord, Kubik was able to make his career exclusively as a composer and circumvented teaching until 1970, when he became composer-in-residence at Scripps College in Claremont and at the Claremont Graduate School.

"Suddenly, the wheel of fortune turned and Kubik's artistic career began a curious decrescendo. At the moment Kubik was at the peak of his profession, the serious music scene took a decisive turn in a direction completely alien to his own musical speech, which was the tonal, neo-classic, neo-romantic 'American' idiom that saw its heyday in the 30s and 40s.

"Suddenly, serialism, 12-tone music, electronic music, and the noise music and experimentalism of John Cage took hold of the influential music centers here and abroad and became the power music, the prestige music.

"When Stravinsky and Copland took up 12-tone writing late in their careers and led many composers down that path, Kubik remained an unreconstructed traditionalist, calling those that crossed over 'camp followers'.

"The unhappy result was that he lost his intellectual cachet.

" 'He found that what his interior voice was was not what people were interested in,' recalls John Lilley, a former Scripps colleague. 'He felt spiritually bereft and demoralized.'

"He did, however, make a strenuous effort to acquaint himself with Schoenberg's music, with that of Webern, Milton Babbitt, *et al.*, to see what was going on, but emerged still sticking to his guns, not feeling any need to change his style.

"Meanwwhile, his film career also began to decline. He was one who wrote 'crazy' music in the view of some studio moguls. It was too strong, too symphonic for their tastes. So, Kubik was caught increasingly between the cracks: too populist for respectful treatment by the intellectual establishment; too abstract for steadily continuing employment in the commercial motion picture medium.

"Another reason for Kubik's eclipse was a tactical error of his own doing. He had become a long-term expatriate in Europe at precisely the wrong time. Between 1950 and 1967, when he should have been in the United States promoting his own music, he lived mostly in France and Italy and became better known there than in the United States. In later years he openly regretted this.

"What does his music sound like?

"Often it is compared to that of Aaron Copland and Roy Harris, but it is really distinctly individual. It's always accessible, always directly expressive in the tradition of the classic and romantic era, but not a bit reactionary. It's unmistakably 20th Century in its crisp angles, jaunty assymmetrical rhythms and unsentimental emotionalism.

"That's not to say that there isn't a strong American cornball side to it, but it's understated and sublimated into a kind of Continental refinement.

"Kubik could write a good tune, though more often the music sounds contrapuntal. He could be eloquent and telling with a few notes in a sparse, almost Webern-like texture, or imposing and grandly dramatic, as in the cantata *A Record for Our Time,* his last big piece played in Los Angeles, in 1976 with Roger Wagner conducting the L.A. Sinfonia and Master Chorale.

"But above all, Kubik's music was marked by an insistent, rattling, skittering energy. 'His personality came out in his music,' notes friend Marilyn Goetsch. 'There's a frantic aspect to it, then suddenly a moment of complete calm and tranquility. All of his works end on a high-pitched, searching kind of feeling. I think his life was that way.'

"To his friends, Kubik was a vivid character who projected, without any affectation, the glamorous aura of the successful composer: elegant, highly intelligent, introverted, and yet he was a *bon vivant*, a world traveler with a house in southern France and membership in New York's exclusive Century Club.

"*Charming, rosy* and *optimistic* are adjectives mentioned by some of his colleagues, but his personal life was far less so. His wives (he was married four times) knew him as a difficult person to live with, and, among other professional musicians, he had a reputation as a short-tempered perfectionist.

"In 1980, Scripps College asked Kubik to retire at the mandatory age of 65. He adamantly refused, asserted that a creative person should be measured by productivity, not age, and with characteristic stubbornness sued the college. The American Civil Liberties Union took his case on a *pro bono* basis, but he lost.

"He seemed to suffer persistent writer's block in his last years. He started a piano concerto in 1974, that was unfinished at his death.

"In 1982, still based in Claremont though no longer at Scripps, he traveled to Africa and India, exchanging his home in Venasque, France, with a home in Harare, Zimbabwe, for three months.

"At some point on his tour he contracted kala azar, an infectious disease caused by a protozoan parasite transmitted by the bite of a sand fly. Kala azar is endemic to Africa, Asia, and the Mediterranean — all regions Kubik had traveled to in his last seven years with his insatiable curiosity.

"At first, he was just not feeling well. He was mysteriously losing weight and losing his appetite. He went for an exhaustive series, suspecting either cancer or leukemia.

"Through the early months of 1984, Kubik became increasingly debilitated. He continued to see doctors but nobody seemed to know what his ailment was. Finally, the doctors confirmed kala azar, but it was too late for the treatment — antimony, a heavy metal — to reverse the effects on his liver, kidneys, and blood. He died only a week after the diagnosis was confirmed, at 69, on July 20, 1984.

"The final irony is that serialism in music is now, in the words of composer Virgil Thomson, 'dead as a doornail,' and the trend of the hour is tonal neo-romanticism—Kubik's kind of music."[63]—Mark Grant, in the *Los Angeles Times*, 11/4/84.

"Gail Kubik is one member of the second generation of the American nationlist persuasion whose accomplishments are far too little known to the general music public and too often taken for granted by the musical profession.... There has always been a foundation of seriousness and warmth, as well as intimations of a virile and reticent tenderness, beneath the busy, playful surface of his major works."—Paul Snook, in *Fanfare: The Magazine for Serious Record Collectors*, 3-4/81.

Magic, Magic, Magic for Solo Voices, Chorus and Piano (or Orchestra). *Pub.*: Lawson-Gould.
1. *Invocation* (*text:* Joan Allred)—SATB with tenor solo, narrator. 2. *Spell to Bring the Longed-for Letter* (*text:* Eugene Walter)—SATB with alto. 3. *E-XU-ZI-NHO*—chorus with tenor.

"This set of three *Incantations...* was commissioned by the San Antonio Bicentennial Committee in 1976. They are published with piano accompaniment, with orchestral parts being available from the publishers. The style of this writing is avantgarde. Well trained musicians would be required to perform these numbers, but they would be highly effective and would have appeal to advance college choirs. Gail Kubik's music is always written in good taste; he is one of our finest American composers."—Ruth J. Brush, in *The American Music Teacher* (Music Teachers National Association), 6-7/82.

Symphony Concertante for Orchestra. 26m *Comm. & prem.*: Little O Society of NY, Thomas Scherman, cond. Winner, 1952 Pulitzer Prize. *Rec.*: RCA Victor (Mono LP; reissued as Composers Recordings Inc. Stereo LP CRI SD 267): Arthur Hanneuse (tpt), Marie-Thérèse Chailley (vla), Frank Glazer (pno), French Radio O, Gail Kubik, cond. *Pub.*: Belwin-Mills.
1. Fast, vigorously. 2. Quietly. 3. Fast, with energy.

"Gail Kubik's music combines two important trends in the contemporary scene. On the one hand he adheres to the neo-classical aesthetic that motivates his preoccupation with the large forms of absolute music. On the other he takes his stand with those who have cultivated the kind of functional music—such as motion picture and

---

[63] Fashions change—"influences" remain—the progress of any art inevitably gives rise to controversies and opposing solutions to common problems. Meanwhile most people would probably agree that what matters most—after all—is the integrity of a given artist. (Ed.)

radio scores—that forces a composer to communicate with a mass audience.

"The *Symphony Concertante* displays Kubik's gifts at their most appealing: his colorful imagination in the choice of orchestral sonorities; his characteristic use of jazz rhythms and other popular elements in a style that is gay, full of movement and gesture, and carried off with enormous verve. The result is very American, yet wholly personal, the work of a musician of wit and sophistication.

"The first movement is in modified sonata form. It opens with an imperious gesture and builds steadily to the exciting fugato passage that constitutes its climax. Rhythm is the form-building element here: a dynamic rhythm of a ballet-like vividness. The slow movement is, as the composer describes it, 'a very long, increasingly dramatic song with a reflective epilogue at the end.' Its contemplative lyricism unfolds in flowing lines. The third movement is a rondo that recaptures, in twentieth-century terms, the steady forward impulse of the *concerto grosso* of Bach's time. With its spare, transparent texture and its stylization of jazz rhythms, this finale is a splendid example of the lithe, sinewy writing of the contemporay American school." —from liner notes for Composers Recordings Inc. LP CRI SD 267.

Fred Lerdahl

B. 1943, Madison WI. *Educ.:* Lawrence Univ, Princeton Univ, Freiburg Hochschule für Musik, Tanglewood. *Taught at:* Univ of CA (Berkeley), Boston Univ, Harvard Univ, Yale Univ, Columbia Univ, Univ of MI. *Awards & grants:* Fulbright grant, Koussevitzky Composition Prize, Guggenheim Fellowship, Natl Inst Arts/Letters Award, ASCAP Composer Award. Composer-in-residence Marlboro Music Festival, IRCAM *(Institut de Recherche et Coordination Acoustique/Musique)*, Wellesley Composers Conf, Amer Acad (Rome). USA editor, *Contemporary Music Review;* bd dirs. Koussevitzky Music Fndn, Ariel Chamber Ens. *Author of: A Generative Theory of Tonal Music* (with Ray Jackendoff), *Prolongations in Pitch Space.* Works incl.: *Beyond the Realm of Bird* (s/chamber orch), *Eros* (m-s/7 insts), *Fantasy Etudes* (fl/cl/vln/vc/perc/pno), orchestral works (*Chords, Cross-Currents*), *Wake* (s/string trio/ hp, 3 perc), *Waltzes* (vln/vla/vc/bs), *Waves* (chamber orch).

A note from the composer (from a letter to the Editor): "I might mention that although you are featuring my two string quartets, the works of mine that are played the most these days are *Waltzes, Fantasy Etudes, Cross-Currents,* and *Waves*. I wish the quartets were played more!"

Fantasy Etudes for Flute, Clarinet, Violin, Cello, Percussion and Piano (1985). 15m Comm. by Musical Elements, Alea III, Arch Ensemble, Contemporary Chamber Players (Univ of Chicago). *Prem.:* Musical Elements, Daniel Asia, Robert Beaser (dirs). *Pub.:* Boelke-Bomart (distr. Jerona Music Corp. — score; parts on rental).

"The form of *Fantasy Etudes* is built up from 12 interlocking 'etudes', each having its own characteristic musical idea and texture. This sequential profusion of material results in an overall sense of 'fantasy'. Against this surface variety there exists an underlying similarity of procedure. Each etude is cast in the form of expanding variations: it starts with a simple event and progressively elaborates into complexity. Each time, as the material of an etude beings to collapse under the weight of its elaborations, a new etude enters. These overlaps produce moments of dramatic tension-changes, if you like, from one fantasy to another." — Fred Lerdahl.

Quartet 1 for Strings (1978). 22m Comm. by Juilliard Quartet & the Josyln Art Museum. *Prem.:* Juilliard Quartet. *Pub.:* Boelke-Bomart (distr. Jerona Music Corp.).

"Lerdahl's one-movement score is a set of geometrically expanding variations in which the built-in drama of the formal idea is ingeniously exploited and powerfully developed—an evolution that grips the ear and makes one long to hear how the composer continued and completed this variational process in his new *Second Quartet* [below]." —Peter G. Davis, in *New York* Magazine.

"The *[First] String Quartet* is a set of variations, but not on a theme. The starting point is an open-fifth chord, G-G-D-G. This is the first of fifteen sections; each subsequent section is a variation and expansion of—approximately one and a half times as long as—its predecessor. Section No, 2 is just two chords, that of No. 1 preceded by a differently spaced G-G-G-D. In No. 3, a new chromatic chord, built of semitone, appoggiaturalike displacements of G and D, intervenes between the two chords based on G. In No. 4, two such chords intervene. In No. 5, further displacements yield a sequence of eight chords, still opening and closing as Nos. 3 and 4 did. So far, all has been in strict homophony and played nonvibrato at an unvarying *piano*, each chord a half-note long. In No. 6, a small rhythmic independence, created by appoggiaturas from the first and the second violin, creeps in. It grows in No. 7, and here there is also a single, sustained vibrato chord within the nonvibrato progression. No. 8 introduces the first dynamic nuance. The most insistent of the intruder notes has been C-sharp, a tritone from the tonic G, and at the close of the next four sections this C-sharp lodges itself in the basic G-D harmony.

"All this sounds schematic, and of course it is, but the effect is not dry or mechanical. The quartet sounds like a composition that demanded to be written, not a clever construction. I recount the details from the score, but the composer's claim, in a program note, that 'the process of expansion is... audible' is justified. Gradually, from his very simple start, he amasses his material. Gradually the harmonies, the rhythms, the variations of timbre, and the range of dynamics grow more intricate, and the listener can hear how they grow — through the first ten sections or so. Nos. 10, 11, and 12 can be heard starting with the same melody in an ever richer form. But, because of the sesquialter increases, detailed following of the process becomes harder, although developments of earlier melodies, moods, and kinds of movement can still be recognized. The first chord lasts less than a second; the final section last some six minutes and is subdivided into contrasting sections of its own. From the seed, stems, branches, and blossoms have sprung. The pit is no longer discernible in the peach tree. But that vegetable metaphor suggested by the quartet's 'organic' growth is not wholly apt. The finale is not the inevitable, the only possible outcome. Throughout the work, one feels that improvisation played a part in its making, that in the earlier sections each progression — and in the later sections each episode — was chosen from many that would have been possible within the schema established for the piece. (Once the selection is made, of course, it becomes a fixed quantity affecting the range of subsequent possibilities.) Moreover, there is what the composer calls a 'psychological' progress running through the quartet, 'from simplicity and repose to their opposites.' The easy, conventional formal ending would have been a restatement of the start; the actual ending is stranger. For a moment, there is a hint of a shining, almost *Lohengrin*-like, A-major apotheosis. Then echoes of the cadence that closed the earlier sections are heard — but after the preceding adventures a return to that simple affirmation cannot be entertained, and the work dissolves instead into disjunct, disturbed chromatic sighs.

"The quartet met that first, simple critical criterion I wrote about last month: 'Do I want to hear the piece again?' Through the courtesy of the Juilliard School, which tape-records Juilliard Theatre concerts for its archive, I was able to do so, and it rewarded further listenings. There are still some episodes — notably, a long passage of 'wave motion' in the finale — whose sense eludes me, but as a whole and in most of its details the quartet, like [the composer's] *Eros*, a rich and beautiful set of variations for mezzo and chamber ensemble, reveals an individual and striking voice, a fertile yet disciplined mind, and a finished, confident technique. The piece is composed for the four isntruments as a piano piece might be for ten fingers: by which I mean that it makes the effect less of a dialogue between four individual players than of a single discourse set out in four — or, with divisions, in up to eight — parts. The composer suggests a timing of twenty minutes; the Juilliard performance lasted about fourteen. I used a stopwatch over the whole, not a metronome to check individual passages, but have the impression that the earlier sections might profit from a more deliberate, spacious exposition, and that, in general, the Juilliard, while already evident masters of the music, may give it a longer breath in subsequent performances. Lerdahl is working on a *Second Quartet*, commissioned for the Pro Arte, which 'will continue the expanding variational process but reverse the psychological course of the *First Quartet* back to its beginning.' I'll be watching for it. The *First Quartet*, he says, 'is both a complete piece in itself and first half of a larger work.' " — Andrew Porter, in *The New Yorker*, 5/14/79.[64]

Quartet 2 for Strings (1980-82). *Prem.:* Pro Arte Quartet (Normal Paulu, Martha Blum, vlns, Richard Blum, vla, Parry Karp, vc). *Rec.:* Laurel Records (Stereo LP) LR-128: Pro Arte Quartet. Commissioned by Pro Arte Quartet, with National Endowment for the Arts assistance. *Pub.:* Boelke-Bomart (distr. Jerona Music Corp.).
Part I (10m) — Part II (13m).

"A first version [of the *Second String Quartet*] was performed by the Pro Arte Quartet in 1981 in Madison, Wisconsin. In 1982 I revised and substantially enlarged the work; this final version was premeiered by the Pro Arte in November, 1983, at a League-Interna-

---

64 Reprinted in *Music of Three More Seasons, 1977-1980* (Alfred A. Knopf, 1981).

tional Society of Contemporary Music (ISCM) concert in New York City.

"The *Second String Quartet* is in one long movement that falls into two parts; Part II is an enlarged elaboration of Part I. Each part in turn breaks down into: (1) a quiet, yearning introductory section; (2) parallel developmental sections of great polyphonic complexity and almost violent expression; (3) a wave-like, whirlwind passage that gradually dissipates the accumulated energy; (4) a slower, more lyrical section followed by a pulsating but subdued scherzando; (5) a chorale-coda. The final chorale retrospectively reveals the underlying harmonic structure of the work and at the same time provides a measure of quizzical peace in response to the turbulent fantasies that have preceded it.

"From another perspective, the *Second String Quartet* is a sequel to the *First String Quartet*. That work takes the form of 15 geometrically expanding variations; the *Second Quartet* constitutes two more variations. In quality, however, the two pieces are different. The *First Quartet* is inward, explorative, given to unexpected changes and silences. The *Second* is otuwardly passionate, developmental, full of energy and sweep.

"Playing my *Second String Quartet* is no easy matter. The Pro Arte has long had an inside reputation among composers for being unusually dedicated to accuracy and to the fulfillment of the composer's intentions. But I never dreamed the Quartet would perform my piece so magnificently, right from the beginning. At the first rehearsal I attended, these performers played the work through without stopping (composers are not used to this). Later rehearsals could thus be devoted entirely to refinements of balance, pacing, and nuance. Working with the Pro Arte was, in its very different way, almost as satisfying as composing the piece in the first place." — Fred Lerdahl.

"[Lerdahl's *Second String Quartet* is] as straightforward as a piece by Brahms, concerned with what it has to say, not with grinding an axe. Once one has been drawn into its unfolding, the experience becomes fascinating, as recurrent patterns and moments of tonal or rhythmic stability serve as points of reference. One is struck by the sophistication with which Lerdahl handles his material, so that one feels that the music sounds exactly as he means it to sound at all times, while an over-arching musical concept lends a sense of direction, purpose, and shape." — Walter G. Simmons, in *Fanfare: The Magazine for Serious Record Collectors*, 3-4/85.

ANDREW LLOYD WEBBER

B. 1948, London (England). *Educ.*: Royal Coll of Music. *Works incl.*: film scores (*Gumshoe, The Odessa File*), stage works (*Aspects of Love, Cats, Evita, Jeeves, Joseph and the Amazing Technicolor Dreamcoat, The Phantom of the Opera, Starlight Express, Tell Me on a Sunday*).

Jesus Christ Superstar (A Rock Opera). *Lyr.*: Tim Rice. *Rec*: MCA Records (Stereo LP) DL7-1503: original Broadway cast (selections); MCA Records (2 Stereo LPs) MCA 2-10000 (formerly DXSA 7206)(complete). *Pub.*: Leeds Music Ltd. (except No. 21 [Norrie Paramor Music Ltd], No. 22 [Superstar Music Ltd]).
9 M, 2 F; chorus
Insts. incl. drums/perc, b gtr, gtr (electric/acoustic), gtr (electric), keyboard (pno/electric pno/organ/positive organ), t sax
1. Overture. 2. Heaven on Their Minds. 3. What's the Buzz. 4. Strange Thing Mystifying. 5. Everything's Alright. 6. This Jesus Must Die. 7. Hosanna. 8. Simon Zealotes. 9. Poor Jerusalem. 10. Pilate's Dream. 11. The Temple. 12. Everything's Alright (reprise). 13. I Don't Know How to Love Him. 14. Damned for All Time. 15. Blood Money. 16. The Last Supper. 17. Gethsemane (I only wanted to say). 18. The Arrest. 19. Peter's Denial. 20. Pilate and Christ. 21. King Herod's Song (Try It and See). 22. Could We Start Again Please (added 1971). 23. Judas' Death. 24. Trial Before Pilate (incl. The 39 Lashes). 25. Superstar. 26. The Crucifixion. 27. John Nineteen: Forty One.

"JESUS ON BROADWAY. It was in Berkhamsted in August of 1970, a little north and west of London. 'You must hear a piece by two young Englishmen,' he said. 'Boys, actually, when they wrote it. One was seventeen and the other nineteen.' The 'it' he referred to was *Joseph and His Amazing Technicolor Dreamcoat*. And so I came for the first time to hear the names of Tim Rice and Andrew Lloyd Webber. The gentleman speaking to me was a verger at St. Paul's and was clearly delighted with the piece which had first been performed at Central Hall, Westminster in 1968. It had been presented as an oratorio, but when I heard it I remember saying that it had much too much life not to be staged. So we brought it back and staged it at our seminary, Cathedral College in Douglaston, New York. Both Tim and Andrew came over for the opening performance. It was their first visit to America, though as events turned out, not their last.

"The story of Joseph and his brothers quite literally leapt from the pages of Genesis with all the freshness of Tim's words and Andrew's quite delightful music. As the Old Testament Joseph was a precursory image of Christ, so was this lark of a musical, with its colorful coat and music, a forerunner of more serious attempts to bring the Gospel to Broadway.

"The sixties were a time of hope and possibilities. John XXIII with his Council had thrown open the windows of the Church; in the political order John Kennedy had gathered that hope, made it a dream and we called the time Camelot. But individual men don't simply change, or with any suddenness radically reshape the world. They see and sense and become the voice of those creative human energies the rest of us have not yet recognized or named. All except of course the artists and the writers who, living to feel, sense the tenor of the times and, living outside of things, tend to see them more clearly.[65]

"*Joseph* is about a dreamer and a dream. It is the story of a young man who lived long ago, by two very modern young men. They have fun in the telling. The story is direct and simple and has all of the delightful, if not even impudent — freshness of youth, And it has the young man's belief in dreams, reminding a receptive audience, an audience of the sixties, that dreams are necessary — in fact '*any* dream will do'....

"During the course of the telling, Andrew Lloyd Webber matches the verbal fun with music that conjures up a Presley-singing, problem-filled Pharaoh, with some 'roaring twenties' courtesans, and a wonderfully tongue-in-cheek reversal or roles for Joseph and his brothers. It is all sprightly and happy and again it echoes the times. But while [Lloyd] Webber and Rice were enjoying this, they were thinking and writing *Jesus Christ, Superstar*....

"In 1971 I had the pleasure of producing and directing *Jesus Christ, Superstar* at the college. I had to study the music and search the text for its visual shape. You always come to know and care for a piece when you have to do that. The words and music seemed a far cry from the tinsel caricatured extravaganza that opened on Broadway that same year....

"In discussing [the show] for this article, a friend of mine was surprised by my calling it 'a serious piece of work.' I do feel that it is quite serious. Clearly it had to get over the hurdle, for most of the public, of having the story of Jesus Christ presented in Rock music. It's a bit of a jolt to hear apostles asking, 'What's the buzz?' and even more of one to have a crowd cry out to the Son of Man, 'Hey, J.C.'

---

65 One tends to think of the sixties in the U.S. *either* as a time of high spirited optimism *or* as a period of numbing disillusionment (Vietnam, Kent State, the assassinations of three national leaders). The curious fact, of course, is that the sixties were a time of *both*. (Ed.)

But reverence can be expressed in different ways. Surely the words of Scripture must go beyond the pages of the Old and New Testaments if they are to be alive in our times. The sower has to know when to *throw* the seed and have the courage to do it. If he merely keeps it in his hand, nothing happens. It is kept intact but it is also kept from life, from giving life. The Word came to us where we were and he has a right to invest his Life in all the things we make.

"*Superstar* is faithful to Scripture. The music shapes universals of feeling and the words place them in Jerusalem, in Judas, in the Apostles, in the priests—in Jesus. The Jesus I thought missing in *Godspell* is very present here. Both Rice and [Lloyd] Webber catch the humanness of Christ. He is a Jesus whose humanity endures the discovery of his mission, and then 'becomes' in its fulfillment. He is the tender, compassionate Christ so wonderfully warm in the words and the music when he weeps over Jerusalem. He is unheedful of the names imposed on Mary Magdalen when she feels comfortable about touching him. For him she is simply a person who is in need. For Judas she is the despisable name. He collapses from exhaustion when the sick and the afflicted keep pulling at his energies and his heart. He explodes in fierce indignation at the abuse of his Father's house. But more than anything else we see him in the Garden searching (for to be truly human is to be uncertain) and embracing his Name. The agony of Gethsemane is powerfully portrayed, magnificent in the music, moving from uncertainty to resolution—then to gift and ultimately to death.

"The play seems to stop at death, but when I was invited to hear the album at St. Thomas' Church (at the time [Lloyd] Webber and Rice first brought it to this country), they accompanied the record with slides. Each slide matched and illuminated a particular moment of the opera. When they got to the John 19 section at the end, they showed all slides of the Resurrection. With that as a clue, when I produced *Superstar* I also ended with a resurrection scene.

"In *Superstar* we are presented with a Jesus who makes a difference. He is significant; he can change our lives. Thus Mary Magdalen doesn't know what to do with him. She doesn't know how to love him but she knows that to be herself, she must. She sings, in our name, most powerfully our sometimes-feelings. The impact of his presence breaks the sleep and the life of Pilate, and in a dream which transcends time (as dreams are wont to do) Pilate shudders at the judgment of history. The music of this breaking dream stops us like a temptation that could cost us life.

"The character of Judas is fascinating for he seems to speak out of a time which was his own and also out of the history that later judged his life. He cries out of a pain which has already named him part of the night, a thing whose life is meant to kill the Light. Though the authors make him human, as indeed they should, we feel in his temptation and his fall (protesting a providence which 'made him do it') a rationalizing insufficiency we are all very familiar with. The insight and the art are all too clear, so that even the priests see through it. He dies at last for silver. It is betrayal. It has more weight than Herod, whose simpering effete superficiality names the energy in our society which mocks innocence with wealth and a jaded exhibitionism. One cannot create a play wherein both words and music portray radical human experience with such power and presents us with so challenging, so compassionate, so loving a Jesus—and not be serious.

"The human energies in the Scripture story are made more real. Perhaps Rock itself was made to sing when all the other stones of art were silent. Jesus will be heard."—Harold Buckley, in *The Catholic World*, 1-2/89.

Requiem. Rec.: Angel Digital LP DFO-38218 (also as CD CDC 7-47146-2): Placido Domingo (t), Sarah Brightman (s), Paul Miles-Kingston (treble), James Lancelot (org), Winchester Cathedral Choir, English Chamber O, Lorin Maazel, cond.

"Only the hardhearted could avoid being moved, moved deeply, by this composition and its first recording.

"That emotional response is, of course, the result of Andrew Lloyd Webber's straightforward if unsubtle reaching for the heartstrings of his listeners. It's a quality possessed by much of his work, but also shared by the big three of theatrical (i.e., unsuitable for liturgical use because tending to overshadow instead of complement the ceremony of the Mass) *Requiems*: those of Verdi, Berlioz, and Britten. Indeed, I can't remember when a new work of this sort has moved me more deeply since the premiere of the *War Requiem*. Now, Lloyd Webber and I have not been thief-thick of late, what I've heard of *Starlight Express* leaves me still thinking of Elgar when I hear the title; and since *Cats* seems to be a one-song show I haven't troubled to choose among the various versions of cast albums.[66] I take it that these two works depend so heavily on sheer theatricality that my response is not unusual; and I remember well that *Evita* left me cold until I had seen it—and acquired a context within which the music suddenly became likable. But what with its characteristically abrupt changes of mood, *Requiem* has a dramatic quality not as evident in

---

66   At the time of writing, *The Phantom of the Opera* had not yet appeared. (Ed.)

Lloyd Webber's works since his Tim Rice days[67] — since *Joseph...* and *Superstar*.

"Lloyd Webber did rather little tinkering with the standard *Requiem* ordering of materials. Indeed, he does even less in the way of sectioning the *"Dies Irae"* than does Verdi. However, after the theatrics of this prayer are over, the composer does liven up the *Offertorium* by suggesting something of a tribal ritual on the words *"Hostias et preces tibi, Domine..."* — a line which follows the musical depiction of hellfire with praise and supplication of the Almighty. Then Lloyd Webber tacks the opening of the *"Sanctus"* onto the *"Offertorium"* so as to allow the rest of the prayer to constitute a new and separate dramatic element: a *"Hosanna"*, the rhythms of which make for what is in effect the insertion of a surrogate *"Gloria"* into the *Requiem*, which of course does not possess one. The interplay of tenor and soprano in the *"Hosanna"* gives way to the enormously affecting *"Pie Jesu"* for soprano and boy treble — a section which, one notes, is already getting a great deal of air play. The last section, *"Lux Aeterna"* and *"Libera me"*, ends where the *Requiem* as a whole began, musically speaking — with one difference. There is a shattering sequence of organ chords after the final *"Requiem"* lines — as if suggesting the end of time — and then the plaintive voice of the boy treble repeating *"perpetua..."*

"Thus the work as a whole seems to end on a note of fragile but everlasting hope for peace. Lloyd Webber tells of how the work began with a news story that came out of the Cambodian conflict — determining his choice of solo voices — and also the desire to commemorate the death of his father William, a composer one of whose pieces was recently included on a cello album by Lloyd Webber's brother Julian....

"[On the recording choices of musical emphases have been made which it would be interesting to know more about.] In the *"Hosanna,"* for instance, the tenor's fervent and joyful chant gives rise to a general celebration reminiscent of a Baptist service, replete with tambourine and Gospel-style keyboard. Yet that keyboard is so distantly miked as to fall well short of having its full effect. Solo voices, however, are always as prominent as one could wish; the important boy treble is never overwhelmed, for instance. Domingo's romantic tenor is used to good effect throughout, while the soprano — Sarah Brightman, Lloyd Webber's wife — brings a power and beauty to the proceedings that is probably only abetted by the fact that she owes most of her experience to the popular theater.

---

67 His librettist for several stage works. (Ed.)

"One is curious, finally, about the future of this work, even as one is absolutely sure of its present impact. Though your reviewer weeps more readily than most men do, even in these permissive times, he found it especially hard to hold back tears from the first hearing of this work onward. Should there by any of you out there still pondering purchase [of the recording], let me urge the deed upon you. For unless you rankle at being included by extension in the so-called 'crossover' audience, there is no shame in participating in a harrowing ritual of this sort, even if its therapeutic effects do not last, like the voice of the boy treble, into perpetuity." — John Ditsky, in *Fanfare: The Magazine for Serious Record Collectors*, 7-8/85.

WITOLD LUTOSLAWSKI

B. 1913, Warsaw (Poland). *Educ.:* Warsaw Cons. *Taught at:* Berkshire Music Ctr, Tanglewood. Composer-in-residence, Dartmouth College. Winner, Grand Prix du Disque, Ravel Prize, Sibelius Prize; honorary member Free Acad of Arts, Hamburg; Acad of Arts, West Berlin; Internatl Soc for Contemp Music; correspond member American Acad of Arts and Letters, Royal Acad of Music, London; honorary degrees Cleveland Inst of Music, Univ of Warsaw, Northwestern Univ. *Works incl.:* chamber works, concertos (orch, pno, vc), orchestral pieces *(5 Dance Preludes, Musique funèbre, Symphonic Variations),* 2 symphonies, voice & instruments *(Les Espaces du Sommeil, Paroles tissées, A Straw Chain, Triptych).*

Novelette for Orchestra (1978-79). 18m *Prem.:* National SO, Mstislav Rostrovich, cond. Commissioned by & ded. to National SO, Mstislav Rostropovich, cond. *Pub.:* Chester (distr. Magnamusic-Baton — score; performance materials on rental).
3-3-3-3; 4-3-3-1; timp, perc, celeste, 2 harps, pno; strings
1. *Announcement.* 2-4. *Events 1-3.* 5. *Conclusion.*

"In 1960 Witold Lutoslawski discovered a compositional technique that was quickly to bring his already ripe musical language to full maturity. That technique — inspired by a brief encounter with the music of John Cage — was a 'controlled' or 'limited aleatorism.' Lutoslawski has incorporated a distinctly original and increasingly refined aleatory dimension into each of his works since *Venetian Games* (1961). Focus on this one dimension of Lutoslawski's style, however, has led to a neglect of his early music and has obscured the full range of compositional techniques integrated into his mature works.

"The achievements of Lutoslawki's maturity can now be understood in a much broader context through Steven Stucky's monograph *Lutoslawski and His Music* (1981). Stucky... examines the effects of political and cultural circumstances on Lutoslawski's development: the hardships and repression suffered during the Nazi occupation of Poland, the artistic straight-jacket imposed under Stalinism, and the artistically liberating events of the post-Stalinist period....

"*Novelette* is an eighteen-minute work in five movements: *Announcement,* three *Events,* and *Conclusion. Announcement* is a terse proclamation which begins with a crisp, emphatic call to attention and then introduces, in an embryonic state, much of the material that will form the events of the next three movements. The first and third

Events, although contrasting in character, are of similar length, weight, and dramatic profile. The central, second *Event* is shorter, more subdued. The *Conclusion* is the only slow movement; it seems to be longer than the combined length of the other four movements and reflects Lutoslawski's preference for saving the weightiest movement for the end of the work. After a *tutti* climax, the movement ends with a brief reference to the opening chords. [This] final reference to the opening announcement seems more like an invitation to turn back to the beginning and listen again than a recapitulation that ties the whole work together.

"*Novelette* incorporates many of the elements associated with Lutoslawski's mature style. The consummate mastery of orchestral resources — both in a sensitivity to the range of timbral possibilities and a gift for creating idiomatic and virtuosic instrumental parts — is everywhere apparent. The 'sound pictures' of Lutoslawski's imagination are realized in rich tapestries of varying textural densities, often based on polychronic layering of musics and on aleatory counterpoint, in which pitch and pitch aggregates are carefully controlled while rhythmic values are flexible. Lutoslawski's enduring concern for generative pitch systems can be traced through the distinctive melodic and harmonic material, which is continually developed and transformed. In *Novelette,* as in each of his works, it is fascinating to see how familiar techniques are further refined, how the relationships between elements are redefined and reinterpreted, and how these elements are integrated into coherent formal designs. The music of each of the movements builds to intense climactic moments, usually culminating in systematically constructed twelve-note aggregates, which have been characteristic of Lutoslawski's mature music.

"Cursory observations cannot do justice to such a rich and complex score. My impression is that, like Lutoslawski's other mature works, the formal and dramatic strategies will be easily grasped, while further study of the music will be still more revealing and rewarding. A socre of this importance belongs in music libraries if budgets at all permit." — Lance W. Brunner, in *Notes* (Music Library Association), 3/83.

Symphony 3 for Orchestra (1983). 30m *Prem.:* Chicago SO, Georg Solti, cond. *Rec.:* Deutsche Grammophon (LP): Berlin PO, Witold Lutoslawski, cond.; CBS Masterworks (Digital Stereo LP) IM 42203: Los Angeles PO, Esa-Pekka Salonen, cond. Commissioned by Chicago SO. Winner, Univ of Louisville Grawemeyer Award. *Pub.:* Chester (distr. Magnamusic-Baton — score; performance materials on rental).

3(2 picc)-3(1 E hn)-3(1 E^b cl, b cl)-3(c bsn); 0-4-4-1; timp, perc, 2 harps, piano 4-hands, celesta; strings
In two movements (played without pause).

"We still hear the same tired old complaints: modern concert music is dry, passionless, uncommunicative, repugnant to performers, aloof from the needs and tastes of the concert-going, record-buying public. Those who persist in this mythology just haven't been paying attention: here is a powerfully persuasive score to prove it.

"For years, of course, Witold Lutoslawski has been giving the lie to the notion that new music is unloveable.. Works like the *Concerto for Orchestra, Musique funèbre, Jeux vénitiens, Livre pour orchestre,* the *Cello Concerto,* and the *Double Concerto* for oboe and harp have won places in orchestral repertories all over the world. The *Third Symphony,* too, has already established itself both with conductors and with the public. At this writing [1986], two-and-a-half years after its premiere, there have been more than thirty sets of performances, covering most of the Western musical world; the work has won the University of Louisville Grawemeyer Award of $150,000; and two recordings are already in the making.

"The *Third Symphony's* immediate success is not difficult to understand. One of the composer's most readily accessible, directly appealing scores, it is at the same time formally perhaps his most ambitious. The work was commissioned in 1972 by the Chicago Symphony but not completed and performed until 1983 (for Lutoslawski an extreme but not atypical time lapse). What finally emerged from this long gestation is half an hour of continuous music comprising three large, linked movements plus introduction and coda. At the heart of the symphony lies the second movement, a musical argument whose size, motivic complexity, and sonata-like aspirations stamp the whole enterprise as unmistakeably 'symphonic', in the full, traditional sense of the word. Everything else in the work revolves about this turbulent center: the episodic first movement cunningly prepares for the second, while the highly charged recitatives and cantilenas of the slow third movement rise out of the aftermath of its catastrophic conclusion.

"Many aspects of the *Third* will be familiar to students of Lutoslawski's work: peremtory gestures of punctuation, chattering woodwinds, plaintive double-reed refrains, glissando strings, splashes for harps, piano, and percussion, sound textures deftly woven, then magically transformed, and everywhere vivid colors. What is unexpected, perhaps, are the resorting to sonata-form procedures, complete with clearcut, memorable themes; the hints of neoclassic rhythm; and the big, full orchestrations, octave doublings and all, reminiscent of much earlier works like Lutoslawski's *Concerto for Orchestra*.

"In fact the *Third Symphony* exemplifies a striking development of the last several years: the perfection of a ripe style harmonizing the composer's best-known devices of the 1960s and 1970s with other techniques that have been with him since the beginning of his career. Hints of this reconciling, synthesizing tendency may also be heard in the *Double Concerto* and especially in the powerful *Partita* for violin and piano, composed in 1985 for Pinchas Zukerman. These works are helping to create a broad, rich context in which we can begin to understand Lutoslawki's creative life as an unbroken whole. Indeed, one would be tempted to declare the *Third Symphony* a crowning achievement, summarizing a lifetime of music-making—except that Lutoslawski is still as vital as ever, and still as likely to produce a new surprise in his next piece." — Steven Stucky, in *Notes* (Music Library Association), 12/86.

"While the score [of Lutoslawski's *Symphony No. 3*] is completely notated, the composer calls for passages of 'aleatory counterpoint'. These are passages in which groups of notes, thematically derived and related, are played by individual instruments or in ensemble groupings. (Aleatory, applied to music since about 1945, is also called 'chance music' or 'music of indeterminacy'. Various composers who have used 'chance' vary in degree of its application—leaving decisions to the performers, for example. Lutoslawski believes that aleatoric passages must be controlled by the composer.) The freedom expressed by the idea of 'chance' is controlled both in the pitch content and in the rhythmic shapes and overall time allotted to a given passage. Aleatory counterpoint is an aspect of the orchestration, of the musical sound, and it is made an elemental part of the total structure.

"The composer wrote the following description of his *Symphony No. 3*:

> I began sketching my Third Symphony as early as in 1972. In the following years I composed the main movement, but subsequently I discarded it completely. It took several years for the idea to become mature, and it was only in January 1983 that the whole score finally was ready. It is true, however, that during that period I composed several other works: *Les Espaces du sommeil [Sleep's Spaces]* for baritone and orchestra, *Mi-parti* for orchestra, *Novelette* for orchestra, the Double Concerto for oboe, harp and chamber orchestra, and some smaller pieces.

The form of my Third Symphony is the result of my experience as a listener to music and particularly to large-scale forms during a period of many years. Although the extraordinary strategy of Beethoven in this realm has always fascinated me and was a supreme lesson of musical architecture, the model of a perfectly balanced large-scale form has been for me the pre-Beethovenian symphony and particularly Haydn's. I am still a lover of Brahms' large-scale works, but I confess I always feel exhausted after a performance of a Brahms symphony, concerto or even a sonata, probably because of there being two main movements (first and last) in each of them.

These considerations made me search for still other possibilities, and finally I found a solution in a two-movement large-scale form where the first movement is but a preparation for the main one that follows. The first is meant barely to interest, to attract, to involve, but never to entirely satisfy the listener. In the course of the first movement the listener is supposed to expect something more important to happen; he may even get impatient. This is exactly the situation when the second movement appears and presents the main idea of the work. This way of distributing the musical substance in time seems to me natural and is in conformity with the psychology of perception of music....

After a short introduction comes the first movement, the "preparatory" one. The music here is never set in motion for a very long time. Many pauses interrupt the musical course. The movement consists of three episodes, the first being the fastest, the third the slowest. As a matter of fact, the tempo remains the same and the difference of speed is achieved only by the use of longer rhythmical values. A short slow section leads to the main movement.

The second movement is composed in a form that may be defined as "an allusion to the sonata-allegro" with its contrasting themes. Toward the end, a series of *tutti* sections is followed by the climax of the work. A separate adagio passage, where dramatic recitatives of the strings alternate with a broad *cantilena*, forms the epilogue of the Symphony. A short and fast coda ends the work. The Symphony is to be played without interruption between movements."

> —Arrand Parsons, from liner notes for CBS Masterworks Digital Stereo LP IM 42203 (portions adapted from the program notes of the Chicago Symphony Orchestra).

TOD MACHOVER

B. 1953, New York NY. *Educ.:* Westchester Cons of Music, Juilliard Schl, Univ of CA (Santa Cruz), Columbia Univ, MIT. *Taught at:* MIT. Principal cellist, Natl Opera of Canada (Toronto); guest composer & dir. research, IRCAM *(Institut de Recherche et Coordination Acoustique/Musique)*. *Awards & grants:* Gershwin Prize, NEA Charles Ives Fellowship, Koussevitzky Fndn. *Works (many with electronics) incl.: Deplacements, Electronic Etudes, Famine* (incl 4 amplified voices), *Flora, Fresh Spring* (vocal), *Fusione Fugace, Soft Morning City!, Spectres Parisiens, Towards the Center* (incl 6 instrs).

Composer statement from a 10/90 letter to the Editor: "Here are two recent articles of mine that have statements concerning my aesthetic and compositional ideas.... Best of luck with your [publication]."

ON MUSIC – AND BEING A COMPOSER – TODAY: "From where I sit, the music world at the end of the 1980s seems enormously complicated and unhomogeneous. Music institutions and commercial distribution networks find themselves in the middle of major transformation and subject to a strong tendency towards retrenchment and hyperconservatism. Never before have artistic media reached so many people, yet never before has commercialism threatened to so trivialize artistic experience. Divisions between traditionally distinct categories of music (classical, jazz, rock, etc.) have become less clear, with both positive and negative consequences.[68] The only simple formula that can describe this era's musical style and language is that there *is no common language or mode of expression* – there has probably never been a time in the history of music when so many different musical attitudes seemed simultaneously valid.

"So what is the composer to do? How does one navigate through such unmarked waters? How does one combine the greatest seriousness of intent with a true contact or relationship with one's society? In which ways is the current creative freedom a boon, and in which ways an almost impossible burden?...

"[I believe that] the main task of the composer, as with every creative artist, has not changed in our time and never could. While public attitudes and stylistic fashion shift and sway, we are all in this for no other reason than to express and communicate something essential about being human, using that peculiar and unique combination of absolute precision of means and ambiguity of meaning that is com-

---

[68] See also remarks by William Bolcom and others, throughout this volume. (Ed.)

mon to all music. It finally only matters that one learns to tap into musical visions that are personal enough to be deeply felt, and objective enough to be universal. I truly believe that any music which satisfies these conditions will find listeners somewhere, someday.

"Concerning the overwhelming diversity of today's artistic landscape, I have chosen to confront it head-on as a major component of my musical language. In fact, my consistent and overriding artistic goal, ever since the earliest compositions of my student days, has been to create musical forms that suggest the search for psychological and spiritual unity beyond seemingly impenetrable veils of confusion and juxtaposition. That such unity exists—*must exist*—is one of my deepest convictions. That modern society presents an unprecedented network of complex parallel worlds, apparently so completely disconnected from each other, only amplifies my feeling that the search for deeper truths lies at the heart of our attempt to keep inter-personal and inter-cultural communication from breaking down and disappearing entirely.

"I strive to compose music that clearly conveys a sense of equilibrium and balance among very diverse elements. But I have not yet found such perfect unity. Therefore, my music represents a *search*, sometimes striving and impatient, once in a while more calm and welcoming. The materials that I use for my work and the forms that give them life are chosen because they seem perfectly suited to this central vision....

"In general, the composer in the United States [today] is more isolated from his society than is his colleague in France, with both positive and negative consequences. Although the new conservative government in France might significantly change the present system (which I tend to doubt), most money there is for institutional support and individual composer's commissions come from the Culture Ministry (in the United States there *is* no Culture Ministry). This tends to centralize the decisions about who gets funded and who doesn't. On the one hand such a system fosters a coherent definition of artistic excellence. But it also has a tendency to encourage an 'official' brand of composer, leaving little room for those who stray from the established norms—for aesthetic or musical/political reasons. If one has been denied the stamp of the Directeur de la Musique and his committees, there are simply not a lot of alternatives for funding and support. I was reminded this past week of a more extreme example of similar strong government support for the arts, when I participated in a Boston-area colloquium with six official Soviet composers. I could not help attributing the sameness in their music, the total lack of artistic risk-taking, to what must be a very state and yet constraining system of cultural politics....

"In the U.S., nobody gets an enormous amount of societal recognition as a composer (compare the public awareness of such Americans as John Cage or Elliott Carter with the French national celebrity of Pierre Boulez), but then there is room for virtually anyone with persistence and something to say. It is impossible to even keep track of all students studying composition at any one time. Besides some fairly meaningless composition prizes and awards, the entire culture does its best *not* to select and promote specific individuals, in many senses leaving the choices up to the laws of the marketplace, even if it be the cultural marketplace....

"The diminishing levels of national government funding have also encouraged a general decentralization of contemporary music activity in [this] country. Only a few years ago, New York was the undisputed capital of new music, but this has changed since 1980. Although artistic activity is still very abundant there, many factors have made composers look elsewhere for work environments. New York has become horrendously expensive; market conditions make it difficult to take true risks in a performance situation; new technology has not been thoroughly integrated into traditional performing ensembles; the musical publics still remain rather polarized. These conditions, plus positive factors in other regions (such as state arts agency funding, independent multi-arts performing centers—like the Walker in Minneapolis—and greater national communication through radio and cable television), have led to a boom in music activity throughout the country. Cities such as Boston, Los Angeles, Houston, Seattle, Cincinnati, and Sante Fe (to name a few) are flourishing, and producing abundant new works of international value. Most interesting about this trend is the fact that each city has tended to produce a musical culture which is unique and quite different from the others...

"[It is important I believe not to isolate 'new' works from the repertory generally.] The Horizon Festival, the major contemporary music event organized by [the composer] Jacob Druckmann for the New York Philharmonic, was a resounding success the first time around, less well received the second time, and a basic bore the third time in 1986, to the point that it may not be continued at all. This is due partly to the repetitive nature of that festival's programming (with a shrill insistence on New Romanticism and a certain feebleness in its critical discourse), but probably more to the lack of integration of that event with the orchestra's normal season.[69]

"[An integration such as that represented by the Composer Residency Program, which has been undertaken by orchestras in many parts of the United States,] marks a major, historic turning in American musical culture. When it works, and in certain cities it really *has* worked, this scheme provides a new model on which adventurous music can become part of an established cultural entity, one of the ways to connect the American composer to his society. I am convinced, for example, that one of the reasons that the Boulez 1986 U.S. tour was such a success was that it was hosted by five major symphony orchestras. Recently I attended a Friday afternoon concert at the Boston Symphony where a work by Peter Lieberson, a relatively young American composer, was premiered by Seiji Ozawa, surrounded by works of Beethoven and Ravel. I was struck by the fact that the audience, mostly made up of elder Boston patrons, reacted much more warmly to the new work (expertly composed, but neither superficial nor easy) than to the old staples....

"[An obviously important 'musical culture' in the United States is] that of *commercial and popular music*. This is the music listened to and 'consumed' by the vast majority of non-music professionals. No one could possibly complain about the financial health of the popular music industry in this country, nor of the technical quality of production. But commercialism pushed to its extreme does often mean a terrible homogenization of artistic content, with the best selling product being that which offends the least amount of people. (The amazingly quick demise of rock music video—from stimulating and innovative fusion of sound and image to unbelievably tired and limited clichés—is the clearest and most recent example.) Reaganian philosophy has stimulated the American tendency to equate quality with financial success, and to encourage therefore the arts to 'go Hollywood'. The negative sides of such pressure are all too clear— serious artistic expression is cheapened in every way. But the positive side has been the capturing of a totally new audience for serious music, at least in many cases. And a blurring of the boundaries between musical genres has been very striking in recent years. It is true that for the time being, the boundaries have been crossed in only one direction, and for obvious reasons—Frank Zappa has been played on 'serious' music concerts, and Laurie Anderson commissioned by symphony orchestras, whereas Elliott Carter or for that matter Or-

---

[69] Without any possibility of a doubt whatsoever, the *most workable solution* can be found in the present Editor's *Modest Proposal*—for which see page *xxii*, above. (Ed.)

nette Coleman have not yet become staples on commercial radio or television stations. There is both hope and danger in such popularism: we may in fact find a way of 'selling' things of great value, but it is equally likely that the passion for accessibility and immediate consumption will make it ever harder to convey deep and demanding vision....

"In the last month I have heard several new works that convince me that a vitality and cross-over [of styles, or genres, might indeed] exist in the United States after all. Anthony Davis, a young New York composer recognized as one of the very best current jazz improvisors, had his opera *X* (based on the life of the black activist Malcolm X) premiered at the New York City Opera. Not only was the opera highly publicized and sold out for all its performances, but it was a score of great seriousness and density, written in a style that combined clarity and directness of expression with subtlety and content.... It was taken seriously by the critics as well. It is interesting to note that the Davis opera was developed over a period of a few years, and is the result of an evolution which is beginning to set a precedent. *X* was produced as a 'workshop' opera in Springfield, Massachusetts. Improvements were made before a presentation at the new annual Music Theater Festival in Philadelphia. A third version was prepared for the Brooklyn Academy of Music's *Next Wave* Festival. These three preliminary runs not only allowed Davis to refine and perfect all aspects of his work before bringing it to Lincoln Center, but also allowed it to attract the attention of the New York City Opera who were impressed enough that they agreed to invest in a completely new production, and raised considerable funds to produce it royally. I am convinced that this process helped Davis produce a work that was described in *The Boston Globe* as 'one of the few American operas ever born alive, kicking and screaming, a work full of fire and anger, conviction and understanding, musical and theatrical vitality'.

"In other developments, David Byrne, the leader of the art-rock band Talking Heads, recently had the premiere (at Boston's American Repertory Theater) of his score for Robert Wilson's *Knee Plays*. The music, written for brass ensemble, draws on American folk music rather than on rock, and is well-constructed, unflashy, subtle yet directly appealing. Morton Subotnik's new work, *The Key to Songs,* was premiered last week at M.I.T. Scored for two pianos, two percussion, violin, viola, and live digital synthesis, it managed to break new ground both technologically and musically (it truly sounded as new and vital as any serious score that I have encountered in a long time, especially in its crisp, sparkling hybridization of acoustic and electronic sounds) while it borrowed from rock music a rhythmic and harmonic directness that made it immediately appealing to non-professional listeners. And two primarily visual works that I encountered in the last few weeks (David Lynch's film *Blue Velvet* and Bill Viola's videotape *I Do Not Know What It Is I Am Like*) used sound in revolutionary ways, radical both in the astonishingly subtle mixture of 'pure' music with descriptive music and background noise, as well as in elevating this music to a level of importance at least equal to visual or narrative language....[70]

"[Speaking very personally I believe it is essential] to push for a wider and deeper definition of the musical art, one that raises it again to a level of equal sophistication and importance with visual forms [including motion pictures, television, and music video]. There are many signs that our culture is more ready for such a re-evaluation of serious music than it has been for a very long time. The predom-inance of rock music has prepared many people (while, admittedly, desensitizing others) for an encounter with more demanding music. New computer-based musical instruments have given a common denominator again to serious composers and researchers, commercial musicians, and even interested amateurs who often buy such material for their homes. Many cognitive theorists, such as Marvin Minsky and Howard Gardner, have highlighted the fundamental importance of music as a human activity *precisely because* it is communicative of human intent while being more ambiguous, and therefore potentially more meaningful, than either language or visual representation. And this same factor may also attract more and more people who seek deeper, less contrived, experiences in this overly materialistic society.

"But we must not be afraid to make the highest demands on this new musical language, if it is to flourish and survive, and be integratable as an equal partner into the new collaborative art works of the future. It is not sufficient to merely 'pick sides' from the stylistic battle of the week, nor is it good enough to get lost in the technical minutiae of formalistic systematizing. We must push farther to

---

[70] Mr. Machover's mention of composers Pierre Boulez, Elliott Carter, John Cage, Jacob Druckmann, Peter Lieberson, Ornette Coleman, Laurie Anderson, Frank Zappa, Anthony Davis, David Byrne, Morton Subotnik and many others is a reminder of the enormous number of composers *not* represented in the present volume—which, of course, includes only a very small selection of contemporary artists. It is hoped that, nevertheless, the complaint which is sometimes voiced that "nothing much of interest" is being done in contemporary fields might be put to rest, merely by perusing the table of contents of this book—or by reflecting on Machover's essay. (Ed.)

ask how we may help derive a music which can have as deep as possible an impact [upon] those [with whom] we wish to communicate.

"On this path, it must be remembered that art that is merely self-referential, that speaks only of its own materials and forms, is sterile and superficial. The elements of artistic language must be carefully adapted by the artist to represent a particular human vision. It is precisely this delicate marriage of deep, original vision with a fitting, concise and expressive form that ultimately determines the value of a work of art. Art *can* and *must* represent human reality, but needs to objectify and elevate this reality by giving it form. Music allows us both to observe reality by understanding the behavior of musical materials in ever-deeper ways, and to express a view of reality through the use of these materials....

"The conviction to which I keep returning is that there exists a degree of unity far deeper than that which is suggested by the surface differences and complexities surrounding us. I love to compose music that conveys clearly this sense of equilibrium and balance. As I have said before, I have not yet found such perfect unity. Therefore, again, my music expresses a *search* [for unity... At the same time,] there exists a powerful, tension-generating paradox in my work. My goal is to achieve unity through *inclusion* rather than *exclusion*. I look to find a place for so many different sounds and melodies and textures and harmonies that each piece hovers on the brink of exploding from too much contrast, too many differences. In this way, I am perhaps a spiritual descendant of such American composers as Charles Ives and Elliott Carter. I will only be satisfied when a place is found for everything in the world that stimulates me, everything that I love; and it is out of this chaos, this sonic jungle, that I attempt to forge unity.

"I am not interested in such restrictive artistic movements as serial, minimal, neo-expressionist, new wave, technological, or 'sound art'.[71] They all simplify the world by choosing a safe and limited corner of it. I am motivated rather by the ideal of Bach, who knew how to find a place for every musical idea that his epoch had discovered. And he knew how to forge a language, a context, in which all of these elements found a natural place. It is surely of this all-encompassing vision that Beethoven thought when he punned on Bach's name: '*Nicht Bach; Meer sollte es heissen* [Not a brook—rather, an *ocean* he ought to be called]'. I am not lucky enough to possess

---

[71] Philip Glass—to take one example—also objects to such (however convenient, sometimes) generalizations regarding musical styles and constructions: protesting that his own music is not merely "minimalist". See Glass composer entry, above. (Ed.)

such a comprehensive and total vision. But my fundamental task is to get as close to one as possible, to try as hard as I can to incorporate in this tapestry every musical element that I find stimulating, and to document this journey in my compositions.

"The personal language that I [am trying to] forge attempts to satisfy these conditions. I look for a set of basic sonic materials, syntactic constructions, expressive states and formal principles that allow me diversity and control simultaneously.

"The main parameters of any musical language are melody, harmony, rhythm and timbre. I attempt to enrich each of these parameters as much as I can. But there are limits to our perception and, specifically, our auditory understanding. If all four elements are simultaneously at a maximum level of intense activity, we perceive only confusion. For instance, it would be easier to perceive the rhythmic distinctness of four musical lines moving at different speeds (a polyrhythm, say, of 4:5:6:7) with complex accented patterns if the general harmonic rhythm is slow, rather than if chords are whizzing by at the speed of the shortest note value. The experience of serial music taught us how quickly one loses track of complexity when it is present at the same time on all musical levels....

"The trick for today's composer is to balance or 'unify' these four elements, to make sure that they complement each other. It is as if the four parameters were four passengers in a rather unstable rowing boat, each seated in one of the four corners. With all four sitting still the boat remains stable and well balanced; when one moves, stands up, or jumps up quickly the others must stay more still than ever, moving only to redistribute weight and avoid capsizing, often leaning over the edge of the boat to do so....

"The composer needs to manipulate and control these parameters to achieve various points on the continuum between independence and interdependence. Diversity and complexity are quickly heard as the activity of each parameter is increased. Unity is achieved in two ways. In the first, one of the parameters is clearly established as being more prominent than the others, which then take the role of embellishers. I have often used this method to allow, for instance, a rich and florid melodic line to express the continuity of a particular musical section (*Nature's Breath*), or alternately harmony (first movement of *String Quartet Nr. 1*), rhythm (last movement of the same piece), or timbre (*Fusione Fugace*). In each of these cases, one parameter is given structural importance and defines the musical shape for a particular span of time.

"The second method for achieving multi-parametric unity is to moderate the activity of *all* parameters, so that none is too dense and all shed light on the others. Since my desire is to create states of imbalance, I tend to use this form of writing as a special case, often appearing near the end of compositions, when the necessary musical elements have had a chance to cohere....

"[One element which ultimately enters into my own compositional process is that of research.] I engage in research to help produce the tools and instruments that I need to create the music that I imagine. In turn I am stimulated on to new musical discoveries through contact with thinkers and inventors from many different disciplines. In fact, I often find, as in the current situation at M.I.T., that I have more to learn from researchers in parallel fields (such as perception, cognitive psychology, computer graphics, video, etc.) than from other composers. The danger of course is that it is all too easy to look at these other [fields and] sciences as metaphors rather than as true disciplines, and to make sloppy and too-literal translations from them to a musical context. But if one avoids this trap, then it is possible to learn of profound principles concerning human expressivity, memory, and mental organization that are of fundamental importance for any new music. If the principles are deep enough, then a truly personal reinterpretation, in light of one's own artistic needs, is possible. How boring it is to remain within the narrow confines of the specific technical issues of an art form. In such a case, discoveries are likely to be made in reference to other music, rather than to nature itself, This goes against the spirit of true creativity, and leads to art which is more and more in-bred, about nothing but itself and therefore further and further from deep human concerns." — Tod Machover. French version published in *Inharmoniques*, Centres Georges Pompidou, Paris, 2/87. Portions of the above version also adapted from a second article by Tod Machover, "A Stubborn Search for Artistic Unity", in Simon Emmerson, ed., *The Language of Electroacoustic Music*.

Bug-Mudra for 2 Guitars, Percussion, and Conductor with Midi-Glove (incl. Electronics) (1989-90). 15m Comm. Fromm Music Fndn (Harvard Univ). *Prem.:* Bunkamura Theatre (Tokyo). *Other perf.:* Ens. with David Starobin, Oren Fader (gtrs), Todd Machover (cond).

"*Bug-Mudra* was composed at the request of guitarist David Starobin, and is dedicated to my dear friend Tomoyuki Sugiyama. *Bug-Mudra* is scored for two guitars (one acoustic and one electric), percussion (KAT electronic mallet controller plus three acoustic suspended cymbals), and conductor. The three instrumentalists are connected to the 'hyper-instrument' system, as is the conductor through the use of a special glove (the EXOS Dexterous Hand Master) worn on the left

Composer/conductor Machover wielding the EXOS Dexterous Hand Master glove, described below. Copyright © 1990 Donna Coveney — courtesy Bridge Records.

hand and adapted for music use under the direction of David Sturman. This glove measures the nuances of the conductor's left-hand gestures, translating them to influence the piece's overall sonic result. The title *Bug-Mudra* comes from two sources put together: *mudra* being the word for hand gesture in classical Indian dance, and *bug* referring to computer 'bugs', a pun on the difficulty of getting such a complex interactive system to work in a live concert situation.

"*Bug-Mudra* is organized into six sections (actually eight, since section four is subdivided into three parts), but in fact is imagined as a dynamic *moto perpetuo*, unfolding in a burst of energy from beginning to end. The first section is a rapid, syncopated and contrapuntal song, whose rhythm and harmony become the subject of development in section two. Section three features a virtuosic electric bass melody, over which acoustic guitar tremolos and electronic percussion washes build up interchanging harmonies and harmonic spectra. Section four is melodic and lyrical, although fragmented guitar tremolos and 'hyper-instrument' arpeggios keep the piece moving forward. The melody and accompaniment move into the highest register as the three instruments approach their first moment of total unity, together playing the triumphal melody that leads to section five. Section five is a vivid fantasy that combines a descending bass line played by 'hyper-' acoustic guitar, an ascending soprano *cantus firmus* played by 'hyper-' percussion, and a virtuosic electric guitar melody (with the live guitar adding timbre and phrase articulation to a pre-sequenced track) that sweeps wildly through all registers. Section six is a recapitulation of section one, with an elaborately accumulating harmonic and rhythmic accompaniment, and with extra music added at each reprise. The piece gathers intensity constantly, and ends on an affirmative unison.

"The hyper-instrument design team for this work is: Tod Machover, Joseph Chung, David Sturman, Andrew Hong, Jim Davis and Casimir Wierzynski." — Tod Machover, from program notes for 10/11/90 Miller Theater (New York) performance.

Editor's notes (written on the subway, following the above performance): "From its bang! of an opening, this is a real roller-coaster of a piece, by turns explosive and trance-like hypnotic... now and then one enters a 'minimalist'-like world, with lots of notes streaming energetically out of the amplifiers spaced all around us. I also found myself thinking, 'rock music stuck fast on a Bach passacaglia... gone mad in an electronic fireworks factory'... In sum — terrifically colorful and exciting."

VALIS (opera) (1987). *Lib.*: after Philip K. Dick novel. 77m *Rec.*: Bridge (CD) BCD 9007 (also as MC: BCS 7007; distr Allegro Imports): soloists, Daniel Ciampolini (perc), Emma Stephenson (pno/keyboards), Tod Machover, cond.
1 spkr, 2 s, 1 m-s, 1 t, 2 bar, 1 b
perc, pno/keyboards; pre-recorded tape & computer
In two acts.

"Electronic technology has come a long way since [the 1960s], and no one has worked harder to humanize its power than Tod Machover.

"Mr. Machover studied at Juilliard with Elliott Carter and Roger Sessions; he then went to Pierre Boulez's organization [IRCAM] in Paris, and finally to M.I.T. He has spent the last decade designing 'hyperinstruments' that can be played conventionally, yet are sonically transformed by live electronic processing. So far, this sounds like an average MIDI computer set-up. But Mr. Machover's goal is an intelligent, interactive process, one in which computers respond to the nuances of each interpretation and create a slightly different 'accompaniment' every time.

"All this techology would be pointless without compelling music. But Mr. Machover is as talented a composer as he is an inventor. On 'Flora' (Bridge BCD-9010; CD only), he includes two works for hyperinstruments and live electronics, *Towards the Center* (1989) and *Bug-Mudra* (1990). Mr. Machover has been keeping his ear tuned to the explosion of electronics in the pop-music world, and these works are a high-intensive mix of rock's bass lines and driving beat, rhapsodic fusion-jazz, dissonant counterpoint and delicate classical filigree. Remarkably, this stylistic combination seems entirely natural, and the computer technology opens up uncharted sonic realms that are explored with clarity and virtuosity....

"It was not until the opera *VALIS* that Mr. Machover's language opened up. Based on the Philip K. Dick science-fiction novel, *VALIS* creates a music-video environment of mystical, hallucinatory intensity. By the year 2000, *VALIS* will probably be seen as the first populist, rock-influenced, computer-driven opera, a worthy successor to *Tommy* — and more innovative than [John Adams'] *Nixon in China*." — K. Robert Schwarz, in *The New York Times*, 8/19/90.

"One of Bach's contemporaries once remarked that it was a pity that this intellectual composer had never had the opportunity to write for the opera, where he could learn the art of crowd pleasing. Well, Tod Machover, who needed such an opportunity, has been given one, and boy, has he ever profited by it.

"The lesson was not an easy one: Machover amputated nearly a third of *VALIS* — a half hour of music — following the opera's December 1987 Paris premiere, and he reworked both the score and the libretto (originally a collaborative effort between Machover, French video artist Catherine Ikam, and American actor/director Bill Raymond) to make the definitive, 77-minute version heard [on the new Bridge recording].[72] It must be said that, whatever the initial travails, *VALIS* in its final form has become a work of bold imagination, strongly individual personality, and undeniable emotional impact — in short, a major contribution to the American musical stage.

---

[72] This well illustrates the importance of live performances of contemporary music. A composer(or other artist) ought to have the feeling that he or she is communicating *with* someone. The interaction may or may not, in turn, prompt structural or other changes in a given piece. (Ed.)

"Those familiar with Machover's previous work should be warned that the composer of *Nature's Breath* and *Spectres parisiens* is barely recognizable in *VALIS*, and the earlier Boulez clone who wrote *Light* and *Soft Morning, City!* cannot be found at all. Indeed, one of the most remarkable things about *VALIS* is its extraordinary stylistic range and depth: each of the opera's 22 numbers is an independently conceived set piece, with its own distinct form, structure, harmonic language, and color, making the whole so diverse as to seem, at first, scattered and unfocused. Repeated hearings, howeverver, reveal an underlying cellular/motivic/thematic unity that is doubly impressive in pulling together such extremely varied — even opposed — materials while serving so well the opera's dramatic theme.

"*VALIS* is based on a bizarrely autobiographical novel by the posthumously famous science fiction author Philip K. Dick. Dick' novels are, by and large, convoluted and disturbing exercises in paranoid solipsism in which everyday life, dreams, madness, and fiction lose their boundaries and blend together, with hints of mysterious outside forces (malevolent? benign?) controlling the breakdown. Machover, however, has stripped *VALIS* down to its bare bones, focusing on its central human drama and reducing the sci-fi elements to veiled allusions and a handful of visual special effects.

"Here, Dick is a character in his own fiction — or rather two characters: the dispassionate, unsympathetic authorial voice *and* his alter ego, Horselove Fat (an etymological 'translation' of Philip Dick). Fat is a weak, unhappy neurotic who, as the story opens, has experienced an unnerving, day-long mystical experience (as the author himself did in 1974), which convinces him that human minds are part of a large 'computer-like thinking system' that has, however, failed to function properly. Distressed by the abyss thus opened and by the suicide of a friend, Gloria, whom he had tried feebly to help, Fat attempts suicide. He is counseled by a psychiatrist, Dr. Stone, who quotes Lao-Tse at him and insists that only he, Fat, can explain the universe to himself.

"He also encounters two faintly sinister rock musicians, Eric and Linda Lampton, who seem to know all about his strange experience and its source, which they call VALIS, an acronymn for Vast Active Living Intelligent System. The Lamptons' house composer — who has been conducting the opera! — now climbs out of the orchestra pit and materializes a computer construct/young girl/angel/god named Sophia who heals Phil/Fat of his duality and vanishes, later bidding him good-bye in a dream — in Gloria's voice. Thus fortified and renewed, the author/protagonist sits down to await life's further challenges in calm readiness.

"All this is not only fantastical but symbolic: note the enlightening 'Lamp'tons and the female personifications of Glory and Wisdom. Underneath the technological whiz-bangery lies a universal and 'ordinary' tale of suffering and redemption—made explicit with a quote from *Parsifal*. With its extensive narration, sketchy characters (only Horselover Fat is fully limned), tableaulike scenes, and essentially religious theme, *VALIS* fits very comfortably into the 20th century's 'opera-oratorio' tradition—a tradition of which *Parsifal* might as well be the ancestor.

"In the extreme compression of Dick's plot, Machover places heavy demands on audience attention. Four of the seven characters are never even named on stage, and many important events and relationships are revealed only by allusion or context—so that several French critics at the premiere, for example, mistook the psychiatrist for a priest. To a certain extent, this must be intentional; shifting and uncertain reality is, after all, what this piece is about. The third time I listed to *VALIS*, I tried to imagine a concert performance of the work, in which all visual cues would be absent, and found that the tale still worked very well—but only if the audience were willing to accept a lot of mystery. I suspect that in any production of this opera, staged or not, there will always be the risk that viewers will supply their own, erroneous connections among the disjunct and puzzling events set before them.

"The various scenes and characters of *VALIS* are assigned individual musical garments, ranging from pure noise and 'sound-poetry', through strict serialism and varying degrees of tonality, to classicized versions of rock (complete with video), rap, and new-age music. The assignments are often tellingly calculated: the psychiatrist, for example, gets a sort of atonal Gregorian chant resembling the vocal line of Varèse's *Ecuatorial*, backed by tolling bass drones. Overall, there is a broad movement, following the dramatic structure, from dissonant to consonant and from the spoken (it is more than 15 minutes into the opera before there is any extended singing) to the lyrical. Superimposed on this transition is a traditional two-act form with trio and quartet finales, and spanning the whole is an S-curved musical curve anchored at its extremes by lengthy arias—the only two items so called—for Dr. Stone (low bass) and Sophia (high soprano).

"The emotional peak of the opera, on the other hand, comes at its center. The Part I finale, in which Fat pours out his misery to alter ego Phil while Gloria commits wordless coloratura suicide unnoticed, leads directly into the Lamptons' rock video, the opening scene of Part II. All the tension of the first scene is poured into the second, magnifying the urgency of the Lamptons' skeletal text ('I want to see you, man...') and developing a rhythmic momentum of chair-gripping intensity.

"Since Part II moves toward a concluding serenity, there is no opportunity for comparable histrionics at the end of the opera. Instead, Sophia's dream-farewell to Phil/Fat packs a considerable wallop in its very simplicity and unexpectedness. It is the strongest possible testimony to Machover's musico-dramatic abilities that he is able to bring this sequence off, tiptoeing as he does right to the edge of treacly sentimentality, introducing the number (in Phil's words) as 'the most beautiful song I ever heard' — and then making you believe it.

"On paper, the 'orchestration' for *VALIS* looks austere: just piano, percussion, prerecorded tape, and computer manipulation. Thanks to the last of these, however, there is no sense of 'chamber opera' about the piece at all. Machover, an IRCAM [*Institut de Recherche et Coordination Acoustique/Musique*] veteran, has a well-earned reputation as the wunderkind of the computer-music world, and his extraordinarily sophisticated software is capable of true ensemble performance, turning individual singers into choruses and single instruments into multitimbred ensembles — contrapuntal, homophonic, or hetereophic, as needed. The computer also provides a wide variety of echo and reverberation effects on an almost line-by-line basis. Moreover, since the characters often appear on video monitors instead of (or in addition to) performing *in propria persona*, the blurring of reality that is central to the plot is extended to all aspects of the performance. Is it live, or is it Memorex? You can't tell the players without a score....

"The plot and theme of *VALIS* bears a remarkable resemblance to those of Philip Glass's *1,000 Airplanes on the Roof*, composed at almost the same time. There, too, we find a tormented loner subject to unsettling mental experiences imposed by an alien intelligence; the potential lover rejected; the psychiatric consultation. There are musical similarities too: the stripped-down, highly electronic instrumentation; the heavy reliance on spoken dialogue.

"This implied comparison [is intended to point to the unusual quality of Machover's compelling new stage piece]." — Andrew Stiller, in *Musical America*, 3/89.

JOHN MADDEN

B. Great Britain.

The Chime Child (6 partsongs) for SATB with divisions. *Text:* Adapted by the composer from Somerset (England) folklore. 14m *Pub.:* Novello.
1. *The Chime Child.* 2. *I took My Dame to a Lambing Feast.* 3. *Nutting on Sunday.* 4. *The Lazy Wave.* 5. *The Green Lady.* 6. *The Carol of Christ's Donkey.*

"The composer's note explains that the work was written for the St. Michael's Singers of Cambridge. It consists of six partsongs, four for SATB (sometimes with soloist), one SSAA, and one TTBB. All the songs are unaccompanied, but a piano reduction is provided for rehearsal purposes. Musically [these] are tuneful pieces skillfully composed, tonal and only occasionally banal in their use of 'enriched' harmonies. Extremes of vocal range are avoided: a variety of textures and rhythms are used (including some passages very attractive in their syncopations). *The Chime Child* is another good choral work, conservative in approach, such as English composers have been producing regularly in recent decades: music pleasing in its use of voices, poetry, tunes, and rhythms."—Robert Gronquist, in *Notes* (Music Library Association), 9/81.

MIKLÓS MAROS

B. 1943 (Hungary). For biographical details see Scandinavian Music Center, *Music from Scandinavia*. Works incl: chamber (incl. *Quartet* for saxophones), orchestral (*Aspectus, Confluentia*), vocal.

Symphony 1. Rec.: Phono Suecia Digital LP PS 23 (distr. Audio Source): Budapest Orchestra, Miklós Maros, cond.
In four movements.

"Like very modern music? Looking for something different? Read on.

"Miklós Maros is the 42-year-old son of the late Hungarian composer Rudolf Maros. Miklós, however, left Hungary with his wife, Ilona, and settled in Stockholm in 1968 to study with Ingvar Lidholm and has taught there since 1971. In 1972 he founded the Maros Ensemble, specializing in avant-garde scores. He is a composer of impressive talents, and diversity.

"Maros' *Symphony 1* is an orchestral *tour de force*. Written in 1973-74 and revised slightly after its 1976 premiere, it is scored for a huge orchestra that includes a hecklephone and guitar. The music is incredibly dense and dissonant in a fashion reminiscent of Ives. Maros called this work a symphony mainly because the first movement 'turned out' to have sonata form, but that form is well disguised: free and constricted rhythms are in opposition; different sections of the orchestra wrestle for control; awesome crescendos are reached; a great darkness prevails; a violence of sound engulfs the movement's conclusion. The work's second movement is a funeral march commemorating the death of Gustaf Adolf VI in September of 1973: a muffled and deeply mournful mood is personified by a solo hecklephone passage; the only strings present are the low ones—violas, cellos, and double basses. A miniscule *Scherzando* movement of merely 12 bars is a whirlwind of a toccata that sets up the finale, wherein musical motion is played out in stupendous dimensions—overlapping pulsations, jagged outbursts, and the like. This is strong stuff. Complex, almost gross, but I found it irresistible." — Stephen W. Ellis, in *Fanfare: The Magazine for Serious Record Collectors*, 9-10/85.

PHILIP P. MARTORELLA

B. 1955, New York (Brooklyn) NY. *Educ.:* Mannes College of Music, Juilliard Schl, Manhattan Schl of Music. *Taught at:* Turtle Bay Music Schl, St. Johns Prep Schl. Pianist. *Works incl.:* concerto (pno), musical shows (*Doctors and Patients, Tar Beach Casino*), piano pieces (*10 Etudes*, preludes, sonata).

Composer statement: "Music is a universal language composed of definite and indefinite sounds. Music can be felt as well as listened to. Our hearts are the miraculous 'metronomes of nature', our footsteps can create wonderful marches of indefinite-sounding rhythm, our speaking voices can create conversations of various inflections of sound: high and low, and the dynamics of such sound. Music can be anything from an orchestral tune-up to one of the great symphonic works. It can evoke so many different emotions, feelings, and has an enormous effect on our moods. One may cringe when listening to dissonance, however this is as much a part of music as are the pleasant sounds of consonance. An interesting analogy: dissonance is to consonance as conflict is to resolution. There is so much conflict and tension that exists during everyday life, why shouldn't it be used in music? Music reflects without denial conflicts and resolutions in our society.

"My music is melodic and structured so that dissonance does not necessarily function as a means to an end, but as an interrogation toward a certain kind of response. My music is like translated conversation, dealing with the possibilities of pre-meditated or pre-conceived dialogue within a very harmonious or polyphonic texture that becomes full of urgency, excitement, and passion, as well as moments of serenity. It is also a yearning for the desirable or unattainable, it is a redefinition of the romantic idiom as I understand it. I try to express the full range of the emotions and expressions of my soul. Should a listener dislike any of it, he or she could be misapprehending either the music itself or my feelings."

Please Come Inside (song) for Solo Voice (or Chorus) and Piano (1987). *Ms.:* Philip P. Martorella, 110-11 Queens Blvd, Forest Hills NY 11375.
Sonata 2 in E^b Major for Viola (or Clarinet) and Piano (1980). *Ms.:* Philip P. Martorella, 110-11 Queens Blvd, Forest Hills NY 11375. 1. Allegro con brio. 2. Adagio espressivo. 3. Allegro vivace.
Starlight Transmissions for Piano (1979). 4m *Ms.:* Philip P. Martorella, 110-11 Queens Blvd, Forest Hills NY 11375.

Typically for this composer, these three works make use of popular idioms: the melodic *Starlight Transmissions* (originally titled *Tropical Overture*) employs a jazz style in its depiction of "sounds of the tropics" (stars, breezes, sea, wildlife, trees); *Please Come Inside* (which politely asks the homeless to "please, come inside this home as a shelter for you") is a slow, flowing popular song; the *Second Sonata* for viola or clarinet also has a strong jazz, contemporary flavor.

WILLIAM MAYER

B. 1925, New York NY. *Educ.:* Yale Univ, Juilliard Schl, Mannes College of Music. *Taught at:* Boston Univ. Chmn., Composers Recordings Inc. *Awards:* 2 NEA grants, Guggenheim & MacDowell Fellowships, grants from Ford Fndn, NY & MI State Arts Councils. *Works incl.:* chamber, choral, *Hello, World!* (for children), operas, orchestral music (*Two Pastels*), piano works, *The Snow Queen* (ballet).

Composer statement: "Beware the phrase 'great composer'. It is true, of course, that composers in this officially sanctioned category have produced wondrous compositions. Unquestionably we'd all be poorer if these giants had failed to produce certain works. But it is a false jump in logic to assume that such composers cannot also turn out drab and banal pieces. Every composer has this right, and it is usually exercised. And here is where the public is suckered. Programmers love to present a neat and all-inclusive package, especially if it is anniversary time for a famous composer. So a marathon is offered with doubtful works sneaking in under the never-to-be questioned umbrella entitled 'great composer'. To even suggest that the little varmits be pushed out from the umbrella into the rain is considered treasonable. So the public pays a double price: they are trapped into hearing these mediocre pieces (which they dare not question because of their pedigree), and they miss hearing some truly great pieces by 'non-great' composers."[73]

A Death in the Family (opera in 3 acts) (1983). *Lib.* composer, after the James Agee novel and Tad Mosel play *All the Way Home.* 2 hrs *Prem.:* Minnesota Opera, 1983. *Other perfs.:* Opera Theatre of St. Louis; broadcast on Natl Public Radio on three occasions, with Dawn Upshaw, Jake Gardner (leads). Winner, 1983 Natl Inst for Music Theatre Award. Full & piano-vocal scores available from American Music Center; Music Associates of America.
1 boy s, 2 s, 4 mez, 1 a, 2 t, 2 bar, 2 b-bar, 2 b; various small parts; several parts permit doubling; chorus
2-1-2-1; 2-1-2-0; timp, perc, harp, piano; strings
In three acts. Setting: Knoxville, Tennessee, 1915.

---

[73] At the risk of betraying a certain kind of bias, I can only add "bravo!" It is not that one does not love—and love well—music from a given source, irrespective of "pedigree". But, one does not want to have all of the adventure squeezed out of the listening experience. (Ed.)

"William Mayer's *A Death in the Family* should immediately become a candidate for regular airings around the country so beautiful and meaningful is it, not only in its James Agee story but in the setting the composer-librettist has provided for it." —Robert Jacobson, in *Opera News*.

"In composer Mayer, James Agree found a kindred soul and Opera Theatre of St. Louis, for the first time in its history, a deeply moving and uniquely American work." —Henry Orland, *St. Louis Globe-Democrat*.

"The music understands the spirit of the book in a remarkable way. Thank you for a beautiful work." —Mia Agee, widow of James Agee.

Inner and Outer Strings for String Quartet and String Orchestra (1982). 8m *Comm. & prem.*: Mendelssohn String Quartet (Laurie Smukler, Nicholas Mann, Ira Weller, Marcy Rosen), The String Revival, Howard Shanet, cond. *Other perf.*: Richard Rood, Martin Agee (vlns), Linda Moss (vla), André Emelianoff (vc), Music Today Ens, Gerard Schwarz, cond. *Pub.*: Boelke-Bomart (distr. Jerona Music Corp. —full score).

"Conductor Milton Katims [has] described *Inner and Outer Strings* as a '20th century version of a concerto grosso'. The piece is structured so that the 'inner strings' (the quartet) are spatially separated from the larger group, the 'outer strings'. In my mind the former represent the intimacy of human life while the latter conjure up the impersonal quality of the universe. In pitch the quartet remains within the middle range while the surrounding string orchestra encompasses sonorities at both extremes, sometimes simultaneously." —William Mayer.

"Mayer's *Inner and Outer Strings* is spunky, unself-conscious, and as rich in humor as it is in substance." —Susan Elliott, in the *New York Post*, 12/1/88.

Octagon for Piano and Orchestra (1971). Also vers. for 2 pianos (parts on rental). 29m *Prem.*: William Masselos (piano), American SO, Leopold Stokowski, cond. *Other perf.*: William Masselos (piano), Milwaukee SO, Kenneth Schermerhorn, cond. *Rec*: Composers Recordings Inc (Stereo LP CRI CD-584): William Masselos (piano), Milwaukee SO, Kenneth Schermerhorn, cond. *Pub.*: MCA (Music Corp. of America).
2-2-2-2; 2-2-2-1; timp, 2 perc, harp; strings [also 2-piano version]
In eight movements.

"1. *Interrotto* (Molto moderato). In *Octagon*, themes are often pitted against each other. In the first movement a fragile and saccharine figure is pounded and eventually pulverized by attacking sonorities, first from the piano and then from the orchestra. This aggressive energy continues to bob up, but more sparingly, in succeeding movements, occasionlly attacking new and more serious material without warning. But, there are also many stretches of simple lyricism, free from attacks. And there are a number of organizing principles totally unrelated to conflict. Each movement, for example, features a different facet of the piano, But certainly a central fact of *Octagon* is the rapid alternation of the gentle with the abrasive.

"All the movements are short except for the opening one. This, as the little *Interotto* indicates, is a series of interruptions, short and violent in character.

"2. *Canzone* (Poco adagio). The second movement is a lament, something between a chorale and a song, with a free inner section.

"3. *Scherzo* (Un poco presto). The third movement, insouciant in spirit, tosses flippancies about between clarinets, brass, xylophone and piano, but is still subject to inerruptions reminiscence of the first movement.

"4. *Toccata* (Molto vivo). The *Toccata*, which follows the third movement without pause, is relentless and a knotty workout for the piano, primarily in its darker registers.

"5. *Fantasia* (Andante misterioso). The fifth movement funtions as the central arch of *Octagon*. The opening sonorities on the piano (a simultaneous sounding of major and minor sixths) reappear throughout the fantasy, walling off episodes as if by a crystal curtain. The movement relates back to the second in its lyricism and looks ahead to the sixth and seventh in its bell sonorities.

"6. *Clangor* (Energico). The title *Clangor* pretty well sums up the sixth movement. Anvils extend the clangorous piano sound. The movement is boisterous, and from time to time jeering, led by the kazoo.

"7. *Points and Lights* (Con moto). The seventh movement reflects bell tones — now their distant and delicate side. This movement, too, contains violent interruptions.

"8. *Finale* (Poco presto). The *Finale* contains fragments of previous movements in new combinations. It concentrates, however, on first-movement sonorities attacking the simple lament of the second movement. A short and steely cadenza follows. The work ends on an entirely new plane with remote piano chords and string harmonies — as if all the turmoil were receding into the galaxies." — William Mayer.

Songs and song cycles for voice and instruments. Scores available from Music Associates of America.
- *Enter Ariel* (6 songs) for Soprano, Clarinet and Piano (1980). 11m *Comm. & prem.:* The Ariel Ensemble (Julia Lovett, s, Jerome Bunke, cl, Michael Fardink, pno). *Other perf.:* Bell'Arte Trio (Elizabeth Pool, s, Charles Stier, cl, Jeffrey Chappell, pno).
  1. *Water-Lilies* (text: Sara Teasdale). 2. *Let It Be Forgotten* (t. Teasdale). 3. *The Flight* (t. Teasdale). 4. *Hist-Wist* (t. e. e. cummings). 6. *Flotsam* (t. Langston Hughes).
- *Passage (Journey Through Time)* (7 songs) for Mezzo-Soprano, Flute and Harp (1981). *Texts:* William Mayer (*Sneak-Thief*), Elizabeth Aleinikoff (*Nights Do Go By*), Carl Sandburg, Edna St. Vincent Mil-

lay (*What Lips My Lips Have Kissed*), Dylan Thomas (*Fern Hill* — for soprano & instruments), Percy Bysshe Shelley. 20m *Comm. & prem:* The Jubal Trio. *Other perf.:* Jane Bryden (s), Mary Feinsinger (m-s), Paul Dunkel (fl), Stacey Shames (hp). *Score available from:* Music Associates of America.

"Mayer's *Enter Ariel* [cycle is] most winning, using the voice and instrumental combination to good effect. Mayer's setting of poems by Crane, cummings, Hughes and Teasdale are sensitive, actually augmenting the poer of the texts, something not always true today." — Byron Belt, in *The Star-Ledger*, 5/19/80.

"*Enter Ariel* treats each of its three performers (a soprano, a clarinettist and pianist) as individual entities. Although *Enter Ariel* is a cyle comprising five songs, instrumental passages are not conceived as accompaniment but have equal billing with the voice. As for the title, I had Shakespeare's character in *The Tempest* in mind, for all the sounds deal with currents: wind, water and human. The last poem he wrote. For me it represents the artist's hope that even after he is gone, his message will find wings on 'the sea wind' and 'be blown along'.

"The concept underlying *Passage* is the inexorable progression of time. The first poem, *Sneak-Thief*, castigates time for stealing youth away in such an invisible and stealthy manner. The next poem, *Nights Do Go By*, takes a kinder view of time, reminding us that no matter how restless and long our nights may be, they do go by.

"Edna St. Vincent Millay, in her poem *What Lips My Lips Have Kissed*, would hardly subscribe to those ferociously optimistic lines of poet Robert Browning 'Grow old along with me. The best is yet to be!' Ms. Millay, as it were, bites the bullet. She closes her poem with the poignant admission 'I cannot say what loves have come and gone; I only know that summer sang in me a little while that sings in me no more.' Whistling heard in the song's opening recalls the 'Sweet Bird of Youth'.

"Dylan Thomas, too, recalls youth in his *Fern Hill*, but in quite a different manner from Ms. Millay. The poem operates in two time frames. Earlier sections recreate the exuberance and ease of youth as freshly as they were once experienced. In later passages these same experiences are filtered through adult awareness. The shifts in perspective translate into abrupt tempo changes and contrasting tessituras for the soprano depending on whether she 'is' the child or is remembering the child. In Ms. Millay's poem, the poet admits that summer no longer sings within her. In Dylan Thomas' poem, however, the poet continues to sing despite mortality. 'Time held me green and dying though I sang in my chains like the sea.' " — William Mayer.

GIAN CARLO MENOTTI

B. 1911, Cadegliano (Italy). *Educ.:* Milan Cons, Curtis Inst. *Taught at:* Curtis Inst. *Awards incl.:* Pulitzer Prizes (2), Drama Critics' Circle Awards (2), New York Music Critics' Circle Award. *Works incl.:* ballets *(Errand into the Maze, Sebastian)*, concertos (db, 3 insts, pno), *The Death of the Bishop of Brindisi* (cantata), operas incl. *Amahl and the Night Visitors, Amelia Goes to the Ball, The Boy Who Grew Too Fast, A Bride from Pluto, The Consul, Le Dernier Sauvage, The Egg, Help, Help, the Gobolinks!, The Hero, The Island God, Labyrinth, Maria Golovin, Martin's Lie, The Medium, The Most Important Man, The Old Maid and the Thief, The Saint of Bleeker Street, The Telephone, The Trial of the Gypsy, The Unicorn, the Gorgon and the Manticore.*

Concerto in A Minor for Violin and Orchestra (1952). *Recs.:* RCA Red Seal: Tossy Spivakovsky (vln), Boston SO, Charles Munch, cond; Varèse Sarabande (CD) VCD 47239: Ruggiero Ricci (vln), Pacific SO, Keith Clark, cond.
In three movements.

"Two of 20th-century America's most conservative composers are beautifully represented [with violin concertos: Samuel Barber's op. 14, and the present work.] I have always greatly preferred Gian Carlo Menotti's purely instrumental efforts to his more famous vocal works, and his 1952 violin concerto stands, in my opinion, as his *chef d'oeuvre*. The stunning opening theme, with its ear-opening major-minor ambiguity, has never failed to elicit gasps from friends for whom I've played the [ancient] recording with Tossy Spivakovsky, Munch and the Boston Symphony. [Ricci and the Pacific Symphony under Keith Clark also offer an absolutely top-flight performance.] In addition to the ingenuous beauty of the concerto's many themes, the work, throughout its three movements (but particularly in the outer two) has a playfulness and spirit that are hard to resist." – Royal S. Brown, in *Fanfare: The Magazine for Serious Record Collectors*, 9-10/86.

The Marriage (opera)(1988).

"By any standards, Gian Carlo Menotti must rank as an original: a 77-year old Italo-American composer living in a remote corner of Scotland writing operas about, among others, a Spanish painter (*Goya*, 1986) and a visitor from outer space (*A Bride from Pluto*, 1982). When he tells you that he once wrote an opera for the Ninth International Congress of Anthropological and Ethnological Sciences and that his latest is for the 1988 Olympics opening in South Korea this weekend,[74] the scenario acquires an air of madness which lacks only a White Rabbit for the finishing touch.

"Maestro Menotti agrees that it is indeed all a little 'crazy'. The work was commissioned by the Seoul Olympics Committee at the behest of a long-standing admirer of his work and *quasi* Mother of Korean operas, Mrs. Kim Jah Kyung, to be sung in Italian by an all-Korean cast. The invitation came when Menotti was returning to Scotland from Australia via South Korea to direct two of his operas, *Amelia Goes to the Ball* and *The Medium* — a fact in itself less surprising than might at first appear: his operas are performed regularly throughout the world, from Cairo to Tokyo to Glasgow, earning him a reputation as the most performed composer this century after Puccini, with whom his talent for luscious melody has frequently been compared.

"'It seemed a strange idea but also rather nice. But then I said rather shyly, look, I'm sorry but I only play tennis, and rather badly, and I only win when people let me. I don't want to write an opera about sport.'

"Fortunately, the Seoul officials had no more desire for an opera with choruses of torch-bearers looking *sportif* than did Mr. Menotti. They stipulated only that the work should not be gloomy like *The Consul* (his 1950 opera about an oppressive bureaucratic state, for which he was awarded the Pulitzer Prize), and that it should be based on an ancient Korean folk story — despite the composer's plea that he should write his own original libretto.

"They permitted him, instead, to adapt the story in question, entitled *The Marriage*. It tells of two people who fall in love but have to lie to others about their feelings. 'The story is simple. It could be the subject of a Roman comedy or *commedia dell'arte*. But it has a bitter undercurrent. They may be surprised at the Menotti twist to it.'

"Menotti twists, in subject or music, have caused trouble before. Most of his operas are cast in a traditional and accessible mould, almost as popular on Broadway as in major opera houses. They have a strong message, usually concerning outcasts in society. The combination of pointed moral and fluent, some say facile, music have earned virulent reviews, and the ultimate from an American critic: 'This man has no talent.' His most recent opera, *Goya*, for Placido Domingo, was a celebrated critical fiasco, described by *The New York Times* as 'a rather stupefying exercise in banality, similar, in its superficiality, to his other recent works, though on a larger canvas.'

---

74   The present article appeared in *The Independent* for September 15, 1988. (Ed.)

"The composer, though clearly hurt by such viciousness, says sanguinely that critics can upset his breakfast but not his lunch — which, judging by the cook's soufflé that day [at his austere Palladian mansion, in the heart of Lothian,] is no small mercy. 'People accuse me of being old-fashioned because I write melodies. But old-fashioned is such a strange phrase. Is Calvino old-fashioned because he wrote perfect Italian grammar? A writer can write a perfectly traditional novel without being insulted. In music, this is impossible. Yet my music is popular because it appeals to a collective unconsciousness and it's simple. You learn that from Schubert.'

"He has enjoyed widespread support since *Amelia* was performed at the Metropolitan Opera, New York, in 1938, followed by some 20 more operas over the next 50 years. Persuaded by the conductor, Toscanini, Menotti had left Italty to study in America at 16 and spent most of his young adult life there, setting up home with the composer Samuel Barber and drawing round him a circle of artists including Cocteau, Rauschenberg, Martha Graham, Cartier-Bresson and Horowitz. When he decided to return to Europe, 'to be a proper part of society, not just what I call the after-dinner mint,' he persuaded some of those friends to visit Spoleto, in the Umbrian hills, where in 1958 he established the Festival of Two Worlds, still one of Italy's leading festivals and almost as dear to Menotti as his work as a composer.

"He settled in Scotland in 1974, in the former home of the Marquesses of Tweedale, attracted by the cool grey skies which, he says, suit his untypical Italian temperament. Locals took time to adjust to their curious new lord, stolidy addressing him as Mr. McNotty and continuing to push their prams around the estate uninvited — a practice on which Menotti smiled until discovering that the prams were filled not with bonny babies but with his best ripe apples and plums. A friendly truce has been established and he intends to stay in Lothian until he dies, forays to Seoul and elsewhere to direct his operas notwithstanding.

"*The Marriage* has already run into unexpected problems: a Korean society for the physically disabled heard of there being a taunted cripple in the opera and lodged an official complaint, despite the character having appeared in the original fourteenth century Korean legend — and though Menotti's most performed work, *Amahl and the Night Visitors*, has a cripple as its hero.

"Then the Koreans objected to a point in the libretto where the two main figures say 'I love you.' This apparently breaks every code of social behavior in Korea, which must make the performance of any Western opera tricky. 'It shocked them. It's crazy. What can they say instead? They're in love. I haven't found an alternative yet.'

"Gian Carlo Menotti is now in Seoul, directing the opera and sorting out final cultural contretemps before tomorrow's première. When he returns to Scotland, he intends to write his memoirs, finish a novel about people who are too clever to be employed and sort out piles of unfinished or unpublished scores. He is also thinking of converting the stables into a theater and starting his own local festival, if he can find a millionaire to help him. All that between composing his next few operas." — Geraint Lewis.

FEDERICO MOMPOU

B. 1893, Barcelona (Spain). *Educ.:* Cons of Barcelona. *Works incl.:* choral works, piano pieces *(6 Impressions intimes, 3 Paisajes, 10 Preludes, Scènes d'enfants), Suite compostelana* (gtr).

Cançons Becquerianas for Voice and Piano. *Text:* Poems by G.A. Bécquer. *Pub.:* Edicions Musicals Tenora (Barcelona).
1. *"Hoy la tierra y los cielo me sonrien"* ("Today the land and the skies will smile on me"). 2. *"Los invisibles atomos del aire"* (The invisible atoms of the air"). 3. *"Yo soy ardiente, yo soy morena"* ("I am ardent, I am dark"). 4. *"Yo se cual el objecto"* ("I know which object"). 5. *"Volveran las oscuras golondrinas"* ("Return of the dark swallows"). 6. *"Olas gigantes"* ("Gigantic waves").

"In the *Canciones Becquerianas,* Frederic Mompou continues to follow the de Falla tradition of coloristic, impressionist writing. The poetry by Bécquer (1836-1870), the Romantic Spanish poet who had a pronounced influence on the imagist school of Spanish poets, is exquisitely handled by Mompou [in this set of six songs].

"Songs 1, 2, 4 and 5 achieve a serene contemplative atmosphere by using delicate melodic lines with close intervals and subtle impressionistic harmonies in the piano. In the third song the 'Ritmo de Polo' (an Andalusian dance in 3/8 meter with frequent syncopation also effectively used in the last song of de Fallas' *Seven Spanish Popular Songs*) relfects the ardor and passion of the text. The last song uses strong, sweeping arpeggios in the piano to depict the gigantic waves. The songs lie well within the range of an octave and a fifth. Where difficult intervals occur in the vocal part the singer is often aided by subtle doubling of the vocal line in the piano accompaniment. The *Canciones Becquerianas* are an effective and beautiful addition to the repertoire for voice and piano." — Ruth L. Drucker, in *Notes* (Music Library Association), 3/82.

JEROME MOROSS

B. 1913, New York (Brooklyn) NY; *d.* 1983, New York NY. *Educ.:* Juilliard Schl of Music. *Works incl.:* dance scores *(American Pattern, Frankie and Johnny, Paul Bunyan)*, film scores, musical shows *(Gentlemen Be Seated, The Golden Apple)*, orchestral *(Paeans, Tall Story)*, sonatinas (brass qnt; cls; strngs, bass & pno; ww qnt), symphony.

Concerto for Flute with String Quartet (1978). *Rec.:* Varèse Sarabande (Stereo LP) VC 81101: Frances Zlotkin (fl), Sortomme Hudson, Benjamin Hudson (vlns), Toby Appel (vla), Frederick Zlotkin (vc).

Sonata for Piano Duet and String Quartet (1975). *Rec:* Varèse Sarabande (Stereo LP) VC 81101: Sahan Arzruni, Ron Gianattosio (pnos), Sortomme Hudson, Benjamin Hudson (vlns), Toby Appel (vla), Frederick Zlotkin (vc).

"For a composer who is known principally for his film and theater accomplishments (*The Big Country* and *The Golden Apple* are the most universally celebrated) to be given recognition on records as a craftsman of music in absolute forms is a notable event in itself. The additional fact that these two recent works [on Varèse Sarabande VC 81101 above] are among the most irresistibly enchanting and exquisitely fashioned you are likely to hear from any American pen nowadays makes this release a genuine double treat.

"Jerome Moross is a member of that kindred group of contemporaneous and fiercely talented New Yorkers (also numbering Elie Siegmeister, Alex North, Bernard Herrmann, and Morton Gould) who, reacting to the 1930s rediscovery of Ives and emulating his example (though not his manner) and that of younger exponents of musical populism such as Harris, Copland, and Cowell, wholeheartedly embraced the American vernacular idiom in all its varied manifestations, with particular emphasis on popular and jazz genres. To a greater or lesser extent, all of these men absorbed and consolidated these elements into what during the 1940s would become recognizably individualistic styles, but Moross stands out for the impact which the rustically regional accents of the South and West had on his basically urban sensibility, resulting in an absolutely inimitable synthesis which I think of as a kind of 'cowboy jazz'. Over the years, unlike some of his generation, Moross has shown the integrity to abide by his original youthful instincts and not abandon a congenial idiom for which he has continued to find fresh and inventive embodiments in works as diverse as the 'minstrel' opera *Gentlemen, Be Seated* and the film score for *The Cardinal*.

"For anyone who is familiar with his previous work, barely a few bars of either [the *Concerto* or the *Sonata*] will be enough to make him feel right at home. The marvelously bountiful and effortless songfulness—sometimes embellished with an almost barcarolle-like lilt—the bouncy, double-gaited syncopations, and the always lucidly close-knit and self-generative harmonic fabric permeate these works from start to finish. It's amazing how much mileage and momentum Moross can engender from his basically very simple, homespun, diatonic tunes and how every component of modulation and shape derives naturally from the same pure initial melodic impulse, carefully tailored to create an inevitable sense of forward motion leading to an always satisfying conclusion.

"The concertante-like *Sonata* is exactly that, rather than a 'concerto', with both the pianists and the quartet sharing almost equally in setting forth the musical argument. The thematic material is perhaps a shade more piquant and the ensembles more pungent than in the *Flute Concerto*. This listener was occasionally reminded of an American equivalent to the elegant rhythms and fluent melodic patterns of Fauré, Poulenc, or Jean-Michel Damase. The *Concerto*, which started life as a flute quintet, is dominated by its mellifluous solo instrument, and thus has a more leisurely, lyrical character, particularly in the meditative slow movement, entitled 'Tune with Four Improvisations'. Each work makes delightful use of recurrent themes as linking devices between movements."—Paul Snook, in *Fanfare: The Magazine for Serious Record Collectors*, 1-2/80.

"Moross's best-known film score was that for the 1958 *Big Country*. [This new Varèse Sarabande recording of his *Concerto* and *Sonata*] reveals another side of Moross. The two lively works heard here in first-rate, bracing performances show him to be something of an American Poulenc, with the same crystal-clear handling of odd instrumental combinations, the same engagingly light touch, the same neatness and wit, the same spontaneous vigor. Then again, the simple, diatonic melodies and pervasive American rhythms give a curious, clean, outdoorsy feeling reminiscent of Copland in his folklike moods."—Irving Lowens, in *High Fidelity*, 3/80.

Frankie and Johnny (ballet) for 3 Female Voices and Orchestra (1938). *Prem.*: Chicago Federal Theatre. *Other performs.*: Ballet Russe de Monte Carlo. *Rec.*: American Recording Society (reissued as Bay Cities CD 1007/Koch International): Vienna SO, Walter Hendl, cond. *Pub.*: Sorom Music.
Orch: 2-2-3-2; 2-2-2-0; piano, timp, perc; strings

Great Northern Theater, Chicago: Ruth Page, Bentley Stone—*Frankie and Johnny*. Photo credit: Candid Illustrators, Chicago IL. Courtesy Ruth Page Foundation, Chicago IL.

"By the Depression Era, Jerome Moross was well on his way to establishing himself as one of the most versatile composers of his generation. By his early twenties he had managed to compose for the theater and radio as well as for the concert hall, to much acclaim. Eventually Moross would add motion picture and television scores to his catalog, receiving an Academy Award nomination for his score to William Wyler's classic *The Big Country*.

"Apart from his 'popular' music such as 'The Big Country Theme' and the song 'Lazy Afternoon' from *The Golden Apple,* one of his most frequently performed works is *Frankie and Johnny*. The score is based on the American folk-tune of the same title and can be referred to as a theme and variations. (It can be and has been performed in concert form without the dancing.)

"The creation of this work sprang from a commission by Ruth Page who, in collaboration with the Chicago Federal Theatre, offered the first performance June 20, 1938 at Chicago's Great Northern Theater. The work caused a sensation and ran for six weeks instead of the few nights originally scheduled. In 1945, the Ballet Russe de Monte Carlo incorporated *Frankie and Johnny* into their active repertoire. When the work was presented in May 1950 by Serge Lifar, it caused a scandal rivalling those of *Le Sacre du Printemps* and *L'après midi d'un faune*. Lifar's supporters used the occasion to demonstrate their anger at the treatment they felt Lifar had received in America. It was reported that an American composition had received the full 'chair-throwing' treatment. After counter-demonstrations following this performance, the work received high praise from Le Corbusier, and was danced 20 times in a single month. Alleged 'extremes' in the ballet's plot kept it from being performed in many communities, however by standards of today the work seems hardly objectionable and has been produced on television.

"It is masterfully scored for full orchestra, and the composer's skill in vocal writing is also clearly in evidence. Functioning as a Greek chorus—'American style'—three female singers costumed as 'Salvation Army lasses' wander through the scenes singing and beating cymbal, tambourine and bass drum respectively.

"Moross himself supplied the following scenario:

> Formally, the ballet score consists of an introduction and a suite of seven dances.
>   1. STOMP—the doings around town
>   2. BLUES—a duet between Frankie and Johnny
>   3. RAG 1—the barroom dance; Johnny goes off with Nellie Bly; Frankie comes looking for him; the local denizens help, Nellie and Johnny get away
>   4. RAG 2—the bartender's dance. The bartender tells Frankie what's what, in the meantime offering himself as a substitute
>   5. TUNE—Frankie whips herself into a frenzy and goes off to get her gun
>   6. FOX-TROT—Frankie catches Johnny with Nellie Bly and shoots Johnny

7. ONE-STEP—the funeral. Everybody gets roaring drunk and Frankie and Nellie end up crying on one another's shoulders.

"At the end, each of the 'Salvation Army lasses' gets a glass of beer and sings the final lyrics with her feet on the coffin, as if it were a bar-rail.

"*Postscript.* In 1979, I was given an opportunity to meet Jerome Moross at his apartment. As a member of the Mannes Percussion Ensemble, I had just performed a concert at John Jay College. When I mentioned that to Mr. Moross, he asked me what work I had played:
 " 'I played on the Varèse *Ionisation*—the guiro part.'
 " 'Oh, yes, I know the piece well—I heard the world premiere of it under Slonimsky. Varèse kept insisting to me that I should have been an 'avant-gardist', but that was never my calling.'
 "For the next two hours he spoke of the 'old days' and the many people he had known, among them close friends and colleagues such as Franz Waxman, Alfred Newman, Elie Siegmeister, Edgard Varèse, Percy Grainger, Henry Cowell, Charles Ives and Bernard Herrmann. He also spoke of the future and what he was working on. At that time he was completing the score to his opera *Sorry, Wrong Number,* and spoke of having revised his *First Symphony* and about his hopes of completing a Second (the latter would remain a dream he did not live to fulfill—only very slight sketches survive). We even exchanged opinions concerning flutists we did/did not admire!
 "He asked to see some of my own music, and was ever encouraging and willing to show approval for what I had done. To a young composer this can mean everything. He told me that he had worked in film as a way of making money but, at heart, was a composer for the theater. ('I'm not going to complain about the royalties I've received for 'The Big Country Theme' [which at that time was being used for a Taylor Wine commercial].)
 "Around 1982 or 1983 I made a choral arrangement of his wonderful song 'Lazy Afternoon', which I had meant to present him with as a 70th birthday gift. Much to my regret he passed away before celebrating that occasion.
 "One can hope that, some day, some opera or theater center (Lincoln Center, Covent Garden) will have the intelligence and taste to mount a retrospective of his outstanding work for the theater. He enriched my own life personally by taking the time to talk so freely with me, and—I am thinking especially of the superb craftsmanship and the unwavering lyricism of his music—I will always think of him as a role model professionally."—Dana Perna.

ANDRZEJ PANUFNIK

B. 1914, Warsaw (Poland). *Educ.:* Warsaw Cons, Vienna Acad. *Cond.* Cracow PO, Warsaw PO, Birmingham (England) SO; vice-pres, UNESCO Intl Music Council. *Awards incl.:* Szymanowski Prize, Chopin Prize, Prince Rainier Competition, Sibelius Centenary Medal. *Works incl.:* choral & other vocal pieces, Concerto in modo antico, Miss Julie (ballet), orchestral works *(Heroic Overture, Nocturne, Polonia, Rhapsody, Tragic Overture).*

"COMPOSING VS. THE GLAMOR OF CONDUCTING. A few weeks ago [in 1988], the composer Andrzej Panufnik conducted a program of his music at the 92nd Street Y, courtesy of the First New York International Festival of the Arts. It was an excellent concert, with Mr. Panufnik's outwardly conservative, accessible yet still searching and original music expertly rendered by the New York Chamber Symphony. I reported on the concert at the time, but there was something about the occasion that set my mind spinning off in another direction that seemed inappropriate for a review.

"When Mr. Panufnik strode onto the stage and ascended the podium, he *looked* like a conductor. He bore himself with the requisite imperiousness; his technique was authoritative, and his flowing white hair and commanding profile bespoke a mighty maestro at work.

"But he's not a conductor—not now. He was one once, but he gave it up to concentrate on composing. And this brought to mind all manner of speculation about the relationship of conducting and composing, of famous conductors of the past who bitterly regretted their lack of success as composers, and of men famous in their time as conductors who are now better remembered as composers.

"It would seem that, had Mr. Panufnik so chosen, he could be a very famous man today. He studied conducting in the 1930s in Vienna, Paris and London with one of the most distinguished conductors of the early years of the century, Felix Weingartner. A staunch anti-Nazi during the war, Mr. Panufnik, who is now 73 years old, was appointed conductor of the Krakow and then the Warsaw Philharmonics in the late 40s, also leading the Berlin and London Philharmonics.

"Yet even then his pursuit of conductorial glory was compromised by his determination to compose. Uncomfortable with artistic repression in Poland, he emigrated to Britain in 1954, where he led the City of Birmingham Symphony Orchestra (now Simon Rattle's) from 1957 to 1959. But since then he has rarely appeared on a podium, except to lead his own scores.

"Conducting seems a grand and satisfying life to the average concertgoer; indeed, abetted by the image-making machinery of the typical orchestra and the dead status of most of the composers performed,[75] the conductor becomes the living symbol of classical music for most people.

"Yet from the composer-conductor's point of view, conducting must often seem like the fleshly temptation of the devil, as opposed to the stern and saintly demands of composing. To give up the glamor and wealth and fame of conducting, even for a summer, must be terribly difficult, especially when the alternative is a lonely battle with one's muse, all to produce music that may not be appreciated by the public....

"Some great conductors never had a problem being recognized above all as composers. Richard Wagner helped shape the very notion of the modern conductor, yet no one ever forgot about his own music; he didn't let them. But Mahler was certainly better known during his life-time as a conductor... More recently, Weingartner composed, and so did Wilhelm Furtwängler and Otto Klemperer, among many notable maestros of this century.[76] Indeed, many of them—Furtwängler and Klemperer in particular—were often bitter and depressed at both the lack of time they could devote to their composing and the lack of recognition accorded their music by an unappreciative world.

"Thus one has to admire Mr. Panufnik for sticking so steadfastly to his own music. Clearly, on the basis of that recent New York concert, he has the talent and the looks—never to be underestimated with any performer as highly visible as a conductor—to have developed a major international conducting career. Had he chosen that path, perhaps today we would be soberly assessing the lastest Panufnik Beethoven symphony recordings and eagerly anticipating the compact-disk reissues of his earliest recordings.

"Instead, we have his music. So far, it cannot be said that he has made himself into a household name as a composer; his music is hardly on every lip, hummed happily by the millions. Maybe he gave up fame and glory in a cruelly ironic bargan that brought him only obscurity as its reward.

"And yet, his music is more and more admired and played, and

---

[75] An aside, perhaps—but worthy of italicizing. (Ed.)
[76] Including also Dorati, Boulez, Bernstein, Koussevitzky (db concerto), Chávez, Schuller, etc. —also Britten, Copland, Grainger, Strauss, Stravinsky (to mention composers who also conducted their own and others' music)— and others represented in this book: Penderecki, Skrowaczewski... (Ed.)

there seems a reasonable chance that posthumously he will be recognized as a minor or even a major master. And even if he doesn't join the immortals in the highest pantheon, maybe he has already found a greater inner, personal satisfaction in the private act of creation than he ever would have enjoyed in the all-too-brilliantly public ritual of re-creation." — John Rockwell, in *The New York Times*, 7/24/88.

Ed.'s sociological footnote: To this sympathetic critic's well-chosen words one might add that Panufnik may, simply, prefer composing to conducting. At the same time I feel there is, overall, a point at issue which deserves to be made at a time when mere "celebrity" and the achieving of economic or other wealth and power over others continue *so much* to be honored as the *ne plus ultra* of an enfolding society's implied value-system. On the one hand isn't the *quality of one's life* of some little importance? On the other hand is it not time at last to distribute the material gains of a given economy as a whole rather more equitably? The ultra benevolent monarchy/socialism practised (it was said) by the citizens of Oz and their loving ruler Princess Ozma may be something of an extreme, still, isn't it a tad obscene that a society should allow certain merchants and a handful of "popular" artists, sports figures and the like to extract from the common hoard astronomical sums when the public *from whom these very same "rewards" have, in fact, been taken* retain a thoroughly inequitable share in the proceeding to which, after all, they continue to make such an obviously essential contribution? In sum it might be asked when will we "the public" make an objection... — Thus Rockwell's musings regarding the "sacrifices" which, apparently, are supposed to be somehow *inevitable* (and — perhaps — even *appropriate?*) even for a musician of Andrzej Panufnik's rank and worth not only seem appalling on an individual case basis but, I should think, have — in the end — larger contemporary relevance... Or don't people care?

Autumn Music for Orchestra (1962). 17m *Rec.:* Unicorn Records (Stereo LP) RHS 306: London SO, Jascha Horenstein, cond.

Symphony 1 (Sinfonia rustica) for Orchestra (1948; rev. 1955). *Rec.:* EMI (reissued as Unicorn Records Stereo LP RHS 315, also as UNI-75026): Monte Carlo Opera O, Andrzej Panufnik, cond. *Pub.:* Boosey & Hawkes. In four movements.

Symphony 2 (Sinfonia elegiaca) for Orchestra (1957, rev. 1966). Sections 1 & 3 also arr. 1957 as ballet *Elegy*. *Rec.:* Louisville Records (LP) LOU 624: Louisville O, Robert Whitney, cond. *Pub.:* Boosey & Hawkes.

Symphony 3 (Sinfonia sacra) for Orchestra (1963). Also perf. 1968 as ballet *Cain and Abel*. *Perfs.:* orch. cond. by Leopold Stokowski; Chicago SO, Georg Solti, cond. *Recs.:* EMI (reissued as Unicorn

Chicago SO, Georg Solti, cond. *Recs.:* EMI (reissued as Unicorn Records Stereo LP RHS 315, also as UNI-75026): Monte Carlo Opera O, Andrzej Panufnik, cond.; Elektra/Nonesuch 79228 (Stereo LP; also as CD & cassette 9 79228-2): Concertgebouw O, Andrzej Panufnik, cond. *Pub.:* Boosey & Hawkes.

1. Visions. 2. Hymn.

Symphony 4 *(Sinfonia concertante)* for Orchestra (1973). *Rec.:* EMI EMD 5525: Aurèle Nicolet (fl), Osian Ellis (hp), Menuhin Festival O, Andrzej Panufnik, cond. *Pub.:* Boosey & Hawkes.

Symphony 5 *(Sinfonia di Sfere)* for Orchestra (1975). 32m *Prem.:* London SO, David Atherton, cond. *Rec.:* Decca Headline (Stereo LP) 22 PSI: London SO, David Atherton, cond. *Pub.:* Boosey & Hawkes.

Symphony 6 *(Sinfonia mistica)* for Orchestra (1977). 21m *Rec.:* Decca Headline (Stereo LP) 22 PSI: London SO, David Atherton, cond. *Pub.:* Boosey & Hawkes.

In six sections.

Symphony 7 *(Metasinfonia)* for Organ, Timpani and Strings (1978). *Rec.:* Unicorn-Kanchanada (Stereo LP) DKP 9049 (distr. Harmonia Mundi): Jennifer Bate (org), Kurt-Hans Goedicke (timp), London SO, Andrzej Panufnik, cond. *Pub.:* Boosey & Hawkes.

Symphony 8 *(Sinfonia votiva)* for Orchestra (1982). 25m *Commissioned & prem.:* Boston SO. *Rec.:* Hyperion Records (Digital Stereo LP) A66050 (also as Musical Heritage Society Digital Stereo LP MHS-4886): Boston SO, Seiji Ozawa, cond.

1. Con devozione. 2. Con passione.

AUTUMN MUSIC: "*Autumn Music* is a haunting 17-minute elegy quite different from any other elegy known to me. Yet it reveals many of the composer's most distinctive qualities, with its obsessive use of the major-minor duality and its meticulously refined orchestration, not to mention the important structural features on both the intervallic and the macro-structural levels. It would be easy, yet insufficient, to cite many instances of breathtakingly subtle effects that abound in the work. But beyond instances of local color, as it were, is a work of profound spiritual content, revealing a sensitive and quite original creative mind capable of producing music of strange, unearthly beauty.

"[The Unicorn recording which features this work and three others] is one of the most important recordings of the 1970s...."
—Walter Simmons, in *Fanfare: The Magazine for Serious Record Collectors,* 11-12/80.

AUTUMN MUSIC: "Although my compositions are extremely diverse in character, I approach each new one in the same manner. I feel somewhat like an architect, tackling my work in three stages, always in the same order: first the purpose, or reason for which the work is

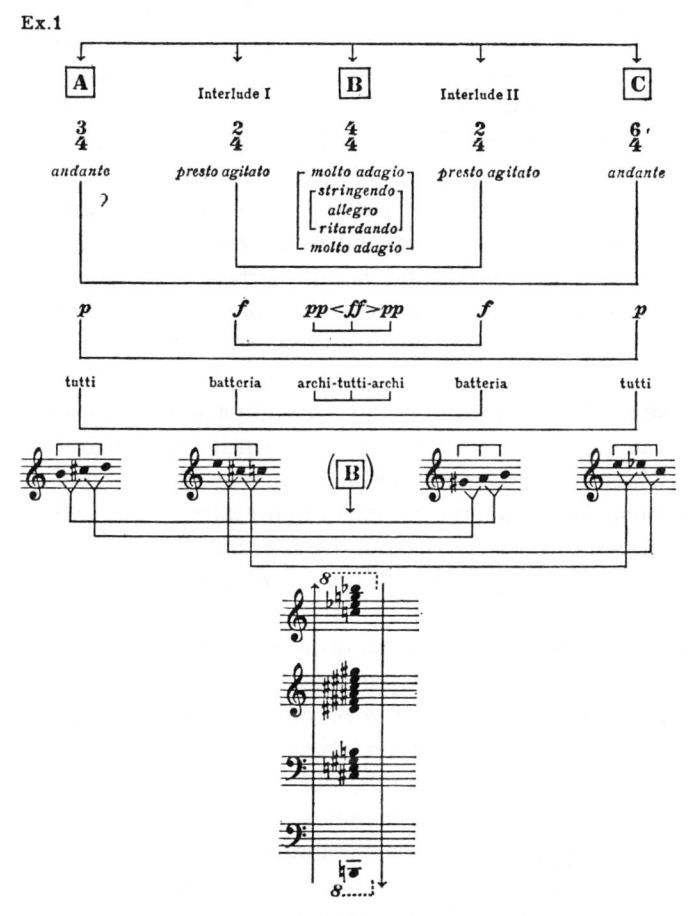

Formal organization of *Autumn Music* — reprinted from
Tempo: A Quarterly Review of Modern Music.

which it is to be built. The purpose of writing my *Autumn Music* was to compose a work in memory of a friend, who, after a long, incurable illness, experienced her last autumn in 1960. Writing this work, I was responding to the end of a suffering human life, and to the season of autumn, with all its manifestations in nature. I made a choice of certain instruments which I found most suitable to express my ideas and feelings. These are: three flutes, three clarinets, a selection of pitched and unpitched percussion, piano, harp, violas, violoncelli and double basses — so in this small orchestra, I have excluded brass instruments and violins. I had two reasons for not using violins — firstly the coloristic factor, because I wished to emphasize the lower register of strings — and secondly, my wish to achieve a transparency of sound, allowing the woodwinds to be rather prominent.

"As to the structure it consists of three main sections, like a triptych, hinged together by two very short interludes. *Autumn Music* is of symmetrical construction, with its climax in the middle of the central section. This symmetrical construction of the whole work is also emphasized by its texture, rhythm, tempo, and dynamics. For example, the first section reflects the last one, as they have the same *andante* tempo, as well as an almost identical rhythm — and the dynamics too are similar. The second, middle section, is the axis of the symmetry, and within itself it is written in mirror form. It starts very slowly, and quietly, with double basses. Then all the other instruments gradually follow, in canonic form. The slow, steady increase of tension is brought about both by a gradual acceleration of tempo and the *crescendo* of all instruments until the climax is reached — at which point the music seems to pause and vibrate statically for a moment, before the reverse image in the mirror starts with the gradual slowing down of speed and the reduction of instruments, until we are back again to just the double basses, as at the beginning of the section.

"Regarding the musical language, in order to achieve a unity of style in *Autumn Music*, I imposed upon myself a particularly strict discipline. The material of the whole work consists of the germ-cells of only three intervals. The first section is based on two of the germ-cell intervals, major and minor seconds, and so is the second short interlude. The last section is based mainly on the minor third and minor second, corresponding with the first interlude. In the middle section, which is contrasting in character to the first and last, the telescoped melodic lines are taken from a chord built on thirds only (Example 1)." — Andrzej Panufnik, in *Tempo: A Quarterly Review of Modern Music*, Spring 1971.[77]

AUTUMN MUSIC; SYMPHONIES 1, 3: "Panufnik's most successful works are among the most extraordinary musical conceptions to emerge from Europe over the past 25 years.... One of the most distinctive elements in [his] music is a virtual obsession with the major-minor triad. Now this is a harmonic structure that has held an almost mystical fascination for composers as diverse as Nielsen, Vaughan Williams, the Czech Miloslav Kabelac, and the Americans Alan Hovhaness, Robert Kurka, and Arnold Rosner. But none of these has made the sound such an essential and pervasive factor as Panufnik has. Another characteristic feature is an exquisite and subtle ap-

---

[77] Copyright © 1971 by Andrzej Panufnik.

proach to orchestration, in which the post-Romantic concept of orchestral sonority is not simply accepted as the basic vehicle for a musical idea, but rather the timbre is treated as an organically inseparable aspect of the musical idea. The other important feature of Panufnik's compositional procedure is the imposition of a particular, usually simple, intervallic scheme as a dominating formal factor over all aspects of the work from the motivic to the macro-structural. (Panufnik is fond of representing these relationships in elaborate, carefully drawn geometric designs that often accompany his program notes).

"*Sinfonia sacra [Symphony No. 3]* was composed in 1963, as a tribute to Poland's millennium—one thousand years of statehood and Christianity. The entire work is based on the first few notes of 'Bogurodzica', an ancient Polish hymn that served both religious and patriotic functions. Thus the symphony reflects this bifurcated significance. The structure of the work is unusual, divided into two movements: the first consists of three *Visions*, the second is entitled *Hymn*. The three visions are martial, ethereal, and violent, respectively; the unfolding of the *Hymn*, which grows with an insinuating deliberateness that is almost painful in its protraction, culminates in one of the most unforgettable climaxes I have ever experienced, as the various essential elements of the work are united.

"*Sinfonia rustica [Symphony No. 1]*, composed 15 years earlier, is a vastly different sort of piece. It has a rather loosely-strung, conventional four-movement structure, and is based on Polish folk melodies. Panufnik's hand is clearly evident through felicities of scoring, and through the omnipresent major-minor juxtapositions, which give the work an incongruously 'American' flavor. This is engaging, lightweight fun."—Walter G. Simmons, in *Fanfare: The Magazine for Serious Record Collectors*, 3-4/79.

SYMPHONIES 1–3: "*Sinfonia rustica* [Nr. 1] (1948), Panufnik's first surviving symphony (there were two previous ones), is partly based on Polish themes. Panufnik's handling of this material is much more original than, say, Lutoslawski's in his roughly contemporary *Mala Suite*. Though much of the music has an open-air freshness (e.g. the bagpiping oboes in the trio-section of the scherzo) this is no mere 'folk rhapsody'. The constituents of the folk melodies are treated as germinal motives and subjected to a rigorous contrapuntal development (emphasized by the antiphonal use of two separate string orchestras) in clear-cut textures and an austerely dissonant harmonic idiom. The treatment may stem from Bartók, but is here applied to wholly personal and invigorating ends.

"The *Sinfonia sacra [Nr. 3]* of 1963 is, I think, Panufnik's finest achievement to date [1973]. It consists of three short, dramatic *Visions* (a heroic fanfare for 4 trumpets, a rapt chorale-like meditation for muted strings, and a warlike *Allegro assai* for full orchestra), followed by an extended orchestral *Hymn* based on the melody of the ancient Gregorian chant *Bogurodzica*. The symphony as a whole unites the best characteristics of Panufnik's art. His paring-down of thematic material to absolute essentials is apparent in *Vision I* (the fanfare, based on a single 5-note motive and its inversion). *Vision III* demonstrates his tight structural control in the expanding and contracting rhythmic symmetries of its percussion refrain, the palindromic forms of its episodes, and the motivic material of its final agitato section (a highly chromatic figure whose descending prhase, Bartóklike, fills in all the notes unsounded by the previous ascending one). The *Hymn*, building up gradually from unaccompanied *flautando* violin harmonics to full orchestra, is Panufnik's most sustained, organic symphonic movement, and has enormous cumulative power; its final combination of the chant melody with the fanfare from the symphony's opening make a superb climax.

"Another Panufnik symphony should be mentioned [here] — *Sinfonia elegiaca [Nr. 2]* (1957), dedicated to the victims of World War II: a triptych in which two intensely lyrical, lucidly-scored slow movements frame a violent, large-scale *Allegro molto* of explosive power. [The version used for the Louisville Orchestra recording] has now been superseded: Panufnik has recently made a completely revised version, amounting to a partial recomposition.[78] It is fascinating to compare the two scores, for although the basic material, overall shape and nature of events are the same, the scoring, balance, motivic detail, harmony, rhythm and even the notation have been completely re-worked: not one bar remains unchanged. I regret the complete disappearance of a plangent horn motive from the opening section, but Panufnik's intention has obviously been to concentrate and more greatly unify his material. The overall effect transforms a rather baldly dramatic work into an even more powerful and far subtler one." — Malcolm MacDonald, in *Tempo: A Quarterly Review of Modern Music*, Nr. 107, 12/73.

SYMPHONY 3: "Trumpet fanfares introduce the *Sinfonia sacra*, and they are followed by brooding strings. Then timpani and percussion lead up to a complete orchestral protest that suddenly ends in

---

[78] A study score of the new version is published by Boosey & Hawkes. In an even earlier (pre-1957) form, the work employed a women's chorus and was entitled *Symphony of Peace*.

silence. The effect is mysterious and quite moving. Part 2 is called *Hymn* and is based on a Gregorian Chant well-known to Poles. The [work] is both religious and patriotic, like the Polish people... [This is] the most appealing of Panufnik's symphonies." — Donald R. Vroon, in *American Record Guide*, 7-8/90.

"Contemporary music from Eastern Europe shares certain traits — an anguished lyricism, a rhythmic vibrancy and a mystical spirituality — that cut across national boundaries and personal styles. The music of the Polish-born Andrzej Panufnik is no exception. Although Mr. Panufnik's tonal, accessible work has always shunned the avant-garde, its darkly colored dissonance and fascination with intricate structure mark it as a product of our era. His *Sinfonia sacra* strikes a balance between romantic fervor and compelling architecture, and in the light of the changed face of Poland this thrilling [composition] — with its militant fanfare, violent percussion and triumphant, climactic hymn — seems positivitely prescient in its faith in the invincibility of the human spirit." — K. Robert Schwarz, in *The New York Times*, 8/5/90.

SYMPHONIES 3, 5, 6: "Unlike two generations of 20th-century American composers — Sessions, Schuman, Piston, Harris, Diamond, and Mennin notably among them — most of the major Europeans after Sibelius and Nielsen discarded the symphony as a viable musical vessel for their ideas. Only Shostakovich, Vaughan Williams, Gustaf Allan Pettersson, Karl Amadeus Hartmann, and Havergal Brian — all of them now dead — plus Andjez Panufnik have composed plurally in that form with sustained commitment and expressive accumulation.[79]

"Panufnik, son of a British mother, fled in 1953 from his native Poland leaving behind all of his music, to settle in England where he has lived since. Although he assimilated a number of avant-garde developments and notational techniques, his music remains essentially conservative, tonally rooted, and subjective in content. If not everything has been of a quality, his long-breathing, lyrical works proclaim a creative personality both eloquent and individual. This is true particularly of *Sinfonia sacra* [No. 3], and more recently of *Sinfonia mistica* [No. 6]. This latter title refers not to a religious experience but to 'mysteries' associated with the number 6 — a work in six sections employing six triads, six melodic patterns (Panufnik's own

---

[79] Raising questions of definition: for example the symphonies of Hans Werner Henze are of considerable interest and importance, although they continue to be infrequently played; Robert Simpson, Lutoslawski, many others surely compose "with sustained commitment". (Ed.)

phrase), six harmonic combinations, and the meter of six. Without its sounding voluptuous or derivative, *Sinfonia mistica* is a Scriabin-related score of richly textured character and haunting afflatus.

"*Sinfonia di Sfere* [No. 5] is not only a longer work—32 minutes in contrast to *Mistica's* 21—but more complex in its structure and linearity. Constructed from a geometric system of three, it sounds more troubled and thereby troubling. Panufnik's triadic scheme includes three sets of timpani, stationed left, rear center, and right, which ultimately duel in a manner presaged by the two sets in Nielsen's *'Inextinguishable' Symphony*, until a piano interrupts their street-corner rumble and silences the grim noise. *Sinfonia di Sfere* has sostenuto passages of noble dignity, but is primarily a non-legato work compounded of passages that stutter or snarl powerfully along with others that may strike the listener on first hearing as discursive. On the surface the *Fifth Symphony* offers less of Panufnik's expressive rapture than other more immediately accessible works, yet underneath a logic is operating that proves riveting once come to grips with. If Panufnik singled out geometry as his *modus operandi* in *Sinfonia di Sfere*, the end product is a balancing act of mind and emotion....

"If Panufnik's music is not yet as familiar as it deserves to be—despite the advocacy of Stokowski and Horenstein—one feels that the best will become repertory pieces when a plentiful supply of new conductors takes over from the incumbents, with less disposition to fly all over the globe leading a mere handful of programs every season. Meanwhile, the already inestimable value of recordings such as [the London SO performances of Panufnik's fifth and sixth symphonies] doubles and redoubles."—Roger Dettmer, in *Fanfare: The Magazine for Serious Record Collectors*, 1-2/83.

SYMPHONY 4: "The two-movement *Sinfonia concertante* [Nr. 4] of 1973 is more of a Concertino than a Symphony, even though [the EMI] recorded performance reveals it as less slight than was my impression at the premiere. The combination of flute, harp and strings could hardly fail to give Panufnik some beautiful sounds—but apart from this area of sonority the music makes no overt play for the listener's sympathies. It is, rather, a little aloof and reserved—though one senses that this is the reserve of a strong and definite character. Moreover it is thematically one of Panufnik's most austere works, deriving all its material from a single three-note cell which, while it ensures a continually euphonious harmonic world, is [perhaps] not itself of compelling interest. Thus in the slow first movement, particularly, one has the impression that for all its poised and frosty beauty the music is like a mobile, some uninvolved and self-sufficient artifact which one can only admire at a distance as it revolves gently in space (an impression enhanced, no doubt intentionally, by the absence of real counterpoint or rhythmic variety). The more capricious finale, with its rapid succession of rhythmical 'microstructures', is an interesting formal innovation which may indicate a fruitful direction for Panufnik to explore in future works. The dance-like music here discloses something of a Stravinskian patrinomy (Panufnik was of course a pupil of Nadia Boulanger), and indeed the whole score has a balletic quality that might act as inspiration for some suitably restrained choreography. One feels that if it were to gain a foothold in the general repertoire, the work would probably remain there, at the very least as a more reflective foil to the Mozart *Flute and Harp Concerto*." — Malcolm MacDonald, in *Tempo: A Quarterly Review of Modern Music*, Nr. 117, 6/76.

SYMPHONY 5: "Since the touching *Autumn Music* of 1962, Andrzej Panufnik has been refining his musical langauge with admirable single-mindedness, in a series of works concerned mainly with symmetrical architecture and tightly controlled motivic unity. The new *Sinfonia di Sfere (Symphony of Spheres)* — his *Fifth Syphony* — is the largest and most successful of these works so far. It maintains the basic characteristics of his style, most notably extreme economy of means and extraordinarily finely etched instrumentation, while it generates more forward drive than was apparent in its immediate predecessors.

"The word 'sphere' is taken as a metaphor for various dimensions of the structure. A small sphere within a large sphere resembles an ABA palindromic shape; spheres of melody are rotations of the basic melodic cell, and so forth. Three sets of membrane drums (12 in all) are placed at the circumference of the orchestra — otherwise normally constituted except that the brass are reduced to four soli, seated immediately in front of the conductor on either side of the piano.

"*Sinfonia di Sfere* is, then, in simplest terms, three palindromic movements fashioned from a single cell, played without pause over a span of about 35 minutes. The intervallic content of this cell (E, F, B) produces a consistently tough harmonic sound, like Panufnik's earlier *Universal Prayer* (1969), which is based on the same triad and is also palindromic — a single gigantic mirror-structure, in fact. A problem with *Universal Prayer* is that once the novel colors (and they are very striking) have become familiar on repeated hearings the lack of real variation on the return journey — while quite justified on paper- tends to work against the fulfilment of expectations aroused by the first half. The new symphony avoids this pitfall by interrelating its three structures, which nonetheless remain discrete entities —

while pre-compositional determinants affect far more dimensions of the music than in the earlier work. (It is to Panufnik's credit that this fact is not immediately apparent on hearing the music before reading the program note.)

"Other possible problems inherent in this type of construction are cunningly avoided: the outer sections of each ternary group are composed to serve different dramatic functions on reappearance. In the first 'movement' the subsections of the initial paragraph are bound together in a seamless lyrical flow, and the pungent staccato sonorities of woodwind and drums in the central section rise and fall from the apex without breaking the expectant atmosphere of the whole movement, which is the most impressively sustained structure to be found anywhere in Panufnik's recent work.

"The central climax of the symphony is a wild episode, with fast repeated-note brass and string figures breaking through the rhythmic counterpoint of the drum groups. To my surprise, I was reminded of Babbitt's *All Set* (of all things), and it may be that the jazzy bit was overdone in [the London SO's premiere] performance. On paper the section looks as if it should be much cooler, although the appearance of Panufnik's scores in general can be rather deceptive.

"Pulse is also handled constructively: the rapid stream of even quavers, slowly oscillating from high to low strings, which opens the final 'movement' is punctuated by sharp syncopated chords spanning the rest of the orchestra in shifting positions (depending on the register of the 'melody'). The chords form a larger pulse filled in by the drums with semiquaver patterns. When this section recurs, it is extended by a short coda which shifts the emphasis wholly onto the chordal pulse, over an ever more relentless battering of drums, bringing the whole work to an exhilarating close.

"Despite the two fast-tempo passages I have singled out, the whole is balanced to favor slow, contemplative music, and it is these passages that most clearly reveal the masterly quality of the orchestration. A disarming facet of Panufnik's scores is the lack of orchestral doublings and superficially 'exotic' coloration, which results in textures which sometimes look dangerously thin on paper. In performance, however, the music is surprisingly rich in timbre, and *Sinfonia di Sfere* abounds in characteristic examples: the brass soli in the opening section, accompanied by violins in two parts; later, a soft unison cello line accompanied only by stark piano chords; some beautifully spaced four-part brass chords in the central section of the third 'movement'; and clear woodwind textures throughout

"The type of control Panufnik imposes on every dimension of the music would cripple a lesser craftsman: the manipulation of a single cell over such a large span, to remain harmonically and rhythmically stable and yet sustain attention, is a tour-de-force. Nevertheless, despite the intricate construction, the warm response of a large audience [at the premiere] indicated that the symphony presents no real problems of assimilation to the casual listener." — Oliver Knussen, in *Tempo: A Quarterly Review of Modern Music*, Nr. 117, 6/76.

SYMPHONY 7: "*Metasinfonia* (No. 7) is a more difficult work to grasp than either Nos. 5 or 8. The consistent impression is of a dark, serious composition, more a contemplation than a drama. Nevertheless, there are dramatic moments: the first entry of the timpani is one, occurring after a fabulous buildup in several long waves. Another is the ferocious ending for the full ensemble [organ, timpani, and strings] after an organ cadenza." — Paul Rapaport, in *Fanfare: The Magazine for Serious Record Collectors*, 9-10/86.

SYMPHONY 8: "[Regarding his eighth symphony, the composer] explains the title *Sinfonia votiva* in part as follows: 'Although my *Eighth Symphony*... is an abstract work without any programmatic content, it nevertheless carries a spiritual and patriotic message. It is a votive offering to the miraculous ikon of the Black Madonna of Czestochowa in my native Poland... said to have been painted by St. Luke on a piece of cypress wood used as a table top by the Holy Family in Nazareth. It was brought to Poland by way of Byzantium and is still preserved at the monastery of Jasna Góra, which is celebrating its 600th anniversary in 1982.... It has always been, and still is, the sacred symbol of Independent Poland.' There are only two movements: the first, *con devozione*, is played at a slow tempo by one or a couple of instruments at a time, in which respect it is a concerto for orchestra, while the concluding *con passione* is a brilliant toccata. It splashes asymmetric rhythmic figures across a tapestry of percussion that grows mightily proclamative—sound that slowly decays after the final chord has been played. If *Sinfonia votiva* hasn't quite the expressive inevitability of Panufnik's earlier *Sacra* or *Mistica* (see above), the substance is managed with superb assurance; Panufnik is neither afraid nor embarassed to share deep feelings with his auditors." — Roger Dettmer, in *Fanfare: The Magazine for Serious Record Collectors*, 3-4/83.

SYMPHONY 8:"[In a composer-conducted performance broadcast by the BBC Transcription Service, Panufnik, at 26:40, takes five minutes more to play the *Symphony No. 8* than does Ozawa on the BSO recording, at 21:25.] Those extra minutes allow him, in the long, awed, reverent first movement, to accustom the hearer, in effect, to the dim light of the shrine that houses the Black Madonna, Poland's historic symbol of freedom. The second movement, characteristically an accretion of motivic fragments that Panufnkik knits and ultimately unfurls, like an arras, becomes uniquely gripping in the composer's performance with the BBC Symphony Orchestra. [His interpretation reveals] a consistently powerful, expressively anguished, but unquenchably hopeful work that descends directly from the *Sinfonia sacra* (No. 3), and *Sinfonia mistica* (No. 6), and before both of those from Szymanowski's best music." — Roger Dettmer, in *Fanfare: The Magazine for Serious Record Collectors*, 3-4/86.

SYMPHONY 8:"Panufnik began work on the symphony in 1980, at the time of the Gdansk shipyard strikes that led to the formation of Solidarity; he finished it a year later. His identification with his country and compatriots is well attested in his music: consider the *Sinfonia rustica [Nr. 1]* which uses fragments of Polish folktunes, the *Sinfonia sacra [Nr. 3]* based on the 'Bogurodzica', the earliest known Polish hymn, and other works such as *Polonia* and the *Katyn Epitaph*. The *Sinfonia votiva [Nr. 8]* is another demonstration of Panufnik's own solidarity with the country he had to leave. The work is in two movements, the first marked *con devozione (andante rubato)*, the second, *con passione (allegro assai)*; and it begins by introducing individual instruments of the orchestra: first solo woodwinds over a vibraphone figure, followed by solo strings backed by the harp; then *tutti* strings provide the background for the introduction of solo brass instruments. The movement builds up into a series of slow climaxes that never quite peak, and dies away in serene eleven-part string writing which, like some of Panufnik's writing for woodwind and brass before it, has a somewhat American sound: the music moves forward in rich textures of block harmony slightly reminiscent of Harris or Schuman. The second movement, over twice as long in score, takes less than half of the first's 18 minutes in performance, as sharp outbursts on brass and woodwind, against a bitter string theme, build up into a nervous, angry climax. The composer refers to it as 'an urgent petition'; it is more an impassioned demand. As with most of Panufnik's music, the *Votiva* is constructed to a rigid plan, this time based on the figure 8, so that the structure of the second movement, different though it sounds, is closely connected with that of the first; and, again as in most of his music, Panufnik's art in concealing his art is considerable." — Martin J. Anderson, in *Tempo: A Quarterly Reviewe of Modern Music*, Nr. 143, 12/82.

STEPHEN PAULUS

B. 1949, Summit NJ. *Educ.:* Macalester Coll, Univ MN. Co-fnd, MN Composers Forum. NEA Composer Fellowship, Tanglewood Composer Fellow, Guggenheim Fellowship. Composer-in-residence, Sante Fe Chamber Music Festival, Minnesota O, Atlanta SO. *Works incl.: American Vignettes* (cello, piano), choral works (*Four Preludes on Playthings of the Wood, Jesu Carols, Madrigali di Michelangelo, North Shore*), *Divertimento* (harp, cham orch), operas (*Harmoonia, The Woodlanders*), orchestral works (*Concerto, Ordway Overture, Reflections, Spectra*), 3 string quartets, voice & insts (*Artsongs* [t/pno], *Bittersuite* [bar/pno], *Letters from Colette* [s/chamb ens]).

Composer statement: "I have enjoyed writing for all kinds of ensembles and instrumental and vocal combinations. These have included opera, chorus, chorus with chamber ensemble and full orchestra, solo voice, chamber groups, and chamber orchestra as well as full orchestra. The diversity of projects and performers I have found to be inspiring and self-renewing.

"The Minnesota Composers Forum (of which I am a co-founder) played a significant part in the development of the early stages of my career. It provided on the job training for such organizational skills as grant writing and managing people. It also provided me with my first performances. Though I am no longer a Board Member or employee of the MCF I continue to support its activities which encourage and nurture younger composers who are starting out on their own careers.

"Another very important aspect in the development of my career has been my position as Composer in Residence with both the orchestras of Minnesota and Atlanta. It has given great exposure to my music and most importantly, it has afforded me countless opportunities for growth as a composer.

"My music is tonally based and lyrical, practical and challenging, and makes liberal use of dissonance where needed. Since the concept of what is 'dissonant' is constantly changing the latter statement is really relative and subject to opinion. I often employ melodies or melodic fragments, in the course of a work, which may be quite angular, i.e. fragmented by octave displacement, wide leaps, etc. Another characteristic of my music is its rhythmic drive. There is in the faster music a rhythmic propulsion and in the slower music an harmonic motion that always keeps the music moving ahead."

Concerto for Violin and Orchestra (1987). 32m Commissioned by Atlanta SO; ded. to William Preucil. Finalist in Friedheim Awards, Kennedy Center, 1988. *Prem.:* William Preucil (vln), Atlanta SO, Robert Shaw, cond. *Rec.:* New World Records NW 363-2 (CD): William Preucil (vln), Atlanta SO, Robert Shaw, cond. *Pub.:* European American.
3(3rd doub.picco)-3-3-3; 4-3-3-1; timp, 3 perc, harp, piano/celeste; strings
1. Allegro con fuoco (13m). 2. Cantabile (11m). 3. Allegro di bravura (8m).

"The *concerto* is in three discrete movements, beginning with a brash *Allegro con fuoco* that is by turns assertive, frenetic, and lyrical. The middle movement's *moderato* section borrows a theme from the first movement and treats it in a slower, more playful manner. The finale, *Allegro di bravura*, emphasizes spirited and brilliant solo work. Mined with virtuosic difficulties in the Paganinian manner, it also contains a brief central interlude in a more idyllic mood." — Nick Jones, from program notes for New World Records CD.

"Stephen Paulus has written his first violin concerto the old-fashioned way: with a particular soloist in mind. That soloist is William Preucil, concert-master of the Atlanta Symphony Orchestra. Paulus conceived the concerto as a vehicle for what he terms Preucil's 'wonderfully sweet tone, even in the highest register, plus his great versatility and flexibility, the ability to do all sorts of athletic things.'

"The result is a 32-minute work of considerable scope and complexity. Dedicated to Preucil, this ASO commission is scored for a large (but economically utilized) orchestra of triple winds, four horns, strings, and a large percussion battery abetted by harp, piano, and celesta. The piece is traditional in form, with three movements, fast-slow-fast. First comes an *Allegro con fuoco* in modified sonata form with an extended cadenza, next a rhapsodic cantabile, and finally an *Allegro di bravura* designed as virtuosic showpiece. Thematic material from the opening movement returns, transformed, in both succeeding movements. The harmonic foundation is solidly tonal, though Paulus is unafraid of bitonal clashes.

"Paulus' neoclassical, clearly demarcated stylistic framework, motoric rhythms, shifting meters, surprising accents, and bracing syncopation suggest Stravinsky. Stravinskian, too, are Paulus' somewhat acerbic harmonies, pungent wind writing, quirky wit, and vividly heterogeneous and lucid orchestration. But Stravinsky is not the only influence. The lyric passages manifest a Romantic flavor; the cadenza is rather Brahmsian, the nostalgic passage before the work's coda Coplandesque.

"In his imaginative and effective writing for solo violin, Paulus adeptly exploits Preucil's sweet tone, acrobatic adroitness, command of the violin's stratosphere, and skill at unfolding a soaring rhapsodic line. [The] new concerto is a piece that merits attention from performers and audiences alike." — Derrick Henry, in *Musical America*, 5/88.

The Postman Always Rings Twice (opera)(1982). *Lib.:* Colin Graham, after James N. Cain novel. *Prem.:* Opera Theater of St. Louis. *Other perfs.:* Washington Opera, Minnesota Opera, Edinburgh Festival, Ft. Worth Opera, Greater Miami Opera. *Pub.:* European American (EA 202 piano-vocal score; performance materials on rental).
1 s, 2 t, 2 bar, 1 b; 1 actor
2(2 pic)-1-1-a.sax-1; 1-2-1-1(b tbn); guitar, harp, piano, 2 perc (incl 2 timp); 6-6-4-3-2
In two acts.

¶*Suite from "The Postman Always Rings Twice* for Orchestra (1986). 22m Comm. by the Minnesota Orchestral Assn under terms of the Exxon/Rockefeller Composer in Residence Program. *Prem.:* Minnesota O, Leonard Slatkin, cond. *Other perfs.:* Civic O of Chicago, Eugene SO, Macon SO. *Pub.:* European American.
3(3rd doub.picc)-3-3-3 + a.sax; 4-3-3-1; timp, 3 perc, harp, piano; strings

"This opera by the young American composer Stephen Paulus has achieved remarkable success since its premiere by the Opera Theater of St. Louis in 1982. It was the first American opera heard at the Edinburgh Festival (1983), and there have been several restagings by important companies, most recently in Washington. *The Postman Always Rings Twice* is attractive for many reasons: it is short (about two hours), it is written in an accessible idiom, it has a small cast whose vocal parts pose no particular problems, it involves no chorus, it is scored for a small orchestra (single and double winds, brass and percussion, plus twenty-one single string players), it demands no elaborate sets, and, most of all, it is based on a story that is familiar and effective.

"James M. Cain's 1934 tale of the adulterous love of Frank and Cora and the murder of her husband Nick has both pulp and intellectual appeal. Camus used it as one of his sources for *The Stranger*, but it is best known to Americans from the 1946 film by Tay Garnett, starring a sultry Lana Turner.[80] Colin Graham has done a reasonable job of constructing a libretto for Paulus. Naturally, much condensation was necessary. The botched first murder attempt in the bathtub is eliminated, as is Frank's infidelity and trip to Mexico....

"The challenge that this text posed for Paulus was finding music for natural, vernacular American speech patterns that, while not monotonous recitative, retains some of the rhythm and tempo of the language. Paulus's 'solution' is to avoid the issue as much as possible: the orchestra supplies affect and coherence by constant repetition of a few melodic fragments, and every opportunity for an orchestral set piece in some sort of closed form is eagerly seized upon. Paulus's best music is in these set pieces, many of which use elements of popular music to help create their ambience. The opening alto saxophone solo includes the most memorable tune in the opera, and Frank's 'Traveling Blues' and Nick's gentle song are clear successes.... [Alongside one's criticisms of the opera it can be said that] *The Postman Always Rings Twice* is a well-organized, well-crafted work with some good music and clear dramatic values." — Fred Hauptman, in *Notes* (Music Library Association), 9/89.

"*The Village Singer* [below] made such a splash that the [Opera Theater of St. Louis] commissioned 32-year-old Stephen Paulus to write his first full-length opera....

"The opera might be described as cinematic in its use of flashbacks, crosscutting and sharp contrasts of mood to link the 20 short scenes. Most of the action takes place at a roadside cafe, where the ill-fated protagonists — Frank Chambers, a drifter, and Cora, the proprietor's wife — play out their pathetic drama of adultery, murder, bitterness and mistrust.

"James M. Cain once said that his crime novels were at heart love stories — a statement that applies to *Postman*, despite its sordid and sometimes violent plot. For all their passion, Frank and Cora never court our pity, and it is a tribute to Colin Graham's literary skills that he preserves the lean, unsentimental quality of Mr. Cain's prose, and that he makes every word tell.

"Mr. Paulus's music is similarly forceful and economical — not every composer could set hard-bitten lines such as 'You like blueberry pie?' so convincingly — but it also has a richly expansive lyricism that many contemporary operas lack. As in *The Village Singer*, the composer peppers his score with Americanisms such as blues, syn-

---

[80] A more recent version featuring William Hurt and another Turner — Kathleen — is also popular. (Ed.)

copated rhythms and honky-tonk piano. Despite these borrowings, his music is personalized and keenly dramatic. For instance, the music for Nick Papadakis, the simple-hearted owner of the Twin Oaks Cafe, has a jauntiness that seems almost too American to be true.

"When Cora desperately tries to send Frank away, slithery strings seem to mirror her unstable emotions. Nick's idealistic aria, first heard with a simple guitar accompaniment, returns in a sparer and more ominous setting just before his death. Even the vaudeville routines for Sackett and Katz, the district attorney and defense lawyer, fit in perfectly." — Harry Haskell, in *The Kansas City Star*, 6/27/82.

"This is 'tonal' music, always in one clearly definable key or another. It uses a four-note melodic figure (G-A-F-E, when it occurs in C Major) as its germinal motif. The orchestration calls for no unusual playing techniques; the harmonic motion is simple enough for a first-year music student to analyze.

"Yet to challenge the score on grounds of 'conservatism' would be a mistake. The only valid criterion for theatrical music is effectiveness. If emotions are amply projected and contrasted in a way that suits the libretto's movement, then the opera works, no matter what the style. If in the bargain the music also happens to be sonically beautiful, as *Postman* is, so much the better.

"In theatrical terms, the *Postman* music is wholly effective. Symbolic sounds are attached deftly to key images: a sharply strummed guitar chord for 'the Greek', single notes on the harp for the genuine love that flows between Frank and Cora, and brutal string sonorities for the purely erotic part of their relationship. Melodic fragments, haunting enough when first heard, return again and again to trigger the listener's memory. The music follows the course of Frank and Cora's love affair; it rises and falls like a barometer in a thunderstorm.

"*Postman* is not for children, but it is for adults who enjoy good theater." — James Wierzbicki, in *St. Louis Globe-Democrat*, 6/19/82.

So Hallow'd Is the Time (A Christmas Cantata) (1985).
Texts: Shakespeare, Dunbar, Milton, Smart, Drummond, Donne, Herrick, Southwell. 33m *Prem.:* Greenwich Choral Society, Richard Vogt, cond. (Aldeburgh Festival). *Other perf.:* Atlanta SO and Chamber Chorus, Robert Shaw, cond. *Rec.:* Pro Arte PAD 257. *Pub.:* European American (piano/vocal score, choral score, full score, parts).
1 s, 1 boy s, 1 t, 1 bar, SATB chorus
1-1-1-1; 1-3-1-0; 2 perc (incl 2 timp), organ, harp; strings

1. *Prelude.* 2. *Proclamation.* 3. *Welcoming.* 4. *The Search.* 5. *The Message.* 6. *The Birth.* 7. *Song of the Mother and Child.* 8. *Ode on the Birth of the Saviour.* 9. *Arrival of the Kings.* 10. *Praise for the Child.* 11. *Postlude.*

"When a major work by a young composer is performed on the same program with that of an 'Old Master' such as Handel, [as it was in recent performances by Robert Shaw and the Atlanta Symphony Orchestra and Chorus,] the work must be very good indeed to avoid being 'lost' in the minds of the audience. Stephen Paulus need have no fear in this respect....

"The listener first hears the baritone solo, 'So Hallow'd Is the Time' (text by Shakespeare), as a *Prelude*. While the text speaks of 'so gracious is the time,' the music conveys a sense of mystery, which develops an undertone of foreboding. The mixing of a 'great wonder' about to occur and 'the world is to be shaken' is done with a confident hand.

"Moving to the *Proclamation*, Paulus uses words by William Dunbar (c.1460-1530), 'Sing, Hevin Imperial, Most of Hicht!' This movement for chorus, tenor and baritone is an unusual mixture of very old English ('Lay out your levis lustily, Fro deid take life'), 20th-century dissonance, and aggressive rhythm. The full resonance of the chorus and the tenor's ringing high-register voice try valiantly to reflect the text ('Be mirthful and mak melody!'), but the continued dissonance in the strings drags the mood into another realm.

"In the *Welcoming*, with text by John Milton (1608-1674), a beautiful, moving, and exquisite women's chorus brings delight to the heart and makes one fervently wish Paulus had not written this to be such a short movement!

"With the *Search*, the tenor sings words by Christopher Smart (1722-1771), while the orchestra provides lovely moods. And yet again Paulus inserts dissonance in the strings, as if to say: 'This was composed in the 20th Century, and don't you forget it!'

"But in *The Message*, there is powerful and compelling music to support the words of William Drummond (1585-1649). The chorus delivers the text 'We bring the best of news, be not dismayed' to engender a great feeling of triumph, rising to the climax of 'the power of Satan broken is.'

"In sharp contrast is *The Birth*. A tympani solo cadenza in the middle of an oratorio is a daring touch, but Paulus begins this movement with that bold stroke, allowing it to lead into the men's chorus. The voices begin in a low but commanding mood, and advance in inexorable steps to a powerful conclusion, as the words of John Donne (1572-1631) proclaim 'Now leave his well-beloved imprisonment.... Seest thou, my Soule, with thy faiths eyes.'

"After such an emotional peak a composer must carefully select the next scene lest it be overcome by that which precedes it. And again Paulus shows his understanding of something even more powerful than triumph: a *Song of the Mother and Child*. Using an intimate quartet of boy soprano, soprano, baritone, and harp, he makes the interesting contrast of a woman's and a boy's voice as they gently sing to one another. One might wonder why a bariton is in this scene, but Paulus uses the male voice to provide a gentle, rich, and unobtrusive background fabric for this special picture.

"In his *Ode on the Birth of the Saviour*, Paulus creates a lullaby effect without the usual coyness. Using words of Robert Herrick (1591-1674), the women's chorus and the orchestra play the phrases back and forth with expert ease ('Thou prettie Babe, borne here').

"But now it is time for the *Arrival of the Kings*, and with a march theme the chorus gives out 'Lordlings, listen to our lay—We have come from far away.' A well-designed (but brief) movement to rouse those who may have nodded off during the previous lullaby. This movement creates the necessary contrast to the preceding 'soft and pretty' movement and the following one.

"In *Praise for the Child*, the chorus displays that unique and glorious sound heard only in *a capella* singing. This setting of a poem by Robert Southwell (1561-1595) is an exquisite piece with delightful dynamics to convey the message: 'His love doth cherish all; His birth our joy, His life our light.'

"Paulus concludes with a lively restatement of 'Sing Hevin Imperial'. This *Postlude* is a fitting capstone to the entire structure, and it closes with a feeling of fulfillment, triumph, and majesty."—Lindsay Cleveland, in *Chorus!* (Duluth GA 30136), 1/90.

Symphony in Three Movements (Soliloquy) for Orchestra (1986).

30m Comm.by MN Orch Assn (Meet the Composer, Exxon Corp, Rockefeller Fndn, NEA grants). *Prem.*: Minnesota O, Neville Marriner, cond. *Rec.*: Electra/ Nonesuch (LP/CD) 79147: Minnesota O, Neville Marriner, cond. *Pub.*: European American.
3(3rd doub. picc)-3-3-3; 4-3-3-1; timp, 3 perc, hp, piano/celeste; strings
1. *Unrestrained*. 2. *Impassioned*. 3. *Volatile*.

"Each of Paulus' operas has had a major orchestral work in its wake, as he explains:

" 'Like two other of my orchestral works, *Spectra* and the *Concerto* for Orchestra, *Soliloquy* has also come on the heels of a completed opera [*The Woodlanders*]. And in all three cases I have felt a certain freedom in not having to worry about covering up singers' voices or "moving the story forward". These are all wonderful elements to contend with when writing for a dramatic situation, but there is also an equal joy in working with instrumentalists in a purely abstract, musical way.

" 'Consequently, there seems to be little need to further explain the title of the first movement of *Soliloquy—Unrestrained*. As in the *Concerto*, I decided to use movement titles which gave a true indication of feeling rather than serve merely as tempo indicators. These titles also worked well to support the concept of the piece. A 'soliloquy' is the act of talking alone, or talking as if alone. I liked this idea because it had theatrical connotations; one thinks of the term most often in connection with theater. This inspired me to write a non-programmatic work that had strong, dramatic overtones. Secondly, it moved me to use a dichotomy to advantage. How was one to take this term, with its idea of speaking alone, and relate it to an ensemble of nearly one hundred musicians? I decided to accomplish that by unifying the players in their projection of an emotion, i.e., to strive to have each player make his or her own musical contribution (sometimes individually and sometimes collectively) to the general emotion indicated by the title of the movement.'

"Thus, while its overall design, tempos and content betray elements of both the concerto and the symphony, such generic terms would not convey the expressive purpose Paulus had in mind. Stylistically, the freely dissonant music gravitates towards tonal centers, which have never hampered the composer's harmonic strategies.[81] From the opening bars, the *Soliloquy* bears the imprint of his rhythmic verve: he unleashes the music with a swift, decisive gesture, establishes an animated pulse, jumps in and out of irregular meters— four, five, seven beats to a bar—and creates phrases that are sparked by syncopation. The result is a fresh, extroverted sound accommodating everyone's notion of an American profile. Beyond a fleshed-out percussion battery, with a lively piano part, the score does not demand extraordinary forces, and all the sections carry equal weight.

"Paulus summarizes the content of each movement:

" 'The first movement, *Unrestrained*, appears at the outset to suggest only anger or a feistiness. But midway into the movement a different kind of unrestrained expression takes hold—a more exhuberant and joyous variety. An unbridled flow of energy permeates the movement with the more aggressive dissonances returning at the close.

---

[81] The contrast between tonality and non- or anti-tonality in contemporary music is a theme which is treated by many composers throughout the present volume, as they discuss both their own music and that of others. See e.g. George Perle essay, below. (Ed.)

" 'The second movement, *Impassioned*, is chiefly romantic and lyrical, albeit often in an angular manner. The major ninth which seems to be the predominant interval throughout the entire work is here presented in the violins at the opening in a high, eerie register. In retaining some of the tension of the first movement, this is a slow movement which takes its time to unfold, but is certainly not leisurely or casual in any respect. The interval of the minor ninth and the constant rise and fall of melodic fragments keep it pressing forward with a certain restlessness.

" 'The final movement, *Volatile*, is more eruptive in nature, and it is the movement with the most internal contrast. In the opening bars, low, quiet strings in octaves are shortly counterbalanced with equally quiet strings in the uppermost registers. All of this unsettling quietude is assuredly interrupted with a force and determination that propels the work to a blustery climax and finale.' " — Mary Ann Feldman, program notes for Marriner/Minnesota Orchestra premiere.

"The movements of *Soliloquy* have titles that describe their natures aptly. *Unrestrained* has the boisterous quality of a large puppy freed from a leash. *Impassioned* is lyrical in a way that Prokofiev's slow movements are lyrical: it's both intense and eerie. The finale, *Volatile*, begins with an air of expectation and proceeds to erupt.

"In scoring *Soliloquy*, Paulus has grouped the several sections of the orchestra—strings, woodwinds, brass and percussion (the latter including piano and celesta)—in families that generally stick together, that is, each section tends to contribute what it has to say as a group.

"The language of *Soliloquy* is fresh and immediately accessible. Although dissonance is much in evidence, Paulus always lets his listeners know where they stand relative to consonance." — Roy M. Close, in *St. Paul (MN) Pioneer Press and Dispatch*, 1/16/86.

"The piano plays an important role, especially in the energetic first movement. The second and longest movement features extremely high and exposed violin writing, such as that found in the slow movement of Copland's *Third Symphony*. Paulus sustains this mood for quite some time, making the outburst all the more surprising when it comes. His atmospheric use of celesta recalls Bartók's in *Music for Strings, Percussion, and Celesta*. In the third movement, an eerie introduction leads into a fanciful and athletic finale that contains one hell of a false ending. Throughout, Paulus's rhythmic urgency is combined with a grace that, while not often encountered today, was a hallmark of such American masters as Copland, Barber, and Piston. Paulus seems a natural successor in this tradition." — John Canarina, in *Opus*, 4/88.

The Village Singer (opera in one act)(1979). *Lib.*: Michael Dennis Browne, after a story by Mary Wilkins Freeman. 60m *Comm. & prem.*: Opera Theatre of St. Louis, with New Music Circle of St. Louis. *Pub.*: European American (EA 454 Vocal Score).
3 s, 1 mezz, 3 t, 1 bar, 1 b; 8-voice choir
2-1-2-1; 1-0-0-0; timp, harp, piano/harm, 2 perc; 3-3-2-2-1

"Richard Gaddes, the general director of the Opera Theatre of St. Louis, liked the way Paulus wrote for voices; thought he detected in him a born opera composer; and (with the New Music Circle of St. Louis) commissioned a one-act piece for the St. Louis company. The result, *The Village Singer*, had its première this month and proved bright testimony to Mr. Gaddes's flair, Paulus's ability, and the prowess of the admirable St. Louis company. Accounts of a successful first opera are usually qualified by the remark that its promising young composer still has a lot to learn. What was striking about *The Village Singer* is how *little* its composer still has to learn about dramatic timing, balancing musical forms and theatrical discourse, creating melodic curves that reveal character or convey emotion, and the other specifically operatic skills. His score is at once fresh and masterly.

"The libretto, by the poet Michael Dennis Browne, is drawn from Mary Wilkins Freeman's short story 'A Village Singer' (1891). For forty years, Miss Candace Whitcomb has been the leading soprano of the church choir in a New England village. Her upper notes have become unreliable. The other members of the choir give her a surprise party and an album of photographs, and she, suspecting nothing, is touched by their tribute. But when they have gone, she finds in the album a letter telling her that her services are no longer needed; a younger soprano, Miss Alma Way, has been engaged. Next Sunday morning, Alma embarks on a solo:

> Her voice rang out piercingly sweet; the people nodded admiringly at each other; but suddenly there was a stir; all the faces turned toward the windows on the south side of the church. Above the din of the wind and the birds, above Alma Way's sweetly straining tones, arose another female voice, singing another hymn to another tune.... Candace Whitcomb's cottage stood close to the south side of the church. She was playing on her parlor organ, and singing, to drown out the voice of her rival.

The minister comes to remonstrate with her, but in vain. 'I'm goin' to let folks see that I ain't trod down quite flat, that there's a little rise left in me.' During the afternoon service, the same antiphonal battle is fought. Now Candace's nephew Wilson Ford, who is engaged to Alma, comes to remonstrate with her, and also in vain. But the fires of ambition and resolution that suddenly blazed in Candace destroy her. Fevered, she takes to her bed. The next Sunday (in the opera, three Sundays later), she asks for Alma to come to sing to her after the service.

> Candace lay and listened. Her face had a holy and radiant expression. When Alma stopped singing it did not disappear, but she looked up and spoke, and it was like a secondary glimpse of the old shape of a forest tree through the smoke and flame of the transfiguring fire the instant before it falls. 'You flatted a little on—soul,' said Candace.

That is all, but it is more than a tragicomic anecdote. Both the story and the opera trace a delicate, touching portrait of 'this obscure woman, kept relentlessly by circumstances in a narrow track, [to whom] singing in the village choir had been as much as Italy was to Napoleon.' Her tender feeling for William Emmons, the elderly leader of the choir, who was wont to walk home with her after rehearsals and sing duets with her to the parlor organ, and who has now acquiesced, even taken a leading role, in her dismissal, adds poignancy to the tale. Thoughts of Prospero, of Verdi's Falstaff, of Isak Dinesen's Pellegrina Leoni, of Strauss's Marschallin, of aging masters in whatever art who find it not easy to hand over leadership to the young deepen a reader's or a listener's apprehension of the story or the opera. It is a good subject for musical treatment, since it can be vividly realized in musical terms, and a fine subject for an American opera with a universal theme and particularity of setting and local color.

"The scenes move between Candace's parlor and the church, visible side by side on the stage, and finally to Candace's bedroom. The score starts as the story does: 'The trees were in full leaf, a heavy south wind was blowing, and there was a loud murmur among the new leaves.' For 'this soft sylvan music—the tender harmony of the leaves and the south wind, and the sweet, desultory whistles of birds,' Paulus has borrowed, developed, and built upon the murmuring figuration that begins the *Così fan tutte* trio *'Soave sia il vento'*. The hymn tunes and their words are traditional: Isaac Watts, Thomas Moore, and Sabine Baring-Gould have contributed to the libretto, and Samuel Webbe, Sir Joseph Barnby, and John Bacchus Dykes to the score. At her surprise party, Candace, asked to sing, obliges with

J.S. Fearis's hymn 'Beautiful Isle' ('Somewhere the sun is shining'), with words by Jessie B. Pounds. It was copyrighted in 1897, and so when Candace says 'I always did like that song' there is a slight chronological awkwardness: since the opera is set 'at the turn of the century,' the piece cannot have been in her repertory very long. But the sentimental tune (William, at Candace's request, joins in the refrain) fits the occasion well, and the other hymn texts are carefully chosen to point the situations. Alma's first solo is Watts' 'In vain we tune our formal songs, In vain we strive to rise', sung to Dykes's 'St. Agnes', in G; the supporting harmonies go terribly awry under the onslaught of Candace's 'Gracious spirit, dwell with me', sung to Richard Redhead's 'Rock of Ages' tune first in E-flat and then soaring up into B-flat. Likewise, the choir's and Alma's 'Come, ye disconsolate' (words by Moore, tune by Webbe), in C, quails before Candace's ringing 'To God my earnest voice I raise', proclaimed to the 'When I survey' tune in A-flat. In each case, one hymn is in 4/4 and the other in 3/4, but the quarter-notes march at the same tempo, and the result is a carefully controlled, not a chance, cacaphony. All Paulus's score is marked by a similar command of harmonic tension that defines the dramatic tensions. The opera is not exactly 'in' any key, but the beginning and the end, where the leafy murmur grows slower and dies at last on the sound of a bell, suggests D major or G major poised above an uneasy tritone alternation of E and B-flat....

"The denomination of the church is left vague, even distractingly contradictory, by all concerned. In the story, the services are called meetings, and Candace refers to the church as a 'meetin' house'. The choir's three hymns in the opera (the third is an offstage 'Now the day is over', accompanying Candace's last monolog) appear, words and music, in the Episcopalian hymnal. Candace's words, however, are taken, no doubt with intent, from Dissenting hymnals. The choir is unsurpliced, informal, but the minister chants the Grace with a positive Tractarian flourish. It is a nice touch that in his fluster at Candace's interventions he leaves out the words 'and the love of God'. There are several such little subtleties, verbal and musical, in the piece. Candace's triumphant last note, on *soul,* is a long, steady G above the staff, *mp-f-pp*. But Alma's note for *soul* had been the A above it....

"An operatic treatment of *A Village Singer* could easily have gone wrong—become broad, larky, or mawkishly sentimental. Paulus's opera is none of these. It shows an uncommon niceness of taste, and delicacy and depth of feeling. The challenge posed to his skills is perfectly met. The piece makes a sure start to an operatic career. Now one would like to see him venture more boldly, into matter still more challenging to his musical invention. Preceded by some New

England melodrama or tragedy, and followed by a high-spirited comedy, *The Village Singer* could well become the central panel of an American *Trittico.*" — Andrew Porter, in *The New Yorker*, 6/25/79.[82]

---

[82] Reprinted in *Music of Three More Seasons, 1977-1980* (Alfred A. Knopf, 1981).

Krzysztof Penderecki

B. 1933, Debica (Poland). *Educ.*: Superior Schl of Music, Cracow. *Taught at:* Folkwang Hochschule für Musik, Essen; Yale Univ; Aspen CO. Honorary member Royal Acad of Music, London; Arts Acad of West Berlin; Arts Acad of German Democratic Republic; Royal Acad of Music, Stockholm. *Works incl.*: cello concerto, chamber works, *De Natura Sonoris 1 & 2* (orch), *The Devils of Loudon* (opera), *Passion According to St. Luke*, *Threnody in Memory of Victims of Hiroshima* (52 strng insts), *Utrenja*.

Concerto for Violin and Orchestra (1976). 35m Commissioned by *Allgemeinen Musikgesellshaft Basel;* ded. to Isaac Stern. *Prem.:* Isaac Stern. *Recs.:* Columbia Records (Stereo LP) M 353150: Isaac Stern (vln), Minnesota O, Stanislaw Skrowaczewski, cond.; Muza 019: Konstanty Andrzej Kulka (vln), Polish Radio O, Krzysztof Penderecki, cond. *Pub.:* Schotts (European American).
3-3-5-3; 4-3-3-1; timp, perc., celesta, harp; strings
In one movement.

"A new violin concerto by a major international composer is an eagerly awaited event, not only because of its potential to broaden the solo literature for this instrument, but even more important in this case because it may signal a decisive change in the creative direction of one of the most influential composers of the past two decades. Krzysztof Penderecki's *Violin Concerto* was commissioned by the *Allgemeinen Musikgesellshaft Basel*. Begun in 1974 and completed in 1976, it was given its world premier in 1977 by no less another musical luminary than Isaac Stern, to whom the work is dedicated. The work is scored for woodwinds and brasses in threes, large percussion section, celesta, harp, and strings.

"Penderecki's interest in string instruments and techniques goes back to his early years; as a matter of fact his early musical training was that of a violinist. In the decade of the sixties he composed a number of works for soli strings, or works in which strings are prominently used. Some of these are his *Threnody, String Quartets No. 1 and 2, Polymorphia, Anaklasis,* and *Capriccio* for solo violin and orchestra. In all of these works there is a consistent attempt to widen the sonorous potential of the instruments, to develop new string devices and articulations, and to develop new notational symbols by which these devices may be represented. Some of these devices are the use of extreme registers, various types of vibrati, tremolos, and percussive effects; playing between the bridge and tailpiece; and microtonal melody and clusteral harmony. He also uses a more flexibile type of notation which dispenses with barlines and instead measures the music in seconds, called proportional notation. And, while many of these devices and procedures may be found in the *Violin Concerto,* they appear there not with the same prominence or intent. Instead technique and device have been placed in the service of higher musical considerations.

"Compared to the earlier works, the mood of the *Violin Concerto* is more somber, rhapsodic, and poetic in nature. It contains passages of haunting and ethereal lyricism, as well as others of angularity and dynamic power. Relatively speaking, the work is quite tonal, and contains much triadic writing, so that elements of new and older harmonic systems coexist side by side or are blended together. The overall form is quite rounded, with the ideas introduced in the opening section periodically brought back to punctuate the various subsections of this single movement work. The way in which ideas are introduced and reappear suggests that the work might even have a philosophical program. In contrast to some of the earlier works, the score is frequently conventionally notated with time signatures and barlines, and proportional notation is only occasionally used.

"The solo violin is explored in all of its registers and shadings, especially in the two cadenzas in the work. Here there are brilliant, technically difficult bravura passages: various types of harmonics, angular arpeggios, complicated trills, double stops in thirds, sevenths and octaves, triple and quadruple stops, and quarter-tone melodies. Thus, the work is only for the very seasoned professional." — Donald Chittum, in *Notes* (Music Library Association), 9/81.

"Krzysztof Penderecki's 1976 *Violin Concerto* is a tremendously impressive piece of music that has great impact on initial exposure and continues to grow with subsequent hearings. It is a lyrical, darkly colored, very intense, and frequently emotional work. With its depth of feeling, the *Violin Concerto* seems to be a spiritual descendant of Penderecki's 1960 *Threnody for the Victims of Hiroshima* for 52 solo strings. However, the unusually colored string-tone, derived from using inexact pitch, and the tone clusters in the earlier work are not present in the *Concerto*. In fact, there are no traces of the tonal experiments that propelled Penderecki to the forefront of the avant-garde. Most noticeable is the often flashy solo part with its hints of Romantic and post-Romantic concertos. Two prominent motives that run through the work are one in which dark strings are heard over the brass choir, and an ominously dirge-like motive with timpani and/or bass-drum beats. The dirge motive also serves as one of the work's three principal themes; the others are one that is songlike and one in the style of a grotesque Mahlerian march. As in Mahler's symphonies, a large orchestra is required but is used sparingly, and much of the music has a chamber orchestra-like clarity. Stern's playing [in the Columbia recording] is superb." — Ben Pernick, in *Fanfare: The Magazine for Serious Record Collectors*, 7-8/79.

George Perle

B. 1915, Bayonne NJ. *Educ.:* DePaul Univ, American Cons of Music, NY Univ. *Taught at:* Univ Louisville, Univ CA (Davis), City Univ NY (Queens College), Yale Univ, State Univ NY (Buffalo), Univ PA, Columbia Univ, Juilliard Schl, Tanglewood. Dir., New Music Group of Chicago; composer-in-residence, Tanglewood Music Center, Bellagio Study and Conference Ctr (Lake Como, Italy). Member, American Acad/Inst of Arts and Letters. *Awards incl.:* 2 Guggenheim Fellowships, MacArthur Fellowship. *Author of: The Operas of Alban Berg* (2v), *Serial Composition and Atonality, Twelve-Tone Tonality*. *Works incl.:* choral pieces, *Concerto* (vc), *Three Movements for Orchestra*, piano pieces, quartets, quintets (wnds, strngs), *Serenades* (chamber ens), sonatas (bsn, cl, vc, vla, vln).

From *The New Grove Dictionary of Music and Musicians:* "During the 1930s Perle was among the first American composers to be attracted by the music and thought of Schoenberg, Berg and Webern. His interest, however, was not so much in the twelve-note system itself as in the idea of a generalized systematic approach to dodecaphonic composition. Using some of the fundamental concepts of the twelve-note system, such as set and inversion, he developed an approach to composition which attempts to incorporate such twelve-note ideas with some of the basic kinds of hierarchical distinction found in tonal practice, such as the concept of a 'key' as a primary point of reference. His 'twelve-tone modal system', developed continuously from 1939 (and in collaboration with Paul Lansky from 1969), is, in simplest terms, an attempt to create useful distinctions and differentiations in a twelve-note context by defining functional characteristics of pitch-class collections, 'chords,' in terms of the intervals formed by component pairs of notes, on the one hand, and the properties of these same pairs with respect to an axis of symmetry, a point about which they are symmetrically disposed, on the other. (In an abstract sense these two concepts are roughly analogous to familiar notions of 'mode' and 'key' in tonal music.) In a composition these kinds of distinction are made useful and noticeable by a consistent use of only a few interval complexes and large-scale references to only a few points of symmetry. Perle's approach does not define explicit procedures for composition but rather outlines a large and highly structured network of pitch-class and formal relations which can then serve as points of reference for compositional development. (In this sense, too, it is like tonal composition in that the composer's 'system' is a general guide to a musi-

> **SPECIAL FEATURE**
>
> An entry on George Perle provides a convenient opportunity to address some of the issues having to do with the tonality/atonality controversy in contemporary music. Whether or not one enjoys—or even approves!—of atonal or serial music, and its various manifestations and derivatives, the debate between traditional tonal or key-centered music and alternative musical structurings and aesthetics comprises one of the essential events in twentieth-century music history. George Perle is an especially thoughtful and articulate spokesperson concerning some of these matters—both as a composer and as a widely-read musical theorist. Here, then, is a small anthology of writings by and about George Perle, intended to illuminate aspects of his work and of the debate itself. (Ed.)

cal language and a given composition constructs a unique interpretation of that language.)...

"In comparison with much music of the time, the 'sound' of Perle's music and the manner in which he unfolds his musical ideas are usually straightforward and relatively uncomplicated. His music eschews the veneer of the avant-garde and what he considers the wrong-headed association of musical complexity with perceptual difficulty. The complexities that concern him are those arising from the many levels on which his pitch, pitch-class and motivic relations interact and interrelate, and for him difficulties are only in making these relations as interesting and understandable as possible. In many of his compositions a few relatively simple musical ideas will appear in different ways and contexts so that the character and quality of these ideas become richer in the process." —Paul Lansky.

On George Perle's *Twelve-Tone Tonality* (Univ of CA Press, 1977): "The disappearance of the normative elements of triadic tonality in 20th century music is one of the most far-reaching and extreme revolutions that the history of music has known. The thesis of [Perle's] book is that the seemingly disparate styles of post-triadic music share common structural elements, and that collectively these elements imply a new tonality, as 'natural' and coherent as the major-minor tonality which has been the basis of a common musical language in the past. [In his study the composer] describes the foundational assumptions of this 'twelve-tone tonality', and illustrates its compositional functions by numerous musical examples.

"'Perle's inquiry may well release creative ideas. In Schoenberg there is little of an explicit model for combining sets or forming vertical systems, whereas Perle has uncovered a wide pre-compositional vocabulary which establishes linear and harmonic relatedness — its strength being the implicit grounding of any one solution in a system that in theory accounts for all solutions.... Schoenberg would have been fascinated by this book, with its outstanding intellectual vision and its steps towards a reconciliation between notions of tonality and twentieth-century pitch structure.' (Jonathan Dunsby, in *Music and Letters*, 7/79).

"'Despite the apparent complexities of Twelve-Tone Tonality, its theories will probably be easier for composers to assimilate than was twelve-tone serialism fifty years ago. It will be interesting to watch this process occur, particularly among today's serialists who may now realize that the twelve-tone system has a newly-revealed other side' (Mark DeVoto, in MLA *Notes*, 12/78)." — Music Associates of America.

" 'A COMPOSER'S MUSIC CATCHES UP TO HIS WORDS': For practically 50 years, George Perle has been known for his ability to unravel in words the intricacies of 12-tone music. Such a classic is his 1962 book *Serial Composition and Atonality*, one of the first attempts to explain how Schoenberg, Berg and Webern could make musical sense out of the chaos of atonality, that it will be published in Beijing, in Chinese, this year [1989]. Especially drawn to Berg, Mr. Perle has also written a definitive two-volume study of Berg's operas.

"Yet for the last three years, George Perle has been better known for writing an elegant, cultivated, often witty and, above all, readily accessible music that sounds nothing like the music he is famous for analyzing. In 1986 he won a Pulitzer Prize for it. The same year, the MacArthur Foundation gave him one of its generous fellowship awards [and] Nonesuch Records devoted a disk to Mr. Perle's music that year.

"And the demand for his music has accelerated. Last weekend, the New York Chamber Orchestra introduced local audiences to Mr. Perle's *Sinfonietta*. The Chamber Music Society of Lincoln Center unveiled the 73-year-old-composer's new *Sextet* for Piano and Winds last night.... Next comes the Juilliard Quartet's premiere of Mr. Perle's lastest string quartet, *Windows of Order*, at the Library of Congress in Washington. On April 9, the American Composer's Orchestra plays Mr. Perle's recent *Dance Overture* at Carnegie Hall, another New York premiere. Finally, the Brooklyn Philharmonic will include *Sonnets of Orpheus*, an a cappella choral piece Mr. Perle wrote in 1974 as a memorial to Noah Greenberg, founder of the pioneering early-music group New York Pro Musica.

"Considering the fact that Mr. Perle has written music as long as he has been writing and theorizing about it, why has the music only lately attracted wide-spread attention? 'I don't know,' the usually talkative Mr. Perle says, when asked the question during a telephone conversation from Berkeley, where he is currently delivering the prestigious Ernest Bloch lectures at the University of California. 'I have to think about it.'

"Mr. Perle acknowledges that there hasn't been a dramatic change in his style, nor would he claim that the quality of his music suddenly got appreciably better than it was. 'I began to get a reputation as a theorist, and I guess people didn't think one could also be a composer at the same time,' he finally concludes....[83]

"Mr. Perle firmly believes that music should speak for itself, and right away, whether one understands it or not. He remembers that his first experience with music was the ecstatic sensation he had, at the age of 6, hearing a cousin play a Chopin etude on the piano.

" 'It was a totally spontaneous, intuitive experience, which has colored my thinking about the relation of a listener to music ever since. So if a child of 6 can have such an experience with a Chopin etude, which is pretty sophisticated music, then an older person listening to a new piece of music for the first time should also be able to make such a connection with it, whether he understands it or not. The first time I heard the Berg *Lyric Suite*, I was totally bowled over by it, although I had no previous acquaintance with that kind of music....

" 'Composers are people like the rest of us,' he [insists]. 'They have to listen to what they compose, and the performer has to listen. And listening is a spontaneous activity. It has to move you in some way.'...

"Mr. Perle has particular fondness for the wind quintet: He has written four. He is also drawn to the solo piano. [Talking about his new string quartet, the composer explains that] he borrowed the title *Windows of Order* from James Gleick's book on developments in mathematical theory, *Chaos*, the expression reminding [him] of the way seemingly chaotic elements in a piece of music can mysterious-

---

[83] Which leaves unanswered the question why his music should generate such interest "overnight". But perhaps this is like puzzling over the "overnight" success of any artist who has continued to labor at his or her craft, year after year, without special recognition, until "all of a sudden..." See also fellow composer Oliver Knussen's remarks, following. (Ed.)

ly come together. That is what the composer hopes happens in the quartet.

" 'I'm just kind of letting things happen without in a way controlling them,' Mr. Perle says, describing how he began the piece, though he could also be talking about how his career as a composer has progressed. "But little by little the sense of a piece emerges, and by the end these things finally gel.' " —Mark Swed, in *The New York Times*, 3/19/89.

"GEORGE PERLE, COMPOSER. The surprise of the 1980 Fromm Festival of Contemporary Music at Tanglewood—to this veteran, at least—was an encounter with two new works by this year's composer-in-residence George Perle. Perle's formidable reputation as a 12-tone theorist and Berg-scholar has almost completely overshadowed his creative work in [Britain]; more suprising, the same was largely true in the United States until relatively recently.

"As could be expected of a relatively fluent composer now aged 66, Perle has amassed a considerable *oeuvre*.

Modesty of gesture, a concentration (though not exclusive) on chamber music, and a quiet integrity of musical speech has, however, militated against 'success' in a headline-dominated musical scene— not to mention the authorship of *Serial Composition and Atonality*. Listeners to the *Fifth Quartet* of 1960 (revised 1967, and recorded by the Composers Quartet on Nonesuch) can hardly fail to have been struck by the 'old-fashioned' clarity and euphoniousness of the sound, however systematic the process of composition; while any suspicion of a limited expressive range can be allayed simply by comparing the surprisingly fierce *Three Movements for Orchestra* and the capricious unaccompanied *Monody I* for Gazzeloni (both available on CRI) with the *Quartet*, all three written in the same year.

"Curiously enough, considering their late date, these works can in a sense be called 'early'. Beginning in 1973 with the *Seventh Quartet*, Perle's music seems to have 'taken off' dramatically, both in technical virtuosity and breadth of vision. This may be attributable to the revelation of hitherto untapped possibilities inherent in his compositional system (see Perle's book *Twelve-Tone Tonality*, though virtually all of the earlier music is founded on his own theoretical discoveries, and has little to do with orthodox 12-tonery), but one cannot avoid the notion that here is another example of a profound 'late flowering', in the sense of Janécek or Gerhard, although Perle would doubtless prefer his beloved Haydn to be invoked, if invoking has to be done. The masterly sequence of works which has subsequently appeared bears the comparison, in any case: a 40-minute chorus and orchestra triptych *Songs of Praise and Lamentation* (1974), which still awaits adequate performance[84] — what about it, BBC?; the virtuoso *Six Etudes* for piano (1975-76); the extraordinarily moving *Thirteen Dickinson Songs* (1977-78), written for and recorded by Bethany Beardslee (CRI); and the two works heard at Tanglewood, *Concertino* for piano, winds and timpani (1979) and *A Short Symphony* (1980).[85]

"The *Concertino* was commissioned by the Fromm Foundation, and first performed in Chicago under Ralph Shapey. Its spiritual roots are in Weber (the working title was *Konzertstück*) and Stravinsky, most apparently the first Allegro of the 1923 *Piano Concerto*, to which Perle's opening 'sneeze' is an obvious, if unconscious, reference. Apparent stylistic models are common in Perle's music — for example, the *Dickinson Songs* are permeated by ghosts of the *Vier Ernste Gesänge* [of Richard Strauss], Schoenberg's op. 15, and Britten's *Donne Sonnets* — but these are radically transformed through the symmetrical chord-formations and interlocking intervallic chains of a harmonically based musical grammar in which every note counts.

"This wonderful scherzo — complete with slow, ruminative trio-substitute — continually impresses striking but simple musical images onto the memory along its bubbling course: piano octave passage-work under strident and immovable minor-third pedals in the upper winds, which briefly get semitonally out-of-kilter to devastating effect in the recapitulation: razor-sharp semiquaver hocketing between pairs of winds and piano — fiendishly difficult, but brought off with tremendous flair by the Tanglewood students under Gunther Schuller; sequences in which the harmony (remarkably these days) stretches *from within*, moving big harmonic distances with virtually no shifts of register (like Tchaikovsky's christmas tree); and a coda which conceals its chordal density in brilliant cheekiness. All this and lots more in barely nine minutes!

"*A Short Symphony*, first performed at Tanglewood by the Boston Symphony Orchestra under Ozawa, similarly encapsulates much contrasted invention in three movements of four to six minutes each. But this is *not* a Carteresque compression involving an extraordinary profusion of simultaneous activity. On the contrary, Perle's *Symphony* must stand unique in recent times, being almost entirely written on 14-stave manuscript paper often containing two systems on a page (!), and even then relatively scant with notes — a fact which

---

[84] Perle's *Cello Concerto* (1966), though long in print, has *never* been performed with orchestra.
[85] To these can now be added a new *Ballade* for piano (1980-81).

should surprise readers who heard the BBC performance earlier this year.[86] For a start, the orchestral economy is masterly: four-part string writing can still sound rich if cunningly spaced; likewise an unearthly sound near the beginning is simply four muted horns, widely spaced in register; and it is the horns and harp which discreetly illuminate the larger choirs for much of the work. It will be noted that both of these examples are nothing if not obvious, but it is precisely the 'simple' orchestration of Haydn and Mozart which is being rediscovered here with larger forces in a (unusually for Perle the composer) near-Bergian sound-world, although the musical content is closer to Stravinskian ideals in its pointedness and concision. It is this subtle balance between warmth and restraint which gives *A Short Symphony* its depth and intimacy.

"The first movement could be characterized as hesitant: a sonata-type movement in which the ideas are always on the way to something which never quite arrives, be they brass articulations which dissipate with a single accent, or rising string 'yearnings' countered by plunging woodwind descents. Temporary fulfilment comes with a magically soft four-bar chorale-coda for clarinets, high muted horns and harp. The second movement, though the most 'note-y' and difficult to play, is even more restrained. It is an intense but submerged scherzo movement for a reduced orchestra, with abrupt brakings into rapt string music of extraordinary stillness. Again the whole movement seems to be a preparation for its last four bars, a wonderfully timed cadence onto C.

"The finale is less restrained but still more elusive. It is the only movement including (discreet) percussion and celesta, and there is a more consistent use of larger orchestral groupings. After a 'short, sharp shock' opening,[87] a rondo-type movement unfolds from curiously short-circuited ostinato figures. The 'episodes' have either the repressed energy of the first movement gestures, or the rapt chorale-like quality of the slow music in both movements, writ large. Neither a near-tutti layering of the ostinato music, nor an increase in the harmonic density of the chorale-like msuic (a very original bit of scoring in which three series of dyads are articulated simultaneously in slow *mezzo-piano* minims by double-reeds with harp, *tutti* strings, and fluttertongued muted brass), prepares one for the sudden catastrophic release of the accumulated pent-up energy of the whole symphy in fourteen devastating bars with which it ends.

---

86   In which one major mistake must be noted — the penultimate chord of the work is a first-inversion D^b major triad with G^b on top, *not* A^b. Listeners to tapes please mentally correct!

87   On a cheap and chippy chopper; reference to the Ko-Ko/Pish-Tush/Pooh-Bah trio in Gilbert & Sullivan's *Mikado*. (Ed.)

(The only comparable ending which comes to mind is the last few pages of Tchaikovsky's *Voyevoda* tone poem.)

"I am, however, at a loss for words to articulate *why* I find George Perle's *A Short Symphony* such genuinely and deeply moving music." — Oliver Knussen, in *Tempo: A Quarterly Review of Modern Music* (No. 136), 3/81.

From "Perle on Perle: The Composer Recalls His Life in Music, in an Interview by Dennis Miller"[88]

"GEORGE PERLE: I wrote my first atonal piece, a molto adagio for string quartet, exactly a year after discovering [Alban Berg's] *Lyric Suite* [in 1937. However] this was more strongly influenced by the first movement of Bartók's *Second String Quartet* than by the Berg, which I didn't know how to assimilate into my own work — as much because of the extraordinary virtuosity of the string writing as for any other reason. A few months after this I began to work on a string quartet in what I thought was Schoenberg's twelve-tone system. All I knew about this was that it defined pitch relations for a given piece by arranging the twelve notes of the chromatic scale in a series that was specific to that piece, that this series could be inverted, and that the original series and its inversion could be stated at any transpositional level. I understood each note in any given form of the series to have a fixed association with the two notes that were neighbor to it in that form. The retrograde operation didn't mean anything to me since it didn't revise the neighbor-note relations. Transposition and inversion were fixed ways of transforming the collection of neighbor-note relations without changing the structure of that collection, but for any particular note new relations would be established because it would have new neighbors in the series. (I am, of course, talking about 'pitch classes', not 'notes', but we didn't know that term in those days, at least not in Chicago.)

"As far as it went, there was nothing 'incorrect' in my understanding of Schoenberg's twelve-tone system, but I had left something out that made a crucial difference. Here is the series of my first, still unfinished, string quartet:

B C D F A A^b G F$^\#$ D$^\#$ E B^b C$^\#$ (B

"I paired this with the following transposition of the inversion:

---

88 Orig. published by League of Composers — International Society for Contemporary Music, Boston Chapter, Northeastern University Division of Fine Arts; reprinted by Music Associates of America. Dennis Miller is himself a composer and Professor of Music at Northeastern University.

B B♭ A♭ F C♯ D D♯ E G F♯ C A (B

"I saw that C, for example, had neighbors B and D in the prime form of the series and F♯ and A in the inverted form, and I assumed that, given these two forms as a basis, C could move to, or be combined with, any of its four neighboring notes at will. This notion of pairing a single P [prime] form of the series with a single I [inversion] form was basic to my assumption of how the system worked. I managed to write fourteen beautiful bars, but then I got hopelessly stuck, since so many possibilities opened up that the series no longer delimited pitch relations.

"It was at this point, in the summer of 1939, which I was spending on our farm in Indiana, that I had my first lesson with Ernest Krenek.... I showed him my fourteen bars in the 'twelve-tone system' at our first meeting, and was dismayed when he explained to me that in Schoenberg's twelve-tone system each element of any form of the series progressed to the next in the given form and was not regarded as intersecting with an element of the same pitch [class] in another form of the same series. I was dismayed not because I had made a 'mistake'—in fact, Krenek was generous enough to call what I had come up with a 'discovery'—but because Schoenberg's idea of the series seemed so primitive compared to mine. I had thought that the series must be something like a scale, functioning as the background structure of a piece, even though, unlike the diatonic scale, it was specific to that piece. The Schoenbergian series was simply a disguised ostinato twelve-tone motive. It was almost like defining the tonality of a piece in E major by simply playing the scale of E major over and over again.

"Krenek was the first person I met with whom I could discuss questions of twelve-tone theory. But why, you may ask, hadn't I discovered that I had misconceived the system before this, through a study of the available twelve-tone scores? For one thing, not that much was available. The first of Schoenberg's twelve-tone compositions that I was able to acquire were two of the American works, the *Fourth Quartet* and the *Violin Concerto*, and they were published only in that same year, 1939.... But above all, I misconceived the twelve-tone system because of my own needs as a composer and because of my own expectations for a post-diatonic musical language. Hitchhiking home from Ann Arbor (my only mode of travel in those days) after my first meeting with Krenek, I had to consider that if I was unwilling to give up my own variant of the twelve-tone system in favor of Schoenberg's, I nevertheless had to admit that I wasn't getting anywhere with it. I speculated that the reason was that my series didn't generate any consistent pattern of neighbor-note relations.

Suppose we were to devise a series in which each pair of neighbor notes formed the same interval? Obviously, the cycle of semitones or fifths would give us this, but it would also eliminate the distinction between prime and inversion and reduce everything to transpositions of the same three-note segment of the chosen cycle. However, if alternate notes of the series unfolded the same cycle in opposite directions a constant neighbor-note interval would recur in a consistently changing relationship around each pivotal (or 'axis') note. I had discovered the cyclic series, or rather rediscovered it, as I subsequently realized, since the twelve-tone series of the first movement of the *Lyric Suite* will be seen to be derived in this way from the cycle of fifths, provided one cyclically permutes the series so that its two hexachords are interchanged.

"As soon as I got home I got out some music paper and paired P and I forms of the cyclic series in the way that I had paired the above P and I forms of the series of my projected quartet, but in a variety of transpositional relationships. The results were spectacular (you can work them out for yourself), but it was some months before I was able to compose anything with my 'twelve-tone modes' and 'twelve-tone keys'. When I came to see Krenek for my second lesson a week or so later, it was with my first 'conventional' twelve-tone piece, a 'Little Suite' for piano, which turned out not to be so conventional after all. It was based on a series whose symmetrical structure (P = RI) brought it around again to the first note, so that it was really a 'thirteen-tone' rather than a 'twelve-tone' piece:

$$B\ A\ C\ F^{\#}\ G\ A^{b}\ F\ D\ E^{b}\ E\ B^{b}\ C^{\#}\ B$$

"Many years later I realized that Alban Berg's last twelve-tone piece, the *Violin Concerto*, is really based on exactly the same kind of symmetrical thirteen-tone set as my first, the twelve-tone theme of the *Concerto* being embedded in that thirteen-tone series:

$$E^{b}\ F\ G\ B^{b}\ D\ F^{\#}\ A\ C\ E\ G^{\#}\ B\ C^{\#}\ E^{b}$$

"So much for influences! One chooses what one wants to be influenced by because of some affinity that is already present, and evidence of that affinity is often mistaken for evidence of an influence....

"It wasn't until August 1940, a year after my discovery of the cyclic series, that I managed to compose three little piano pieces in what I then called the 'twelve-tone modal system'. I had first of all to assimilate the implications of the fact that the cyclic series, when employed as a source of 'neighbor-note chords' as described above, represented a revolutionary departure from earlier concepts of twelve-tone composition in that, like the diatonic scale and its derived triads, it could function as a general set on which any number of pieces could be based. This *Suite in the Second Twelve-Tone Mode* was published in Montevideo in the following year, in the musical supplement of a special issue of the *Boletin Latino-Americano de Musica* dedicated to '*la creacion estadounidense*', along with compositions by thirty-four other composers, among them Luening, Copland, Diamond, Carter, Cowell, Riegger, Piston, Crawford, Schuman, and Ives.... My first article, in which I set forth my theory in the context of a critique of the twelve-tone system, was published at the same time. I wasn't ready to admit that the whole thing had originated in a misconception so I pretended that I had evolved my theory as a consequence of that critique, where in actuality the opposite was the case. I felt vaguely guilty about this piece of deceitfulness until a few years ago, when I read an essay by the British Nobel laureate Peter Medawar in which he shows that this is a regular and accepted procedure in the presentation of new scientific theories. That first paper of mine is embarrassingly naive in some ways, what with its attempts, fortunately brief and only in passing, to justify what I was doing in terms of 'overtones' and other nonsense, but I still consider its discussion of the problematical relation between the motivic and the extra-motivic functions of the series as valid and, considering when it was written, perceptive. This was, after all, still a time when there was hardly any interest in, let along understanding of, the basic Schoenbergian concepts, and here I was already moving on in an entirely new direction from those same concepts. So perhaps there is nothing to be embarrassed about, especially when one considers the writings on the subject of twelve-tone music that were to be published in *die Reihe* and elsewhere some twenty years later.

"In fact, the concept of the cyclic series as a means of defining harmonic structure arises quite naturally out of Schoenberg's *own* concept of the harmonic function of the series as expressed in some brief notes that he wrote shortly before his death and that were published for the first time in 1975: 'Every tone appears always in the neighbourhood of two other tones in an unchanging combination which produces an intimate relationship most similar to the relationship of a third and a fifth to its root.' But the two neighbouring tones do not appear 'in an unchanging combination' in Schoenberg's series. The combination changes when the series is transposed or inverted. Moreover, there is no coherent system of relations among the different neighbor-note combinations within the series. It is the cyclic series which provides an 'unchanging combination' of neighbor notes, and it does so in an ordered system of changing relations to each note of the series.

"DENNIS MILLER: Would you elaborate on the degree to which 'twelve-tone tonality' is involved in your work? Is it strictly a pitch/harmonic control? Does it function short and long range? Are there works which abandon the process?

"PERLE: Everything I've written since 1969 is in the system. It wasn't until then that anyone turned up who was interested in collaborating with me in a further development of the theory. This was a former pupil, Paul Lansky. We worked together very intensively for the next four years, since which time he has given his full attention to computer composition. Our collaboration resulted in a radical expansion of the original theory and a vast enlargement of its compositional possibilities. It led eventually, in 1977, to the publication of my second book, *Twelve-Tone Tonality*. A lot has happened since then and I'm now working on a revised and much enlarged second edition. Most of my compositions from 1940 to 1969 were also in the system.... Quite a number of pieces in the system that I composed before 1969 — three symphonies, two string quartets, etc. — were eventually withdrawn, but there are a few that I think are quite successful, especially the *Serenade No. 1* for solo viola and chamber orchestra, the *Fifth Quartet*, and the *Three Movements for Orchestra*.

"As for your other questions, I would answer them in exactly the same way a tonal composer 100 years ago might have answered them. A piece is either totally in the system or it isn't in it at all. In a twelve-tone tonal piece, at least as I understand it, every simultaneity is referable to the cyclic series and to the harmonic structures that are derivable from the cyclic series, just as every simultaneity is referable to the triad and the diatonic scale in the major-minor system. In both systems a short-range pitch/harmonic control immediately affects rhythm and phrase structure and has the most far-reaching implications for every component of the formal design. I should add, however, that I've always had a special and independent interest in questions of tempo and rhythm and have always tended to work with proportional relations among different tempi, so that within a given basic tempo the tempi of other sections might be expressed or implied by means of different metrical units and groupings.

"MILLER: Surely you must have numered some twelve-tone composers among your friends and colleagues before Paul Lansky came along. Weren't any of them interested in what you were doing?

"PERLE: Paul was never a twelve-tone composer, which may have something to do with the fact that he was interested.... Between August 1943 and February 1946 I was in the Army. [But after the war,] I met [Milton] Babbitt soon after moving to New York early in 1946.

He was the first person I ever met who seemed to share my ideal of an autonomous and self-contained twelve-tone language, but where my notion of this language implied a radical revision of the basic axioms of Schoenberg's system, his implied a radical extension of these axioms, and in particular of Schoenberg's principle of associating inversionally related set-forms by the pairing of hexachords that are mutually exclusive as to pitch-class content. I imagine my article, 'The Harmonic Problem in Twelve-Tone Music', in the November 1954 issue of *The Music Review*, was the earliest to discuss Babbitt's approach to twelve-tone composition apart from Babbitts's own writing at the time.... The impression that Babbitt's work made on me at the time is summed up in my evaluation of his extension of Schoenberg's method: '[H]ere we have the key to an autonomous method of twelve-tone composition, in which all aspects of the musical work—form, the constitution and interrelation of linear and vertical details, even rhythm—will be referable to a basic set, just as these elements are refereable to the triad in tonal composition.'

"MILLER: In other words, you realized that there was an alternative to the direction that you had followed in resolving what you had seen as problematical and ambiguous in Schoenberg's system. Where did this leave you as a composer, this realization that there was another way, very different from the one that you had chosen, of arriving at 'an autonomous and self-contained twelve-tone language'?

"PERLE: As a composer, it left me exactly where I was before. On those rare occasions when I worked on a twelve-tone serial piece I had never, in any case, worked in an *ad hoc*, improvisatory, rule-of-thumb fashion. I was never interested in employing the tone row as an easy way of deciding what the next note in a piece should be. I always looked for invariant relations among different forms of the series as a basis for choosing among these different forms, as I had seen Berg do in the first twelve-tone piece I ever looked at. What interested me in 'combinatoriality' was that the precompositional structure which it provided seemed to be comprehensive, consistent, and self-contained. The same thing is true of the precompositional structure provided by what I called in those days the 'twelve-tone modal system'. The same thing is true also of music in the major-minor system. If it weren't we wouldn't be able to say of two different pieces that they are in the same key. In a general way I would say that the relation between the compositional process and the precompositional structure in twelve-tone tonality is more congenial to me than what I, both as a listener and as a composer, find it to be in other kinds of 'twelve-tone composition'—more, in a way, like what it is in the traditional tonal system....

"MILLER: By the time your article on 'the harmonic problem' appeared in 1954 composers like yourself and Babbitt were no longer so isolated. Isn't that so? Weren't many more people working in the twelve-tone system by then? How did this affect your work?

"PERLE: Things began to change very soon after the war. We even heard of a circle of twelve-tone composers in Paris, the last place anyone expected this 'central European tendency' to find a following. An article by Virgil Thomson in the New York *Herald Tribune*, January 29, 1950, served notice that twelve-tone composition was 'in' and emphasized its practical advantages: 'The device of arranging these twelve tones in a special order, particular to each piece and consistent throughout it, is not an added complication of twelve-tone writing but a simplification, a rule of thumb that speeds up the composition.' I summed up this development in the opening paragraph of the preface to my book, *Serial Composition and Atonality* (1962): 'In the very recent past the twelve-tone movement was regarded as the concern only of a few sectarians. Today it is no novelty to find the modern jazz artist improvising on a tone row, the young music student writing a twelve-tone piece for his composition class, the choreographer converting a twelve-tone classic into ballet music. It is only in the most backward circles that the mere use of a tone row will secure a composer's position as a member of the avant-garde, as it was sure to do only a few years ago.' I concluded my preface with the hope that my book would make twelve-tone composition more difficult.

"As to the question of how this development affected my work, if by this you mean was more attention paid to it, did I begin to get more performances? — how else could it affect my work? — the answer is yes and no. There was much more interest in general in the performance of new music, or to put it more precisely, in first performances of new music. In 1949 I moved to Louisville to take up my first full-time academic appointment.... [There] the experience of hearing one's work rehearsed and performed by an orchestra[89] was an invaluable one [which was] exceedingly difficult to come by in those days.

"In describing the twelve-tone system as a 'rule-of-thumb' method, Thomson's article showed only one side of the coin. On the other side there were the European 'total serialists' who, according to the technical articles which began to make their appearance a few years later in *die Reihe*—a special journal devoted to *Information über serielle Musik*—derived their principles of twelve-tone composition

---

[89] The Louisville Orchestra, which then and subsequently commissioned many new compositions. (Ed.)

from 'mathematical basic research', 'cybernetics', 'information theory', 'sound quanta', 'integral variation- and connection-models', 'conceptual systematization', and so on. I did not find it worthwhile to distinguish between the two sides, as I pointed out in the preface to my book, because for both of them the analysis of a twelve-tone work consisted in 'labelling the notes with their appropriate order numbers, the only distinction being the added "complexity" that results from the serialization not only of pitches but also of dynamics, rhythm, and other "parameters", and from plotting the elements not only in their original serial order from one to twelve but also in various rotations and permutations,' something which for me was as meaningless as 'the labelling of the notes of a tonal composition to indicate their scale degrees.'

"Needless to say, neither side showed the slightest interest in, or even awareness of, my own early contribution to twelve-tone theory. I was more isolated in my work than ever, and I found it more and more disturbing to be identified as a 'twelve-tone composer', an appelation that hadn't bothered me at all in the old days. Some years later, when the twelve-tone system was again out of style, I registered my first protest against that appelation in the notes to Robert Miller's 1974 recording of my *Toccata* (composed in 1969): 'Ever since my first article on twelve-tone music was published, more than thirty years ago, it has been obvious to almost every critic who has been called upon to comment on my work that I must be a composer of "twelve-tone" or "serial" music. Thirty years ago that made me "avant-garde", and today that makes me "academic". But the fact is that in all these years I've written only three pieces in which one can discover tone-rows or serial procedures, and of these I've discarded one and the other two have never been published or performed. The *Toccata*, like almost everything I've written but rather more decisively than many of the pieces that precede it, I think, reflects my preoccupation through all these years with something one might provisionally call "post-diatonic tonality". If I tried to say anything more about this concept in this brief note, it would be misunderstood. Besides, I hesitate to tell listeners in advance what they ought to hear in a new work of mine, beyond what is already implied in the title itself. The piece was originally called *Toccata in D*, but I thought this might imply too much, and perhaps some things that I didn't want to imply. When a colleague told me that he considered this title inflammatory, I decided that I would simply call the piece *Toccata*.' In these days, when the 'return to tonality' is celebrated in the pages of the magazine supplement of the Sunday *Times*, the original title would no longer be considered inflammatory, but it would still be misunderstood.

"MILLER: What, in fact, is your position in respect to the current revial of traditional tonality?

"PERLE: There hasn't been a revival of traditional tonality. The first thing that anyone who wants to revive tonality must do is find out what happened to it that it should need to be revived. One doesn't choose a tradition. Just what vintage tonality are you going to choose? How much of the tonal tradition are you going to revive? Are you going to stop before or after Schoenberg's *First Chamber Symphony* in E Major? The tonal revivalists must avoid such questions at all costs. Without a connection with the past we wouldn't even be able to talk, we wouldn't have any language at all, but you don't establish continuity with the past with a collage of long quotations from tonal composers who have been dead long enough so that their music is in the public domain, or by repeating the same conventional harmonic progression 500 times. These things are parodies of tonality, not revivals....

"Increasing familiarity with Schoenberg's twelve-tone music [through the development of the long-playing record in particular] forced me to confront it critically for the first time. With good reason, we stood in awe of this great man, 'the most significant musician of our age,' as I call him in my 1952 article, 'Schoenberg's Late Style'—'one of Hegel's Heroes, who, beyond any of his contemporaries, "had an insight into the requirements of the time—what was ripe for development".' If there was anything in his music that didn't seem to 'work' we [had] assumed that this could only be because of our own failure of comprehension, a deficiency which we would overcome in time. But now, where the late tonal and most of the pre-serial atonal works struck me as masterly achievements of the first order, I found myself increasingly disturbed by what seemed to me serious flaws in much of the twelve-tone music, and I discussed these flaws and tried to explain them in the same article. Schoenberg had died the year before; it was something I neither could, nor would have written, were he still alive. In his 1941 article, 'Composition with Twelve Tones', Schoenberg has explained his motivations in devising his twelve-tone method as follows: 'After many unsuccessful attempts during a period of approximately twelve years, I laid the foundations for a new procedure in musical construction which seemed fitted to replace those structural differentiations provided formerly by tonal harmonies.' It seemed to me, however, that in texture, rhythmic character, phrase structure, cadential patterns, formal design, the twelve-tone works tended to unfold by way of surface analogy with the corresponding elements of older music, rather than on the basis of 'structural differentiations' that might be in some way integral to the 'new procedure in musical construction.' The analyses that led to this conclusion proceeded in the first instance from an intuitive response to this music. It sounded 'wrong' to me, and I wanted to find out why. It still sounds 'wrong' to me. The means of harmonic differentiation and structure that Babbitt was the first to describe in this music are simply too primitive and too incompletely developed to support the implications of the surface relations. I was distressed to have to come to these conclusions about 'Schoenberg's Late Style', and still am.

"Though I had always been interested in the Bartók string quartets, I had never subjected any of them to any analysis in depth. I did so for the first time while I was still teaching at the University of Louisville, in my article 'Symmetrical Formations in the String Quartets of Bela Bartók'. I realized that in some way this music was as revolutionary as that of the twelve-tone school, in spite of its very different and more traditional surface character. As in the twelve-tone system, inversional complementation was a fundamental principle which established a new kind of equivalence relation. This connection with the twelve-tone system seemed more important to me than the fact that Bartók's music wasn't based on serially ordered twelve-tone sets. I found myself speaking of 'tonalities', 'keys', and 'modulation' in discussing this music. I sensed that it was related in some special way to my theory of a 'twelve-tone tonality', but I was not able to explain how. My article ended with a question which I was only able to answer fifteen years later: 'Can symmetrical formations generate a total musical structure, as triadic relations have done traditionally? The implications of Bartók's work in this, as in other respects, remain problematical.'...

"MILLER: Did your dissatisfaction with [some] of your own compositions ever lead you to question the value, or the validity, of your system of 'twelve-tone tonality'?

"PERLE: It only led me to question the adequacy of my experience in composing with my twelve-tone 'modes' and 'keys'. I had only to try some other way of composing with twelve-tone sets to be convinced of the relative virtues of the 'twelve-tone modal system'. I was disappointed that there hadn't been any more big breakthroughs, like my discovery of the system in the first place, or my first composition in the system. But I anticipated that there would be. After all, only about twenty years had passed since I first hit upon the notion that adjacency relations of the cyclic series pointed toward a new system of tonality based upon the semitonal scale. That's not such a long time, as such things go. I had in the meantime studied the music of the Viennese school in some depth, and nothing that I found there suggested another more viable line of development. And as I said a moment ago, from my more recent studies of Bartók's music I somehow inferred a significant connection between his work and mine. In fact, in the first edition of *Serial Composition and Atonality* I concluded a brief exposition of the 'twelve-tone modal system' with a reference to my article on the Bartók quartets.

"But probably the main reason it never occurred to me to give up on the system was that I had already written some pieces in which it seemed to work very well, pieces in which I felt as indubitable a sense of harmonic progression as there had been in the system of diatonic tonality, and in which the implications of this for other 'parameters' seemed to be realized, if only on a miniature scale. The very first piece ever written in the system, the first movement of the little suite that was published in South America in 1941 (reproduced on p. 32 of *Twelve-Tone Tonality*) is an example. Another early example is the *Two Rilke Songs*, composed in 1941 but only published last year. Other examples are the *Six Preludes* for piano and the *Lyric Piece* for cello and piano (both composed in 1946), and the *Solemn Procession* for band (arranged from a movement of a discarded string quartet composed in 1947), which brings us to the above mentioned 1950 *Sonata* for piano. I felt that the system had worked well in these, admittedly small-scale, pieces, so why shouldn't it work for me again, perhaps even in works that were more substantial in duration and scope. And it did, in the *Fifth Quartet* and the *Three Movements for Orchestra*, both composed in 1960 while I was teaching at the University of California at Davis, and in the *Serenades Nos. 1 and 2* for eleven players, the *Six Bagatelles for Orchestra*, and the *Cello Concerto*, all composed between 1962 and 1968 after my return to New York.

"Which brings us to 1969 and the next big breakthrough. It was in that year that I found my first collaborator, Paul Lansky. I was at the MacDowell Colony that summer when I received a brief note in which he pointed out something that should have been quite obvious but that had never occurred to me. I had derived my three 'twelve-tone modes' by pairing inversionally related set-forms of the cyclic series. But one could derive other equally consistent collections of cyclic chords by pairing transpositionally related set-forms, i.e., two prime set-forms, or two inverted set-forms. In the 'twelve-tone modal system' three types of 'neighbor-note' or 'cyclic' chords were formed when one combined, around a shared pivotal pitch-class, three-note segments of inversionally related forms of the cyclic series based on the perfect fifth: in what I called 'Mode I' the two interval-7 dyads of the respective set-forms were separated by interval-7 or -5 (for example, C-G/G-D or C-G/F-C); in 'Mode II' they were separated by interval-3 or -9 (for example, C-G, E^b-B^b, or C-G, A-E); in 'Mode III' they were separted by interval-1 or -11 (for example, C-G/D^b-A^b, or C-G/B-$F^\#$). The four new modes based on parallel set-forms provided the heretofore missing cyclic chords based on the remaining intervallic distances: interval-zero (e.g., C-G/C-G), interval-2 or -10 (e.g., C-G/D-A or C-G/B^b-F), interval-4 or -8 (e.g., C-G/E-B or C-G/A^b-E^b), and interval-6 (e.g., C-G/F$^\#$-C$^\#$). It had been a sort of frustration for me that I could see no logical means of 'modulating' from one of the three modes derived from inversionally related set-forms to another. I now saw at once that the new modes could serve as such a means. They provided the missing 'gears'. I also saw that where every pitch-class operation in the P/I modes could be inverted within the same array, in the modes that Paul had discovrred it took two complementary arrays to unfold the same symmetrical relations: i.e., an array generated by transpositionally related P sets would be reflected in an array generated by correspondingly transposed I sets, and vice versa. Paul responded to the letter in which I reported the important consequences that I had immediately derived from his discovery with some further considerations along these lines on his part, and so began an interchange that continued for about four years.

"MILLER: If Mr. Lansky's idea was 'obvious' why didn't it ever occur to you during the preceding thirty years?

"PERLE: For the same reason that no one ever thought of interpreting each pitch-class as an intersection of inversionally related set-forms until this 'obvious' notion occurred to me in the summer of 1939. Someone coming in from outside will see things in a fresh way, will see 'obvious' connections that the insiders have overlooked.

"MILLER: It seems that the theory of 'twelve-tone tonality' evolved considerably in the time between your receipt of Mr. Lansky's first letter and your reply. Could you give us some idea of the consequences of your four-year interchange?

"PERLE: I'll try to suggest something about this—I can hardly offer more than a hint in the context of this interview—by pointing to some of the different ways in which the first bar of my first piece in the system might be interpreted, and some of the implications of these different interpretations. This bar unfolds a six-note chord, A^b E G B D A^b, which I derived by combining segments of two inversionally related forms of the cyclic series of interval-7: E A^b B/G A^b D. (Since all the criteria that define a set are given in any one of its three-note segments, I can immediately deduce, from this first chord, the eleven remaining chords that are similarly derived from a shared axis-note. Each of these can provide a symmetrical variant of the first bar: G F A^b C E^b G, G^b F$^\#$ A C$^\#$ E G^b, etc. In moving from one chord to another I'm concerned with questions of voice-leading, octave displacement, presentation of motives and themes, etc., just like any other tonal composer. I don't feel in the least constrained to progress along the notes of the row according to conventional twelve-tone principles, any more than a tonal composer would feel constrained always to move by root progressions of the perfect fifth. All this was settled for me in the 'breakthrough' that led to my first twelve-tone tonal composition.) If I were to look at that first chord today, and were told that it was based on the shared axis-note A^b, I wouldn't know whether it was derived from the cyclic series of interval-7, as shown above, or the cyclic series of interval-3 (which would give us the segments E A^b G/B A^b D), or one cyclic series of interval-2 and another of interval-4 (which would give us the segments E A^b D/G A^b B). So long as I limited myself to chords based on unison axis-notes, there would be no way to distinguish among these three 'interval systems'. But I no longer limit myself to unison axis-notes. Let's suppose that we substitute G for the first A^b and A for the second A^b. This would give us new symmetrical variants of the first bar, and these would differ from one another, depending on the interval system. If we remain within the original interval-7 array, this revises the first bar as follows: G F G^b C D^b A from segments F G C/G^b A D^b. The interval-3 system would give us G F A^b B^b D^b A from F G A^b/B^b A D^b. The interval-2/4 system would give us G F G^b B^b E^b A from F G E^b/G^b A B^b. Each of these chords could again be symmetrically transformed by transposing its axis-note interval. Where in a given array I formerly had twelve axis/neighbor-note chords, I now have 144, and the latter are as easily and spontaneously comprehended as the original twelve were when all I had was what I used to call the 'twelve-tone modal system'.

"All this can only give you the sketchiest notion of what I mean by 'twelve-tone tonality'. For example, I haven't said anything at all about 'tonic chords', something that I've had from the very beginning, but a concept that has been vastly enlarged, like everything else, as a result of the collaboration with Lansky. Perhaps the best summation is given in the concluding chapter of my book, *Twelve-Tone Tonality* (the quotation within the quotation is from *Serial Composition and Atonality*:)

> The early years of the present century bring us, in consequence of the disappearance of conventional normative elements in the atonal music of Schoenberg and his school, to "an ultimate expansion of possible relations to include the whole range of combinations contained in the semitonal scale". We have shown how the convergence of the concepts of the interval cycle and (through the twelve-tone system) of strict inversional complementation leads to a comprehensive *system* of tone relations that permits us to define and classify every one of these combinations in terms of its sums and in-

tervals, and consequently to establish differentiations, associations, and progressions between and among all these combinations.

"MILLER: Your book was published in 1977. Do you feel that you've reached some sort of plateau with this, that things have settled down somewhat? I should think you would welcome a change of pace.

"PERLE: I reached a kind of equilibrium, thank God, in 1973 with my *Seventh Quartet*. I think I would call this, if I may be so bold, my first 'mature' work. There have been new developments and discoveries since then, but the basic structure of twelve-tone tonality, at least as far as I understand it, is there I think, and in the works that follow.

"MILLER: What are these 'mature' works that followed the *Seventh Quartet*?

"PERLE: *Songs of Praise and Lamentation*, a forty-minute piece for orchestra, chorus, and soloists which is my biggest work to date, *Six Etudes* for piano, *Thirteen Dickinson Songs*, *Concertino for Piano, Winds, and Timpani*, *A Short Symphony*, *Ballad* for piano, *Sonata a quattro* for flute, violin, clarinet, and cello, *Serenade No. 3* for piano and chamber orchestra, *Wind Quintet IV* (which won the Pulizter Prize in 1986), *Six New Etudes* for piano, *Sonata* for cello and piano, *Sonatina* for piano, *Sonata a cinque* for clarinet, violin, cello, bass trombone, and piano, and—just finished—*Dance Overture* for orchestra.

"MILLER: This seems like a reasonably good output considering that in addition to *Twelve-Tone Tonality* you also produced your two-volume study of *The Operas of Alban Berg* during this period. You said that you were preparing a 'revised and much enlarged second edition' of *Twelve-Tone Tonality*. In what ways will this differ from the first edition?

"PERLE: I said earlier that one of the things that sustained me during the long years that I worked alone was the sense that there was some significant connection between Bartók's use of symmetrical pitch-class relations and my 'twelve-tone modal system'. The original text of *Twelve-Tone Tonality* develops the system out of a Schoenbergian context, beginning with the notion of the twelve-tone series, just as I have done here. This will remain essentially unaltered in the revised edition, but it will be followed by new chapters in which the same system of pitch-class relations is derived from another direction, from the symmetrical formations that play such an important structural role in the music of Bartók. Aside from this re-examination of the system from another angle, some recent developments will be discussed. The most interesting of these is the recognition of criteria for the definition of certain types of 'dissonance' in the system, so that we can now speak of, and hear, passing notes, suspensions, and anticipations in twelve-tone tonal music.

"In the last chapter of my book I tried, in a very few words, to place twelve-tone tonality in the larger context of post-diatonic music in general. The whole basis of the system is in the interrelation of two different types of symmetry, both of which emerge as a consequence of the replacement of a diatonic scale of unequal intervals and functionally differentiated notes by a twelve-tone scale of equal intervals and functionally undifferentiated notes. One of these is the symmetrical partitioning of musical space by means of interval cycles — the whole-tone scale, the diminished-seventh chord, the augmented triad, the tritone, or the semitonal scale itself. I and others have written of the role that cyclically derived symmetrical formations play in the music of Scriabin, Debussy, Stravinsky, and Bartók. The other type of symmetry is represented by inversional complementation, the fundamental role of which in certain music of Bartók's was stressed in my 1955 article and which is axiomatic in Schoenberg's twelve-tone system. There is a good deal more to be said about all this, but I don't think I'll enlarge my closing chapter in order to say it, since others are doing very good work along these lines. Elliott Antokoletz's definitive book, *The Music of Béla Bartók*, discusses Bartók's work with reference to the system of twelve-tone tonality in a really consequential way, and he is currently doing equally interesting and important work on Stravinsky.

"MILLER: Then you could say that Antokoletz, too, is a collaborator in the development of your theory, in the sense that he is elaborating its historical context and connections. Are there others?

"PERLE: Yes. Charles Porter is composing some excellent music in the system, and his work is attracting attention and getting more and more widely performed. Another talented young composer, with an astonishing grasp of the theoretical ramifications of twelve-tone tonality, is Pat Carrabre. He is interested in its implications for larger disciplines — linguistics, semiotics, etc. Unfortunately, I don't have the background to understand the work he is doing along these lines. Very recently there has been a new and exciting practical development. I indicated earlier that a whole array of 144 axis/neighbor-note chords could be deduced from any one chord of the array. There are thousands of such arrays, and James Carr has developed a computer program which will instantly unfold, in musical notation, any one of these.

"MILLER: One of the questions that I had intended to ask you was on the relevance of your work as a theorist, scholar, and educator to your work as a composer. This whole discussion has been an answer to that question. Still, you've published four books and about seventy-five articles and I can't help but wonder, have you ever felt that there was some conflict between all this prose writing and your composing?

"PERLE: All my work as a theorist and Berg specialist, the two activities that have resulted in 'all this prose writing', has been in response to needs and interests that arose in the course of my work as a composer, so I've never felt that there was a conflict, except in the competition between them for time. But it has been only too obvious that there was a conflict as far as others were concerned. My articles were published as soon as I had written them; the compositions often had to wait for years. People who knew my work as a theorist, and more particularly as a Berg scholar, might learn that I was 'also' a composer, but they assumed that I regarded this as a peripheral activity. Thus when my early piano sonata was reviewed in a British quarterly that had published many of my articles I was identified as 'an American music critic who has recently taken up composition.' A few years ago my *Concertino for Piano, Winds, and Timpani* was performed in Vienna, probably the first performance of any work of mine in that city. One of the papers described it as 'a composition by the American musicologist, George Perle.'... I am pleased with the way things have developed recently, however. I am beginning to be identified as a composer who is 'also' a musicologist."

Ballade for Piano Solo (1981). 9m *Ded. to & prem.:* Richad Goode. *Rec.:* Nonesuch (Digital Stereo LP) 9 79108-1 F (also CD and cassette vers.): Richard Goode.
Concertino for Piano, Winds and Timpani (1979). 9m Comm. by Fromm Fndn. *Prem.:* ens. cond. by Ralph Shapey. *Rec.:* Nonesuch (Digital Stereo LP) 9 79108-1 F (also CD and cassette vers.): Richard Goode (pno), Music Today Ens, Gerard Schwarz, cond. *Pub.:* Boelke-Bomart (Jerona) (score; parts on rental).
2-2(1 eh)-2-2; 2-2-2-0; timp, pno

"[Perle's *Concertino* is] an infectious piece that should quickly establish itself in the contemporary repertory." — *Chicago Tribune*. [See also notes by Oliver Knussen, above.]

"Perle has done more than anyone else to clarify [the early 20th-century composer Alban] Berg's achievement. In view of this prolonged labor of love, it is worth pointing out how little Perle's music sounds like Berg's. The Viennese composer is always vocal and theatrical, the Op. 5 clarinet miniatures and the *Three Orchestral Pieces* no less so than *Wozzeck* and *Lulu*. In his hyper-expressivity Berg is one with the writers he loved: Strindberg, Wedekind, Peter Altenberg. The jungle-like luxuriance of his imagination coexists with the most Byzantine formal complications in a fascinating and uneasy relationship. The labyrinthine structures of his later works mingle fantastic ingenuities of craft – e.g., the large-scale palindromes in the *Chamber Concerto*, *Lulu*, and other works; personal confessions disguised in code; and elaborate number systems. There is little of the confessional and nothing of the occult in George Perle's music. In its sobriety and playfulness, its rhythmic unpredictability, its delicate balance of harmonic and contrapuntal energies, it often brings Haydn to mind. The free flow of ideas can seem as witty and allusive as good conversation, or as 'stream of consciousness' as Molly Bloom, and there is a constant pleasure for the listener in following the unexpected twists and turns of the narrative, and actually *hearing* the design take shape (this is not 'music for the eye'[90]). Whatever the emotional intensities expressed – and such works as *Songs of Praise and Lamentation* (1974) and *Thirteen Dickinson Songs* (1979) convey a powerful emotional charge – one feels a language has been found that is exactly suited to its expressive requirements. Perle's development is, to a large extent, the story of his gradual discovery of this language, which he calls 'twelve-tone tonality'.

"Twelve-tone tonality is not to be equated with Schoenberg's 'method of writing with twelve tones', though this is one of its sources and it arises out of the same dilemma: the increasing richness of semitonal (chromatic) harmony and weakening of the diatonic hierarchy in the latter part of the nineteenth century. The difference between the relative weight of a modulation in Brahms and one in Reger or early Schoenberg measures the weakening of tonality's gravitational field. To bring order to the wildly expanded range of possibility, composers have pressed into service everything from polymodality to the Fibonacci series. Some have done this in public, with all the appearance of logic (Schoenberg and his school), while others have kept their recipes secret (Varèse, Bartók). But what makes a certain order feel natural, another imposed? Or, to put the question differently, is there an order analogous to tonality, which is a natural outgrowth of the properties of the twelve semitones, and that can be discerned in certain works of Scriabin, Stravinsky, Schoenberg, Bartók, Berg, Webern, and Varèse, among others, despite their differences in methodology and style? Perle thinks of twelve-tone tonality in this way, and has devoted his most important theoretical writings to explaining it.

---

90   A reference to the literally marvel-ous notational schemes devised by some modern composers whose music itself may be of a lesser interest. (Ed.)

"If the foregoing has given the impression that Perle the theorist dominates the composer, the *Concertino* (1979) and other works prove the contrary. The *Concertino* packs a lot of music into barely nine minutes. It is full of striking musical images: the opening 'sneeze' for brass and piano, and the succeeding toccata passage, with the piano galloping in octaves under persistent woodwind thirds in the treble; the chattering dialogues between solo and winds in constantly changing meters; the sultry middle section, in which the piano embroiders variations on the English horn's torch song; and the dramatic outburst of the coda, urged on by the entrance of the timpanist, who has patiently waited 236 bars for this moment.

"This profusion of events is contained in a kind of motoric rondo, with a contrasting lyric interlude. The various *scherzando* elements that make up the main section keep on reappearing in slightly altered but always recognizable forms. For example, about a quarter of the way through the piece (bar 67), after a flute trill, we hear a descending passage of sixteenth-note thirds, against more static eighth-notes in the bassoons. When this recurs (bar 90) the shape and texture are similar (bassoon eighth-notes, piano descent, soft dynamic level), but the pitches and intervals are altered, the rhythms are shifted, and the whole episode is shortened. Its third appearance (bar 183) is, audibly, the inversion of the first—now the piano ascends, and the bassoons have turned into oboes. There is a pleasing economy in all this. Neater yet is the way the octave, third, and major seventh which permeate the texture of the whole piece are contained and expelled in that first explosion in bar 1, which also serves as the 'motto' that firmly nails the closing section together. The interplay of clarity of the larger shapes with constant minute variations in all the details is distinctive in Perle's music; firm in outline yet alway in flux, as if mercury were set flowing through crystal containers.

"In the *Ballade* (1981) Perle broke the containers and wrote a piece looser in form, lusher in sonority, emotionally more wayward and demonstrative. It is a kind of homage to nineteenth-century Romantic piano music, evoked through its textures, which sound far richer than they look on the page, its 'painless' dissonance, saturated with thirds and sixths (was this a partial concession to this pianist's harmonic sweet tooth?), and its constant wave-like surging up and falling back. The improvisatory stream, with its carefully planned subliminal structure of seven interrelated tempi, shapes itself into five areas, defined by movement and sound-character rather than theme. The first opens hesitatingly in thirds and minor sevenths, establishing the basic four-voice texture. The second, a dry, scuttling *scherzando*, builds to a big climax, then slowly subsides. After a pause comes the turbulent third section, with a short contrasting trio. A wandering fantasy in triplets, à la Scriabin follows, then the sudden eruptive coda, with its two dramatic double-note descents, the first *forte*, the second *pianissimo misterioso*. The most distinctive formal feature lies in what has been left out—there is no recapitulation of sections, carrying-over of motives, or 'circular form'. The narrative, except for one dreamily reminiscent bar near the end, never looks back, and the journey ends, in the air, with the final *pppp* E^b."—Richard Goode, from liner notes for Nonesuch Digital Recording 9 79108-1 F.

"Why is George Perle's music so easy to understand? There are a number of reasons. First, it is gratifying and rewarding to play, as I can attest and as [the New World recordings of the *Six New Etudes, Ballade, Concertino* and other instrumental pieces] demonstrate, and the devotion and effort Perle consequently earns from performers has led to a lively and productive relationship. One gets the sense that his music is accurately and cleverly sculpted and scripted for human performance. Second, it is self-referential. Its consistencies, its quirks and oddities, its points of departure, and its logic are all evident and self-explanatory. It never seems necessary to invoke prior conceptual bases or metaphors to understand its sense and consequence. This may seem a surprising assertion in view of his well-known theoretical formalisms, but in Perle's view, and to my ears as well, the sense of his theory is that it enables the construction of a lucid, self-referential musical context. Finally, it is often fun and funny. Whimsy, intentional awkwardnesses, and cute consequences combine in endlessly interesting ways, much in the spirit of Haydn and middle-period Beethoven."—Paul Lansky, in *American Music*, Winter 1988.

"Pianist Richard Goode, the excellent annotator of [the Nonesuch recording of the *Ballade* and *Concertino*], claims that Perle's version of Berg's sort of music—what the former calls 'twelve-tone tonality', or making the Viennese construct conform more or less to the rules of conventional tonality—doesn't really resemble Berg's in finished form. If I disagree, it is not in the terms Goode establishes that I do so; Perle and Berg, to my ears, resemble one another uncannily in the very way both men combine their instrumental colors. And instrumental color is one of the means by which [these pieces] communicate themselves on first hearing as music that is enjoyable, followable, if by by no means also 'easy'.

"Color, and recognizably consistent and engaging rhythms, are the means by which George Perle can be said to have 'humanized' his twelve-tone inventions. Goode compares Perle's *Serenade No. 3* for Piano and Chamber Orchestra, quite rightly, to those of the Classical era; but the present century's fans of Stravinsky and Bartók—note the ingredients of the *Concertino*—should have no difficulty with [either the *Serenade* or *Concertino*, or the *Ballade*—] a remarkable compendium, true to its title in its hosed-down romanticism." —John Ditsky, in *Fanfare: The Magazine for Serious Record Collectors*, 11-12/85.

Six Etudes for Piano (1976). 11m *Rec.:* New World Records: Bradford Gowan. *Pub.:* Magnum Music.

Six New Etudes for Piano (1984). *Rec.:* New World Records (Digital Stereo LP) NW 342: Michael Boriskin. *Pub.:* GunMar Music Inc. 1. 1. *Praeludium* (1m). 2. *Gigue* (2m). 3. *Papillons* (1m). 4. *Romance* (2m). 5. *Variations* (2m) 6. *Perpetuum mobile* (2m).

"[The *Six Etudes* are] among the most significant recent compositions in the American piano literature." —*Piano Quarterly*.

"[Perle's *Six Etudes* are] among the finest works for piano written in a generation." —Paul Hume, *The Washington Post*. [See also comments by Paul Lansky for *Concertino* entry, above.]

"[In the *Six New Etudes*,] brilliant piano writing, wonderfully unusual and odd motivic profiles, and extremely consistent and interesting harmonic language converge in different and fascinating ways in each of the six movements.... [Earlier works such as the *Suite in C* and the *Fantasy Variations*,] both written in the early 1970s during the period when Perle was formulating significant new developments in his theoretical thinking, seem exploratory. I have the feeling that in the *New Etudes* (and the first set as well) Perle has come upon what he was searching for in the earlier pieces or, more generally, that they have been made possible only by extensive exploration....

"George Perle is often described as one who has achieved 'belated' recognition. Rather than lamenting this fact, however, we should all be encouraged by the model of a composer who, in his seventies, continues to grow, develop, and change with the energy and fervor usually associated with much younger composers. It will be interesting to see what the next twenty years bring." —Paul Lansky, in *American Music*, Winter 1988.

"If George Perle's reputation as a composer is no longer overshadowed by his world-wide renown as a musicologist and theorist, it may be thanks to pieces like *Six New Etudes*. Completed at the end of 1984, this work is an important contribution to the contemporary piano literature. It is also a worthy complement to Perle's already popular *Six Etudes*; both sets deserve to occupy firm and lasting places in the repertory.

"While the new studies naturally focus upon technical considerations (not only the 'usual' mechanical challenges, but also more subtle difficulties involving articulation, pedalling, nuance, phrasing, and rhythm), the pieces are devoid of meaningless digital display. The music's considerable demands are always motivated by expressive values, and Perle conveys his sophisticated musical ideas in a deft, poised, elegant, and totally engaging manner. The etudes are brilliant and enormously effective. Although they contain many fiendishly difficult passages, the writing never goes against the instrument or the hand, and the score is extremely well crafted. Perle's characteristically lucid textures are lean, crisp, and piquant. While the meters are fluid throughout (time signatures are generally absent or, when present, change frequently), the rhythmic syntax here is much more straightforward than in many of his other scores.

"The etudes are all brief, ranging in duration from thirty seconds to scarely more than two minutes. The technical and expressive aims are clearly defined at the outset of each study, and the forms are likewise direct and easily grasped. The pieces have titles, which imply that the six etudes may be thought of collectively as a kind of suite. These headings, however, were appended only after the work was completed, and are intended to convey something of the character and form of each piece. The *Praeludium*", with its treacherous double notes and daredevil stretches, serves as a dashing curtain-raiser to the set. It is followed by a light, whirling *Gigue*, written in an extended rondo, in which the recurring material becomes abbreviated in successive appearances. The third etude, *Papillons*, depicts perhaps the only polyrhythmic butterflies in music, quietly fluttering along in threes against four. The sensitive *Romance* is the most ruminative and poetic of the pieces; it is a rich, yet delicate, study in controlled rubato and subtle dynamic inflection, in which every expressive gesture has been carefully indicated. *Variations* is by far the most involved and difficult etude, a real *tour-de-force* of rapid chordal passages, wide leaps, and sudden changes in dynamics and articulation; any of its eleven interconnected sections (there is no real, independent 'theme' here) might be regarded as the main material, with the remaining sections offering different perspectives and views, somewhat like a prism which reveals a variety of facets when observed from slightly altered positions. With the eerie, yet exhilarating, *Perpetuum mobile* and its darting, ethereal scales, *Six New Etudes* does not so much end as drift away into silence; this final etude is the solo version of the identically-titled movement of *Serenade No. 3* for piano and small ensemble....

"*Six New Etudes* belongs in any serious collection of twentieth-century instrumental music." —Michael Boriskin, in *Notes* (Music Library Association), 9/86.

Quintets 1-4 for Winds. *Rec.:* New World (Stereo LP) NW 359 (also CD vers.): Dorian Wind Quintet (Elizabeth Mann, fl, Gerard Reuter, ob, Jerry Kirkbride, cl, Jane Taylor, bsn, David Jolley, hn).
Quintet 1 (1959). 1. (3m). 2. (6m). 3. (3m). *Pub.:* Theodore Presser. *Quintet 2* (1960). 1. (5m). 2. (4m). 3. (2m). *Pub.:* Boelke-Bomart. *Quintet 3* (1967). 1. *Fantasia* (3m). 2. *Scherzo* (4m). 3. *Recitative* (3m). 4. *Finale* (4m). *Pub.:* Boelke-Bomart. **Quintet 4** (1984). 1. *Invention* (3m). 2. *Scherzo* (5m). 3. *Pastorale* (6m) 4. *Finale* (5m). Winner, 1986 Pulitzer Prize. *Prem.:* Dorian Wind Quintet. *Pub.:* Galaxy Music.

"One danger with 'isms', Theodore Adorno wrote in his *Aesthetic Theory*, is that, initially, artists who follow the 'ism' less religiously tend to be underrated in favor of those whose allegiance is more dramatic. Few composers better exemplify that phenomenon than George Perle, who for much of his career has stood in the shadow of the serialist composers with whom he is dubiously associated. Only gradually has the music world come to realize how individual his music is, what a flexible musical language he has developed, and how different that language is from serialism. Thus the 1986 Pulitzer Prize Perle received for [his] *Wind Quintet Nr. 4* seemed not so much an award for an isolated achievement as an overdue tribute to someone who has upheld the highest musical standards for over a quarter-century.

"Perle's divergence from mainstream twelve-tone music came early, through one of those happy 'misunderstandings' on which so much historical progress depends. In 1937 he borrowed the score to Alban Berg's *Lyric Suite*. Through it he discovered Schoenberg's twelve-tone system; but instead of regarding the row as an inviolable ordering of the twelve pitches, he considered it a modified scale that the composer could move around in at will. By the time he realized his mistake, he had discovered so many possibilities in his own, more flexible system that, as he said, 'Schoenberg's idea of the series seemed so primitive compared to mine.' Perle persevered in developing a 'twelve-tone tonality', a method of using the entire chromatic spectrum that corresponds closely to the major/minor system of traditional tonality. In recent years younger composers have been influenced by Perle's 'misunderstanding' of the system, and have extended twelve-tone tonality to a larger body of work.

"The differences between Perle's system and serial music may look abstruse on paper, but they are quite obvious to the ear. Clearly, his technique allows for a melodiousness foreign to serial music's angular, discontinuous lines. More remarkable is the way in which the music defuses a pernicious distinction between tonality and atonality by hovering ambiguously in between; it continually skirts reference to a particular tonal center. Perle's harmony glides between the simplest and most complex sonorities with unique fluidity. If serialism retains a vestige of romanticism's angst, Perle has invented a chromatic classicism in which opposites are seamlessly reconciled.

"These qualities are nowhere more apparent than in Perle's wind quintets. This medium, so neglected by most composers (apparently, except for the German Tilo Medek, no one else has written so many of them since the early nineteenth century), seems well suited to Perle's language: the instruments' varied colors clarify his stratified harmonies, their staccato attacks nicely articulate his tempo structures, and their breathing requirements fit his classically proportioned phrases. Though each quintet has its own distinctive personality, Perle's conception of the genre is well defined. For example, the clarinet seems to be his preferred solo instrument, as witness extended solos in the *Second* and *Third Quintets*, and each quintet begins with a 'winding-up' motive for that instrument, from which the succeeding movement is generated.

"The *First Quintet* (1959) closely follows an eight-year period during which Perle wrote nothing he still acknowledges; at the time, he was teaching at the University of California at Davis. Though Berg and Bartók were the first composers with whom Perle felt strong affinities, this quintet's juxtaposed panels of sound, recurring in new combinations, seem distinctly Stravinskian, the second movement in particular calling to mind that composer's *Symphonies of Wind Instruments*. However, in the *Second Quintet*, written only a year later, we are in another world. Its melting harmonies and evanescent melodies look to no other composer, but only to Perle's later music.

"Rhythm in Perle's music, an aspect not often discussed by commentators, is largely a function of tempo relationships, and the quintets conveniently demonstrate four different stages of his tempo conception. The *First* suggests accelerando through decreasing duration values, following half-notes (listen particularly to the French horn) with dotted quarters, quarters, dotted eighths, and eighths. The *Second* experiments with the related idea of metric modulation, which is more clearly audible here than in the more heavily layered music of Elliott Carter. Except in the last movement, Perle limits his metronomic relationships to ratios of two to three.

"Soon after writing the *Second Quintet*, Perle moved to the City University of New York (Queens College), where he taught until

1985. In the *Third Quintet* (1967) he expanded metric modulation to a more complex system in which tempos are related by ratios of four to five, four to seven, five to eight, etc. This is the quintet in which such relationships are most audible, especially in the final movement, where staccato, reiterated chords keep track of the fluid meter and tempo changes. This quintet also contains the most unusually textured movement of the group, the *Recitative*, whose atmospheric chords appear and evaporate one note at a time.

"For the record, the *Fourth Quartet* (1984) is the only one written strictly in Perle's system, though the system informs all of his writing, and the ear is hard put to tell the difference. The piece abandons the strictures of metric modulation for a freer conception of tempo with frequent ritards and accelerandos. Like so many late works of important composers, this quintet possesses a greater smoothness and cohesiveness of language than the earlier ones, for which some of the style's more picturesque idiosyncrasies have been sacrificed (one thinks of the late Beethoven sonatas, or Wagner's counterpoint in *Parsifal*). The work's most fascinating feature is possibly the arrhythmically contrapuntal texture of the *Scherzo* (forever interrupted by the rabble-rousing horn), unique in the genre's literature. Symmetry on every level is an increasingly important aspect of Perle's later music, and the finale quotes heavily from the opening movement.

"Less dramatic than that of Boulez, Wuorinen, or even Babbitt, Perle's music usually sounds simpler than it is. If his surfaces seem uncomplicated, one can listen *through* the texture to hear the background irregularities that keep the music interesting—a changing note in a held chord, a beat quietly dropped or added—much as one does in Mozart or Schubert. Repetition is common and never literal. Perle never writes down to an audience and never worries about 'accessibility', but he is a firm believer that a 'piece that "makes sense" will reach one, at some intuitive level, even at first hearing'. Such is certainly true of [his wind] quintets, which place Perle alongside Schoenberg, Nielsen, and Jolivet as composers who have raised the wind quintet above its utilitarian origins to make an enduring personal statement." —Kyle Gann, from program notes for New World NW 359 recording.

"George Perle's four wind quintets are a substantial and engaging addition to the twentieth-century repertory for that ensemble, which is sometimes maligned for its five discrete, seemingly immiscible, timbral zones. Perle's polyphonic treatment of the timbres of the ensemble boldly displays 'pure' individual instrumental colors while exulting in the combinations and overlappings of timbres. The timbral polyphony associates with the pitch polyphony and with formal musical events, using timbres to clarify and to characterize textures and structures.

"The first three quintets are 'tone centered', in Arthur Berger's term (see this writer's 'A Tonal Analog', *Perspectives of New Music* XXI/1-2 [1982-83], pp. 257-84, for a fuller discussion). The tone centers may be heard as projected by intersecting complementary whole-tone collections, by intersecting octagonic collections, or by some combination of both collection classes. At the beginning of the *First Quintet*, for example, the clarinet plays a repeated motive whose pitches suggest the intersection of segments from two whole-tone collections: $C-D^b-E^b-(F)-G$ and $D-E$. The second segment is continued by the pitches in the horn and bassoon: $F^\#-G^\#$. This dyad becomes a constant in the first movement, serving as the point of departure and of closure. The tone centers in the second and third movements are projected similarly.

"There are motivic links between the *First* and *Second* Quintets, but the polyphony in the three movements of the latter work is even more finely wrought and the tempo shifts are more richly conceived than in the former. The *Third Quintet* has four movements: a brief opening section, a scherzo, a slow movement ('Recitative') and a vigorous *Finale* that has some motivic links with the first two quintets. As in the *Second Quintet*, the tempo shifts are subtly elaborated. (The tempo relations in Perle's music would repay careful study.)

"The *Fourth Quintet* was awarded the Pulitzer Prize in 1986. Its pitch structure, like that of Perle's music since the early 1970s, is derived from his twelve-tone tonal system [see Perle's study of *Twelve-Tone Tonality*, 1977], whose basic element is a set generated by an interval cycle (for example, interval-class 7) that is combined with its complimentary inversion. The sums of pitch-class numbers between P and I and the intervals of those collections provide resources of association and combination that can be defined objectively and systematically in both theoretical and compositional contexts. The intimate relationships between Perle's music generated by symmetrical interval cycles (in this case, complementary 'whole-tone' cycles) and by twelve-tone tonality can be heard [with particular clarity by comparing] the *Fourth* and *First* Quintets." —Richard G. Swift, in *American Music*, Summer 1989.

Songs of Praise and Lamentation for Solo Voices, Chorus and Orchestra (1974). 40m Ded. Noah Greenberg. *Prem.:* Desoff Choirs, members of the Concordia CHoir (Bronxville), National Orchestral Assn, Michael Hammond, cond. *Pub.:* Boelke-Bomart (Jerona)(rental).

1. *From the 18th Psalm* for Mixed Chorus and Orchestra. *Text:* Hebrew. 9m
4-3-3-3; 4-2-4-1; timp, perc, cel, harp; strings
2. *Sonnets to Orpheus* for Mixed Chorus a capella. *Text:* Rilke, German. 12m
3. *In Eius Memoriam* for Soli, Double Chorus and Orchestra. *Text:* John Hollander, English and Latin. 19m
2-2-2-2; 4-2-4-0; timp, perc, cel, harp; strings (no basses)

"*Songs of Praise and Lamentation*[91] is an extended choral composition dedicated to the late Noah Greenberg. The first part is twelve verses of Psalm 18, set in Hebrew for four-part chorus with large orchestra. The second is four of Rilke's *Orpheus* sonnets set in the original German, two for single and two for double chorus, unaccompanied. The third, specifically an elegy for Mr. Greenberg, includes quotations from Ockeghem's lament on the death of Binchois, Josquin's on the death of Ockeghem, and Vinders's on the death of Josquin. Quatrains by John Hollander grow from them, with the refrain *'Timor mortis conturbat me'* (as in Dunbar's *Lament for the Makaris*). There is a salute to Auden, Greenberg's collaborator, 'the best shaper of words'; and, finally, the opening verses of Psalm 1 are refashioned: 'His ever-fruitful life shall stand, A tree in a well-watered land; Winds through unwithered leaves will play; *Laus musicae componet me.*' This movement is for soloists, double chorus, a smaller orchestra, and, in the Renaissance *déplorations*, Renaissance instruments such as used to play in Mr. Greenberg's New York Pro Musica." — Andrew Porter, in *The New Yorker*, 3/3/75.[92]

A Short Symphony for Orchestra (1980). 15m *Prem:* Boston SO, Seiji Ozawa, cond. *Perf.:* BBC SO, Oliver Knussen, cond.; Orchestra Bayerischer Rundfunk, Gunther Schuller, cond.; American Composers O, Gunther Schuller, cond. *Pub.:* Boelke-Bomart (Jerona)(score; rental).
3-3-2-3; 4-2-3-1; timp, perc, harp; strings
In three movements.

"One cannot call George Perle's music shallow, and his *Short Symphony,* composed in 1980, is a typical example of the intense concentration of urgent musical ideas that has characterized his work. For years Perle has worked the mines of serialism, evolving his own personal approach to musical organization, which he refers to as twelve-tone modality. The three movements of this symphony en-

---

91 For additional comments, see notes by Oliver Knussen, above. (Ed.)
92 Reprinted in *Music of Three Seasons, 1974-1977* (Farrar Straus Giroux, 1978).

compass a playing time of only fifteen minutes; yet, they are all so compact in gesture and intense in musical syntax that they seem much longer. The first movement, of a relatively moderate tempo, is a sonata-allegro form. The second movement, faster with almost continuous sixteenth-note movement, is a rondo with a recapitulation. The final movement fluctuates between four tempos, each relatively fast, but with many ritards and accelerations. The form may be described as 'sonatina' (sonata-allegro without development) which, as a coda, brings back the opening motive from the first movement. The musical language is atonal and uncompromisingly dissonant. As an example of musical structure, it is impressive — musical details mesh and meld into intellectually intriguing relationships." — Karl Kroeger, in *Notes* (Music Library Association), 9/85. [See also notes by Oliver Knussen, above.]

DANA PERNA

B. 1958, Garden City NY. *Educ.:* Mannes College of Music, Long Island Univ, Northwestern Univ Schl of Music. Founder Holzbläser NY/Chicago. *Works incl.:* electronic music, music for brasses, winds, band, guitar, organ, piano, strings; arrangements & editions. Music by Dana Perna available from Bardic Edition.

Composer statement: "When I work I do not feel the need to compose for any specific audience, in any particular trend or 'ism', or as a way of telling the world that my music will put food on someone's table, a roof over their heads, or bring about world peace; but, my hope is to live in a better world. Apart from composing I wish to draw greater attention to important music that remains unknown, neglected or unperformed.

"I believe that we live in a time when the very meaning of 'what is art' and the freedoms that should be guaranteed to all who practice the arts are being questioned. Art, by nature, is an act of conscience. It is ironic that we see walls of injustice coming down all over the world at the very same time that so many other 'walls' are being erected in their place. To censor an artist's work is to destroy more than some people can possibly imagine, because—without the enlightment that culture offers to all of the world's peoples—there can only be darkness in its stead."

Deux Berceuses for Flute and Piano (or Orchestra)(1983).
Three Conversations Between Two Flutists (1980).
Fantasy-Sonata for Unaccompanied Flute (1978).

Dana Perna has composed extensively for the flute. His *Deux Berceuses* have an especially lyrical quality. The work exists in two versions—the piano version being a separate accompaniment of its own, and not merely a reduction of the orchestral score. In *Three Conversations Between Two Flutists*, both performers are required to play equally matched, moody, contrapuntally treated music. The *Fantasy-Sonata*, in three movements, grows organically from a series of pitches heard at the beginning.

Two Early Ayres for Woodwind Quintet (1976-77).
Nonet (In Memoriam—Charles T. Griffes) for Winds (1981, rev. 1985). 6m
Two Preludes for Wind Ensemble (1971/1980).
  1 pic, 2 fl, 2 ob (2 Engl hn), 1 E^b cl, 3 B^b cl, 1 alto cl, 2 b cl, 2 bsns, 2 alto

sax, 1 t sax, 1 bar sax, 3 hn, 3 tpt, 3 tbn, 1 bar hn (Euphonium), 1 tuba, 4 perc

Two Early Ayres is light and lyrical—meant to entertain. The *Nonet (In Memoriam—Charles T. Griffes)*, originally for brass quintet and saxophone quartet (1981), was rescored in 1985 for piccolo, flute, oboe, English horn, clarinet, bass clarinet, bassoon, contra-bassoon (or second bassoon) and French horn. This memorial to the American composer Charles Tomlinson Griffes (1884-1920) abounds in dissonant clashes and kaleidoscopic coloration. The *Two Preludes* for Wind Ensemble are based on recognizable tunes: Christmas songs and carols in *Christmas Prelude* (treated dissonantly to express the composer's consternation at the commercialism which surrounds contemporary religious celebration), folksongs in *Hillsong Prelude*. This second *Prelude* was inspired, in part, by a trip to the Adirondack Mountains in New York State, among which splendid surroundings the composer first heard the *Hill Song Nr. 2* by the Australian-American composer-pianist, Percy Grainger (1882-1961).

VINCENT PERSICHETTI

B. 1915, Philadelphia PA; *d.* 1987. *Educ.:* Combs Cons, Philadelphia Cons. *Taught at:* Philadelphia Cons, Juilliard Schl of Music. *Author:* Dir. publns, Elkan-Vogel Co. *Author of: Twentieth Century Harmony, William Schuman* (with F. R. Schreiber). *Works incl.:* band pieces, choral works *(The Creation* oratorio, *Spring Cantata, Winter Cantata),* concertos (E hn, pno), quartets (strngs), 5 parables (var insts), 13 serenades (var insts), sonatas (pno, 2 pnos, vc, vln), 9 symphonies.

"VIEWS OF THE COMPOSER. Vincent Persichetti sits at the desk in the spartan studio he shares at Juilliard with fellow composer and teacher David Diamond. Spread out before Persichetti is a score by one of his composition students. While he creates the musical progress of the past week in his head, Persichetti is oblivious to the competing phrases of Chopin and Bach that float through the open door from practice rooms down the hall.

"His words come in staccato bursts, but without the hard edge that can so easily inflect the teacher's criticism of student work. He speaks *con amore.* 'That's a really beautiful phrase,' he says. He pauses at another measure and asks, 'Can you consider adding a chord here?' He softens the questions with humor. 'You know what a chord is?' As the student weighs the suggestion, Persichetti makes certain that the young composer's artistic sense is not being overwhelmed by his own. He has no desire to turn out carbon-copy Persichettis. 'Well, just promise me that you'll think about it this week. See if it makes sense.'

"Throughout the thirty-minute lesson, Persichetti supports his suggestions with a bar from Carl Orff or a prhase from Darius Milhaud or a line from Juilliard colleague Roger Sessions. He draws on what music critic Martin Bookspan admiringly calls an 'encyclopedic knowledge' of music history and repertory. 'Vincent,' says Bookspan, 'has every score in his bloodstream,' and can recall almost anything from the literature and execute it right on the spot....

"Persichetti is, at 64, a first-rate pianist and sight reader, as well as a conductor, music editor, musicologist, and, of course, a prolific American composer. A former ASCAP Board member,[93] he is author of the leading text on twentieth century harmony, which has dominated the field for the last 18 years. [He] has been a member of the composition faculty at Juilliard since 1947. His students range from Peter Schickele (otherwise known as P.D.Q. Bach) to Jacob

---

93 American Society of Composers, Authors and Publishers. (Ed.)

Druckman. He visits the school two days a week to see a dozen composition students plus some hold-over doctoral candidates who are finishing major orchestral scores as dissertations....

"In addition to his Juilliard duties, Persichetti spends a few hours each week at Elkan-Vogel, the music publishers, where he serves as principal outside advisor on publication. Periodically, he visits other schools to lead workshops devoted to his music. The rest of the time, 'definitely more than half,' he says, is for composing. In an era when a single important score in a year from a composer is unusual, Persichetti is now working on some piano etudes which will have an opus number in the 140s. His *Opus 1* (a serenade for ten wind instruments) was written in 1929 when he was 14. It is still available from Elkan-Vogel and has recently been recorded in a university performance....

"Just as Persichetti has encouraged the independence of his students, he has always been his own man as a composer. He has turned down offers to write television music for amounts of money that make his expressive eyebrows dance, and he has never accepted a commission for a piece he did not want to write....

"With an accurate self-perception, Persichetti assesses his role in modern American music: 'I've never been a part of an avante garde or any particular camp,' he told an interviewer in 1973. 'What I am, I guess, is an amalgamator—I use everything that's around me.' The Cowell clusters, the Penderecki textures, and the other devices of avant-garde composers 'contribute something to the total vocabulary of music,' he says. 'But it is when it all comes together that really counts... When all of these ideas are synthesized, they become the language of the century. I think I'm part of the new renaissance of music.'

"Perhaps because of this eclecticism and his reluctance to adopt trendy compositional styles, Persichetti has never been a 'fashionable' composer or one much in the public eye. The closest he came to this was in 1972 when he was asked by the Nixon Inaugural Committee to write a short piece for the inaugural concert using as a text Abraham Lincoln's second inaugural address. The text appealed to him and he wrote the music in a couple of hectic weeks. At the last moment the performance of the work was cancelled because Nixon advisors felt the Lincoln text might be interpreted as anti-war and thus an attack on President Nixon, who had just embarked on the Christmas bombing of Hanoi. Persichetti remained calm during this controvery even though *The New York Times* and news magazines tried to whip up a feud between the composer and the White House. 'I just wrote the piece out of respect for the office of the President,' Persichetti says with a shrug. And indeed, it is hard to imagine a less political musician to have been dragged into the mess. Shortly after the Nixon cancellation, the piece was played by the St. Louis Symphony.

"Mario di Bonaventura, Director of Publications for G. Schirmer, compares Persichetti with Paul Hindemith, in that both made an effort to write a large body of 'useful music' for neglected instruments. Few other twentieth century composers have been interested in the creation of such a literature. 'The difference between the two,' says Arizona State's Prof. Cohen, 'is that Hindemith had a set style. The uniqueness of Persichetti is not just that his pieces have a range of difficulty, but also a wide range of harmonic idioms. You can't predict what his next piece will sound like.' " — David M. Rubin, in *ASCAP in Action*, Spring 1980.

Concerto for Piano, Four Hands, Op. 56 (1952). *Recs.*: Columbia (Mono LP) ML-4989: composer and his wife; Grenadilla (Stereo LP) GS-1050: Jean Wentworth, Kenneth Wentworth; Melodiya (Stereo LP) C10161334: Alexander Bakhchiev, Elena Sorokina.

"The *Concerto for Piano, Four Hands* was performed many times during our stay in India as Fulbright scholars in 1964-65. After one concert in Calcutta, a local journalist came back to speak to us. She had never heard of Mozart and Schubert, but was enchanted by the Persichetti. Here is her description of the work:

> First, you are waiting,
> Then it comes,
> Then, a question,
> Then it is finished.

"The poetic quality of the lady's response is touching, and the lines, while scarcely comprehensive, confirm the enduring sense of traditional order which is a Persichetti trait. The tempo/section indications, listed on the opening page [of the score], are in fact *Lento — andante — presto — larghissimo — coda.*

"The flamboyant *presto*, which contains a large A B A, has many developmental qualities, particularly in a psychological sense. However, the work is based throughout on various permutations of its opening subject, which may have been heard first in various portions of Schoenberg's *Pierrot Lunaire*. In two rising intervals, often a 3rd and 5th, it outlines a major or minor 7th, then falls a minor 3rd. The transformations may be successive rhythmic diminutions — as in the fugue *(andante)* or the dramatic opening of the *presto;* or, later, in that section, in the mixed-meter *più mosso*, may become 4- or 5-note cells freely related to the original. Another time-honored device closely associated with Persichetti's writing—the canon—is employed just after the opening of the *presto* and again in the exciting beginning of the coda, where the material is spun out over 30 bars in a stunning *accelerando* and *crescendo*. The delicately haunting passage which leads to the *presto* is realized by yet another contrapuntal technique, the mirror image. Finally, while the opening theme contains 11 of the 12 chromatic pitches, the work never strays far from a firm tonal center of D minor (the *andante* suggests A minor/major, its dominant), and, despite some massive dissonance, there is a pervasive use of logical diatonic, even triadic, harmonic progressions.

"The *Concerto* is replete with characteristically American references and with idiomatic *concertante* writing. From the suggestion of a single cello-bass line in the somber opening bars to an analogous passage which leads into the *andante*, full symphonic forces seem to have been marshalled; similar and even more powerful effects are felt thereafter. To these, and to the mighty plateau of implied unison strings at the *presto* opening, are opposed myriad *concertino* timbres. One can imagine wind and brazz, *pizzicato* strings, and percussion combinations suggestive of the open prairie, the steam train, the Charleston: a panorama of nostalgic national images."—Jean & Kenneth Wentworth, from liner notes for Grenadilla Stereo LP GS-1050.

"The tremendous recording activity involving music by Vincent Persichetti continues apace in [his] 65th year with [this release by Jean and Kenneth Wentworth], bringing the number of pieces currently available on disc to 35. The new installment returns to currency one of Persichetti's unquestionable masterpieces: the *Concerto for Piano, Four Hands*. This 1952 composition boasts one of the composer's most successful formal plans (and one that he used also in the equally brilliant *Symphony No. 5*): a continuous, multi-sectional design growing from one initial thematic idea. This answer to the perennial unity/diversity question seemed to provide Persichetti with an ideal medium through which to explore a boundless developmental fertility. The *Four Hands Concerto* is an enormously stimulating and fully satisfying virtuoso work that bristles with exciting rhythmic, textural, and contrapuntal interplays. True, the genesis of these stylistic features can be traced easily enough to Stravinsky. Yet perhaps it is not too heretical to question whether the latter composer ever demonstrated the sort of graceful fluency and compressed integration found in this *Concerto*. Two particularly distinctive traits in Persichetti's best music are present in this work: a childlike innocence and ingratiating impishness as the spiritual core of the music, whatever the degree of complexity, or surface harshness and angularity; an emotional tone wholly free of *angst*, despite interactions of considerable tension within the fabric of the music. It is probable that the latter trait enables one to listen to a work like this *Concerto* countless times in succession without tiring of it. Like the *"Jupiter" Symphony* it is a comprehensive tour de force of compositional virtuosity, reveling in the ecstatic delight of the developmental process itself." — Walter G. Simmons, in *Fanfare: The Magazine for Serious Record Collectors*, 9-10/80.

Dryden Liturgical Suite for Organ, Op. 144. *Pub.:* Elkan-Vogel (Presser).
1. *Prelude* ("By whose aid the world's foundations first were laid").
2. *Response* ("Give us Thy self, that we may see"). 3. *Psalm* ("From sin and sorrow set us free"). 4. *Prayer* ("Make us eternal truths receive").
5. *Toccata* ("Inflame and fire our hearts").

"Vincent Persichetti's *Dryden Liturgical Suite* is based on the composer's own hymn tune setting of John Dryden's hymn to the Holy Spirit, 'Creator Spirit, by whose aid the world's foundations first were laid'. (The tune is from the collection *Hymns and Responses for the Church Year*, published in 1956.)

"The *Suite* consists of five movements. Each movement is subtitled with a fragment of the Dryden hymn [see above]. The emphasis of the quotations, interestingly, is not that of the Dryden Pentecost text. The third movement's title and quotation are incongruous; 'from sin and sorrow set us free' implies the redemption of the soul, a concept found in the New Testament rather than in the Old Testament.

"The hymn tune is stated twice in the *Prelude* and reappears, triumphantly, near the end of the *Toccata*. Otherwise, it forms the basis of fantasy-like movements. Each movement has a contrasting character of its own related to its title. For example, the *Prelude* is soft and introduces the tune. The fourth movement, *Prayer*, is quiet and meditative, and the *Toccata* is fiery and brilliant.

"The *Dryden Liturgical Suite* is superbly crafted, as is always the case with Persichetti, and the music possesses drive and direction. The organ is used idiomatically throughout the work. The music lays well under the fingers and feet.

"Vincent Persichetti's contribution to the organ literature is significant. Over the years, he has written a number of major works for the organ, one of the few composers of our time to do so. There has, in general though, been no particular direction of development in his music, as the organ works demonstrate. *Shimah B'Koli*, Op. 62 (1962) and *Parable (VI)*, Op. 117 (1972) are large, imaginative and virtuosic one-movement works that stand as major contributions to

American organ literature. But this adventuresome style has given way to a more tonal and less complex idiom found in the *Dryden Suite* and *Auden Variations,* Op. 136 (1977), both based on hymn tunes by Persichetti."[94] —David Shuler, in *Notes* (Music Library Association), 6/82.

Parable for Solo Trombone. *Pub.:* Elkan-Vogel.

"Persichetti's *Parable* for unaccompanied trombone is similar to works by the same name for solo trumpet and solo horn. It juxtaposes shifts of melodic and rhythmic style, tempos, dynamics, and tone colors throughout and is a good example of carefully thought out contemporary music which projects strong emotional content when convincingly performed. It demands a performer of advanced technical development, and especially a player with enough musical imagination to strongly project Persichetti's carefully marked score. A fine piece for teaching (and expressing) an important approach to contemporary composition." —Peter Schmalz, in *The American Music Teacher* (Music Teachers National Association), 4-5/83.

Reflective Keyboard Studies for Piano, Op. 138. *Pub.:* Elkan-Vogel.

"There are 48 brief studies in this work, divided into three sets of 16 each. The studies are each only two or three lines long. In the Composer's Note we are told that these are 'exercises designed to develop both hands at the same time, giving fingers, wrists and arms strength and flexibility.' Some of the technical aspects covered in the *Studies* are: scales, scales with leaps, arpeggios, double notes, alternating octaves, chords by seconds and fourths, finger repetition, and ornamental patterns. The score includes indications for tempo, dynamics, phrasing, and pedaling, all of which turns them into very attractive musical tid-bits which are great fun to play. The composer tells us that the studies 'will help in attaining manual dexterity and virtuosity, and in preparing for performances of my *Mirror Etudes* and *Twelfth Piano Sonata (Mirror Sonata)* [described below].' Medium difficulty." —Evelyn Garvey, in *The American Music Teacher* (Music Teachers National Association), 6-7/84.

Serenade 4 for Violin and Piano. *Pub.:* Elkan-Vogel.

---

94 For the composer's own response of sorts to the charge that he demonstrated "no particular direction of development", see his distinction between "*grazioso*" and "grit" in the Shackelford interview following (at the end of the *Sonatas* section). (Ed.)

Serenade 7 for Piano, Op. 55 (1952). 7m *Rec:* Owl Records OWL-29: Ellen Burmeister. *Pub.:* Elkan-Vogel.
1. *Walk.* 2. *Waltz.* 3. *Play.* 4. *Sing.* 5. *Chase.* 6. *Sleep.*

SERENADE 4: "This *Serenade* is a fine example of Persichetti's masterly composing technic. The first-movement *Pastorale* expresses a gentle mood in legato 6/8 flowing passages. The fast, loud, rather brusque manner of the next *Episode* is in complete contrast—percussive chords alternate with fast runs. The *Interlude* is an andante cantabile movement that flows along in a rather serene manner. The finale *Capriccio* is very fast and brilliant. High passages of 16th notes starting very high and dashing down are its predominating feature.

"Although basically tonal, it is never dull and has flashes of unexpected color in its free use of accidentals. The form is concise and well planned. The moods are vividly portrayed, resulting in a very attractive new work for advanced musicians. The piano part is of equal importance and the contrapuntal elements are always effective." —Catherine L. Petersen, in *The American Music Teacher* (Music Teachers National Association), 2-3/84.

SERENADE 7: " 'Although *Serenade Nr. 7* is often referred to as a group of teaching pieces, I must say that I have never written teaching pieces as such. I write music, all of which can be taught, but some to students younger than others. The *Serenade* contains some of my favorite music, and seeds from this work are sprouting in my first opera, *The Sibyl (A Parable of Chicken Little).*' —Vincent Persichetti.

"These vignettes are vintage Persichetti. Schumann and Bartók, for instance, wrote similar piano pieces which, partly through their simplicity, capture an essence of childhood and youthfulness. Their miniatures, like Persichetti's, may speak to the less developed technique, but with no modification of musical quality or artistic expression. Mrs. Persichetti has said that these pieces 'are distillations of a musical expression that has undergone clarification to the point of great simplicity.' " —Ellen Burmeister, from program notes for Owl OWL-29 recording.

Sonatas 1-12 for Piano. *Pub.:* Elkan-Vogel.
Sonata 1, Op. 3 (1939). In 4 movements. 16m *Sonata 2,* Op. 6. In 4 movements. 11m *Sonata 3,* (1943). *Rec.:* Chandos (DDD Stereo LP) CHAN-8761: David Allen Wehr. *Sonata 9,* Op. 58 (1952). 9m *Recs.:* American Gramaphone (LP) AG-361: Jackson Berkey; Melodiya (LP) C10161334: Alexander Bakhchiev. *Sonata 10,* Op. 67 (1955). Comm. by Juilliard Fndn. *Prem.:* Joseph Raieff. *Recs.:* SPF Records (LP) 41203/4: James Ruccolo; Owl Recordings (Stereo LP) OWL-29: Ellen Burmeister. Adagio—Presto—Andante—Vivace. 23m *Pub.:* Elkan-

Vogel. *Sonata 11,* Op. 101 (1965). *Ded. & prem.:* Dorothea Persichetti. *Rec.:* Owl Recordings (Stereo LP) OWL-29: Ellen Burmeister. *Risoluto—Articolato—Sostenuto—Leggero—Conclusivo.* 17m *Pub.:* Elkan-Vogel. *Sonata 12 (Mirror Sonata),* Op. 145. In 4 movements. 13m *Rec.:* Orion (Stereo LP) ORS-84473: Jeffrey Jacob.

"The first complete edition of Vincent Persichetti's twelve piano sonatas constitutes a monument of American piano music. For that reason alone it belongs in the library of every teacher of advanced students.

"The sonatas span Persichetti's creative career, from the *First Sonata,* Op. 3, through one of his last works, Op. 145. As these works amply show, the piano was integral to his compositional style and musical personality. Throughout the sonatas one finds the rhythmic vitality and idiomatic fleetness that characterized his piano music. The *Twelfth Sonata,* in the 'mirror style' that Persichetti adopted in his last several years, recalls Rudolf Ganz's late etudes based on the same principle."—Mark Wait, in *The American Music Teacher* (Music Teachers National Association), 10-11/89.

SONATA 1: "The four-movement, 16-minute *Sonata 1* is in the conservative harmonic idiom which has always been a trademark of Persichetti's style, and which seems to be making a comeback these days, even among composers who were once considered among the avant-garde. The first movement is bright, cheerful, and rhythmic; the second is an *Adagio* with beautiful, rich harmonies; the third movement is a bounding *Scherzo,* fully living up to the literal meaning of the word; the fourth is a *Passacaglia* which begins with a thin, gentle sound and which, after several metamorphoses, brings the *Sonata* to a close with a full energy and a bravura style. The work is an absolute delight and is moderately difficult."—Evelyn Garvey, in *The American Music Teacher* (Music Teachers National Association), 6-7/84.

SONATA 2: "This beautifully-crafted eleven minute *Sonata* is in four movements. The first movement has a lovely, bucolic air; the second movement is slow and wistful; the third movement has a quickened pace, but remains low-key dramatically; the fourth movement lets loose with a fast, bouncy, syncopated beat. Except for the last movement, the texture is genreally rather thin. Much use is made, both harmonically and melodically, of the intervals of fourths, sevenths, and ninths. It is this that gives the work its own distinctive sound. It is moderately difficult."—Evelyn Garvey, in *The American Music Teacher* (Music Teachers National Association), 6-7/84.

SONATA 3: "The *Sonata No. 3* is probably the simplest and most accessible of the twelve. Its outer movements are warmly yet vigously affirmative, while the second movement displays a gentle sweetness and nostalgic poignancy that are quite moving. Greatly resembling the *String Quartet No. 2* (composed the following year) in style and concept, the sonata is overtly American in sound, with the influence of Roy Harris's formal thinking in evidence. " — Walter Simmons, in *Fanfare: The Magazine for Serious Record Collectors*, 1-2/90.

SONATA 9: "[Persichetti's *Sonata 9* is] the first of his twelve essays in the medium to appear on record. Composed in 1952, the same year as the *Concerto for Piano, Four Hands*, this 8-1/2 minute work is similar in its integrated multi-sectional design. Yet its unfolding is somewhat less concentrated, offering a more relaxed 'American neo-classical' sound, but with engaging sparkle, vitality, and rhythmic punch." — Walter Simmons, in *Fanfare: The Magazine for Serious Record Collectors*, 11-12/80.

SONATA 10: " 'My *Tenth Piano Sonata* belongs to a series of one-movement compositions that are generated by a single source motive. The music is closely related in some ways to the *Piano Quintet* with its falling motive, and more generally to the *Concerto* for Piano Four-Hands, *Symphony* for Strings, *Fourth String Quartet* and *Sinfonia: Janiculum*.' — Vincent Percsichetti.

"The composer has suggested that the dramatic opening phrase of descending thirds is, in a sense, the entire sonata. The development unfolds continuously from the opening declaration which is also presented literally at points throughout the sonata. Two other features make special contributions to the brilliance of the sonata. Persichetti employs a keyboard device found in toccata writing from Bach through Ravel, that of dividing a horizontal figure between the hands. This creates an articulate sound and often a sparse texture. One hears virtuoso passage work, chords, octaves, and opposing hands. Themes, however, are not used in the usual sonata fashion. Second, within the tonal structure of the sonata are passages in which modes in dorian, lydian, mixolydian, and aeolian, melodic, minor, chromatic, and whole-tone scales are self-contained within one or two measures. This hovering and shifting of prevailing pitches is not only colorful but vaguely unsettling.

"The sonata is ingeniously balanced around the *Andante* movement. The fast movements introduce phrases of lament, sections of exultation, bits of ragtime, lightning-fast jazz licks, and passages of the smoothest gliding. In its central position, the slow movement could be considered a love song that is by turns flirtatious, affectionate, pleading, and shy. Amazing in its degree of intimacy and tenderness, the *Andante* lends stability to the whole work.

"The *Tenth Sonata* is one of the important contributions to the literature of the genre." — Ellen Burmeister, from program notes for Owl OWL-29 recording.

SONATA 11: " 'My *Eleventh Piano Sonata* was written for my wife, Dorothea, a fabulous pianist and musician. She understands my music as no one else does and knows how to project and shape what I have written. At one point I decided that I wanted to write for her a gracious and restful piece, a kind of relaxing after-dinner piece because she had braved the sharp nails and skids of the terrorizing *Concerto* for Piano Four-Hands. But early in the piece a sudden *dolce* surprised a rude *sforzando* and particles of sound began to fly. In this work she was on her own with just two hands. Her new B Steinway was moved from our home to the Art Alliance in town and she premiered this technically and emotionally demanding work with clarity, control and love.

" 'The sonata has thick and thin sonorities, elusive and direct thematic material, objecting rhythms and gestures of approval, and graciousness and grit. The final truce is reserved for the close of this five section, one movement sound piece.' — Vincent Persichetti.

"Listeners who know a cross-section of Persichetti's music hear a kind of Florestan and Eusebius opposition of styles. The composer himself acknowledges two strains within his music, that of a graceful character and that of more serious substance. Persichetti has referred to the *Eleventh Sonata* as 'very gravelly'. Many view it as a radical departure from any of his previous styles. While there is an element of truth to this view, more than a casual study of the work reveals many of Persichetti's traits which were employed before this sonata's composition. Such characteristics as short, fragmentary phrase parts, fast tempos at the brink of unplayableness (but which always work), slow tempos that defy control, attention to the beauty of long notes on the piano and their influence and sensitivity to surrounding pitch activity, massiveness countered by spritely counterpoint, severe intensity balanced by timid questioning, sections of dance-like activity, and generous good humor are all as intrinsic to this work as they are in the other sonatas.

"The sonata *is* more bristly than the others. It uses various combinations of twelve pitches differently than the other sonatas, but it is a single set of twelve tones that provides the binding between the movements and that is seen repeatedly in the main themes. This is not to infer that the sonata is twelve-tone in Schoenbergian terms but rather to suggest that the work is tightly molded in its original thought.

"The opening gesture, probably the work's moment of greatest tension, is a more immediate point of reference throughout the sonata, and it is this motif that develops into long periods of cadential references. It is presented percussively, sparsely, with shimmer and gleam, in layered trills, and in brilliant chord-cluster tremulos; yet it remains a mysterious presence, at times haunting and at times predatory." — Ellen Burmeister, from program notes for Owl OWL-29 recording.

SONATAS 10-11: "Vincent Persichetti is one of the most fertile, profoundly creative, and intrinsically musical minds of our time. A virtuoso pianist, he has demonstrated in his piano music an imaginative and individual application of the full gamut of keyboard possibilities.... the instrument becomes for him an entire universe of aesthetic possibilities. [In fact,] one aspect of Persichetti's output that has baffled many who have attempted to concepualize it is its omnivorous stylistic range — the way his music appears to move unsystematically and unpredictably from simple, diatonic pieces to the most rigorous and complex treatment of material that is quite knotty and harsh. Most casual listeners seem to associate him with a neoclassicism of the sort that flourished in this country during the 1940s — indeed, a Stravinsky/Hindemith/Copland stylstic axis does serve as Persichetti's basic frame of reference, but his work ranges far and in many directions from that central fulcrum. Yet an essential unity of temperament — a childlike innocence and ingratiating impishness wholly free of angst — lies at the spiritual core of the music, whatever the degree of complexity, surface harshness, or angularity, and despite internal interactions of considerable tension.

"Centrally located along Persichetti's stylistic spectrum is the *Sonata No. 10*, the longest and possibly the most elaborate of the composer's piano sonatas. Composed in 1955, during Persichetti's richest and most fertile period, it resembles his other major works of the decade: a continuous, multisectional movement of about twenty minutes duration, in which a minimum of motivic material is developed into a varied and integrated large-scale work. A spontaneous, inmprovisatory spirit pervades, despite the definitiveness of total premeditation, creating, in effect, a summation of modern classicism within the boundaries of a single composition. The result is highly cerebral music with charm, wit, grace, tenderness, and dynamism. (Similar works are the *Concerto for Piano, Four Hands*, Op. 56; *Symphony No. 5*, Op. 61; *Piano Quintet*, Op. 66; and *String Quartet No. 3.*, Op. 81.)

"The *Sonata No. 11*, Op. 101, was composed ten years later and is among Persichetti's most complex and rarified works, along with the *Symphony No. 9*, Op. 113 *(Janiculum)*, and the *String Quartet No. 4*, Op. 122. Without actually employing the twelve-tone technique, these works use quasi-serial procedures to create a similar impression of severity, irregularity, instability, and disjointedness in texture, rhythm, and tonality." — Walter Simmons, in *American Music*, Winter 1987.

SONATA 12: "This is the sonata for which the *Reflective Keyboard Studies*, Op. 138 [above], is the preparation. The first movement begins with a slow introduction, then goes into the main body of the movement which is fast, energetic, and syncopated. The insertion of material from the introduction on two brief occasions allows both the performer and the listener a brief respite from the surrounding fury. The second movement is a beautiful *Amabile* with a great deal of chromaticism and many parallel minor sevenths and tritones. The third movement contains a rapid though quiet scherzo and a more relaxed waltz-like trio whose configurations include many written-out trills. After a few slow opening chords, the finale is off in a blaze of fast double sixths and octaves. There is a big, crashing ending. A most attractive piece requiring a fairly hefty technique." — Evelyn Garvey, in *The American Music Teacher* (Music Teachers National Association), 2-3/84.

"The piano music of Vincent Persichetti, especially the twelve sonatas, comprises the most penetrating lens through which to view the formidable output of one of the most profoundly creative and intrinsically musical minds of our time....

"Although his music is almost wholly abstract, i.e., non-referential (with the exception of vocal works with texts), one begins to realize with greater familiarity that there is a sense in which it *is* referential — not in the sense of the typical late-Romantic symphony, for example, with its 'abstract program', in which the music presents an abstract analog in sound to an emotional drama. Rather, Persichetti's vocabulary of gestures and figures and the rather objective, detached way they unfold and interact form a kind of private language, from which he has created his own little universe of expression. Seen in this way, the music begins to emerge as a personal metaphor, with cross-references and elaborations of ideas from other pieces winking slyly at the listener, conveying a wealth of enigmatic allusions that call for a particularly intuitive level of apprehension. All this is carried out with a light touch, devoid of pomposity or solemnity, yet by no means trivial. The impression is of an imaginary world, peopled by a large cast of cartoon-like characters, created by an eccentric master-puppeteer who amuses himself by portraying his own metaphysical vision through the interactions of his puppets. This admittedly strange interpretation is confirmed [not only by the *sonatas* but] by several other items. One is Persichetti's ongoing series, begun during the late 1960s and now numbering almost 30, of *Parables* — pieces that 'convey a meaning indirectly by the use of comparisons or analogies'. These are abstract pieces — many of them brief essays for unaccompanied monophonic instruments, such as trumpet, oboe, etc. — which function in an allegorical way, usually by developing a motif that may have appeared originally in another work. The *Parable* then becomes a sort of footnote or commentary to an aspect of the earlier work. This notion became more apparent with the recent [1987] appearance of the composer's first opera, *The Sibyl*, which bears the subtitle 'Parable XX'. And what is *The Sibyl*? A cute, witty, musically ingratiating but thoroughly bizarre, nightmarishly pessimistic piece, set to the composer's own libretto, brimming with references to previous Persichetti works, based on the story of 'Chicken Litle', with a cast comprising Henny Penny, Duck Lucky, Turkey Lurkey, etc. In a way, *The Sibyl* is the quintessential Persichetti work." — Walter Simmons, in *Fanfare: The Magazine for Serious Record Collectors*, 1-2/87.

FROM AN 1982 INTERVIEW: "RUDY SHACKELFORD: The solo sonatas [for piano] form quite a large body of music: do they in any way reflect your personal and musical evolution as a composer-pianist or pianist-composer?

"VINCENT PERSICHETTI: Viewed in perspective, [they] do reveal the portrait of a composer coming to grips with the complexities and enigmas of his times. The *First Piano Sonata*, Op. 3, contains some of the overexuberance and chromaticism of my 'silent decade', which ended with its composition in 1939. My creative life during this hiatus was far from a quiet one. I wrote reams of aggressively adolescent, unsophisticated music: a verbose Sibeliusian piano concerto, a pitifully sad Scriabinesque poem for violin and piano, a twisted Ravelish orchestra piece, a chorus and orchestra work concerned with the transcendentalism of Emerson, an unruly Messiaenic organ fantasy, a restless piano suite about the Barnegat Bay, and a fabricated Brahmsian quintet for piano and strings. At best, my 'Brahms' work resembled those the master himself discarded, or possibly was more like a portrait of his lady friends — though not of their top-flight professionalism. There *was* some significant music, but none of it mine.

"The *Third Piano Sonata* is one of two 'war pieces'; the other is the *Third Symphony* of 1946. The *Sonata's* first movement echoes the frightening implications of a war declaration; the second is a quiet episode of introspection during war; and the third, a psalm of prayer and peace. For John Kirkpatrick, its most faithful performer, the *Third Sonata*... 'seems to be a vision of mankind's relation to the divine, inspired by the Old Testament, but stated in the athletic forthrightness of modern dance.' As the *First Sonata* is close in size to the *Fourth,* so is the *Third* akin to the *Ninth* in transparency of texture. The *Fifth, Seventh,* and *Eighth* are baby sonatas, while the *Second* has a German flavor and the *Sixth,* a Viennese bouquet. The *Tenth* is the largest, and the *Eleventh,* written for and premiered by [my wife] Dorothea, very gravelly....

"SHACKELFORD: The remark about the 'gravelly' quality of your *Eleventh Piano Sonata* reminds me of the distinction you acknowledge in all your music between what you call 'grit'—the severe, serious works—and the more 'graceful' compositions. Does this kind of classification supplant the customary divisions of an artist's work into periods?

"PERSICHETTI: From my earliest days, there seem to have been strands of *grazioso* and grit present in my music. Some pieces contain one or the other of the ingredients, while some have both. At eleven, I wrote a very hospitable intermezzo, set politely in an E-flat modal area, alongside a razor-sharp keyless scherzo, whose 'mijor; and 'manor' chord structures were whipped into a tonicless batter. So I set the tone right from the start. No, my music doesn't fall into periods. I feel sure that somewhere within me there must be a female gene, but I happen to be strongly male—with no periods or variants.

"There are some who know only my 'graceful' music, and others only my 'gritty' music. Then there are those who know my early 'gracious' works and later 'gravelly' ones, and think I am changing—or possibly 'progressing'?

"SHACKELFORD: In what ways are your compositions 'American' rather than, say, 'international'? Do you have in music what Copland once called his 'vernacular' style?

"PERSICHETTI: The composer is a gregarious musical being. He wants no boundaries; he desires whatever truth may come from communication. Composers write significant music because they're individual, not because they are local. Most of us are international—not only national—and it makes little difference in what subway, town, or country our music is composed, or where the *cantus firmus* substance originated.

"It's true that some composers allow their musical souls to be seduced by attractive new sounds, while others become spatially disoriented. There are those who work themselves into a fanciful bind and 'freak out' with the joy of the surface of the sound images, as well as those who sleep through musical life in mesmeric bliss. Some composers wallow in the goo of mixed dissonant saucery, as others go directly to the past and rob themselves of the *influence* of the rich past. There are even some who work through the electronic maze without giving a thought to medium repairs, and those who are so full of solidity and weightiness that creative mobility ceases as a fog of scholarship envelops them.

"Although Milhaud stood so heavily on his music it became sluggish, and Webern called down the light of the universe too soon, I enjoy listening to most of the music of our century. Some of it is satisfying, some is creatively stimulating. It is *our* music, and it is *my* music; I am deeply affected by it, one way or another.

"There is Schoenberg, who speaks through the black amnesias of heaven, and Shostakovich whose thin fraud I wink at privily; Sessions whose leathery textures unroll the flicker's rousing drum, and Barber whose tunes can be as soft as the collied night; Stravinsky whose music makes me drunken with deep red torrents of joy, and Milhaud who brings dust in sunlight and memory in corners; Ives whose radiant spirals crease our outer night, and Webern whose loneliness includes me unawares; Satie whose melodic tones hang like those top jewels of the night, and Chavez who gathers for festival bright weed and purple shell; Berg who rears the frondings, sighing in aetherial folds, and Prokofiev who puffs out marching upon a blue sky; Britten whose subtler dreams touch me nigh to tears, and Harris whose shadow dancers are alive in my blood; Bartók whose ravished lute sings to virgin ears, and Poulenc whose warm winds spill fragrance into our solitudes; Copland to whose more clear than crystal voice the frost has joined a crystal spell, and Gershwin who sets a beat where at midnight motion stays.

"If you listen to our century's music very carefully, you will hear the cotton sky shaking jewels into orchards, and witness the jewels turning to stars. If you play our music very sensitively, you can touch a flower without troubling a star. If you sing our music very softly, no lonely flower will ever blush unseen.

"I'm not sure that the English horn's lower range should be extended, nor am I certain just how long music can sit as a prism to be admired for its colors. I am, however, sure of the validity of the Sanskrit line which will stir each composer's soul:

> Should fancy cease, the world would be a desert, dead and dry.[95]"
>
> > — from Rudy Shackelford, "Conversation with Vincent Persichetti", in *Perspectives of New Music*, Fall-Winter 1981/Spring-Summer 1982.

Three Toccatinas for Piano. 6m Comm. by Univ of MD. *Pub.:* Elkan-Vogel.

"This attractive set of pieces was commissioned by the University of Maryland for the 1980 International Piano Festival and Competition. The pieces move essentially in a single line, with the motion being divided between the hands. They all move swiftly along, in a 'fast, less fast, very fast' sequence. The first piece is bubbly and exciting; the second one chuckles along liltingly; and the third is a jolly, perpetual motion. A note from the composer tells us that the piece 'should be played with a gentle touch.' This produces a wonderful effect, something like a subterranean bubbling that never really erupts until the last few measures of each piece. Although they are on an advanced level, the pieces are not enormously difficult because they are so cleverly written. One especially needs a strong rhythmic sense and the ability to control passage-work that alternates between the hands." — Evelyn Garvey, in *The American Music Teacher* (Music Teachers National Association), 1/82.

---

95 Text from *Three Canons for Voices* (1947); the sources of poetic lines paraphrased in the three preceding paragraphs will be found in Persichetti's *Poems for Piano* (volumes I-III), *Night Dances* for orchestra, and *The Creation*.

TOBIAS PICKER

B. 1954, New York NY. *Educ.:* Manhattan Schl of Music, Juilliard Schl. Composer-in-residence, Houston SO. *Awards & grants incl.:* Guggenheim Fellowship, Amer Acad Arts/Letters Charles Ives Award, NEA fellowships, Rockefeller Fndn, Bearns Prize. *Works incl.:* concertos (ob, pno, vla, vln), *New Memories* (strng qt), piano solo (*Old and Lost Rivers, When Soft Voices Die*), *Pianorama* (2 pnos), 3 sextets, songs, 3 symphonies.

Composer statement: "For me, composition is de-composition. In order to compose it is first necessary to religiously tear away and discard that which encases the thing which must be—which will be—revealed, freed from within."

The Encantadas for Speaker and Orchestra (full & chamber orch versions). *Text:* Herman Melville. 30m *Prem.:* Albany SO, Julius Hedgyi, cond. *Rec.:* Virgin Classics: Sir John Gielgud (spkr), Houston SO, Christoph Eschenbach, cond. *Pub.:* European American.
1. *Dream.* 2. *Desolation.* 3. *Delusion.* 4. *Diversity.* 5. *Din.* 6. *Dawn.*

"Picker's *The Encantadas* is a picturesque work, but a rich one that I've now heard several times with pleasure. It's for speaker and orchestra—a combination that is seldom effective but is here brought off. At the second performance, in Springfield, Picker himself recited the text, with inflections and timing that made it seem part of the composition, not a distraction. The words are descriptive passages from Melville's Piazza Tale, telling of the mysterious islands' desolation, of the ponderous tortoises, of Rock Rodondo, rising towerlike from the sea, with its tiered population of birds.... Melville's charged prose spins exotic metaphors of the human condition; Prospero, Caliban, and Ariel seem not far away. Picker responds with romantic, colorful music. His materials are conventional, often Mahlerian in cut; his use of them is fresh and imaginative."—Andrew Porter, in *The New Yorker,* 9/3/84.

Octet for Oboe, Bass Clarinet, Horn, Violin, Cello, Double Bass, Harp and Vibraphone/Marimba (ca.1979). 9m Ded. to Parnassus ens., Anthony Korf, cond. *Prem.:* Parnassus ens., Anthony Korf, cond. *Pub.:* European American.

"Tobias Picker's *Octet...* happily confirmed the favorable impression made by Picker's *Rhapsody* for violin and piano [see below]. The forces of the *Octet...* are skilfully and imaginatively handled. The start of the piece suggests that of *Tristan* in the way motif steals upon motif to build into chords, but instead of Wagner's clinging semitones there is a gentle, open whole-tone flow — or, rather, a series of flows so directed that, while a cross-section through any point of the opening measures may reveal a common triad, one hears a web of lines and timbres instead of a chord progression. The scoring is smooth. Voice laps over or enters upon voice; coincidence on crossing points lends color and emphasis to the moments of unison; the texture is active but not dense or lumpy. A whole-tone melody implicity in the opening measures, later drawn out in a single thread by the horn, is never far away, but the moods and the motion of the music change freely, as if in a set of improvisations spun from that basic theme. The ending comes suddenly, perhaps too suddenly — but better that than a welcome outstayed. I find Picker's music hard to describe. I can't point to influences. Sometimes I think he may have been listening to Varèse timbres. Carter may have encouraged his feeling for inner rhythmic vitality. (Picker's music 'keeps going' in an organic way, generating its own energy, not relying on motor or *moto perpetuo* pulses.) The harmony seems to have been arrived at by intuition. My intuition tells me that he is one of the most gifted, individual, and unschematic of our young composers. He is twenty-four." — Andrew Porter, in *The New Yorker*.[96]

Rhapsody for Violin and Piano (1978). *Prem.*: Group for Contemporary Music (Benjamin Hudson, vln, Tobias Picker, pno). *Rec.*: Composers Recordings Inc. (Stereo LP) CRI SD 427. *Pub.*: European American.

"Tobias Picker's *Rhapsody*, for violin and piano, introduces a young composer who should be worth watching: a genuine creator, with a fertile, unforced vein of invention and the ability to hold one's attention on everything that he made happen. [It] has stood up well to further hearing." — Andrew Porter, in *The New Yorker*.[97]

---

[96] Reprinted in *Music of Three More Seasons, 1977-19080* (Alfred A. Knopf, 1981).
[97] Ibid.

MÁXIMO DIEGO PUJO

B. 1957 (Argentina).

Cinco [5] Preludios for Solo Guitar. *Publ.*: Australian Universal Edition (distr. European American Music; ed. John W. Duarte).

"It is a pleasure to experience South American guitar music which takes into consideration works by the likes of Barrios, Carlevaro, and Villa-Lobos without aping any of them. The preludes of Máximo Diego Pujol are refreshing and new-sounding—frequently changing in texture, yet always guitaristic. This young guitarist-composer works mainly in his native Argentine forms and rhythms, such as the *triste, tango,* and *candombe.* He at times combines two of these as in the third prelude *Tristango en vos.* However, these folk influences merely provide the composer with a framework to which he adds his own tonal but untraditional harmonic palette. The result is a delightful, accessible set of pieces which are only moderately difficult.

"Everything in the *Cinco preludios* lies well for the left hand. Fingerings are complete enough and well done [in the published score, which also includes] an explanatory table on the notation and brief remarks by Pujo himself regarding each prelude." —Michael Fink, in *Notes* (Music Library Association), 9/86.

ALFRED REED

B. 1921, New York NY. *Educ.:* Juilliard Schl, Baylor Univ. *Taught at:* Univ of Miami Schl of Music. Exec. ed., Hansen Publications. *Awards & grants incl.:* Luria Prize. *Works incl.: Armenian Dances,* concert overtures *(The Hounds of Spring, The Music-makers), Greensleeves* (fantasia), *Russian Christmas Music, Symphonic Prelude on "Black is the color of My True Love's Hair".*

A Festival Prelude for Symphonic Band. *Rec.:* Golden Crest Records (Stereo LP) ATH-5057: Michigan State Univ Symphonic Band.

¶For commentary, see *Symphony 2,* below — composer letter to critic Walter Simmons.

The Garden of Proserpine (symphonic pastorale) for Wind Band. 8m *Rec.:* Cornell Wind Ensemble Records (Stereo LP) CUWE-31: Cornell Univ Wind Ens, Alfred Reed, cond. *Pub.:* Piedmont (distr. Marks/Belwin)(concert band set; full score; condensed score; extra parts).

"Alfred Reed has more than 200 works published in all categories, with many fine examples in the medium of the symphonic and concert band. His music may be said to be very conservative and traditional. The other side of the coin, however, is that his music is always well crafted, melodic, solid, and immediately approachable by audience and performers alike. *The Garden of Proserpine* is a gently moving portrait of Proserpine, Roman counterpart of the Greek Persephone, who became associated with the unconscious world of sleep, goddess of peacefulness, quiet, slumber, and rest for the weary spirits of men. The work is in three-part ABA form, with the third part becoming a continuing development of the first. It is scored for full symphonic band, including English horn, contrabass clarinet, and harp. The gently undulating triplet figurations that weave around the main melodic line do much to keep the work moving, yet sustain the peaceful mood set by the poetic excerpt from Algernon Swinburne quoted at the head of the score. The reaction of this reviewer's own group upon reading through the work was immediate and heartfelt: let's play it at our next concert. (The full score is clear and understandable, and parts are cued for instruments that may be lacking so that bands with incomplete instrumentation may also enjoy performing this work.)" — Raoul F. Camus, in *Notes* (Music Library Association), 9/83.

Symphony 1 for Symphonic Band.16m *Rec.:* USC Sound Enterprises (Stereo LP) KM 4971: Tennessee Tech Symphonic Band, R. Winston Morris, cond.

Symphony 2 for Symphonic Band (1978). *Recs.:* Golden Crest Records (Stereo LP) ATH-5057: Michigan State Univ Symphonic Band, Kenneth G. Bloomquist, cond.; USC Sound Enterprises (Stereo LP) KM 4971: Tennessee Tech Symphonic Band, Alfred Reed, cond.

"Alfred Reed is one of America's most prolific and successful composers of music for the high school and college band, an immense but segregated musical sub-culure. With well over 200 works to his credit, his name is virutally unknown to most mainstream music lovers, even to those inclined toward the esoteric. The aetheticosociological aspects of American band music and the composers who write it comprise one more fascinating chapter in the denigration and neglect of our own serious musical culture.[98]

"Reed's *Symphony No. 2* is a thoroughly serious and instantly compelling work that makes a powerful and individual impression. Growing directly from the neo-romantic lineage of Giannini and Hanson, but darker and grimmer than the latter, the *Symphony* demonstrates how convincingly a fresh and personally-styled work can still be created from purely traditional materials. This new work, much more mature and sophisticated than Reed's *Symphony No. 1* for brass and percussion, is a real powerhouse progression from a grippingly funereal *passacaglia* to a wildly ferocious *tarantella* to a concluding hymn of resignation. While extremely consonant harmonically, the idiom is freely atonal, contributing to the restless intensity that permeates the work. The [recording] performance by the Michigan State University Symphonic Band is superb, offering the kind of rock-solid sonority and high-voltage virtuosity demanded by this kind of music." — Walter G. Simmons, in *Fanfare: The Magazine for Serious Record Collectors*, 1-2/79.

---

[98] A composer who remains popular with band and wind ensembles (with Frederick Fennell's wonderful Cleveland group, for example) but is less frequently performed by full orchestra is the Australian-born Percy Grainger, who lived and concertized in the United States from 1921 until his death in White Plains, New York in 1961. Since so many of Grainger's original compositions and his arrangements are equally short and sweet — and/or lively — they would contribute an interesting balance to either "pop" or more serious concert programs. A number of Grainger works (such as *"In a Nutshell" Suite, Lincolnshire Posy,* and *The Warriors* — this last performed by the Chicago SO at Orchestra Hall, 1/90) are more substantial. (Ed.)

LETTER FROM THE COMPOSER TO WALTER SIMMONS, PUBLISHED IN *FANFARE* 9-10/80:

"...You have raised certain issues and questions that I would dearly love to see argued in print—and as publicly as possible. For instance, in the review of my Golden Crest recording you state: 'The aesthetico-sociological aspects of American band music and the composers who write it comprise one more fascinating chapter in the denigration and neglect of our own serious musical culture.' I could not agree more, although perhaps not from precisely the same point of view. This prompts me to suggest to you that it is the 'band' (using the word generically, to include such diverse terms as 'concert band', 'symphonic band', 'wind ensemble', 'wind orchestra', etc.), rather than the traditional orchestra, that today provides the most widespread opportunities in the field of large-scale ensemble performance for both composers and performers in the country, and that this must, of necessity, be one of the strongest (if not *the* strongest) factors in the generating of both repertoire and audiences for the future. After all, consider that there are only about 1,400 orchestras in the country (*including* all high school, junior high school, college, and community groups—most of which cannot really perform too much of the standard repertoire too well) as against some 25,000 'bands' of every shape and size—some of whom don't do too well, either! Still, the disparity in numbers is formidable—particularly since it is here, I do believe, that despite the availability of fine recordings and playback equipment for listening to the standard orchestral and chamber-music works, the taste of a major portion of the next generation of listeners/supporters/audience in the area of large-scale ensemble music is being formed. Therefore, to refer to this area, as you did in the review, as a 'segregated musical subculture', is to raise a question of real moment indeed....

"I am certain you will agree when I say that, to the composer, a piece of music not performed might just as well not be written.... Performance is the name of the game; it has never been any different, is not today, and will not be tomorrow. Regardless of the length of hair of the work (if I may so put it), it is performance, again and again, and consequent acceptance (or rejection) of the work by the widest possible audience time and time again that ultimately counts in the final value judgment of the composer and the music, whether it is Beethoven or Berlin—at least in this country. Regardless of how any one of us feels about it, we have to be prepared to look this question squarely in the face and, in turn, face up to the only possible answer in a supposedly free, competitive society: If you are going to give people the right (among other rights) to read, see, and listen to what they please, are you prepared to put up with what they freely choose if what they choose does not happen to agree with your own taste and judgment?

"For myself, as a composer, it is somewhat ironic that I, who received the most stringent, classical upbringing (musically), to whom the 'band' didn't even exist prior to my receiving a letter from Uncle Sam beginning, 'Greetings!'... have become one of the leading contemporary composers of band music, with over 50 commissions to date and more on the way, and with more invitations to conduct my own music than I can possibly accept.

"No one knows better than I... that there are many mediocre talents, and even no-talents, on the conductor's stand (and at the writing desk), and whether it is the New York Philharmonic or the Podunk Junior High School Band, the whole validity of what is being done, musically, artistically, aesthetically, and otherwise, all hinges on the conductor's taste and ability.... But we must carry on despite all this and do our thing to the best of our ability, instead of sitting around and waiting for the millenium (which, especially in musical matters, seems to have a habit of never showing up) or wasting precious time and energy in decrying the state of things and trying to influence the audience by exhortation rather than example.

"So, what it comes down to, for me, at any rate, is that the opportunities for performances of large-scale instrumental ensemble music on a continuing basis lie with the wind orchestra rather than the traditional orchestra, and that from every other point of view: meeting audiences (especially the younger audiences who are the audiences of the future), publications, recordings, etc., any composer alive today who is either ignorant of this, or, having been made aware of this denies it on the grounds that it doesn't matter what those local yokels out there in the hinterlands are doing, is very effectively drawing a very sharp knife across his own throat, certainly in this country, even if every one of his works gets its three performacnes by the Boston Symphony or the New York Philharmonic. Strongly put, perhaps, but true to life and consistent with what is actually happening in this huge country.

"All of which brings me to, if I may, one of the five... works on the Crest Recording that you characterized as 'pretty pedestrian affairs (that) often verge on the idioms of the military march or the commercial arrangement,' *A Festival Prelude*. This has turned out to be one of the most frequently performed pieces in the entire modern repertoire (it has sold, according to my royalty statements from the publisher, over 12,000 *sets* to date, and with each set accounting for an average of seven performances, which is the accepted figure among publishing firms as a basis for such computations, has had well over 80,000 performances in the 19 years of its published life thus far) and has even been transcribed for orchestra, in which form it is also becoming a best-seller in sales and performances. This raises a fascinating point. Is a work to be down-rated just because it is almost entirely tonal in conception and has strong melodic lines? I think you will find that the workmanship and handling of materials in this score are on a par with that of the *Second Symphony*, and that the only real differences between them are the length, and therefore general structural organization of the textures, and the fact that the *Symphony* is so largely non-tonal. I do, of course, defend to the death your absolute right *not* to be impressed with anything that I or any other composer may write, but supposing that I myself were to agree with you, that compared to the *Second Symphony*, *A Festival Prelude* is of comparatively negligible musical value, what is there to be said? Perhaps what George Bernard Shaw said when he was called to the stage at the conclusion of the premiere performance of one of his early plays, and amid the general applause there was one loud and insistent 'boo'. Shaw turned towards the source of this dissatisfaction and called out, 'My dear fellow, I quite agree with you, but what are we two against so many?' But on the other hand, did not Beethoven once say, '*Vox populi, vox Dei*? That you will never get me to believe.' All in all, a fascinating question. Whose voice counts for what in such matters. Do *I* know, even for myself? But I am trying to find out, all the time....

"Need I add that none of the above is to be taken as an attack on your position or on yourself, but merely as a hopeful stimulus towards continuing examination of what has to be a crucial matter in the development of so-called serious music and audience generation in our time. Princes, kings, emperors, and, today, even government bodies and foundations cannot, in a free society, ever take the place of the audience. I would not wish to live and work in a society in which they ever do."

A DIALOGUE CONTINUES. "In the Letters section of *Fanfare* IV:1, Alfred Reed offered an eloquent and cogent plea on behalf of the legitimacy of the symphonic band and its more refined adjunct, the wind ensemble, as significant—indeed voracious—media for the representation of creative musical activity in our society today. [The recent appearance of a second recording of his *Symphony 2*, together with a performance of *Symphony 1*, gives one another opportunity to judge his own music in this sphere.]

"Reed's *Symphony No. 1* is a compact, 16-minute work for brass and percussion only. Generally traditional in style, its two outer movements are highly extroverted, and are scored to achieve effects of great brilliance and excitement. The opener is generally martial in character while the finale bristles with Latin rhythms. The slow movement is solemn and dramatic, offering the expected contrast. Imposing no unfulfilled pretensions, the symphony is a neat, efficient, and flashy showpiece....

"Reed's *Symphony No. 2* represents a considerable broadening and deepening of aesthetic concern in comparison with the earlier symphony. In reviewing the Golden Crest release I singled out this work for rather extravagant praise, which drew the aforementioned response from the composer... I might add that several of my associates, to whom I submitted Reed's *Second Symphony*, corroborated my general impression. And hearing this new recording only reinforces my conviction that it ranks, along with Persichetti's *Symphony No. 6* and Flagello's *Symphony No. 2*, among the finest American symphonies for winds. Far deeper in substance and more subtle in workmanship than Reed's [own] *Symphony No. 1*, the later work applies a Hindemithian clarity and objectivity to darkly powerful expressive content reminiscent of his teacher [Vittorio] Giannini, or Hanson. The result is a well-proportioned statement that is neither shallow nor obscure." — Walter Simmons, in *Fanfare: The Magazine for Serious Record Collectors*, 1-2/81.

JAY REISE

B. 1950. *Educ.:* Hamilton College, McGill Univ, Univ PA, Tanglewood. *Taught at:* Kirkland College, Hamilton College, Univ PA. NEA awards, Guggenheim Fellowship, Fromm Fndn and Koussevitzky Tanglewood Prize in Composition, Yaddo Fellowship. Composer-in-residence, Grand Teton Music Festival. *Works incl.: Bagatelles* (vln/pno), *Fantasy* (vc/pno), *Prelude* (strng orch), 2 string quartets, 3 symphonies, vocal works.

Composer statement: "It seems to me that the single greatest influence on our musical consciousness from the mid-century has to be the advance in media. This has enabled music to reach a mass audience. For the first time in history, the expressive symbols of several centuries of music have become a part of the mass culture. Composition up to the time of the post-war serialists involved the quest for a personal musical idiom or even language to establish artistic legitimacy. With the almost inevitable advent of atonality in the early part of the century, this trend resulted in increasingly limited musical symbols. *Angst* and alienation gained a death-grip on music, while such things as joy and nobility of spirit were impossible to express, and atonal humor was not able to be sustained.

"In my music, I have chosen to go the 'expressive route'. This involves willingly re-embracing the widely accepted symbols of tonality, and using them in the contexts of intense conflict with atonality, and irony. Expression of alienation cannot forever exclude the further experiences and expressions of joy and humor. Loss of innocence hopefully implies maturity rather than degredation; and so I strive for a fresh and original synthesis. In this post-Freudian age, we recognize the tremendous conflicts of violence and love present in our inner psyches; our contemporary world is one of both great barbarity and unprecedented human concern. This schizophrenia, which is responsible for both our triumph and our tragedy, can and should be expressed in our music."

Rasputin (opera)(1988). *Lib.:* composer. *Prem.:* New York City Opera, Christopher Keene, cond.
2 female solo, 7 male solo; chorus of servants, courtiers, peasants, revolutionaries
Act I. Scene 1: A cellar in Siberia; early twentieth century. Scene 2: A ballroom in the Winter Palace, St. Petersburg. Scene 3: Alexandra's boudoir. Scene 4: The boudoir, shortly thereafter. Act II. Prologue: A public place. Scene 1: A nightclub. Scene 2: A room in Rasputin's

apartment. Scene 3: A stateroom in the palace. Scene 4: A room in Yusupov's palace on the Neva River. Scene 5: The Assassination — 1918.

"The controversy [over the music and staging of Jay Reise's *Rasputin*] will linger, but one thing is clear: this new opera is a spellbinding, challenging and profoundly beautiful creation.

"The nudity and violence that upset some of the audience at Lincoln Center's New York State Theater were an integral part of a score whose seriousness and effectiveness are beyond question. The 38-year-old composer's first opera works.

"The beginning was striking. Out of the darkness were heard voices in chaos, shouting 'Where is he?' again and again. A shaft of light crashed in from upstage and the holy man was revealed. Rasputin slowly descended to the crowd — who were undressing by now — as icons rose from the ground and the music began. Huge throbbing orchestral gestures punctuated a wild orgy that left little to the imagination. This holy man, you see, preached that salvation can be reached only through mortal sin.

"Rasputin's peculiar theology changed a bit as the Siberian peasant learned the ways of power and came in touch with the Romanovs, Russia's last royal family. The opera describes his strange relation with Nicolas and Alexandra, and the role he played in bringing down an empire.

"In the devastating final scene, the 1918 murder of the royal family took place in full view of the audience. The lights went down as Lenin's words 'the bodies must pile high, the rivers must run red' blared from every corner of the theater and Bolshevik henchmen took aim at the audience.

"The libretto, by Mr. Reise and [director] Frank Corsaro, is concise and episodic. There is much to tell here as well as much that is left to the music. Mr. Reise's musical language is eclectic and conservative by today's standards. A brilliant orchestrator, he obtained myriad colors from forces that surrounded and supported flattering vocal lines. His frequent atonalism is of the Bergian variety — longing for a lost romanticism. Like Giuseppe Sinopoli's recent *Lou Salome*, *Rasputin* also has whole stretches of vocal music that would not be out of place in a score by Korngold.

"The lyricism of the scene when the two monarchs hold up their newborn boy, and the horror of the baby's sudden hemophiliac bleeding, are mirrored in striking musical invention.

"Tchaikovsky's 'Waltz' from Act I of *Swan Lake* is sent up and fractured in the first scene of the Russian court. A hysterical drag cabaret song for Prince Yusupov was followed by the suicide of Yusupov's friend. In one of the few instances in which the opera departed from history, the motivation for his murder of Rasputin became clear. The musical textures varied from lush to rough and arid, but all were cut from one distinctive cloth.

"[Bass-baritone] John Cheek was a mesmerizing Rasputin, filling out the demanding role with a column of dark sounds. His muscular presence made the holy man's sensuality palpable. As Yusupov, Henry Price camped it up shamelessly in the best Marlene Dietrich drag since Helmut Berger. The tenor also sang in glorious voice and created a complex character with superb economy of means. Christopher Keene led the whole affair with obvious commitment to the music and awesome control over the vast forces." — Octavio Roca, in *The Washington Times*, 9/19/88.

"Historical context is suggested musically in several ways. For a royal ball scene, there's a shrewd distortion of the first of the many waltzes in Tchaikovsky's *Swan Lake*. Violent cross-rhythms remindful of Stravinsky's *Rite of Spring* (1913) serve for an orchestral interlude depicting the growing revolution. Massive choral-orchestral utterances manage to avoid imitating either Mussorgsky or Shostakovich, although the latter's operatic style is quite naturally not far from Reise's. The score as a whole thus gives you a variety of weight and style that keeps the ear alert from scene to scene." — Leighton Kerner, *The Village Voice*, 10/4/88.

"[This] opera about the power-worshipping monk who advised the last Tsarist family in Russia leaves one with a greater sense of its unity than any new opera we've attended in years. It isn't simplistic but a listener feels able to grasp the plot and the music....

"The staging, by Frank Corsaro, is direct and powerful. The nightclub scene in which [Henry] Price's character, Prince Felix Yusupov, sings that he's 'Bebe d'Amour' is meant to indicate a decadent society just before it falls.

"There is wonderful use of stylized staging. Erick Avari, in a non-singing role as Lenin, gives a speech behind a brightly lighted, transparent screen. His profile and listeners facing him from across the stage are silhouetted. There are silhouettes from time to time throughout the opera. In one scene, silhouetted couples dance at stage rear establishing a ballroom setting and allowing major characters uncluttered use of the stage front.

"This uncluttered staging looks more German expressionistic than Russian but it suits the opera." — Mary Campbell, *Associated Press (AP)*, 9/18/88.

"FROM CLASSES IN PHILADELPHIA TO A PREMIERE IN NEW YORK. Reise teaches two days a week at [the University of Pennsylvania], in his first-floor office. Its glaring yellow brick walls are relieved only by a broken thermostat that is plugged up with paper towels. His archaic Hermes Rocket manual typewriter might be worth something—in a couple of years, as an antique—and there is a huge and ugly fan that, he says, throws mustard gas and makes coffee.

"Reise doesn't compose there, however—life at home is much more conducive to creativity. He lives in Swarthmore with his wife and their two children. It is a comfortable Victorian place, piled high with old 78 rpm photograph records, children's wind-up toys and books reflecting Reise's reading binges—Proust and Beckett, Walt Whitman, and Lewis Carroll. He reads in one area—like philosophy or history—for a year or two, then moves on to another.

"He composes almost all day, every day, except on the two days a week he's teaching; often he has middle-of-the-night spells of creativity as well. In the less than two decades he has been composing, Reise has produced a lot—some three dozen works. The breadth, too, is impressive: from preludes, caprices and an 'imaginary ballet' to string quartets and symphonies. His work has been praised by critics for its 'exceptional stylistic assurance,' 'deeply felt lyrical strain' and 'rare balance between accessibility and complexity.' You hear the word 'eclectic' often in connection with Reise's music, meaning that you can't categorize him as a 'post-Romantic' composer or any of the other easy pigeonholes. The style grows out of the material....

"Composer Reise remains buoyantly enthusiastic about [*Rasputin*] and claims he enjoyed opening night from beginning to end. That end was very late, for after the opera was over Reise, his wife, conductor Keene and some 60 friends took off for the Troika Restaurant, a few blocks from the New York State Theater. Here they had a private party with blini and gypsy violin music. After about the tenth rendition of '*Ochi Chernye* (Dark Eyes)', Dick Wernick [also one of America's most important composers of serious music, who, with Reise and their fellow composer George Crumb, is also a member of the University of Pennsylvania's music department,] decided it was time for a toast.

" 'Fifteen years ago, after first meeting Jay Reise,' he said, raising his glass to the composer, 'I came home to my wife Bea, and I told her, 'I think the university caught a big fish.' Tonight I *know* we did.' " —Diana Burgwyn, in *Philadelphia*, 11/88.

* * *

"PUTTING ON *RASPUTIN*: It is the first day of staging rehearsals for Jay Reise's new opera *Rasputin*. In a New York City Opera basement rehearsal room, Frank Corsaro, the director, finishes blocking the first orgy scene (there are two), minus the chorus and supers who will supply writhing, naked flesh and simulated copulation. 'It's going to be a melee at the end,' the director cheerfully tells the cast. To John Cheek, the bass who sings the title role, he says, 'Let's change that last word, "Rise," to "Chr-i-i-st,"' dragging out the vowel. 'It's much more sexual.'

"Then the rehearsal moves on to Scene Two, which opens with a fractured, drooping version of the big waltz from *Swan Lake*. Two men in military uniform dance formally together, carrying on a sardonic, bitchy conversation. 'The waltz should be bent,' Mr. Corsaro calls to the pianist. 'Ground into the ground. Like they're already dead.'

"The 38-year-old composer looks on with interest, ready to change a line or offer an opinion. *Rasputin*, which opens on Saturday evening [September 17, 1988], is his first opera, but the process of getting it on stage seems to hold little terror for him. He has already been working with Mr. Corsaro for several years on the shaping of the libretto, paring down volumes of history—the collapse of the Romanov dynasty, the Russian Revolution—into a tight, hallucinatory sequence of events.

"Mr. Corsaro plans to go all out to depict the decadence and unraveling of the society. 'We mean business,' the director says, dismissing the usual American treatment of operatic sex scenes as 'body-stocking orgies'. 'You have to. Anything less is really pandering. When people do that, it's more debauched than anything you put on stage.'

"For both the composer and the director, this combination of high tension and explicitness is part of what makes the opera contemporary. Mr. Reise chose a cataclysmic moment of the 20th century—the events culminating in the assassination of the highly placed Russian monk Rasputin in December 1916—for a purely theatrical reason. 'It was the death scene that grabbed me,' he says. 'You know how in opera the singer is always getting up and singing again as he's dying? With Rasputin, that really happened. They kept poisoning him, shooting him, and he kept rising up again.' Rasputin also seemed a perfect, larger-than-life operatic character in the traditional mold. Yet Mr. Reise's working-out of this material is unlikely to remind audiences of 19th-century spectacles.

"For one thing, the opera has no heroes. 'It's like a lot of 20th-century novels, where everybody is, at best, neutral,' says the composer, who lists William Gass, Samuel Becket, Gabriel Garcia Marquez and

New York City Opera production—*Rasputin*.
Photo by Carol Rosegg / Martha Swope Associates.

Marcel Proust among his favorite writers. In Mr. Reise's broadly historical portrayal, Rasputin, a Siberian peasant, gains control of Czarina Alexandra by stemming the bleeding of her hemophiliac child. To the decadent Russian aristocracy, Rasputin preaches—and practices—a doctrine of salvation through sexual license. Czar Nicholas is powerless. Prince Felix Yusupov, who murders Rasputin, is not a simple patriot, but a bored, bisexual aristocrat who does a drag-queen number in a private nightclub and is fascinated by the monk. Lenin, who delivers a rabble-rousing speech, is a tyrant in the making.

" 'Generally, there's no release,' Mr. Reise says. 'That's one of the things that's very contemporary about the piece: its pacing and sense of drive are relentless. Even with the lushest, most romantic E-flat-major music, it never seems real, never seems that you've reached the oasis, the symphonic slow movement where you can relax. Even in those passages—such as the big duet in the second act, where Nicholas is so spaced out that he doesn't know what's going on—there's a sense that they're doomed, surrounded by disaster. You know that this is not some point of stability, but an illusion.

"Mr. Reise found a musical equivalent of this historical chaos that comported with his own compositional philosophy. 'I'm influenced by all facets of 20th-century music, and my composition has been highly eclectic,' he says. 'I'm very interested in all of the clashes that occurred in this century, and that continue to occur. Here you have a sectarian monk with old ideas, coming into a monarchy that is rotten to the core, overripe, ready to fall off the tree. And yet you've got the 20th century, with its airplanes and telephones, so you end up with the clash of two different periods. What I do in the opera is make an analogy, a metaphor in the music, giving the Romanovs very tonal-sounding Russian music, and juxtaposing that against the angst-ridden, atonal, violent kind of music characteristic of Serialism and beyond.'

"Writing an opera, the composer found, made special demands that no single school of composition could fulfill to his satisfaction. 'One thing I'm trying to do is provide emotional contrast. The styles Schoenberg and Berg developed tend to limit the kind of expression possible. You don't find in *Wozzeck* and *Lulu* the kind of free joy that you find in Mozart. That's why I incorporate all the available musical symbols that we already know. Major and minor scales, for example, tell people a lot about what's going on.'

"*Rasputin*, Mr. Reise says, is much more tonal than his instrumental works. 'To have Rasputin singing Serial music with Alexandra, when they're basically singing love music—it just doesn't gel.'

"Christopher Keene, the music director of City Opera from 1982 to 1986, first brought Mr. Reise to the attention of Beverly Sills. 'Beverly and I were trying to put a program in place whereby we would commission a work or present a New York premiere every year,' says Mr. Keene, who will conduct *Rasputin*. 'I think that's what we're here for—to give talented composers a chance to grow.'

* * *

"Mr. Keene was the music director of the Syracuse Symphony when he met Mr. Reise, who was then teaching at Hamilton College, in Clinton, N.Y. (he is now at the University of Pennsylvania). The conductor commissioned and introduced two of Mr. Reise's symphonies—the *Second* with the Syracuse Symphony (he repeated it with the Philadelphia Orchestra), the *Third* with the Long Island Philharmonic. When the composer broached the idea for *Rasputin*, Mr. Keene was interested, and he wasn't particularly worried about Mr. Reise's inexperience in opera.

" 'He's a superb orchestrator, so he commands the whole palette of theatrical possibilities,' Mr. Keene says. 'His kind of ecstatic lyric gift is just what we need in operatic writing. And he has an amazing intellect; he is alive at once to the dramatic possibilities and the black humor. The subject is half terrifying and half hilariously funny because of the absolute insanity that was going on at the highest level of the Russian government. One of the most important powers in the world was being run in a vacuum by charlatans, madmen, transvestites. I thought Jay had the intellect to put together a work that would be challenging and fun to work with.'

* * *

"To the extent that Mr. Reise's style recalls any earlier composer's, Mr. Keene says, it is Berg's, at least in the lyric sections. Mr. Keene, who has conducted many new operas, finds that *Rasputin* works well. 'He's written big, marvelous roles—Rasputin, the Empress and Yusupov are extraordinary parts. And this isn't the donkey-bray school of modern vocal music. The cast has enjoyed working on it, which is very important. When you have a bunch of disgruntled singers who hate their parts, it's difficult to get much of a performance out of them.'

"Three years in the works, the opera went through numerous revisions. First came the construction of the libretto, which Mr. Reise decided to write himself. Increasingly consumed with Romanov lore, Mr. Reise and Mr. Corsaro read everying they could about the period. Either can pontificate on the subject at the drop of a hat—

one rehearsal ended with a discussion about new evidence on the fate of the royal family.

"Such catholicity has its dangers. 'The temptation with material like this is to pile it all in, all your book learning,' says Mr. Corsaro. 'But you've got to compress it, throw history out and reinvent it for yourself. In reinvention you're creating the atmosphere, condensing and projecting events. Essentially, the composer has to deal with events that are nonfactual. Facts don't sing.'

* * *

"To make it theater, Mr. Reise collapsed the time span of events from 20 years to about 2, tooks some historical license (the Czarevich is an infant rather than a young boy) and invented a character who would provide motivation for Yusupov's murder of Rasputin ('what really does trigger him is not operatic,' says Mr. Corsaro).

"The music, too, went through several versions. 'He totally revised the full score,' says Mr. Keene. 'I had to replace all my markings.'

"The changes continued during the rehearsal period. Some of the Czarina's '300 high Cs' were adjusted, Mr. Keene says, as was the orchestration. During the waltz scene, lines of dialogue were cut, words changed, emphases altered. Contrary to the stereotype of the adamant composer, Mr. Reise has no objection to making changes. 'There's been a sense of exactness in contempory music that was beneficial in some ways, but a kind of preciosity went with it,' he says; 'I'm looking for what's going to be most effective.' Mr. Corsaro adds, 'Nothing is done until it's done on stage. I don't care what playwrights or composers have in their heads. No one is that clairvoyant.'

* * *

"Mr. Corsaro hopes to capture the piece's hallucinatory mood through stylized direction ('like Eisenstein films, historical tableaux'), ghostly lighting, larger-than-life gestures, and of course, sex and violence. 'I want the audience to be aghast with excitement,' he says. 'There is a ferocious excitement in all of these events, in their awful, diabolic, sado-masochistic way. Unless you feel that excitement, fear, even sort of prurient fascination, you're not getting the point. Because of these elements, that country fell apart.'...

"Mr. Reise would like to write an opera about another kind of 20th-century antihero, a 'truly likeable' character who is a victim of circumstance. *Rasputin*, he says, 'is a myth, a fairy tale. An adult fairy tale. Frank will make sure its adult.' " — Heidi Waleson, *The New York Times*, Sep 11 1988, II p.29.

Symphony 2 for Orchestra (1981). 20m *Ded. & prem.:* Syracuse (NY) SO, Christopher Keene, cond. *Other perf.:* Philadelphia O, Christopher Keene, cond.
1. *Prelude.* 2. *Aria.*

"Jay Reise's gripping *Symphony No. 2* is a twenty-minute work for very large orchestra incorporating both tonality and what the composer calls 'the searing gestures of post-Webern serialism.' That combination may be common these days [1981], but this score is far more compelling than most comparable works. First, Reise—a composer as attuned to Fauré and Rachmaninoff as to Boulez—has a deeply felt lyrical strain; few contemporary composers could match the bittersweet melancholy of his rich string outpourings. Second, although it is an expansive work (tempos are often slow, ideas develop over broad spans), every note tells. The structure is tight (a short *Prelude* in sonata form, followed by an *Aria* with variations uniting slow and fast movements in the manner of Beethoven's Op. 111); and the transitions are paced so that the climaxes seem inevitable—cataclysmic rather than merely brutal.

"Most important, Reise has achieved a rare balance between accessiblity and complexity. As the warm audience response [at the Syracuse Symphony Orchestra premiere] demonstrated, *Symphony No. 2* hits hard. Yet each rehearing yields a deeper appreciation of the dense counterpoint, the metric modulations, and the intricate motivic interrelationships: this is music whose beauties go well beneath the surface." — Peter J. Rabinowitz, in *Musical America*, 3/81.

"The Reise *Symphony No. 2* is a two-movement work for large orchestra, which uses large forces for lucid expression. The music makes its point through instrumental clarity, rather than through masses of sound, and it draws the boundaries of its expression by use of melodic lines, an instrumental aria. That is not a 'old-fashioned' device, but a highly workable one since it leaves listeners satisfied at the completeness of the music.

"It is also music for a virtuoso orchestra, almost a concerto, which gives the solo violin, oboe, cello and the brass players star roles. Any such concerto is bound to evoke the ways other composers have celebrated the orchestra. Reise finds some echoes in his, and there are sections that point to this as the logical next step after Ravel's *Daphnis and Chloe.*

"But a very long step. Reise keeps in reserve resources for two immense climaxes and, in the second movement, one cascade of sound that starts in the high register and plunges into the bass in a gesture that is pure celebration of orchestral sound and done with winning high spirit.

"His music has a way of claiming kinship with that of other writers without quoting them. His symphony takes its place in the grand march of music but without surrendering personality or contemporaneity." — Daniel Webster, in *The Philadelphia Inquirer*, 10/20/84.

"Reise's background includes study with master jazz pianist Jimmy Giuffre. His catalogue includes jazz compositions, and his view of symphonic music is anything but that of the elitist. He is part of a generation of composers trying to heal the breach between composer and listener, a gap that opened in the 1950s and 60s.

" 'I don't think this is the age of the new romanticism,' he says with characteristic vigor. 'It's the age of new emotionalism. At least, that's what I'm trying for with the gestures I use.'

"Emotion in music is difficult to define or to manufacture, but composers agree that music somehow can define emotion, stir emotion and express emotion as no other art can hope to do. That's the quarry; the pursuit is the lifetime's involvement.

"The means of writing in the age of the new emotionalism are without limits, Reise says. His *Symphony No. 2* incorporates serial writing, harmonic events, soaring melodies for oboe, trumpet and cello, and allusions to music by other composers. 'For people who say they recognize influences in my music, I acknowledge them all: Ravel, Tchaikovsky, Brahms, Rochberg — even the composers I don't know. I don't believe any music comes from space. We are all influenced by what we know and have heard.'

"Reise has patterned his symphony after Beethoven's *Piano Sonata (Op. 111)*, a work in two movements, with the larger second movement being a set of variations on a theme that makes an early appearance in the first movement. The form is both homage and a practical recognition that Beethoven had hit on something that has application today. Reise does not insist that his listeners know or care about that use of an older form; the choice, however, provided him with the means of writing the work.

"Beethoven had his own models, and, working with a tonal system of music, had a clear view of the way to form his music. It had to do with progress from one key to related keys and eventually back to the original key. That process is not so clear today. 'The big problem we face,' Reise says, 'is finding the way to develop those tensions in our music which can give the music form.'

"Reise struggles with that reality every day [not only as a composer but also] in his role as teacher of composition at the University of Pennsylvania....

"Reise's inclination toward the operatic gesture in his music has made him eager to try his hand at composing opera.

" 'I have a couple of ideas now [1984],' he says enthusiastically. 'Rasputin is one, but George Rochberg suggested that, and I have to talk to him to know if he actually wanted to use it. I've [also] been thinking about an opera about the castrati (the male sopranos who were the superstars of the 17th- and 18th-century opera). That would be an opera about music-making, a little like *Die Meistersinger*, and would open itself to references to music from other eras. I've started my libretto.' " — Daniel Webster, in *The Philadelphia Inquirer*, 1984.

SILVESTRE REVUELTAS

B. 1899, Santiago Papasquiaro, Durango (Mexico); d. 1940, Mexico City (Mexico). *Educ.:* Juárez Inst, St. Edwards Coll, Chicago Musical Coll. *Taught at:* Mexico Cons. Asst. cond, Mexico SO. *Works incl.:* string quartets, orchestral pieces *(Colorines, Cuauhnahuac, Esquinas, Ventanas, Redes), El Renacuajo paseador* (ballet)

COMMENTARY: "Europe has often produced composers like the late Silvestre Revueltas, the Americas rarely. Our music writers are most likely to do the light touch with a heavy hand. Revueltas's music reminds one of Erik Satie's and of Emmanuel Chabrier's. It is both racy and distinguished. Familiar in style and full of references to Hispanic musical formulas, it seeks not to impress folklorists nor to please audiences by salting up a work with nationalist material. Neither does it make any pretense of going native. He wrote Mexican music that sounds like Spanish Mexico, and he wrote it in the best Parisian syntax. No Indians around and no illiteracy.

"The model is a familiar one of the nationalist composer whose compositional procedures are conservative and unoriginal but whose musical material consists of all the rarest and most beautiful melodies that grow in his land. Villa-Lobos is like that and Percy Grainger; so was Dvorák. The contraries of that model are Josef Haydn and Satie and a little bit Georges Auric — certainly Darius Milhaud. These writers use the vernacular for its expressivity. But their musical structure and syntax are of the most elegant. Their music, in consequence, has an international carrying power among all who love truly imaginative musical construction.

"Revueltas's music could never be mistaken for French music. It is none the less made with French post-Impressionist technique, amplified and adapted to his own clime. It is static harmonically, generously flowing melodically, piquant and dainty in instrumentation, daring as to rhythm. He loves ostinato accompanying figures and carries them on longer than a more timid writer would. He orchestrates à la Satie, without doubling. He fears neither unexpected rhythmic contrasts nor familiar melodic turns. His music has grace, grandeur, delicacy, charm, and enormous distinction." — Virgil Thomson (1941), reprinted in *A Virgil Thomson Reader* (Houghton Mifflin Company, 1981).

La noche de los mayas [The Night of the Mayas] for Orchestra
(1939 film score arr. 1960 for concert perf. by José Ives Limantour). 31m *Perf.:* Compton (CA) SO, Hans Lampl, cond.; Orquesta

Filarmónica de la Ciudad de México, Fernando Lozano, cond. *Recs.*: Desto (Stereo LP) DC 7215: Orquesta Filarmónica de la Ciudad de México, Fernando Lozano, cond.; Musart (LP) EMCD 3022: Guadalajara SO, José Limantour, cond.; Mexican RCA (LP) MRS.021: Xalapa SO, Luis Herrera de la Fuente, cond.; Angel EMI (CD) CDC 49785: Orquesta Filarmónica de la Ciudad de México, Enrique Bátiz, cond. *Pub.*: Southern Music.

1. *Noche de los mayas [Night of the Mayas]* (Molto sostenuto). 2. *Noche de jarana [Night of the Jaranas (Night of Merrymaking)]* (Scherzo). 3. *Noche de Yucatán* (Andante espressivo). 4. *Noche de encantimiento [Night of Enchantment]*.

"The music of Revueltas is a glory of his nation beyond any by a contemporary or successor to date: the equivalent in sound of canvases and murals by Diego Rivera or José Clemente Orozco.... The four movements [of the *Noche de los mayas* suite] incorporate music of the pre-Colombians, the Mestizo and Creole cultures, and Mexico's Afro-West Indian 'tropicals', so-called.... " — Roger Dettmer, in *Fanfare: The Magazine for Serious Record Collectors*, 9-10/82.

"A number of years ago, the Viennese-born conductor Hans Lampl, then conductor of California's Compton Symphony Orchestra, ran across [Revueltas' incomparable music to the film *La noche de los mayas*] and programmed it. The audience response was so overwhelming that he and the orchestra had to schedule an impromptu repeat of the concert the following week. Since the work is a born crowd-pleaser, it is doubly strange how little opportunity it has had to impact on Northern audiences — in spite of the fact that there are now *four* recordings of it (only two of them, however, have ever been available in the United States). Anyone who is Mexican and who knows anything about contemporary concert music already looks upon this piece as a classic. Beyond Lampl's performances, the music has been played once at the United Nations and has been broadcast on American television by the Orquesta Filarmónica de la Ciudad de México under Fernando Lozano, who has also made one of the recordings of the score....

"The man responsible for arranging the score for concert performance, the Mexican conductor and musicologist José Limantour (b.1919), also made the first recording of the music, about which more later. The music comes from 36 cues that Revueltas wrote in 1939 — the last year of his life and the same year that produced his masterpiece, *Sensemayá* — for a film directed by Chano Ureta with a script by Antonio Médiz Bolio. Limantour juxtaposed these cues in a most imaginative way. *La noche de los mayas* still sounds like film music — which is what it is and will always rightly be — but it moves extremely spontaneously and naturally from one episode to the next. Few have ever seen the original cues, and I cannot believe that Limantour did not, properly, engage in some out-and-out composition here and there in order to make things work as well as they do.

"The music is simpler in line and texture than *Sensemayá*. As always with Revueltas, there is very little padding. Every gesture is exposed—and every gesture works....

"The writer [of the liner notes for the Lozano and Herrera de la Fuente LPs, José Antonio Álcaraz,] properly compares this music to the frescos by such painters as Rivera, Orozco, and Siqueiros (and Revueltas' own brother, Fermín, who, according to Robert Stevenson in *Grove*, painted 'bold simplistic designs limned in bright colors")—murals that adorn so many Mexican walls and buildings. Revueltas paints in broad strokes, too, and each idea is so true and borne straight from the heart that it cannot fail to touch the listener. The lyrical parts—much music in thirds in the Mexican manner—contain harmonies that have totally personal and original twists to them. At first hearing, they surprise, but they make sense, and they make us want to hear them happen again.

"The opening movement (also called *"Noche de los mayas"*) is title music in the grand manner. It used to be played through loudspeakers to introduce audiences to the Tiffany glass curtain in Mexico City's Palacio de Belles Artes, which depicts a grand Mexican landscape. Perhaps it still is. I have never seen the film, but the music seems to suit such a scene.

"The following scherzo, *"Noche de jarana"* ("Night of Merrymaking"), mostly in 5/8 time, is the trickiest and most sophisticated of the movements. It obviously is meant to accompany a folk-festival scene, and it reflects a great enjoyment of such goings-on. It has some wonderful tunes for the brass, in particular certain life-threatening moments for high horns that could devastatingly change the course of any horn player's career—but they are worth the risk.

"Both in this movement and in the next, *"Noche de Yucatán"*, where the lyricism is the simplest, there are wonderful passages for the tuba, an instrument that Revueltas understood completely and for which he had great affection. More than once he leaves the instrument alone, at the bottom of the texture, in sole support of the orchestra. It is at moments like these that the tuba is given those especially telling intervals—often, touchingly simple descending chromatic halfsteps—that hit just right and against which there is no defense. The tuba, by the way, is often the concertmaster in the excellent Sinaloese brass band one finds everywhere in Mazatlán. In Revueltas, too, the tuba player is given his dignity, in the most sensitive passages imaginable—and in the most droll. For one, listen to the lyrical section closing the third movement. For the other, listen to the very end of the second movement—the very last note.

"But the Devil is here, too, worming his way into Revueltas. The story has yet to be told about this composer, an alcoholic at times violently out of control, and one who could have the darkest and most convoluted of visions. In the final movement, *"Noche de encantimiento"* ("Night of Enchantment"), a monster percussion section erupts, attendant upon a sacrificial ritual involving the whole orchestra in a series of gargantuan and dissonant explosions, each one more terrifying than the last. Once this section has begun, it is time to abandon all hope. And, yet, of course, it is this section that is the most fun for live audiences and for the ambitious audiophile who is willing to risk the fury of landlords and neighbors. At the very end, the grand opening title music returns, welded together with the hellish percussion music. Crude—and monstrously effective."—William Malloch, in *Musical America*, 1/90.

"In this work, the composer has recovered and combined various tendencies which contribute to nourish the vital roots of Mexican folklore, particularly from the point of view of expressiveness and essential meaning. Revueltas knew how to create, unfold and typify sonorous actions endowed with aspects which at the same time are *pre-Columbian* (utilization of a Maya melody in the third movement and the use of big sonorous conches in the final section), *Mestizo* (in the *'jarana'*, which is a dance expressing Spanish reminiscences but is tinged and animated by melodic passages, turns of feeling and local instruments), *Creole* (in the second movement, through the use of the rhythmic construction of the most well-known Mexican forms of strophic songs, because, although these forms have Spanish origins, they were created during the colonial period in the region which is Mexican today), and even *tropical* (in its incisive compulsiveness which takes on an Afro-West Indian contour in the final movement). In addition, in the first part of the score, the composer dramatically throws into relief purely imagined archaeological forms.

"The link between these different expressions is naturally Revueltas' warm, exuberant and incredible inventiveness. At the same time he is capable of elaborating and producing passages of delicate sensitivity which combine with melodramatic, heart-rending atmospheres. There are also kinds of musical interjections which are sometimes rasping and at other times joyful, as well as broad sequences of great purity which do not abandon, for all that, the dazzling colors of popular gaiety.

"In the sphere of colors, his character blends those of Mussorgsky and Mahler, as René Leibowitz so pertinently remarked....

"[Some additional notes on the individual movements:]

"1. *The Night of the Mayas:* structured exposition and basis from the music orginally written for the film.

"2. *The Night of the 'Jaranas':* a lively and refreshing scherzo in which the character of the popular dances is just as obvious as successful.

"3. *The Night of Yucatán:* an expressive nucleus which at the same time achieves a contrast with the preceding and following movements through its idyllic atmosphere. The flute solo which brings out the native people's traditional song: *'Konex Konex Palexén'* ('Come on, come on boys, the sun is about to set') constitutes the essential part of this movement which is connected with the fourth without interruption.

"4. *The Night of Sorcery:* pre-eminently magical music of which the nature and character are magnificently delineated by Revueltas through the obsessive, rhythmic reiteration, characteristic of pre-Columbian rituals.

"The final result, which is both nationalist and modern, tempts one to consider *La Noche de los Mayas* as the musical equivalent of the great Mexican frescoes: assertive, socio-aesthetic customs; subjugating plasticity indissolubly interwoven with a certain Brechtian dialectic spirit—as shown in the ethnic-artistic expression—the obvious result of the Mexican Revolution of 1910 as the product of a living and dynamic culture which does not disregard contradiction, antagonism or heterogeneity as constituent elements which are even modular."—José Antonio Alcaraz (transl. by David Giles), from program notes for Desto DC 7215 recording.

Sensemayá for Voice and Orchestra (1939). Recs.: CBS: orch. cond. by Leonard Bernstein; RCA Red Seal (LP) ARL 1-2320: New Philharmonia O., Eduardo Mata, cond.; Varèse-Sarabande (Digital Stereo LP) VCDM 1000.220: Orquesta Sinfonica del Estado de México, Enrique Bátiz, cond.; Vox Cum Laude (LP) D-VCL 9033: Xalapa SO, Luis Herrera de la Fuente, cond.; Desto (Stereo LP) DC 7218: Orquesta Filarmónica de la Ciudad de México, Fernando Lozano, cond.

"Had it not been for his death at age 40, [Revueltas] might have been acclaimed Mexico's most celebrated and influential composer. Although the roots of *Sensemayá* are Afro-Cuban, his idiom is powerfully and inimitably Mexican, and beyond that eminently individualistic."—Roger Dettmer, in *Fanfare: The Magazine for Serious Record Collectors,* 3-4/82.

"Besides their ethnic significance, [pieces by Revueltas] are individual, exotic, and often melodramatically powerful — for example, the relatively familiar *Sensemayá (Chant to Kill a Snake)*." — R. D. Darrell, in *High Fidelity*, 9/78.

ROGER REYNOLDS

B. 1934, Detroit MI. *Educ.:* Univ of MI. Taught at: Univ of CA (San Diego), Yale Univ, Brooklyn Coll, Amherst Coll, Univ of IL. *Awards & grants:* Guggenheim, Rockefeller, Ford, Natl Inst Arts/Ltrs, 1989 Pulitzer Prize. Board member, American Music Ctr, Meet the Composr, Composers' Forum. *Author of: Mind Models; A Searcher's Path; A Composer's Ways. Works incl.:* chamber (*Ambages, Coconino... a shattered landscape, Dionyus, Fantasy for Pianist, Gathering, Less than Two, Mosaic, Personae, The Promises of Darkness, Shadowed Narrative, Transfigured Wind III, Traces*), choral (*Blind Men, Masks*), orchestral (*Dream of the Infinite Rooms, Fiery Wind, Graffiti, Symphony [Vertigo], Threshhold, Wedge*), stage (*The Emperor of Ice Cream, The Tempest* [tape], vocal (*Again, Compass, The Palace*).

Composer statement: "Music involves the application of the composer's ear and mind to the uses of sound. Sometimes the ear leads, at others the mind (or heart), but for me the world of possibly interesting engagements is a very large one. My output is not as varied as it is because I try to be different but because there seem to me so many interesting occasions on which and ways in which to engage things musical. In an era when musical language is itself so varied, so lacking in common practices, the composer has a freer hand. The reciprocal reality is that there is even more than normally the obligation to be consistent and thorough in devising the materials and methods that one uses within a particular composition. Thus, composers now are in a state which entails both extra-ordinary latitude for our work, and at the same time an unusually urgent obligation to consider each element in the making of a piece using always the total resources of mind and spirit."

Additional comments: Embodying a distinctive blend of art and science which seems appropriate to our times, Roger Reynolds' music expresses that spirit of adventure and openness to new modes which characterizes much of contemporary music. For example, the composer has been a leader in combining live and computer-processed vocal and instrumental lines, and in mixing quadraphonic tape and concert performance to produce a music which surrounds the audience with larger-than-life sonic impressions. He has characterized his creative goal as the fusion of musical structure, language and movement—an effort to extend the scope of musical composition toward theater but without sacrificing its own integrity. He writes: "I am a dedicated polyglot... but it is important to me to maintain a concern with vivid, luminous moments and with a strongly integrated overall structure." Alan Rich wrote in *New York Magazine*: "At UCSD [University of California at San Diego] Roger Reynolds continues to produce a dynamic, tense music whose form seems to derive from unwritten poetry... O Brave, new, noisy world!" Leighton Kerner, surveying Reynolds' career in *The Village Voice*, observed that "[his] sophistication as a composer, orchestrator, manipulator of electronic equipment constructs musical metaphors in space that's sometimes fixed, sometimes shifting around the listener—music that moves physically as well as emotionally and intellectually."

American music historian Gilbert Chase adds: "It would be a mistake to assume that avant-garde composers such as Roger Reynolds necessarily repudiate the music of the past. Although they are working in a different socio-cultural and scientific-technological environment, they find elements of continuity and individual affinity in certain of their predecessors. For example, the overall shape of time could be plotted by the sequence: rebellion—innovation—acceptance. As expressed by Reynolds: 'Each generation of initially frightening innovations in art is soon proved docile.' Does this 'docility' seem like an anticlimax? Is it a let-down to pass from the frightening to the tamed? Not necessarily; many of the great masterpieces of music that we cherish have gone through that process: familiary has bred acceptance. Now we are faced with any and all the sounds from our total sonic environment as possible components of musical composition. To what extent they will prove to be docile remains a fascinating question for the future.

"Of one thing we can be certain: Roger Reynolds will be a leading participant in the search for meaningful new forms of musical experience."[99]

Quick Are the Mouths of Earth for Chamber Ensemble (13 players) (1964-65). 18m *Prem.*: Contemporary Chamber Ens, Arthur Weisberg, cond. *Rec.*: Nonesuch H-71219: Contemporary Chamber Ens, Arthur Weisberg, cond. *Pub.*: C. F. Peters (score).
3 (3 pic)-1-0-0; 0-1-1-1 b trb; perc (2), pno; 3 vc
In six sections.

" 'Quick are the mouths of earth, and quick the teeth that feed upon this loveliness...' is a quote from Thomas Wolfe that intrigued Roger Reynolds and which, in his own words, 'had the capacity of generating musical images for me.' The work is divided into six sections, each

---

[99] "Additional comments" adapted from Don Gillespie, ed., *Roger Reynolds: Profile of a Composer* (C. F. Peters, 1982), and other sources. (Ed.)

subdivided into six parts which are in turn further subdivided according to a system of proportions. The music is composed in 'moments' (i.e., a series of events of distinct character) and textures — the latter based on diverse, complex and fanciful ways of playing familiar instruments. The score contains two full pages of instructions for the instrumentalists on how to read and realize the various slides, rasps, hisses, whistles, wails, raps, clicks, and knocks required. A certain amount of spatial manipulation of sound is also built into the work. The notation might be described as adapted-traditional. While everything is written out, the exact proportions and ensemble effect may vary somewhat: a certain freedom and flexibility is built in. Thus, the overall shape of the piece is relatively fixed but many of the details are left to the players' immediate responses and may vary from performance to performance." — Eric Salzman.[100]

"*Quick are the Mouths of Earth* [is] a real blockbuster of a work.... Reybnolds won his degree in engineering at the University of Michigan and later studied with Ross Lee Finney and Roberto Gerhard. The work is in six sections and is based on a quotation from Thomas Wolfe that apparently had the capacity of generating musical images for Reynolds.... This is an utterly fascinating piece that unfolds with an almost self-conscious sense of architecture. Stylistically, it is part of the mainstream of today's new writers, but it is unfettered by any prescribed system. Reynolds provides a clue to things in his score. He says: 'There are three types of spatial interplay between the instrumental groups: clusters of marked entrances occurring across the entire span of the ensemble; the passing of similar materials from group to group; or the continuous flow of one sound (a particular pitch or noise) from right to left.' " — Oliver Daniel, in *Saturday Review*, 9/13/69.

"[Like *Wedge* (1970) for chamber orchestra,] *Quick are the Mouths of Earth* makes great use of antiphonal interplay of sub-units in opposition to one another, rhythmically and texturally. The small orchestra of *Wedge* continually breaks up into two laters of interacting material; in *Quick Are the Mouths of Earth*, the ensemble has been subdivided into three groups distinctly separated from one another on stage. Such considerations have obviously influenced the musical material, which stresses the overlapping of static motivic fragments, telegraphed repeated notes, intense rhythmic crossplay and a brilliant handling of vivid, memorable sonorities — all reminiscent of Varèse, only (if possible) more so. Reynold's sense of instrumental

---

[100] In Gillespie, ed., *ibid.*

balance is most acute, and his control over 'time' in all its aspects—durational unfolding, interaction of varying pulses, abrupt rhythmic articulations—equally adroit....

"Performances of [the two] Reynolds works will require maximum effort and rehearsal time, and highly skilled players, but the results should more than justify the expenditure of energy."—Elliott Schwartz, in *Notes* (Music Library Association), 12/67.

"*...the serpent-snapping eye*" for Trumpet, Percussion, Piano and 4-Channel Computer-Synthesized Tape (1978). 18m

Prem.: Edwin Harkins (tpt), Jean-Charles François (perc), Cecil Lytle (pno). *Perf.*: Curtis Nash (tpt), William Winant (perc), Nohema Fernandez (pno). *Rec.*: CRI: Edwin Harkins (tpt), Jean-Charles François (perc), Cecil Lytle (pno). *Pub.*: C. F. Peters (score).
In three sections.

" '*...the serpent-snapping eye*' is the second composition of mine for soloists and four-channel tape to result from the suggestive images in Melville's *Moby Dick*. The first, '*...from behind the unreasoning mask*', dealt with the tensions set up by performance activity of varying autonomy set against a monolithic tape. The present work explores the various ways in which performers can join with a rich and sonorous fabric of computer-generated sound. '*...the serpent-snapping eye*' divides into three roughly equal portions. In the first, the primary aim of the performers is to match, to submit to and intensify the taped sound. The second, in which the synthesized sounds are sparse, allows greater independence as the performers respond, reflecting on models provided by the tape. In the final section, the live performers complement and elaborate upon, then attempt to augment, the synthesized sound.

"The phrase quoted as a title comes from 'The Quarterdeck' chapter of *Moby Dick*, where Ahab, distributing grog to the crew, draws all into a directed abandon. My intention, then, is to explore those situations in which a certain lack of orientation leads us more deeply into the moment itself. There is a rather aquatic feel to the work.

"The structure of '*...the serpent-snapping eye*' follows closely the expanding and contracting time proportions upon which the earlier composition was built. In addition, the shape of each component phrase parallels one of the three models used to program the computer in computing the sounds that appear on the tape (all of which are synthesized). Thus, the models for the electronic sounds find a second, more flexible expression in the activity of the live performers.

There is, I hope, at every level, an evident concern for matching and conformation." — Roger Reynolds.[101]

"Scored for a battery of 11 percussion instrumets, trumpet, piano, and computer-generated tape sounds, '...*the serpent-snapping eye*' provided a kaleidoscopic array of sounds in a varied and appealing setting.
"The computer sounds were based on the natural harmonic overtone series and the writing for instruments often provided simple triadic harmonies with the tape. In each of this work's three sections there were instances of exquisite blending of the taped and performed tones, each emerging from the other in a finely honed, mellifluous fashion." — Francis Thumm, in *The San Diego Union*, 2/1/79.

"The percussionist [Jean-Charles François] was a delight to watch as he circulated among the battery of instruments hitting and stroking with controlled precision. The trumpet created a spectrum of articulations — a wealth of percussive and aspirated resources which provided multi-colored ideas. One of the fascinations of [this] piece is the echoing of similar timbres back and forth between the different instruments." — Richard Ames, in *Santa Barbara News Press*, 2/2/79.

Transfigured Wind II (concerto) for Flute, Orchestra and 4-Channel Computer-Processed Tape (1984). 35m *Prem.*: Harvey Sollberger (fl), American Composers O, Charles Wuorinen, cond. *Rec.*: New World Records: John Fonville (fl), San Diego SO, Harvey Sollberger, cond. *Pub.*: C. F. Peters.
In one movement.

On composing and producing "Transfigured Wind II": "Musical variation has always fascinated me, and recent engagements in Paris and California with large computer systems have led me toward a formal ideal that might be called the 'transformational mosaic'. I apologize for dropping this locution into the analysis — the idea is clear to me, but I find it difficult to put into words succinctly. It is my suspicion that this confirms its essentially *musical* nature.
"Computers allow us to recast musical materials, to transform them in ways that are intriguing and let one retain that delicious and mysterious *sense* with which a fine performer imbues a musical line. One instance of what I mean might be captured by referring to the [instant play-back] slow-motion imagery that television has made available. We are all now able to share the magical grace inherent in the movements of an athlete, a dancer at his work. There is a poetic

---

[101] Gillespie, ed., *ibid*.

evolution, an inevitability to these slowed-down experiences that can now have a direct parallel in the world of sound. In short, aspects of our experience that were always there, but to which we had no access, now can form a part of our (repeatable) aesthetic opportunities.

"In composing *Transfigured Wind II*, I began with a four-part solo for flute. It was recorded *as performed*. That is, all the directional, musical intelligence that the soloist brought to my phrases was captured and became, along with pitch, duration and dynamics, a part of the compositional materials. Once inside the computer, it could undergo a host of transformations before re-emerging on the tape you will hear.

"The making of this central aspect of the work would not have been possible without the formidable support of my musical assistant on this project, Richard Boulanger. Mark Dolson of the staff at the Computer Audio Research Laboratory, on the University of California at San Diego campus, was also of great importance to my work. I am deeply grateful to them, to Lee Ray and to the entire CARL facility at UCSD, where this work was realized.

"The four solo-flute sections, in the context of an actual performance, function as proposals, each longer and with a new character. To the soloist's proposals, the ensemble responds with transformations, elaborations of what has been offered. On tape, a rather 'painterly' montage of the soloist's elements and lines is contributed. It would, of course, have been ungracious to conceive the computer-processed materials so that they challenged the capacities of the live soloist. My aim was rather to provide unexpected, perhaps otherworldly reflections of and upon the soloist's specifics, elaborations that might serve to enlarge the range of our understanding as listeners (and, perhaps, to instill fresh impetus into the soloist's successive statements).

"The work (like its predecessor, *Archipelago*, commissioned by IRCAM in Paris) is primarily concerned with the way in which transformations may allow music a more subtle and far-reaching engagement with the wonders of our temporal experiences as human beings. We anticipate, reflect, recall. We are sometimes absorbed in specifics, at other times we wander in larger, less-defined worlds of impressionism. My aim in devising the idea of 'transformational mosaic' was to invite back into music recognizable but not literal repetition of materials, while at the same time providing a basis for the role of the pre-cursor—that which acts as a premonition of musical ideas that have not yet appeared in definitive form but do so as the work progresses.

"Admittedly these are speculative notions.... Such intentions are, as I have said, for me quite clear in the music but are still difficult to communicate outside of it. John Cage once remarked to me, in response to some probing, 'I am, perhaps, still too young to these ideas'. It did not prevent him from a practical engagement with them. My circumstance is similar. I hope that listeners will find the computer to be a more evocative, less severe musical instrument in this work than sometimes it is thought to be. Computers can, I believe, extend the reach of our musical imaginations, of our experience as human beings." — Roger Reynolds.

"Reynolds [has] used the flute first as an instrument of analysis and dissection — rather as one uses field glasses to scan and marvel at details of drawing and paint in the Sistine ceiling — and then as a projector. Computers, he wrote in his program note [for the 1984 premiere]. 'allow us to recast musical materials, to transform them in ways that are intriguing and let one retain that delicious and mysterious *sense* with which a fine performer imbues a musical line.' *Transfigured Wind II* began with flute solos played by a live performer and recorded; that way, composer and performer together provided material that 'once inside the computer... could undergo a host of transformations before reemerging on the tape.' With computers, one can dissect and examine them both 'horizontally', in time, separating attack — of breath upon mouthpiece, string upon bow — from the note that follows, and 'vertically', in their timbre structures. One can then prolong, emphasize, transform, or remove any of the elements. The sounds that music is made of, we have learned, are far more complicated than once was thought. There were sounds in Reynolds' piece — the soft sizzle of the player's breath seemed to be one — that have long been a part of music although not before prominently heard. New sounds can in themselves be eloquent, and the discovery of new instruments and new sounds is important. But what matters more is the use that composers make of them. The eighteenth-century clarinet with downward extension would be forgotten today had Mozart not composed a quintet for it. Reynolds is at once an explorer and a visionary composer, whose works can lead listeners to follow him into new regions of emotion and imagination." — Andrew Porter, in *The New Yorker*, 7/9/84.

"More extroverted and expansive than *Whispers Out of Time* [below], this earlier opus is a virtuoso fantasy in a single movement, as rich and demanding as a giant Jackson Pollock oil painting.

"Vibrant brass and percussion underscore the work's pointillistic idiom... Reynolds' evocative tape part, as winning an electronic construction as I have heard in many years of electronic music auditing, acted as a buffer between the assertive solo and the intense orchestra sections. Reynolds integrated these three forces skillfully, allowing the tape solo to appear to emanate from the flute's subtle cadence." — Kenneth Herman, in *Los Angeles Times*, 2/17/90.

Whispers Out of Time for Violin, Viola, Cello, Double Bass and String Orchestra (1988). 16m Winner, 1989 Pulitzer Prize. *Prem.:* Amherst College Ens, Harvey Sollberger, cond. *Rec.:* New World Records: Janos Negysesy (vln), Yun-Jie Liu (vla), Peter Farrell (vc), Bertram Turetzky (db), San Diego SO, Harvey Sollberger, cond. *Pub.:* C. F. Peters.
In six movements.

Composer's note: "In 1524, the mannerist painter Parmigianino using a convex barber's mirror to find his image, conceived the bravura notion of reproducing not only his likeness but that of the mirror itself. He asked a carpenter to fashion a wooden ball and then cut it to size. Across its surface he reproduced his own distorted likeness and that of his room. In 1959, John Ashbery saw the *Self Portrait in a Convex Mirror* in Vienna and responded with a long and particularly rich poem by the same name. My encounter with Ashbery's unsettling, elusive commentary affected me as no other poetry has. Stumbling over its improbable landscape of ideas and images, each time finding new paths, and losing them, I decided that my most effective 'reading' might be accomplished through a musical composition, an analog in sound. My intention was to examine the circumstance that had stimulated the poet and to follow where possible the processes that his words suggested.

"Ashbery mentions Berg's report that a theme in the first movement of Mahler's *Ninth Symphony* was 'death itself', and I went to that score only to find that Mahler was himself quoting Beethoven's *'Lebewohl'* (farewell) opening to the *Sonata* Opus 81a. In several nested contexts, then, content was distanced by time as well as by individual perspective. I reduced the introduction of the Beethoven *Sonata* to a two-line skeleton, but then stretched out, phrase by phrase, its original rhythmic proportions. (The effect is of temporal convexity.) A similar but more extensive procedure was followed with an ominous and otherworldly passage from Mahler.

"The poem is in six sections of markedly differing lengths. Critic Helen Vendler observes that Ashbery uses changes in mood to define structure, and I took note of its fluctuations, mirroring them not literally, of course, but in his manner. I composed a series of six interrelated movements which parallel the poem in varying degrees. My work is a mirror, a sonic one, which selectively recasts and translates into its own world Ashbery's vision. While he has been content with one reference, Parmigianino's portrait, I have included as a thematic basis, two. The first is the skeletonized Beethoven cocooned within two new lines of my invention. Its influence is felt primarily during the first three movements. The second thematic source is based on the later Mahler, and begins my fourth movement with a jagged, appassionata solo line against an insistent pedal on F-sharp and C. The last three movements, most strongly shadowed by Mahler, also include references to the earlier Beethoven source.

"Because the stretched quotations (contrapuntal residues of their originals) are placed in a linearly layered relationship to my added parts, it is possible to 'weigh' the degree to which a citation reveals or shrouds its identity. Removing my cloakings brings one into direct contact with the source, while removing the traditionally derived materials provides only the contemporary context (against which the influence of the musical past may still be sensed). Further harmonic and figurative elements were needed almost as theatrical sets—for preparation, relief, transition—and these were independently composed.

"I have always resisted the venerable tradition of borrowing from the work of other composers, seeing its practical attractions, but preferring to say what I had to offer with my own voice. In this case, however, the distance between our contemporary circumstance and an earlier artist's statement is fundamental to the weighing and relishing of the subject.[102] The medium of the string orchestra seemed ideal for the dark, lyrical world of inference aroused in me." —Roger Reynolds.

"True to its title, *Whispers Out of Time* does not shout but, despite its sparse texture and austere, monochromatic timbre, it is densely packed with ideas. Divided into six carefully balanced movements, *Whispers* insinuates Gustav Mahler's melancholy resignation—Mahler is obliquely quoted—and invites comparison to the spiritual

---

[102] This is an interesting comment on the "borrowing" or simply quoting of other composer's themes, or materials generally. In defense of an "eclectic" use of art materials themselves, one might plausibly argue that the world that one represents through his or her art includes many "artificial" constructions—including (that is to say) not only man-made buildings, appliances, institutions, but also other works of art. Thus someone else's musical composition would appear to be a legitimate subject for one's own musical composition. But there is obviously more to it than that. In a given work of art, one expresses a kind of *personality*. Thus, in absorbing another work of art, one absorbs (in part) another's personality. But what *is* a given "personality"—if not the manner in which a given being comes to be known? Thus the "borrower" has, himself, contributed to the very "personality" of that of which he makes some use. One's *own* identity (or personality), indeed, seems rather fluid. (Ed.)

Composer Roger Reynolds, conductor Harvey Sollberger—*Whispers Out of Time*. Recording session, New World Records.

aspirations of late Beethoven. Its unrelieved intensity... places great demands on the listener.

"Working with small, fragmentary motifs, Reynolds either suspends them in a delicate—albeit atonal—tapestry or unravels them in layered but rarely contrapuntal strata. Although he structured *Whispers* like a concerto grosso, the interplay between the solo group and the orchestra seemed less codified than any Baroque of neoclassical concerto grosso."—Kenneth Herman, in *Los Angeles Times*, 2/17/90.

VITTORIO RIETI

B. 1898, Alexandria (Egypt). *Taught at:* Peabody Cons, Chicago Musical Coll, Queen's Coll (NY), New York Coll of Music. *Works incl.:* ballets (*Bacco e Arianna [The Triumph of Bacchus and Ariadne], Indiana, Kaleidoscope, A Sylvan Dream* — see also below), chamber works (*Partita*), choral pieces, concertos (cello, 2 pnos, strng qt, vln [2], 5 wws), inc. music for plays, *Madrigal* (12 insts), operas (*Don Perimplin, The Pet Shop, Teresa nel Bosco*), 5 string quartets, symphonic suites (*L'Arca di Noè, Conundrum, Hippolyte*), 11 symphonies.

NOTES ON THE COMPOSER. "[Vittorio Rieti, an] American composer of Italian descent, studied music with [Giuseppe] Frugatta in Milan (1912-1917) as well as economics at the University of Milan, where he obtained a doctorate in 1917. After brief war service in the Italian army, he [continued] studies with Respighi in Rome (until 1920). In the early 1920s he was associated with Massarani and Labroca in a group that called itself *I Tre*, in imitation of *Les Six*. His first international success came at the ISCM Festival in Prague in 1924 with his *Concerto* for wind and orchestra, conducted by Casella, who continued to befriend his younger colleague. From 1925 to 1940 Rieti divided his time between Rome and Paris, where he formed close ties with *Les Six*. He wrote ballet music for Dyagilev (*Barabau* being particularly successful) and much incidental music for the Parisian theatre of Louis Jouvet. He was also one of the founder-directors of the Paris group *La Sérénade*, dedicated to modern chamber music (1931-40). In 1940 he moved to the USA (he became a citizen in 1944). There his ballet music was choreographed by Balanchin, his orchestral music conducted by, among others, Toscanini and Mitropoulos. He [has] continued to be productive; on his 75th birthday a number of new works were presented to the public. As a teacher of composition, he was active at the Peabody Conservatory (1948-49), the Chicago Musical College (1950-53), Queens College (1955-60) and the New York College of Music (1960-64).

"Rieti's musical style has been fairly consistent throughout his long career. After early experiments with atonality, he evolved an idiom akin to neo-classicism, which remained his characteristic trait. He said in 1973: 'I maintain the same aesthetic assumptions I have always had; I have kept evolving in the sense that one keeps on perfecting the same ground.' His music has a natural, unaffected fluency, elegant charm, controlled feeling, sophisticated humor and impeccable technical mastery; his textures are clear and limpid, his orchestration transparent and sensitive. Casella's praise (see Cobbett) has lost none of its relevance; elsewhere he wrote: 'Rieti's *oeuvre* stands apart in its specific clarity, gaiety and sophistication of a kind only he possesses; yet it hides a good deal of melancholia.' " — Boris Schwarz, in *The New Grove Dictionary of Music and Musicians* (1980).

"Vittorio Rieti is a true cosmopolitan. Born in Egypt of Italian background, he began his musical studies in [Alexandria and later in] Rome with Respighi [orchestration — though the composer is largely self-taught], spent the period between the two World Wars in Paris, came to the United States in 1940, and has remained here since. Paris in the 20s and 30s seems to have had the greatest impact on his musical style (as it did with Casella), for he was a major figure in French artistic circles of the time. He has written in every form and for almost every medium, from opera and ballet to chamber music. On the whole, his music has the clarity of his French contemporaries and leans to witticism rather than to depth, characteristics that often reflect the superrefined atmosphere of the Paris Conservatoire. He is never, to use the French term with so many connotations, *'vulgaire'*." — Albert Seay, in *Notes* (Music Library Association), 9/82.

AN INTERVIEW WITH THE COMPOSER. On 10/3/90 composers Mark Grant and Dana Perna, and the Editor, interviewed Mr. Rieti in his New York apartment, finding him (at 92) to be utterly charming, gracious, hospitable — not fond of generalities, preferring to deal with specifics instead, often with a wry smile, and economical turn of phrase.

"EDITOR: How would you respond to a conductor whom you like very much, who is sincere, whose opinions you respect, who complains, 'I can't program contemporary music because nobody will come'?

"VITTORIO RIETI: I'd say well don't.

"ED. (laughing): I think that's a good answer.

"VR: What can you say.

"ED.: I wish performers would do *something* at every concert. Don't put the blame on the audience. I had an opportunity to ask André Watts once why, for the most part, he only played Schubert and so on — he said that's because those are the people he liked the most. He was honest.

"VR: He's right — music that he likes, he should play that.

"ED.: What would you say to a talented young composer who asks you how to go about getting a hearing for his or her music?

"VR: Well, I'm not very good at 'PR'! I have not much experience in that line.

"MARK GRANT: Earlier in your career, when you were working on commission for ballets, when you worked with Louis Jouvet and others, there might have been more respect for hiring serious composers to supply incidental music for ballets and so on, than there is today in this country.

"VR: Yes, I think the situation's changed. I worked with Balanchine. My first ballet, *Barabau*, was also *his* first ballet, for Diaghilev. We worked together [many times].

"DANA PERNA: Have you had many commissions since then?

"VR: Oh yes, many. The Indianapolis Ballet Theatre, for *Kaleidoscope* (the last one) and others. Also they revived *Barabau* and others. But today a lot is done with music written before, for other purposes... there are no so many original ballets today. And ballet should be a *drama*—much of it now is very abstract.

"ED.: What attracts you to ballet?

"VR: Only that they say that my music generally speaking is very apt for the dance.

"DP: Have you conducted?

"VR: Occasionally, but not the ballet. I also played the piano occasionally. I played one of the four pianos for [Stravinsky's] *Les Noces*, in Paris, in London.

"ED.: Do you compose at the piano?

"VR: Yes, but by this I do not mean I improvise at the piano. I *check* with the piano—everything in my mind—before I write it down. Stravinsky used the piano. Hindemith, no—Hindemith could write on the train. Stravinsky asked Rimsky about this—Rimsky told him, there are some composers who use the piano, and some who do not. You are among those who use the piano. That's all. It doesn't mean anything.

"MG: Composers of the last thirty years or so have tried many different styles.

"VR: With Stravinsky, it's very clear that the first part of his career is the Russian, the second part is the neo-classical, and finally he tried also atonal, serial.... In my case I think I have not changed very much. My music has been described as neo-classical.

"DP: Are you working on any new scores now?

"VR: I have just finished my *Symphony 10*. I am working on number eleven.

"DP: A new Havergal Brian.

Igor Stravinsky, Vittorio Rieti. Photo by Henri Cartier-Bresson.

"VR: I beat Beethoven by two points! You can't beat Haydn though. My tenth is going to be performed this winter by the St. Luke's. The eleventh I hope Dick will do....[103]

"DP: I understand you studied with Respighi?

"VR: Not so much. I was on very good terms with Respighi. Perhaps he gave me one or two lessons in orchestration, but I consider myself self-taught. The only musical education I had was piano. When they ask me, whom did I study composition with, well I

---

[103] Richard Kapp, composer and director of the Philharmonia Virtuosi, who premiered Rieti's *Symphony 9*, when the composer was 90, in 1988. Rieti's *Symphony 4* received a memorable performance by Arturo Toscanini and the NBC Symphony Orchestra, in 1945.

studied with Bach, with Mozart, with Beethoven, Rossini, Verdi, Debussy.... Casella sponsored me, very much. Casella conducted my music when I was very young and unknown.

"DP: Do you have any favorite contemporary composers? Like Elliott Carter?

"VR: Oh yes, he is a great friend of mine. It is hard to say—there are so many.

"MG: Boulez?

"VR: I think Boulez is an extremely competent musician.

"DP: I don't know anyone who actually knew Diaghilev. Is there anything you could say about him of a personal nature?

"VR: He was really the first in history to persuade first-rate composers to write their best music for the ballet—Stravinsky, the *The Three Cornered Hat* of De Falla, the Ravel *Daphnis*. Usually this does not happen. Diaghilev put the music first. In his youth he wished to be a composer himself. He wrote something and showed it to Rimsky-Korsakov. Rimsky-Korsakov wrote him a letter and said, yes it's all right, but I would suggest a cut... from the beginning to the end. [*The interviewers laugh.*] That was the beginning of the end for Diaghilev as a composer.

"DP: Did Stravinsky encourage your composition?

"VR: Yes very much.

"DP: The violinist Nathan Milstein said that Stravinsky had a very changeable personality. Did you find that to be true?

"VR: He also changed his opinions on things. At the same time he wouldn't admit that he had changed. There was a conflict some times, between changing his opinions and not admitting that he had. [*Smiles.*]

"ED: Is this a good time to be a composer, do you think?

"VR: Sometimes I think there are too *many* composers! I was once on a jury for the state of Illinois—for the string quartet. The string quartet is one of the most difficult—do you know how many we received [to judge]? More than one hundred. One state, for no more than a five year period. Over one hundred. How many piano pieces must there be? Then multiply by fifty states—then so many countries, all over the world. How many compositions must there be? Tens of millions...

"ED: I know what you mean, but I would say also I am so glad. It shows a lot of people care about music. A lot of people are—or would like to be—involved.

"VR: [The musical culture] may be much more extensive now because of technology... the phonograph record, TV. At the same time there is much that is superficial... amateurish.

"INTERVIEWERS: We've had a wonderful time talking with you. Thank you!"

Ballets.

Le Bal (1929). *Prem.:* Diaghilev's Ballets Russes (Alexandra Danilova, Anton Dolin), George Balanchine (choreogr.). ***Barabau*** (1925). *Prem.:* Diaghilev's Ballets Russes (Woidzikowsky, Tatiana Chamié, Lifar), George Balanchine (choreogr). *Other perf.:* Indiana Ballet Theater. ***Native Dancers*** (arr. of *Symphony 5*) (1959). *Prem.:* NY City Ballet (Patricia Wilde, Jacques d'Amboise), George Balanchine (choreogr), Robert Irving, cond. ***La Sonnambula [The Night Shadow]*** (after music by Bellini) (1941). *Prem.:* Ballet Russe de Monte Carlo (Alexandra Danilova, Nicholas Magallanes, Maria Tallchief, Michel Katcharoff), George Balanchine (choreogr.). *Other perfs.:* NY City Ballet, Washington Natl Ballet, Royal Danish Ballet, Ballet Rambert (London). ***Waltz Academy*** (arr. of *Second Avenue Waltzes* for 2 pianos) (1944). *Prem.:* New York City Ballet.

"[In the early 1920s] Rieti's music tended clearly toward the Stravinskian mode. In 1924, a major piece of his, a concerto for woodwinds and orchestra, had been performed in Paris, and attracted Diaghilev's attention. 'Our of a blue sky, I received a telegram asking me if I could meet him in Venice in September,' Rieti has said of his first meeting with Diaghilev. 'I was exactly twenty-seven.' Although Rieti had no connection with ballet at that time, he had been composing music for ballet. 'Just for fun,' he said. 'I had three ballets, three scores. One was about Noah's Ark. One was about Robinson Crusoe. And the third one was *Barabau*, which is based on a Tuscan nursery rhyme. Diaghilev chose that one. Then he asked me to revamp, to cut this and that and that and that, and so on, and finally it was ready. It was performed in London in December of 1925, and that was the beginning of my being introduced to the ballet world. And from then on I worked in the ballet more than in any other form.'

"*Barabau* was about a peasant:

> Barabau, Barabau, why did you die
> You'd wine in my cellar, your
>   bread was not dry,
> And salad you grew in your garden nearby.
> Barabau, Barabau, why did you die?

"Rieti embellished this whisper of a plot by inventing a prosperous peasant and his friends who live a life of simple, earthly pleasures and are suddenly destroyed by soldiers who appear out of nowhere. Barabau seems to be killed, but when the soldiers go away he comes back to life, to carry on as before. (*Barabau* was later interpreted in London as an anti-Fascist piece.) In *Barabau*, the ladies wore false bosoms and bottoms and the men wore false noses, and the action included lots of lusty innuendo. 'When the curtain rose, there was a line of peasants standing parallel to the footlights and with their backs to the audience laboriously wriggling their buttocks,' one incensed English critic wrote. 'Their movements, inspired by drunkeness and other attributes of low comedy, were correspondingly coarse and ugly.' The choreographer was George Balanchine, who was then twenty-one years old, and *Barabau* was his first original choreography for Diaghilev. Balanchine and Rieti would remain friends for life. 'It was pure garlic,' Balanchine said of *Barabau* many years later. 'It was a very funny ballet. It was the first time I'd heard people laugh non-stop all through a ballet.' The sets for *Barabau* were done by Maurice Utrillo. Alexandra Danilova, who was then twenty-one, danced the part of one of three peasant girls who star in it. The critics did not approve of the unconventional ambiance, but in London, Paris, and Monte Carlo the audiences laughed. *Barabau* was a popular success....

"Rieti's second score for Diaghilev was *Le Bal*, for which he chose the most conventional setting possible — an aristocratic ball. With the librettist, Boris Kochno, he worked on the plot for two years. '*Le Bal* is about a young man who falls in love with a woman, but then it turns out that she is an old woman,' Rieti told me. 'When she takes her mask off, the young man is horribly shocked. Then it turns out that there is a second mask, and she is really a young woman, and there is also an old man, who is masked, and really young, and the two go off together, leaving the first young man in a state of total collapse.' Diaghilev pestered Rieti for so many changes in *Le Bal* that when he finally delivered the score, in February of 1929, he included a note that said:

> Dear Mr. Diaghilev:
> Here is *Le Bal*. It is dedicated to you; it is for you; do what you want with it, but above all do not hope that I will work on it any more![104]

"*Le Bal* had its premiere that May. The sets were by de Chirico. It was choreographed by Balanchine, and Alexandra Danilova danced the female lead. The ballet was performed in Monte Carlo, Paris, and London, to good reviews....

---

104 *Cher Monsieur Diaghilev, / Voice Le Bal. Il vous est dédié; il est à vous; faites-en ce que vous voulez, mais surtout n'espérez pas que j'y travaille encore! / Toujours à vous, / Vittorio Rieti.*

"In 1944, Rieti developed *The Second Avenue Waltzes* [for two pianos] into a score for Balanchine called *Waltz Academy*—a mostly abstract ballet, held together by the idea of a competition among students in a dance school. In America, Rieti also wrote *La Sonnambula*, the most successful work of his career. He is modest about it, because the music is [based on themes freely elaborated from Bellin's operas. Another contribution—and a] reason the work has remained so popular—is the story.

"The ballet starts with an conventional ball, given by the Baron in a courtyard. The Poet arrives and falls in love with the Baron's mistress. When the guests go in to dinner, leaving the Poet behind, a sleepwalking woman descends from a tower. The Poet tries to get a reaction from the Sleepwalker, who floats around holding a candle in front of her, although she appears unable to see. Still, as if with a sixth sense, she unerringly avoids him. Even when he throws himself in her path, she steps over him. When the Baron's mistress discovers that the Poet has fallen in love with the Sleepwalker, she is jealous. She tells the Baron that the Poet has been trying to seduce her, with the result that the Baron kills the Poet. In death, the Poet gets the Sleepwalker's attention. She floats up to his body, and this time is stopped by it. Then, in a very strange theatrical moment, she picks up the Poet's body and carries him away with her into the tower.

"Two other Rieti ballets—*Native Dancers* and *The Triumph of Bacchus and Ariadne*—were choreographed by Balanchine in America. But it is *Sonnambula* that has endured. It was performed by the New York City Ballet last season, and also, in another version, by the American Ballet Theatre—a performance broadcast on the Public Broadcasting System, with Mikhail Baryshnikov and Alessandra Ferri in the leading roles. Rieti estimates that *La Sonnambula* has had between two and three thousand performances."—Suzannah Lessard, in *The New Yorker*, 1/9/89.

BARABAU:"The next notable event of [Diaghilev's 1925 London season] was another return to our ranks of Lydia Lopokova. She returned from nowhere and imported her usual gaiety into our lives and performances alike. And then Diaghilev announced a new ballet. It was to be done at once, while we were still in London. He asked me to go round to his hotel and showed me a sketch, asking whether I liked it. I saw that it was signed 'Utrillo'—a painter whose work I greatly admired—and said, yes, I did. 'This is for the scenery of our new ballet, *Barabau*,' said Diaghilev. I had already heard that the young Italian composer Vittorio Rieti had written the music; and what Diaghilev had summoned me for was to allot the parts. The choreography was to be by Balanchine, of whom Diaghilev now had high hopes as a result of his success with *Le Chant du Rossingol*.

"*Barabau* in fact turned out very well. Utrillo's sketch for the scenery was beautifully interpreted by a remarkable scenic artist, Prince A. Shervashidze; the music, consisting of simple Italian tunes, partly sung by a choir placed on the stage itself, was delightful; and Balanchine's choreography, apart from a not altogether satisfactory *finale*, was most interesting and original. There were three chief parts: Barabau himself, danced by Woidzikowsky—in this as always marvellously precise in his movements; the Peasant Woman, danced by Tatiana Chamié—an excellent comedy role; and a smart young Sergeant, danced by Lifar. Unfortunately we were unable to give *Barabau* as often as we should have liked on account of the chorus, who were very expensive."—S. L. Grigoriev, in *The Diaghilev Ballet, 1909-1929*, transl. by Vera Bowen (Constable & Co. Ltd., 1953).

NATIVE DANCERS: "*Native Dancers*... has something to do with race horses but, fortunately, not too much. The title, of course, has its derivation in the name of one of the greatest of American horses, Native Dancer, but Mr. Balanchine, one of the greatest of all choreographers, has presented his dancers as humans and has elected to find his parallel in the fact that there are champions in both breeds, equine and man. A finely bred race horse has no equal in matters of beauty, strength and skill; neither does a finely bred dancer.

"In *Native Dancers*, the dance champions are put through a fantastic array of choreographic challenges and they emerge triumphant. Never has Patricia Wilde, in the principal female role [at the 1959 premiere with the New York City Ballet company], danced more excitingly. With the bells on her costume tinkling and her pony tail flying, she sped through some marvelous leaps and spins, prancings and agile steppings, mercurial shifts in direction with the beauty and dash of a thoroughbred. The ballet itself was a delight....

"As the chief jockey, Jacques d'Amboise also had his moments of glory. In an unguarded moment, perhaps, Mr. Balanchine once stated that there were a limited number of steps and patterns for the male dancer. Well, in *Native Dancer* he has gallantly disproved his point by giving Mr. d'Amboise some spectacular movements, all balletic in base but fresh and athletic and loaded with kinetic impact. And so, there were two champions on stage in *Native Dancers*, Miss Wilde and Mr. d'Amboise.

"To return to Mr. Balanchine's danced tribute to the race horse, let me say that he has skillfully avoided those equine-like maneuvers which have destroyed several other ballets dealing with fillies, races and the like. He has been content with equivalents and thus, he has called for special qualities of alertness, nimbleness and speed from his dancers. Occasionally, with wit, he makes a closer analogy, such as when Mr. d'Amboise appears to be shoeing Miss Wilde or when she, as a free and spirited creature, tries to elude his grasp or when the two dance part of a duet in and out of hoops. But these are humans dancing and Mr. Balanchine has celebrated this inescapable fact in his bright and brisk choreography.

"[The ballet is supported also by corps of male and female dancers.] The score, by Vittorio Rieti (*Symphony Nr. 5*), serves the dance and the dancers superbly." — Walter Terry, in *The New York Times*, 1/15/59.

> LA SONNAMBULA (THE NIGHT SHADOW): "This dramatic ballet was suggested by the opera *La Sonnambula (The Sleepwalker)* by Vincenzo Bellini. *Night Shadows* has a dark, romantic mood appropriate to the suppressed and clandestine loves that dominate the story. The time is long ago, a time of rigid conventions that the romantic spirit aimed to destroy....
>
> "[The Bellini opera] merely provided the subject matter for the ballet and not its plot. The opera tells the story of a romance between a farmer and a miller's daughter who is addicted to walking in her sleep. The score for the ballet is an [elaboration of music from *La Sonnambula* and *I Puritani* and other works] by the same composer....
>
> "Soon after the ballet was first presented [in New York City, by the Ballet Russe de Monte Carlo,] the American critic Edwin Denby wrote, in *Looking at the Dance:* 'Mysterious in the interaction of its elements; the vapid ballroom dances; the winsome exhibition numbers that have a perverse and cruel undertone; the elaborate, encircling artifices of the coquette's *pas de deux*; the directness and space of the sleepwalking scene.... The progress of the piece is "romantic" — it is disconcerting, absurd and disproportionate; but its effect when it is over is powerful and exact. It gives you a sense — as Poe does — of losing your bearings, the feeling of an elastic sort of time and a heaving floor. As a friend of mine remarked, "When it's over, you don't know what hit you." ' " — George Balanchine and Francis Mason, in *Balanchine's Complete Stories of the Great Ballets*, Rev. & Enl. Ed. (Doubleday & Company, 1977).

Dodici Preludi for Piano (c.1982). *Pub.:* General Music.

> "Another set of preludes — this time twelve rather than twenty-four. Yet certainly there is room for this set by Italian composer and now American citizen Vittorio Rieti who has already given us a fairly sizable number of piano works.

"In keeping with Rieti's affinity for neo-classic style and the character piece, the preludes are tiny miniatures with sparse textures and with prominent lyrical melodic lines. The majority seem to dance—rhythmic buoyancy is inherent in Rieti's style. The slower preludes all have a warmth and lyricism that tests a student's legato. Phrase lengths are frequently predictable and symmetrical, and the contemporary harmonic palette incorporates frequent modulation and key changes prior to the inevitable return to a tonal center.

"Selections especially to be noted include No. 2 in march style, No. 5 with its impressionistic sounds, No. 7 with carneval references, No. 11, a gigue, and No. 12 which is subtitled 'Passacaglia'. Several of the preludes in the full set are short, just slightly over a page long, and all are idiomatic and fit well into the pianist's hand. The score is easy to read as a result of Rieti's fondness for triadic outlines and typical keyboard figurations.

"The music is infectious and technically and musically appropriate for the lower-division college pianist or a talented high-school pianist. Either as an entire set or with groupings of preludes from the set, these Rieti preludes would be effective on a solo recital program. They are accessible and ingratiating!"—Jane Magrath, in *The American Music Teacher* (Music Teachers National Association), 6-7/83.

Second Avenue Waltzes for 2 Pianos (1941). (Also arr. as ballet *Waltz Academy*). 15m *Recs.:* Arthur Gold, Robert Fizdale; Serenus Stereo LP SRS 12073: Elda Beretta, Maria Madini-Moretti. *Pub.:* General Music.
1. *Innocent.* 2. *Elaborate.* 3. *Feminine.* 4. *Masculine.* 5. *Romantic.* 6. *Episodic and Brilliant.*

"*Second Avenue Waltzes* is a set of six waltzes inspired by and during the composer's early residence in the neighborhood of Second Avenue in New York. In those days Second Avenue was a street filled with decrepit old buildings and tenements, the incessant noise and rumble of the Second Avenue Elevated Railroad and all the detritus that goes with a run-down neighborhood in a violent, congested city. Second Avenue was also the avenue along which many artists and impoverished persons of artistic sensibilities lived with reality. Rieti lived here and so did a number of his friends and relatives, so that *Second Avenue Waltzes* is dedicated to these associates, to each his own waltz."—J. Tucker Batsford, from program notes for Serenus SRS 12073 recording.

NED ROREM

B. 1923, Richmond IN. *Educ.*: American Cons, Chicago; Northwestern Univ; Curtis Inst; Juilliard Shl of Music. Composer-in-residence Univ of Buffalo, Univ of UT. Winner, Pulitzer Prize (for *Air Music* for orchestra, 1976). *Books incl.*: *Critical Affairs, Nantucket Diary, New York Diary, Paris Diary, Settling the Score*. *Works incl.*: *Book of Hours* (fl, hp), piano pieces, operas *(Miss Julie)*, orchestral pieces, more than 200 songs & song cycles, incl. *Schuyler Songs* (prem. 11/90).

Eagles for Orchestra (1958). 9m *Prem.*: Philadelphia O, Eugene Ormandy, cond. *Rec.*: New World Records (Digital Stereo LP) NW 353 (also CD vers./NW 353-2): Atlanta SO, Louis Lane, cond.
1 picc-2-2-1 E hn-4-2-1 c bsn; 4-3-3-1; timp, 15 other perc insts (incl pno, ratchet, woodblocks, whip), harp; strings

String Symphony for String Orchestra (1985). *Prem.*: Atlanta SO, Robert Shaw, cond. *Rec.*: New World Records (Digital Stereo LP) NW 353 (also CD vers./NW 353-2): Atlanta SO, Robert Shaw, cond. Commissioned by Atlanta SO American Music Project.
1. *Waltz*. 2. *Berceuse*. 3. *Scherzo*. 4. *Nocturne*. 5. *Rondo*.

Sunday Morning for Orchestra (1977). *Prem.*: Philadelphia O, Eugene Ormandy, cond. *Rec.*: New World Records (Digital Stereo LP) NW 353 (also CD vers./NW 353-2): Atlanta SO, Louis Lane, cond. Commissioned by Saratoga Performing Arts Ctr.
3-3-3-3; 6-3-3-1; perc, mandolin, harp, piano/celesta; strings
In eight movements (see below).

"Some composers are lucky. Blessed with careers of many decades, they live long enough to see their music come into—or come *back* into—fashion. Ned Rorem is one. Active for more than 40 years, Rorem refused to jump on the 12-tone band-wagon and consequently saw his compositions scorned as tonal anachronisms. But during the past decade, tonality has been revived, and Rorem's brand of French-perfumed neo-Romanticism has returned triumphant.

"Rorem's 65th birthday provoked a veritable orgy of performances, along with a collection of his essays on music entitled *Settling the Score* and the present recording. Although often pegged as an art-song composer,[105] Rorem has paid considerable attention to instrumental music, and it is to three works in this genre that New World's recording is devoted.

"Rorem's music, like his prose, is characterized by the French virtues of lucidity, concision, and simplicity. The five-movement *String*

---

[105] Quite properly, of course. (Ed.)

Symphony, really a suite of dance and character pieces, exemplifies the refreshing clarity of Rorem's formal thinking. At times angular and dissonant, at times graceful and consonant, its emotional range is broad. The violence of its opening pages provides an anguished context for what turns out to be its most striking feature, a waltz theme that recurs during the course of the piece. Bathed in Parisian cafeé harmonies, this waltz might seem sentimental if wrenched out of context; but placed in an atmosphere of longing and regret, it becomes a nostalgic, even bittersweet evocation of a lost era.

"*Sunday Morning*, inspired by a Wallace Stevens poem, is scored for full orchestra. Cast in eight brief movements, each prefaced by a phrase of poetry, it is more overtly coloristic than the *String Symphony*, but it is just as varied in expressive range. The brief *Eagles* also arises from a literary impulse, in this case a poem by Walt Whitman. All three works, whether or not poetic in origin, are graced with lyrical melodic contours that reflect the innate vocal quality of Rorem's creative gift.

"Those who fear new music will find this recording utterly user-friendly. And those who love new music will be grateful that Rorem kept composing throughout those decades of public neglect." — K. Robert Schwarz, in *Musical America*, 3/89.

The composer on *String Symphony*, *Sunday Morning*, and *Eagles* for orchestra:

"Such reputation as I may have in the musical world has always seemed to revolve around sung settings — songs in particular, but choral works too, and some small operas. So I am especially thrilled by the present [New World recording], which represents my less familiar, strictly symphonic, side, since non-vocal orchestral and chamber works do account for the bulk of my output. However, even when building so-called abstract structures I've always felt most at ease when guided by a concrete program, as the tone poems *Eagles* and *Sunday Morning* indicate. But if the impulse for *String Symphony* was also poetic, it was unconscious and non-verbal; I was aiming (always difficult for me) toward un-literary meaning.

"*String Symphony*: The composition of *String Symphony* was begun on May 26, 1985, in Nantucket, and completed there just eight weeks later. The product of this shortish parturition (shortish, considering that other large projects involved me at the same time) is not bedecked with extramusical teases. I have so often been chided for the literary or visual names of my non-vocal compositions (*Remembering Tommy*, *Green Music*, *Sunday Morning*, and so on) that I decided in this case to fall back on just the lean term 'symphony', even as I composed for just a clean choir of bowed instruments rather than for full orchestra.

"Like most symphonies of the past half-century, the piece is called that *faute de mieux:* the term has become so all-encompassing as to be meaningless. By textbook standards this piece is probably less faithful to classical definitions than are my previous three symphonies (each for big orchestra). Indeed, it could as easily be named *Suite,* as hinted by the Chopinesque titles of its five sections: *Waltz, Berceuse, Scherzo, Nocturne, Rondo.*

"I'm seldom interested in what composers say technically about their finished work, and this particular work is so formally clear as to need no verbal exegesis. For you who like to learn such things, however, I'll allow that the various movements share their tunes, and that those tunes seem mostly shaped (I myself realized this *ex post facto*) from minor thirds.

"*Sunday Morning:* Wallace Stevens (1879-1955), among the greatest modern American poets, is also one of the most influential, his art touching not only other authors, but three generations of composers, here and abroad, who have drawn from his verse for their song settings. I myself first made musical versions in 1971 with *Last Poems,* for soprano, cello and piano.

"This symphonic suite, however, is a non-literal, dreamlike recollection of Stevens' long poem *Sunday Morning* (1915). Like the poem the music is divided into eight sections; the words, as I comprehend them, are not expressed through a human voice but through the colors of instruments, alone and together.

"The piece was... composed in Nantucket and New York City during the summer and fall of 1977, and premiered by [the Philadlephia Orchestra] the following August. Each movement contains different components of the standard symphony orchestra:

    1. "...green freedom" (Full orchestra)

    2. "Passions of rain" (Six horns and strings)

    3. "...indifferent blue" (Clarinet and cello solos, with harp and muted strings)

    4. "...birds, Before they fly" (Three flutes and muted strings)

    5. "Death is the mother of beauty" (Full orchestra)

    6. "...our insipid lutes" (Full orchestra with mandolin solo)

    7. "...a ring of men" (Timpani solo with full orchestra)

    8. "...to darkness, on extended wings" (Two solo violas against the full orchestra)

"*Eagles:* The musical seed for *Eagles* was planted when, in the early 1950s, I came across Walt Whitman's "The Dalliance of the Eagles":

    Skirting the river road, (my forenoon walk, my rest)

> Skyward in air a sudden muffled sound, the dalliance of the eagles,
> The rushing amorous contact high in space together,
> The clinching interlocking claws, a living, fierce, gyrating wheel,
> Four beating wings, two beaks, a swirling mass tight grappling,
> In tumbling turning clustering loops, straight downward falling,
> Till o'er the river pois'd, the twain yet one, a moment's lull,
> A motionless still balance in the air, then parting, talons loosing,
> Upward again on slow-firm pinions slanting, their separte diverse flight,
> She hers, he his, pursuing.

"In September of 1958, at the MacDowell Colony, I composed a nine-minute instrumental interpretation—a memory, rather—of those verses. It purports to relate, in tone, the calm of a poet's country stroll interrupted by an intense sensual disturbance which ultimately subsides, leaving the dreamer alone again—but not quite. Eugene Ormandy gave the first performance the following year, with the Philadelphia Orchestra, on my birthday. (In 1962 I wrote a complementary work called *Lions*, but have yet to realize the final panel of the triptych, *Whales*.)"—from liner notes for New World Records Digital Stereo LP NW 353.

Serenade on Five English Poems for Mezzo-Soprano, Violin, Viola, and Piano. *Text:* Fletcher, Shakespeare, Tennyson, Hopkins, Campion. *Rec.:* Grenadilla (Stereo LP) GS-1031: Elaine Bonazzi (m-s), Cantilena Chamber Players (Frank Glazer, pno; Edna Mitchell, vln; Harry Zaratzian, vla).

"Ned Rorem's much-deserved fame as a writer for the human voice has often tended to eclipse his prowess as an instrumental composer. Although his creative instincts have always remained courageously tonal, in recent years he has produced a rich series of substantial works—such as the Pulitzer-Prize-winning orchestral *Air Music*, the pair of pieces for violin and piano entitled *Day Music* and *Night Music*, and the ravishing set of symphonic pictures *Sunday Morning* [see above] inspired by the poetry of Wallace Stevens—which have shown him striving systematically to expand his harmonic palette by incorporating influences from sources as far-flung as Henze and Messiaen. However, the incredibly fluent, fertile, and communicative lyricism lying at the core of his gift has never been obscured by these new dimensions, as is conclusively demonstrated by this recent *Serenade* for mezzo voice, piano, violin, and viola.

"Instead of a group of individual vocal numbers, Rorem has given us a completely integrated concert work which in some respects almost constitutes a chamber concerto for four solo musicians. Cast in a continuous, rhapsodic form, the work offers virtuosic cadenza-like passages for all three instrumentalists in between and surrounding vocal settings of five carefully chosen poems about love, salvation, and death by first-rank English poets.... The introduction and transitional sections as well as the actual accompaniments all display Rorem's infallible talent for embodying the essence of a verbal utterance in effortlessly natural and appropriate musical imagery, as, for instance, in the piano's restless arpeggios throughout Shakespeare's tortured reflections *(Sonnet No. 129)* on the turmoil and abasement attendant upon the promptings of lust, or the simple, berçeuse-like rhythm established for Tennyson's philosophic musings on a flower blooming forlornly in a stone wall, or the dramatic intermittencies of Hopkins' clotted language and disjointed prosody about the violent overthrow of a reluctant soul by a bird-like harbinger of religious peace. And for the two end-pieces — Fletcher's unsentimental invocation of Night to disguise and protect the act of love, and Campion's gentle, pious acceptance of the deliverance of death — Rorem has created thematically echoing settings which are almost ironic mirror-images of one another. This splendid work is given an eloquent interpretation [in the Bonazzi/Cantilena recording]." — Paul Snook, in *Fanfare: The Magazine for Serious Record Collectors*, 9-10/79.

Three Choruses for Christmas, and other choral works.

From an interview with Ned Rorem, conducted by Deborah Davis in *The Musical Quarterly*, 7/82:

"DAVIS: Suppose I divide your choral works into two groups. I notice in your early works what I would call traditional harmony — more major and minor triads with occasional added seconds or added sixths. Your later works seem to be more dissonant in that you use chords built on seconds and fourths, ten-part extended tertian sonorities, etc. Could you comment on this?

"ROREM: I'm flattered by your scholarly approach and will be glad to read the results. However, a musicologist's conclusions are never quite recognizable to the composer, commenting as they do, after the fact, on something conceived before the fact. Of course, if musicologist and composer saw eye to eye, wouldn't one of them be dispensable? A composer tries to be tolerant, but never knows quite what the historian is after. I don't think of my own music as problematic and am always surprised when people tell me that it is. Partly it's because the general public reads prose with less difficulty than they hear music, and more people read books than go to concerts. The musical public is far more specialized than the literary public—though there's not a very big public for either in America today. And a writer of the same age and reputation as a composer earns maybe ten times more, and a painter twenty times more, because they write and paint things that can be bought and sold. I published my first book, a diary, in 1966, and in the six months that followed I had more reaction from strangers than I have had in twenty years as a professional composer. I always thought of my music as pristine, clear, direct, pure, and portraying the unsullied and stable side of myself, whereas my diaries were messy and bloody and neurotic and spoiled and hysterical and expressed a more diabolical, more infantile, side of myself. With the ensuing years, as I realized that total strangers were going to read my prose, that prose began to take on the aspects of my music, becoming ever more pristine, clear, direct, pure, and above all objective, while the music, like Doctor Hyde, grew gradually tougher, more virile, more violent, and, I hope, more ugly—for all art must contain ugliness within its beauty. These two aspects of myself crossed each other, as though I were entering a mirror, or like two amebas merging, then separating. Therefore, if my musical palette is more 'dissonant', as you would say, I think it's that I now aim higher, at least as far as forms are concerned. If my two professions have replaced each other, it's not the result of a conscious decision but of a fomenting need. Other people besides you have pointed out that the kind of poetry I choose is different today, and, for the most part, contemporary and American, with a few exceptions, like *Three Motets* on Gerard Manley Hopkins. Meanwhile, I don't hear my musical work as 'dissonant' or 'difficult'—I just hear it.

"DAVIS: You do, however, have certain pieces that seem to go back into the old style.

"ROREM: Sometimes I'll do that because a style is needed for an occasion. My *Three Choruses for Christmas (The Oxen, O Magnum Mysterium,* and *Shout the Glad Tidings*) were commissioned, for instance, by St. Stephen's Church on 69th Street. They said, 'We want a piece that is brief, as easy as *Sing My Soul,* and that will be specifically for Christmas.' So I wrote not one, but three, to be sung *a capella* without much rehearsal. Obviously I'm not going to give them a lot of parallel major sevenths. The choral music of say, Webern, or indeed of any professional composer, is always simpler than their instrumental music because it's harder for choruses to stay in tune than it is for string quartets. I take that into consideration. It's not that I revert in the abstract, but for what the occasion demands. And the texts that I chose also happen to be direct statements.

"DAVIS: Do you think of yourself as a tonal writer?

"ROREM: Oh, definitely. I think of all music as tonal, because I hear all music according to my conditioning, just as you hear the same music according to your conditioning. I was raised on contemporary concert music as well as on American pop music of the forties, and as fate would have it, I knew all that music—the air of my epoch— long before I knew the classics, even Chopin or Tchaikovsky. I had to accustom myself (the way most people have to accustom themselves to the so-called moderns) to Bach and Beethoven, while I took the music of my own time for granted. Now, no matter how 'modern' that music was, I always heard it tonally; and no matter how chromatic my own music becomes, I hear it forever with a key base, sometimes even with a pedal point from beginning to end.

"DAVIS: In some of your most dissonant sections you suddenly end with a major triad. Are you trying to establish the tonal center?

"ROREM: I generally try to get back where I came from. That's arbitrary, because I was told very early by somebody—by Leo Sowerby, actually—that a piece has to end where it began. That's a compositional device that stuck, no matter how mad the music may be in between. Or, if I end in a key remote from where I began, I usually have to come reasonably close. I don't think that's either right or wrong.

"DAVIS: You seem to like parallel intervals. You use a lot of parallel fifths and fourths, particularly in a soprano-tenor or alto-bass combination. Is there any particular effect you're trying to get out of that?

"ROREM: The particular effect that I'm trying to get is of parallel fifths and fourths.

"DAVIS: Your choral music is basically homophonic rather than contrapuntal. Is that for textual reasons?

"ROREM: I've been criticized for that and so have coldly tried for more counterpoint in some pieces. For example, the piece on Colette. I'm not a contrapuntalist by nature, anymore than any French composers. My choral music inclines to want to be in blocks.

"DAVIS: Why is that?

"ROREM: I don't know. I hear choral music as blends, as layers of many voices, and to write block music in that way is so very different in sonority than the solo voice. I suppose it's in immediate contrast to the solo voice.

"DAVIS: When you use counterpoint, it's usually in the form of a canon.

"ROREM: And usually quite simple.

"DAVIS: Most of your early choral works utilize fairly even rhythms in comparison to later works.

"ROREM: Yes but lots of times, many composers will tell you, somebody will say something cruelly true to them and if that somebody is somebody they respect, they'll think it over. I remember just before I wrote *Praises for the Nativity*, a person close to me and musically knowledgeable said, 'Try to write a piece that's a little less stodgy, less square rhythmically.' Now, *Praises for the Nativity* turned out so madly difficult it never gets sung. It's for two choruses, with a lot of good ideas and good tunes. But it's tougher than it should be, tougher than its worth. I learned a lesson. Now I'd like to keep my music rhythmically vital without it being all that difficult. I agree with you. It is true that my pieces tend to be a little more square.

"DAVIS: Your choral works also contain much use of rests on the first beat of a measure. Is there a special effect you're trying to get with that technique?

"ROREM: Probably I feel it's more interesting. Precisely to get away from ponderousness. It's still the same music, but easier for the chorus. Most Bach fugues begin on an offbeat, so that the entrance of the second subject can be on the strong beat. It's not an inspirational but a tactical decision. Indeed, none of my music has much to do with inspiration. Nobody's does. You assume inspiration. You wouldn't be a composer in the first place if you weren't inspired. The urge that made you give up your whole life to the folly of being an artist already implies that you think you're good enough to condense and package and finally impart your inspirations to others. The vanity of that decision is such that you'd certainly better have enough technique that you can get away with it. A composer sits down, then, strictly with technical problems in front of him and hopes to God that the piece will sound inspired when it's finished.

"DAVIS: Has anyone influenced you in the writing of your choral works?

"ROREM: The question of influence is one that composers avoid. It's like confessing to be a thief, when thievery is a noble pursuit. If you know who has influenced you, you try to disguise, and the act of disguise is the act of artistry. Unconscious influences are more pernicious. Radiguet said: A real artist cannot help but be original; he has only to copy to prove his originality.[106] Novelty is less important

---

[106] Similarly, Ravel once advised young composers to imitate the work of admired fellow composers, because at worst one would arrive at a poor imitation—one's special individuality would come through, if one had any—one would, in any event, learn something. (Ed.)

than quality, and composers themselves aren't much concerned with tracing influences. That's your field.

"DAVIS: How about the other way around? How have you had influence on other composers of the twentieth century?

"ROREM: That's not for me to say or know. I hope so."

Arnold Rosner

B. 1945, New York NY. *Educ.:* NY Univ, State Univ NY (Buffalo). *Taught at:* Wagner College, Brooklyn College (City Univ NY), Kingsborough Community College (CUNY), Composer-in-residence, Colorado PO. *Works incl.:* choral works, *Concertino* (harp, hpsd, celesta, piano), *Of Numbers and of Bells* (2 pnos), qnt (ww), sonatas (ob [or vln], pno, vc, vln), 6 symphonies.

Composer statement: "Mahler said, 'When I make a symphony I try to create a universe.' When I write a piece—symphony or otherwise—I try to create a *part* of a universe. What kind of universe? A universe of feelings, passions, fears, ecstasies, dreams, revelations, obsessions, perhaps even catharses. To write music that merely entertains, or even soothes or stimulates, without any individual character, is merely to increase the already colossal glut of composition on paper or in our ears.

"The early composers of our century were correct, I think, when they considered the Classical tonal system to be played out. But they discarded the baby with the bath-water—many of them, at least—when they further eliminated from their pallettes all consonant or 'rooted' sounds, and later, anything recognizable as melody, counterpoint, or chord-progression. In their place, we have permitted relatively narrow devices to dominate the aesthetics of entire generations of music, and as a consequence, we have suffered. For example, the hyper-expressive, dissonant atonal style reached its peak in Schoenberg's fantastic *Erwartung*, which predated the actual formulation of serial procedures. The style was past its prime and nearly spent by the time it was formulated into a system. As for minimalism, the Javanese gamelan predates and overshadows our candy-striped Euro-American stuff. (But within more varied styles some quasi-minimal sections or pieces may be wonderful.)

"I think my own music reveals more love—it's almost an obsession—for the nonstandard treatment of simple harmony (major-minor clashes included!) than any composer since Gesualdo. Gesualdo works because no piece is longer than five minutes. But every listener familiar with Gesualdo knows the hazard: Before long the ear becomes so accustomed to chromatic and modal harmonic connections that they lose their potency. This can be prevented by buttressing the harmony with a full arsenal of structural and contrapuntal techniques, memorable melodies, and effective scoring.

"While I believe expressiveness is foremost, there is no doubt that richness, substance, and complexity are necessary to avoid cheapness and enable the music to endure more than one or two hearings. I hope that my music has enough strength and fabric to carry everything through so that my 'part' of a universe may one day be inhabited by some component of the fraternity of listeners."

From *The New Grove Dictionary of Music and Musicians*: "Rosner began writing music at an early age, developing his own individual style before receiving formal instruction. He was awarded the Ph.D. degree by the State University of NY (Buffalo) in 1972, successfully resisting all attempts to impose on him the dominant compositional trends of the day. Rosner composes prolifically in a primitivistic style characterized by the extensive use of modal counterpoint, *cantus firmus*, and ground bass. Repudiating many of the complexities of the past 300 years, Rosner favors clear, straightforward — if robust — textures and simple rhythmic patterns, preferring to concentrate on the expressive possibilities of a consonant, triadic harmony liberated from tonal expectations. Within its limited syntax, his music is capable of a surprising emotional gamut — at times gentle, serene, or even ecstatic; at others, brooding, harsh, or violent." — Walter Simmons.

The Chronicle of Nine (opera), Op. 81 (1984). *Lib.*: Florence Stevenson, after her play *The Chronicle of Queen Jane*. 2 hrs *Rec*. (Prelude to Act II): Laurel (Stereo LP) LR-849 CD: Jerusalem SO, David Amos, cond. *Pub.*: Arnold Rosner, c/o Kingsborough College Music Dept., 2001 Oriental Blvd, Brooklyn NY 11235.
7 M, 2 F; chorus, dancers
2-2-2-2; 4-3-3-1; perc., harp; strings
In three acts.
¶*The Tragedy of Queen Jane* (suite) for Orchestra.

"*The Chronicle of Nine* belongs to the tradition of operas concerning thrones and those who vie for them. In this case, the central character is Lady Jane Grey, an unfortunate victim whose marrige, ascendancy to the [English] throne, overthrow, and ultimate execution all result from the ambitions and actions of others.

"Florence Stevenson's libretto is a straightforward dramatization of the actual events, but reflects considerable sensitivity towards the people who lived them. The opera's title refers to the number of days in Jane's reign, as well as to the number of active singing roles and to the number of scenes in which there is vocal activity.

"Much of the text is set in impassioned recitative, calling to mind the operas of Monteverdi. Perhaps the closest English language comparison is Vaughan Williams' *Riders to the Sea*. A minstrel appears after the prelude to each act, setting the mood with a ballad something in the manner of an Elizabethan lute song. Several key scenes in the opera are duets, which the composer intensifies through striking instrumental effects: the love duet between Jane and her bethrothed highlights harp and vibraphone; the dialogue between Mary (the rightful Queen) and Jane, before the latter's execution, is accompanied only by six cellos. There are also grand crowd scenes and powerful orchestral preludes." — Walter Simmons.

¶**Prelude to Act II.** "Like many others of today's composers for whom there seems to be an active and receptive audience, Arnold Rosner writes music that is extremely straightforward, accessible, and rooted in traditional sounds and formal structures. Echoes and reminiscences of other composers abound, from Josquin and Gesualdo to Vaughan Williams, Shostakovich, and Hovhaness. Yet the cumulative impact of his music—with regard both to external style and inner meaning—is unmistakably unique and unquestionably original.

"The story of the teenage girl who—caught in a political web woven by others—became Queen of England for nine days before being dethroned and executed, is ideal for Rosner, providing the opportunity for an intense emotional experience within the historical context of sixteenth-century England—a natural setting for Rosner's musical language, with its many deliberately archaic usages. This unusual stylistic interpretation is apparent in the stunning six-minute Prelude to Act II— also included in *The Tragedy of Queen Jane*, the four-movement orchestral suite drawn from the opera—a solemn dirge of tremendous power, eloquence, and majesty, prompting great interest in *The Chronicle of Nine* as a whole." — Walter Simmons, in *Fanfare: The Magazine for Serious Record Collectors*, 1-2/90.

From a review of Laurel LR-849 recording: "Arnold Rosner was born in 1945, thereby missing by a hair the most disturbing event of our time and glad of it, judging by his music, which combines the gentler aspects of contemporary harmony with a feel for modality recalling the Renaissance and little that would seem overtly American in tone. He has managed to isolate himself from the mainstream to some extent, which may also constitute a form of defense against living in Brooklyn. At any rate, his music recalls the styles of Rubbra and Vaughan Williams.... Like those composers, religion appears to play a strong role in his choice of subject matter, while his liner notes [to this recording, which also includes the *Concerto Grosso Nr. 1, Five Meditations, A Gentle Musicke* and *Magnificat,*] also make reference to a love of the Renaissance and baroque as well as the late romantics. It is lovely and deeply felt music with a strong sense of inner peace about it.... [The *Chronicle of Nine* Act II Prelude] contains a moving melody, unusual in today's music where gestures and possibly harmony seem the moving forces." — David W. Moore, in *American Record Guide*, 7-8/90.

Quartet 4 for Strings, Op. 56 (1972). 20m *Pub.:* Arnold Rosner, c/o Kingsborough College Music Dept., 2001 Oriental Blvd, Brooklyn NY 11235.
1. Overture (Grave). 2. *Isorhythmic Motet*. 3. *Passacaglia* (Adagio sostenuto e misterioso).

"An unearthly combination of archaic and modern features in a work of extreme gravity. In the first movement, a stark French Overture is followed by a savage *allegro tempetuoso e marcato;* the second movement applies an ancient variation technique to eerily harrowing effect; the third movement, a passacaglia, builds cumulatively to a grim conclusion." — Walter Simmons.

Requiem for Solo Voices, Chorus and Orchestra, Op. 59 (1973). 62m *Pub.:* Arnold Rosner, c/o Kingsborough College Music Dept., 2001 Oriental Blvd, Brooklyn NY 11235.
1 s, 2 t, 1 b-bar, SATB
3-3-3-3; 4-3-3-1; perc, celesta, hpsd, pno; strings
1. Overture: *"The Seventh Seal"* (*t*. Liturgical). 2. Recitative: *"Ein Wort, ein Satz"* (*t*. Gottfried Benn). 3. Toccata: *Musica Satanica" (orch. only)*. 4. *Ballade: "Les neiges d'antan"* (*t*. François Villon). 5. Sutra: *Enmei Jukko Kannon Gyo* (*t*. Tibetan Book of the Dead). 6. Madrigal: "To All, To Each" (*t*. Whitman). 7. Organum: *"Lasciate ogni"* (*t*. Dante). 8. Prayer: "Kaddish" (*t*. Hebrew Liturgical). 9. Passacaglia: *"Libera me"* (*t*. Liturgical). 10. Nocturne: *"Und wieder dunkel ungeheuer"* (orch. only).
¶Nos. 2, 4 and 8 also arr. as *Three Elegiac Songs* for High Voice & Piano.

Sonata 2 for Cello and Piano (1968). *Rec.:* Opus One (Stereo LP) 108: Maxine Neuman (vc), Joan Stein (pno).

"A 40-year-old composer from New York City, Arnold Rosner has developed his own personal musical language based on a direct, traditional, easily accessible vocabulary. Like his *Sonata for Horn and Piano* [below], Rosner's cello sonata makes a powerful impact, ranging between the austere intensity of a Shostakovich quartet and a spiritual, ecstatic quality reminiscent of Hovhaness. Despite its indebtedness to the aforementioned composers, and to others as well — Vaughan Williams, for example — Rosner exhibits that rare quality (how rare can be appreciated only by those who spend a good deal of time listening to new music): a truly strong, unique musical personality. Despite conventional assumptions, this highly desired quality does not depend on being free of 'influences': it comes far more from a desperate urgency to express something—to communicate—which gives authenticity to the articulation and overshadows self-conscious considerations of originality, technical ostentation, etc. For Rosner, this urgency has resulted in more than 80 works in a variety of standard forms, although his music is only now beginning to attract anything like the attention it deserves.

"Like all composers with a dominating musical personality, Rosner is not for everyone—the simplicity of his means, a rather dogged adherence to his own peculiar syntax, and a relentlessness that borders on heavy-handedness, have alienated some listeners. But those who enjoy the horn sonata are not likely to be disappointed by this earlier work, which it resembles in large measure. And listeners favorably disposed toward the more conservative 20th-century styles and interested in discovering a fascinating new voice might well appreciate the music of Rosner—one of the true individuals of his generation [note, for example, the almost hysterical frenzy of the second movement—a wild, tempestuous fugue]."—Walter Simmons, in *Fanfare: The Magazine for Serious Record Collectors*, 5-6/86.

Sonata for Horn and Piano, Op. 71 (1979). 18m Winner, Harvey Gaul Award. *Prem.:* M. Sptealnik (hn), A. Brewster (pno). *Rec.:* Opus One (Stereo LP) 91: Heidi Garson (hn), Yolanda Liepa (pno). *Pub.:* Arnold Rosner, c/o Kingsborough College Music Dept., 2001 Oriental Blvd, Brooklyn NY 11235.
1. Lento. 2. Allegro. 3. Andante sostenuto.

"A work of uncompromising musical substance for an instrument whose repertoire of such works is limited. The first movement is a passacaglia of ominous majesty, based on an angular, wide-arching ground bass; the second movement is scherzo-like, with much syncopated rhythmic interplay, building to an exultant, affirmative climax; the third movement is based on a modal incantation that culminates in a ceremonial hymn of praise."—Walter Simmons.

Critic Simmons has also written: "In its beatific moments, the music [of Rosner] often reminds ones of Hovhaness, but unpredictable harmonic successions also suggest Gesualdo. However, the music is capable of a wild ferocity at times, not unlike Shostakovich. The result of all this is a rather broad spectrum of emotions—often ecstatic and violent elements juxtaposed—contained within a strictly defined rhetoric. Within these parameters Rosner pursues his individual course, preserving a stylistic purity utterly impervious to the influence of alien syntax....

"The *passacaglia*, with its capacity for slow and solemn contrapuntal development to a powerful climax, is a favorite form of Rosner's, and the one which opens this 1979 horn sonata causes one to forget the slight oddness of the instrumental combination, as one is immediately drawn into a musical experience of larger proportions. The vigorous *allegro* that follows offers a convincingly organic contrast, and the third movement is a characteristic neo-Renaissance hymn. Rosner's music has much to offer many listeners and this [sonata] provides a fine opportunity for discovering it." —Walter Simmons, in *Fanfare: The Magazine for Serious Record Collectors*, 9-10/84.

Symphony 5 ("Missa sine cantoribus super Salve Regina") for Orchestra, Op. 57 (1973). 35m *Prem:* Colorado PO, Arnold Rosner, cond., 1975. *Pub.:* Arnold Rosner, c/o Kingsborough College Music Dept., 2001 Oriental Blvd, Brooklyn NY 11235.
2-2-2-2; 4-3-3-1; perc., harp; strings
1. *Kyrie.* 2. *Gloria.* 3. *Credo.* 4. *Sanctus. Agnus Dei.*

"The composer's idiosyncratic adaptation of Renaissance polyphony applied to the Mass, in a powerful, robust treatment for modern symphony orchestra; each movement is based on the Gregorian hymn, *Salve Regina.*" —Walter G. Simmons.

CHRISTOPHER ROUSE

B.1949, Baltimore MD. *Educ.:* Oberlin Cons, Cornell Univ. *Taught at:* Univ of MI, Eastman Schl of Music. *Awards:* League of Composers/ISCM, Kennedy Ctr Friedheim Awards, NEA, Rockefeller Fndtn, American Music Ctr, Warner Brothers, BMI, Pitney-Bowes; Composer-in-residence, Baltimore SO. Active as a writer on musical subjects incl. rock music. *Works incl.:* concertos (db, strings), *Jagannath* (orch), *Lares Hercii* (vln, hpsd), *Mitternachtlieder* (bar, chamb ens), works (4) for percussion ens., *Phaeton* (orch), string quartets (2), *Surma Ritornelli* (chamber ens.), *Thor* (wind ens).

Composer statement: "My essential belief about music is put most simply by saying that any art, including that of sound, has no interest for me unless it has been created primarily to communicate to the open-minded reader/viewer/listener what might be termed an 'expressive state', and that the purpose of technique or craft is fundamentally to make that expressive statement intelligible and coherent. In music, I disagree with any aesthetic which elevates the craft of a work to the *raison d'être* in composing it. If a composition is only about the materials which make it up, without regard for their impact on the listener's emotional sensitivities, it ceases to be true art.

"Beyond this, I do not care whether a work is serial or aleatoric, tonal or atonal, minimalist or maximalist. Though my own music has been categorized as 'futurist', 'neo-expressionist', 'new romantic', and 'reactionary', these labels are really less important than whether or not I have tried and succeeded in conveying to my audience a valid and meaningful expressive message, and it is my firm conviction that this goal can be achieved using virtually any musical language available today."

Gorgon for Orchestra (1984). 17m *Prem.:* Rochester PO, David Zinman, cond. *Perf.:* Indianapolis SO, John Nelson, cond.; American Composers O, Nelson, cond.; Dallas SO, Richard Dufallo, cond. *Pub.:* Helicon Music Corp (European American).
1. *Stheno.* 2. *Euryale.* 3. *Medusa.*

"When David Zinman asked me to compose a work for the Rochester Philharmonic in commemoration of the Rochester, New York Sesquicentennial, my immediate concern was that an 'occasional' score dealing with some aspect of Rochester history or life might not be of interest beyond a very small geographical area, but his assurances that he wanted me simply to write any sort of piece I liked led me back to an idea which I'd long been attracted to, that of the three sisters of ancient Greek myth, the gorgons. So hideous were they—with snakes for hair, brass claws, and immense tusks for teeth—that one glance from any of them would turn a human to stone. For some years I had been concerned with the apparently ever-slowing metabolism of new music, with the result that many composers seemed either uninterested in or unwilling to consider the traditional sustained *allegro*. Earlier works such as *The Infernal Machine* for orchestra, *The Surma Ritornelli* for chamber ensemble, and my first string quartet had explored the possibilities inherent in composing connected fast movements, and in *Gorgon* I decided to carry this notion to its logical extreme—a score entirely composed of music in the same fast tempo. The myth of the gorgons, with its intensity and capacity for brutality, seemed a good choice for subject matter.

"*Gorgon* is cast in three connected movements, each named for one of the sisters. Between the movements is a brief percussion interlude entitled 'Perseus' Spell' after Medusa's killer. The tempo is unremittingly 176 to the quarter note. The result is a virtuoso display piece for orchestra which makes hefty demands upon the dexterity and stamina of the performers. On a surface level, *Gorgon* may be listened to as an orchestral 'rave-up' inspired by the legend of these notorious monsters. But on a deeper level, I intended the *symbol* of the gorgons—that of a horror too terrible to face directly—as a dialectic for all of our private monsters which we bury deep in our subconscious to avoid confronting for fear of *our* being destroyed. The overall impact of *Gorgon* is one of exorcistic rage and almost unbearable savagery, and it was my hope that my score might force sensitive listeners to face the very real terrors and despairs of their own existences.

"Because of the substantial demands *Gorgon* makes upon players, it has perhaps scared off potential conductors. However, on those occasions when it has been performed, audience reaction has consistently been overwhelmingly enthusiastic. Because it is a work which can be enjoyed on a visceral level, it has proven popular with listeners, and of all my scores it is the one for which I retain the most special fondness, both as the ultimate example of my 'allegro style' but also as a piece which distills most clearly my fascination with the darkest side of human experience.

"Though *Gorgon* has proven somewhat controversial, due largely to its obsessively violent character, many writers have found it invigorating. John Ardoin in the Dallas *Morning News* said, 'a monster of a piece, a score than is relentless in its demand for attention and empathy... a sort of orchestral perpetual motion, its textures are varied to fascinating degrees. The music never lets up; it drives from first note to last. It is a virtuoso rhythmic achievement, a true discovery.' Robert Palmer in the Rochester *Democrat and Chronicle* called it simply a 'monster smash'." —Christopher Rouse.

Phantasmata for Orchestra (1981-85). 18m *Comm. & prem. by:* St. Louis SO, Leonard Slatkin, cond. *Perf.:* Detroit SO, David Zinman, cond.; Denver SO, Philippe Entremont, cond.; Honolulu SO, Donald Johanos, cond.; Baltimore SO (incl. European-Soviet tour, 1987). *Rec.:* Nonesuch (LP) 79118-1: St. Louis SO, Leonard Slatkin, cond. ("The Infernal Machine"); Nonesuch: Baltimore SO, David Zinman, cond. *Pub.:* Helicon Music Corp (European American).
1. *The Evestrum of Juan de la Cruz in the Sagrada Familia 3 AM*. 2. *The Infernal Machine*. 3. *Bump*.

" 'The Infernal Machine' (Movement 2) was composed in 1981 originally as a concert opener for the University of Michigan Symphony Orchestra's French tour performances that May, and it went on subsequently to be performed by over fifty (to date) major orchestras around the world. One of its most ardent champions has been Leonard Slatkin, music director of the St. Louis Symphony Orchestra, who heard of my wish to compose two other movements around 'The Infernal Machine' and decided to commission the complete triptych for his orchestra. The remainder of the work was composed in 1985 and the whole entitled *Phantasmata* (Paracelsus' term meaning 'hallucinations created by thought'). Of the three movements, only the first cannot be performed as a separate entity.

"All three were inspired by dreams—hence, the work's title. The first movement represents an imagined out-of-body experience as the astral body of Saint John of the Cross floats through Antoni Gaudi's Cathedral of the Holy Family in Barcelona at 3 AM. As such, it is music imbued with the spirits of Spanish mysticism and surrealism; scored for strings and percussion, it is an *adagio* which gradually swells to one large climax and then subsides, and its overall harmonic language might be described as 'diatonically dissonant'. 'The Infernal Machine' is a *presto* inspired by the vision of an immense self-sufficient machine eternally in motion for no particular purpose. It takes its title from the play of Jean Cocteau but is not in any other way connected to that drama. Rather, it is a *perpetuum mobile* of 'atonal' character seeking to depict the leviathan as, sometimes, it whirs along in contented fashion, and at others throws off sparks or grinds as it changes gears; at the end, the machine self-destructs. 'Bump' derives from a dreamt tour of the Boston Pops in hell, in which the various ghouls and demons emerge from the crevasses at the concert's beginning to dance a 'nightmare conga', and 'Bump' imagines the music to which they dance; the characteristic throwing out of the hips or buttocks characteristic of the conga dance (knowing as 'bumping' on the dance floor), gives the work its title. The music is characterized by a bass drum stroke on every fourth beat to underline the conga flavoring, and there is also further evidence, notwithstanding the work's atonal language, of popular music influences from the big band style of Stan Kenton to references to such rock groups as Led Zeppelin and Canned Heat. Though 'Bump' is an *allegro moderato* notably slower than 'The Infernal Machine', its greater feeling of weight and power make it a more suitable finale.

"Popular and critical response to *Phantasmata*, in whole or in part, has been positive. In the *Suddeutsche Zeitung* (Munich), Karl Schumann referred to 'black humor of its wild rhythms, impudent melodies, and piercing tones of this... lavish orchestral piece ["Bump"],' while 'The Infernal Machine' has been praised as 'a total delight' by both the *New York Times* and Chicago *Tribune*. Though *Phantasmata* might seem, with the exception of the first movement, to be a lightweight comic work, I intend a somewhat darker undercurrent to the score. Much of the wit is quite sardonic, and the work with which I most closely associate the triptych in my own mind is Carl Nielsen's *Symphony No. 6*." —Christopher Rouse.

Symphony 1 for Orchestra (1986). 28m Comm. by Meet the Composer for the Baltimore SO. Winner, 1st Prize for orchestral composition, Kennedy Center Friedheim Awards. *Prem.*: Baltimore SO, David Zinman, cond. *Perf.*: San Francisco SO, Minnesota O, Dallas SO, Rochester PO, Milwaukee SO (all with Zinman). *Pub.*: Helicon Music Corp (European American).
In one movement.

"My long-held fascination for fast-tempo music led many, perhaps including myself, to wonder whether I was capable of writing a convincing *adagio*, and I decided to find out with my first symphony, composed in the summer of 1986. The original impetus for the composition was a passage for strings I had composed in 1976 as part of my doctoral dissertation for Cornell University. I wanted to re-use this excerpt from a piece with which I was otherwise ultimately dissatisfied, and I elected to construct a one-movement *adagio* around it; my first symphony was the outcome. Unlike most of my works since 1978, my symphony makes much use of recognizably tonal harmony, beginning in E minor, and finally concluding in E^b minor. There are other parts of the score which are more atonal in nature, and it was one of my goals to attempt the construction of a harmonic world in which I could move convincingly from 'tonal' to 'atonal' musics and back. Though the symphony is in one connected movement, it can be further divided into four slow sections—a *lamentoso* introduction which presents the principal material, a string fugato which is followed by a gradual climax built upon a ostinato, the serene D major string passage detailed above (which leads, perhaps unexpectedly, to a tortured and dissonant *tutti* outburst), and a concluding *doloroso* epilogue serving as a summation.

"My *Symphony No. 1* has come to function in my mind as yang to the yin of *Gorgon*. While *Gorgon* is an astringently dissonant *perpetuum mobile* at a very fast speed, the symphony is a single-movement *adagio* which makes much reference to tonal music. However, both concern themselves with issues of human suffering, with *Gorgon*'s hysteria and overwhelming violence here replaced by music more somber and tragic in tone. Though my first symphony possesses no program—at least not one nearly so specific as that of most other of my works—it does take as its subject the romantic-era notion of the tormented human spirit. Here, though, there is no romantic salvation or transfiguration; instead, the imaginary protagonist is utterly defeated and destroyed. To those who have accused me of an overly disturbing pessimism in this work, my only reply is that I believe the duty of the creative artist is not necessarily to uplift but rather to observe. It would be my hope that the observations contained in this darkly elegiac symphony, however harsh, might ultimately provide consolation."—Christopher Rouse.

"The fear of appearing foolish demands that a critic, hearing a remarkable new work for the first time, eschew what may later seem to have been over-lavish praise. It was no less a critic than Schumann, after all, who responded to Chopin's relatively insubstantial *Variations on 'Là ci darem la mano'* with 'Hats off, gentlemen, a genius!'

"But Christopher Rouse's *Symphony No. 1* is a work that is so rich, so allusive and masterly in its textures, and—ultimately—so moving, that it is hard to resist superlatives. With this splendid new score, Rouse has... produced music that is largely tonal and yearning, rather than screaming, in its expressiveness. The symphony is not 'symphonic' in the conventional four-movement sense. It is an immense (the orchestration calls for four Wagner tubas), 28-minute adagio in four sections: a keening introduction that is interrupted by Mahler-like explosions; a second section introduced by a tolling motive that leads into a fugato and finally is dominated by a Shostakovich-like ostinato; a transfigured passage that is bathed in almost mystical light; and—after yet another shouting climax—a final section, highlighted by a haunting oboe d'amore solo, which ends in yearning and painful ambiguity. This is a work that alludes to some of the most harrowing symphonic adagios ever written — those of the Sibelius No. 4, the Shostakovich No. 8, and the Bruckner No. 7 — yet it does not seem derivative. Rouse uses these fragments as a shore against the anarchic and ruinous dread that his music here attempts to confront. That the *Symphony No. 1* finds its own voice amid those of such distinguished predecessors speaks to the composer's achievement." — Stephen Wigler, in *Musical America*, 7/88.

"Rouse's symphony is an atmospheric, cinematic, ingenious, deeply personal, accessible, brilliantly crafted essay." — Scott Duncan, Baltimore *Evening Sun*.

MIKLÓS RÓZSA

B. 1907, Budapest (Hungary). Winner, Oscars for 3 film scores *(Ben Hur, A Double Life, Spellbound)*. Works incl.: concertos (pno, strngs, vc), film scores *(Ivanhoe, Julius Caesar, Quo Vadis)*, *Sinfonia concertante* (vln/vc/orch).

Quartet 1 for Strings, Op. 22 (1950). *Rec.:* Laurel (CD) LR 842 CD (Consortium Recordings/Allegro Imports): Pro Arte Quartet.
Quartet 2 for Strings, Op. 38 (1981). *Rec.:* Laurel (CD) LR 842 CD (Consortium Recordings/Allegro Imports): Pro Arte Quartet.
Rhapsody for Cello and Piano, Op. 3 (1929). *Rec.:* Laurel (CD) LR 842 CD (Consortium Recordings/Allegro Imports): Parry Karp (cello), Howard Karp (pno).

"More than 30 years separate Miklós Rózsa's *String Quartet No. 1* from his second essay in the medium, yet in that time the 'serious music' style of this well-known Hungarian-American film composer has hardly changed. Not that there aren't differences in mood between the two works. The first quartet teems with spicy dissonances and wonderfully propulsive, lopsided rhythms borrowed — like so many in the Bartók literature — from the treasury of Magyar folksong, but on the whole it seems just a warmup for the outpouring of intensity that marks its successor. What has remained impressively consistent over the decades is Rózsa's choice of materials and the way he shapes them for his highly personal expressive ends.

"The short, sharp chord that launches *Quartet No. 2* is harmonically and gesturally so compatible with the resolution of the first quartet's finale that the unsuspecting listener is tempted to hear it as a continuation of the earlier piece.[107] Perhaps a better way to hear it would be as the start of yet another chapter in a life's work that has been in-progress ever since Rózsa's student days in the 1920s, in Budapest and subsequently at the Leipzig Conservatory. With that image in mind, the 1929 *Rhapsody* for cello and piano — more tonal in

---

[107] The Johnston third and fourth string quartets have this kind of relationship — see above; also, of course, there is the "Ring" cycle. For this listener, the four Brahms symphonies equally display an uncanny unity, suggesting a sort of grand symphony in four parts. Each follows naturally from the one before, it seems to me — each takes its place in the four-part balance of the whole. It begins with a very definite, assertive, welcoming, openly expansive movement (symphony) 1; then a smooth, bucolic movement 2; followed by the somewhat jagged, not-quite-on-center, not-quite-conclusive movement (symphony) 3; concluding with an at-first-pensive, and then triumphantly consummative — with a fine, stirring *passacaglia* — movement 4. These four make a very full evening! (Ed.)

its language, more lyrical in expression, but no less forceful in its statement — comes across as a sort of prologue.

"This is solid, determined music, and it has very little in common — except for its completely unblemished craftsmanship — with Rózsa's memorable scores for Hollywood's *Quo Vadis?*, *Ben Hur*, *El Cid*, and *The Golden Voyage of Sinbad*. [In the Laurel CD recording] the performances by the Pro Arte Quartet are as probing as the works themselves." — James Wierzbicki, in *Musical America*, 9/89.

Sonata for Piano (1948). *Recs.:* Capitol: Leonard Pennario; Orion (LP) ORS 74137: Albert Dominguez.

"Rózsa's 1948 piano sonata is the kind of piece you would expect to hear more often. Besides its pianistic panache, it has enough energy, drive, and rhythmic pulse to last an audience an entire evening. Working within fairly classical forms, Rózsa probably reaches more exciting climaxes in a brief period than any other composer I can think of.

"But one reason for the effectiveness of the Rózsa excitement lies in the nature of the surrounding material, whether in the tranquil, almost Hindemithian opening of the first movement or the Hungarian-folksong quality that sets the second theme of the last movement against the frenetic syncopations that open it. The composer also sets up a harmonic idiom, making strong use of open fourths and fifths but also of some rich polytonal chord structures, that strongly enhances the somewhat percussive, Bartókian piano sonorities that pervade the work." — Royal S. Brown, in *High Fidelity*, 7/74.

Toccata capricciosa for Violoncello Solo, Op. 36. 8m *Pub.:* Breitkopf & Härtel (ed. by Jeffrey Solow).

"The *Toccata* by Miklós Rózsa, a composer well known for his motion picture scores, is immediately rewarding to performer and listener. It is a brilliant piece in a conservative style, well constructed and easily comprehensible, which makes effective use of musical events which naturally sound well on the cello." — Peter Farrell, in *Notes* (Music Library Association), 6/82.

EDMUND RUBBRA

B. 1901, Northampton (England); d. 1986. *Taught at:* Oxford Univ. *Works incl.:* choral pieces *(La Belle Dame sans merci, The Sacred Hymnody, Te Deum)*, concertos (vla), *Fantasy* (2 vlns/pno), songs with orchestra, 2 string quartets, *Sinfonia concertante,* 11 symphonies.

"Rubbra and [Michael] Tippett have shared certain formative influences; each however has produced his own individual result. Both have shown a great interest in Elizabethan religious and secular vocal music and the monodic music of the seventeenth century. To this Rubbra adds a strong influence from his teachers, Holst and R.O. Morris, and from Vaughan Williams, although he has never shown in his own music the slightest desire to use folksong material or style.

"A strong religious belief, intellectual rather than emotional, has perhaps had the most influence of all upon Rubbra's music. This has shown itself from the beginning in a fondness for setting the words of mystical peots such as Henry Vaughan and John Donne. The general leaning towards the motet and madrigal has had a considerable influence on Rubbra's music as a whole, instrumental as well as vocal. Early works such as the *Fantasy* for two violins and piano (one of the finest of his compositions to this day [1967]), by expanding ideas of the same type as may be found in the shorter unaccompanied choral works, show the fitness of his naturally vocal invention for extended development. An occasional leaning towards impressionism (he greatly admires Ravel) resulted curiously in superficial impressionistic effects producing an entirely unimpressionistic sound, because he could not disregard his desire for cogent musical form and shape. However, the potentiality of his music for growth to great stature became more and more apparent through such works as the *Fantasy* already mentioned (which is not a fantasy), the first string quartet, in F minor, Op. 35, and the *Sinfonia concertante* for piano and orchestra, a magnificent piece of integrated musical thinking with a fugal finale dedicated to Holst. It was inevitable that such a musical nature should come eventually to the symphony, and this he did in 1936 when he began his *First*. It is a fine work....

"[Rubbra] will never have Mahler's orchestral sense, but a Rubbra symphony scored in Mahler's manner would be ridiculous. In his *Third* and *Fourth Symphonies,* he wrote one near and one actual masterpiece. There are no finer symphonic ideas in the whole range of English (and much Continental) symphonic writing than the opening passages of these two works." — Harold Truscott, in Robert

Simpson, ed., *The Symphony; Vol. 2: Elgar to the Present Day* (Penguin Books, 1967).

"[In contrast to a composer such as William Walton,] despite his wide reading, historical knowledge, and interest in the graphic arts, Rubbra cannot be described as urbane. His music almost excludes epigram, impressionistic digressions or sudden brilliance; most of its ideas have high lyrical potential and may be suffused with lyrical sentiment from the beginning (as at the opening of the *Fourth Symphony*) but they usually need ample time to become impassioned. The rhetoric moves steadily to its climaxes, where emotion glows to full incandescence as in filaments at some distance from their source of power. Rubbra's achievement has been to combine the classical principle of expanding variation with a continuously polyphonic texture — polyphonic not just in the Wagnerian sense, but in a sense that has made people regard some of his movements as gigantic motets. Indeed, the claim to have linked renaissance with modern musical organisms, falsely made for composers whose texture was at least half impressionistic (Vaughan Williams's *Mass*, for instance, has more of Debussy than Byrd in it) can be sensibly made for Rubbra and only for him. Rubbra does not seek incidental color for its own sake. Most of his ideas are song-like and grow by polyphonic texture wherein the long phrases reach inexorably forward into big paragraphs — not of balanced sequences and patterns of figuration, but of asymmetrical sentences." —Arthur Hutchings, "Music in Britain 1916-1960", in Martin Cooper, ed., *The New Oxford History of Music: The Modern Age, 1890-1960* (Oxford University Press, 1974).

Symphony 2 in D for Orchestra, Op. 45 (1937). *Rec.:* Lyrita Edition SRCS 96 / HNH Records (Stereo LP) 4081: New Philharmonia O, Vernon Handley, cond.
1. Lento-rubato – 2. *Scherzo* (Vivace assai). (16m) 3. Adagio tranquillo. (11m) 4. *Rondo* (Allegro amabile). (8m)

"Rubbra [as a symphonist] certainly ranks with the best, having established his own grippingly personal identity through his [11] endeavors in this form. From my vantage point, the composers with whom Rubbra most demonstrates an affinity are the Dane Vagn Holmboe and the American Peter Mennnin, with whom he shares a propensity for violent rhythmic and tonal emphasis within an unrelievedly grim polyphonic context. All three approach the symphony as an abstract metaphorical framework through which to treat metaphysical preoccupations of uncompromising gravity. In comparison with Holmboe and Mennin, both of whom incline towards almost hysterical frenzy, Rubbra retains a more sweeping, expansive tone, soberly striving toward epiphanies of majestic grandeur. On the other hand, Vaughan Williams, often mentioned as an influence on Rubbra, has a softer center, a warmer, more humanistic identification.

"Rubbra's *Symphony No. 2* is a powerful realization of these general traits, the sort of work that compels one with its importance from the very first note, and pursues its relentless course to the end without faltering. This is an essential installment of the output of a composer indispensable to any consideration of the symphony in the 20th century." —Walter Simmons, in *Fanfare: The Magazine for Serious Record Collectors,"* 7-8/79.

"Polyphonic thought informs most of [Rubbra's] music, his symphonies included, and is perhaps the major part of his complex musical personality; and, in spite of his very real stature as a symphonist, and the [eleven] examples of this style he has produced, it would be of little use to study the classical symphony in order to find a clue to Rubbra's methods. His symphonic thought, far from reducing the contrapuntal approach, increases and intensifies it, so that, genuinely symphonic though his symphonies are, their approach is both different from the classical, or even the romantic, where the use of counterpoint, while important, is largely incidental to a basically homophonic texture, and from Sibelius, who has sometimes been quoted as an influence. Largely, Sibelius's symphonies, excluding such things as the first movements of the *First* and *Third,* which are plainly sonata movements, are extensions of his tone-poem approach (Sir Donald Tovey, in a letter to me, once described them as 'symphonic poems without programme'), requiring, except for the *Seventh,* more than a single design—and the *Seventh* was first conceived and announced at its first performance as a *Fantasia.* There may be, here and there, a Sibelian touch in a Rubbra turn of phrase, but counterpoint rarely appears in Sibelius's symphonies, and is rarely absent from Rubbra's. The two attitudes are fundamentally different.

"It was primarily the contrapuntal texture which caused problems in the first movement of the *First Symphony,* composed in 1936; problems innate in the music, and which just have to be accepted. Once they are, mists clear, and the whole thing becomes much more pertinent and clearly delineated. As so often happens once a composer has taken the symphonic plunge, the *Second* followed, in 1937, close on the heels of the *First.* With this, too, there were some problems, but these were solvable, and later Rubbra made some alterations, which included ending the work in D instead of E-flat, as originally, and re-scoring the first two movements to some extent.

"The first movement of the *First Symphony* is mainly a matter of extracting every ounce of contrapuntal meaning from one short semi-tonal figure, first announced energetically by a choir of brass, the upper part mirrored in the bass. The first movement of the *Second* begins *Lento rubato*, with a long melody in unison for all strings except double-basses, which is treated at first as though the movement were going to be a slow fugue. Fugal treatment abounds in the piece, but a fugue it is not—other elements are mixed with it; primarily extended development of ideas on a sonata form basis, although the piece is far from being a sonata movement. There *is* a certain link with Haydn, in that everything that happens is in some way derived from that initial melody, and the movement consists of continous development. There are two main parts to the theme, the second involving repeated notes and dotten rhythm. Episodes are built at times from these parts of the single line in counterpoint with each other, and rarely do they come exactly as before—but they grow with every appearance.

"Two qualities, apart from the counterpoint, are fairly persistent in any Rubbra symphony: the use of bi-, and at times tri-tonality, and the use of a dual tempo, made of fast and slow, or slower, running simultaneously. Both of these are much in evidence in the *Second Symphony*, and both are bound up with the composer's habit of maintaining a bi-tonal passage over many bars and suddenly allowing the music to pick a new harmony, often arrived at from a note used enharmonically; the effect is of a sudden soaring jump from a springboard, and the music sounds at such moments as though it suddenly strides into the middle of next week. Fast tempi grow almost imperceptibly from slow, but it is the slow tempo that controls the music. B-tonal passages are not difficult to find. Figure 2 in the score shows a prominent B minor-D minor bass against A-flat minor; around figure 4 we have a sort of A minor-F-sharp minor against E-flat minor, held together by a pedal D. This kind of writing informs the whole conduct of the first movement, where the strings say the key is D, but the oboe says it is A minor.

"The Rubbra *scherzo* is one of the most remarkable creations in twentieth century music. That in the *Fifth Symphony* has become a particularly noted movement among those who know his music, and yet, delightful though it is, and although many of Rubbra's most characteristic methods of movement and thought are present, in some ways this is the least characteristic example in his work,. About most of them there is something much more energetic, and at times, as in the present case, something almost demoniacal. Rubbra is a very religious man, and everyone has his or her own particular demons with which to wrestle. I have somethimes thought that the *scherzo* of the *Second Symphony* could record some such encounter. Most characteristically, Rubbra's *scherzi* move at varying tempi but usually in compound times — 6/8, 9/8, even, as in the *Second String Quartet*, 12/8 against 21/8. They seem to stem from the genial Perigourdine middle movement of the *First Symphony*, and the most rapid and vivid are those in the *Second* and *Seventh Symphonies* and that in the sonata for cello and piano, although the individual character of these three movements varies enormously. In the *Second Symphony*, from a rapid but harmonically energetic start on an oblique C-sharp minor which lands firmly on C minor, the movement pursues its way with a number of themes through various harmonies, 9/8 at times becoming 3/4, with slower effect, and collecting a 2/4 on the way, harmonically twisting and turning, but ultimately resolving itself into a battle between C major and C-sharp minor; C-sharp minor wins.

"The *Adagio tranquillo* is a profound meditation on three ideas, the initial viola melody, with its anticipation of the variation theme which went into the finale of the *Third Symphony*, a dotted rhythm derivative and an electrifying theme of contrary motion thirds on oboes, clarinets and bassoons. As always the surrounding counterpoint adds to the mood and the profundity.

"The final chord of the *Adagio* is a characteristic Rubbra surprise — B major in this case. The prominent D-sharp becomes, enharmonically, the tonic of the E-flat minor in which the *Rondo*-finale breaks out. The initial dancing 6/8 tune has a sting in the end of its phrases, in a sudden 2/4, which is extended at times and usually connects the music to a new harmonic springboard. This sting grows, too, with each appearance of the rondo theme. A lilting theme moving up and down in fourths and fifths (another Perigourdine type) joins the throng and is developed in combination with theme A for some time, leading by way of the sting in the tail to the first episode, a 2/4 pitched around A but with D major inflections. The rhythm of the 2/4 sting plays a large part here. The middle episode is largely development of theme A, the first episode returns, now on D with G major inflections, and the work ends with a triumphant D major apotheosis coda. Everyting is fulfilled, including the listener." — Harold Truscott, from program notes for Lyrita Edition/HNH 4081 recording.

Symphony 5 in B^b for Orchestra, Op. 63 (1948). *Rec.*: HMV DB-21384-87 (78 rpm)/ HMV BLP-1021 (10" LP) / RCA LHMV-1011 (LP) / RCA WHMV-1011 (45 rpm): Halle O, John Barbirolli, cond; Chandos (Stereo LP) ABR-1018 / Musical Heritage Society Stereo LP MHS-827285Y: Melbourne SO, Hans-Hubert Schönzeler, cond.
In four movements.

"Prof. Louis Blois has observed, 'Of all non-liturgical works in the literature, the symphonies of Rubbra and Bruckner are the most direct trajectories to a divine presence.' Such a strong statement certainly provokes consideration, though some may dispute it. However, after those of Vaughan Williams, for me Rubbra's are the most imposing symphonies composed by an Englishman, with a lofty grandeur and spiritual integrity that gives credit to the symphonic medium.

"Completed in 1948, the *Fifth Symphony* is one of the most highly regarded works in Rubbra's estimable canon — in fact, the distinguished composer Herbert Howells found it 'a work with the power to make one fall in love with music all over again.' It is also one of Rubbra's most accessible symphonies, with a lyrical warmth missing from the sterner *Second* and *Seventh*.[108] Its long, beautifully shaped, flowing lines evoke a mood of great nobility, dignity, and reverence; the slow, majestic unfolding of the first movement and the elegiac third are especially moving, [revealing] moments of an almost Mahlerian elegiac lyricism that haunt the listener long after the work is done. A gently rollicking scherzo and robust finale provide comfortable contrast, although my own preference for overall continuity does not dispose me toward conventional approaches to formal balance." — Walter Simmons, in *Fanfare: The Magazine for Serious Record Collectors*, 7-8/81 & 7-8/86.

Symphony 6 for Orchestra, Op 80 (1953-54). Comm. Royal P Society. *Prem.:* BBC SO, Malcolm Sargent, cond. *Rec.:* Lyrita (Stereo LP) SRCS-127: Philharmonia O, Norman Del Mar, cond.
1. Lento–Allegretto. 2. *Canto* (Largo e sereno). 3. Vivace impetuoso. 4. Poco andante–Allegro moderato.

Symphony 8 (Hommage à Teilhard de Chardin) for Orchestra, Op 132 (1966-68). *Prem.:* Royal Liverpool PO, Charles Groves, cond. *Rec.:* Lyrita (Stereo LP) SRCS-127: Philharmonia O, Norman Del Mar, cond.
1. Moderato. 2. Allegretto con brio. 3. Poco lento.

"Although they straddle the *Seventh Symphony*, the *Sixth* and *Eighth* can be said to have more in common with each other than with that work — even though a decade and a half elapsed between the beginning of work on the *Sixth* and completion of the *Eighth*. For instance, the propulsive energies of the second movement of the *Eighth* strongly resemble those of the surging first and third movements of

---

[108] The *Seventh* has been recorded as Lyrita SRCS 119, available in the U.S. on the Musical Heritage Society label.

the *Sixth*. The *Sixth* is, in fact, built around four recurring notes the permutations of which are easily recognizable to the listener; the result is a strongly unified whole which leaves the hearer with a sense of the composer's ultimate optimism. In the second movement of the *Sixth*, for instance, there is a gradual build-up of power which then recedes towards a point of acceptance or affirmation; in the finale — originally meant to be the first movement — initial uncertainties are resolved with a chorale-like restatement of materials.

"The *Eighth* is meant as a tribute to the late Teilhard de Chardin, and though the annotation makes no attempt to connect the music *directly* with the ideas of this remarkable thinker whose death only slightly eased a growing nervousness about him in some parts of the hierarchy of the Roman Catholic Church, the analysis provided in Robert Layton's succinct summary does in fact complement Teilhard's notions of an evolutionary progress by all created matter upwards towards some final point of fusion — the 'Omega Point' — with the Creator. That upward rising, that quasi-Oriental notion of an ultimate and universal acceptance, can be felt throughout Rubbra's musical design — this time one of three movements merely, with the fastest coming in the middle, and with the entire work progressing towards some final, blissful silence." — John Ditsky, in *Fanfare: The Magazine for Serious Record Collectors*, 9-10/82.

"It is often said that the music of Edmund Rubbra could be written in no time other than our own, and yet that it is not of our time. Certainly, his music is deeply rooted in England and its musical heritage through his is a far from insular outlook. The poetry he has set ranges from the Chinese T'ang dynasty, Icelandic ballads, medieval Latin and French verse, and his interest in Eastern cultures has been lifelong. His music does not readily surrender its secrets: the quiet integrity his art exhibits holds no appeal for those who are only drawn to gleaming surface brilliance, vivid colors and orchestral spices, and a high norm of dissonance. In Rubbra's music these would be out-of-place, for they would draw attention away from his quietist depths. There is nothing in Rubbra's music for people in a hurry, or for those who set greater store by exciting *sounds* rather than profound *sense*. If matter rather than manner is his central concern, this does not mean that the two are unrelated. In time one comes to appreciate that the substance of Rubbra's music and its presentation are indivisible, just as they are in the symphonies of Brahms....

"In all, the symphonies span five decades: the *First* (1935-37) could hardly be thought of as a 'motet for orchestra'.[109] It reflects much of the tension we encounter in the *First Symphony* of Walton or the *Fourth* of Vaughan Williams in whose wake it appeared. Three symphonies followed in quick succession and established him as a force to be reckoned with. The *Fourth Symphony* (1941-42) has a purity of spirit, and the simplicity of the opening idea speaks with rare directness of utterance. For many admirers of the composer it is one of the most searching and inspired moments in English music. With the *Fifth Symphony* (1947-48) he achieves a synthesis of the linear and the dramatic that leaves no doubt as to his purely symphonic credentials.

"Rubbra prefaces the score... of his *Sixth Symphony* (1953-54) with the four notes E, F, A and B, the first three of which are heard in the opening chord on harp, horns and bassoon and timpani. The four notes are heard thematically on the cor anglais at the beginning of the *finale,* which the composer had originally planned as a first movement. It was only when work on the symphony was well advanced that he realised its true place in the scheme. Each of the other movements draws on two or three of the four notes: the first is in a well-defined sonata design prefaced by a glowing, thoughtful introduction, and has two firmly contrasted musical themes. Yet, for all that, the whole argument is borne along by a strong sense of linear continuity: the burden of the melodic line remains virtually unbroken. The second movement, *Canto,* is preceded by some lines of Leopardi:

> *Sempre caro mi fu quest'ermo colle,*
> *E questa siepe, che da tante parte*
> *Dell'ultimo orizzonte il guardo esclude.*

> Always was this lonely hill dear to me
> And this hedge which shuts out
> So much of the distant horizon.

This is a powerfully serene movement which grows from the open fifth, A and E, and its tranquillity of spirit and language almost recall the composer's *Missa in honorem Sancti Dominici* (1948). This is possibly the most beautiful single movement in any of the Rubbra symphonies. In the *scherzo*, Rubbra sets out from the first two notes of his motto but the texture is soon lightened by a carolling figure on harp and celeste and clarinets. As the late Hugh Ottaway put it, the primary impulse in the symphony 'remains melodic and contrapun-

---

[109] Such is the eloquence and the quality of his output for *voices* that some critics have been tempted to speak of the symphonies as 'motets for orchestra'.

tal, but with greater emphasis on harmonic texture and therefore colour'.

"A *Seventh Symphony* (1956-57)[110] soon followed but a decade elapsed before Rubbra returned to the symphonic challenge. The *Eighth* (1966-68) bears a high opus number, so that the intervening years were in no sense creatively sterile. Rubbra was undoubtedly determined not to traverse the same terrain. The symphony was first performed by the Royal Liverpool Philharmonic Orchestra under Sir Charles Groves on January 5th, 1971. It bears the sub-title, *Hommage à Teilhard de Chardin*, the controversial Catholic thinker whose writings have had a great influence on Rubbra. It has something of the mystical intensity that inspires the *Ninth* (1971-72), arguably his masterpiece and certainly his most visionary utterance. Writing in *The Listener* (31 December 1970), Rubbra mentioned that instead of his usual preliminary short score, he wrote the *Eighth* directly in full score. 'The tonal centres of all three movements have their origins in the widely-spaced chord' heard at the outset, and the emphasis shifts from line (as in the *Sixth* and *Seventh*) to an increasing awareness of color. Each movement takes as its starting point an interval generated by the chord. In the second movement, for example, the concluding flute fragment of the first movement sets the pattern not only for the thematic substance of the *allegretto* but also its harmonic support. Rubbra's sense of organic continuity is in no way diminished. In his *Listener* article, the composer drew an interesting analogy when he spoke of the 'intensity generated by the progressive contraction of intervals as comparable to the energy engendered by the astronomical phenomenon of star contraction'. The emotional center of gravity is the *finale* whose textures and lines are permeated by the three-note figure that comprises both the opening chord and the ascending string line." — Robert Layton, from program notes for Lyrita Edition SRCS 127 recording.

"For the most part, Rubbra's symphonies are solemn, dignified works that develop their thematic material by weaving an introspective polyphony, slowly building momentum to climaxes of considerable grandeur. There is little contrast or conflict in the conventional symphonic sense, as changes of mood and tempo within a movement occur gradually and inevitably, despite an impression of open-endedness. The tone is consistently lofty and often beautiful, with never a vulgar or meretricious lapse. Thanks to the richness and

---

[110] *Symphony 7* in C Major, Op. 88. Recorded on Lyrita Edition SRCS-41 / Musical Heritage Society MHS-1397: London PO, Adrian Boult, cond. (Ed.)

depth of Rubbra's personality, the music compels attention throughout.

"The early symphonies have been criticized by some as concentrating relentlessly on the development of a musical idea to the point of exhaustion. (Not by me, though. This quality of relentlessness, while perhaps to some degree psychologically eccentric, generates a sense of majestic exhilaration as it proceeds on its uncompromising course.)

"However, the *Symphony No. 5* and *Symphony No. 6* are more 'humanized', offering an ingratiating lyricism and greater emotional variety. Thus perhaps these two works represent a better introduction to the symphonies of Rubbra. Annotator Robert Layton suggests that the second movement of *No. 6* may be the most beautiful movement in a Rubbra symphony; I might give that honor to the third movement of *No. 5*. But on the whole, the *Sixth* is at least as fine a work as the *Fifth*, exhibiting a jubilant nobility of rare conviction.

"The *Symphony No. 8, 'Hommage à Teilhard de Chardin'*, was completed in 1968, some 14 years after *No. 6*. Like the *Seventh*, it retreats somewhat from the overtly lyrical quality of the preceding two, yet becoming in no way forbidding. In fact, it is perhaps somewhat less demanding of the listener, with a greater emphasis on orchestral color and a more relaxed, fluid quality. The scherzo, in particular, is breezy, inventive, and quite effective." —Walter Simmons, in *Fanfare: The Magazine for Serious Record Collectors*, 9-10/82.

Symphony 10 (Sinfonia da Camera) for Orchestra, Op. 145 (1974). 17m *Rec.:* Chandos (Stereo LP) CBR-1023 (also as CHAN-8378) / Musical Heritage Society Stereo LP MHS-827285Y / RCA (UK) RL-25027: Bournemouth Sinfonietta, Hans-Hubert Schönzeler, cond.
In one movement.

"At the age of 84, Edmund Rubbra remains one of the most distinguished living exponents of the symphony as a primary medium for metaphysical reflection, expressed through the development of musical ideas. In the wake of the recent departure of such comparable figures as Pettersson, Mennin, and Shostakovich, Rubbra is a composer whose work continues to assert the durability of the symphony as a vital, relevant musical genre, when shaped by a composer of personality, artistry, and vision.

"As has often been stated, Rubbra's symphonies grow not from the Austro-German symphonic tradition, with its emphasis on duality, conflict, and resolution, but from Renaissance choral polyphony, with its focus on open-ended linear metamorphosis. Rubbra's symphonies are reflections on the ebb and flow of life and the cosmos, delivered by a compassionate but somewhat removed observer—unhurried without being prolix, improvisatory without being digressive. These contemplations may be tender or tempestuous, but they are always gracefully articulated, devoid of extravagence or abruptness, with a pervasive spirit of dignity, nobility, and humanity. Their somber tone and lofty perspective are likely to suggest Sibelius to the unfamiliar listener, though Rubbra achieves a linear coherence that eluded his Finnish predecessor. In fact, one might argue that Sibelius' inability to free himself completely from Beethovenian notions of motivic fragmentation, despite the very different nature of his spiritual content, prevented him from developing the formal procedures best suited to his artistic needs.[111] Perhaps one of Rubbra's most impressive achievements is his discovery of just such procedures—similar to those devised at about the same time in this country—though with infinitely less scope, vision, or sheer craftsmanship—by Roy Harris.[112]

"The reference to Sibelius is prompted by Rubbra's *Symphony No. 10*, in which the resemblance is particularly strong. Scored for chamber orchestra, it is modest in stature, its content compressed into one 17-minute movement. Composed in 1974, it is more subdued in tone than the earlier symphonies, and its thorough exploration of germinal material culminates in a sense of gentle serenity."—Walter Simmons, in *Fanfare: The Magazine for Serious Record Collectors*, 1-2/85.

* * *

THE SYMPHONIES OF EDMUND RUBBRA: A PERSPECTIVE. "The music of the British composer Edmund Rubbra (born 1901) bears a direct resonance with our times. Many composers have responded to our inhospitable century with jagged, cataclysmic, or alienating music. What makes Rubbra's music vital is that it is predicated on a positive, harmonious world view. His is a powerful, yet warm-hearted style

---

[111] A fascinating and intriguingly debatable point by a good friend. I happened to hear a Cleveland Orchestra performance of the Sibelius *Second* recently, and was reminded once again of the astonishing effects achieved by just this "fragmentation"—this special breaking things up which somehow—almost in a teasing way—contributes to (accents) the majestic, unified sweep of the whole. I think of the finale in particular, but the point applies to the work generally. (Ed)

[112] Yet, as I know Walter would agree, the works of Roy Harris have a zest and other characteristics which are thoroughly distinctive of the composer—and also seem distinctively American. One's "vision" sometimes *is* one's voice, I should think—with respect to music, having to do e.g. with the very *sound* of a given composer's work. (Ed.)

whose sturdy lyricism abstains from tough and cynical rhetoric. Rubbra's many works, especially the symphonies, offer tender compassion and, in a religious sense, nourishment to the contemporary spirit. Whether their theme is troubled or celebratory, they call upon an intense resource of affirmative perseverance.

"Like some other great inventions of Western civilization, the symphony seems destined to thrive in our century. Some still hold to the fanciful and rather provincial notion that the symphonic tradition died with Mahler. Such an assertion overlooks the major contributions of figures such as Shostakovich, Vaughan Williams, Mennin, and Rubbra. The quality and variety of their accomplishments speak for the viability of the symphonic form.[113] If Mahler is a landmark in this legacy, it is both as the closing voice of one era and the fountainhead of the next.

"Along with these other composers, Edmund Rubbra has made the symphony the central skeleton of his output. He has pursued his own voice apart from the tonal and atonal thickets our century has denoted as 'mainstream'. His loftiness is characteristically British, but his music is different from the folk-oriented modality of Vaughan Williams as well as from the urbanity of Britten and Tippett. In contrast to his countrymen, his attitudes toward color and content place him within a sphere of Scandinavian influence. The difficulty in categorizing Rubbra may contribute partially to his undeserved neglect.

"The most salient feature of Rubbra's music is its smooth melodic flow and generous counterpoint. Its impetus does not depend on the rhythmic, textural or thematic contrasts which have been commonly used since the origin of the sonata. These would be too disruptive for his intentions. Rather, Rubbra seeks a purely lyric and polyphonic realization of musical form, one which is shaped by the sheer growth of melody. The mainspring for such a style is a powerful sense of spontaneous melodic expansion, harnessed by disciplined formal organization. It seems natural that the continuous dialectic of a Palestrina- and Bach-like counterpoint occupies the foundation of his musical thinking.

"Rubbra's movements are typically 'arch' structures, logically motivated at every point. 'When I begin, my only concern is with finding a starting point that I can be sure of.' His melodies, which too often have been likened to those of Sibelius, show his connection to both Elizabethan and neo-Romantic attitudes. Their small in-

---

[113] The novel, apparently, is not dead, either. However, the concepts and indeed forms of both novel and symphony have — undoubtedly — been worked over a good deal. (Ed.)

tervallic motion gives them an ingratiating vocal quality, a feature not unrelated to his many works for voice and chorus. Although his triadically resolving harmonies and tonal centers are allowed to move with expressive freedom, his music is founded on the unwritten doctrine of cooperation — in both the aesthetic and formal sense of this word. Even when sonata strategy is executed, the tonal centers and thematic groups become allied rather than opposing participants. The dichotomy of conflict and resolution, then, is absorbed into a fabric of graduated harmonic and textural stress within the musical discourse. The first movements of his symphonies are the primary representatives of Rubbra's potent and contemporary idiom, an idiom that reflects a unique fusion of sixteenth- and twentieth-century tonal resources.

"Rubbra's works fall almost exclusively into two categories — vocal settings and abstract forms. Both share the same lyrical essence. The avoidance of theater music, even the declamatory manner of oratorio and cantata, is consistent with the kind of internal experience his music usually compels. His active interests in literature and religion, both Eastern and Western, have constantly broadened his creative perspective. As a student of Holst he acquired a fascination for the East and at times has incorporated its colors into his non-symphonic work. Rubbra seems to have been concerned with the meditative aspects of these elements and thus the occasional exotic indulgence is not totally divorced from his symphonic attitudes. His study of Buddhism and Taoism led to many vocal settings of oriental texts. Yet, one is just as likely to find settings of Elizabethan poets and Medieval Christian theologians. His four masses and other liturgical works reflect his intimacy with Catholicism.

"A portrait emerges of a composer for whom musical exposition is a vital extension of a broad commitment to philosophical, religious and aesthetic matters. In this regard the symphonies of Rubbra and Bruckner share common ground. Their canvases are both drawn from cooperative, rather than antagonistic musical material, toward climaxes which are expressions of ecstasy rather than confrontation. Through his musical form Rubbra has always shown a concern for wholeness, for mending man's disunity both individually and collectively. Even in works written during the second World War his dialectics have been sternly restorative, never bitter or violent (as we find in so many great 'war works' of other composers). His canon of eleven symphonies is sophisticated and attractive, and at the same time offers challenge and reward to the enterprising listener.

"Rubbra's symphonies trace a continuous growth and in some way each represents a reaction to the previous one. One may group the first four as a strict contrapuntal revamping of the symphony, from a different vantage point. A softened lyricism in the *Third* and *Fourth* replaces an earlier severity. Subsequent to that, an increasing tone poise and use of homophonic texture leads his development in the direction of harmonic and structural variety.

"At thirty-five, Rubbra brought a spiritual and intellectual maturity to his first works in the form. The first two symphonies were composed within a year of each other and share a zealous contrapuntal fervor. The principal material is sundered into phrases which are meshed, transmogrified, and reassembled in an environment of bursting contrapuntal activity. Their thick orchestraton is appropriate to the intended effects. A wide range of devices is explored which would become permanent to his style: fluctuations of texture, sequencing, cross-rhythms, and the climactic use of ostinati and pedal points.

"In the first movement of *Symphony Nr. 1* (1936), Rubbra tends to thread short motifs into longer periods with a congested abandon that some listeners find thrilling. The 'Perigroudine' movement establishes what would become a generic component of future symphonies, the 'Rubbra *scherzo*': a polyphonic tour-de-force built around a chipper tune. The lengthy final movement has impressive passages, yet it makes overly exhaustive use of its sparse motivic material.

"Almost as a gesture of compensation, in each of the four movements of the next symphony the composer elaborates long initial material which is then used in a piecemeal fashion. A particular austerity and breadth of expression belongs to this *Symphony Nr. 2*, whose grandeur is distributed throughout. In the *Adagio tranquillo* one finds the monastic transport and climactic epiphany that is special to his slow movements.

"These symphonies are both works of considerable moment and ambition. Yet Rubbra soon was to strive for a different kind of melodic impact which would require a moderation of texture.

"In the next symphony, *Nr. 3* (1939), we find the composer's intellect less in competition with his lyrical gift. With a less crowded canvas Rubbra relaxed the tenor of his symphonic writing by endowing it with a mellifluous vocal quality, as well as interspersions of homophony. His prolific music for voice and recent orchestration of the Brahms-Handel variations were apparent influences. The first movement's songful allure, antiphonal exchanges, and development through contrasting episodes are evidence of this, as is the *finale*, a set of variations and fugue. The slow movement is particularly touching for its delicate cross-rhythms and unbroken *melos*. Rubbra seems to have been guided by a straightforwardness and a poetic-religious valor, in which the quest for stylistic and spiritual purity seem to be at one. It is worth repeating the remark of the composer Herbert Howells, who wrote, 'Now and again there comes a work with the power to make one fall in love with music all over again. In such a mood I found myself when listening to your [3rd] symphony.' With a lyrical quality both innocent and in the British sense, noble, Rubbra shaped the melodic character of his successive symphonies.

"In contrast to the idealism of the *Third*, the grim probing of the *Fourth Symphony* (1941) was more of a direct response to the war-torn world. The composer, who was stationed with the Army in Wales at the time, must have physically enhanced this impression as he conducted the première in battle dress. The work is a masterpiece of his amassed disciplines. The opening *Con moto* is the most singularly focused, monothematic movement of the Rubbra canon. It develops by a layered succession of broad, nearly regular breath-long phrases which elaborate on an initial three-note motif. Its searching lyricism, as well as the composer's own use of harmony, is underscored with rhythmic throbbings of unresolved seventh chords. Thus, the somber atmosphere of accumulation is supported by two laters of activity—one contrapuntal and the other homophonic—each with its own obsessive behavior. The climax is one of his finest contrapuntal passages. The slow movement is incorporated into the *finale*, a stirring and weighty tract of contrapuntal shaping. Throughout the symphony Rubbra exhibits his uncanny ability to transmit intense psychological and meditative states. In this context the tragically beautiful *Soliloquy* for Cello and Strings, begun a year later, should be mentioned.

"Rubbra's next symphony, the *Fifth* (1947-48), was a resounding success which brought him much attention. In it he achieves a triumphant synthesis of his contrapuntal foundation and classical procedures. Rubbra's performing involvement with his own Trio, which he had formed during the war years, had a pronounced influence on the new symphony. His use of contrasting tonal centers, crisp rhythms, and lucid instrumentaion shows his concertizing exposure to the repertoire of Haydn, Mozart and Beethoven. This new tonal stability resulted in his organizing the first movement, as well as those of the next two symphonies, around sonata form. The *Fifth* is Rubbra's celebration of lyrical abundance. The opening four-note motif undergoes a remarkable transformation of identitites, complying with the music's rhythmic variety and charismatic reflexes. The *Scherzo* is the most charming representative of its kind, the flow movement a monumental benediction. Wilfrid Mellers, who has written much about Rubbra, praises the *Fifth* as having 'a positive power and serenity which implies religious assent, however painfully it may have been won.' It was the first Rubbra symphony to have been recorded.

"Between the *Fifth* and *Sixth Symphonies* Rubbra, who was raised as a Non-conformist (Congregational), converted to Roman Catholicism. This immediately led to the celebrated *St. Dominic Mass*, as well as a quantity of sacred Latin vocal cycles during successive years. Such behavior again evidences the continuity and conviction of his spiritual-musical world.

"Harmonic texture becomes more prominent in the next symphonies. As a result, Rubbra's style converges on a new contrapuntal-homophonic synthesis (in the *Third* and *Fourth* they were used as distinct textures). This indicated a greater focus on harmonic thinking, and a shift to longer basic materials as opposed to terse motifs. Also, all successive symphonies have technical and/or dramatic relationships which unify their movements beyond the usual consistency of style and attitude. In the *Sixth* (1953-54) this happened on both a conscious and subconscious level. Not only do its four movements share deliberate intervallic derivations, but after they were written Rubbra decided to arrange them in the exact reverse order of their composition. This is particularly unusual for a Rubbra symphony, whose disposition is so dependent on that of the first movement. Yet, there is a pastoral and vigorous benevolence that the movements share so that none presides over the artistic tenor. It is probably this temper of spiritual equilibrium which disposed the magic *Canto* movement, one of his most blessed and metaphysical visions.

"The *Seventh* (1957) is the symphony probably best known in America for its one time appearance on the Musical Heritage Society label (MHS-1397). More than any other, its use of harmony is the most stirring and varied, inducing ethereal effects in one passage and emotionally charged tension in the next. Diametric to the homogeneity of the *Sixth*, its three movements are built around the dynamics of conflict. The first movement is one of exceptional concentration and economy. Its sonata subjects are unusually antithetic for a Rubbra work. Yearning, scalewise material is plotted against a rising chromatic figure which, as it drops by fourths, increases in urgency. Its spellbinding power derives from a double axis of motivic tension in which the antagonism of harmonic severity is harnessed by a gripping melodic logic. The *Scherzo* inherits this agitation (as well as motivic similarities), and culminates in an electrifying collision of extremes. In the final *Lento* this crescendo of opposites is neutralized in the oneness of a transcendent *Passacaglia and Fugue*. The radiant harmonies within, and the transfer of tension across each movement, make a profound impression laden with philosophical overtones. Whatever dark forces the *Seventh* reconciled in Rubbra's soul, a full decade would pass before the next symphony appeared.

"With the *Eighth Symphony* (1966-68) Rubbra emerged at a new stage of development. The work is dedicated to Pierre Teilhard de Chardin, the controversial Catholic thinker whose writings intrigued the composer. Teilhard sought within Christian dogma a rational theory of human and cosmic evolution yeilding an ultimate 'omega point'. The musical relationship is not intuitive, but the symphony does give the impression of great expanse and structural solidity. The reason for this is the eventful, yet static nature of the landscape in which, as Robert Layton points out [see above—Ed.], 'emphasis shifts from line to an increasing awareness of color'. The *Eighth* is virtually an offering of sonorities as natural wonders. The orchestration takes on a new, vivid transparency. In the first movement Rubbra attaches expressive importance to the chordal progressions and intervals associated with certain motifs. As a result, the expected development is inhibited and instead, the motifs juxtapose and overlap in massive, climactic summits. Similarly, the enchantment of the final *Poco lento* owes much to its varying spiritual riches. There is plenty in this symphony to provoke the listener's mind and ear, such as half-buried harmonic and intervallic bonds between movements, and in particular, the cryptic appearance of the closing tune in each of the three movements. It remains a work filled with panoramic luster and opulence which has drawn specific attention from British critics.

"In the *Symphony Nr. 9*, the *'Sinfonia Sacra'* (1973), Rubbra makes another departure from symphonic tradition, combining his vocal and orchestral idioms with his sympathies for Christianity. It is conceived in the spirit of the Bach *Passions*, and it is his longest symphony (45 minutes). It presents a soundscape of the events from Christ's death to the Resurrection, scored for soloists, male and female choruses, and orchestra. All resources are pooled to create a pungent evocation of the ancient Middle-East along with the sepulchral darkness of Catholic mythology. The ariosos are based on narrations from the New Testament Gospels. The undulating contralto carries much of the forward symphonic tension. In the orchestral and choral installments Rubbra's new sound palette reclaims the pathos suspended in the *Eighth Symphony*. The *finale* portrays the Resurrection itself where latent ecstasy is absorbed in a glowing hymn conceived in the Church tradition. As in the previous symphony, Rubbra shows a tendency away from cumulative and toward episodic rhetoric.

"His latest two symphonies are also his shortest, about a quarter of an hour each. In them Rubbra continues his formal innovations.

Their somber ebb and flow are digressively guided with the vivid timbres of their predecessors.

"In the *Symphony Nr. 10* (1974), the *'Sinfonia da Camera'*, Rubbra fulfilled a long contemplated desire to disjoin the subdivisions of the sonata into individually contained movements. Its pale motifs and occasional Sibelian phrase contribute to its searching nature.

"The *Eleventh* (1978-79), according to Rubbra, is 'a culmination of all my symphonies compressed into one movement'. While no explicit reference to previous symphonies is evident, it is a tighter musical drama than the *Tenth*, punctuated by more frequent musical events. Its melancholy is wrapped in tones more luxurious than troubled.

"With the *Eleventh*, the canon of Rubbra's symphonies to date is complete. They chronicle a life rich in internal activity with an apparently boundless source of inquiry and innovation. They are excellent candidates for conductors looking for appealing new works to incorporate into the standard repertoire. While Rubbra's conservatism may have put him temporarily out of fashion, currency of style has never been a trustworthy measure of musical quality.

"Rubbra's context is a theistic one which is both lofty and humane. His values have never been inhibited by trends of the avant-garde, nor have they been compromised by a public seeking immediate apprehension. His music deserves celebration for the imposing quality of its thought and for the strength and individuality of its vision.

"But perhaps most important, Edmund Rubbra has demonstrated with great depth and beauty that the twentieth century is able to support music that conveys reverence and affection, music which pauses to look inward from many perspectives of human experience. Rubbra's music, in its own tenacious way, espouses the harmonious cooperation out of which it is built. Such music must secure an esteemed position in the symphonic tradition of which Mahler represents not an end, but a crossroads." — Louis Blois, in *The American Record Guide*, 5/84.

HARALD SAEVERUD

B. 1897, Bergen (Norway). *Educ.:* Bergen Music Acad; Hochschule für Musik, Berlin. *Works incl.:* concertos (ob, pno, vln), inc music *(Peer Gynt, The Rape of Lucretia)*, orchestral *(50 Small Variations)*, piano pieces (sonatas, sonatinas), *Ridder Blaskjeggs mareritt [Bluebeard's Nightmare]* (ballet), 9 symphonies.

Symphony 5 (Quasi una fantasia) for Orchestra, Op. 16 (1941).
  Publ.: Musikk-Huset (Oslo)(miniature score; performance materials on rental).
3-2-2-3; 4-3-3-1; timp, perc, harp; strings
In one movement.

"Harald Saeverud is one of Norway's most prominent composers. His recognition as a leader of modern Norwegian music came during the 1940s and 50s, particularly after his incidental music for Ibsen's *Peer Gynt* in 1948. Although Saeverud is regarded by many of his countrymen as one of the most truly Norwegian of composers, according to Kristian Lange he began his career as a musical internationalist with elements in his music ranging from Mahler to Krenek. In the latter half of the 1930s, phrases reminiscent of Norwegian folk music formed a part of Saeverud's compositional palette. However the years of the German occupation brought out the most nationalistic elements in Saeverud's music. 'A real rage of productivity was immediately released in me,' said the composer. 'I felt that my work had to be a personal war with Germany.'

"During the war, Saeverud wrote a symphonic trilogy dealing with struggle and faith. This consists of the *Symphony No. 5*, with the subtitle 'Resistance Movement Symphony', the *Symphony No. 6* also known as the *Sinfonia dolorosa*, and the *Symphony No. 7*, 'Salme [Hymn]'. Norwegian elements are apparent in the fifth symphony. Although Saeverud does not quote folk melodies, he is clearly influenced by them. For example, the persistent dotted rhythms of the Norwegian *Slatter* (dance melodies) are heard throughout the piece. Much modal writing in the symphony must be due to the influence of folk music and the Hardanger fiddle, a Norwegian folk instrument, whose melodies are often cast in the Lydian mode. This mode occurs most noticeably in the violin statement of the second theme. The Mixolydian mode and the whole-tone scale appear less frequently. The themes themselves are generally diatonic; dissonant harmonies are placed within a tonal framework. The use of various modes and scales makes the tonality fresh and modern for its day.

"The form of this one-movement symphony defies easy categorization. There are six main sections: exposition, a set of variations, development, a second exposition and development with a third theme, and a long coda. The bold and angry first theme sets the mood for the work. A second theme is heard before a set of twenty-six variations on the first theme come into play. In the later variations, Saeverud uses only fragments and motives from the main theme; the result is a series of interrelated motives resembling the *vek* technique of Norwegian folk music.

"The orchestration is careful and occasionally complex. One instrument often plays alone for a few measures to be joined later by the other members of the section. In the case of the first violins, one to four instruments are used in solo sections. This chamber quality provides a nice contrast to the fuller *tuttis*. The composer is meticulous in indicating what bow strokes string players should use.

"Saeverud's *Symphony No. 5* is a vital addition to the symphonic literature, and [its] score will be a worthwhile addition to any music library." — Patrick Hardish, in *Notes* (Music Library Association), 6/84.

Symphony 6 (Sinfonia Dolorosa) for Orchestra (1942). 12m Rec.: Norwegian Philips (LP) 6507 007: Bergen SO, Karsten Andersen, cond.
In one movement.

Symphony 7 (Salme [Psalm]) for Orchestra (1944–45). 19m Rec.: Norwegian Philips (LP) 6507 063: Bergen SO, Karsen Andersen, cond.
In one movement.

"The 82-year-old Harald Saeverud is the towering, lonely genius of modern Norwegian music and one of the most exceptional and peculiar figures in all of the 20th century. After nearly two decades of experimenting with various very individualistic combinations of neo-Romanticism and dodecaphony, under the impact of Germany's occupation of his beloved country during World War II, his mature style crystallized into a craggy, muscular, contrapuntal lyricism — obstinately dissonant but decisively tonal — which, like Roy Harris' in this country, fused the distilled ethos of nationalism with the super-structure of Renaissance polyphony into a supple, rugged, visionary engine of self-expression.

"Also like Harris, the creatively eccentric Saeverud delights in spikey, asymmetric ostinato rhythms with obsessively repetitive phrases, crab-like, parallel and contrariwise harmonic motions, and dour, plangent chorale melodies which graphically conjure up the unique Hardanger folk idiom Saeverud must have absorbed into his subconscious during the many years he has lived in his native Bergen. Yet this music also shows an amazing sophistication in its delineation of psychological states ranging from the childlike to the demonic, in its spartan directness of facture, and in its aphoristic, almost circular self-sufficiency, for Saeverud is one of the masters of the intensely concentrated and organically conceived single-movement form, as, for example, in his 12-minute *Sixth*—and possibly greatest—*Sinfonia Dolorosa*.

"The *Seventh*—or 'Psalm'—*Symphony* of 1944-45 reflects a slight slackening of the almost Sysiphean atmosphere of dark affliction and desolation prevailing in the *Fifth* and *Sixth*, written in the depths of the war years. Subtitled 'A symphony of hardship, struggle, faith and gratitude. Mother's and Father's symphony.' its heroic 19-minute frame encompasses an exhortation to the impending victory of Norway over the invading foe, and as such has a kind of mythic, bard-like aura of solemn Nordic commemoration. Built around two chorales, a hymn-tune, and a 'chime' motif—all of which are original and intervallically related—the symphony builds gradually but unrelentingly, through an interlocking web of elaborate variation techniques, into a weighty peroration or 'Glorification' in which all the various strands are superimposed in a conclusion of transfiguring light and benediction."—Paul Snook, in *Fanfare: The Magazine for Serious Record Collectors*, 5-6/79.

Symphony 9 for Orchestra, Op. 45 (1966). *Rec.:* Norwegian Composers (CD) NCD 4913: Royal PO, Per Dreier, cond.

ON CONTEMPORARY COMPOSERS IN SCANDINAVIA: "The abundance of first-rate symphonic music produced by Scandinavia in the 20th century is a mysterious secret to most music lovers. Is there life after Sibelius and Nielsen? Try: Vagn Holmboe, Herman Koppel, Niels Bentzon, Aare Merikanto, Einar Englund, Klaus Egge, Fartein Valen, Hilding Rosenberg, Gösta Nystroem, or Lars-Erik Larsson. These are certainly among the better known Scandinavian composers of the present day, which is to say that they are hardly known at all outside Scandinavia itself. This is our loss, which can be particularly acute when it comes to a symphonist of such stature and integrity as the Dane, Holmboe. Perhaps the same might be said of the Norwegian composer Harald Saeverud, who this year [1988] celebrates his 90th birthday.

"Saeverud is very well known in Norway, where some of his compositions from the World War II years [such as *Ballad of Revolt* for orchestra], epitomizing the resistance, have become part of the fabric of Norwegian national consciousness....

"Saeverud's music is generously spiced with dance rhythms. It is most imaginatively and piquantly orchestrated, and possesses a multitude of very affective and expressive melodies. The canvas onto which these components are splashed in bold and original ways is a large one, though woven in a traditionally tonal and thoroughly accessible manner. There is a free-wheeling, unfettered, almost improvisatory air to the way ideas are developed which is quite exciting and fascinating....

"*Galdreslåtten [Symphonic Dance]* is a good example of the fun Saeverud can have with dance rhythms. So is the *Poco lento* movement of the *Ninth Symphony*. I have not heard such a delectable treatment of the waltz since the second of Lars-Erik Larsson's *Due Auguri*, as beautiful an apotheosis of the dance as has been written in modern times." — Robert R. Reilly, in *Musical America*, 1/88.

ALFRED SCHNITTKE

B. 1934, Engels (German Volga Republic). *Educ.:* Moscow Cons. *Taught at:* Moscow Cons, Vienna Hochschule für Musik. Author essays on Shostakovich, Prokofiev, Stravinsky, Bartók, Webern, Berio, Ligeti, others. *Works incl.:* 6 ballets *(Othello, Peer Gynt)*, concertos (ob/hp/strngs, pno, vc, vln), more than 60 film scores, piano pieces, 3 string quartets, *Requiem, Suite in the Old Style* (vln/pno), 3 symphonies, trio (vln/vla/vc).

" 'For me, Alfred Schnittke is probably the greatest composer [alive],' the pianist Vladimir Feltsman confidently told an interviewer recently. 'That does not mean I ignore Ligeti, Messiaen or Cage, but I find Alfred's music is particularly interesting. And in the Soviet Union, he has inherited the stature that Shostakovich had before his death. He does not have a lot of official titles, like People's Artist or any of that, but for musicians and music lovers in the Soviet Union, he is definitely No. 1, no question about it.'...

"In an interview at Mr. Feltsman's apartment [in New York, Mr. Schnittke himself said], 'In the beginning, I composed in a distinct style, but as I see it now, my personality was not coming through. More recently, I have used many different styles, and quotations from many periods of musical history, but my own voice comes through them clearly now.'

"Mr. Schnittke's music is, as he suggests, an eclectic mix, with elements of Baroque, Classic and Romantic style refracted through a decidedly contemporary prism. In some cases, these references to other eras are humorous; in others they have a wistful quality, and in still others they seem merely to provide a formal platform from which Mr. Schnittke launches his own explorations. He is also not averse to using patches of 12-tone writing, dense tone clusters or even jazz allusions, side by side with Baroque dance forms or rich 19th-century lyricism.

" 'It is not just eclecticism for its own sake,' he explains. 'When I use elements of, say, Baroque music, I do it not simply because I want to juxtapose different styles, but because I feel it's what I have to do in the piece at hand. Sometimes I'm tweaking the listener. And sometimes I'm thinking about earlier music as a beautiful way of writing that has disappeared and will never come back; and in that sense, it has a tragic feeling for me. I see no conflict in being both serious and comic in the same piece. In fact, I cannot have one without the other. They are two sides of the same consciousness.'

"Now 54, Mr. Schnittke came to music comparatively late. He was born in Engels, in the U.S.S.R., in 1934. 'During the war years,' he recalled, 'we didn't have a radio; I don't think I heard any music at all. One of the first pieces I heard, in 1946, was the Shostakovich *Ninth Symphony*, which was very refreshing, but also very strange.'

"It was around that time, he says, that he first felt the urge to compose, but at 12 years old, he did not play any instruments. That year, his parents were posted to Vienna (his father was in the foreign service), where he began studying the piano. And when they returned to the Soviet Union, in 1948, he entered a music preparatory school and, in 1953, the Moscow Conservatory.

"Mr. Schnittke remained at the conservatory as an instructor after completing his studies in 1958, and he began writing concertos and chamber works on commission. He also embarked on a flourishing career as a film-score composer: between 1961 and 1984, he score 60 films. But from the start there was a wide gulf between his film scores and his concert music, his concert works often being couched in a severe atonal style.

"He reached a turning point in 1968, with his *Second Violin Concerto*, a work he now looks at as his first 'polystylistic' piece. 'I was influenced by three things,' he explains. 'The first was the music of Mahler and Ives. The second was Henri Pousseur's total serialism — the serial arrangement not only of pitches, but dynamics, durations and other elements too. And the third was my work in the cinema. In writing for films, I was often writing music that suggested other eras. So I adopted that for my other works.'

"Mr. Schnittke's reputation as an innovator grew quickly, but given the changing winds of Soviet officialdom, that was not necessarily a good thing. 'Alfred was a leader of the so-called "non-conformist" school,' Mr. Feltsman recalls, citing Edison Denisov, Arvo Part and Sofia Gubaidulina as others in that camp. 'When these people were young, they were finding their way, and because they used techniques that were not approved — serialism, for instance — life was made very difficult for them.' Among their principal adversaries was Tikhon Khrennikov, chief of the Composer's Union since Stalin's time (and still in office), who declared that 12-tone writing, for instance, was an alien influence that had no place in Soviet music....

"By the late 1970s, some players — most notably the violinist Gidon Kremer — began performing and recording Mr. Schnittke's music in the West, and citing him in interviews as one of the best Soviet composers. In the United States, these frequent citations have aroused considerable curiosity, and in 1982, Continuum offered a Schnittke retrospective. Thereafter, Orpheus and the New York Philharmonic offered works of his, and recordings by Mr. Kremer, members of the Borodin Trio and other players began to arrive more frequently. In Boston this March, Mr. Schnittke's music figured prominently in the programming [of Sarah Caldwell's 'Making Music Together' cultural exchange festival]....

" 'The situation in the Soviet Union is much better now than it has been for many, many decades,' says Mr. Schnittke, who is at work on his *Fifth Symphony* and an opera on the Faust legend. 'I am also very pleased that my music is being performed in the West. But I must say that none of this has any effect on my philosophy or motivations. Whether or not my music is widely performed, I will continue to write the music I think needs to be written.' " —Allan Kozinn, in *The New York Times*, 5/22/88.

Concerto 3 for Violin and Chamber Orchestra (1978). 28m *Ded. & prem.:* Oleg Kagan (vln), Chamber Ens of Moscow Cons Students, Yuri Nikolayevsky, cond. *Recs.:* Eurodisc (Stereo LP) 201 234-405: Gidon Kramer (vln), Berlin P Chamber Ens, Woldemar Nelsson, cond.; Melodiya (Stereo LP) S10-15681-82: Oleg Kagan (vln), Soloist's Ens, Yuri Nikolayevsky, cond. *Pub.:* Universal Edition (Philharmonic Pocket score series No. 496)
violin solo; 2 (1 picc)-1 (+ 1 eh)-3 (1 picc cl, 1 b cl)-1 (+1 cbsn); 2-1-1-0; strings (1-0-1-1-1)
1. Moderato. 2. Agitato—3. Moderato.

Concerto Grosso 1 for Two Violins, Strings, Cembalo, and Prepared Piano (1976-77). 25m *Prem.:* Gidon Kremer, Tatiana Grindenko, Yuri Smirnov (soloists), Leningrad Chamber O, Eri Klas, cond. *Recs.:* Melodia C10 21225 004: Liana Isakadze, Olego Krysa, Natalia Mandenova, Alfred Schnittke (soloiosts), Georgian State Chamber O, S. Sondeckis, cond.; Melodia/Eurodisc (Stereo LP) S 10 13135-6 (also as Vanguard Stereo LP VSD 71255): Gidon Kremer, Tatiana Grindenko (vlns), London SO, Gennadi Rozhdestvensky, cond.; BIS (CD) 377: Christian Bergvist, Patrik Swedrup (vlns), Roland Pöntinen (hpsd/pno), New Stockholm Chamber O, Lev Markiz, cond.
strings (6-6-4-4-1)
1. *Preludio* — 2. *Toccata* — 3. *Recitative.* 4. *Cadenza* — 5. *Rondo* — 6. *Postludio.*

"There is no better evidence of the maturity of advanced Soviet music than the music of Alfred Schnittke. And thanks to Eurodisc, you can look in *Schwann* and find two examples of Schnittke at his finest: the *Concerto Grosso* and the *Violin Concerto No. 3.*

"Schnittke came to his modernism through his contact with Nono during the latter's visit to Moscow in 1963. Thus, in 1964, Schnittke wrote two orthodox serial pieces and has been a leading, if not *the* leading, Soviet avant-gardist since then. But serialism did not remain a creative lodestone for Schnittke. By 1970 he was producing collages, with quotations from old music à la Berio, Hambraeus, and Druckman. His *Concerto Grosso* (1977), his prime work in this polystylistic spirit, is one of my favorite works of the decade—a haunting vista of the Baroque, with Vivaldi, Corelli, and Handel resurrected amidst aleatorality, microtonality, and a touch of the tango. It was also his last work in that style of overt musical collage.

"Since 1977 Schnittke has written in a style that incorporates elements of old and new music into a more homogeneous web, 'a monostyle', as Schnittke has put it. The *Violin Concerto No. 3* of 1978 is his first work in this latest style, wherein traditional 'composition' has been more and more 'displaced by what I would like to call "deciphering work"; I try to capture as precisely as possible in notes the aural visions which occur to me,' eschewing traditional symphonic development and tension-release linearity. The concerto begins with a 75-measure *Prolog*, the first 51 being a solo cadenza of trilled, incantory-like notes and then 23 measures of further introductory material accompanied by the 13 winds. (The work's chamber orchestra consists of 13 winds and four strings—the strings being held back until the end of the second movement.) The *Prolog* sets up the intervallic and motivic material for the concerto, its closely seguing three movements forming a sort of condensed sonata movement of exposition, dialogue-development and quasi-recapitulation. The harmony is chromatically atonal, frequently microtonal, though 'tonal bases' are secured. The soloist is not the expected dramatic protagonist, instead adopting a *cantus firmus* role that is simply enthralling."—Stephen W. Ellis, in *Fanfare: The Magazine for Serious Record Collectors*, 3-4/83.

"The [*Third Violin Concerto's*] chamber orchestra is largish, [featuring] winds, brass and strings. There is no percussion, which figured heavily in the preceding violin concertos. Although the work breaks down into three movements, one hears the work as a single sequence, basically a sonata form arising from the tensely trilled opening cadenza and orchestral introduction, proceeding through numerous contrasting but thematically and motivically linked sections, and eventually rounded off with a moving and very quiet extended coda. Along the way one discovers passages palpably 12-tone, dovetailed together with some episodes that are serial, some aleatoric. The language includes extended diatonic passages, modality, microtones, and a subtle array of metrical devices. It could well have been a complete *gribouillage*, but it is not. I believe that the open-minded hearer—that is, one who accepts the validity of all the compositional devices here employed—will find this music an unusually absorbing experience."—John D. Wiser, in *Fanfare: The Magazine for Serious Record Collectors*, 3-4/83.

"Alfred Schnittke's *Concerto Grosso*... offers a fascinating indication of the kind of music being written in Russia today [c.1980] by an extremely competent and relatively adventurous composer....

"The term 'concerto grosso' applies both to the cooperative and complementary relationship of the soloists to the ensemble and to the sequence of movements (*Preludio, Toccata, Recitative, Cadenza, Rondo* and *Postludio*). Moreover, the work relies heavily upon characteristic melodic gestures and formal devices of baroque music, as well as the sort of motoric rhythmic drive typical of that period.

"Yet the concerto is in no sense a dry academic exercise. Each movement has an unmistakable character, and the various neologisms are filtered through a distinctly contemporary sensibility. Only rarely does the music become openly triadic in structure; when this happens, the intent is often humorous, as in a very funny and clever tangolike episode in the *Rondo*. One occasionally hears echoes of other contemporary composers (there are some striking similarities, though perhaps coincidental, between the *Toccata* and the third of Lukas Foss's *Baroque* Variations), but on the whole the work sounds fresh and personal. It is brilliantly written for the instruments and must be a joy to play."—Robert P. Morgan, in *High Fidelity*, 3/80.

In Memoriam... for Orchestra (1972-78). Arr. of *Quintet* for Piano and Strings. 25m *Prem.:* Moscow PSO, Gennadi Rozhdestvensky, cond. *Rec.:* BIS 447 (distr. Qualiton): Malmo SO, Lev Markiz, cond. *Pub.:* C. F. Peters (Miniature score).
3-3 (1 eh)-3 (1 b cl)-3 (1 cbsn); 4-4-4-1; perc (timp, 2 tam-tams, mar, vibr, glock, bells), electr gtr, hp, celesta, hpsd, 2 pnos, organ; strings (min. 7-6-5-4-3) [arr. from 1972-76 piano quintet]
1. Moderato—2. Tempo di Valse. 3. Andante. 4. Lento—5. Moderato pastorale.

"In the year 3111 AD, when a musicological microchip scans the compositional achievements of the far-distant past, the printout may well characterize the music of the twentieth century as essentially synthetic: music carefully crafted using pieces of and references to the musical past. Our omniscient megabyte might retrieve descriptions of a constant, twentieth-century passion for recycling music of earlier times. Whether stemming from the ideas of collage, Neo-Classicism, Neo-Romanticism, Referentialism, Neo-Serialism, or Neo-Modernism, the description of our current music would center on the cross-cultural and cross-temporal synthesis that catalyzes compositional creativity in the twentieth century.[114]

"The works of the extraordinary Soviet composer Alfred Schnittke, only now becoming known in the West, typify recent developments in Referential music, music that constantly refers to diverse historic and contemporary styles and traditions. Schnittke has long been associated with the Moscow Conservatory, first as a student and then as a teacher of instrumentation, score-reading, counterpoint, and composition. He has also worked at the Experimental Studio of Electronic Music in Moscow.

"Intense, dramatic, brooding, and brilliant, Schnittke's *In Memoriam...*, a five-movement piece for large orchestra, is the apotheosis of Referentialism.... [His] musical materials include quarter-tones, clusters, and unmetered sections of music placed side by side with tonal sections, waltz rhythms, and passacaglia themes. In fact, *In Memoriam...* can be legitimately viewed as a monument to the whole history of Western art music. Specific references abound: the *idée fixe* of the semi-tone, often D and E^b, the musical motto of Dmitri Shostakovich, is found in each movement. The second movement, an evocative waltz, has for its basic pitch material the motive B-A-C-H. Here, the semitone of the 'Shostakovich' motto has been slyly expanded to embrace an homage to Papa Bach, as well as all those many composers who have also used the B-A-C-H theme. The fifth and final movement of the work, a *Moderato pastorale*, which has a constant D^b pedal, is based on a tonal passacaglia theme that is rhythmically and melodically reminiscent of Beethoven's *'Pastoral' Symphony* and the horn calls of Mahler. By using a passacaglia in the final movement of *In Memoriam...*, Schnittke pays fond respects to Brahms as well as Beethoven and Mahler. The shifting and juxtaposition of many diverse elements and references imbue *In Memoriam...* with intensity and dramatic thrust. The nuances of memory and emotion are allowed to combine and recombine as the nuances of styles and traditions are allowed to interact.

"[Like Peter Maxwell Davies in Britain,] living in and expanding upon the traditions of his native country, Schnittke is a master of revivifying music and is producing some of the most well-crafted, extraordinary, inventive music of our time. Certainly *In Memoriam...*

---

114 Or, making a similar point, but with a somewhat startling difference, "our omniscient megabyte" might discover in this same "synethsis" etc. an amazing vitality demonstrated *by* it varieties, irreverences, extensions of (and breaking-downs of) forms and traditions, tendencies to mock and to revere simultaneously, and also to look forward and backward in much the same breath (see e.g. Stravinsky's 1905-07 *Symphony No. 1* — at once a kind of homage to Rimsky-Korsakov and, incipiently at least, angular and quirky in the best "modern" sense). (Ed.)

should merit the attention of the musically sensitive and alert." —
David Noon, in *Notes* (Music Library Association), 3/85.

Quartet 2 for Strings (1980). 20m Comm. by Universal Edition (Vienna); ded. to Larisa Shepitko. *Prem.:* Muir Quartet. *Rec.:* Preciosa Aulos (Digital Stereo LP) PRE 68-508 (distr. German News): Leonardo Quartet (Johannes Prelle, Gabriele Sassenscheidt, vlns, Jörne-Uwe Ender, vla, Klaus Marx, vc). *Pub.:* Universal Edition (Vienna). 1. Moderato — 2. Agitato — 3. Mesto — 4. Moderato.

"For those who tuned in late, Alfred Schnittke is one of the most interesting and eventually developing of all living Soviet composers. He is a freelancer in a society that doesn't ordinarily tolerate such unstructured existences, apparently making most of his living as a film composer. It's unfortunate that we don't get to hear much of his work in that area, a situation unlikely to improve in the near future.

"The *String Quartet No. 2* is a much rangier, more ambitious, more intensely communicative piece than its twelve-tone 1966 forerunner. (The *String Quartet No. 1* was once available in a boxed set from Ariola/Eurodisc, performed by the Borodin Quartet.) Schnittke dedicated his *Second Quartet* to the memory of Soviet film director Larisa Shepitko, a close friend for whose last two films he had composed the score.

"The quartet is punctilious in formal symmetry, not always an important consideration in Schnittke's music. It is based on the dissonant heterophony of old Russian sacred music. The range of texture is enormous, ranging from close rhythmic and harmonic-intervalled canonic statement of thematic material through tremendously powerful sections in a unison near-*bariolage*, to high-tension melodic statements in which every element is trilled upon. Dissonance and consonance are used in contrast but not in relief; tonal centers dissolve and reform almost too quickly to follow. Pacing tends to be mercurially variable. Schnittke clearly has an ear of Schoenbergian sensitivity to string color. On the basis of this and other recently heard works, I feel that we're confronting the spectacle of a composer of world importance emerging from a singularly provincial and unpromising mileu." — John D. Wiser, in *Fanfare: The Magazine for Serious Record Collectors*, 1-2/85.

Ruth Schonthal

B. 1924, Hamburg (Germany). *Educ.:* Stern Cons (Berlin), Royal Acad of Music (Stockholm), Conservatorio Nacional (Mexico), Yale Univ. *Taught at:* Adelphi Univ, New York Univ, Westchester (NY) Cons. *Works incl.:* concertos, *4 Epiphanies* (vla), *Fantasia* (gtr), *Love Letters* (cl/vc), operas *(The Courtship of Camilla)*, orchestral suites, piano works *(Fragments from a Woman's Diary, In Homage of..., Miniatures, Nachklänge [Reverberations], Sonatas)*, quartets (2), sonatas (vc, vln), songs & song cycles *(By the Roadside,* Lorca songs, *The Solitary Reaper, Songs of Love and Sorrow), The Young Dead Soldiers* (cantata).

Composer statement: "I am never without music going through my head. I think about it constantly. Writing music is central to my life and as such obsessive. As the music floats through my head, I dig for the 'ultimate version', shaping, reshaping, developing phrases, harmonies, shapes and textures sometimes hundreds of times until I have found the 'absolute right' way. This I do on paper at the piano, and away from it in my head. My ideal is to write music for people who love music. Although this proved to be, for most of my composing life, an unfashionable objective. I want my music to be well-crafted, beautiful and expressing the full range of human emotions. Through my own background I feel a special kinship to the European, especially the German and Viennese musical tradition, and often use this as the foundation of my own musical creativity. This I expand by fusing the old with the new, using contemporary techniques and expressing contemporary sensitivities, shaped by my own individual concerns, esthetic and temperament."

The Canticles of Hieronymus for Piano (1987). 18m *Ded. & prem.:* Margaret Mills. *Other perfs.:* New York, Florida, Heidelberg. *Pub.:* Fine Arts Music.

"In *Canticles*, the composer has created a piece that yields the full emotional range and Medieval atmosphere that are portrayed in the famous Triptych by Hieronymus Bosch, *The Garden of Earthly Delights*, on which the piece is loosely based. Like the painting, *Canticles* forms three sections or panels: 'Creation-Paradise', 'The Garden of Earthly Delights', and 'Hell'. The painting's symbolisms are here replaced by musical symbolisms. Tempo, register, and contour help to underscore the intellectual aspects. Modes, intervals, and harmony underscore the emotional content.

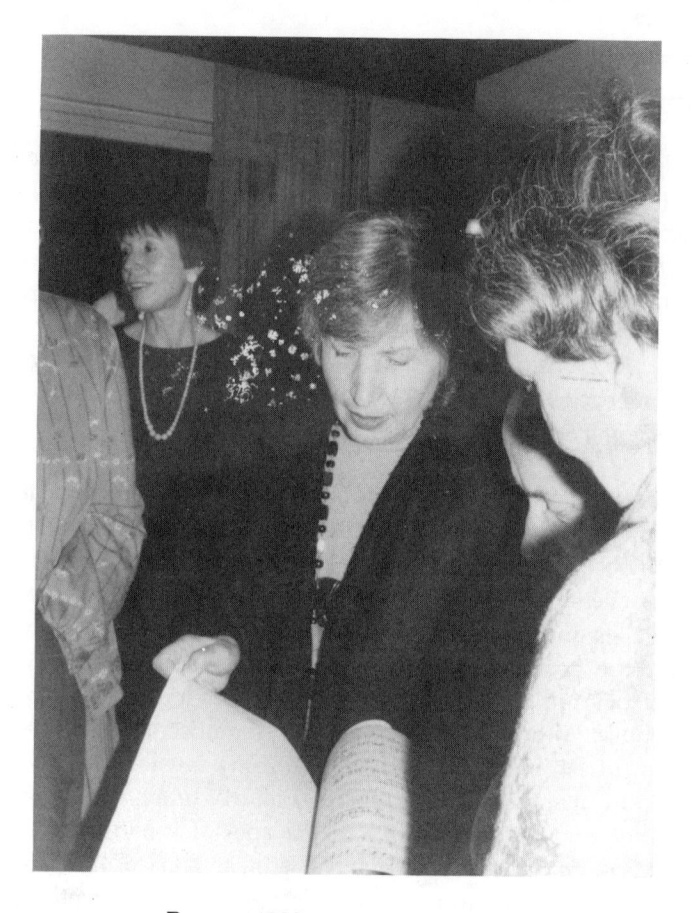

Bonn — 1989.

"The 'Creation' presents fragments composed of dissonant and consonant elements. The creation of life is suggested with a motiv of sequentially ascending fourths, which is contrapuntally bitonal, creating different tonal and rhythmic relationships. The same intervals (ascending fourths), transformed in tempo and register, suggest the menacing 'evil forces' — according to the tenet that contrasts (good-bad, beautiful-ugly, etc.) are made of the same matter but in constant conflict — attracting, repelling, and influencing each other. The angelic section is created by further transforming the interval of the fourth into undulating thirds performed pianissimo in the upper register by the right hand, and undulating fifths in the left hand, with a built-in chorale. Gradually even this angelic section is affected and influenced by new chordal dissonances, containing clashing fourths and fifths.

"The 'Garden' section is conveyed by shimmering, multi-rhythmic, slowly varying figurations, gradually becoming more intensely

Hochheim, near Frankfurt—1989.

passionate. After building to a climax, the previously heard Chorale interrupts with gently descending thirds.

" 'Hell' is portrayed as an ongoing battle between the forces of Darkness and Light with transformations and interrelationships of previously heard material. Towards the end, there is a short reprise of the fragmented material from the opening section."—Margaret Mills.

Music for Horn and Chamber Orchestra (1978). 12m *Prem.:* Brooks Tillotson (hn), orch. cond. by Dale Monson. *Other perfs.:* Robert Johnson (hn), White Plains SO, Siegfried Landau, cond.; Robert Johnson (hn), New Amsterdam O, Rachel Worby, cond.; Joel Winter (hn), Ridgefield (CT) SO, Beatrice Brown, cond. *Rec.:* Crystal Records (Stereo LP) 5673: Meir Rimon (hn), Israel PO, Shalom Ronly-Riklis, cond.

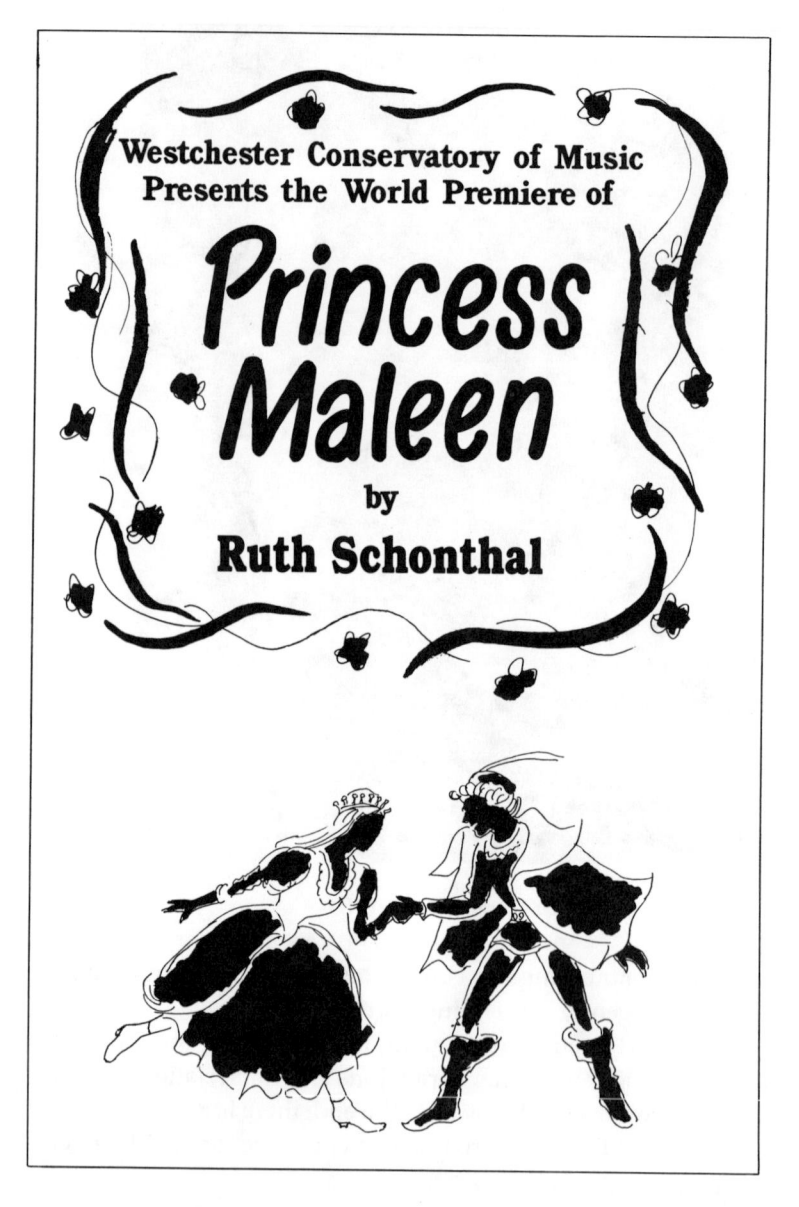

¶Also vers. for horn and piano (1978). *Perfs.:* New York, Tel Aviv, Jerusalem.

"*Music for Horn and Chamber Orchestra* is intended to convey an Alpine mood in its six short sections, which feature variation and contrast. The work opens with a folk-like theme introduced by the horn, accompanied by gentle triplets in the strings. The peaceful theme, in C major, is briefly interrupted by a passage in E major. In the second section, yodel-like motives are introduced by the woodwinds and responded to by the horn. The third section contains 'rounded' contrapuntal lines that capitalize on the horn motive. The fifth section begins with gypsy-like figures in the orchestra, but after the orchestra comes to a halt, the horn takes over with an extended cadenza that recaptures some of the previous material. The closing section returns to the tranquil mood of the opening." — Claude K. Sluder, in liner notes for Stereo LP.

"Ms. Schonthal treats both the horn and the orchestra in a manner frankly reminiscent of late German Romanticism, particularly of the writing of Richard Strauss. The tonal horn theme, which unifies the work, could almost be said to evoke images of the Alps. Such associations, plus the well-conceived and richly orchestrated background, makes for a piece that offers no resistance to audience enjoyment." — Courtenay V. Cauble, *Ridgefield (CT) Press*, 3/11/82.

Princess Maleen (fairytale love story for "children of all ages")(1988-89). *Lib.*: Ruth Schonthal & Wallis E. Wood, after the Brothers Grimm. 90m *Comm. & prem.*: Westchester (NY) Cons of Music, with grant from Texaco Philanthropic Fndn: soloists, chorus & orchestra, Elliot Magaziner, cond. *Ms.*: available from composer, c/o Westchester Conservatory of Music, Soundview Avenue, White Plains NY 10606.
3 female (s; m-s, a [may be staged as double role]) 3 male (high t, 2 bar [or triple role for 1 bar]), chorus (incl. 7 "additional character" roles) 2-2-2-2, c-bsn; 2-3-3-0; perc, synthesizer; strings [also vers. for synthesizer or piano]
Prologue: A garden in the castle of the King of the North. Act I. Scene 1: Years later in the same garden. Scene 2: The tower prison. Scene 3: The tower, seven years later. Act II. Scene 1: The courtyard of the King of the South. Scene 2: The bedroom of the Ugly Princess. Scene 3: The Wedding Chapel. Scene 4: The bedroom of the Ugly Princess. Scene 5: The courtyard of the King of the South.

" 'You know, most adults have never even seen an opera,' asserted Laura Calzolari, executive director of the Westchester Conservatory of Music. 'Unfortunately, opera has so many negative stereotypes, like the fat lady in the helmet in the dying scene that goes on for four hours. *Prince Maleen* is an opportunity to give children an accessible experience in opera. It's in English, and it's a story with all kinds of fabulous elements: war, unrequited love, mistaken identity, power struggles.'

"Ms. Schonthal, who wrote the libretto in collaboration with [the professional writer and publisher] Wallis Wood, believes that children should be able to identify with the various characters on every level. 'There is a great deal of symbolism and substance, and the idea of Fate intervening. Laura had said that it shouldn't just appeal to young children, but to children of all ages, including adults.'

"Once the composer decided on the story, she completed the work in a whirlwind effort of about three weeks. She improvised most of the music on the synthesizer, recording as she went along, and then backtracking to transcribe the notes. Sometimes, she created the words and the music at the same time, a feat Ms. Calzolari referred to as 'divine inspiration... the music is very compelling, and very successfully brings you into the drama of the story.' The synthesizer's dramatic effects are an integral part of the orchestration.

" 'I tried to create a kind of Rossini-like atmosphere in the happy parts, which I transform into avant-garde effects when Fate intervenes,' explained Ms. Schonthal. 'It's extremely melodious and has many arias.' Ms. Schonthal carries specific musical elements throughout the opera. 'I made myself psychological outlines for every character, total portraits which I translated into musical language. Each character has his own way of speaking, so you recognize them musically. As the opera progresses, the characters experience transformations that Fate imposes on them.'

"Ms. Schonthal had special considerations in tailoring the opera for children, both as audience members and as participants. 'Rhythmically, I had to write more simply than I usually do. I tried to use the quarter-note as the basic measurement. It's based on many things children can do, like scales and Alberti bass. The avant-garde effects are easy. It's very tuneful and there are many arias, none of which are too extended. I wanted to always keep their interest, so the action goes very quickly, giving the work a tremendous tension.'

"The opera's director [for its initial performances], Norma Bruce, added: 'It's both very challenging and very difficult to work with children. They tend to have short attention spans, but they can get very excited if they are properly challenged.' " —Karen Campbell, *Westchester Artsnews*, 5/89.

"Ruth Schonthal knows what it means to succeed in an artistic field traditionally dominated by men. She is a concert pianist and prize-winning composer of sophisticated orchestral, chamber and choral works which have been recorded and performed worldwide. Last spring an audience of 2,000 attended the American premiere of her anti-war cantata, *The Young Dead Soldiers*, performed by the New Orchestra of Westchester. In addition to teaching and lecturing at the [Westchester] Conservatory and elsewhere, Schonthal is a frequent guest on New York area radio programs, and an active member of the International Congress of Women in Music and American Women Composers. She has lived in New Rochelle [NY] for 30 years.

"Says Schonthal, 'Fairy tales have great power and suspense. They show how fate can create havoc in people's lives and then straighten it out at the end so that everyone is happy.' She says the Princess Maleen story intrigued her as a composer because 'it has all the operatic elements: action, suspense, and characters who inspire empathy. It even has several villains, both male and female.'

"Schonthal and Laura Calzolari, executive director of the Westchester Conservatory, feel there is a tremendous need for children to be educated in the arts, and that opera is unique in bringing together several art forms—vocal, choral and orchestral music, drama and fine art.

" 'Opera has great psychodrama,' says the composer. 'It develops great identification and empathy in children. It is about human qualities—goodness, meanness, scariness. Children love to be scared! And it's all there on stage for them to digest.' As a composer, she finds opera the perfect vehicle for expressing the complex range of human emotions which children, as well as adolescents and adults, experience.

"To make *Princess Maleen* accessible to young audiences who have never seen or heard an opera before, Schonthal used unifying musical themes that are easy to recognize, and short 'mini-arias' interrupted by frequent changes in action. She also employed a variety of humorous devices to hold younger children's (and parents') interest." — Lora Friedman, in Harrison (NY) *Women's News*, 5/89.

Quartet 1 for Strings (1962). 13m *Prem.*: York Quartet (A. Schiller, A. Fryer, vlns, L. Fader, vla, R. Gardner, vc). *Other perfs.*: Frankfurt, Mexico City. *Rec.*: Leonarda Productions (Stereo LP) LPI 111: Crescent Quartet (A. Edelberg, N. McAlhany Diggs, vlns, Jill Jaffe, vla, Maxine Neumann, vc).
In 10 brief continuous sections (Very slow and expressive–Moderato–Tempo di recitativo–Allegro molto, un poco scherzando–Moderato–Slow Valse–Allegro molto agitato–Lento–Allegro con spirito–Lento moderato [dancelike]).

"Of this quartet, the composer writes:

> [It] consists of many brief, contrasting connected movements. Often the ending phrase of one movement serves as the inspiration of the next one in a 'stream of consciousness' fashion. Towards the end there are some allusions to *Tristan* and Schubert, meant to be understood as tongue-in-cheek homage.

"Beginning slowly, progressing from low to high register, the tempo changes frequently, as Schonthal utilizes special effects and special timbres. Throughout the entire work many melodies and/or melodic fragments dominate. The texture is, for the most part, more that of accompanied melody than of contrapuntal density.

"The middle section is often reminiscent of early twentieth-century Romantic wanderings within a vague key center. Schonthal also makes abundant use of the first violin in spinning out her melodies, and the references to Wagner's *Tristan* occur here.

"In the section that follows immediately, Schonthal makes use of Spanish dance rhythms, with the melody in the first violin and the rhythmic accompaniment in the other strings. Ending on a tonal open fifth cadence on D, this rhythmic section leads to the final one, which is somewhat similar to the beginning. The cello here assumes a lyrical solo.

"References to Schubert occur in dotted rhythms just before the final ending, again on a tonal open fifth cadence on D."[115] — Diane Peacock Jezic, in *Women Composers: The Lost Tradition Found* (The Feminist Press, 1988).

Totengesänge [Songs of Death] for Soprano and Piano (1963).
Text: composer. Prem.: Bethany Beardslee (s), Ruth Schonthal (pno). *Other perfs.:* Helen Lightner, Catherine Rowe. *Rec.:* Leonarda Productions (Stereo LP) LPI 106: Berenice Bramson (s), Ruth Schonthal (pno).
1. *Totenglocken* [Bells of death]. 3m 2. *Die ewige Liebe* [Eternal love]. 3m 3. *Wiegenlied an ein krankes Kind* [Cradle song for a sick child]. 7m 4. *Tod einer Jungfrau* [Death of a maiden]. 3m 5. *Totentanz* [Dance of death]. 2m 6. *Totenreigen* [Round-dance of death]. 3m 7. *Hurenlied* [Song of a whore]. 1m 8. *Die Spanierin* [The Spanish lady]. 1m

"In *Totengesänge*, life's ironies and suffering are expressed in Ruth Schonthal's own words and music.

"(1) The slow tension-filled introduction of 'Bells of Death' prepares the leaping melodic phrase that states that life's great suffering has passed. The accompaniment introduces the death bells which the trembling soprano — now longing for death — sings of hearing in her dreams. (2) 'The Eternal Love' is a bitingly sardonic but also tragic song. Its jagged accompaniment and disjunct soprano line culminate in a passionate outburst, where, finally, Death is the Redeemer. (3) 'Cradle Song for a Sick Child'. The mother's tender '*Aya Popaya*' alternates with tension-filled chords and screaming outbursts of fright as the thought flashes through her mind that Death may wrestle her child from her arms. There is a long postlude in which the listeners keep vigil with the mother through the long night, ending with a shimmer of hope. (4) 'Death of a Virgin' is deliberately reminiscent of '*Gretchen am Spinnrad*'. In her fever, the virgin imagines Death as her approaching lover and revels in the ecstasy of her passion. (5) 'Dance of Death'. A slow, deceptively inviting theme challenges the woman to a dance. The sudden, ugly

---

115 I recently (3/90) attended an alert and moving performance of this splendid work, given by the Crescent Quartet at the United Nations in New York, as a part of celebrations of the International Conference of Women in Music (ICWM). This program, which also included the 1951 *String Quartet Nr. 4* of Grazyna Bacewicz and a 1983 *Fantasy* for Clarinet and Piano by Joan Tower, reminded one once again of the incredible richness of 20th-century music — of which composers themselves deserve to be proud. (Ed.)

tuning of the fiddle prepares for this insanely wild dance, which is interrupted by a great clash of clusters and finishes after an extended peaceful cadence. (6) *'Valse'*. A waltz with an often repeated catchy tune finally winds down like a worn-out record. (7) 'Song of a Whore'. This short song portrays a whore who seems more alive in her grave than many of the living. (8) The Spanish rhythm in 'The Spanish Woman' underscores the fiesta mood of the bullfight and mocks the 'sensuous' effect of violence; it ends tongue in cheek." — Liner notes for Leonarda Stereo LP LPI-106.

"It is risky to attach the title 'masterpiece' to contemporary work, but for works [such as] Ruth Schonthal's *Totengesänge* I think no smaller word will do. No serious collection of contemporary music should be without [Leonarda's recording of this cycle]." — Joseph McLellan, in *The Washington Post*, 4/3/83.

"Ruth Schonthal's settings of her own words [are] dramatic, yet tenderly lyrical at times. In short, this [Leonarda's new recording] is an uncommonly attractive song disc." — John Ditsky, in *Fanfare: The Magazine for Serious Record Collectors*, 5-6/81.

Variations in Search of a Theme for Piano (1974). 16m *Prem.*: Gary Steigerwalt. *Perf.*: NY, Berlin, Heidelberg, Mexico City, Sydney. *Rec.*: Orion (Stereo LP) ORS 81413: Gary Steigerwalt. *Pub.*: Oxford Univ Press.

"The first 'variation' presents various elements: interval combinations, melodic fragments, timbres, rhythms. In the ensuing variations some of these elements undergo kaleidoscopic changes, and new fragments are added and gradually reenforced. From Variation 7 onwards, many melodic fragments have been welded into longer lines. At the end the listener is left with the feeling that the theme was presented in the course of the variations through accumulation of recognizable and reenforced elements. The beginning of the piece presents a world of friction and fission, whereas the ending is one of fusion, harmony and infinite tenderness." — Liner notes for Orion Stereo LP ORS 81413.

WILLIAM SCHUMAN

B. 1910, New York NY. *Educ.:* Columbia Univ Teacher's College, Mozarteum Acad (Salzburg), Juilliard Schl of Music. *Taught at:* Sarah Lawrence College. Dir. publications, G. Schirmer, Inc.; pres., Juilliard Schl; pres., Lincoln Center NY. Winner, Pulitzer Prize; Composition Award, Amer Acad Arts and Letters; 2 Guggenheim Fellowships. *Works incl.: Awake Thou Wintry Earth* (cl/pno [or fl/bsn]), choral pieces, concertos (pno, vln), *New England Triptych* (orch), overtures *(American Festival, William Billings)*, 5 string quartets, *Song of Orpheus* (vc/orch), 10 symphonies.

Three Colloquies for Horn and Orchestra (1979). 23m *Prem.:* Philip Meyers (hn), New York PO, Zubin Mehta, cond. *Rec.:* New World (Stereo LP) NW 326: Meyers (hn), New York PO, Zubin Mehta, cond.
1. *Rumination.* 2. *Renewal.* 3. *Remembrance.*

"William Schuman has received a special Pulitzer citation for his half-century of contribution to American music. Winner of the first Pulitzer Prize in music back in 1943, his body of works certainly deserve this *tutti* recognition....

"We get few brass concertos from our major composers and fewer yet horn concertos. So this work is especially welcome. The *Three Colloquies* are a thinly disguised concerto, giving the hornist plenty of solo opportunities, including two sections where he duets with himself by way of alternately open and stopped passages. Like [George] Crumb, Schuman is a prime musical colorist—but with the difference that Schuman's effect is produced by the grouping and contrasting of blocks of related instruments. Here, however, Schuman eliminated horns, trombones, and tubas from the orchestra, but assigns important lines to a group of three trumpets.

"The first movement begins with clangorous chords framing doleful, held notes on the horn. Soon strings encourage the horn to play phrases, and the entrance of the woodwinds and percussion inspires the soloist into much activity. Clangorous chording returns briefly, followed eventually by soft timpani alone that accompanies the soloist without a break into the second movement, where typically Schuman wind-and-string sections, plus the three trumpets, play lively games of musical tag with the horn. Passages of wistfulness and storminess are traded back and forth in this *scherzo-trio-scherzo* setup, and the timbral variations here are impressive and memorable. The third movement begins hauntingly with a slow horn and cello duet. They are soon joined by an oboe and then other woodwinds. The whole movement is marked by expressive exchanges with a chamber-music intimacy that effectively contrasts with the *tutti* material that has preceded this. The movement makes a fan of Schuman's music long for all the instrumental sonatas he has ever written." —Stephen W. Ellis, in *Fanfare: The Magazine for Serious Record Collectors*, 7-8/85.

"Long recognized as one of this century's greatest symphonic composers, William Schuman evinces throughout his oeuvre an intimate familiarity with orchestral technique. *Three Colloquies*, scored for standard woodwinds and strings, a brass section of three trumpets plus the solo horn, and an extensive percussion section, contains typical Schuman traits such as arching melodies, vibrant syncopations, piquant dissonances, lush string chorales, and frequent parallelisms. In three continuous movements, the nearly twenty-three-minute work exploits the entire range of the horn. [In the recording] Philip Myers, principal hornist of the [New York] Philharmonic, masterfully handles the abrupt register shifts, virtuoso flourishes, and rapidly shifting open and stopped tones with aplomb." —Craig B. Parker, in *American Music*, Summer 1987.

"Schuman's *Three Colloquies* is a major effort by a major American composer for horn and orchestra. It is available, published in a very readable manuscript, for horn with piano reduction. The piece is not intended to be performed with piano, and even an accurate reading of the reduction will take two pianists. This is a very large scale work of [approx.] 24 minutes, set in three movements to be played without pause. Schuman's stylistic hand is readily identifiable throughout and it is obvious that he took this commission by the New York Philharmonic very seriously. All performers, orchestra, conductor, and especially solo hornist, must be of the very finest professional caliber. This is a piece worth every effort of the horn player with the necessary technical and musical equipment, as well as access to a first-rate orchestra and sympathetic conductor." —Peter Schmalz, in *The American Music Teacher* (Music Teachers National Association), 4-5/83.

"William Schuman's *Three Colloquies* represent an important addition to the woefully small body of concerted works for French horn and orchestra....

"While the familiar trademarks of Schuman's style are here present (polyharmony, orchestration by choirs, skittishly syncopated rhythms, virtuosic timpani solos), there is much that is new as well. Schuman continues to search for unique syntheses of third-based polyphony with more simple triadic tonal functions, particularly evident here in the *Colloquies's* final movement; the composer also maintains his interest in bell sounds, which can be traced back through the *Tenth Symphony* and the *Concerto on Old English Rounds* to the *Eighth Symphony*.

"The orchestral parts, while challenging, are straightforward and should be manageable by a good university-level orchestra. The solo horn part, however, is extremely demanding both in terms of dexterity and tessitura and requires an excellent performer.... All in all, the *Three Colloquies* are a major new contribution to the twentieth century's concerted repertoire for wind instruments." — Christopher Rouse, in *Notes* (Music Library Association), 9/82.

Concerto for Violin and Orchestra (1947; rev. 1954, 1959). *Prem.:* Isaac Stern (vln), Boston SO, Charles Munch, cond. *Rec.:* Angel EMI (CD) CDC 49464: Robert McDuffie (vln), St. Louis SO, Leonard Slatkin, cond. *Pub.:* G. Schirmer.

"Few American violin concertos have entered the repertory, so it is a special treat to rediscover William Schuman's — and an even greater pleasure to realize that it is a first-rate work, on a par with the best of his symphonies. Written in 1947 (and revised in 1954 and 1959), it was once championed by Isaac Stern, but has had few performances in recent years. With its expansive, soaring melodic lines, rhythmic vibrancy, and darkly hued, tonally rooted dissonance, the concerto would seem to be an accessible work that has languished for lack of an ideal interpreter.

"Enter Robert McDuffie, who has poured himself into this unfamiiar score with such intensity as to transform it into his personal vehicle. McDuffie negotiates the score's sweeping lines with impassioned fervor, and he succeeds in sustaining the broad arches of its endless melodic curves. The leaping, wide-ranging violin part can be devilishly awkward; even McDuffie, with technique to spare, is forced to cheat here and there. But his seething Romantic fire is perfectly matched to the concerto's pervasive agitation, and his occasional roughness of attack derives only from his desire to wring every expressive drop from this emotive work." — K. Robert Schwarz, in *Musical America*, 1/90.

The Mighty Casey (1-act opera) (1951-53). *Lib.:* Jeremy Gury, after Ernest L. Thayer poem "Casey at the Bat". Also concert vers. *Prem.:* Julius Hartt Musical Fndn (Hartford CT), Moshe Paranov, cond. *Other perf.:* Gene Shalit (narr), Pittsburgh SO, Leonard Slatkin, cond. *Pub.:* G. Schirmer.

A Question of Taste (opera) (1989). *Lib.*: J.D. McClatchy, after Roald Dahl story. 50m *Prem.*: Glimmerglass Theater company, Stewart Robertson, cond.
In one act.

"The Mudville of William Schuman's endearing one-act opera *The Mighty Casey* is surely Cooperstown, New York, the Victorian village where baseball's Hall of Fame is celebrating its 50th year [1989]. *Casey* was an apt choice to open the Glimmerglass summer season, paired with Schuman's new companion piece, *A Question of Taste*.

"Based on a vignette by the contemporary short-story writer Roald Dahl, *A Question of Taste* has a wealthy, turn-of-the-century businessman betting the hand of his daughter, Louise, that their oenophile dinner guest can't name the wine being served. The 50-minute opera sweeps along in major triads, tritones, and sunny bitonality, its neo-Forties overture waltz becoming dinner music, Louise's aria, and a love duet with her boy-friend—whom her parents won't let her marry because he didn't go to Yale. J.D. McClatchy's clever libretto is sensitive to the score, with such easygoing lines as 'Let's go to the table and look at the label.' It renames the smarmy guest [in Dahl's story] Phillisto—some sort of Philistine Mephisto, no doubt. This scoundrel... has a suspenseful eight-minute guessing solo full of French wine names, accompanied by lively percussion and low-pitched instruments.

"Cooperstown is the Bayreuth for performances of *The Mighty Casey*, Schuman's 1953 expansion, with librettist Jeremy Gury, of Ernest L. Thayer's poem *Casey at the Bat*. The work looks and sounds something like a golden-age Broadway musical; villainy (which in this happy hamlet consists of the catcher informing the pitcher that Casey can't resist a high-insider) is spiced with snatches of the whole-tone scale.... At intermission, Schuman told us that his current interest is melodic line, for which singing about love provides much opportunity. To that end he has created characters—Casey's girl, Louise's fellow—[who do not appear] in the two original plots."—Leslie Kandell, in *Musical America*, 11/89.

"Two major works composed recently gave Mr. Schuman an opportunity he relishes—to work with poets. *On Freedom's Ground*, a cantata for baritone, chorus and orchestra, was composed for the 100th anniversary of the Statue of Liberty. The text is by Richard Wilbur. *A Question of Taste*, a new opera, has a libretto by J. D. McClatchy and is based on a story by Roald Dahl. 'Setting poetry is not a matter of thinking you can improve a poem,' Mr. Schuman says. 'You can add a dimension. Some works are more capable of that kind of treatment than others. I set a lot of Whitman. When I was very young, I found it difficult to set things with "I" rather than "we", so I would change the "I's" to "we's". In my older age I find it easier to set "I". People think young people are prone to bare their emotional selves more easily. That's not necessarily true. It's harder to imagine anything more emotionally available than the last works of Beethoven.'

"Mr. Schuman stresses the importance of words and is determined that they be heard and understood in his work. 'The words are basic in opera, and I'm all for supertitles when it's in another language.'

* * *

"At a rehearsal of [the composer's] cantata version of the baseball opera, *The Mighty Casey*, for a performance during the Great Woods Festival of American music in Mansfield, Mass., the conductor, Leonard Slatkin, ran from the podium out to the hall and back several times to check the balance between the Pittsburgh Symphony, the narration by Gene Shalit, and the performers, many in borrowed [Boston] Red Sox uniforms.

"Mr. Slatkin, music director of the St. Louis Symphony, and a staunch supporter of American composers, especially those who were searching for the Great American Symphony in the 1930s and 40s, talked about Mr. Schuman during rehearsals of *Casey*.

" 'The first thing to remember is that Bill qualifies as one of the handful of true symphonists who produced an extraordinary body of works trying to maintain the performance structure of the classic symphony. He and his contemporaries can be thought of in American culture as the great symphonists of Europe in the last century. Where Bill differs from his colleagues is that he has a highly urban style of writing. It smacks of city life. There's an urgency, even though there's great lyricism. You can't go two or three bars without recognizing Bill's voice. That's what I think will stand him in good stead as years go by. There are certain signature moments—using a bass clarinet solo, a timpani solo, the use of percussion as an independent force. He writes in a kind of block style with the brass, woodwinds and strings having separate musics for the most part, and when they engage constantly with each other, they tend to be as opposing forces rather than unifying ones. The style and the sound are very recognizable, and that's what should carry them very well in terms of the totality of history, not just of American music but of all music.'

"To questions about his own status, Mr. Schuman says, 'One thing I love about being a composer is that I don't have to evaluate anybody's music, even my own. My job is to write the best music that

I can write, and there are always people around who will evaluate it. It might be flattering or demeaning, but it doesn't matter, because in the long pull there's a body of opinion that creates a consensus. There's nothing much you can do about that. It's rather a comforting thought.'

"Mr. Slatkin, who has probably conducted more Schuman than anyone, with the possible exceptions of Serge Koussevitzky and Leonard Bernstein, sheds some light on the situation from a conductor's standpoint. He thinks much American music did not get into the repertory because of jealousy over symphonic works among conductors. He points out that one conductor would not want to be associated with works that might be connected with another conductor.

"Stokowski and Koussevitzky fought over the rights of pieces and stayed away from each other's repertory,' Mr. Slatkin explained. 'There was an emphasis on first performances that also prevented a lot of music from being heard with any degree of regularity.' As for the current scene, Mr. Slatkin views what is happening as a natural historical assessment of a century as we near its close. 'Now we see the contemporary composers looking back, and all of a sudden we look on Schuman as an influence. It's continuing the historical line.'...

"Mr. Schuman, romanticist, says, 'the composition of music is the glory road,' but Mr. Schuman the realist immediately follows up with, 'But as a profession it's a joke. Almost nobody wants to play new music, or listen to it, or buy the records. It's not commercial. I smile when I say that, because it has nothing to do with being a composer or with wanting to write the next piece.'

* * *

"While looking for an idea for the new opera commissioned by the Glimmerglass Opera in Cooperstown, N.Y., Mr. Schuman's wife, Frances, came across a tale by Roald Dahl. After Mr. Dahl gave permission to adapt the story, 'Taste', the search for a librettist began. At one time, the composer considered writing the libretto himself. 'I wrote a little of it,' he said, laughing, 'submitted it to myself, and turned it down.'

"The poet J. D. McClatchy was suggested, but when he sent a volume of poetry, Mr. Schuman found it difficult. 'Then McClatchy said he wouldn't be writing poetry but verse for a libretto. He made wonderful suggestions, and said he'd never had anyone read his work so carefully as I did when we worked together. It was a marvelous experience.' " — Vivian Perlis, in *The New York Times*, 8/12/90.

Quartet 4 for Strings (1950). *Rec.:* Columbia (Mono LP) ML 4493: Juilliard String Quartet.

"*String Quartet No. 4* is mature Schuman, exciting, fresh, and ingenious. It is a landmark both in his musical development and in contemporary chamber literature. This is Schuman of a wider harmonic palette and unfailing urgency." — Vincent Persichetti, in *The Musical Quarterly*, 7/54.

Symphony 3 for Orchestra (1941). *Prem.:* Boston SO, Serge Koussevitzky, cond. *Rec.:* Columbia (Mono LP) ML 4413: Philadelphia O, Eugene Ormandy, cond. *Pub.:* G. Schirmer.
1. *Passacaglia and Fugue.* 2. *Chorale and Toccata.*

Symphony 6 for Orchestra (1948). *Prem.:* Dallas SO, Antal Dorati, cond. *Rec.:* Columbia: Philadelphia O, Eugene Ormandy, cond. *Pub.:* G. Schirmer.

"The vigorous *Third Symphony* is the most brilliantly written work of Schuman's early period. A robust athleticism has built its unique architecture; its virility extends even to the lyricism, which is strong and nonsubjective.

"The symphony is divided into two parts with two connected movements in each: *Passacaglia and Fugue,* and *Chorale and Toccata.* Passacaglias, canons, and fugues appear in many of Schuman's works. So far as he is concerned the possibilities of older forms have not been thoroughly explored. The essence of these forms is the thing that attracts him, and while he employs many of the standard devices, the manner in which they are developed and changed under his hands causes a surprisingly new plan to evolve. He regards these forms as natural foundations for supporting musical organisms, and believes that if freed from contrapuntal artifice they can be fresh and alive, and worthy of any musical expression.

"The Fugue is a set of free variations on its canonic opening, which is derived from the Passacaglia theme; and the Passacaglia is a linear prelude to the Fugue. The entire work is based upon the Passacaglia theme and a remarkably unified whole is achieved. The most important feature of the theme are its salient intervallic traits. The violas state the theme:

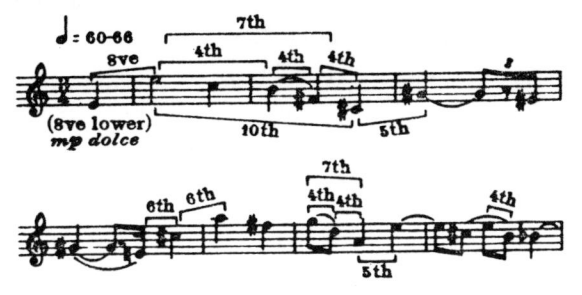

These melodic characteristics form the basis of the entire thematic structure of the symphony, and are prominent in the detailed development of each movement. Among the distinguishing qualities of the theme are the octave leaps; the fourths combining to form a seventh; the rising sixths and fifths; and the fall over-all tenth at the beginning.

"The viola statement on E is followed canonically (on rising semi-tones to B-flat) by entrances of the second violins, 'cellos, first violins, double basses with low woodwinds, horns, and high woodwinds. These seven entrances unfold a strict four-part canon and avoid a seven-voice structure. When the violas, second violins, and 'cellos reach the end of their canonic line they jump to the aid of the winds with a clarifying pizzicato reinforcement. This doubling insures that there are never more than four contrapuntal voices. As the instruments pile up on rising semitones, the symphony gains force quickly. Accompanying counterpoint adds to the tense opening by employing the melodic features of the theme in diminution. The climbing octave and occasional fifth reaching for a firmer grip dominate the counterpoint. At relaxed places, descending fourths enable the multi-moving lines to breathe...

"Part II opens with a Chorale derived from the Passacaglia theme. Violas and 'cellos divided begin molding the shape of the chorale melody. The chorale proper is sung by a solo trumpet:

As in the Fugue, the falling over-all tenth is picked up by the rising octave, thereby regaining the original register. In measure three, the tenth is inverted to prepare for the high G hold. Again, fourths combine to form the characteristic interval of the seventh.

"The solo flute carries the trumpet line up into its own highest register, then drops gradually to form a luminous arc of light. As the flute falls out of sight a harmonic string background takes over. Descending melodic fourths direct the strings to a variant of the chorale. Embellishment resulting in melodic seconds produces an inversion of the Fugue's first variation. Second violins and violas unfold free diminution of the figure the first violins and 'cellos are playing:

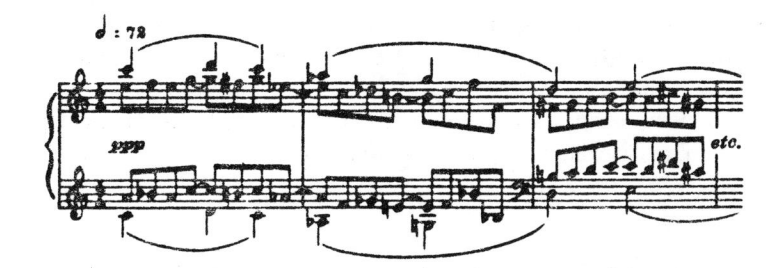

"A sudden crescendo brings a loud but hollow sounding chorale statement in two bare lines played by the woodwinds and strings. In coupled two-part counterpoint, four horns wend their way (via the melodic second) down to a dark close. Divided violas and 'cellos waver on the interval of the second and soon nothing is left but the bassoons' lowest B-flats.

"The Toccata begins while the low B-flats are held. The complete rhythm of the principal theme (fourteen measures) is taken by a quiet snare drum. Then the bass clarinet exposes the melodic contour of the theme while the snare intersperses comments:

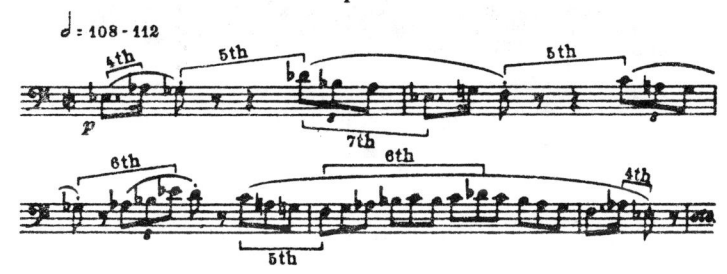

The Toccata is a display piece full of virtuoso passages for solo instruments and groups of instruments, and each player is challenged by the thematic material. The intervallic structure of the melody is derived from the Passacaglia; the octave characteristic is held back until its release in the ninth measure. The bass clarinet runs from its lowest E-flat up three octaves to its highest E-flat, swoops down, and involves all the woodwinds in a wild game. As in Part I, the voices enter canonically. Each member of the woodwinds is compelled to try the theme. When the oboe cannot make the swoop the piccolo helps out. The total effect is one of extreme brilliance and speed, with a bustle of buzzes and shrieks.

"The oboe tries singing the bass-clarinet tune in long notes, but the rest soon crowd him out. A short transition leads to a cadenza section for all the strings where the first variation of the Fugue is given a workout.

"The closing sections continue to bring the symphony's material together. The Chorale is given a rhythmic massage:

[musical notation: Strings, ♩ = 108]

The Toccata theme is augmented against the dialogue material of the final section of the Fugue:

[musical notation: Strings and Muted Brass, ♩ = 108]

Rhythmic blocks from the Passacaglia's first variation are inserted:

[musical notation: ♩ = 108]

and the resultant minor-third motif from the Passacaglia development is shouted by the brass while the remaining choirs drum out the underlying Toccata rhythms." — Flora Rheta Schreiber and Vincent Persichetti, from *William Schuman* (G. Schirmer, 1954).

JOHN CLARK INTERVIEWS THE COMPOSER ON HIS SYMPHONIES: "William Schuman has been a prominent figure in American music for more than four decades. He was part of an extraordinary group of American composers that emerged in the 1930s and 1940s, and his contributions to the musical life of this country extend well beyond the concert hall. Appointed president of the Juilliard School of Music in 1954, he left that position to become the first president of Lincoln

Center for the Performing Arts. Schuman retired from Lincoln Center in 1969 in order to devote more time to composing.

"The symphonies are an essential part of Schuman's work, and he has composed ten of them to date [1986]. The first two, composed in 1935 and 1937, were never published and were withdrawn from performance nearly forty years ago. His *Third Symphony* (1941) enjoyed a resounding critical and popular triumph. Along with the *Sixth*, it is still one of his most frequently performed works.

"JOHN CLARK: In your mind, what distinguishes a symphony from other types of orchestral works; do you adopt a specific musical stance when composing a symphony as opposed to some other kind of extended orchestral piece, especially a one-movement work? How are they different from your ballets, *Undertow* or *Judith*, for example?

"WILLIAM SCHUMAN: Or *Credendum;* that's an interesting question. I have often wondered why I didn't call *Credendum* a symphony. It's almost a symphony. So that suggests to you that I have some criteria in mind. I have never tried to articulate them, even to myself, but I have often wondered why I didn't call that particular work a symphony. I guess I still don't think of it as a symphony even though it's played without pause between movements; although I did use the same bridge passage to link the movements. But the *Seventh Symphony*, which is similar in some respects, I call a symphony.

"I think of the symphony as the musical equivalent of the novel: a work requiring large forces. In the case of a literary work, multiple characters, complexity of theme, subsidiary ideas, main ideas, developmental devices, and it all comes out as a unified whole in some way. To me symphonies will always be written as long as composers wish to use large instrumental forces to say what they have to say, as distinguished from a string quartet, in which you can say something different. I think of a symphony as being complex, not necessarily complicated, but complex in that it has these multiple aspects to it. Whether it's a one-movement symphony or several movements to me is a matter of what you plan to get within an entity. My *Sixth* and *Ninth Symphonies* are definitely one-movement works in the sense that there is a continuum, and that to me is the essence of it: there is a continuum. Then you have another work such as the *Seventh*, which is in separate movements without pause because I wanted the juxtapositions not to lag. In order to make the musical point in that work, there had to be an immediate *attaca*.

"In the *New England Triptych*, I made a mistake. There should be an *attaca* after the slow movement into the chorale which begins the last movement. That was a great musical lesson to me. At the end of the second movement of the *Triptych*, when that minor chord dies away, you should immediately hear the following chorale. Now I am so convinced of that in my own mind, when I don't hear the *attaca*, it's an insult to my musical sensibilities. Yet when I composed it, I didn't sense that, or I wouldn't have written it.

"It's really the juxtaposition of tempi and moods that is important. In the *Seventh Symphony* if you pause you lose a great deal, because when you have the long duet for clarinets—I guess that's the first movement—and then you go into the fanfare, if you had a pause it would absolutely kill the fanfare and the fading away effect of it. With something like the *Third Symphony*, which is very well integrated thematically, you definitely feel the end of the first half. I never said that the work was in four movements; I always said that it was in two parts.

"CLARK: So your concern is with juxtaposing elements or with continuum, which might be equivalent to flow.

"SCHUMAN: No, I think continuum is different from flow. I think that flow in a one-movement symphony means that there is a constant autogenetic development of the materials, which are constantly turning on themselves in some way, and spreading out or contrasting. You may have the equivalent of a number of different movements within a one-movement symphony, but they are all so related that there is never time for a pause; it's an ongoing thing. The other thing, the *attaca* idea that I mentioned, has to do more with what follows next and whether what follows next is better served by a pause or not. That's the only thing that I'm concerned with.

"CLARK: In the *Sixth Symphony* I would say there is more than a hint of the classical four-movement structure with a slow introduction and postlude added on.

"SCHUMAN: Maybe, it never occurred to me while I was doing it. I guess that's for someone else to say. It certainly wasn't conscious on my part. I thought of it as two great big anchors at the beginning and end. I didn't think that when I was starting it. It just came as I was writing it....

"CLARK: What role, if any, does sonata form play in the design of your symphonies? Also, what about any of the elements that we usually associate with that form—recapitulation, tonal schemes, etc.?

"SCHUMAN: Absolutely none. When I write I have no idea of a tonal scheme. People are always telling me about my harmonic organization, but I have absolutely no idea of a tonal scheme. It's all instinctive. I mean I know what I'm doing while I'm doing it, but I never think of it as a tonal scheme. I think of where that particular section is going. I don't think in terms of a tonal scheme because I can make a convincing ending at any place in the chromatic scale, and it doesn't matter where I began. That's number one. Number two, I never think of sonata form or any other form. I think of my own form for each work, and that's the reason the forms differ so greatly. Sometimes when I hear the first movement of the *Symphony for Strings,* I think that that is the most classical movement I've written. I don't know if that's true. That's hindsight. But I never think of it that way when I'm doing it. To me form is the most important element there is in music.

"CLARK: But for you it's a totally instinctive matter.

"SCHUMAN: Yes, with me it's instinctive. It's the most important element, and I write it instinctively. I write long musical essays, and I have an instinctive feeling about it. I don't mean that it always works. I'm not praising it; I'm describing it. I think that form is the most important thing because no matter how brilliant the materials are, if the form isn't convincing, you don't have a convincing concept because it violates a human need. It's the form that satisfies the human need. There's that marvelous thing in Beethoven of not expecting what comes next, but it's always right. I've never said this before, but if you want to know the most brilliant example of twelve-tone writing, that has nothing to do with twelve-tone writing, it is in the *Fifth Symphony* of Beethoven. The principle of not repeating a note in twelve-tone writing until you've sounded the other eleven is basically that of conserving a tone to make it fresh. I think Beethoven gave the greatest example of that in the little passage in the second movement of the *Fifth* [mm. 10-14] which is repeated over and over. Then just before the end of the movement, he adds a little extension to it [mm. 223-27]. That's the genius, that's saving it. Now, I can't believe for a minute that he saved it on purpose or consciously, but he saved it. When you hear it you can't believe it. I think a good composer saves by instinct. I can't think of a single great composer who hasn't had a sense of economy in building his forms and using his orchestra.

"CLARK: You have composed several symphonies in one movement. What attracts you to the single-movement form, and what problems does it solve or create? Also, you might address the question of what are the roots of the one-movement symphonic form, and how does this differ from the multimovement form?

"SCHUMAN: To answer the last part of the question first, I don't know what the roots are.... The great problem with an extended one-movement symphony—for example, my *Ninth,* which is half an hour—is that it has to interest an audience for that length of time. This means that there has to be more highs and lows and dramatic attention-getting devices within the material itself; not just theatrics, because they never work, or at best they only work the first time. Theatrics is an interesting subject all by itself. For example, Bartók's string quartets. Someday those nailed pizzicati are going to hurt that music, because the music is so much better than that effect. If you have an effect that you use all of the time, it becomes apparent as an effect. Now I don't think it's serious in the those quartets, because they are so remarkable. But to get back to the one-movement idea, the thing that I think is so extraordinarily difficult is to find a way of being intriguing musically. After all, you have nothing else but music going on without giving the audience a rest. The purpose of the one-movement thing is not only to say what you have to say in a single utterance, but it is also like an act of a play. It's like going to the theater for an hour-and-a-half continuum or [to] Eugene O'Neill's *Mourning Becomes Electra,* where you go out for dinner and come back two hours later to finish the play. To go on, I think the principal problems with a one-movement symphony are those of form and audience interest. I think the particular reason for doing it is that you have materials that you do not wish to be interrupted. Your musical invention just goes on, and you want to do a whole evening's play or a half-hour symphony without an intermission. The only people who object to not having an intermission are the concessionaires.... Let me ask you a question. How far back do one-movement symphonies go?

"CLARK: For symphonies I can't think of a truly organic one-movement work before the Sibelius *Seventh*. There are the Schumann *Fourth* and Mendelssohn *Third*, but they are multimovement works played without pause. The true predecessor is, I think, the Liszt B-Minor *Sonata*. All roads seem to lead there.

"SCHUMAN: Very interesting. You mean in terms of form in a large work.

"CLARK: Right, a large-scale one-movement work.

"SCHUMAN: Later taken up by Strauss and the rest.

"CLARK: Yes, then you have the Sibelius *Seventh*.... What, in your mind, are the principal unifying elements in your symphonies? Would it be a germinal theme or melodic idea, some kind of harmonic structure, rhythm, or any of the above?

"SCHUMAN: No, it can be any or all of those, but the unifying idea must be found in the form, and only in the form. It's the form that gives it the unity. If it's a one-movement work, it has to have a *raison d'être* in those terms, and that has to be found in the structure rather than these other things which could contain some or all of them....

"CLARK: In looking at your catalogue of works, it's certainly varied, but with the exception of the four string quartets, I think there is a noticeable absence of chamber music.

"SCHUMAN: Nobody wants to commission any chamber music, and I'm accustomed to functioning as a professional composer. It's not just the money, but I like to write because people ask me for something. I don't know; it does something for me because I'm writing on request. Now this year I wrote some songs that nobody asked me for, because I couldn't resist. I have the four string quartets, but of those the *First* is withdrawn and the *Second* should be. The *Third* I still love, and that's played once in a while. The *Fourth* is too difficult to be played, especially the middle movement with all of the double stops.... Some of the things just don't work terribly well. But I love chamber music. It is one of my great passions in the world, but that's quite aside from whether I write it....

"I find it very difficult to write for piano and very easy to write for the symphony orchestra. Of course there's *Voyage* for piano. André Previn told me that someday he was going to have the nerve to play *Voyage* for me, and then I said I wonder why that isn't played more. He said because it's a virtuoso work but doesn't sound like one.

"CLARK: I agree, it's much more difficult than it sounds.[116]

"SCHUMAN: All in all, the piano has not been a special love of mine. I find it very difficult to write for, whereas Copland finds it very easy." — from John W. Clark, "William Schuman on His Symphonies: An Interview", in *American Music*, Fall 1986.

---

116 *Editorial aside:* Every performer makes an essential contribution to bringing every piece of music into being — obviously; thus, no performer's contribution to a piece of music should ever be slighted. However, it is precisely *as* collaborators that performers (like critics) surely have a responsibility to present new works to the public. However, not all players accept this responsibility with equal grace, or enthusiasm. Two complaints commonly heard are (1) new works require too much effort in exchange for too little of musical substance — raising the interesting question of how this could be known, if the work has not been performed in the first place; and (2) audiences may not sufficiently appreciate the performance, having nothing (or little) with which to compare it. In the end it is perhaps a matter of conscience, for each performer to consider for himself or herself. I should only ask that if — alas — composers do not derive any benefit from performances of their works (if performances do not take place in their own lifetime, for example) — then in what strange way has the performer's debt to composers been satisfied?

JOSEPH SCHWANTNER

B. 1943, Chicago IL. *Educ.:* Chicago Cons, Northwest Univ. *Taught at:* Eastman Schl of Music. Comp-in-res St. Louis SO. Charles Ives Scholarship; winner ISCM Natl Comp Competitions, Kennedy Ctr Friedheim Award; winner, 1979 Pulitzer Prize. *Works incl.:* And the Mountains Rising Nowhere (wind ens), chamb *(In Aeternum, Diaphonia intervallum, Music of Amber)*, orch *(Aftertones of Infinity, A Sudden Rainbow)*, voice & insts *(Dreamcaller, Sparrows, Wild Angels of the Open Hills)*.

Composer statement: "For as long as I can remember, I have been inexplicably attracted to music. This all consuming passion for and preoccupation with music has remained with me for the greater part of my life. It is a world that completely and pervasively engrosses me for I continue to be imbued with a sense of wonder at musics' many mysteries. My notions about music are reflected, quite naturally, in my work, and the musical issues they engage change as the nature of my work inevitably changes. This is the way I live my life, with each new work illuminating and defining, hopefully with ever greater clarity and precision, those uniquely individual elements that constitute a personal voice. For me, music becomes an enticing journey through unchartered sonic worlds—a creative encounter advancing myriad musical possibilities that totally engage my ear, mind and spirit."

Magabunda (4 Poems of Agueda Pizarro) (cycle) for Soprano and Orchestra (1983). 32m *Comm. & prem.:* Lucy Shelton (s), St. Louis SO, Leonard Slatkin, cond. *Other perfs.:* Boston SO. *Rec.:* Nonesuch Digital LP D-79072: Lucy Shelton (s), St. Louis SO, Leonard Slatkin, cond. *Pub.:* Helicon Music (European American).
4(1 picc)-3(1 E hn)-3 cl-3(1 cbsn); 4-3-3-1; ampl pno/celesta, harp, 3 perc, timp; strings
1. *Shadowinnower (Sombraventadora)*. 2. *Blancolvido (White Oblivion)*. 3. *Black Anemones*. 4. *Magabunda (Witch-nomad)*.

"The richness and dreamlike quality of [Pizarro's] verbal images is echoed in the striking, theatrical gestures of the music, which makes varied use of the orchestra (often deployed in families, with the percussion taking a role at least equal in prominence to that of the others) and a rhapsodic vocal part that is often sustained in the higher register for extended periods, though also requiring rapid changes of register, lavish ornamental gestures, and the vaguely pitched speech of *Sprechtstimme* here and there. Throughout the score the varied colors, the alternation of tiny, obsessive ostinato figures with great swashes of sound, the delicate hues of instrumentation, and the broad cantilena of the vocal part invite the listener to be seduced into an enchanted world, where magic is at work and both dreams and nightmares seem to exist simultaneously." — Steven Ledbetter, from 1/86 program notes for the Boston Symphony Orchestra.

"[Schwantner's *Magabunda* is] an elaborately colorful setting of poetic texts [which] are by turns incantatory, brooding, minatory and fiercely aggressive. [They] make enormous demands on the vocal soloist in terms of great leaps from end to end of the soprano register and utilization of the entire expressive gamut of which the human voice is capable within the bounds of music, ranging from *parlando* to dramatic *coloratura*. Schwantner's orchestral scoring calls upon all available orchestral resources short of overt electronic means, with the percussion section, including tuned glasses, water gong and amplified celesta, playing a major role." — David Hall, *Ovation* 2/85.

New Morning for the World: "Daybreak of Freedom" for Speaker and Orchestra (1982). *Text:* Martin Luther King, Jr. 27m *Prem.:* with Willie Stargell (spkr). *Rec.:* Mercury (Stereo LP) 289-411 031-1: Willie Stargell (spkr), Eastman Philharmonia, David Effron, cond. *Pub.:* Helicon Music (European American)
3 (2 picc)-3 (1 eh)-3 (3 b cl)-3; 4-3-4-1; timp, 4 perc, ampl celesta, ampl pno; strings

"Joseph Schwantner's *New Morning for the World* for narrator and orchestra is anything but 'abstract'. The circumstances of its composition and of its premiere — the use of texts by Martin Luther King, Jr., and the performance (and subsequent recording) with sports star Willie Stargell — lend the work an immediate appeal. Those who come upon the score after having first experienced the piece as listeners may be surprised by Schwantner's economy of means. A great array of dramatic gestures is built from only a few patterns, most of these complex ostinatos, which are then repeated throughout the work. Contrast is achieved by altering their context, both in their means of musical articulation (dynamic level, register, phrasing) and their relationship to the spoken text. The relationship between narrator and instruments is — wisely — kept simple; usually the two forces alternate, and during those passages where both are employed together the orchestra is held to sustained (or repetitive) background sonorities. The orchestration often relies upon heavy brass, piano, and tuned percussion for its dramatically brilliant *tutti* textures. As effective as these are, one senses a more imaginative — and especially evocative — quality in the delicate chamber-like ensemble groupings." — Elliott Schwartz, in *Notes* (Music Library Association), 12/86.

Toward Light for Orchestra (1987). 22m *Comm. & prem.:* Canton (OH) SO, Gerhardt Zimmermann, cond.
3 (1 picc)-3-3-3; 4-3-3-1; 2 pnos, hp, timp, 3 perc; strings
1. *Someday Memories.* 2. *Toward Light.* 3. *Shadowed Images.*

"*Toward Light* is perhaps Schwantner's most lyrical work to date — a sunny tone-painting of youth and innocence. The composer acknowledges influences of Debussy, Stravinsky, Bartók, and Britten, but has assimilated them thoroughly: the bright tones, clean intervals, and rhythmic design are unmistakably his own.

" 'Someday Memories,' the first part of the work, grows from a brief, agitated introduction to a singing, pensive melody, and includes a dancing motif in a dozen different colorations. Plucked arpeggios and shifting timbres create the imagery of running water in a gentle, introspective second part for strings only, bearing the title of the work. Percussion, winds, and brass return for a third, dramatic section, 'Shadowed Images'. Twittering winds and chiming bells sing over sustained low strings, and earlier motifs return.

"The work continues Schwantner's preoccupation with shifting sonorities, light, and the effects of overtones. It's a score which merits attention. [The premiere] was played to a packed, appreciative house." — Philippa Kiraly, in *Musical America*, 1/88.

Veiled Autumn (Kindertodeslied) for Piano (c.1987). *Publ.:* Helicon Music Corp/European Music Corp (score).

"*Veiled Autum* is a brief elegiac character piece for piano. The title provides the poetic backdrop for the introspective, reflective and somewhat dark-hued tone and character of the piece. The overall design is rondo-like with the melodic material lyric and expressive and the harmonic material essentially modal." — Joseph Schwantner.

Performance notes by Maurice Hinson: "This impressionistic piece is full of subtle sonorities that require careful use of the damper pedal. Even though the composer has added some pedal marks, pedals should be used much more than indicated. Lyrical gestures permeate *Veiled Autumn* and clear, but changing tonal centers undergird the logical structure. Ringing sonorities brought about by sharply attacked chords that are left to die away slowly, or sharply accented notes left to ring, add much color and atmosphere. A few of these sonorities are heard at measures 2, 4, 5 and 52. The composer attributes his continuing interest in ringing sonorities to his early experience as a guitarist. Metrical changes should flow smoothly from one into the other. The Coda (measures 53 to the end), with its repeated motives, ends unresolved tonally, and the pedal should be held until all the sound has disappeared."

Robert Simpson

B. 1921, Leamington (England). *Educ.:* Durham Univ. *Author of: Bruckner and the Symphony; Carl Nielsen, Symphonist; Sibelius and Nielsen.* *Works incl.:* concertos (pno, vln), piano, quartets, 6 symphonies, trio (cl/vc/pno), *Variations and Fugue* (rec/string qt).

A character sketch of Robert Simpson's music: "Robert Simpson's sense of rhythm is organic, not motoric. Rhythm for him is not an infantile drumming, but the proportion of paragraphs of large harmonic thinking. This he shares with Sibelius.

"Simpson's melody is not ingratiating. He is no miniature lyricist: that is why he is a true symphonist. But he has the ability to write a simple tune; and he says 'When I write a tune, I bloody well mean it' — a gutsy conviction lacking in [many] contemporary composers.

"His harmonic vocabulary includes the most prosaic chords, sometimes in unrelated and unexpected progressions; like a plain man uttering his own philosophy in common parlance. His harmony also contains uncompromising dissonance of a stark, rather than sumptuous nature.

"He has worked at counterpoint; something fewer and fewer composers are doing (to music's detriment, for polyphony has been till now the continuing language of great music). It is his contrapuntal prowess that gives his music its symphonic current.[117]

"His orchestration is that of a constructor, not that of a colorist. Its function is to clarify his form. His brass writing is written 'from the inside', and he was formerly a trumpeter. Before that, as a boy, he participated in Salvation Army band music; a first bond between himself and the boy Carl Nielsen, who played bugle and trombone in the Odense military band in Denmark.

"Simpson never conceives of his music as 'programmatic', though he does compose with *analogies* to music in mind — often analogies drawn from biological or astronomic processes (he is a keen amateur astronomer).

"The intonations of his music are certainly Nordic. Anyone who knows the common language of very different Scandinavian composers will recognise their kinship to the sound of Simpson's music....

---

[117] In this respect see also the symphonies of Edmund Rubbra, above. (Ed.)

"If I were to characterize Simpson's work in one epithet it would be: integrity. In a fragmented age, those who still value the humanistic tradition will prize this quality and the music which expresses it.

"Our knowledge of the nature of genius is limited, but I am convinced that one of its essentials is energy. Simpson has this (one of his works for brass band is entitled *Energy*). The energy basic to his industriousness, his intuitions plus the craftsmanship needed to embody them in musical forms, his aggressive anti-pessimism — all these things indicate his genius. He is congenitally incapable of experiencing or transmitting boredom.

"Simpson's music will live and its significance will be increasingly perceived, if only mankind does not destroy itself. If the graph of modern history, from its trough of despond, can take an upward turn, his music will come into its own." — Ronald Stevenson, essay insert accompanying Hyperion A66117 recording of the Simpson Quartets 7-8.[118]

Quartet 7 for Strings (1977). 19m *Prem.:* Gabrieli String Quartet. *Rec:* Hyperion (LP) A66117/Harmonia Mundi: Delmé String Quartet (Galina Solodchin, Jeremy Williams, vlns, John Underwood, vla, Stephen Orton, vc).
Tranquillo — Vivace — Tempo primo.

Quartet 8 for Strings (1979). Comm. by Brunel P Society. *Prem:* Delmé String Quartet. *Rec:* Hyperion (LP) A66117/Harmonia Mundi: Delmé String Quartet.
1. Grave, molto intensivo (11m). 2. Molto vivace (*Eretmapodites giletti*) (3m). 3. Allegretto grazioso (5m). 4. Risoluto e concentrato (12m).

"Although [Simpson] may be known to many as a most knowledgeable and engaging writer on composers such as Bruckner, Nielsen, Sibelius, Beethoven, and Brian (through his books, articles, and broadcasts), he would probably consider himself primarily a composer. This he could do with justification, for he has been writing music for about 40 years. If his output seems small, we must remember that he also held a position for 30 years in the BBC music division. Nonetheless, that output, which includes eight symphonies and 11 string quartets, is a solid one. Of the more than dozen works I've heard I find [almost all] worthy indeed: beautifully crafted, expressive, often very exciting, always justifiably demanding of our concentration and repeated listening.

---

118 Ronald Stevenson, the eminent pianist, is himself a composer and the subject of Malcolm MacDonald's *Ronald Stevenson: A Musical Biography*, published in 1989 by the National Library of Scotland and, in 1990, by Pro/Am Music Resources, Inc. in the United States. (Ed.)

"These two quartets are fine works. In *Nr. 7*, the repetition of certain melodic figures near the start may be slightly overdone, but the remainder of this highly inventive, long-breathed work provides some validity for that. Each half of the fast mid-section of this continuous quartet attains a magnificent climax by means of what are essentially no more than scales and similar 'empty' figures like partial triads. But rarely has 'empty' been fuller than here. Simpson is most adept at creating powerful music out of material which out of context *looks* quite undistinguished.

"The first movement of the longer *Eighth Quartet* contains an intriguing fugue which often digresses to ponder different things and eventually disintegrates into a beautiful bell-like pasage in the violins. The second movement is a mosquito-like scherzo, full of adroit tonal shifts. The slower third movement, which seems to reflect on the second, is in some ways more relaxed, in others more unsettled. The final movement, like so much of Simpson's music, is thoroughly contrapuntal, full of energy, and really propulsive in its drive. The use of scales is particularly imaginative; their form and function towards the end are more diverse than those of the scales found near the end of the *Seventh Quartet*.

"Simpson's music has often been criticized for sounding like that of Carl Nielsen. If that were all it did, the criticism could stand. But Simpson has *internalized* the essence of much of Nielsen; the links between the two are profound and positive, not superficial and negative. I am as sure that Nielsen would have understood the last movement of Simpson's Eighth Quartet as I am that he could never have written it." — Paul Rapoport, *Fanfare: The Magazine for Serious Record Collectors*, 1-2/85.

"[Both the *Quartet 7* and *Quartet 8*—] highly contrasted and mature [works]—have scientific associations: the earlier astronomical by its commission to mark the Centenary of the former Astronomer Royal, Sir James Jeans; the latter entomological by its dedication to Professor David Gillet, discoverer of the mosquito species *Eretmapodites gilletti* (is the second movement of the *Eighth Quartet*, in its depiction of the insect, the first known piece of specifically mosquito-inspired music?).

"*Quartet Nr. 7* is a tripartite single movement. 119 bars of *Tranquillo* music, virtually all *pp* and *ppp*, begin it. Given the celestial connotations, it is easy to imagine depicted here the silent immensity of space; but the purposeful unfolding of a design whose backbone is very clearly exposed in the repetiion and development of a rising idea first heard on the first violin only five bars in, gives the lie to any notion that the eternal void is going to be described by any meandering about, however atmospheric; Simpson's cosmos is as musically shapely as Haydn's Chaos. The center of the quartet is a powerful *vivace*, propelled throughout (with the exception of a withdrawn middle passage), by a torrent of triplet figures, eventually rising to an immensely powerful statement, throttled back at the *tempo primo*, of the rising figure from the opening section. After this, the music falls back in on itself, like a collapsing sun, to a short recapitulation of the opening mood, but now dotted with gentle rising scales that are so reminiscent of moments in Haydn's *Representation of Chaos* that one wonders if they are a deliberate homage by Simpson to an acknowledged master.

"Nr. 8 is in four movements: a massive fugue, and a finale whose nature is well described by its marking *Risoluto e concentrato*, flank the much smaller mosquitoid scherzo already mentioned and a diminutive, muted *Allegretto grazioso*....

"Professor Lionel Pike calls both works masterpieces. Certainly they are as wonderfully coherent musical designs, [however], the work of Simpson's which is for me unquestionably a masterpiece from every point of view is his tremendous *Ninth Quartet*, the 32 *Variations and Finale on a Theme of Haydn* [below]." — David J. Brown, in *Tempo: The Quarterly Review of Modern Music*, Nr. 150, 9/84.

"Like those of two predecessors, Beethoven and Bartók, Simpson's quartets span his whole composing life. He has so far written ten. Not only do they contain music of a most attractive and exciting kind, but they also illustrate this composer's abiding interest in organic development and the problems of organising large musical structures. Increasingly, too, they reflect his fascination with musical motion and with energy. In particular, the seventh and eighth quartets illustrate Simpson's interest in the possibilities of everyday musical sounds when approached as if one had never heard them before. We have here two powerful masterworks which must surely take their place in the quartet literature of the second half of the present century as did those of Bartók in the literature of the first....

"The *String Quartet Nr. 7* was written in 1977 at the request of Lady Jeans (Susi Jeans, the organist), and it is dedicated to her. The work was completed quickly and was first played by the Gabrieli String Quartet at a concert in Lady Jeans' home, Cleveland Lodge, Dorking, during a concert celebrating the centenary of her husband. The composer, himself a keen astronomer and a Fellow of the Royal Astronomical Society, draws parallels between the music of this work and aspects of the universe — quiet and mysterious and yet pulsating with energy. There is only one movement, which falls into three distinct sections, slow—fast—slow. At the beginning of the work the first violin introduces a stationary line on the note D which is crossed by an upward moving one: from this material all the remainder of the piece grows quite logically. At first the vastnesses of space are invoked: progress is occasionally held in check by the sustained bottom note of the cello—a readily identifiable and memorable sound of which Robert Simpson is very fond. Indeed, the various open strings of all four instruments, tuned in fifths, play an important role in the quartet and provide a force which one might compare to gravitation, controlling the movement of stars in space. The music may seem to move slowly in various directions but it always remains under this tonal-gravitational control; this circle of fifths has different effects according to the way we seem to be facing. The energy of the universe is suggested in the central fast section which contains a tremendous climax of an intensity rare in string quartet literature. The slow music returns to end the work as it began, with the note D, contemplating immensities.

"The *String Quartet Nr. 8*, funded in part by the Greater London Arts Association, was first performed on 21 June 1980 by the Delmé String Quartet at Brunel University. The diminutive *Scherzo* of this quartet gives an impression of the 'formidable delicacy' (the composer's words) of a mosquito, and its subtitle, '*Eretmapodites gilletti*', refers to the species named after its discoverer, Professor Gillet, director of Biological Sciences at Brunel University, the dedicatee of the work.

"There are four movements, each of which is in some way unconventional. The first is a large, slow fugue whose intensity is mitigated at times by more reflective material: the fugue subject is a great span of melody that crosses all the strings of each of the instruments in turn and embodies the elements from which the rest of the music grows. But the subject is itself continually changed and transformed, gaining all the while in power and energy. At the climax of the fugue the scurrying motion of the viola and cello, and the inexorable increase in latent momentum which has been gradually built up, are such that the two violins are suddenly left with a steady chiming passage, which then fades into the distance. It is as if a band of campanologists[119] has worked up such power, speed and propulsion in their ringing that they can leave the bells to continue sounding alone under the motion generated.

"The second movement illustrates the mosquito in a little *Scherzo* of A-B-A form. Professor Gillett, on being asked whether the music of the piece is what the insects sound like, replied, 'No—but it's what

---

119 Campanology—the art or study of bell casting and ringing. (Ed.)

they behave like', and he indicated that D. H. Lawrence's little poem 'The mosquito knows—' is also an accurate account of the insect:

> The mosquito knows full well, small as he is
> he's a beast of prey.
> But after all
> he only takes his bellyful,
> he doesn't put my blood in the bank.

"The third movement is for muted strings and is all elusive half-shades. It is cast in very small-scale sonata form. The *Finale*—whose size balances that of the opening fugue—is a highly original movement, being for part of its length a variation of the first movement, but without the fugal texture. It is tumultuous, yet deliberate, and the tempo is not fast. Pungency rather than speed creates the intense feeling of activity. In the first movement the calmer, more reserved music eventually prevailed; but in the *Finale* it is the sense of concentrated energy that ultimately triumphs, with scales of all kinds evolving from the texture and becoming dominant. Superlatives of all kinds are frequently overused, but no one need have any hesitation in describing these two quartets as masterpieces." — Lionel Pike, from program notes for Hyperion A66117 recording.

Quartet 9 for Strings. 58m *Prem.*: Delmé String Quartet. *Rec*: Hyperion A66127 (distr. Harmonia Mundi): Delmé String Quartet.

"The Robert Simpson Society and Hyperion [Records] have now given us the huge *Ninth Quartet*, 58 minutes of continuous music which happen to be based on a theme of Haydn. 'Based on' is really too simple a way of putting it; 'springing from' might be more accurate. The palindromic theme itself is found in the minuet of Haydn's symphony in G known as No. 47; on it, from it, inside it, and against it, Simpson has written 32 variations and a fugue, with every one of the variations a palindrome.

"His style is hard to describe. Its starting point is surely the harmonic/contrapuntal organicism of Beethoven; it is related too to the more recent worlds of Shostakovich, Britten, and Nielsen, without sounding like any of them. And while the dimensions of the work may suggest another composer highly regarded by Simpson — namely Bruckner, it is more the essence of some of the individual variations (rather than the sound or scope of the piece) that may be called Brucknerian. The variations I have in mind have an obsessive urge and concentration which are typified by much of Bruckner. For that reason, this quartet will not be to everyone's taste: some of the longer explorations of some really imaginative figuration are hard to place in the context of the whole. This is a problem with which some listeners may deal successfully but others may not. Although the success of the entire quartet in this regard is hard to judge, there is certainly an abundance of magnificent music in it.

"Another thing is certain: those who listen repeatedly to[120] this gigantic work will find more and more in it. The subtle contrast of musical worlds, for example, is something Simpson handles so easily that one may be misled at first into thinking nothing of it. Deft contrasts of types of motion, even in the simpler early variations, are notable for projecting both emotional depth and emotional control. This is the sort of thing which gives the whole quartet a vastness of projection. Even the wonderful ending of the quartet suggests something quite beyond itself: it contains both a finality and a freshness, both resolving and not resolving what has preceded. So be it! This is the kind of paradox which art must contain and continually grapple with.... [Simpson's *Ninth Quartet* is] highly recommended to the adventurous sort eager for a traditional work which is not traditional at all." — Paul Rapaport, in *Fanfare: The Magazine for Serious Record Collectors*, 3-4/85.

"This is a 'ninth' and no mistake. In that number there was, surely, a challenge to a composer so acutely aware of its significance in the output of more than one great and admired predecessor, and Robert Simpson tackles it head-on with all the power and originality that have characterized the products of his marvellously fruitful 'retirement' [from his BBC producing career]. No explicit parallel, therefore, with 'the' *Ninth Symphony*, nor with any Beethoven quartet, but instead a design to match another Beethovenian masterpiece, and one coeval with the *Ninth Symphony* — the *'Diabelli' Variations*.

"It must be fairly well-known by now that each variation of Simpson's 32 (is this number another Beethoven salute?) is a palindrome, as is the original theme from the minuet of Haydn's *Symphony 47*, and one might well pause at the sheer constructional ingenuity this represents: any old set of notes does *not* sound just as good, but different, played backwards! Simpson's ideas are so characterful that their reverses almost always are not only fascinating in themselves but throw more and different light on the original forms. What might to some composers have been an intolerable strait-jacket is to him a liberating tool. He uses, in particular, the turnround point of his aural mirror in a multitude of ways: pivots of increasing tension or relaxation, climbing or falling, receding or advancing, points of stasis, maximum activity or in some case a con-

---

120 And, presumably, perform. (Ed.)

tinuity so smooth that without the score one would be hard pressed to discern the point at which the reverse starts. Simpson's nodepoints glitter all over this work like the facets of a diamond.

"The larger design, too, is wonderfully conceived, with many of the variations being grouped so that they form virtually continuous larger entities within the whole. There is a tendency, also, for these groupings to get bigger as the *Quartet* proceeds, and with more extreme contrasts between their characters. There are two 'slow movements': firstly Variations XV and XVI a little before the half-way mark, and secondly a bigger one near the end, consisting of Variations XXX, XXXI, XXXII and, so far as the unbroken effect is concerned, the first four minutes or so of the *Fugue*. The second of these two, in particular, has an intensity and wholly unsentimental depth of feeling that matches anything in the quartets of Shostakovich, to look no further. The *Fugue* quickens and grows in contrapuntal activity until it overflows in a boiling energy surpassing anything that has gone before: the demands on the sheer stamina of the players are heavy indeed, but [the Hyperion recording demonstrates that] the Delmé Quartet, as they [also] demonstrated at the Wigmore Hall premiere, are the equal of anything that the composer puts before them. He makes the utmost use of every expressive device offered by the quartet medium, but never abuses it. However, perhaps the most remarkable thing about this remarkable work is that Simpson's response to his self-imposed intellectual challenge is full of *emotional* power as well — mind serving heart and vice versa in a rare way." — David J. Brown, in *Tempo: The Quarterly Review of Modern Music*, Nr. 152, 3/85.

Quartet 10 (For Peace) for Strings. *Rec:* Hyperion (CD) CDA 66225 (distr. Harmonia Mundi): Coull Quartet.

Quartet 11 for Strings. *Rec:* Hyperion (CD) CDA 66225 (distr. Harmonia Mundi): Coull Quartet.

"Simpson's music is worth getting to know, especially for contemporary-music afficionados who subscribe to the idea that the 'validity' of a new piece is dependent on its form and content being somehow on the cutting edge. It's worth getting to know because Simpson — who produces well-wrought and compelling music that is valid in every way — represents the very antithesis of the avantgarde.

"He did have a flirtation with serialism, but that was way back in the 1940s, before he wrote his *First Symphony* and before he began what amounted to a 30-year career as programmer and host for the BBC in London. Since 1951, as the laudatory article in *The New Grove Dictionary of Music and Musicians* tells us, 'all his music... has been firmly based in tonality, and he has shown no desire to experiment with newly evolved techniques or methods of composition.' That, however, is not to suggest that Simpson's style has not changed over the years. I can't comment on his entire oeuvre, but there are certainly differences in vocabulary and approach to be noted between the 1977 *Symphony No. 6*, on the one hand, and, on the other, the *Symphony No. 7* of the same year and the 1984 *String Quartet No. 11*. The *Sixth Symphony* generates the same tonal atmosphere and seems driven by the same techniques of motivic development as the later symphonies of Sibelius, while relatively grinding dissonances and relatively angular melodic lines make the *Seventh Symphony* and the *String Quartet No. 11* sound almost 'modernistic'.

"In at least one sense, Simpson *is* a modernist, that is, an artist whose work suggests he is a man acutely aware of the state of mankind in the modern world. The subtitle of the *String Quartet No. 10*, 'For Peace', summarizes his basic position, and all of his compositions that I've heard seem to be attempts to articulate that position through music. Simpson's music is not without tension or friction; almost always, though, the elements of tension and friction serve only to make their opposites seem all the more desirable. This is music of conviction and integrity, music based on traditional values and traditional methods, and the fact that it is patently old-fashioned diminishes neither its solidity nor its effectiveness." — James Wierzbicki, in *Musical America*, 11/88.

STANISLAW SKROWACZEWSKI

B. 1923, Lwów (Poland). *Educ.:* Univ Lwoów, Univ Cracow. *Cond.* Wroclaw (Breslau) PO, Katowice PO, Krakow PO, Warsaw PO, Minneapolis S/Minnesota O. *Awards*: Kennedy Center Friedheim Award (*Ricercari Notturni*, sax[cl]/orch). *Works incl.:* concertos (cl, sax, vln), *Fantasie per quattro* (cl/vln/vc/pno), *Ricercare* (sax & orch), *Trio* (cl/bsn/pno), orch. transcriptions, 4 symphonies.

Concerto for English Horn & Orchestra (1969). 17m *Rec:* Desto Records (Stereo LP) DC 7126: Thomas Stacy (E hn), Minnesota O, Stanislaw Skrowaczewski, cond. Ded. to Thomas Stacy. *Pub.:* European American.
3(1 picc)-0-0-0; 3-3-3-0; 5 timp, 3 perc, pno (keyboard not used); strings (10-0-8-8-6)
1. Quarter Note Equals 100. 2. *Aria*— 3. Quarter Note Equals 144.

"The *Concerto* consists of three movements that are alternately fast, slow (an aria) and again fast. The spiritual climax of the finale breaks into a chorale of four triads, each of three different notes so that all twelve tones of the octave are used. The choice of these chords is such that any order of them gives the B-A-C-H pattern—a kind of hommage to Bach. Nevertheless, the work does not proceed from any particular school or 'ism'. Whatever aspects of twelve-tone technique it has absorbed are almost accidental, for they function as a byproduct of expressive development of melody. By eliminating all other reeds, the scoring focuses on the [English horn's] distinctive timbre. The only other representative of the woodwind family are three flutes (the third doubling piccolo).

"According to its composer, the purpose of the *Concerto* is not merely to provide a vehicle for English horn but to show off the orchestra in relation to the solo instrument; in its way, the work is a miniscule concerto for orchestra. The strings play not as sections but as persons. Much of the time each player is allotted different musical material. The *Concerto* exploits some possibilities for English horn that have never before been used, such as *multiphonic-fingerings* (producing chord-like sounds), *harmonics* and *sympathetic vibrations* (effected by playing directly into the sounding board of the piano, causing sympathetic vibrations in its strings)." — from liner notes for Desto Stereo LP DC 7126.

Concerto for Orchestra (1985). 32m *Pub.:* Boelke-Bomart (distr. Jerona Music Corp.).
4-4-4-4; 4-4-3-1; timp, 4 perc, hp, pno (cel); strings
1. Adagio (Misterioso)(Quarter note = 56). 2. Adagio (*"Anton Bruckners Himmelfahrt [Anton Bruckner's Ascension]"* (Quarter note = 42-44).

"The *Concerto for Orchestra* is Skrowaczewski's strongest work to date, certainly his most deeply felt. Perhaps, too, it is his most personal statement. At the end of the work, hearing the mighty Bruckner-like theme in the brasses poke through the busy cacophony of the entire orchestra—and the sweet tone of consolation that ensues—who can avoid seeing this as a statement from a man who has always seen music as a consoling, ennobling, transcendent force?" — *Minneapolis Star and Tribune.*

"[The *Concerto* is] a wonderful essay, radiant and full of feeling." — *St. Paul Pioneer Press and Dispatch.*

Music at Night for Orchestra (1949; rev. 1977). 17m *Prem. (rev. vers.)* 1977 Cabrillo Music Festival (CA), Stanislaw Skrowaczewski, cond. *Pub.:* Boelke-Bomart (distr. Jerona Music Corp.).
2(pic)-2(E.hn)-2(a.sax)-2; 4-2-3-1; timp, 2 perc, harp, piano; strings
In 4 continuous sections.

"*Music at Night* is a synopsis of material from a ballet which Skrowaczewski wrote in 1943 and revised in 1960.

"The work is in four sections, but is performed without interruption. Its dramatic theme is a love story whose tragic circumstances are clearly audible.... Its strong Slavic antecedents are clearly evident, too." —Jack Benson, Aptos (CA) *Sunday Morning News*, 8/28/77.

"[This] engaging piece, along with Lou Harrison's *Suite for Violin, Piano and Small Orchestra* the best of the contempory music played at this year's [Cabrillo Music Festival], opens with a rumbling of basses and cellos, soon followed by an anguished cry from the violins. At times there are sounds coming from the strings which make your teeth hurt, but they quickly diminish into incredibly soft threads of tone. Some of the effects [which the composer] extracts from novel pairings of instruments are but eerie fragments which he uses to stitch together massive blocs of music coming from the full orchestra. In writing this [the composer] runs the whole spectrum of musical expression: there are Debussy-like moods, some menacing moments, the throb of plucked basses sounding like heartbeats, and angry outbursts punctuated by snare-drum rolls...." —Bill Akers, *Watsonville (CA) Register-Pajaronian*, 8/27/77.

"Skrowaczewski's greatest achievement comes in creating a dream-like atmosphere of sound that envelops the listener, allowing each member of the audience to create his own fantasy world. As the final coda slowly evaporated, it was clear that [the Cabrillo Music Festival performance] was one world premiere that deserved the honor." — *Sentinel*.

"[Skrowaczewski's] *Music at Night* is full of big gestures, sharp evocations and such subtle instrumental combinations that it is plainly the work of a romanticist." — *The Philadelphia Inquirer*.

"*Music at Night* is authentic, solid, well-orchestrated and has a sweep beyond the casual interest of mere novelty..... [It is] one of those occasional new works one would truly want to hear again and again." — The (Philadelphia) Bulletin.

Symphony for Strings (1947-49). 22m *Score:* Music Associates of America.
1. Adagio (Eighth note = 54) — Allegro (Dotted quarter note = 84). 2. Adagio (Quarter note = 52). 3. Presto (Quarter note = 152).

"I wrote my *Symphony for Strings* during my residence in Paris between 1947-49. This composition is a certain reaction to my other works of this period written for a large orchestra, thick in instrumental, harmonic, and formal texture and overloaded with polyphony. This time period marked in many cases my departure from postromantic tonality and first experiences with the twelve-tone method. However, the twelve-tone idea never appealed to me as a 'total' solution or any historical necessity; I considered it rather a possibility for further extension of romantic expressiveness. There is extensive use of this sort of serialism in my *Symphony for Strings* but the way I employ it sounds more as a melodic theme or sort of leitmotif which is more proper for the traditional way I built sonata form in the first and third movements and for the broad usage of polyphony. Interestingly enough, this frequent use of polyphony sounds not linearly but more harmonically, vertically. The harmony — the vertical sound — of chords has always been for me a matter of utmost importance.

"The slow introduction to the first movement sets not only thematic, serial, and harmonic material, but the mood and color for the entire work. Then follows the Allegro, based on the same theme, built in sonata form with two themes, development section, recapitulation and coda." — Stanislaw Skrowaczewski, 10/16/77.

Trio for Clarinet, Bassoon and Piano (1983-84. 17m *Perf.:* Philadelphia Chamber Ens (Donald Montanaro, cl, Bernard Garfield, bsn, Kiyoko Takeuti, pno). *Rec.:* Minnesota Composers Forum: Joseph Longo (cl), John Miller (bsn), Paul Schoenfield (pno). *Pub.:* Boelke-Bomart (distr. Jerona Music Corp. — score with parts).
In 3 movements.

"A playful, highly virtuosic work, this piece combines a Stravinskyan sense of color and rhythm with harmonic materials derived from Schoenberg — plus a touch of piano-interior and bassoon multiphonics as a bow to contemporaneity.

"[Members of the Philadelphia Chamber Ensemble performed this] immensely difficult work with the greatest assurance and understanding — the two winds being especially admirable in showering so much skill upon the music while refusing to treat it as a mere display vehicle." — Andrew Stiller, *The Philadelphia Inquirer*, 1/13/90.

"Skrowaczewski's *Trio* features expressive virtuosic writing for the wind instruments as well as the piano. Its style is modern but very dramatic, expressive but far from severe. Played to perfection by the Longo/Miller/Schoenfield team [on the Minnesota Composers Forum recording, it] is a fine addition to contemporary wind literature." — *The Double Reed*, Spring 1985.

STEPHEN SONDHEIM

B. 1930, New York NY. *Educ.:* Williams Coll. Pres., Dramatists Guild; member, Amer Acad/Inst of Arts and Letters. *Lyr. for shows:* Do I Hear a Waltz?, Gypsy, West Side Story. *Inc. music: Girls of Summer, Invitation to a March, Twigs. Film scores: Reds, Stavisky.*

NOTE: Some of the following data also derived from David Hummel, *The Collector's Guide to the American Musical Theatre* (2 vols)(Metuchen NJ: The Scarecrow Press, 1984). Since Stephen Sondheim is surely among the two or three most written-about composers of theater music today, no attempt has been made to add to the critical literature here. Instead, miscellaneous production notes for each of the shows are provided, along with lists of song titles and selected recording and publication data, which, it is hoped, will interest and be of some use to lovers of Broadway show music, playgoers, and local theater groups.

Anyone Can Whistle (musical play) (1964). *Book:* Arthur Laurents; *lyr.:* composer. *Licensing agent:* Music Theatre International. *Rec.:* Columbia (Mono LP) KOL-6080 (Stereo LP KOS-2480; reissued as CSP AS 32608: original cast. *Pub.:* Random House (libretto), Chappell (piano-vocal score), Chappell (vocal selections).
5 M, 3 F; variable chorus, dancers
5 reeds; 2-3-2-0; accordion, pno/celeste; 0-0-5-1
Numbers: I'm Like a Bluebird. Me and My Town. Miracle Song. Simple. A-One March. Come Play Wiz Me. Anyone Can Whistle.* A Parade in Town. Everybody Says Don't.* Ballet. I've Got You to Lean On. See What It Gets You. The Cookie Chase (waltzes). With So Little to Be Sure Of (rev. version). *Cut prior to New York opening:* There Won't Be Trumpets.*† There's Always a Woman. The Natives Are Restless. The Lame, the Halt, and the Blind. A Hero Is Coming. With So Little to Be Sure of (orig. version.) *Also used in *Side by Side by Sondheim,* below. †Also used in *Marry Me a Little,* below.

"Initially this show was a failure, but over the years and with the subsequent career of Sondheim it has become more and more respected. It takes place in an imaginary township under the control of a corrupt Mayor and her evil aides. A phony miracle is concocted to attract tourists to the area. There is also a plot dealing with madness. The local insane asylum is called 'The Cookie Jar', and some of the staff there become involved in the town's activities. This is an interesting and challenging property."—Richard Chigley Lynch,

Musicals! A Directory of Musical Properties Available for Production (American Library Association, 1984).

NOTES ON THE PRODUCTION: "*Anyone Can Whistle* was an innovative musical not destined for a long Broadway run. The show is best described by the term 'alienation/theatre of the absurd', a form that commercial audiences of the sixties could not accept. Its small cast makes it ideal for adventurous community theatres; the musical is memorable and the characters well drawn.

"Technically it isn't too complex and may be inexpensively mounted. Some production companies with limited offstage space and funds have kept the town square and its buildings onstage throughout the production, rolled on the bed and the rock and relocated Cora's message area to the town square. There are few props necessary to the play; the waterfall is the only technical aspect which is a bit complex, but a good electrician and utilization of waterproof paint should alleviate any problems.

"The costumes are modern and may be 'pulled' from the everyday wardrobe. Cora's costumes are more elaborate than others but are still of modern vintage. The four 'chorus' boys, who dance well, should probably be costumed alike, but this may be left to the discretion of the designer.

'The song 'There Won't Be Trumpets', although in the published version of the script and score, was eventually cut from the original production. The song may be heard on the album *Marry Me a Little* (RCA)." —Carol Lucha-Burns, *Musical Notes* (Greenwood Press, 1986).

Company (musical play)(1970). *Book:* George Furth; *lyr.:* composer. Winner, Tony Award (best musical), NY Drama Critics' Circle Award. *Licensing agent:* Music Theatre International. *Rec.:* Columbia (Stereo LP) OS 3550 (also Quad vers. SQ-30993), Time-Life (Stereo LP) P-16385 (also STL-AM12): orginal cast; selections also on Warner Bros. (2 Stereo LPs) 2WS-2705. *Pub.:* Random House (libretto); Otis L. Guernsey, Jr., ed., *The Best Plays of 1969-1970*, Dodd, Mead (condensation); *American Musicals: Sondheim*, Time-Life (condensation); Stanley Richards, ed., *Ten Great Musicals of the American Stage*, Chilton (anthology); Valando (piano-vocal score); Valando (vocal selections).
6 M, 8 F; small chorus (incl. 4 female pit singers)
5 reeds; 2-3-2-0; electric kybd/pno, 2 guit, 2 perc; 3-0-2-1
Numbers: Company.* The Little Things You Do Together.* Sorry-Grateful. You Could Drive a Person Crazy.* Have I Got a Girl for You. Someone Is Waiting. Another Hundred People.* Getting Married Today.* Side by Side by Side.* What Would We Do Without You? Poor Baby. Tick Tock (dance music by David Shire). Barcelona.*

The Ladies Who Lunch. Being Alive.* *Cut prior to New York opening:* The Wedding Is Off. Multitudes of Amys. Marry Me a Little.*† Happily Ever After.† *Also used in various versions of *Side by Side by Sondheim,* below. †Also used in *Marry Me a Little,* below.

"This musical takes a stinging look at the state of matrimony, particularly in a big city — New York City. Various married couples try to convince a 35-year-old bachelor that he should marry, but they do not present very good role models for marriage. This musical has been hailed as a landmark in American theater. The original set resembled a modern building skeleton with many different levels, stairs, and two elevators." — Richard Chigley Lynch, *Musicals! A Directory of Musical Properties Available for Production* (American Library Association, 1984).

"Almost all the critics, including those who were not partial to the production, wrote in superlatives about Stephen Sondheim/s score and brilliant lyrics. Moreover, although Sondheim's songs were integrated into the plot, often serving as comments on the action, they had variety and revealed his talent in creating a versatile score. Critics said it would be difficult to take Sondheim;s songs out of context, but, nevertheless, they cited two numbers for their excellence. 'Another Hundred People' dealt with some of the inanities and ironies of contemporary urban life. The best song, 'The Ladies Who Lunch', ridiculed the dull ladies who go to luncheons, continually drink too much, and fritter their lives away on trifles. The critics also commended George Furth for his original and striking plot." — Abe Laufe, *Broadway's Greatest Musicals,* Rev. Ed. (Funk & Wagnalls, 1977).

NOTES ON THE PRODUCTION: "Those looking for good audition monologues may want to examine April's speech in Act I, as it shows character and is comedic.

"A synopsis of *Company* doesn't do justice to the excellence of the script for the plot seems rather disjointed. The play traces the life of a New York bachelor who realizes his friends are jaded and not happy in their relationships.

"The show may be inexpensively played on a small unit set with simple props to established specific location where necessary, for example, a bed, to delineate Robert's bedroom. It is also possible to use one costume per actor and enhance Amy's wedding scene with a veil rather than a full costume. The cast is very balanced, which makes the show a good choice for community groups that want to give opportunities to a variety of their better female performers. Special attention should be given to casting April and Marta, who have precise, rapid diction numbers. One cast member must dance well. The only major company number, 'Side by Side', requires basic soft-shoe." — Carol Lucha-Burns, *Musical Notes* (Greenwood Press, 1986).

Follies (musical play)(1971). *Book:* James Goldman; *lyr.:* composer. Winner, Tony Award (best composer & lyricist), NY Drama Critics' Circle Award. *Licensing agent:* Music Theatre International. *Rec.:* Capitol (Stereo LP) SO 761: original cast; selections also on Warner Bros. (2 Stereo LPs) 2WS-2705. *Pub.:* Random House (libretto); Otis L. Guernsey, Jr., ed., *The Best Plays of 1970-1971,* Dodd, Mead (condensation); Columbia Pictures/Charles Hansen (piano-vocal score); Valando (vocal selections).
4 M, 8 F; large mixed cast
5 reeds; 1-3-3-0; harp, perc, pno; vlns-1-1-1
Scene: A party on the stage of the Weismann Theatre. Time: Tonight. No intermission. 1. The Folly of Love. 2. The Folly of Youth (scene: A Bower in Loveland). 3. Buddy's Folly (scene: A Thoroughfare in Loveland). 4. Sally's Folly (scene: A Boudoir in Loveland). 5. Phyllis's Folly (scene: A Honky-Tonk in Loveland). 6. Ben's Folly (scene: A Supper Club in Loveland).
Number: Overture. Beautiful Girls. Don't Look at Me. Waiting for the Girls Upstairs.* (Listen to the) Rain on the Roof. Ah, Paris!* Broadway Baby.* The Road You Didn't Take. Bolero d'Amour (theme by SS, dance development by John Berkman).‡ In Buddy's Eyes. Who's That Woman? I'm Still Here.* Too Many Mornings.* The Right Girl. One More Kiss. Could I Leave You?* Loveland. You're Gonna Love Tomorrow.¤ Love Will See Us Through.¤ Buddy's Blues (The God-Why-Don't You-Love-Me-Blues).¤ Losing My Mind.*¤ The Story of Lucy and Jessie.¤ Live, Laugh, Love.¤ *Cut prior to New York opening:* Opening Montage (medley of songs from show). All Things Bright and Beautiful (song dropped but music retained for overture).† Bring on the Girls.* Can That Boy Fox Trot!* It Wasn't Meant to Happen.† Pleasant Little Kingdom. That Old Piano Roll (song dropped but music retained for instrumental background). The World's Full of Boys/Girls. In Someone's Eyes. Uptown, Downtown.*† Little White House.† Who Could Be Blue.† *Also used in various versions of *Side by Side by Sondheim,* below.†Also used in *Marry Me a Little,* below.
¶Also 1985 vers. as *Follies in Concert. Book & new continuity:* James Goldman. ‡not included in this version; ¤added for this version. *Perf.:* principals, New York PO. *Rec.:* RCA (2 Digital Stereo LPs) HBC2-7128 (also CD vers. as RCD2-7128).

"Various cast members of the old Weismann shows gather at a reunion just before the theater is to be torn down and replaced with a parking lot. As they recall their youth, we see them as young performers doing their numbers. We also find out about their lives, as the title of the show has a double meaning. For most of the action, the set is a stage of a decrepit theater, but suddenly it is transformed into a Ziegfeld Follies-type setting for the finale. One appeal of the original Broadway production was seeing old stars return to the spotlight. Sondheim's score has been described as 'an incredible display of musical virtuosity'. One of the popular songs from the score is 'Losing My Mind'." — Richard Chigley Lynch, *Musicals! A Directory of Musical Properties Available for Production* (American Library Association, 1984).

"Stylistically, James Goldman's book for *Follies* runs the course from near-realism to a finale of metaphorical, fantastic surrealism. The four principal characters — two former Follies girls and their husbands, each a former stage-door Johnny — meet at a Follies reunion. As the party chatter gives way to deeper and more introspective reflection, we discover in these four a microcosm of middle-aged disappointment, frustration, and bitterness.

"The present appears bleak and frightening to these people and so, falling into the very trap that *Follies* warns against, they attempt to flee from the present by running into a past that seems safer, marked by a time when — as they see it today — their love was sincere, their ambitions were noble, and their motives were pure.

"However, the four main characters are denied the chance to escape into the past, for in *Follies* the past comes to them: ghosts of their former selves appear throughout the course of the evening, hovering about them, shadowing them, echoing [1]confronting them.

"As the evening moves on, the hysteria mounts: faced with a present filled with pain, and a past that is even more painful in what it ultimately reveals, the two couples become increasingly desparate in their attempt to outrun it all. Instead, they fall into the follies created by their own self-deluding dreams, and along with their younger selves, are hurled into an overwhelming, Wonderland-like Follies production of their own.

"*Follies* is not only a metaphorical examination of our approach to the past. Through its particular choice of genre, *Follies* is also a statement critical of an art form, the platitudinous musical, which endorses, even legitimizes, our love affair with the past. As much as it exposes the myth of the past, so *Follies* exposes the myth propagated by the musicals of a bygone era, which celebrated and reflected the naivete of their own time.

"The exaggerated production numbers, then, serve not only to emphasize the distorted perspective of our nostalgia, but to highlight the flaws inherent in the musical genre itself. In *The Village Voice,* John Lahr said that '*Follies* is the first Broadway musical to examine its genre as the myth machine. This is a brutal business, but the effects can only be healthy.'

"Stephen Sondheim's Tony Award-winning score for *Follies* draws its inspiration from an era many consider to be the heyday of American musical comedy — specifically that time between the wars when men such as Irving Berlin, Jerome Kern, and George Gershwin wrote Broadway's melodies. He discussed his score for *Follies* in a *Time Magazine* cover story on the musical in May of 1971:

> I truly love the body of musical comedy of that period.... *[Follies]* could be parody, but obviously it's done with such affection and... in each of the pastiche songs there's always something of me added to the imitation of Kern or Arlen or whoever it is. That's something I couldn't avoid — my own comments on the style.

A contradiction once again: while it is deeply immersed in the distinct musical styles of the past, *Follies* is very much a contemporary score and, like the thrust of the show itself, achieves its powerful effect by bringing a bygone world into ours....

"*Follies* has survived. There is poetic justice in that, for the message of *Follies* is one of survival. In concept, in theme and in story, *Follies* is passionate, often angry, in its eradication of the past. The final effect, however, is neither grim nor defeatist; it is, in fact, quite exhilarating, for when the past is removed, what is left? The present, of course, and the future." — Bert Fink, from liner notes for RCA Digital Stereo recording HBC2-7128.

"Playwright Goldman created the literate book that looked on unblinkingly as illusions were destroyed, and Stephen Sondheim the songs. Sondheim's tunes were frequently gentle parodies of melodies that had graced long-gone shows, but his lyrics had the expected Sondheim brilliance, a brilliance lyrics from the old annuals rarely approached. One girl, describing the years that followed her Follies glamor rhymed 'Abie's Irish Rose' with 'Dionne-babies, Major Bowes'." — Gerald Bordman, *American Musical Theatre: A Chronicle* (Oxford University Press, 1978).

NOTES ON THE PRODUCTION: "The work is a magnificent and challenging theatrical endeavor with interesting and well-drawn characters. There are many strong female roles which will give older community theatre actresses something more exciting than the usual character chorus parts.

"The score varies from simple vaudeville to vocally complex. The younger principal counterparts should all sing well.

"The costumes are period or present-day evening clothes. The 'Follies Girls' sequence costumes are extremely lavish as are the 'Loveland' ones. They will probably need to be rented for they must have an opulently theatrical look that isn't easy to whip up by home seamstresses with limited fabric selection.

"The set is that of an old theatre, but the 'Follies' sequence is reminiscent of the twenties and thirties and probably will require at least one painted drop with some painted wing pieces. There are companies listed in the *Simon's Directory* that rent drops quite inexpensively.

"*Follies* requires a quality director and choreographer who must work closely together to achieve a strong unity in production. This is a show that needs more than blocking to make it work. The director and actors must examine the character relationships and re-create with clarity and understanding the ugliness, bitterness and love that exist among these couples. The show will not survive without motivated actors who have the emotional maturity to portray these middle-aged characters who have lost so much.

"The show is excellent, complex, challenging and worth the effort. It is one that should be seen more often. Do not let the cast size be a deterrent. Many of the characters only have a few lines and one featured song, which means the early rehearsals can be broken up into smaller sections." —Carol Lucha-Burns, *Musical Notes* (Greenwood Press, 1986).

The Frogs (musical comedy)(1984). *Book:* Burt Shevelove, freely adapted from Aristophanes' comedy; *lyr.:* composer. *Licensing agent:* Dramatic. *Rec.:* RCA Records (2 Stereo LPs) CBL 2-4745: 2 selections only in album *Sondheim Evening*. *Pub.:* Dramatic (libretto).
10 M, 2 F; large chorus, dancers, swimmers
Numbers: Prologus (Invocation to the Gods and Instructions to the Audience). Parodos (The Frogs). Hymnos (Evoie!). Parabasis (It's Only a Play). Paean (Evoe for the Dead). Exodus (The Sound of Poets). Fear No More (added for 1975 Cleveland revival).

"The plot concerns the god Dionysus, dissatisfied with the current crop of playwrights, going down into Hades to bring back Bernard Shaw and restore him to life. This 90-minute farce was originally staged at Yale around a swimming pool and was later produced in New York City. Reviews indicate that there were various water ballets *à la* Busby Berkeley. There was also dancing at poolside, and the actors were sometimes out in the pool in a rowboat. The Yale production was quite spectacular, with about 125 people involved in the show." — Richard Chigley Lynch, *Musicals! A Directory of Musical Properties Available for Production* (American Library Association, 1984).

A Funny Thing Happened on the Way to the Forum (musical comedy)(1962). *Book:* Burt Shevelove and Larry Gelbart, based on the plays of Plautus; *lyr.:* composer. Winner, Tony Award (best musical). *Licensing agent:* Music Theatre International. *Rec.:* Capitol (Mono LP) WAO-1717 (also as Stereo LP SWAO-1717; reissued as Capitol Mono W-1717, Stereo SW 1717), Time-Life (Stereo LP) P-16385 (also STL-AM12): original cast; selections also on Warner Bros. (2 Stereo LPs) 2WS-2705; United Artists (Mono LP) UAL-4144 (also as Stereo LP UAS-5144)(selections for film vers. with new inc. music by Sondheim and Ken Thorne). *Pub.:* Dodd, Mead (libretto); *American Musicals: Sondheim,* Time-Life (condensation); Chappell (piano-vocal score).
Large mixed cast
5 reeds; 0-3-3-0; perc, 3 drums, hp; 3-1-1-1 (also smaller arrangement)
Numbers: Overture. Comedy Tonight.* Love, I Hear. Free. The House of Marcus Lycus (rev. version, no lyrics). Lovely. Pretty Little Picture. Everybody Ought to Have a Maid. I'm Calm. Impossible. Bring Me My Bride. That Dirty Old Man. That'll Show Him. Lovely (reprise). Funeral Sequence. Finale. *Cut prior to New York opening:* Love Is in the Air.* Your Eyes Are Blue.† Echo Song. Invocation. I Do Like You. The House of Marcus Lycus (orig. vers. with lyrics). Something About a War. The Gaggle of Geese. Window Across the Way. Miles Gloriosus. *Added for 1972 revival:* Farewell. *Also used in various versions of *Side by Side by Sondheim,* below. †Additional vers. used in *Marry Me a Little,* below.

"Hero, in love with a slave girl he cannot afford to buy, turns his problems over to a fast-talking slave, Pseudolus, who is the real star of the show. After a good deal of low comedy and confusion, all is straightened out — lovers are united and Pseudolus is set free. Zero Mostel starred on Broadway and in the film version and Phil Silvers later starred in a revival. Set in ancient Rome, this show is very funny and popular. It is physical, energetic, unpretentious, and for adults only! Audiences love it." — Richard Chigley Lynch, *Musicals! A Directory of Musical Properties Available for Production* (American Library Association, 1984).

"[For the first time] the songs not only had lyrics by Stephen Sondheim, they had music by him as well. His tunes — from the opening 'Comedy Tonight' to the finale—were light and easy on the ear, with a distinct hint of Rodgers and Hart. One of them, 'Lovely', has remained popular. Yet it was Sondheim's masterful way with words that was most telling. The love-sick Hero in 'Love, I Hear' wakes 'too weak to walk'. Pseudolus promises that in his gratitude for being made 'Free', 'I'll be so conscientious I may vote twice,' while Senex suggests 'Evrybody Ought to Have a Maid'. Later Senex and Hero find it outrageously 'Impossible' that the other could be in love. Some of Broadway's funniest comedians assisted in the antics with Zero Mostel leading a contingent that also boasted Jack Gilford as a farcically hysterical Hysterium. The show rocked Broadway with laughter for two years." —Gerald Bordman, *American Musical Theatre: A Chronicle* (Oxford University Press, 1978).

NOTES ON THE PRODUCTION: "This comedic show is easy to produce as there is only one set that consists of the exterior of three Roman houses. Philia in the original was often seen on the rooftop, but she could be seen in an upper window. The costumes, one per actor plus Domina and Hysterium's disguises, are period Roman. Miles is in Roman armor but his entourage may be costumed as servants if necessary.

"The music is in keeping with the comedy and should be played cleanly and broadly. The actors and director need to have a solid background in comedy and be versed in standard comedic bits of business. The script is witty and calls for a knowledge of 'playing the audience'." —Carol Lucha-Burns, *Musical Notes* (Greenwood Press, 1986).

Into the Woods (musical play) (1988). *Book:* James Lapine; *lyr.:* composer. Winner, Drama Critics Circle Award, Drama Desk Award. *Licensing agent:* Geffen Music. *Rec.:* RCA Records (LP, CD, Cassette versions): original cast. *Pub.:* Rilting Music (vocal selections).
7 M, 12 M
Numbers: Act I: Prologue (Into the Woods). Hello, Little Girl. I Guess This Is Goodbye. Maybe They're Magic. I Know Things Now. A Very Nice Prince. Giants in the Sky. Agony. It Takes Two. Stay with Me. On the Steps of the Palace. Ever After. Act II: Prologue (So Happy). Agony [reprise]. Lament. Any Moment. Moments in the Woods. Your Fault. Last Midnight. No More. No One Is Alone. Finale (Children Will Listen).

"*Into the Woods* brings to musical life Cinderella, Jack and the Beanstalk, Little Red Ridinghood and other well-known fairy-tale characters. Interwoven with these classic tales is the story of the baker and his wife, whose longing for a child is thwarted by a mischievous witch who lives next door. James Lapine and Stephen Sondheim have fashioned a musical which goes beyond mere Broadway razzmatazz. Sondheim's songs, seamlessly melded to Lapine's text, are perfect expressions of character and action which reflect the complications of living in modern society and the difficult choices we encounter on the paths of our lives." —Notes to the published edition of the libretto.

A Little Night Music (musical play)(1973). *Book:* Hugh Wheeler, suggested by the Ingmar Bergman film *Smiles of a Summer Night; lyr.:* composer. Winner, Tony Award (best musical), NY Drama Critics' Circle Award. *Licensing agent:* Music Theatre International. *Rec.:* Columbia (Stereo LP) KS 32265 (also as Quad SQ-32265; selections also on Columbia Stereo LP HS-35333), Time-Life (Stereo LP) P-16385 (also STL-AM12): original cast; RCA (Stereo LP) LRL1-5090: London cast; selections also on Warner Bros. (2 Stereo LPs) 2WS-2705. *Pub.:* Dodd, Mead (libretto); Otis L. Guernsey, Jr., ed., *The Best Plays of 1972-1973* (condensation); *American Musicals: Sondheim,* Time-Life (condensation); Stanley Richards, etc., *The Great Musicals of the American Theatre,* vol. 2, Chilton (anthology); Clive Barnes, ed., *Best American Plays,* 8th series, Crown (anthology); Revelation Music/Rilting Music (piano-vocal score); Revelation Music (vocal selections). Large mixed cast
5 reeds; 3-2-1-0; perc, hp, celeste/pno 1, pno 2; 3-1-1-1
Numbers: Act I: Overture (vocal). Night Waltz. Piano Practice. Now (rev. version). Later. Soon. The Glamorous Life. Remember? You Must Meet My Wife.* Liaisons. In Praise of Women. Every Day a Little Death. A Weekend in the Country. Entr'Acte. Act II: Night Waltz (The Sun Won't Set). Night Waltz II. It Would Have Been Wonderful. Perpetual Anticipation. Dinner Table Scene. Night Waltz (piano solo). Underscoring. Send in the Clowns.* The Miller's Son. Underscore. Reprises. Last Waltz. Bows. *Cut prior to New York opening:* Bang!† Silly People.† Two Fairy Tales (portion retained for Frederika's piano exercise).† Not Quite Night. My Husband the Pig. Now (orig. vers; different music & lyrics). Night Waltz II (restored in some versions). *Also used in various versions of *Side by Side by Sondheim,* below. †Also used in *Marry Me a Little,* below.

"Called a musical with elegance, this show is set in Sweden at the turn of the century. The central character is a middle-aged actress, and the plot concerns her family and loves. Most of the music is in three-quarter time, and there is almost no dancing. This show was highly praised for its style and imagination and its combination of humor and sadness. The big song is 'Send in the Clowns'. There was a film version in 1977 with Elizabeth Taylor. An opulent production is recommended." —Richard Chigley Lynch, *Musicals! A Directory of Musical Properties Available for Production* (American Library Association, 1984).

"Critics agreed on the excellence of Sondheim's clever rhyme schemes and score, particularly since all the songs were written as waltzes or as waltz variations.... Although Sondheim's songs were integrated into the action, one number, 'Send in the Clowns', has become a favorite with many of the top-ranking vocalists in the country because it demonstrates Sondheim's askill in using an enchanting melody to emphasize dramatic lyrics." —Abe Laufe, *Broadway's Greatest Musicals*, Rev. Ed. (Funk & Wagnalls, 1977).

NOTES ON THE PRODUCTION: "The show is a charming one and is a musical pastiche that captures the flavor of turn-of-the-century Sweden. The actors must be superb or the show shouldn't be considered. It is musically quite difficult and there are quite a few period costumes for each character, including formal dinner wear. The sets may be simplified by using the wing and border system if the stage is proscenium. In fact, the sets aren't as important as the performances or the costumes.

"The production must be extremely fluid, and the movement must be smooth and flowing. While there are no 'dance numbers' per se, a choreographer should be utilized to train the performers in the act of movement and period decorum. In order for the show to be successful and interesting, the audience must experience the 'evening' as an entirely believable theatrical entity." —Carol Lucha-Burns, *Musical Notes* (Greenwood Press, 1986).

Marry Me a Little (musical show)(1980). *Conceived and developed by:* Craig Lucas and Norman Rene; *lyr.*: composer. *Licensing agent:* Music Theatre International. *Rec.:* RCA (Stereo LP) ABL1-4159: original cast.
1 M, 1 F
Numbers: Two Fairy Tales (from *A Little Night Music*, above). Saturday Night (from *Saturday Night*, below). Call That Boy Fox Trot! (from *Follies*, above). All Things Bright and Beautiful (from *Follies*, above). Bang! (from *A Little Night Music*, above). The Girls of Summer (as inc. music for play of same title, lyrics added). Uptown, Downtown (from *Follies*, above). So Many People (from *Saturday Night*, below). Your Eyes Are Blue (from *A Funny Thing Happened on the Way to the Forum*, above). A Moment with You (from *Saturday Night*, below). Marry Me a Little (from *Company*, above). Happily Ever After (from *Company*, above). Pour Le Sport (from unproduced show *The Last Resorts*). Silly People (from *A Little Night Music*, above). There Won't Be Trumpets

(from *Anyone Can Whistle,* above). It Wasn't Meant to Happen (from *Follies,* above). *Cut prior to New York opening:* Who Could Be Blue? (from *Follies,* above). Little White House (from *Follies,* above). *Added to London production:* That Old Piano Roll (from *Follies,* above). Class (from *Saturday Night,* below). I Do Like You (from *A Funny Thing Happened on the Way to the Forum,* above).

"A one-hour musical (without intermission) made up of bits and pieces of Sondheim scores dropped from other shows. The set is a run-down studio apartment and the cast of two are both on stage, although they are both meant to be alone in their own apartments. There is no spoken dialogue. Through the songs we learn of their lives and loneliness. The 16 Sondheim songs are the main reason for this show. It can be simply staged with only a piano accompaniment." — Richard Chigley Lynch, *Musicals! A Directory of Musical Properties Available for Production* (American Library Association, 1984).

Merrily We Roll Along (musical play)(1981). *Book:* George Furth, after a George S. Kaufman and Moss Hart play; *lyr.:* composer. *Licensing agent:* Music Theatre International. *Rec.:* RCA Records (Stereo LP) CBL 1-4197: original cast. *Pub.:* Dodd, Mead (libretto), Revelation Music/Valando (vocal selections).
Cast of 27
Numbers: The Hills of Tomorrow. Merrily We Roll Along. Rich and Happy. Old Friends. Like It Was. Franklin Shepard, Inc. Not a Day Goes By. Now You Know. It's a Hit. The Blob. Good Thing Going. Bobby and Jackie and Jack. Opening Doors. Our Time. *Cut during previews:* Honey. Darling! Thank You for Coming.
"Based on a 1934 play, this musical tells the story of some young hopefuls (song writers and novelist) and their careers over a 25-year period. An unusual technique of going backwards in time is used. The story begins when one of the leads comes back to address the graduating class at his old high school; the plot continues in reverse until he is graduating. The Broadway set was 'high tech' style bleachers with skyline projections. Members of the young cast wore T-shirts with their names or titles on them. 'Not a Day Goes By' is one of the better songs from the Sondheim score." — Richard Chigley Lynch, *Musicals! A Directory of Musical Properties Available for Production* (American Library Association, 1984).

Pacific Overtures (musical play)(1976). *Book:* John Weidman, additional material by Hugh Wheeler; *lyr.* composer. Winner, NY Drama Critics' Circle Award. *Licensing agent:* Music Theatre International. *Rec:* RCA Records (Stereo LP) ARL 1-1367 (also as CD vers.

RCD1-4407): original cast. *Pub.:* Dodd, Mead (libretto); Otis L. Guernsey, Jr., ed., *The Best Plays of 1975-1976*, Dodd, Mead (condensation); Revealtion Music (piano-vocal score).
Large male cast
5 reeds; 2-2-1-0; 2 perc, shamisen (onstage), Oriental perc (onstage), hp, keybd-RMI celeste; 0-1-1-1
Numbers: The Advantage of Floating in the Middle of the Sea. There Is No Other Way. Four Black Dragons. Chrysanthemum Tea (rev. version). Poems. Welcome to Kanagawa. Someone in a Tree. Lion Dance. Please Hello. A Bowler Hat. Pretty Lady. Next. *Cut prior to New York opening:* Prayers. Chyysanthemum Tea (orig. vers. with different music & lyrics). We Float.

"Performed in the style of the Japanese Kabuki theater, this is the story of Commodore Perry's 'opening up' of Japan in 1853. The original production (with an all-male cast, some in female roles) was highly praised for its costumes and sets. The Sondheim score commands a great deal of attention. A jump at the finale brings the story to the present. This is a real challenge." — Richard Chigley Lynch, *Musicals! A Directory of Musical Properties Available for Production* (American Library Association, 1984).

"Sondheim and Weidman attempted to portray Commodore Perry's opening of Japan from a Japanese viewpoint. The entire cast was Asian — even the Americans were played by Asians. (All the players took several roles.) At first the Japanese are frightened and reluctant, but at the very end the scene switches to 20th-century Japan, and the American intrusion is seen as justificaton for Japanese expansionist policies. Sondheim used not only Oriental instruments to convey his moods, but poetry highly suggestive of Japanese haiku. The mounting drew strongly on the Japanese Kabuki Theatre. Boris Aronson's poetic sets had a distinctly Oriental tinge. He designed Perry's ship to resemble a dragon as much as a vessel. Accordingly, the 'Americans' used makeup that suggested they wre not only foreign, but possibly fearful monsters." — Gerald Bordman, *American Musical Theatre: A Chronicle* (Oxford University Press, 1978).

NOTES ON THE PRODUCTION: "The show is more interesting than its short run indicates. In the original production, all the roles were played by men, for the director wanted to stylize the show in the Kabuki manner. This is unnecessary and would normally be detrimental to the quality of any American production because it takes years of training for a male to accurately portray a female in the traditional Japanese theatre. In fact, in America the final product would appear *more* accurate if the female roles were played by females.

"The music is challenging and the show worthy of study if the director has some knowledge of Japanese dance, theatre and manners.

"The costumes include court brocades, peasant Yukatas, modern costumes, and 1860s period European military. The visual style is maintained through the costumes and they should be accurate and designed for stylized movement.

"Sets may be comprised of small pieces or presented on a very large scale, depending on the director's needs and the budget allowed. The acting and the style are more essential in creating the mood than the sets."—Carol Lucha-Burns, *Musical Notes* (Greenwood Press, 1986).

Saturday Night (unproduced musical show)(1954.)*Book:* Julius J. Epstein & Philip G. Epstein, based on their play *Front Porch in Flatbush; lyr.:* composer.
Numbers: Saturday Night.† Class. Love's a Bond. Isn't It? Delighted, I'm Sure. Exhibit "A". A Moment with You.† I Remember That. So Many People.† One Wonderful Day. In the Movies. All for You. It's That Kind of a Neighborhood. What More Do I Need? †Also used in *Marry Me a Little*, above.

Side by Side by Sondheim (musical revue)(1977). *Continuity:* Ned Sherrin; *lyr.:* composer (with additional music by various collaborators). *Licensing agent:* Music Theatre International. *Rec.:* RCA Records (2 Stereo LPs) CBL 2-1851: original cast; Australian RCA (2 Stereo LPs) VRL2-0156: original Australian cast (1977). *Pub.: The Hansen Treasury of Stephen Sondheim Songs*, Hansen (music).
2 M, 2 F
Numbers: Comedy Tonight (from *A Funny Thing Happened on the Way to the Forum*, above). Love Is in the Air (from *A Funny Thing...*, above). If Momma Was Married (from *Gypsy* [music by Jule Styne]). You Must Meet My Wife (from *A Little Night Music*, above). The Little Things You Do Together (from *Company*, above). Getting Married Today (from *Company*, above). I Remember (from TV producing *Evening Primrose*). Can That Boy Fox Trot (from *Follies*, above). Company (from *Company*, above). Another Hundred People (from *Company*, above). Barcelona (from *Company*, above). Marry Me a Little (from *Company*, above). I Never Do Anything Twice (from film *The Seven Percent Solution*). Beautiful Girls (from *Follies*, above). Ah, Paris! (from *Follies*, above). Buddy's Blues (from *Follies*, above). Broadway Baby (from *Follies*, above). You Could Drive a Person Crazy (from *Company*, above). Everybody Says Don't (from *Anyone Can Whistle*, above).

Anyone Can Whistle (from *Anyone Can Whistle,* above). Send in the Clowns (from *A Little Night Music,* above). We're Gonna Be All Right (from *Do I Hear a Waltz* [music by Richard Rodgers]). A Boy Like That/I Have a Love (from *West Side Story [music by Leonard Bernstein]*). *The Boy from... (from The Mad Show* [music by Mary Rodgers]). Pretty Lady (from *Pacific Overtures,* above). You Gotta Have a Gimmick (from *Gypsy* [music by Jule Styne]). Losing My Mind (from *Follies,* above). Could I Leave You (from *Follies,* above). I'm Still Here (from *Follies,* above). Conversation Piece (bits of Sondheim songs arranged by Carl Brahms and Stuart Pedlar). Side by Side by Side (from *Company,* above). *Used in productions:* Too Many Mornings (from *Follies,* above). Being Alive (from *Company,* above). There Won't Be Trumpets (from *Anyone Can Whistle,* above). Everybody Ought to Have a Maid (from *A Funny Thing Happened on the Way to the Forum,* above). Waiting Around for the Girl Upstairs (from *Follies,* above). I've Got You to Lean On (from *Anyone Can Whistle,* above). Sorry-Grateful (from *Company,* above). There Is No Other Way (from *Pacific Overtures,* above). Little Lamb (from *Gypsy* [music by Jule Styne]). I Feel Pretty (from *West Side Story* [music by Leonard Bernstein]). The Ladies Who Lunch (from *Company,* above). The Miller's Son (from *A Little Night Music,* above). Impossible (from *A Funny Thing...,* above). *Added for revival (orig. written for 1952 Kukla, Fran and Ollie TV show):* The Two of You.

"This revue was conceived and first presented in Great Britain. It was a great success on Broadway, however, and has been presented in many locations since that time. There is a cast of four—three singers and a 'wry narration' and perhaps a song by the fourth. According to the director and star Ned Sherrin, 'We wanted to explore three propositions. Sondheim as the best lyric writer... the most adventurous composer of musicals, and the most considerable musical dramatist.' *Company, Follies,* and *Anyone Can Whistle* are the main sources of material, although such obscure titles as *The Seven Percent Solution* and *Evening Primrose* are included. A simple set with stools and two pianos is all that is required."—Richard Chigley Lynch, *Musicals! A Directory of Musical Properties Available for Production* (American Library Association, 1984).

Sunday in the Park with George (musical show)(1984). *Book:* James Lapine; lyr.: composer. Winner, 1985 Pulitzer Prize, NY Drama Critics' Circle Award. *Rec:* RCA Stereo LP HBC 1-5042: orig cast. Pub.: Revelation Music/Rilting Music (vocal selections).
Act I takes place on a series of Sundays from 1884 to 1886 and alternates between a park on an island in the Seine just outside of Paris

and George's studio. Act II takes place in 1984 at an American art museum and on the island.

Act I: Sunday in the Park with George. No Life. Color and Light. Gossip. The Day Off. Everybody Loves Louis. Finishing the Hat. We Do Not Belong Together. Beautiful. Sunday. Act II: It's Hot Up Here. Chromolume #7. Putting It Together. Children and Art. Lesson #8. Move On. Sunday (reprise).

"As befits a show whose subject is the creation of a landmark in modernist painting—Georges Seurat's *Sunday Afternoon on the Island of La Grande Jatte* (1886)—*Sunday* is itself a modernist creation, perhaps the first truly modernist work of musical theater that Broadway has produced. Instead of mimicking reality through a conventional, naturalistic story, the authors of *Sunday* deploy music and language in nonlinear patterns that, like Seurat's tiny brushstrokes, become meaningful only when refracted through a contemplative observer's mind.... *Sunday* is a watershed event that demands nothing less than a retrospective, even revisionist, look at the development of the serious Broadway musical."—Frank Rich, *The New York Times Magazine*.

Sweeney Todd the Demon of Fleet Street (musical play)(1979).
Book: Hugh Wheeler, based on a version of *Sweeney Todd* by Christopher Bond; *lyr.:* composer. Winner, Tony Award (best musical), NY Drama Critics' Circle Award. *Licensing agent:* Music Theatre International. *Rec.:* RCA Records (2 Stereo LPs) CBL 2-3379: original cast. *Pub.:* Dodd, Mead (libretto); Otis L. Guernsey, Jr., ed., *The Best Plays of 1978-1979*, Dodd, Mead (condensation); Revelation Music (piano-vocal score); Revelation Music (vocal selections).
Large mixed cast
5 reeds; 1-2-3-0; 2 perc, hp, org; 1-1-1-1
Scene: London—Fleet Street and environs. Time: the 19th century.
Numbers: Act I: Prelude. The Ballad of Sweeney Todd (Attend the Tale of Sweeney Todd). No Place Like London. The Barber and His Wife. The Worst Pies in London. Poor Thing. My Friends. The Ballad of Sweeney Todd (Lift Your Razor High, Sweeney!). Green Finch and Linnet Bird. Ah, Miss. Johanna. Pirelli's Miracle Elixir. The Contest. The Ballad of Sweeney Todd (Sweeney Pondered and Sweeney Planned). Wait. The Ballad of Sweeney Todd (His Hands Were Quick, His Fingers Strong). Kiss Me! Ladies in Their Sensitivies. Quartet. Pretty Women. Epiphany. A Little Priest. Act II: God, That's Good! Johanna (reprise). By the Sea. Wigmaker Sequence. The Ballad of Sweeney Todd (Sweeney'd Waited Too Long Before...). The Letter. Not While I'm Around. Parlor Songs. City on Fire! Final Sequence. The Ballad of Sweeney Todd (Attend the Tale of Sweeney

Todd: reprise). *Cut during previews:* Johanna (Judge's version, orig. after The Ballad of Sweeney Todd (His Hands Were Quick, His Fingers Strong).

"A cut-throat barber practices above a pie shop supplying it with cheap and easy meat! Todd is an escaped convict who was unjustly sentenced so that the Judge could have Mrs. Todd. He returns to find his wife a suicide and his daughter the ward of the Judge. Victorian London is presented as a plague-spot—a dark grotesque underworld. This needs to be awesome, staggering, epic, monumental—a huge factory signifying the Industrial Revolution covers the stage and center stage becomes the pie shop, a lunatic asylum, the wharf, the basement furnace, the barber shop, and the street. There is no choreography. It is almost completely sung. This is one of the more challenging shows to produce; it is also a challenge vocally. There was a cable telecast in 1982 with Angela Lansbury."—Richard Chigley Lynch, *Musicals! A Directory of Musical Properties Available for Production* (American Library Association, 1984).

NOTES ON THE PRODUCTION: "It is a musically demanding show whose cast requirements include four tenors in leading roles and a vocally talented chorus. The set requires no drops and may be performed with the pie shop, usually a revolve from exterior to interior, and a location for Judge Turpin's home. The costumes are period, Industrial Revolution, England. It is possible for each cast member to have one costume although it gives more visual variety if Mrs. Lovett has several.

"The trick barber chair must be rigged and timed to allow the bodies to fall, via a trapdoor, to the area below. It is an extremely important part of the action which must be smoothly controlled. Another consideration is the handling of the throat-slashing sequences and the use of blood pellets, or squirter, either on the razor or hidden on the actors' necks. The costume crew must be prepared for daily laundering.

"Both Todd and Tobias visually deteriorate through the show, as each grows more and more insane. Some backstage help should be waiting to assist the performers in the makeup changes.

"The show is extremely exciting and can be occasionally seen on cable TV. It would help a company considering the show to purchase or rent the [Angela] Lansbury touring tape."—Carol Lucha-Burns, *Musical Notes* (Greenwood Press, 1986).

AUGUSTA READ THOMAS

B. 1964, Glen Cove NY. *Educ.*: Juilliard Schl Prep Div, Northwestern Univ, L'École normal (Fountainbleau), Yale Schl of Music, Royal Acad of Music. *Fellowships:* Fontainbleau Schl of Music, Tanglewood Music Ctr, Aspen Music Schl, Radcliff Coll Bunting Inst; *awards & grants:* ASCAP, BMI, NEA, Amer Acad/Inst Arts & Ltrs, Guggenheim Fndn, Univ IL Kate Neal Kinley Fndn, Columbia Univ Bearns Prize. *Works incl.: aria* (fl/ob/vln/vc/pno), orchestral (*Crystal Planet, Partita* (brass qt), *Ritual* [overture concertante], *Under the Sun*), *Psychles* (an opera of groupings and juxtapositions), *Red Moon* (fl/cl/vln/vc), *Sonata* (solo tpt), *Sonnet* (vla/pno), *Streams of Illusion* (strng qt), *Wheatfield with Lark* (fl/wind orch). Concert music published by Theodore Presser.

Composer statement: "The orchestra has a wealth of repertoire and history and through an understanding of this history and its music, one can discover the foundation for developing a new era of orchestral music.

"For several years I have been devoted to the composition of orchestral music. Defining and organizing my concepts of specifically contemporary thought, I attempt to apply these concepts to all of the parameters of orchestral composition."

Black Moon (Cantata 2) for Chamber Orchestra (1987). 9m
Prem.: Cleveland Chamber S. *Other perf.*: Berio Festival (London).

"*Black Moon* is constructed entirely out of its opening brass fanfare. Nine and ten note 'tone-rows' are derived and they structure the work in both a linear and vertical manner. The final section of the work is a fugue the subject of which is the opening brass fanfare and the countersubject of which is a trill sequence."—Augusta Read Thomas.

echos for Soprano, Mezzo-Soprano and Chamber Orchestra (1989). *Text:* poems *Sonnet 123* (Shakespeare), *Inside* (Joseph McLean). 13m *Prem.*: Tanglewood Music Center.

"Miss Thomas was looking for poems that captured the mood of basic emotions and raw experience without the intervening structure of concrete images or story. Her use of 'Inside' enchances its meaning by breaking it up, moving lines around, the idea of the observer's final inability to describe and the higher experience of being in unity is put across with greater strength. *echos* expresses a relationship with beauty, 'a relationship of being' consumed with that which (one) was nourished by, the 'web song of mystery'." — Joseph McLean.

"The echoes are of two kinds — musical, of course, but also verbal. The soloist sings fragments from two poems — one by Shakespeare, the other by Joseph McLean — to create what Thomas describes as a 'dreamlike' montage of words and sounds.

"Thomas's music... is uncompromisingly modern, reflecting her study with such composers as Jacob Druckman and Oliver Knussen. In place of melody, there are fragments and figures; in place of traditional harmony, sound clusters. Underneath, there is a current of feeling that breaks through most readily in her vocal writing....

"Thomas credits her family with igniting her love of music. She grew up as the youngest of 10 children from two marriages. Some of her brothers and sisters were taking piano lessons. They would perform for the family.

" 'We would listen to music almost every night — classical music,' she recalled.

" 'I heard Bach and Beethoven and Brahms — everybody — when I was 5. It was almost a concert situation. We would just sit and listen. That's what we did after dinner.'...

"She finds there are two kinds of composers — the 'highly trained' ones 'who can talk you around in circles', and the 'massively emotional' ones whose music 'has just got life and spirit'. She clearly identifies herself with the latter.

"She found [George] Perle 'very intellectual and inspiring', and she enjoyed [Lukas] Foss for his 'energy' — for example, his way of 'playing Mozart symphonies at the piano and making music alive'.

"It is Knussen to whom she feels the greatest debt. The Briton, she said, gave her [an] opportunity at Tanglewood, took her music seriously and helped her to 'grow during the summers, rather than just sitting out in Chicago waitressing'.

"Becoming a composer is like becoming a poet. 'Nobody asks you to do it, and the chances of publication — and recognition — are slight. She has worked hard to get herself performed, mailing out scores (at $40 a pop) and tapes to concert artists even when the chances of performance look dim.

"She has been rewarded by performers' liking and then promoting her music. In London, for instance, a string quartet liked a piece and did it twice. A cellist played a piece in a school program, won a competition and repeated the performance in his prize recital in London's prestigious South Bank complex.

New York Philharmonic
ONE HUNDRED FORTY-EIGHTH SEASON 1989-90

ZUBIN MEHTA, Music Director

Friday, July 27, 1990, at 6:30 p.m.　　　　　　　11,547th Concert

LAWRENCE LEIGHTON SMITH, Conductor
(New York Philharmonic Debut)

HORIZONS '90: NEW MUSIC FOR ORCHESTRA

WILSON	"Lumina"
KNIGHT	"Total Eclipse" (World Premiere)
DRATTELL	"Lilith" (World Premiere)

Intermission

THOMAS	"Wind Dance" (World Premiere)
HAGEN	"Common Ground" (New York Premiere)
DAUGHERTY	"Oh Lois!"

" 'I've been very fortunate,' Thomas said. 'But I also spend almost 10 hours a day on music, like seven days a week. I'm really devoted to it.' " —Andrew L. Pincus, in *The Eagle*.

Haiku for Violin, Cello and Chamber Orchestra (1990). 20m
Comm. & prem.: StonyBrook Contemporary Chamber Players.

"*Haiku* is a double concerto in 5 movements. Each of the movements is based on a different Haiku by Basho. The musics of each of the movements are closely related to one another while at the same time, each movement attempts to recreate or to 'paint' the image of its corresponding Haiku." —Augusta Read Thomas.

Two Pieces for Orchestra (1988). *Perfs. (Glass Moon):* Young Musicians SO (London); Philadelphia O, Hans Vonk, cond.
3-2-2-2; 4-3-3-1; 4 perc, timp, hp, pno; strings (16-14-12-10-8)
1. *Glass Moon* (11m) (with solo clarinet 1 and string quartet). 2. *Sunset of Empire* (11m) (with solo trumpet 1 and entire trumpet section).

"As a nocturne, *Glass Moon* attempts to create a glazed and smooth night-piece while investigating glassy, silken, transparent textures. The movement is constructed from four chords, each consisting of seven to ten pitches. From these collections of chordal notes, small tone rows and motivic cells are derived. The original four chords are combined to create nine new ones, forming a harmonic palette of thirteen.

"*Sunset of Empire* explores a far more violent, rhythmic and percussive music than *Glass Moon*.

"Although *Glass Moon* and its sibling movement, *Sunset of Empire*, can stand alone, there are relationships between the two. What the former gently outlines, the latter expresses passionately." — Augusta Read Thomas.

Requiem for Children's Chorus and Youth Symphony (1984). Text: *Requiem Mass* segment (in Latin). 9m *Comm. & prem.:* Glen Ellyn Children's Chorus, Suburban Youth SO (Chicago).
3-2-2-2; 4-3-3-1; 3 perc; strings

"I am very concerned about involving young children in the process of 'new music'. This work is a statement for world peace presented to all generations by young children." — Augusta Read Thomas.

Vigil for Cello and Chamber Orchestra (1990). 12m *Comm. & prem.:* Norman Fisher (vc), Cleveland Chamber S.

"*Vigil* expresses an abstract or metaphorical vision of a vigil. The work juxtaposes ceremonial and nocturnal musics, throughout which the cellist is in constant dialogue with the orchestra." — August Read Thomas.

Wind Dance for Large Orchestra (1989). 18m *Prem.:* New York P, Lawrence Leighton Smith, cond.
In two connected movements.

"Among the primary concerns in the compositional process [for *Wind Dance*] was a preoccupation with a desire to organize the musical material and expression into a shape or form that was organically its own. The work's architecture has reminiscences of symphonic form, theme and variation form, concerto form and shapes that are characteristic of a tone-poem form. The piece is constructed in two movements although, because of their structural interrelationships, it is performed without a pause.

"The primary musical material which serves as the core source for all of the music in the work is not exposed until halfway through the second movement. Until that point, all of the materials, which are headed toward their most primary expression, are, in a sense, variations of transformations of this core material. Small melodic fragments are transformed and later grouped into two scales which are juxtaposed throughout the development of the work.

"The programmatic aspect of the work—a 'landscape' of a *Wind Dance*—can be heard in the transformation of melodic and harmonic structures as well as in aspects of the orchestration. Highly intricate orchestration which involves multiple string divisions (frequent 10-part string writing and often 18-part string writing) and solo passages of all lengths for the entire orchestra combine to form a texture and fabric in which the musical material can be organized." —Augusta Read Thomas.

"Ms. Thomas is in full command of the orchestra's textures and colors, and she used them to create a vivid 18-minute work that paints the swirling picture suggested in the title.

"But there was more to the work than tone painting. Using a rich language that skirted around tonal clusters but that rarely lighted on them, she couched the piece in a mysterious, shifting atmosphere that supported the picturesque elements with a sense of emotional dimension." —Allan Kozinn, in *The New York Times*.

VIRGIL THOMSON

B. 1896, Kansas City MO; *d.* Educ.: Harvard Univ. Organist, King's Chapel, Boston. Music critic, *New York Herald Tribune;* author *American Music Since 1910, The Art of Judging Music, The State of Music.* Works *incl.:* chamber pieces, choral pieces, concertos (fl, vc), film scores, operas *(Four Saints in Three Acts, The Mother of Us All),* Portraits (vars insts).

Ballet and Film Scores Transcribed for Piano: *The Plough That Broke the Plains, Filling Station, Lord Byron on the Continent, Louisiana Story* (#1-3 arr. by composer, #4 by Andor Foldes). *Rec:* Musical Heritage Society (Stereo LP) 7458T (also as cassette MHS 9458W): Jacquelyn Helin.

"[These] delightful [works] re-prove a point made by Baroque composers centuries ago: that a good piece of music is good in many guises. Virgil Thomson, whose ballet and film scores are famous in their deft, uncluttered use of hymns, folk songs, cowboy tunes, and dance rhythms, has opened a fresh avenue of accessibility with these piano transcriptions. *Lord Byron on the Continent,* in fact, is in its fourth mutation here, having started as the *String Quartet No. 2* (1932), found its way (orchestrated) into the opera *Lord Byron,* and subsequently emerged as *Symphony No. 3* (1972). All these piano versions... work wonderfully well on the keyboard. If you didn't know better, you would swear that they originated there.

"What makes them work, among other factors, is Thomson's clear linear writing: one is struck repeatedly by the pure, Bach-like counterpoint—whether in the real fugatos of *Plough* and *Filling Station* or in the toccata spirit of the opening and the minuet of *Lord Byron.* The linear character of the music is often more pronounced on the keyboard than in orchestral form, where instrumental colors divert the ear. Of course, some attractive sounds are sacrificed—the pianist can't duplicate the *Plough's* banjo, guitar, or alto and tenor saxophones or the *Third Symphony's* snare drums. But to a remarkable degree, the lilt, pungency, and spaciousness of the music are preserved and take on their own dynamism."—Shirley Fleming, in *Musical America,* 1/89.

MICHAEL TIPPETT

B. 1905, London (England). *Educ.:* Royal College of Music. CBE 1959, knighthood 1966. *Works incl.:* operas *(The Ice Break, King Priam, The Knot Garden, The Midsummer Marriage)*, oratorios *A Child in Our Time, The Vision of Saint Augustine)*, sonatas (4 hns, pno), 4 symphonies.

Concerto for Double String Orchestra (1939). *Rec.:* EMI Angel (2 Stereo LPs) EX 29-0228-3: Moscow Chamber O, Bath Festival Chamber O, Rudolf Barshai, cond.; Argo: orch. cond. by Neville Marriner.

"[Tippett is widely regarded as] England's greatest post-Vaughan Williams composer... His is a deeply rooted and organically determined gift which matured relatively late in life in a burst of furious creativity centering about the opera *The Midsummer Marriage* [1955]....

"The *Concerto* for Double String Orchestra of 1939 is Tippett's first major statement—a synthesis of all his fascinations and susceptibilities up to that time: Tudor polyphony and Beethovenian mass and *gravitas* freely combined with the dancing, singing spontaneity of the English nationalist mode. The concerto is an assured and exhilarating work whose rhythmic displacements and open harmonies oddly have much in common with the American nativist idiom of the 30s—a fortuitous parallel which carries intermittently up until the *Second Symphony*. And at the heart of this music is a clarity and sweetness and light which are almost childlike and mystical at the same time."—Paul Snook, in *Fanfare: The Magazine for Serious Record Collectors*, 11-12/85.

The Mask of Time (oratorio) for Soprano, Mezzo-Soprano, Tenor, Bass, Chorus and Orchestra (1984). 90m *Comm. & prem.:* Faye Robinson (s), Yvonne Minton (ms), Robert Tear (t), John Cheek (b), Tanglewood Festival Chorus (John Oliver, cond), Boston SO, Colin Davis, cond.
Part I: 1. *Presence*. 2. *Creation of the World by Music*. 3. *Jungle*. 4. *The Icecap Moves South-North*. 5. *Dream of the Paradise Garden*. Part II: 6. *The Triumph of Light*. 7. *The Mirror of Whitening Light*. 8. *Hiroshima, mon amour*. 9. *Three Songs*. 10. *The Singing Will Never Be Done*.
In 10 movements.

"*The Mask of Time* should fulfill most of the expectations aroused when it was known that Tippett was working on a grand synthesis of his life's work in the form of a creation myth.... Here is the authentic early Tippett, the lyricist of *The Midsummer Marriage* come back with a stock of age's freshness and insights to replenish the freshness of his youth.

"*The Mask of Time* enables us to see [such] recent works as *The Ice Break*, the *Fourth Symphony*, the *Fourth String Quartet*, and the *Triple Concerto* as studies for and satellites of the new work: ideas are quoted in *The Mask* from the *Fourth Symphony* and *Triple Concerto*; and the 'birth to death' musical program of the *Symphony* and *Fourth Quartet* is obviously refelected in the *Mask*. But the *Mask* is not just one of the 'planets' in the solar system of Tippett's oeuvre (as are his first three operas and *A Child of Time*[121]) It is more like the sun itself. At 90 minutes duration (in two parts of five movements each) it is his longest non-operatic work; and it seems massier, more fierce, more readily throwing off light and heat than the other major works; more compendious and inclusive; a sort of immoveable center comprehending the worlds both of *The Midsummer Marriage* and *The Vision of Saint Augustine*; drawing into itself the different genres — oratorio, cantata, opera, and symphony[122] — to unite them under the rubric of 'masque', or 'Mask'.

"The solar analogy is not inadvertent. The work is literally about the solar system, and its narrative plunges us through space and time, from the first *Presence* ('Sound / Where no airs blow'), through the *Creation of the World by Music*, the development of plant and animal life on earth, the movement of the ice-cap, and the emergence of man, his moral defeat, acquisition of destructive knowledge, and search for a basis of affirmation in an 'expanding universe' where he can be at best (quoting, as Tippett does, from Loren Eiseley's *The Invisible Pyramid*) 'a gladiator ringed by the indifference of the watching stars'. The presiding metaphor is Halley's comet (which both Tippett and Eiseley saw as little boys in 1910), 'the great wild satellite' that reverses its course. A concept of 'reversal', opposing a concept of the 'fixed' (which Nature so largely appears to be — Tippett derives evidence from Annie Dillard's extraordinary observations in *Pilgrim at Tinker Creek*), dominates the philosophy of the work. It is the possibility of a second chance, metaphorically of a 'second coming', in the imminent Age of Aquarius, that draws Tippett on. One of the rejected fragments of the text — compiled by the composer himself,

---

121 *The Mask of Time* comes full circle from *A Child of Our Time*, whose 'argument', sung by alto soloist, ran: 'Man has measured the heavens with a telescope, driven the gods from their thrones. But the soul, watching the chaotic mirror, knows that the gods return. Truly, the living god consumes within and turns the flesh to cancer.'
122 'Symphony' probably construed in the sense of Berlioz' *Romeo and Juliet*. The movement-titles of Mahler's *Third Symphony* (which Tippett allegedly has never heard) were the inspiration for his own chapter-headings.

in his usual brilliantly eclectic fashion—was a couplet from the Czech biochemist-poet, Miroslav Hclub:

> You ask the question:
> It has one name: again.

I was struck by a similar remark made by Rabbi Leo Baack and quoted in Paul Grattan Guiness's *Hear O Israel:*

> The hope that the Messiah will come again has not always been officially recognized by the Church; but it remains, nevertheless, a living hope. The difference between Jewish and Christian hope finds its focus in this one word, *again.*

'Maybe', Tippett writes in the commentary to his text, 'the messengers, even the angels, will return...'. His contemplation of such matters has resulted in a work both apocalyptic and sceptical, full of yearning and bizarre irony, drawing affirmation only out of the dark. It offers itself not as a confident choral-orchestral oratorio in the tradition of Haydn's *Creation,* Beethoven's *Missa Solemnis,* Delius's *A Mass of Life,* and Mahler's *Eighth Symphony,* but guardedly as 'fragments or scenes' (simply designated 'for voices and instruments') 'from a possible "epiphany" for today'.

"The genre is intriguingly novel. I can think of few if any musical precedents for it[123] (but Berlioz is never far away). The Renaissance masque itself—a theatrical pageant of ideas—is always a presence but, except in the quasi-theatrical *Dream of the Paradise Garden* (movement 5), a somewhat shadowy one. Perhaps the best analogy would be with Shaw's 'metabiological pentateuch', *Back to Methusaleh,* a work to which Tippett has been indebted all his creative life. (For instance, its last part, *As Far as Thought Can Reach,* has more or less the same *mise-en-scène* as *The Midsummer Marriage* and its characters include a Strephon, a He-Ancient, and a She-Ancient.[124]) Shaw's five-part drama begins with Adam, Eve, and the Serpent, and zooms on to a satirical condemnation of the First World War, and ends in 31,920 AD with the postulation of superhuman existence that has scientifically triumphed over matter and death. Tippett's creed, if it can be called that, is *au fond* not perhaps so different from Shaw's pleasantly exaggerated rationalist belief in renewal: though Tippett insists that he 'could not come down on the side of one God or associate

---

[123] Andrew Porter has suggested (*New Yorker,* 23 April 1984), as a 'partial analogue', Henze's Giordano Bruno setting *Novae de Infinito Laudes* of 1963.

[124] Also, the egg from which the Newly Born hatches in *As Far as Thought Can Reach* suggested the plaster encasement of Yuri in the last scenes of *The Ice Break.* Cf. Tippett's little article in *Shaw Review,* Vol XXI Nr. 2, May 1978.

[himself] with any specific ideology or intellectual stance'; that he had to 'accommodate a plurality of co-existing viewpoints'.

"A host of other writers have influenced the work's content. An image from a late poem by the author who, with Shaw and T. S. Eliot, has had most impact on Tippett's creative life, W. B. Yeats—his whiffler or artist-figure, 'stalking on' into 'the terrible novelty of light' (from 'High Talk')—provides the composer with a starting point and a putative self-dramatization. The tenor soloist sings (*Presence*—movement 1):

> All metaphor, Malachi, stilts and all.
> Malachi, Malachi, all metaphor.[125]

"And the chorus, in one of the work's sonorous 'archetypal' motifs (deployed almost Wagnerianly, with great effectiveness), enclose him within their singing of the word 'Sound'.[126] 'Time' and 'Space' are presently bodied forth in a similar treatment; the space motif is in fact the opening of the *Fourth Symphony*. Another line from Yeats, 'Measurement began our might'—it has fascinated Tippett at least since he wrote his *Moving into Aquarius* essay, 'What Do We Perceive in Modern Art?'—figures in the second movement, a brisk, explosive, yet breezy *Creation of the World by Music*. Assorted bits of text are blithely run together (Wallace Stevens's 'My ear rehearses river noises' a leading image); and the eventuation is a vague parody of Haydn—'Achieved is the glorious work'—which soars a while then descends with a bump.

"The third movement, *Jungle*, is based on chapters from Annie Dillard's book. Soloists give us disarming facts from the insect world, making for strange pieces of word-setting, as in the line about the lacewing's 'juices excreted by her own ovipositor'. The chorus chants animal noises ('Crokiokiax', 'Bizzwazz', etc.) in a side-line drama of predator and prey, whose choral manner is not far from that of *The Shires Suite*. And for sure, no previous piece by Tippett is too 'minor' not to be acknowledged and embraced by *The Mask of Time*; even *Crown of the Year*[127] and *The Weeping Babe* are here. The end of *Jungle* is an exquisite Monteverdian duet for soprano and mezzo soloists

---

125 Who is Malachi? *Vide* Richard J. Fenneran's new edition of Yeats's complete poems (Macmillan, New York, 1983). Malachi ('my messenger'): supposed author of the last book of the Old Testament; Irish saint (1095-1148) known for his reforms; Joyce's nickname for Buck Mulligan (Yeats's friend Oliver St. John Gogarty) in *Ulysses*.

126 David Cairns likened the 'sound' motif to 'a pair of cosmic billows' (*Sunday Times*, 8 April 1984).

127 Cf. the second chorale prelude in Tippett's *Mirror of Whitening Light*.

depicting 'the tree with the lights in it', time unfurling 'across space like an oriflame'.

"*The Ice-cap moves South-North* (using texts by Jacob Bronowski — *The Ascent of Man*, both book and BBC series — G. M. Hopkins, Thomas Traherne, and T. S. Eliot) is a superbly inventive, cleverly sustained long movement. Tippett's self-vindicating literal-mindedness is well evidenced here. When we are told about primitive man's sacred 'images of bison running', tom-toms and xylophone make sure we actually hear their hooves; when a human heart is being torn out for sacrifice, we seem to hear it throbbing; and the sun to which it is to be offered then shines out with almost visible brilliance. Tippett's pervasive use of electric organ in florid patterns is instanced at the line 'found a strange grain'; the 'genetic accidents' that produced the grain are two words cutely set, with an idiosyncrasy that recalls the first movement's fission of 'eternal' into 'e-ter-ter-ter-ter-' as well as this movement's lovely echo treatment of 'touch' and its numinous double repetition of 'with our' in the line 'Touch the sacred with our hand?'. The movement also contains fabulous Eliotic speech of thunder.

"*A Dream of the Paradise Garden*, movement 5, is the centerpiece of the work, as it is at the center of *The Ice Break* and *Triple Concerto*. Tippett has devised a drily humorous and at the same time affectingly nostalgic commentary on Milton, lines from Book 4 of whose *Paradise Lost* he quotes and misquotes at the beginning and end. His misquotation is 'This was the place' for 'Thus was the place'; and whether or not caused by Tippett's poor eyesight, it is felicitous. It is set to a memorable descending phrase for chamber choir, and leads to the loveliest single passage in the work, a dewy sarabande for three flutes and harp, condensing all the magical moments in Tippett. The scene that follows—it could come out of *The Knot Garden*—shows Tippett at his zaniest:

> MAN: Come, Ancestor, and take a seat.
> ANCESTOR: I thank you; and the air is cool.
> WOMAN: Dragons don't sit, I suppose.
> DRAGON: I'll poise myself upon the grass.

"Absurd, garish electric organ chords (not without vibrato) represent the Ancestor. A radiant horn quartet evokes meadows of peace. Paradise slips away as the chamber chorus intones an ominous verse from the *I Ching*. The mellifluous Miltonic setting returns in cool symmetry, with the added line, to end Part I, 'This was the everlasting place of dream'.

"The complex, extended sixth movement, *The Triumph of Life*, is one of the best things Tippett has achieved. It is a setting of part of

Shelley's unfinished poem, in which the dawn sun is imagined as a 'great chariot rolling on, carrying a mass of humans, all of whom eventually get thrown off' (the composer's words). A heavy and slow, once-heard-inevitably-there ground bass leads full chorus and beleaguered tenor soloist through a deafening apocalyptic phantasmagoria that is measured by clattering drums and fringed by trumpets of doom. A C major choral climax on the word 'life' marks the switch to the appended depiction of Shelley's own death by water, where Tippett manages to evoke the reeling motion of a yacht and somehow the very smell of sail and rigging.

"*The Mirror of Whitening Light* seventh movement steals its title from Maxwell Davies, and quite obviously (though this has been denied) its method too. It comprises three instrumental preludes on *'Veni creator spiritus'* and three much shorter choral verses (with accompaniments that feature the sound of an anvil) taking their texts about mathematics and alchemy from two chapters, headed 'The Hidden Structure' and 'The Music of the Spheres', in Bronowski. The total form is orginal; and the invention in the preludes, particularly the metallic ostinato of the third, which seems to presage nuclear calamity, spellbinding.

"*Hiroshima, mon amour* — a title taken from an [Alan] Resnais movie the composer has never seen — is a setting of lines from Anna Akhmatova's *Requiem* and *Poem Without a Hero*, initially for pungent soprano soloist against male humming chorus at a tempo marked M.M. 29 to the crotchet. In genre this first part resembles the blues songs of Tippett's *Third Symphony* rather than, as one could have expected, *The Midsummer Marriage*'s Sosostris aria and its descendants (Denise's and Hannah's set pieces from *Knot Garden* and *Ice Break*) with their formal pathos. But it is also a new departure in sonority for Tippett and requires an exceptionally careful dynamic balance. The subsequent choral threnody, diversely orchestrated, retaining fanfares from Act II of *King Priam*, often sounds strangely gleeful, suggesting that the victims of mass-brutality would always wear their tribulation like a rose.

"The ninth movement, *Three Songs* that focus on individuals, opens with an energizing snippet from the *Triple Concerto;* the first song's rendition of exhortations from Rilke's *Sonnets to Orpheus* (Nr. 9 from the first series, Nr. 26 from the second; both excerpts in a vividly literal English translation by Tippett himself) also embraces a musical quotation from John Dowland. The second song, 'The Beleaguered Friends', drawing on Helmut Wilhelm's *I Ching* lectures, is musically and scenically the weakest section of *The Mask of Time*. But the third, 'The Young Actor Steps Out', after Mary Renault's novel *The Mask of Apollo,* builds up quickly and convincingly to the work's memorable culmination in a full choral surge to the words (supposedly uttered by the 'face of power' on a statue of Zeus): 'O man, make peace with your mortality, for this too is God'. The brief wordless last movement, entitled *The singing will never be done*, follows immediately with its vocal melismata outstripping in complexity even *The Vision of Saint Augustine* and its ever-widening harmonic space reminiscent of the ecstatic climaxes of *The Midsummer Marriage*. It is like doors opening and shutting on eternity; the door is open when the work suddenly ends.

"From the start, apparently, Tippett was sceptical about the optimism as to man's destiny maintained in Bronowski's *Ascent of Man*. The message of his own work, not so clearly ascertainable, and, as I said, not at bottom unoptimistic, certainly excludes easy consolation. Meirion Bowen, the dedicatee of *The Mask of Time* and closely involved in its gestation, said in a lecture the day after the first performance that he had come to find the work dark and humbling, its vision one in which human individuals are remorselessly swept away by an unchanging cosmos. I myself find it a celebratory work, not only for its Rilkean extremism:

> Order the screamers, O singing God!
> That they may wake flowing,
> bearing on the river-race the head and the lyre.

but because of its sheer Blakean energy, its late reaffirmation of Tippett's deepest creavity.

"But I have one especial criticism of the work: In its scheme of things no place is assigned to erotic love. While *agape* is enshrined in the Akhmatova setting, *eros* does not particularly figure in *Dream of the Paradise Garden* nor anywhere else, and is in fact kept under the floor. A movement on erotic or romantic love could be conceived of; if it were to be added, a twelfth movement too would probably have to be found, in respect to epic patterns. Such an increase from ten to 12 parts would, oddly enough, make another parallel with *Paradise Lost*, which Milton reorganized in like fashion between its first and second printings." —Paul Driver, in *Tempo: A Quarterly Review of Modern Music*, Nr. 149, 6/84.

Quartets 1-3 for Strings. *Rec.:* Decca L'Oiseau-Lyre LP DSLO 10: Lindsay Quartet (Peter Cropper, Ronald Birks, vlns, Roger Bigley, vla, Bernard Gregor-Smith, vc).
Quartet 1 (1934-35; rev. 1943). 1. Allegro. 2. Lento cantabile. 3. Allegro assai. (19m) **Quartet 2** (1941-42). 1. Allegro grazioso. 2. Andante. 3. Presto. 4. Allegro appassionato. (36m) **Quartet 3** (1944-45). 1. Grave e

sostenuto—Allegro moderato. 2. Andante. 3. Allegro molto e con brio. 4. Lento. 5. Allegro comodo. (31m)

"British composers seem to turn to the string quartet less often than do Americans. Britten wrote two string quartets in the early Forties, and only last year [1976] a third. Michael Tippett's three quartets are early works; since [the opera] *A Midsummer Marriage*, which occupied him from 1947 to 1952, he has written more operas, concertos, symphonies, piano and vocal music, but no more quartets....

"Tippet was drawn to the medium early, in his Royal College days, when the Busch and the Léner Quartets played regular cycles; and he has said that he also got to know the Léner's Columbia recordings of Beethoven so well that he was in danger of building the turnovers of those 78-rpm sides into his idea of the music. It is tempting to trace Busch influences in the rhythmic vigor of Tippett's fast movements and Léner influence in the poetic refinement of his lyrical melodies—with Beethoven behind both. Another strand in Tippett's musical makeup is the Tudor polyphony of madrigal and of viol fancies. In the first movement of *Quartet No. 2*, the bar lines are there only for notational convenience; each instrument may be singing its own melody with its own rhythmic patterns, propelled by differing accents.

"One talks of influences—and Beethoven has remained a constant influence on Tippett, most patently on the piano concerto, the *Third Symphony*, and the *Third Piano Sonata*—but Tippett's style is all his own, hard to describe and very easy to recognize. Anyone who has heard *A Midsummer Marriage* knows it. One element is an exhuberant, joyful, dancing quality of rhythm, achieved sometimes by cross-accents within a regular meter (as in the finale of *No. 2*), sometimes by an impetuous flow of lively movement that defies regular barring (as in the finale of *No. 1* and the scherzo of *No. 2*, where the time signatures on the page keep changing while the ear is carried forward without restraint). Another element is the resolution, often unexpected, of tonally independent lines into concord, with an effect sometimes poignant, sometimes wonderfully consoling.

"Tippett seems to be incapable of writing a dull or routine line. If anything, there can be at times too much musical energy. (Someone once remarked that his *Third Quartet* must contain more notes than all Shostakovich's quartets together.) This can lead to a contrapuntal busy-ness that has prompted comparisons with middle Hindemith at his most remorselessly active. It makes Tippett hard to play: like Berlioz, he used to be accused of lacking instrumental dexterity—until performances such as those Colin Davis has put on record made everything clear. The *Third Quartet* has had some currency in Britain, but I own that my admiration for it remained qualified until the Lindsay Quartet, [in its Oiseau Lyre recording] — well, one cannot exactly say made *light* of its difficulties, for it is not a light piece, but at any rate showed the necessity for the writing's being as energetically florid as it is.

"The young [Lindsay] quartet (formed at the Royal Academy in 1967) has forged the kind of special relationship with Tippett that the young Fitzwilliam Quartet (formed in Cambridge in 1969) had with Shostakovich. Its players possess the buoyancy, the energy, and the passion that Tippett's music needs." — Andrew Porter, in *High Fidelity*, 4/77.

"The three string quartets all come in the first period of composition. If we add at least two previous, immature and unsuccessful attempts at this genre, then it's clear how close the quartet form was to me at that early time. It still remains close, but circumstances have drawn me constantly away into other fields.

"This early provenance of all the three published quartets makes them a different grouping from the three [later four] *Piano Sonatas*, or the three [later four] *Symphonies*. Different, that is, in their relationship to each other. I felt them then to be in a consciously evolving sequence and I intended to pursue the sequence with certainly a fourth, at not too long a distance. Since the fourth never got written, the sequence was closed — by the prolonged composition of *The Midsummer Marriage* and everything that happened after.

"*The Midsummer Marriage* broke with all that had gone before (except *A Child of Our Time*) because it was dramatic not symphonic. The quartets, with the *First Piano Sonata, Concerto for Double String Orchestra* and the *First Symphony* were all concerned with my almost total preoccupation then with matters of form. The main questions were: How many movements in a work? What sort of movements? How are the chosen movements to be made successful (both in themselves and in contrast and complement)?

"The *First Quartet* is the best example of the initial struggles, for it alone of the three goes back to the period when I often needed to rewrite what had seemed to be a finished work. In its original version, as performed publicly by the Brosa Quartet in 1935, there were four movements (where now there are three). I think I felt the first two movements, of this original version, to be potentially successful in complement and contrast to the two that followed; but I felt them to be failures in themselves. So I discarded them. (The manuscript shows now that I was quite right as to the second movement, but less right as to the first.) Some years later, after the completion indeed of

Quartet 2, I wrote a new single movement to replace the two discarded—and thus radically changed the original conception!

"I have never had to be as extreme as that since.

"So the *First Quartet* as finally published is a three movement work: and the movements can be shortly described thus:

"1. A Sonata-form allegro—meaning: A^1 Statement of musical material, ending with an upward-striving, then calming, passage for solo cello. B. Discussion or development of this material. A^2. Re-statement of A^1, this time ending with a downward-striving, then calming passage for the cello. (I mention these cello passages because the second is note-for-note how the very original conception thought the slow movement should be entered upon.)

"2. A slow Lento of almost unbroken lines of lyric song for all the instruments in harmony. The shape is that of a Pavane, i.e. A-B-C, and each of the three sections divides, as in huge breaths, into two. (The earliest, and one of the most sustained, example of this long-lined lyricism.)

"3. A vigorous Allegro: which in form accurately speaking is a fugue; but a fugue harking less back to Bach in feeling than to Beethoven. (The earliest example of additive rhythm and cross-rhythm polyphony.)

"*Quartet* 2 remains the most classically balanced of the three, the closest to a 'standard' four-movement piece. What happens, in fact, is that the supposed 'standard' is slightly juggled with and moved around. Thus—

"1. A lyrical Allegro; where the basic sonata-form is deliberately loosened to keep the lyricism above the dramatics.

"2. An intense Andante; a formally strict, rhythmically uniform fugue with a chromatic subject. (One of the very rare occasions where a theme-subject came ahead of the work; I noted it down during the Munich days of 1938).

"3. A Presto Scherzo: $A^1 A^2 A^3$. (Additive rhythm in tighter style.)

"4. A passionate sonata-form Allegro; a deliberate attempt, I remember, to shift the dramatics from first movement to last—as opposed to lightening everything at the end with some kind of Rondo.

"With *Quartet 3* the 'standard' shifts again: from four movements to five—and with no sonata-form movement at all. Instead, three fastish fugues divided by two slow 'lyrics' (for want of a better word). The whole conception is larger.

"1. A slow introduction followed by the first of the fugues; the fugue subject is extended and the statement by all four instruments lengthy. The two later statements are proportionate and the intervening sections likewise.

"2. A song-form first slow movement; the song-line is long-breathed, appearing four times: on Violin 1, Violin 2, Viola, Cello; in that order.

"3. The second fugue (with two subjects) as a short, fast, rhythmically rigorous middle point in the scheme.

"4. The second slow movement is two-part; atmospheric and rhetorical (I think it may show the direct influence of hearing the six Bartók quartets). For the [Lindsay Quartet] recording I have asked the players to enforce the attaca to the last movement by letting that begin on the last note of the fourth.

"5. The third fugue is lyrical and its gentle 9/8 subject is emotionally subordinate to a 3/4 'motto' embedded in the texture.

"I was invincibly drawn to the quartet medium as soon as I came to the Royal College of Music, London, in 1923, and heard the top-ranking players of those days. The two ensembles I remember best were the Busch and the Léner. The Busch was held to be more virile and the Léner more polished. I liked them both. Both gave complete cycles of all the Beethoven Quartets annually, and the Léner made a cycle on 78s for Columbia. I had access to a set of these records and got to know them so well, including such details of where the turnovers of the disc sides came in the longer movements, that I had to stop listening. But their influence was decisive (in matters of style and form); and while I got to know, of course, all the rest of the normal quartet repertory, nothing so decisive happened further until the first London performances of the Bartóks in the war and after. I had heard all six before I wrote *Quartet 3*." — Michael Tippett, from program notes for Decca L'Oiseau-Lyre DSLO 10 recording.

Sonata 4 for Piano (1984). 35m Commissioned by the Los Angeles P Assn. *Prem.:* Paul Crossley. *Rec.:* CRD (2 Digital Stereo LPs) 11301: Paul Crossley. *Pub.:* Schott.
In five continous movements.

"This powerful work, comissioned in celebration of the eightieth birthday of the composer (January 1985) was composed in 1984. Sir Michael is an eclectic. It is safe to say that the outstanding composers we know selected from various sources during their formative compositional years, but Tippett, one of England's leading composers, developed his individual style while remaining an eclectic. Typically, one finds in this sonata a variety of melodic, harmonic and rhythmic idioms that nevertheless carry his trademark.

"A large five-movement work, it is mildly dissonant, of composite modality, dramatic, lyric, technically challenging and pianistic, rhythmically complex but flowing and appealing. There are abrupt changes of mood and dynamics, almost Ivesian, and yet there is unity. Although he is better known as a composer of choral works, Tippett's instrumental compositions demonstrate a continuous interest in traditional structural processes, contrapuntal textures and widely different idioms. There are many suggestions for interpretation, but tempo directions are vague, and there are no metronomic guides. Fortunately, there are authoritative recordings of the piano sonatas by Paul Crossley, who premiered this work." — Benning Dexter, in *The American Music Teacher* (Music Teachers National Association), 11-12/88.

"Unlike Messiaen or Shostakovich, Tippett has never been a performing pianist, but throughout his life he has written for the piano. Since the *Piano Concerto* (1953-55) he has regularly included it in his orchestral tapestry, blending it beautifully with harp, chimes, bells, gongs, xylophones, and marimbas. In the *Third Symphony*'s slow movement and other soft passages Tippett uses the piano as a percussion instrument, combining its high octaves with the other instruments of the section. Percussive chords are rare. Most of the writing is linear, as one would expect from so contrapuntal a composer, but the effect is never dry.

"In addition to his extensive orchestral use of the instrument, Tippett has composed six major piano works, one for each decade of his career. The *First Sonata* appeared in 1938, the *Fantasia on a Theme of Handel* for piano and orchestra in 1941, the *Piano Concerto* in 1955, the *Second Sonata* in 1962, the *Third Sonata* in 1973, and the *Fourth Sonata* in 1984, following the completion of the ambitious 10-movement oratorio *The Mask of Time*....

"At 35 minutes the *Fourth* is the longest of the four sonatas; its structure follows the arch form of Bartók's quartets. After the structural rigor and fierce virtuosity of the *Third Sonata*, the *Fourth* sounds more rhapsodic and leisurely, although the fourth movement's technical difficulties are considerable. Tippett orginally conceived the piece as a series of bagatelles in the manner of Beethoven's Op. 126, but he cast four of the five movements in traditional molds. The exception is the central slow movement, which contains some of the work's most beautiful music; it is divided into five section, A-B-C-B-A, reflecting the palindromic shape of the sonata as a whole. The second and fourth movements are both in scherzo-and-trio form, the first light and dancing, the second stormy and full of robust, jazzy rhythms. The first movement is in sonata form, and the finale is a series of variations of disarming simplicity, in striking contrast to the elaborate variations of the *Third Sonata*.

"The *Fourth Sonata* contains some of Tippett's most effective piano sonorities. As always, these are achieved by traditional methods, without such devices as tone clusters, plucked strings, or playing with the forearm or fist. He uses the sostenuto pedal extensively, especially in the middle movement, where six-part Messiaenic chord progressions ring out in the high treble over booming octaves held in the low bass. This new emphasis on sonority is also seen in a more characteristically contrapuntal passage in the first movement, where a motto theme in octaves underpins the rapturous pealing of bells in the treble.

"In the slow movement, as usual the longest of the work, the B section is a languorous blues-inspired passage, with the melancholy melody accompanied both above and below by wide-ranging, rhythmically independent lines. The texture is quartet-like, but the sound is supremely pianistic.

"In this sonata Tippett uses such markings as 'ring', 'ping', 'like a bell', and 'like a marimba'. Knowing the orchestral works of this period is an advantage in trying to capture these sounds. In the *Triple Concerto*, for example, he uses tuned gongs, vibraphone, and marimba to magical effect to evoke the peace and serenity of Bali.

"The sonata ends with a variation of stunning beauty, a reflective two-part invention in which the hands spin delicate lines at opposite ends of the piano, leading to a climax before descending to a final restatement of the simple original theme that recalls the end of the variations of Beethoven's *Sonata*, Op. 109.

"I hope the celebrations honoring Sir Michael Tippett's 85th birthday [January 1990] will help bring his piano music the attention, recognition, and study it deserves. With time and more widespread performances, both live and recorded, these works will be acknowledged as masterpieces of 20th-century piano literature." — Clive Swansbourne, "The Piano Music of Michael Tippett", in *Clavier*, 1/90.

EDUARD TUBIN

B.1905, Kallaste (near Tartu [Dorpat])(Estonia); d. 1982. Cond. Tartu SO. *Works incl.*: concertos (balalaika, db), operas *(Barbara von Tisenhusen, Prosten från Reigi [The priest from Reigi])*, piano pieces (folk dances, preludes, 2 sonatas, suite), sonatas (sax, vla, vln), songs.

Symphony 1 for Orchestra. *Rec.*: Bis Records (CD BIS 351): Swedish Radio SO, Neeme Järvi, cond.

Symphony 2 (Legendary) for Orchestra (1937). *Rec.*: Bis Records (Stereo LP) LP-314 (also as CD BIS 314): Swedish Radio O, Neeme Järvi, cond.

Symphony 3 for Orchestra (1942). *Rec.*: Bis Records (CD BIS 342): Swedish Radio SO, Neeme Järvi, cond.

Symphony 4 (Sinfonia lirica) for Orchestra (1943). *Rec.*: Bis Records (Stereo LP) BIS LP-227: Harmonien O of Bergen, Neeme Järvi, cond.

Symphony 5 in B Minor for Orchestra (1946). *Rec:* Bis Records (Digital Stereo LP) BIS LP-306 (also as CD BIS 306): Bamberg SO, Neeme Järvi, cond.
In three movements.

Symphony 6 for Orchestra (1952-54). *Recs.*: MK (10" Mono LP): Estonian Radio O, Eduard Tubin, cond.; Bis Records (Stereo LP) LP-314 (also as CD BIS 314): Swedish Radio O, Neeme Järvi, cond.
1. Andante sostenuto ma ritmico. 2. Molto allegro. 3. Festoso.

Symphony 7 for Orchestra (1959). *Recs.*: Big Ben (Stereo LP) 601 851-002: Helsingborg SO, Hans-Peter Frank, cond.; Bis Records (CD BIS 401): Gothenburg SO, Neeme Järvi, cond.
In three movements.

Symphony 8 for Orchestra (1966). *Rec.*: Bis Records (CD BIS 342): Swedish Radio SO, Neeme Järvi, cond.

Symphony 9 for Orchestra (1969). *Rec:* Bis Records (Stereo LP) BIS LP-264: orch. cond. by Neeme Järvi.

Symphony 10 for Orchestra (1973). *Rec.*: Bis Records (CD BIS 297): Gothenburg SO, Neeme Järvi, cond.
In one movement.

"If someone told this writer, even a few years ago, that all ten of the symphonies by Estonia's greatest composer—and one of our century's major symphonists—would probably be recorded within his own lifetime, he would have scoffed in disbelief. And yet along comes the magnificent Neeme Järvi, a political refugee from the Soviet Union and a master conductor whose sympathies for turn-of-the-century and mainstream-modern repertoire seem unlimited—

and who will probably someday head one of America's major orchestras — to prove me quite marvelously wrong!

"For those listeners who are coming to Tubin fresh, the [BIS LP] pairing of [Nos. 2 and 6], an early and a mature symphony, is the recommended starting-point. The *Second* — subtitled 'Legendary' — was written in 1937, during the composer's halcyon years in his native land before his forced relocation to Sweden as a result of the war. And yet in spite of some residual Sibelianisms (which were much more noticeable in the milder 'Lyric' *Fourth Symphony*), it exhibits in embryonic form so many of the distinctive character-traits heard in full dress in the *Sixth* postwar symphony (1954): the growing structural massiveness (several movements run nearly to 15 minutes in length), the increasingly sombre-hued brass textures, the gradual minatory crescendos and enigmatic diminuendos, and — most readily apparent — the obsession with dark and melodramatic ostinati, over which the strings and sometimes an abruptly spotlighted solo instrument — such as a saxophone or viola — intones a doleful tune with few if any ethnic connotations — that this listener (who has never heard the *Third Symphony*) asks himself whether the composer might not have come back to the *Second* and made revisions in the light of his experiences and accomplishments during the postwar period.

"While the *Fifth Symphony* of 1946 is both stylistically and psychologically a kind of transitional work, the *Sixth* is a full-blown example of Tubin's finally coming into his own voice after the disruption triggered by the war years had been digested. The *Sixth* is the first of those three remarkable middle-period symphonies when the composer's awareness of unavoidable human waste and folly is captured in music with an almost brash and frenetic pulse: the rhythmic aspect is a predominant factor in three movements whose tempo markings tell the tale — *Andante sostenuto ma ritmico, Molto allegro,* and *Festoso*. The middle movement in particular is a kind of compulsive fandango (the liner-notes identify it as a 'rhumba') that approaches Paul Creston in its metric complexity and restlessness. The finale is a set of variations on a chaconne theme that bodies forth all the fatalistic, juggernaut-like qualities of Tubin's harsh, unblinking vision, in which the 'festive' element has a forced and bleak irresolution about it. This may be relatively simple music but it certainly packs plenty of character and power.... Once again, this [coupling of *Symphonies 2 and 6* in performances by the Swedish Radio Orchestra under Neeme Järvi] is the best place [on records] to make first acquaintance with one of the truly outstanding symphonists of the postward period." — Paul Snook, in *Fanfare: The Magazine for Serious Record Collectors*, 3-4/86.

"Not surprisingly, Tubin's *First Symphony* is very much in the lyrical, highly rhapsodic vein of his other early symphonies, which culminate in the extremely beautiful and Sibelian *Fourth Symphony*. Surprisingly, the *First* is a stronger composition than the overly descriptive and somewhat meandering *Second Symphony*. Like Sibelius's *First*, Tubin's *First Symphony* is amazingly self-confident and large in scale for a composer's first essay of the symphonic form. Neeme Järvi and the Swedish Radio Symphony give it a stunning performance.

"Tubin's *Third Symphony*, like his *Second*, has a good deal of marching in it (too much so in its last movement) and is primarily martial in character. It has grand themes, propulsive rhythms, and heroic vistas; the full complement of orchestral resources is deployed in some rousing, Sibelian moments of real sweep and grandeur. The last movement, however, tends toward the grandiose.... While I prefer the *Third Symphony* to its predecessor, I find it too extroverted and not quite at the level of the very lovely *Fourth*. Tubin's *Eighth Symphony* is music of a knottier sort, far more introspective and infused with a sense of tragedy. A fascinating and enigmatic work....

"The *Seventh Symphony* is clearly part of Tubin's symphonic sound world. The same kind of formal thinking evident in his early symphonies is present here, but in leaner form—less lush and ecstatic, more mature and melancholic, but still quite beautiful and full of longing. It's also without the violence and sense of catastrophe of the *Fifth* and *Sixth* symphonies.

"Tubin's last symphony, the *Tenth*, is written in one movement. It begins with a somber adagio in the strings, which is soon punctuated by recurring horn calls that attempt to summon the music from its melancholic brooding. The adagio gives way to a more energetic and uplifting theme, which is, if not triumphant, at least enlivened by a note of optimism. The two themes alternate effectively, creating a weighty feel for both the powerful inertial pull of melancholy and the great strength needed to overcome it. The spirited theme finally prevails in the *Adagio festivo*, which builds to the symphony's powerful and magnificent climax, after which comes a long orchestral fade to the end. It would be an overstatement to call Tubin's last symphony elegiac, but it is pervaded by a strong sense of mortality and by the feeling of sadness that comes with the knowledge that triumph is always temporary. Järvi's performance with the Gothenburg Symphony Orchestra is superb."—Robert R. Reilly, in *Musical America*, 5/90.

SYMPHONY 4. "Underneath this unforced blend of Sibelian sound, Slavic soul, and Brucknerian span, one can detect the seed of Tubin's driving fascination with cellular motifs, persistent ostinatos, and cumulative crescendos, all interfused with his Kokkonen-like restrained sense of proportion and almost pantheistic reverence for the expressive weight and economic of sonic structure. The freshly minted and soaring melodies in this score are absolutely ravishing in a totally unostentatious way: weaving in and out of each other, they build a web of shared roots and cross-references with a narrative impetus that is exceptionally forthright, resilient, spontaneous, and communicative." — Paul Snook, in *Fanfare: The Magazine for Serious Record Collectors*, 9-10/83.

"Tubin's *Fifth Symphony* is the first composition completed upon his taking refuge in Sweden after the War. Though he denied that the work had any particular program to it, the War and its effects on his homeland loom large here, beyond any doubt. The driving first movement seems to reflect the triple invasion Estonia suffered at Soviet and German hands; and in the work as a whole, Tubin's usual Sibelian textures seem underscored by the apparent influence of Shostakovich. The slow — but not quite tranquil — second movement makes effective use of Estonian folk material interwoven with musical sophistication so as to rise above mere local color folklorism. The finale reaches a martial crescendo seemingly meant to prophesy the eventual triumph of the Estonian spirit.... [This] highly recommended [recording of Tubin's *Fifth Symphony* is] probably one of the year's best.

"With the Tubin's symphonies now available on records, it begins to seem possible to sense something of a progression in these works — from the ghostly, macabre, but possibly nature-oriented *Second;* to the *Fourth,* an elegiac refuge-taking out of a time of War; through this assertive nationalistic *Fifth;* on to the exotically rhythmical (and almost American-sounding) *Sixth,* which uses saxophone prominently in a symphony a good four years before Vaughan Williams' more famous effort; the darkly brooding *Seventh* (even its scherzo is couched amid the sobriety of its slow second movement); and the penultimate, relatively straight-forward *Ninth.* In all these works, Tubin's characteristic vitality appears — a vitality which often finds expression in some of the most imaginative reliance on percussion employed since Nielsen (who just may be, after all the names I have suggested as influences over the years, the major one upon Tubin after all, assuming the latter could have known the former's compositions). We wait for more. This most interesting emergence from the shadows may take many more years to complete and assess, but for now it can hardly fail to bring cheers from [record] collectors." — John Ditsky, in *Fanfare: The Magazine for Serious Record Collectors*, 9-10/86.

GEORGE WALKER

B. 1922, Washington DC. *Educ.*: Oberlin College, Curtis Inst, American Cons (Fontainebleau), Eastman Schl of Music. *Taught at:* Dillard Univ, New Schl for Soc Research, Dalcroze Schl, Smith College, Univ of Boulder, Peabody Cons, Univ of DE, Rutgers Univ. *Awards & grants:* Fulbright Comm, Guggenheim, Rockefeller, John Hay Whitney Fellowships, Koussevitsky Prize; honorary doctorates Lafayette Coll, Oberlin Coll. *Works incl.:* choral (*Cantata, Mass*), concertos (pno, vc, vln), *Dialogus* (vc/orch), orchestra (2 *Sinfonias, Variations*), quintet (brass), sonatas (pno, vc, vla, vln), vocal works (*15 Songs, Spirituals*).

Composer statement: "Musical composition has provided me with the challenge of creating interesting works to augment the standard repertory of diverse mediums."

Address for Orchestra (1959). *18m Prem.:* Atlanta SO, Robert Shaw, cond. *Other perfs.:* New World SO, Benjamin Steinberg, cond. (2 movts only); Baltimore SO, Sergiu Commissiona, cond.; Mons (Belgium) festival o, James Depreist, cond.; Oakland SO, Richard Buckley, cond. *Rec.:* Desto Records DC 7107 (movt 3 [*Passacaglia*] only): Oakland Youth O, Robert Hughes, cond. *Pub.:* MMB Music. In 3 movements.

"The *Address for Orchestra* is the work of a sophisticated craftsman whose rhetoric is individual, powerful and communicative. It begins urgently with a succint four-note motive dramatically stated and punctuated by the xylophone.

"The initial idea is then subjected to involved fugal treatment of the most metrical complexity, leading eventually into a lovely lyrical passage in which Walker's orchestral palette is tinged with the voluptuousness of the late romantics.

"It ends with a restatement of the original material whose rhythms once more become increasingly animated, culminating in a brilliant perpetual motion section." — Elliott W. Galkin, in the *Baltimore Sun*.

"The Walker *Address* is a major piece of great energy and thrust, whose three movements are culminated by a moving *Passacaglia*, which has often stood on its own in concerts. The enthusiastic reception [at the Oakland Symphony performance] of this handsome work should inspire further hearings." — Marilyn Tucker, in the *San Francisco Chronicle*, 2/20/86.

Concerto for Trombone and Orchestra (1957). 17m *Rec.:* Columbia (LP) M-32783: Denis Wick (tbn), London SO, Paul Freeman, cond.

"Belongs in the standard modern repertory.... [This is] a tremendous contribution to the meager trombone literature, a bold virtuoso vehicle of considerable melodic and rhythmic power that speaks with a deeply personal voice. The concluding *Allegro* is a special delight." — Kenneth Furie, in *High Fidelity*, 6/74.

"I would send out an all-points bulletin to conductors on behalf of George Walker, [the composer-pianist who is also] a professor of music at Rutgers University. He [has] emerged not merely as a leader of his black colleagues but as one of the ablest composers in the American community, occupying a place between the older circle of Copland-Schuman-Carter and the younger coterie of Crumb-Wuorinen-Druckman. [In each work] he addresses himself confidently to his problem, possesses a sure sense of direction, and works energetically toward his objective.... I would recommend that conductors interested in a colorful, concise example of Walker's abilities listen to his concerto for trombone and orchestra, included in Columbia's 'Black Composers' recordings." — Irving Kolodin, in *Saturday Review*, 10/15/77.

Lyric for Strings (1946). 6m *Perf.:* New York P, Paul Freeman, cond. *Rec.:* Columbia LP M-33433: London SO, Paul Freeman, cond.; Orion (Stereo LP) ORS-83461: Joyce Flissler, Gregory Walker (vlns), Robert Glaser (vla), Avron Coleman (vc). *Score available from:* composer.

Prelude and Caprice for Piano (1945). *Rec.:* Orion Stereo LP ORS-83461: George Walker. *Pub.:* MMB Music.

Sonata 4 for Piano Solo (1985). 14m *Prem.:* Frederick Moyer. *Rec.:* GM Recordings CD GM 2016: Frederick Moyer. *Pub.:* MMB Music. In three movements.

Spatials for Piano. 4m *Recs.:* Composers Recordings Inc (Stereo LP CRI SD-270): George Walker; Orion Records (Stereo LP ORS-83451): George Walker. *Pub.:* MMB Music.

Variations on a Kentucky Folk Song for Piano. 5m *Rec.:* Orion Records (Stereo LP ORS-83461): George Walker. *Pub.:* MMB Music.

"The *Lyric for Strings* is a bittersweet, transparent, beautifully-textured piece, written as a memorial to Walker's grandmother, and it possesses many of the same endearing qualities as Samuel Barber's youthful *Adagio*. It is a very touching and attractive piece.... [Although the composer is, of course, frequently identified as a major 'black' composer, his] music should be played more often by *all* musicians, white, black, brown [or whatever]." — Irving Lowens, in *The Washington Star*, 9/2/77.

"Walker is... a conscientious craftsman with a true gift for musical communication. The *Lyric for Strings* (1946), perhaps his most popular work, is a warm, emotive elegy very much in the style and spirit of Barber's *Adagio* of a few years earlier, though for my taste it's a less sentimental and therefore better piece. The *Prelude and Caprice,* also from the 40s, are pretty examples of an updated impressionist genre, the *Caprice* especially exquisite in its sprightly chromatic filagree. *Spatials* is a fiery, Webernesque vignette dotted with moments of introspection." — Kyle Gann, in *Fanfare: The Magazine for Serious Record Collectors,* 1-2/87.

"Walker's *Piano Sonata 4* [is] an ambitious work that seems to owe a debt to Ginastera and Barber's famous sonatas, but is itself a distinctive work of American Modernism — complex, yet immediately appealing, built, for the most part, on the contrast between stark proclamations and more lyrical passages, leading to a rousing toccata." — Tim Page, in *The New York Times,* 9/27/85.

"[Walker's *Lyric for Strings* is] an absolutely marvelous piece, very short but intensely moving and beautiful.... It is a little in the vein of Samuel Barber's famous *Adagio,* but bigger in thrust and deeper in content. A truly magnificent moment." — Alred Frankenstein, in *High Fidelity,* 10/75.

"George Walker is first and foremost a gifted composer whose works are bold and dramatic. He is also a prodigious pianist whose sonatas reflect his affinity for the instrument.
"The *Fourth Piano Sonata* is a relatively brief three-movement work. Its brevity, however, should not be misleading. The drama infuses this sonata with great energy and vitality.
"As with Walker's earlier piano works, the atonal style contains dramatic lyricism in its wide-ranging texture. The bold gesture is very much a part of the composer's vocabulary, from the driving motoric rhythms to the angular strings of sixteenth notes and dotted rhythms.
"Perhaps it is unfair to suggest comparisons, but one is reminded in this music of the progressive music of Aaron Copland's *Piano Fantasy,* but with a thicker texture. Copland's work is one of the great piano masterworks of our time, and Walker's *Fourth Sonata* has much of its rugged, heroic quality.
"The *Fourth Sonata* is difficult, but an advanced college student (or even one in high school, given the high degree of talent one finds today) could, with the right dramatic temperament, find great

pleasure in this brilliant work." — Mark Wait, in *The American Music Teacher* (Music Teachers National Association), 11-12/88.

Dan Welcher

B. 1948, Rochester NY. *Educ.:* Eastman Schl of Music, Manhattan Schl of Music. *Taught at:* Univ of Louisville, Univ of Texas, Eastman Schl of Music, Aspen Music Fest. *Performer:* Principal Bassoonist, Louisville O, 1972-78; also positions in Rochester PO, Hudson Valley PO, Aspen Music Fest. Asst. Cond, Austin SO. *Awards:* Fellowships from Natl Endowmnt Arts, MacDowell Colony, American Music Cntr. *Works incl.: Concerto da camera* (bsn, small chamb orch), *Dervishes* (orch), piano music, songs, string quartets, woodwind quintets (3), vocal chamber music.

Composer's statement: "Music is a means of communication. No less than literature, motion pictures, the visual arts or theater, serious music must speak immediately and directly to audiences. The most exciting feature of music of the 1980s (and, presumably, music of the 90s) is the total rejection of the 'art for art's sake' mentality that governed composers from the 1950s through the 1970s. Music which is difficult to comprehend is no longer automatically considered profound or advanced, and music which contains the old-fashioned values of audible counterpoint, rhythmic clarity, melodic recognition or harmonic sense is no longer pigeonholed as 'conservative'.

"My own music has benefited from the multiplicity of choices available to this new aesthetic. I have employed serial techniques in many of my works, but always in tonally organized methods. My orchestral music (probably the best-known of my works) is often praised for its colorful and skillful orchestration. I credit this to my long years as a professional bassoonist and conductor, and continue to teach my students that composers *must* be performers in some capacity. It is essential that composers remain 'hands-on' practitioners of their art, because when this closeness to performance disappears the music becomes, in subtle ways, artificial. I have not sought prizes as a composer, but commissions[128] and performances. I feel that it is far more important that I write music that people *want* to play, sing, or conduct than for scholars to analyze or for foundations to endow. In the long run, the music that stays in active performance due to its own value and its ability to communicate to audiences and performers is the music that will endure."

---

[128] Dan Welcher has received commissions from Jan DeGaetani, the Louisville Orchestra, American Brass Quintet, Cleveland Quartet, others. (Ed.)

Concerto for Flute and Orchestra (1973). 25m *Comm. & rec.*: Louisville (Stereo LP) LS-742: Francis Fuge (fl), Louisville O, Jorge Mester, cond. *Pub.*: Carl Fischer (available on rental)
1 picc-1-1-1 b cl-1; 2-2-1-0; timp, perc, harp, piano-celesta; strings
1. Andante—Andante con moto—Allegro vivo—Andante mosso. 2. Theme and Variations: Moderato doloroso—Allegro moderato—Allegretto—Con fuoco—Broad—Allegro alla marcia.

"The idea of writing a flute concerto was suggested to me by the Music Director of the Louisville Orchestra, Jorge Mester. He had been seeking a suitable new work for France Fuge, the Orchestra's Principal Flutist since 1959, to perform and record. I had come to Louisville in 1972 as Principal Bassoonist in the Orchestra and Instructor of Theory and Bassoon at the University of Louisville School of Music, and one of the things that impressed me the most soon after arriving was the extraordinary caliber of virtuosity the orchestra possessed in its principal wind players, most notably Mr. Fuge. Having become very familiar with his playing in the Orchestra (and numerous chamber music sessions together), I was eager to write a piece for this occasion that would suit his particular artistic needs, and equally important for me, that would be direct and engaging for the audience. I have for some time been uncomfortable about the growing gap between the contemporary composer and his audience: out of mistaken insecurity, the typical concert-goer will lamely applaud an avant-garde piece that he finds boring or static, rather than give in to his real feelings and hiss at it, as if he really isn't sure what he should or shouldn't like. This is not to say that music should regress, or that what we need is a spirit of condescension to the audience's collective taste (whatever that may be); but that a very essential part of music should be its effect on an audience. This aspect of music is often overlooked by contemporary 'serious' composers, and I feel it is the main reason that so much new music seems relatively unimportant to everyone except the composer. Music is, after all, a communication: it involves active participation on both ends. Audiences, too, have a responsibility to be discriminating and should, I think, voice genuine disapproval as well as approval (provided, of course, that they approach each new piece with optimism and receptive ears[129]).

---

[129] Which requires that audiences be given an opportunity to *hear* new music, in the first place, in order to develop and exercise any discrimination at all. Perhaps most people would admit that, in the end, "public taste" will out, and that, perhaps, few enough "masterpieces" do slip through the cracks; nevertheless—to emphasize a point which can scarcely be overworked—music, obviously, *must first be heard...* before judgments can be made. (Ed.)

"The *Concerto for Flute and Orchestra* is scored for a rather small orchestra. The composition falls into two lengthy movements, each of which divides into several sections. The first movement is itself in two parts. It begins with a nervous figure in the xylophone (which becomes a unifying factor throughout the movement) and, after a tentative series of statements by the flute, leads into the main theme, a lyrical *Andante con moto*. Muted brass contribute a secondary theme over which the flute continues to sing, and, after an extensive buildup in which the soloist is subjected to vigorous exercise, the main theme returns *fortissimo*, subsides, and moves on. A sudden restatement of the xylophone figure interrupts and heralds a brief cadenza, and the solo horn's answer to that cadenza becomes transformed into a dancelike, rhythmic theme marked *Allegro vivo*. This second section of the movement contains all of the themes presented earlier, but in more spirited settings, including the muted brass theme of the previous section which is cast as a capricious little waltz. The movement ends slowly and reflectively with the flute's final word to the xylophone.

"The second movement is a *Theme and Variations* and is written in a fairly strict serial format. Only the theme contains non-serial elements, and while this may seem a reversed application of the variation formula (that of varying elements present in the theme), it is actually quite natural: the theme 'discovers' a twelve-tone row within itself, and the variations expand upon it. There are five variations, arranged in three sections. The first three variations are connected without pause: one in which the flute is supported mainly by pizzicato lower strings, one in 6/8 time with a brooding quality in horn and violins, and a very excited third variation punctuated unpredictably by brass and percussion. The fourth variation is in a broad 3/2 meter and begins as a dialogue between the orchestra's statements and the flute's inversions and improvisations on those statements. A chorale follows; not 'in the Bach style' as Berg had done in his *Violin Concerto*, but simply the row-theme divided into chorale phrases. Celesta and tremolo strings provide a variation-within-the-variation as the flute pecks out an eerie staccato counterpoint. The chorale floats upward into solo strings, and the last variation begins with the banal thumpings of bass drum and cymbals. Marked *Allegro alla marcia*, this variation provides a stimulating contrast to the solemnity of the previous one. For the first time, the entire orchestra is used to challenge the flute, which is put to a real test of virtuosity. The *Concerto* ends with a brilliant flash." — Dan Welcher, liner notes for Louisville Stereo LP LS-742.

"The flute concerto written for Francis Fuge, the Louisville Orchestra's principal flutist, is as serious and brooding as the Dello Joio *Hommage to Haydn* [with which it is coupled on the Louisville recording] is carefree and vivacious, and it is composed in a style that is much more international in character. Yet not only is it an exceptionally well-crafted work in which a line-against-line tension is constantly maintained between the flute and various elements of the orchestra, but the music communicates on a deep emotional level falling somewhere between the polished severity of a Frank Martin and the almost morbid despair of an Alban Berg. Welcher also masterfully evokes atmosphere and mood, both through his rich, basically nontonal harmonic language and through a truly virtuoso and yet subtle manipulation of instrumental color.

"On the basis of this work, I would say that Welcher is one of the most promising of young American composers I have heard, for he has managed to attain, in a complex, finely developed musical idiom, a profundity of expression [many] recent composers seem to shun like the plague." — Royal S. Brown, in *High Fidelity*, 8/75.

Dance Variations for Piano (1979). 20m *Prem.:* Bradford Gowen. *Pub.:* Elkan-Vogel (distr. Theodore Presser).

"Commissioned by pianist Bradford Gowen upon his winning the Kennedy Centre/Friedheim Prize for Excellence in Performing American Music, this work is a tour-de-force for a virtuoso pianist. It features inside-the-piano effects, but is largely written for conventional technique (albeit of the Lisztian variety!). Serial and tonal elements at first clash with each other, then merge in a transcendental final variation/epilogue with a Debussian suspension of time." — Dan Welcher.

"Dan Welcher's *Dance Variations* is a twenty-minute virtuoso work with a strong rhythmic component, a variety of interesting piano textures (both keyboard and inside the piano), and a very clearly delineated structure.

"Based on two themes, or more appropriately, two kinds of music — one serial, the other pentatonic — the work is actually a contrast between the two, which sometimes apepar separately as in the lengthy exposition, sometimes together as in the beautiful Debussy-like section of the epilogue (Var. VI). There are six continuous variations, each with a separate character, but all sharing a strong rhythmic thrust. Although only one variation is an actual dance (Var. III is a waltz), all are dance-like in spirit, and the pulse, whether steady or in shifting meter, is always apparent. The entire work is in the shape of an arch centering on Var. III (which is in itself an ABA form), the opening being reinstated at the end before a presto coda.

"Robert C. Marsh of the Chicago *Sun-Times* [wrote that] 'Gowen's performance of the *Dance Variations* was a thoroughly convincing statement of a fine, original work from the mainstream of American keyboard writing.' Welcher, who is on the faculty of the University of Texas at Austin, has written one other work for solo piano, a *sonatina*. Of moderate difficulty, it has been used recently as the required twentieth-century work in several American piano competitions. Both works are beautifully engraved by Elkan-Vogel." —Lois Svard, in *Notes* (Music Library Association), 12/86.

Della's Gift (opera)(1986). *Lib.*: Paul Woodruff, after O. Henry story "Gifts of the Magi". 70m *Prem.*: Univ of Texas Opera Theater, Dan Welcher, cond. *Pub.*: Theodore Presser (perf. materials on rental).
1 s, 3 mez, 3 t, 1 bar, optional tripling of mez & t roles by same two singers
1-1-2-1; 2-2-1-0; harp, piano, 1 perc; strings
In two acts.

Written for the University of Texas Opera Theater. "The chances of a new opera's surviving long after its opening night are remote, to put it kindly. But I'd be willing to risk money that *Della's Gift*, by composer Dan Welcher and librettist Paul Woodruff, is going to be a welcome exception. The reasons are good and much deserved. The music is disarming in its charm and eminently singable. And as theater, *Della's Gift* is uncomplicated and affecting.... Welcher has not hesitated to express sentiment, but in doing so, he has skillfully avoided the trap of being sentimental. Around the 'magical children' of O. Henry's familiar story, he has constructed a musical aura that evokes a bygone American era in a gentle, loving way." —John Ardoin, *Dallas Morning News*.

Prairie Light: Three Texas Watercolors of Georgia O'Keefe for Orchestra (1985). 14m *Comm. & prem.*: Sherman (Texas) SO, Cecil Isaac, cond. *Pub.*: Theodore Presser.
1. *Light Coming on the Plains*. 2. *Canyon with Crows*. 3. *Starlight Night*. (Played without interruption.)
3-2-2-2; 4-3-3-1; timpani, 3 perc, piano, harp; strings

A sound-picture of three primitive early paintings of Georgia O'Keeffe, all of the same landscape in the Palo Duro Canyon near Amarillo. The light varies with the time of day, and the three movements take the listener through a 24-hour cycle. The music is gentle, simple in texture, yet very affecting. "*Prairie Light*, a succinct, impressionistic piece inspired by three watercolors by Southwestern artist Georgia O'Keeffe, opened the program.... The music moved in gentle, almost pastel progressions, much in keeping with the watercolors done in 1917 in Canyon, Texas, by the artist. Eastern elements and non-linear melodic ideas appeared, but the work was easily accessible to hard-core fans of strict classical repertoire." —Michael Point, *Austin American-Statesman*.

Quartet 1 for Strings (1987). 26m *Comm. & prem.:* Cleveland Quartet. *Pub.:* Elkan-Vogel.
In 4 movements.

A semi-serialized work, highly dramatic and energetic, for a virtuoso quartet. In length, seriousness of intent, and communicative spirit it resembles the quartets of Bartók. "Who knows? Perhaps the string quartet is, for all practical purposes, dead. But, apparently, Dan E. Welcher has not heard about its demise. The Rochester-born, Texas-based composer's *String Quartet No. 1*, which received its West Coast premiere by Chamber Music West Thursday evening... sounds like the genuine article. What came through first in the Cleveland Quartet's dedicated performance was the sheer élan Welcher exhibits in writing for the four classical string players. The composer so capitalizes on the possibilities of mutual interplay between the musicians that the traditional ritual experience of 200 years of string quartet writing seems preserved, not in amber, but in some more volatile medium." —Allan Ulrich, *San Francisco Examiner*.

Sonatina for Piano. 10m Ded. to Bradford Gowen. *Pub.:* Elkan-Vogel.
In 3 movements.

"This *Sonatina*, dedicated to Bradford Gowen, who was the first prize winner in the Kennedy Center-Rockefeller Foundation Piano Competition three years ago, is, like Gowen, also a winner. The dissonance is mild, and much of the texture of the two outer movements is contrapuntal. The middle movement is a lovely, quiet oasis that is a perfect foil for the restlessness and hyperactivity that pervades the other movements. The piece is fairly difficult, but it is rhythmically uncomplicated."—Evelyn Garvey, in *The American Music Teacher* (Music Teachers National Association), 4-5/82.

The Visions of Merlin (tone poem) for Orchestra (1980). 24m *Comm.* by the Sunriver Music Festival, Lawrence Leighton Smith, mus. dir. *Perf.:* Dallas SO, Eduardo Mata, cond. *Rec.:* Louisville First Edition (LP): Louisville O, Akira Endo, cond. *Pub.:* Theodore Presser.

Prologue *(Merlin the Enchanter)*. *The Sight 1 (The Red and White Dragons)*. *The Sight 2 (Stonehenge, the Giants' Dance)*. *The Crystal Cave*. 2-2-2-2; 3-2-0-0; piano, celesta, timpani, 3 perc; strings

In several connected sections. Organized with leitmotifs and a specific program, not unlike the longer tone poems of Strauss, but with the harmonic language of a Berg or Frank Martin. "The Dallas Symphony does not often perform very new music, so it was a treat to hear, as the opening work of 1987, a substantial, attractive piece by a composer not only living but young. He is Dan Welcher, and his composition *The Visions of Merlin* was performed by Eduardo Mata and the orchestra.... [It] is a musical depiction of three scenes from the legend of King Arthur's magician. Welcher uses exotic, evocative sounds to create an air of mystery. The work is colorfully orchestrated, and though it is spiced up with sounds that are not conventionally pretty, the overall impression is of an ingratiating piece that never overstays its welcome despite its considerable length." —Olin Chism, *Dallas Times Herald*. "*The Visions of Merlin* is dramatic, lyrical, and romantic, with much spectacular writing." — Dewey Faulkner, *San Antonio Express*.

ALEC WILDER

B. 1907, Rochester NY. "Wrote popular songs and arranged music for Frank Sinatra, Judy Garland, Perry Como, Peggy Lee, and the bands of Benny Goodman and Jimmy Dorsey. Wilder excels particularly in short operas scored for a limited ensemble of singers and instruments and suitable for performance in schools." — *Baker's Biographical Dictionary of Musicians*. Works incl.: chamber works, concertos (hn, ob, sax, tpt) & various ensembles, piano pieces, sonatas (bsn, vc, E hn,, hn, ob, tpt, trb, vla), songs & other vocal pieces.

Sonata for Clarinet and Piano. 11m *Pub.:* Margun (score & part; ed. by Gunther Schuller).
1. Allegro moderato. 2. Andante. 3. Grazioso. 4. Allegro con fuoco.

"The *Sonata* for clarinet and piano illustrates well [Wilder's] development of a highly personal language and a strong and versatile technique which enabled him to use that language with great flexibility for a variety of purposes. The basic idiom is like what one might hear in the best Broadway shows: swinging rhythms, broad lyric phrases, lots of parallel tenths and altered dominants. These elements are shaped into unpretentious yet convincing forms. The first of the four movements, *Allegro moderato,* lies somewhere between a traditional sonata-allegro and a three-part invention. The second, *Andante,* is a blue-mood song; relaxed and expansive, it never sags. Wilder uses the simplest of materials to build a large and beautiful movement. The third, *Grazioso,* is a graceful dance, and the finale, *Allegro con fuoco* — the most overtly jazz influenced — is a rhythm-piece which grows out of a four-to-the-bar bass pattern.

"The demands on the performers are not extreme, but fast fingers and a feel for jazz phrasing would be useful. For the latter, the editing indications of Gunther Schuller are very helpful." — Jerome Rosen, in *Notes* (Music Library Association), 12/84.

Suite 1 (Effie Suite) for Tuba and Piano. *Prem.:* Harvey Phillips (tba). *Pub.:* Margun (score & part).
In six movements.

"The 'Effie Suite' by Alec Wilder is one of the most engaging and virtuosic works in the solo tuba repertoire. The *Suite* was written for tuba soloist Harvey Phillips and is only one of many tuba works composed by Wilder. The work is in six movements, each describing the humorous escapades of Effie the Elephant. The music is highly descriptive, following Effie as she chases a monkey, falls in love, takes a dancing lesson, joins the carnival, goes folk dancing, and, finally, sings a lullaby.

"Both the piano and tuba writing are ambitious, particularly in terms of velocity and range for the solo tuba. Although the mood is light, there is ample room for interpretive expression, which makes this a fine showcase for the advanced player." — Frank Byrne, in *Notes* (Music Library Association), 6/85.

Ellen Taaffe Zwilich

B. 1939, Miami FL. *Educ.:* FL State Univ, Juilliard Schl of Music. Member of American SO, Leopold Stokowski, cond. Winner, Elizabeth Sprague Coolidge Chamber Music Prize, Guggenheim Fellowship, Ernst von Dohnanyi Citation, American Acad/Inst of Arts and Letters award, Pulitzer Prize. *Works incl.: Celebration* (orch), *Chamber Symphony,* concertos (pno, tpt/5 players), *Images* (2 pno/orch), quartets, *Trio* (pno/vln/ vc).

Composer statement (courtesy George Sturm, Music Associates of America): "It seems to me that there is something very deep about music, in the same category as falling in love or a religious experience. People do things they feel to be deeply enriching, because they are totally pulled along, because they *want to.* I have other preoccupations that go back many years, but music for me is different. I remember my musical toys when I was a child. I can't imagine life without music at the center of it. But I don't know *why.*"

"[Ellen Taaffe Zwilich has created some] exquisitely honed works in a variety of mediums from string trio to symphony. She writes in an idiosyncratic style that, without ostentation or gimmickry, is always recognizably hers.... Mrs. Zwilich's compositions reflect a concision and craft that appeal to both professional musicians and the general audience. Her music is complex, yet should prove accessible to those willing to listen closely. It is directly emotive, yet devoid of vulgarity, and characterized by a taut chromatic intensity that stretches the limits of tonality while rarely venturing outside them....

"Like many composers, Mrs. Zwilich, the daughter of an airplane pilot, was writing music before she formally knew how. 'I used to simply make things up on the piano, and play them again and again; I didn't write anything down until I was about 10. By that point, I had begun studying with the neighborhood piano teacher in Miami, where I was born and brought up. It was an unhappy relationship; she made me play all these silly children's pieces, and I thought my own compositions were better.'

"By the time she was in her teens, Mrs. Zwilich was proficient on three instruments—piano, violin, and trumpet. She wrote a highschool fight song, was the concertmaster of the orchestra, first trumpet in the band, and a student conductor as well. She continued to compose, and, by the age of 18, she was turning out full-scale orchestral works....

> Copyright © 1990 United Features Syndicate Inc.
> National syndication; published Gannett Westchester Newspapers 10/13/90.

"She became the first woman to receive a doctorate in composition from Juilliard, in 1975. Shortly thereafter, Pierre Boulez programmed her *Symposium for Orchestra* (1973) in New York, and she began to receive awards, commissions, and critical praise. She produced a *String Quartet* (1974), a *Sonata in Three Movements* for Violin and Piano (1973-74) [below], and the *Chamber Symphony* in 1979....

" 'I only spend a few hours a day actively engaged in writing music, but I think that being a composer is like being a writer of any sort—there's never really a moment when you're not working. I attend concerts as a composer, listen to records as a composer, think about life as a composer, and everything adds to the music, one way or another.

" 'There's a funny story behind my string trio. Somebody I hadn't seen in quite a while called me, and asked me if I would be interested in doing a work for their first concert. I said that I didn't have the time, but we kept talking for a while, and during the conversation I started to hear music. The trio was already beginning to take shape in my head. So I said I'd think it over, and I did, throughout the rest of the day, and, I guess, through the night as well. In any event, I woke up the next morning, and the whole opening section was waiting to be written down.' "—Tim Page, in *The New York Times Magazine*, 7/14/85.

"[Conductor John] Nelson says he was drawn to Zwilich's music right away. 'I don't feel that new music has to be out of reach of contemporary ears,' he says. 'It's not true historically that new music is never appreciated by its early listeners—it's about fifty-fifty. Her music is very genuine, very natural—it just pours out of her. I'm a very structurally conscious person, yet at the same time I have a passionate desire to communicate, and her music does both of those things. She has dramatic ideas that she builds with great reason. Look at the *Prologue and Variations* [for String Orchestra]: there is a minor second, which inverted becomes a major seventh, and that's the structure of the whole thing, with tremendously exciting variations. And having been an orchestral player she knows the sound of strings—which is refreshing for the string players, who feel left out by many contemporary composers.' Nelson says his audiences also respond to Zwilich's music.

"Her music has been compared to Shostakovich and Bartók, but it is indeed written in her own idiom. It is very vertical and, in some of the later scores particularly, often unsettled or even violent. There is tremendous rhythmic vitality and imaginative use of percussion. Violins in the highest register are contrasted with low rumblings in the bass; a line will start, to be interrupted suddenly by a burst of brass, then begin again, only to be interrupted anew. Zwilich does not talk about her sources, except to say that she has grown less inhibited over the years about 'letting go in my music,' and that music 'is about passion and adventure, and all the human experiences. It's something that comes from very deep inside me, and it's got all of me in it. I think that if we're good artists, our work is always more interesting than we are in a certain way.'

"All the more reason, she says, that concertgoing should not be routine. 'We need to retain a sense of adventure in the concert hall. You can't write either words or music if you start by eliminating this and that; you get everything flowing by doing a lot of things that you will later reject. The more free and open you are, the better your final product.' Appreciation of new music requires similar openness on the part of the audiences, and the composer's presence at concerts encourages this. 'The audience must see that the composer is not a marble bust, is not only not dead but looks like one of them, went to high school, and so on. It *means* something to them. It reminds them of what music has always been, which is a form of human communication, not someone coming into a concert hall and saying, "I want to know exactly what I'm going to hear, what it's going to sound like." Music is about life and death, and it should not become a set commodity. That stands in the way of people perceiving what it's all about....

"'Anyone who lives in America in the late 20th Century and is sensitive to the world around them has got to relish diversity,' she maintains. 'It's our national character. I think we're beginning to see audiences and performers and composers who no longer talk about how you must do only this or that. My composer colleagues run the gamut from so-called minimalism to total serialism. I welcome the existence of all kinds of music. I don't want to shut anything off. And I think you're seeing more and more of this [eclecticism] among conductors and composers and audiences.'

"Zwilich's love of diversity shows in her own music. Powerful rhythms remind one that she was once a jazz band performer. Her percussion parts sometimes sound like rock and roll. And yet the string writing speaks of a long love affair with the violin and the classical tradition. 'I'm not trying to throw out the past,' she says. 'Notice how the term "angry young man" doesn't work for women? And I don't feel the need to say I must not like rock music or go disco dancing. In my music, what I want to do is draw all the threads of my life together. And I wish this for all of my friends who are composers too.' " — Heidi Waleson, "Composer Living Her Dream", in *Symphony* Magazine, 4-5/86.

Concerto for Flute and Orchestra (1990). 16m *Comm. & prem.*: Doriot Anthony Dwyer (fl), Boston SO, Seiji Ozawa, cond.
1. Allegro. 2. Lento. 3. Allegro.

"Zwilich's concerto, one in a series she has been writing for wind instruments, is a dazzler. It is in her familiar style, at once challenging, individual, and accessible. The three movements, which last 16 minutes in a more or less continuous arch, begin with a bright, virtuosic Allegro. A cadenza helps to usher in a Lento in which the flute sings a silvery melody over slowly changing chords in the orchestra. The Allegro finale is driven by highly charged, sometimes syncopated rhythms. Zwilich and [retiring BSO flutist Doriot Anthony] Dwyer worked together in the crafting of the concerto, and the resulting orchestration cushions and flatters the solo part. There are no competing flutes in the orchestra, though other woodwinds have a good bit to say. Exotic percussion instruments, including four suspended cymbals, a conga drum, and crotales, add spice. In key places the flute must blend with cornets, which Zwilich specifies in place of trumpets." — Andrew L. Pincus, in *Musical America*, 9/90.

Concerto Grosso 1985 (to Handel's *Sonata in D* for Violin and Continuo, First Movement) for Orchestra (1985). 15m Comm. by Washington Friends of Handel. *Prem.*: Handel Festival O, Stephen Simon, cond. *Rec.*: New World Records (Stereo LP) NW 372: New York P, Zubin Mehta, cond. *Pub:* Mobart Music (distr. Jerona Music Corp. — full score; parts on rental).
1-2(E hn)-0-1; 2-0-0-0; hpsd; strings
1. Maestoso. 2. Presto. 3. Largo. 4. Presto. 5. Maestoso.

CONCERTO GROSSO 1985
I

Ellen Taaffe Zwilich

"Ms. Zwilich, when asked to write a commemorative work in honor of Handel, almost immediately thought to base her own work on that composer's D-major Violin Sonata. 'I performed the work many years ago,' she said recently. 'And I especially love the opening theme of the first movement—the striking head motive and the beauty of the generative tension between the theme and the elegant bass line.' The resulting composition, she says, is a 'twentieth-century response to the spirit of George Frideric Handel. My concerto is both inspired by Handel's sonata and, I hope, imbued with his spirit.'

"The concerto is in five movements, in an overall arch form. The first and fifth, and the second and fourth movements are pairs, with the middle movement functioning as the keystone in the arch. It is in the first and fifth movements, both marked *Maestoso*, that the Handelian 'spirit' is most obvious. The two, in fact, can almost be regarded as the ornate Baroque frame around the edges of the *Concerto's* three middle movements. The first movement of the Violin Sonata, as pointed out above, is in a rough binary form. Zwilich's first movement has imbedded within it—in the form of numerous quotations—the entire A section of Handel's work; her fifth movement contains the entire B section. Each of the two movements is written in a musical language that is undeniably hers, but she has woven into the texture—almost like the dominant colors of a tapestry—the Handel quotations. The result is somewhat sectional, the old contrasting with the new. The composer, in fact, wants the differences to be as marked as possible, and has instructed the instrumentalists, when playing the Handel sections, to perform in obvious Baroque continuo style.

"The three inner movements are freely composed, with no interpolated quotations. Movements two and four, both marked *Presto*, are a pair of free fantasias; the fourth, in fact, is essentially a *da capo* repetition of the second. These two function as an inner frame for the middle *Largo* movement which, according to the composer, is the most important of the work. 'The third movement is the emotional peak, the most personal movement of the concerto,' she says. 'It, too, is a free fantasy, inspired by Handel's theme, but without the direct quotations I used in movements one and five. I found myself using compositional techniques typical of the Baroque period, including terraced dynamics, repeated melodic phrases, and suspension-like constructions. These are techniques I would not normally use, but I felt inspired to do so because of the fact that this piece was based on Handel.' " —Program notes, 1985 premiere.

Double Quartet for Strings (1984). 21m *Comm. & prem.:* Chamber Music Soc of Lincoln Center. *Rec.:* New World Records (Stereo LP) NW 372: New York P members, Ellen Taafe Zwilich, cond. *Pub.:* Merion Music (distr. Theodore Presser — score; parts on rental).
In three movements.

"If the kind of lamentation we hear in the great Shostakovich slow movements hovers in the background of the trumpet concerto and the *Concerto Grosso 1985*, in the *Double Quartet* it becomes the central principle: even the allegro vivo of the third movement is interrupted by a threnody that bears most of the music's emotional weight. From the first pages (where uneasy but obsessive ostinatos unsettle the music's soaring lines) to the last (stark, almost motionless), this is a constantly troubling work; harsh, intense, compelling, it reminds us that contemporary tonal music — even contemporary neo-Romantic tonal music — need not be slick." — Peter J. Rabinowitz, in *Fanfare: The Magazine for Serious Record Collectors*, 11-12/89.

"Throughout [the] piece Mrs. Zwilich displays clear-eyed maturity and a rare sense of balance. She writes music that pleases the ear and yet has spine." — Donal Henahan, *The New York Times*.

"I become as fully acquainted with a new composition as possible before I begin writing it [the composer says]. For example, when I began my *Double Quartet*, I went to Alice Tully Hall [at New York's Lincoln Center] to find out exactly where the players would be sitting, and how their sound would reach the audience. By the time I actually started composing, I dind't have to just jot down a disembodied, arbitrary B-flat. I knew that it was a specific B-flat for viola, in this register or that, this context or that. In the case of my *Double Quartet*, I even knew whether it would sound from the right or the left side of the stage....

"I wanted the audience to realize that this was not just a piece for two cellos, two violas, and four violins, but two separate string quartets, simultaneously competitive and cooperative. Chamber music demands a continual trade-off in its musical hierarchy. Now the first violin has the melody, now it's taken by the cello; now the one quartet leads the way, now the other." — Ellen Taaffe Zwilich, in *The New York Times Magazine*, 7/14/85 [quoted as a part of Tim Page's article excerpted above].

Sonata in Three Movements for Violin and Piano. 11m *Rec.:* Cambridge Records (Stereo LP) CRS 2834: Joseph Zwilich (vln), James Gemmell (pno). *Pub.:* Elkan-Vogel (distr. Theodore Presser).

"The *Sonata in Three Movements,* widely performed here and abroad, was selected for the repertoire list of the Kennedy Center-Rockefeller Foundation Competition for Excellence in the performance of American music, held in 1980 for violinists.

"The composer writes: '*Sonata in Three Movements* was written for my late husband, violinist Joseph Zwilich, who premiered it on a tour of European capitals. Writing for the violin has always held special meaning for me (it is my own instrument), but this composition grew out of my feelings for Joseph as well as from my particular fondness for the wonderfully dramatic and expressive powers of the violin.

" 'It is cast in three movements, of which the first is the most complex, with contrast between lyrical and vigorous material, and contrast between relatively free, recitative-like material (culminating in a cadenza for the violin) and the otherwise strict tempi. The second movement is slow and lyrical; the third movement short, fast, and rhythmically propulsive.' " — Liner notes for Cambridge Stereo LP CRS 2834.

"Well-made, concentrated, knowing about sonorous values, and intensely personal, this music has a direct singing humanness to it." — Richard Buell, *The Boston Globe.*

Symphony 1 (Three Movements for Orchestra) (1982). Grammy nominee; Arturo Toscanini Music Critics Award; winner, 1983 Pulitzer Prize. *Comm. & prem.:* American Composers O, Gunther Schuller, cond. *Rec.:* New World Records (Digital Stereo LP) NW 336: Indianapolis SO, John Nelson, cond. (Arturo Toscanini Music Critics Award). *Pub.:* Margun (score; performance materials on rental). 2(pic)-1 E.hn-1 b.cl-2(cbsn); 4-2-3-1; timp, 3 perc, pno, harp; strings 1. (7m) 2. (6m) 3. (4m)

"The excellent premiere recording now provides an opportunity to discover what a treasure we have in this work and this composer." — Andrew L. Pincus, *The New York Times.*

"Like other recent pieces by this distinguished composer *(String Trio, Cello Symphony),* this work is sturdy, idiomatic, straightforward, and very conservative; it has little in common stylistically with her earlier, more chromatic pieces (the 1974 *String Quartet,* for example). In most of her works, Zwilich shows a fondness for large structures growing from simple intervallic cells, and the *Symphony No. 1* is no exception with its almost complete dependence on the minor third as the central sound and primary building block.

"The three movements range in mood and gesture from quiet and serene to robust and highly rhythmic. The instruments are always handled effectively..., but timbral concerns do not seem to be of great interest to the composer in this piece. Rather, motivic unity and exploration of very simple materials are at the heart of this music. The instrumentaion used is large but standard, with no unusual additions to any section. The work could be played with enjoyment by orchestras ranging in proficiency from high school to professional." — Andrew Frank, in *Notes* (Music Library Association), 12/86.

"[Zwilich's *Symphony No. 1*] aims at emotional directness rather than abstractions of any kind, preferring clarity and comprehensibility at the risk of repetitiousness and overcoherence. [The] symphony has a strenuous first movement, a slow movement that is... an elegy, and a brisk rondo finale. Interestingly enough, sonata form, the traditional vehicle for symphonic expression, is nowhere in evidence — all movements are either 'cellular' and ongoing or simply sectional in structure. Conventional tonality does not play a large part, but the work is clearly centered on a particular pitch, and has occasional expressive recourse to elements of triadic harmony. The composer makes frequent use of long pedals, particularly in [the] slow movement, and ostinatos in the fast movements. [This is a work of] solid orchestral craftsmanship. It 'sounds'....

"The music of Ellen Taaffe Zwilich is notable for its intimacy, sincerity, and clear suggestions of personal feeling. Her *First Symphony* is most effective in its middle movement, with its long, arching string melody over pulsating thirds. The finale, brief, inconclusive, and totally lacking in brutality, is also engaging.... The whole work is eminently clear to the ear, consistently stressing minor thirds and centered on the pitch A." — Fred Hauptman, in *American Music*, Fall 1987.

"In her preface to the printed score of [the *Symphony No. 1*], Zwilich speaks of some of her central musical concerns — concerns that link her music to the past and the present and send it searching into the future. She addresses formal and harmonic issues that appear in more than one period of the history of music; she speaks of her commitment to the joy of performing and to the musicians who perform her music. Out of her personal synthesis of these and other factors comes music that is her own:

> First, I have long been interested in the elaboration of large-scale works from the initial material. This "organic" approach to musical form fascinates me both in the development of the material and in the fashioning of a musical idea that contains the "seeds" of the work to follow.

> Second, in my recent works I have been developing techniques that combine modern principles of continuous variation with older (but still immensely satisfying) principles, such as melodic recurrence and clearly defined areas of contrast.
>
> Finally, *Symphony No. 1* was written with great affection for the modern orchestra, not only for its indescribable richness and variety of color, but also for the virtuosity and artistry of its players.

"Zwilich accepts commissions only when they fit what she wants to compose next. She began the symphony, however, before she had a commission, which came from the American Composers Orchestra and the National Endowment for the Arts. Everything in the work arises from the melodic and harmonic implications of the first fifteen bars, music Zwilich says she felt compelled to write. Over a rustle of percussion, the violas, clarified by the harp, sound a minor third, which is then taken up, *accelerando*, by flute and cellos. This makes a kind of motto that signals evolutions of tempo and musical character; these work up to a sustained allegro that ultimately subsides into an ending as quiet as the beginning. All the most complex harmonies come from piling third upon third upon third. Although the structure of the movement is not conventional, the generative use of the interval is perhaps not remote from Brahms' procedures.

"The second and third movements are more traditional in their origins: the second movement is a song form; the third is a rondo. But they are not traditional in either sound or form. The slow movement contains an important part for vibraphone and an eloquent *cantabile* solo for tuba; bells—a characteristic sound in much of Zwilich's music—keep tolling the music home. The last movement combines the functions of scherzo and finale, though the edgy rondo lacks the traditional reassurances of that form: the material retains its chameleon capacity for continuous development and for surprise."—Richard Dyer, from liner notes for New World Records Digital Stereo LP NW 336.

"When Richard Dyer, author of the liner notes [for the New World Records] disc, writes that 'Zwilich accepts commissions only when they fit what she wants to compose next,' he underplays one of the musical phenomenons of the 1980s. In the last six years this very accomplished composer has risen from relative obscurity to gain a Pulitzer Prize and arrive at a point where she is even turning down commissions! Now, I ask you, how many American composers are in a position to do that? She has apparently become one of the few American composers making a living exclusively from commissions.

"And it is no wonder. Zwilich (prounce the *ch* as *k*) writes music for audiences—and for performers. Her music is readily accessible to virtually any assembled throng. At the same time, the expressiveness and finesse of her lines, frequently given over to solo instruments even in large ensembles, are surely welcomed by instrumentalists. Her music is an outgrowth of the performance tradition."—Stephen W. Ellis, in *Fanfare: The Magazine for Serious Record Collectors*, 9-10/86.

Symphony 2 (Cello Symphony) (1985). 24m *Comm. & prem.*: San Francisco SO, Edo de Waart, cond. *Rec.*: New World Records: Louisville O, Lawrence Leighton Smith, cond. *Pub.*: Merion Music (distr. Theodore Presser—score; parts on rental).
3-3-3-3; 4-3-3-1; timp, 3 perc, pno; strings
In three movements.

"It is refreshing to find a composer of this decade whose music is both accessible to audiences and yet challenging to the technique and intellect of the professional musician. Such a composer is Ellen Taaffee Zwilich, the first woman to earn a doctorate in composition from Juilliard. Dedicated to communicating something about life and living through her music, she exhibits in her work an uncommon rhythmic vitality that seems to appeal to contemporary listeners. Since her *First Symphony*, for which she won the Pulitzer Prize, Zwilich has explored various genres in works such as the *Double String Quartet* for strings, the *Trio* for piano, violin and cello, the *Piano Concerto*, and *Tanzspiel*, commissioned by the New York City Ballet.

"Her *Second Symphony* is dedicated to Edo de Waart, who conducted the world premiere. Written to showcase the outstanding violoncello section of the San Francisco Symphony, the work makes full use of the cello's wide range (from $C^\#$ to a''') and is aptly subtitled the 'Cello Symphony'. More somber in mood than Zwilich's *First Symphony* or her more recent *Celebration* for orchestra, this piece sets singing cello lines against a dark backdrop of rumbling brass, and makes use of sharply contrasted orchestral colors to delineate motives and themes. Though the work is decidedly tonal, its consistent use of a minor second (and its octave displacements) as a germinal motive throughout all three movements places it squarely in the tradition of twentieth-century musical chromaticism.

"The first movement, in a tightly constructed sonata form, is written as a concerto for the orchestra's cello section. Each of the two main lyrical themes presented in the exposition by the cellos is announced by a violent rhythmic motive; these motives permeate the fabric of the movement. Beginning with the short, staccato accompaniment to the second theme, the development fragments both themes and their rhythmic motives, creating a sparse texture. The recapitulation is heralded by the reappearance of the first rythmic motive, in canon between the upper and lower winds and strings. This penchant for extreme registers is also evident in the cadenza for the cello section, where both unison and divisi writing fully exploit the instrument's capabilities.

"The stark, emotional quality of the second movement contrasts with the fierce drive of the first. The second movement is written in a loose three-part form, with its smaller sub-sections delineated by meter changes and motivic contrast. The larger sections are defined by passages of suspension, where Zwilich explores the expressive power of the violins, trumpets, and clarinets, respectively. At the end of the first larger section a Stravinskian use of ostinato is coupled with a Shostakovich-like use of octaves in the violin melody. A passage reminiscent of a funeral march (mm. 34-38) adds to the pervasive feeling of grief, and a haunting violin solo closes the movement.

"The third movement, a tightly-woven rondo, begins as a frenzied, macabre dance in triple meter. The opening pizzicato figure in the cellos is a transformation of the first rhythmic motive of the work. Themes from previous movements are interspersed throughout the dance, and sections are defined by meter changes. An unmistakeable, fully orchestrated return of the beginning of the first movement occurs in m. 282, with the lyrical cello passage now given to the violins. The spectral mood is altered in m. 303, with new lyric material for the middle range of the cellos. A short coda concludes the work, its final ten measures hammering out the rhythm of the germinal motive in octaves.

"The score is an extremely legible reproduction of the composer's manuscript, and includes pertinent bowings along with other specific indications for the cellists. Because of the high technical demands placed upon the cello section, performances of this work will be limited to university or professional orchestras." — Suzanne Kimberly Barber, in *Notes* (Music Library Association), 9/89.

"Ellen Taaffe Zwilich's swift rise to popularity... provides a significant comment on the direction of American symphonic music, for she relies heavily on the language and gestures of neo-Classicism, exploring the orchestra traditionally with the exception, perhaps, of instrumental range. There is little hint in [her *Second Symphony* of Fred Lerdahl's complex textures, for example], despite the ample percussion section and the occasional multiple division of the strings.... Zwilich's appeal, however, is not superficial; beyond the medium lies a significant, though often frustratingly elusive, subtext. In her music, a minimum of material frequently provides a complicated network of cross-relationships; at a crucial point in the work—a cadenza, perhaps—a revelation may challenge the listener to unravel the web. Such is the simplicity of the medium that deciphering the message becomes paramount.

"In the *Second Symphony*, true to form, Zwilich permutates thematic relationships within a straightforward formal organization, challenging the audience to perceive a larger plan...

"Serialism has been an important factor in the evolution of Zwilich's style. But for all its chromatic melodies built on abstract interval patterns, and long-term devices such as dominant substitutions, the *Second Symphony* may be described as tonal; a D/A axis supports the work. The formal scheme is simple: three movements, the first binary, with a nod to sonata form, the second slow and rhapsodic, and the last a rondo of sorts whose refrain is a triple-meter scherzo. The basic thematic materials are laid out in the first movement: an opening, fanfare-like melodic line based on A with a distinctive rhythm reminiscent of the double-dotted French overture style; a rising arpeggio, romantic cello melody, and accented, irregular crotchets against a pounding, regular background. They produce a strange mixture; used synchronously, the first two ideas prevent the music from being either rousing or lyrical. Almost at the end of the movement, however, before completing their cadenza, the cellos slowly intone a curious, unaccompanied line, like a fragment of plainsong: E-F-E-D-C-B-A. This is the only truly diatonic moment in the symphony.

"In the second movement, contrapuntal melodies unfold, but as in a dream so that we are never brought closer to the source. Beneath the counterpoint, and sometimes substituting for it, full sustained chords are articulated by rich piano arpeggios. Fragments of the haunting plainsong descent occur, often distorted, in Ivesian reminiscence, occasionally interrupted by vaguely irritating trumpet reminders of the fanfare rhythm.

"The irregular tonal treatment of the first movement (where the second subject returns transposed up a minor third) is echoed in the third: the expository material in D, which recalls the fanfare motif, returns down a tone in C and later, in truncated form as a coda, back in D. Between these major sections, shorter, contrasting ones recall the lyricism of the slow movement. The plainsong material makes an extended though distorted appearance on the cellos just before the coda. A few bars later it appears contrapuntally on violins doubled by upper winds; the two parts pause on $C^{\#}$ and B^{b} respectively before resolving with the whole orchestra on to a resounding, sustained and triumphant A.

"But what of the subtext? The economy of material in this work creates a maze from which the listener may extract him/herself by assembling a hierarchy of motifs. Tonally oriented listeners, undoubtedly Zwilich's intended audience, will be drawn primarily to the plainsong material, though its appearance is belated and hardly ubiquitous. Its original, pure diatonicism never returns; in the second movement it snakes through all kinds of chromaticism, and in the third it arrives only with some difficulty at its goal. But on its arrival it proves a joyous affirmation of the tonality of the work while presenting its audience with a parable of twentieth-century tonality itself." — Rhian Samuel, in *Music and Letters*, 5/89.

INDEX OF COMPOSITIONS

VOCAL

Choral
    Argento: *Te Deum*, 31
    Bolcom: *Songs of Innocence and of Experience* for Solo Voices, Chorus and Orchestra, 106
    Brant: *Western Springs: A Spatial Assembly* for 2 Orchestras, 2 Choruses and 2 Jazz Combos, 112
    Carter: *Prayers of the People* for Speaker, Alto, Tenor, Chorus and Orchestra, 132
    Finney: *Spherical Madrigals*, 180
    Flagello: *Te Deum for All Mankind* for Chorus and Orchestra, 185
    Henze: *Orpheus Behind the Wire*, 204
    Hovhaness: *Magnificat* for Soprano, Alto, Tenor, Baritone, Chorus & Orchestra, 210
    Husa: *Apotheosis of This Earth* for Orchestra with Chorus, 220
    Johnston: *Journeys*, for Contralto, Chorus and Orchestra, 236
    Johnston: *Sonnets of Desolation*, 236
    Josephs: *Requiem* for Bass-Baritone, Chorus, String Quintet and Orchestra, 250
    Kubik: *Magic, Magic, Magic* for Solo Voices, Chorus and Piano (or Orchestra), 258
    Lloyd Webber: *Requiem* for Tenor, Contralto, Chorus and Orchestra, 268
    Madden: *The Chime Child*, 291
    Martorella: *Please Come Inside* for Chorus (or Solo Voice) and Piano, 293
    Paulus: *So Hallow'd Is the Time* (Christmas cantata), 329
    Perle: *Songs of Praise and Lamentation* for Solo Voices, Chorus and Orchestra, 372
    Rorem: *Three Choruses for Christmas*, 445
    Rosner: *Requiem*, 453
    Thomas: *Requiem for Children's Chorus and Youth Symphony*, 555
    Tippett: *The Mask of Time* (oratorio), 558

Stage Works
    Adams: *Nixon in China* (opera), 2
    Amram: *Twelfth Night* (opera), 29
    Eaton: *Danton and Robespierre* (opera), 160
    Glass: *Einstein on the Beach* (opera), 194
    Lloyd Webber: *Jesus Christ Superstar* (rock opera), 265
    Machover: *VALIS* (opera), 286
    Mayer: *A Death in the Family* (opera), 295
    Menotti: *The Marriage* (opera), 301

INDEX OF COMPOSITIONS

Paulus: *The Postman Always Rings Twice* (opera), 327
Paulus: *The Village Singer* (opera), 334
Reise: *Rasputin* (opera), 402
Rosner: *The Chronicle of Nine* (opera), 451
Schonthal: *Princess Maleen* (fairytale love story for children), 497
Schuman: *The Mighty Casey* (1-act opera), 505
Schuman: *A Question of Taste* (1-act opera), 506
Sondheim: *Anyone Can Whistle* (musical play), 535
Sondheim: *Company* (musical play), 536
Sondheim: *Follies* (musical play), 538
Sondheim: *The Frogs* (musical comedy), 541
Sondheim: *A Funny Thing Happened on the Way to the Forum* (musical comedy), 542
Sondheim: *Into the Woods* (musical play), 543
Sondheim: *A Little Night Music* (musical show), 544
Sondheim: *Marry Me a Little* (musical show), 545
Sondheim: *Merrily We Roll Along* (musical play), 546
Sondheim: *Pacific Overtures* (musical play), 546
Sondheim: *Saturday Night* (musical show), 548
Sondheim: *Side by Side by Sondheim* (musical revue), 548
Sondheim: *Sunday in the Park with George* (musical show), 549
Sondheim: *Sweeney Todd, the Demon Barber of Fleet Street* (musical play), 550
Welcher: *Della's Gift* (opera), 584

Voice(s) & Instruments
Amram: *The Trail of Beauty* for Mezzo-Soprano, Oboe and Orchestra, 25
Carter: *Night Scenes* for Speaker, Flute, Clarinet, Two Percussionists, Piano and Celesta, 132
Carter: *Symphony* for Medium Voice and Orchestra, 132
Flagello: *Contemplazioni di Michelangelo* for Soprano and Orchestra, 183
Gideon: *Creature to Creature* for Voice, Flute and Harp, 187
Gideon: *The Resounding Lyre* for Tenor and Instruments, 187
Gideon: *Sonnets from Shakespeare* for Baritone, Trumpet and Strings, 188
Gideon: *Spirit Above the Dust* for Mezzo-Soprano and Instruments, 188
Gideon: *Wing'd Hour* for Tenor, Flute, Oboe, Violin, Cello and Vibraphone, 189
Hovhaness: *Avak the Healer* for Soprano, Trumpet and Strings, 208
Martorella: *Please Come Inside* for Solo Voice (or Chorus) and Piano, 293
Mayer: *Enter Ariel* (6 songs) for Soprano, Clarinet and Piano, 298
Mayer: *Passage* (7 songs) for Mezzo-Soprano (Soprano), Flute and Harp, 298
Mompou: *Cançons Becquerianas* for Voice and Piano, 305

Rorem: *Serenade on Five English Poems* for Mezzo-Soprano, Violin, Viola and Piano, 444
Schonthal: *Totengesänge* for Soprano and Piano, 501
Schwantner: *New Morning for the World: "Daybreak of Freedom"* for Speaker and Orchestra, 518
Thomas: *echos* for Soprano, Mezzo-Soprano and Chamber Orchestra, 552

CHAMBER (10 or Fewer Instruments)

General chamber
    Beck: *Scherzo* for Clarinet, Violin and Cello, 67
    Beck: *Sonata* for Cello and Piano, 67
    Briccetti: *Sonata* for Flute and Piano, 115
    Carter: *Variations* for 2 Flutes, Oboe, English Horn, 2 B^b Clarinets, 2 Horns and 2 Bassoons, 133
    Corea: *Inside Out* (jazz quintet), 135
    Erb: *Sonata* for Clarinet and Percussion, 173
    Finney: *Two Studies* for Saxophones (1 player) and Piano, 180
    Grant: *Echoes of a Lost Serenade* for Flute, Guitar and Harp, 200
    Grant: *Epiphanies: A Childhood Album* for 10 Winds, 200
    Machover: *Bug-Mudra* for 2 Guitars, Percussion, Conductor and Electronics, 284
    Martorella: *Sonata 2* for Viola (or Clarinet) and Piano, 293
    Perna: *Deux Berceuses* for Flute and Piano (or Orchestra), 375
    Perna: *Three Conversations Between Two Flutists*, 375
    Perna: *Fantasy-Sonata* for Unaccompanied Flute, 375
    Perna: *Nonet (In Memoriam Charles T. Griffes)* for Winds, 375
    Persichetti: *Parable* for Solo Trombone, 382
    Persichetti: *Serenade 4* for Violin and Piano, 382
    Picker: *Octet* for Oboe, Bass Clarinet, Horn, Violin, Cello, Double Bass, Harp and Vibraphone/Marimba, 393
    Picker: *Rhapsody* for Violin and Piano, 394
    Pujo: *Cinco [5] Preludios* for Solo Guitar, 395
    Rosner: *Sonata 2* for Cello and Piano, 453
    Rosner: *Sonata* for Horn and Piano, 454
    Rózsa: *Rhapsody* for Cello and Piano, 462
    Rózsa: *Toccata capricciosa* for Cello Solo, 463
    Schonthal: *Music for Horn and Piano*, 495
    Wilder: *Sonata* for Clarinet and Piano, 587
    Wilder: *Suite 1 (Effie Suite)* for Tuba and Piano, 587
    Zwilich: *Double Quartet* for Strings, 595
    Zwilich: *Sonata in Three Movements* for Violin and Piano, 595

Organ
    Persichetti: *Dryden Liturgical Suite*, 381

INDEX OF COMPOSITIONS

Piano four-hands
   Grant: *Overture to "Chautauqua"*, 200
   Ince: *Cross Scintillations*, 230
   Josephs: *Doubles* for 2 Pianos, 249
   Mayer: *Octagon* for 2 Pianos (or Piano and Orchestra), 296
   Persichetti: *Concerto* for Piano, Four Hands, 379

Piano solo
   Albright: *Five Chromatic Dances*, 7
   Bassett: *Preludes*, 34
   Bentzon: *Sonata 18*, 72
   Bentzon: *Sonata 19*, 72
   Bentzon: *Sonata 20*, 72
   Bolcom: *Twelve New Etudes*, 102
   Flagello: *Sonata*, 184
   Ince: *My Friend Mozart*, 233
   Martorella: *Starlight Transmissions*, 293
   Perle: *Ballade*, 363
   Perle: *Six Etudes*, 367
   Perle: *Six New Etudes*, 367
   Persichetti: *Reflective Keyboard Studies*, 382
   Persichetti: *Serenade 7*, 383
   Persichetti: *Sonatas 1-12*, 383
   Persichetti: *Three Toccatinas*, 392
   Rieti: *Dodici Preludi*, 439
   Rózsa: *Sonata*, 463
   Schonthal: *The Canticles of Hieronymus*, 493
   Schonthal: *Variations in Search of a Theme*, 502
   Schwantner: *Veiled Autumn (Kindertodeslied)*, 520
   Thomson: Ballet and Film Scores Transcribed for Piano: *The Plough That Broke the Plains, Filling Station, Lord Byron on the Continent, Louisiana Story*, 557
   Tippett: *Sonata 4*, 568
   Walker: *Prelude and Caprice*, 577
   Walker: *Sonata 4*, 577
   Walker: *Spatials*, 577
   Walker: *Variations on a Kentucky Folk Song*, 577
   Welcher: *Dance Variations*, 583
   Welcher: *Sonatina*, 585

Quartets (for strings unless otherwise specified)
   Beck: *Quartet 2*, 66
   Bloch: *Quartet 1*, 75
   Bloch: *Quartet 2*, 80
   Bloch: *Quartet 3*, 85
   Bloch: *Quartet 4*, 88
   Bloch: *Quartet 5*, 90
   Finney: *Quartet* for Oboe, Cello, Percussion and Piano, 179

Hovhaness: *Upon Enchanted Ground* for Flute, Cello, Harp & Tantam, 212
Husa: *Quartet 3*, 227
Johnston: *Quartet 2*, 236
Johnston: *Quartet 3*, 236
Johnston: *Quartet 4*, 236
Lerdahl: *Quartet 1*, 260
Lerdahl: *Quartet 2*, 263
Rosner: *Quartet 4*, 453
Rózsa: *Quartet 1*, 462
Rózsa: *Quartet 2*, 462
Schnittke: *Quartet 2*, 492
Schonthal: *Quartet 1*, 499
Schuman: *Quartet 4*, 509
Simpson: *Quartet 7*, 522
Simpson: *Quartet 8*, 522
Simpson: *Quartet 9*, 526
Simpson: *Quartet 10 (For Peace)*, 528
Simpson: *Quartet 11*, 528
Tippett: *Quartets 1-3*, 564
Welcher: *Quartet 1*, 585

Quintets
  Moross: *Concerto* for Flute with String Quartet, 306
  Perle: *Quintets 1-4* for Winds, 369
  Perna: *Two Early Ayres* for Winds, 375

Sextets
  Bassett: *Sextet* for Piano & Strings, 34
  Ince: *Waves of Talya* for Flute, Clarinet, Piano, Percussion, Violin and Cello, 234
  Lerdahl: *Fantasy Etudes* for Flute, Clarinet, Violin, Cello, Percussion and Piano, 260
  Moross: *Sonata* for Piano Duet and String Quartet, 306

Trios
  Erb: *Trio* for Violin, Keyboards, and Percussion, 174
  Finney: *Two Acts for Three Players* for Clarinet, Percussion and Piano, 181
  Reynolds: "*...the serpent-snapping eye*" for Trumpet, Percussion, Piano and 4-Channel Tape, 423
  Skrowaczewski: *Trio* for Clarinet, Bassoon and Piano, 534

ORCHESTRAL

Ballet
  Moross: *Frankie and Johnny*, 307

INDEX OF COMPOSITIONS

Panufnik: *Cain and Abel:* see *Symphony 3,* 313
Panufnik: *Elegy:* see *Symphony 2,* 313
Rieti: *Le Bal,* 435
Rieti: *Barabau,* 435
Rieti: *Native Dancers,* 435
Rieti: *La Sonnambula,* 435
Rieti: *Waltz Academy,* 435

Band (Symphonic or Other)
Brant: *An American Requiem* for Wind Symphony Orchestra, 111
Erb: *The Hawk* (concertino) for Alto Saxophone, Brass, Percussion, and Saxophone Ensemble, 172
Finney: *Skating on the Sheyenne* for Symphonic Band, 179
Flagello: *Symphony 2 (Symphony of the Winds)* for Wind Orchestra, 184
Hovhaness: *Symphony 4* for Wind Symphony Orchestra, 211
Hovhaness: *Symphony 7 (Nanga Parvat)* for Wind Symphony Orchestra, 211
Husa: *Apotheosis of This Earth* for Wind Ensemble (also for Orchestra with Chorus), 220
Husa: *Concerto for Wind Ensemble,* 224
Husa: *Music for Prague, 1968* (also orchestral vers.), 226
Josephs: *Concerto* for Brass, 247
Perle: *Concertino* for Piano, Winds and Timpani, 363
Perna: *Two Preludes* for Wind Ensemble, 375
Reed: *A Festival Prelude* for Symphonic Band, 396
Reed: *The Garden of Prosperpine* (symphonic pastorale) for Wind Band, 396
Reed: *Symphony 1* for Symphonic Band, 397
Reed: *Symphony 2* for Symphonic Band, 397

Concertos, etc.
Amram: *Concerto* for Violin and Orchestra, 22
Amram: *Shakespearean Concerto* for Chamber Orchestra, 23
Beck: *Ballade* for Piano and Orchestra, 65
Brubeck: *Dialogues* for Jazz Combo and Orchestra, 126
Corea: *Concerto* for Piano and Orchestra, 134
Corigliano: *Concerto* for Clarinet and Orchestra, 139
Corigliano: *Pied Piper Fantasy (Concerto)* for Flute and Orchestra, 141
Erb: *The Hawk* (concertino) — see Band
Flagello: *Capriccio* for Cello and Orchestra, 183
Hovhaness: *Concerto 1 (Arevakal)* for Orchestra, 208
Hovhaness: *Concerto 7* for Orchestra, 209
Hovhaness: *Concerto 8* for Orchestra, 209
Hovhaness: *Elibris (Dawn God of Urardu)* for Flute and Strings, 209
Hovhaness: *Khaldis* for Piano, Four Trumpets [or any multiple thereof], and Percussion, 209

Hovhaness: *Lousadzak (The Coming of Light)* for Piano and Orchestra, 209
Hovhaness: *Talin* for Viola (Clarinet) and Strings, 212
Husa: *Concerto for Wind Ensemble* — see Band
Josephs: *Concerto for Brass* — see Band
Josephs: *Concerto 1* for Piano and Orchestra, 248
Mayer: *Inner and Outer Strings* for String Quartet and String Orchestra, 296
Mayer: *Octagon* for Piano and Orchestra (or 2 Pianos), 296
Menotti: *Concerto* in A Minor for Violin and Orchestra, 301
Paulus: *Concerto* for Violin and Orchestra, 326
Penderecki: *Concerto* for Violin and Orchestra, 338
Perle: *Concertino* — see Band
Perna: *Deux Berceuses:* see Chamber — General
Reynolds: *Transfigured Wind 2* for Flute, Orchestra and 2-Channel Tape, 424
Reynolds: *Whispers Out of Time* for Violin, Viola, Cello, Double Bass and String Orchestra, 427
Schnittke: *Concerto 3* for Violin and Chamber Orchestra, 488
Schnittke: *Concerto Grosso* for Two Violins, Strings, Cembalo, and Prepared Piano, 488
Schonthal: *Music for Horn and Chamber Orchestra*, 495
Schuman: *Three Colloquies* for Horn and Orchestra, 503
Schuman: *Concerto* for Violin and Orchestra, 505
Skrowaczewski: *Concerto* for English Horn and Orchestra, 530
Skrowaczewski: *Concerto* for Orchestra, 531
Thomas: *Haiku* for Violin, Cello and Chamber Orchestra, 554
Thomas: *Vigil* for Cello and Chamber Orchestra, 555
Tippett: *Concerto* for Double String Orchestra, 558
Walker: *Concerto* for Trombone and Orchestra, 577
Welcher: *Concerto* for Flute and Orchestra, 581
Zwilich: *Concerto* for Flute and Orchestra, 592
Zwilich: *Concerto Grosso 1985* for Orchestra, 592

General orchestral
Adams: *Chairman Dances from "Nixon in China"*, 3
Amram: *American Dance Suite* for Chamber Orchestra, 20
Bassett: *Echoes from an Invisible World*, 35
Bassett: *Variations*, 35
Brubeck: *California Suite*, 130
Brubeck: *Overture to "The Devil's Disciple"*, 130
Crumb: *Variazioni*, 158
Erb: *The Seventh Trumpet* for Orchestra, 173
Finney: *Landscapes Remembered*, 178
Grant: *Overture to "Chautauqua"*, 200
Hovhaness: *Alleluia and Fugue* for String Orchestra, 208
Hovhaness: *Anahid (Fantasy)* for String Orchestra, 208

INDEX OF COMPOSITIONS

Hovhaness: *And God Created Whales* for Orchestra and (Pre-Recorded) Whales, 208
Hovhaness: *Celestial Fantasy* for Strings, 208
Hovhaness: *Floating World (Ukiyo),* 209
Hovhaness: *Fra Angelico,* 209
Husa: *Music for Prague, 1968* (also band vers.), 226
Husa: *Two Sonnets from Michelangelo,* 228
Ince: *Ebullient Shadows,* 230
Ince: *Infrared,* 231
Kubik: *Symphony Concertante,* 258
Lutoslawski: *Novelette,* 171
Panufnik: *Autumn Music,* 313
Revueltas: *La noche de los mayas,* 414
Revueltas: *Sensemayá,* 418
Reynolds: *Quick Are the Mouths of Earth* for Chamber Ensemble (13 players), 421
Rorem: *Eagles,* 441
Rorem: *Sunday Morning,* 441
Rouse: *Gorgon,* 456
Rouse: *Phantasmata,* 458
Schnittke: *In Memoriam...,* 490
Schonthal: *Music for Horn and Chamber Orchestra,* 495
Schwantner: *Toward Light,* 519
Skrowaczewski: *Music at Night* for Strings, 531
Thomas: *Black Moon (Cantata 2)* for Chamber Orchestra, 552
Thomas: *Two Pieces for Orchestra,* 555
Walker: *Address for Orchestra,* 576
Walker: *Lyric for Strings,* 577
Welcher: *Prairie Light: Three Texas Watercolors of Georgia O'Keeffe,* 584
Welcher: *The Visions of Merlin* (tone poem), 585

Symphonies
Amram: *Songs of the Soul,* 24
Bax: *Spring Fire,* 39
Bax: *Symphony 1,* 42
Bax: *Symphony 2,* 45
Bax: *Symphony 3,* 48
Bax: *Symphony 4,* 49
Bax: *Symphony 5,* 54
Bax: *Symphony 6,* 56
Bax: *Symphony 7,* 58
Becker: *Symphony 3 (Symphonia brevis),* 69
Blomdahl: *Symphony 3,* 95
Brian: *Symphony 3,* 117
Brian: *Symphony 10,* 124
Carter: *Symphony* for Medium Voice and Orchestra — see Voice & Instrument(s)
Flagello: *Symphony 1,* 184

INDEX OF COMPOSITIONS

Flagello: *Symphony 2*—see Band
Hovhaness: *Symphony 2 (Mysterious Mountain)*, 211
Hovhaness: *Symphony 4*—see Band
Hovhaness: *Symphony 6 (Celestial Gate)* for Small Orchestra, 211
Hovhaness: *Symphony 7 (Nanga Parvat)*—see Band
Hovhaness: *Symphony 9 (Saint Vartan)*, 211
Hovhaness: *Symphony 25 (Odysseus)*, 212
Lutoslawski: *Symphony 3*, 272
Maros: *Symphony 1*, 292
Panufnik: *Symphony 1 (Sinfonia rustica)*, 313
Panufnik: *Symphony 2 (Sinfonia elegiaca)*, 313
Panufnik: *Symphony 3 (Sinfonia sacra)*, 313
Panufnik: *Symphony 4 (Sinfonia concertante)*, 314
Panufnik: *Symphony 5 (Sinfonia di Sfere)*, 314
Panufnik: *Symphony 6 (Sinfonia mistica)*, 314
Panufnik: *Symphony 7 (Metasinfonia)* for Organ, Timpani & strings, 314
Panufnik: *Symphony 8 (Sinfonia votiva)*, 314
Paulus: *Symphony in Three Movements (Soliloquy)*, 331
Perle: *A Short Symphony*, 373
Reed: *Symphony 1*—see Band
Reed: *Symphony 2*—see Band
Reise: *Symphony 2*, 411
Rorem: *String Symphony*, 441
Rosner: *Symphony 5*, 455
Rouse: *Symphony 1*, 459
Rubbra: *Symphony 2*, 465
Rubbra: *Symphony 5*, 468
Rubbra: *Symphony 6*, 469
Rubbra: *Symphony 8*, 469
Rubbra: *Symphony 10*, 473
Saeverud: *Symphony 5 (Quasi una fantasia)*, 482
Saeverud: *Symphony 6 (Sinfonia Dolorosa)*, 483
Saeverud: *Symphony 7 (Psalm)*, 483
Saeverud: *Symphony 9*, 484
Schuman: *Symphony 3*, 509
Schuman: *Symphony 6*, 509
Skrowaczewski: *Symphony* for Strings, 533
Tubin: *Symphony 1*, 571
Tubin: *Symphony 2 (Legendary)*, 571
Tubin: *Symphony 3*, 571
Tubin: *Symphony 4 (Sinfonia lirica)*, 571
Tubin: *Symphony 5*, 571
Tubin: *Symphony 6*, 571
Tubin: *Symphony 7*, 571
Tubin: *Symphony 8*, 571
Tubin: *Symphony 9*, 571
Tubin: *Symphony 10*, 571

INDEX OF COMPOSITIONS

Zwilich: *Symphony 1 (Three Movements for Orchestra)*, 596
Zwilich: *Symphony 2 (Cello Symphony)*, 599

DIRECTORY

OF SELECTED ARTS INSTITUTIONS, LICENSING AGENTS, MUSIC PUBLISHERS AND SUPPLIERS, NATIONAL MUSIC CENTERS AND RECORDING COMPANIES

Note: National music centers (signified with a ●) offer a great deal of useful biographical and compositional information concerning local composers. See also publication *How to Find the Music: A Guide to the Members of the International Association of Music Information Centers,* available from the AMERICAN MUSIC CENTER.

Alfred Publishing Company – 16380 Roscoe Boulevard – P.O. Box 10003 – Van Nuys CA 91410
Alphonse Leduc – c/o Theodore Presser Company
American Academy of Arts and Sciences – 280 Newton Street – Brookline Station – Boston MA 02146
American Composers Alliance – American Composers Edition – 170 West 74th Street – New York NY 10023
● American Music Center – 30 West 26th Street – Suite 1001 – New York NY 10010
American Society of Composers, Authors and Publishers (ASCAP) – 1 Lincoln Plaza – New York NY 10023
The Ashmere Music Group – 154 Bradley Street – New Haven CT 06511
Associated Music Publishers, Inc. – c/o Hal Leonard
Augsburg Publishing House – 57 Main Street – Columbus OH 43215
● Australian Music Centre Ltd. – P. O. Box 49, – Broadway, N.S. W. 2007
● [Austrian Music Center] – Österreichische Gesellschaft für Musik – Hanuschgasse 3 – A-1010 Wien
Bardic Edition – 6 Fairfax Crescent – Aylesbury, Buckinghamshire – England HP20 2ES
● [Belgian Music Center] – Centre Begle de Documentation Musicale – CeBeDeM – Rue d'Arlon 75-77 – B-1040 Bruxelles
Belwin-Mills Publishing Corp. – c/o Columbia Pictures Publications
Bertelsman Music Group (BMG) – 1133 Avenue of the Americas – New York NY 10036
Birch Tree Group Ltd. – 180 Alexander Road – Princeton NJ 08540
Birchard Music Co. – *see:* Birch Tree Group Ltd.
Boelke-Bomart, Inc. – c/o Jerona Music Corporation
Boosey & Hawkes, Inc. – 24 West 57th Street (serious music/perform) – New York NY 10019 – *also* 200 Smith Street (publishing/sales) – Farmingdale NY 11735
The Boston Music Co. – 116 Boylston Street – Boston MA 02116

DIRECTORY

- British Music Information Centre – 10, Stratford Place – GB-London W1N 9AE – *See also:* Irish Music Center – Scottish Music Center – Welsh Music Center

Broadcast Music, Inc. – 589 Fifth Avenue – New York NY 10017

Broude Brothers – 141 White Oaks Road – Williamstown MA 01267

- Canadian Music Centre – Chalmers House – 20 St. Joseph Street – Toronto, Ontario M4Y 1J9

Capitol Records Inc. – 1750 North Vine Street – Hollywood CA 90028

CBS Records Inc. – 51 West 52nd Street – New York NY 10019

Chappell/Intersong Music Group – 810 Seventh Avenue – New York NY 10019

Cherry Lane Music Co. Inc. – 110 Midland Avenue – Port Chester NY 10573

Chester Music Inc. – c/o Music Sales Corp.

CMS Records Inc. – 226 Washington Street – Mt. Vernon NY 10553

- [Colombian Music Center] – Centro Documentacion Musical – Calle 11, No. 5-51 – Bogota 1

Columbia Broadcasting System – *see:* CBS Records Inc.

Columbia Pictures Publications – 15800 NW 48th Avenue – Miami FL 33014

Composers Recordings Inc. – 170 West 74th Street – New York NY 10023

Concordia Publishing House – 3558 South Jefferson Avenue – St. Louis MO 63118

The Conductors Guild – P.O. Box 3361 – West Chester PA 19381

Chick Corea Productions – 2635 Griffith Park Boulevard – Los Angeles CA 90039

- [Czech Music Center] – Hudebni Informacni Strediscko / – Ceského hudebniho fondu – Busedni 3 – CS-11800 Praha 1 – *also:* Slovensky Hudobny Fond / – Music Information Centre – Fucikova 29 – CS-81102 Bratislava

Danacord Records – Gernersgade 35 – DK – 1319 Copenhagen – Denmark

- [Danish Music Center] – Dansk Musik Informations Centre – Vimmelskaftet 48 – DK--1161 Copenhagen K

Derry Music Company – 240 Stockton Street – San Francisco CA

Desto Records – c/o CMS Records Inc.

Deutsche Grammophon – *see:* Polygram Classics Inc.

Oliver Ditson Co. – c/o Theodore Presser Co.

Dover Publications Inc. – 31 East Second Street – Mineola NY 11501

Dramatic Publishing Company – 4150 North Milwaukee Avenue – Chicago IL 60641

Elektra International Classics – 75 Rockefeller Plaza – New York NY 10019

Elektra/Nonesuch – c/o Elektra International Classics

Elkan-Vogel, Inc. – Bryn Mawr PA 19010

English Music Center – *see:* British Music Centre

European American Music – P.O. Box 850 – Valley Forge PA 19482

- [Finnish Music Center] – Suomalaisen Musiikin Tiedotuskeskus – Runeberginkatu 15A – SF-00100 Helsinki 10

Carl Fischer, Inc. – 62 Cooper Square – New York NY 10003

- [French Music Center] – Centre de Documentation de la Musique Contemporaine – 225, Avenue Charles de Gaulle – F-92521 Neuilly-sur-Seine Dedex

Galaxy Music Corp. – 131 West 86th Street – New York NY 10024

Geffen Music – c/o Warner Bros.

General Music Publishing Co., Inc. – 145 Palisade – Dobbs Ferry NY 10533

- [German Music Center] – Internationales Musikinstitut Darmstadt – Nieder-Ramstädter Strasse 190 – D-6100 Darmstadt

GunMar Music Inc. – c/o Margun Music, Inc.

Edition Wilhelm Hansen/Chester Music NY Inc. – 30 West 61st Street – #12B – New York NY 10023 – *also:* c/o MMB Music

Helicon Music Corporation – c/o European American Music

G. Henle USA Inc. – c/o MMB Music

Henmar Press – c/o C. F. Peters Corp.

Highgate Press – c/o Galaxy Music Corp.

- [Hungarian Music Center] – Music Information Centre of Hungary – Magyar Zeneművészek Szövetsége – P.O. Box 47 – H-1364 Budapest

- [Icelandic Music Center] – Islensk Tónverkamiostoo – Box 978 – IS-121 Reykjavík

- [Irish Music Center] – Contemporary Music Centre – 95 Lower Baggot Street – Dublin 2

- Israel Music Institute – P. O. Box 3004 – 61030 Tel Aviv

Jerona Music Corp. – 81 Trinity Place – Hackensack NJ 07601 – *also:* P.O. Box 5010 – Hackensack NJ 07606

Robert King Music Co. – 7 Canton Street – North Easton MA 02356

Neil A. Kjos Music Co. – 4382 Jutland Drive – San Diego CA 92117

Lawson-Gould, Inc. – c/o Alfred Publishing Company (sales) – or G. Schirmer, Inc. (rentals)

Leeds Music Ltd. – *see:* Belwin-Mills

Hal Leonard Publishing Company – 8112 West Bluemount Road – Box 13819 – Milwaukee WI 53123 – *also:* 960 East Mark Street – Winona MN 55987

Leonarda Productions – P.O. Box 1736, Cathedral Station – New York NY 10025

Margun Music, Inc. / GunMar Music Inc. – 167 Dudley Road – Newton Centre MA 02159

Edward B. Marks Music Corp. – c/o Hal Leonard Publishing Corp. – or Theodore Presser (rentals)

MCA Records Inc. – *see:* Music Corp. of America

McGinnis and Marx Music Publishers – P.O. Box 229 – Planetarium Station – New York NY 10024

Merion Music, Inc. – c/o Theodore Presser Company

DIRECTORY

Minnesota Composers Forum – 289 East 5th Street – St Paul MN 55101
MMB Music (Magna Music Baton) – 10370 Page Industrial Boulevard – St. Louis MO 63132
Mobart Music Publications – c/o Jerona Music Corporation
Music Associates of America – 224 King Street – Englewood NJ 07631
Music Corp. of America (MCA)) – c/o Hal Leonard Publishing Corp. (sales) – or Theodore Presser Company (rentals) – *also:* MCA Records Inc. – 70 Universal City Plaza – Universal City CA 91608
Music Sales Corp. – 5 Bellvale Road – Chester NY 10918
Music Theatre International – 1350 Avenue of the Americas – New York NY 10019
Musical Heritage Society / Musicmasters – 1710 Highway 35 – Ocean NJ 07712
National Academy of Recording Arts and Sciences – 21 West 58th Street – New York NY 10019
National Association for American Composers and Conductors – 15 West 67th Street – New York NY 10023
National Endowment for the Arts – Washington DC 20506
National Institute for Arts and Letters – 633 West 155th Street – New York NY 10032
National School Orchestra Association / NSOA Composition Competition – NSOA Service Office – 345 Maxwell Drive – Pittsburgh PA 15236
● [Netherland Music Center] – Donemus – Paulus Potterstraat 14 – NL-1071 CZ Amsterdam
New World Records – 701 Seventh Avenue – New York NY 10036
Northeastern Records – P.O. Box 3589 – Saxonville MA 01701
● [Norwegian Music Center] – Norsk Musikkinformasjon – Toftesgate 69 – N-0552 Oslo 5
Orpheus Publications – 4th Floor – Centro House, Mandela Street – London NW1 ODU
Oxford University Press – 200 Madison Avenue – New York NY 10016
Owl Records – P.O. Box 4536 – Boulder CO 80306
Paganiniana – 1 TFH Plaza – Third and Union – Neptune City NJ 07753
Joseph Patelson Music House Ltd. – 160 West 56th Street – New York NY 10019
Peer-Southern Organization – c/o Theodore Presser Co.
C. F. Peters Corp. – 373 Park Avenue South – New York NY 10016
● [Polish Music Center] – Polskie Centrum Muzyczne – Rynek Starego Miasta 27 – PL-00-272 Warszawa
Polygram Classics Inc. – 825 Eighth Avenue – New York NY 10019
Theodore Presser Company – Presser Place – Bryn Mawr PA 19010
Pulitzer Prize in Music – 702 Journalism – Columbia University – New York NY 10027
Random House, Inc. – 201 East 50th Street – New York 10022

DIRECTORY

RCA Records – *see:* Bertelsman Music Group (BMG)
Record Industry Association of America – 1 East 57th Street – New York NY 10022
Revelation Music Publishing Corp. – 1270 Avenue of the Americas – New York NY 10019
E. C. Schirmer Music Co. – 138 Ipswich Street – Boston MA 02215
G. Schirmer, Inc. – c/o Hal Leonard (sales) – *or* Music Sales Corp. (rentals)
Schott Music Corp. – c/o European American Music
● Scottish Music Information Centre – 1, Bowmont Gardens – GB-Glasgow G12 9LR
Shawnee Press Inc. – Waring Drive – Delaware Water Gap PA 18327
Smith Publications – 2617 Gwynndale Avenue – Baltimore MD 21207
Sorom Music – 6951 S.W. 134th Street – Miami FL 33156
Southern Music Publishing Company – c/o Theodore Presser Co.
● [Spanish Music Center] – Centro de Documentacion Musical – Torregalindo 10 – E-28016 Madrid
Summy-Birchard Music – *see:* Birch Tree Group Ltd.
● [Swedish Music Center] – Svensk Musik – P. O. Box 27327 – S-10254 Stockholm
● [Swiss Music Center] – SUISA Foundation – P. O. Box 409 – CH-2001 Neuchatel
Universal Edition Publishing Inc. – c/o European American
USC Sound Enterprises – P.O. Box 11211 – Memphis TN 38111
Valando Music Publishing Group, Inc. – 1270 Avenue of the Americas – New York NY 10019
Warner Bros. Music – 9000 Sunset Boulevard – Penthouse – Los Angeles CA 90069 – *also:* 3300 Warner Boulevard (records) – Burbank CA 91510
● Welsh Music Information Centre – Music Department – University College, Box 78 – GB-Cardiff CF1 1XL
Young Concert Artists Inc. – 75 East 55th Street – New York NY 10027
● [Yugoslav Music Center] – SOKOJ / Documentation and Information – P.O. Box 213 – JU-11000 Beograd

INDEX OF ANNOTATORS

Agee, Mia / Mayer (*A Death in the Family*)
Albright, William / Albright, W.
Akers, Bill / Skrowaczewski (*Music at Night*)
Alcaraz, José Antonio / Revueltas (*La Noche de los Mayas*)
Anderson, Martin J. / Panufnik (*Symphony 8*)
Ardoin, John / Welcher (*Della's Gift*)
Balanchine, George / Rieti (*La Sonnambula*)
Barber, Suzanne Kimberly / Zwilich (*Symphony 2*)
Bassett, Leslie / Bassett (*Echoes from an Invisible World, Preludes, Sextet, Variations* for Orchestra)
Batsford, J. Tucker / Rieti (*Second Avenue Waltzes*)
Beck, Jeremy / Beck (*Ballade* for Piano and Orchestra, *Quartet 2* for Strings, *Scherzo* for Clarinet, Violin and Cello, *Sonata* for Cello and Piano)
Belt, Byron / Mayer (*Enter Ariel*)
Benson, Jack / Skrowaczewski (*Music at Night*)
Bentzon, Niels Viggo / Bentzon (*Sonatas 18-20*)
Berrett, Joshua / Bolcom (*Twelve New Etudes*)
Bloch, Suzanne / Bloch (*Quartets 1-5* for Strings)
Blois, Louis / Rubbra (*Symphonies 1-11*)
Bolcom, William / Bolcom, W.
Bordman, Gerald / Sondheim (*Follies, A Funny Thing Happened on the Way to the Forum, Pacific Overtures*)
Boriskin, Michael / Perle (*Six New Etudes*)
Boroff, Edith / Finney, R. L.
Brancaleone, Francis / Amram (*Shakespearean Concerto*), Briccetti (*Sonata* for Flute and Piano)
Brian, David J. / Brian (*Symphony 3*), Simpson (*Quartets 7-9* for Strings)
Briccetti, Thomas / Briccetti (*Sonata* for Flute and Piano)
Brown, Royal S. / Menotti (*Concerto* for Violin and Orchestra), Rózsa (*Sonata* for Piano), Welcher (*Concerto* for Flute and Orchestra)
Brunner, Lance W. / Lutoslawski (*Novelette*)
Brush, Ruth J. / Kubik (*Magic, Magic, Magic*)
Buell, Richard / Zwilich (*Sonata in Three Movements*)
Burge, David / Albright (*Five Chromatic Dances*)
Burgwyn, Diana / Reise (*Rasputin*)
Burmeister, Ellen / Persichetti (*Serenade 7, Sonatas 10-11*)
Byrne, Frank / Wilder (*Suite 1* for Tuba and Piano)
Campbell, Karen / Schonthal (*Princess Maleen*)
Campbell, Mary / Reise (*Rasputin*)
Camus, Raoul F. / Erb (*The Hawk*), Finney (*Skating on the Sheyenne*), Reed (*The Garden of Proserpine*)
Canarina, John / Paulus (*Symphony in Three Movements*)
Cantrell, Scott / Bax, A.

INDEX OF ANNOTATORS

Caras, Tracy / Finney (*Landscapes Remembered*), Glass, P.
Carter, Chandler / Carter (*Night Scenes, Prayers of the People, Symphony, Variations*)
Cauble, Courtenay V. / Schonthal (*Music for Horn and Chamber Orchestra*)
Caudle, Todd / Corea (*Inside Out*)
Chism, Olin / Welcher (*The Visions of Merlin*)
Chittum, Donald / Penderecki (*Concerto* for Violin and Orchestra)
Clark, John / Schuman, W.
Clarkson, Austin / Bolcom (*Twelve New Etudes*)
Cleveland, Lindsay / Paulus (*So Hallow'd Is the Time*)
Close, Roy M. / Paulus (*Symphony in Three Movements*)
Cole, Edward / Hovhaness (*Symphony 9*)
Cope, David / Brant (*An American Requiem*)
Cox, David / Bax (*Symphonies 1-7*)
Darrell, R.D. / Revueltas (*Sensemayá*)
Davidson, Mary Wallace / Johnston (*Quartets 3-4*)
Davis, Deborah / Rorem, N.
Davis, Peter G. / Lerdahl (*Quartet 1 for Strings*)
Dettmer, Roger / Bassett (*Echoes from an Invisible World*), Panufnik (*Symphonies 5, 6 & 8*), Revueltas (*Sensemayá*)
DeVoto, Mark / Perle, G.
Dexter, Benning / Tippett (*Sonata 4 for Piano*)
Ditsky, John / Hovhaness, A., Lloyd Webber (*Requiem*), Perle (*Ballade, Concertino*), Schonthal (*Totengesänge*), Tubin (*Symphonies*)
Douguay, Robert / Bassett (*Variations for Orchestra*)
Downes, Olin / Hovhaness, A.
Driver, Paul / Tippett (*The Mask of Time*)
Drucker, Ruth L. / Mompou (*Cançons Becquerianas*)
Dyer, Richard / Zwilich (*Symphony 1*)
Eaton, John / Eaton (*Danton and Robespierre*), Erb (*The Seventh Trumpet*)
Ellis, Stephen W. / Bentzon (*Sonatas 18-20* for Piano), Crumb (*Variazioni for Orchestra*), Erb (*Trio for Violin, Keyboards, and Percussion*), Maros (*Symphony 1*), Schnittke (*Concerto 3 for Violin and Chamber Orchestra, Concerto Grosso*), Schuman (*Three Colloquies*), Zwilich (*Symphony 1*)
Erling, John / Bloch (*Quartets 1-2 for Strings*)
Farrell, Peter / Rózsa (*Toccata capricciosa*)
Faulkner, Dewey / Welcher (*The Visions of Merlin*)
Feldman, Mary Ann / Paulus (*Symphony in Three Movements*)
Ferriter, Gene / Corea (*Inside Out*)
Fink, Bert / Sondheim (*Follies*)
Fink, Michael / Pujo (*Cinco Preludios* for Guitar)
Finney, Ross Lee / Finney (*Landscapes Remembered, Quartet* for Oboe, Cello, Percussion and Piano, *Two Acts for Three Players*)
Flagello, Nicolas / Flagello, N.
Fleming, Shirley / Thomson (Piano reductions)
Foreman, Lewis / Bax (*Spring Fire, Symphonies 1-4, 7*)

INDEX OF ANNOTATORS

François, Jean-Charles / Erb (*Sonata* for Clarinet and Percussion)
Frank, Andrew / Zwilich (*Symphony 1*)
Frank, Peter / Albright (*Five Chromatic Dances*)
Frankenstein, Alfred / Brubeck (*California Suite*), Walker (*Lyric for Strings*)
Freed, Richard / Corigliano (*Concerto* for Clarinet and Orchestra)
Friedman, Lora / Schonthal (*Princess Maleen*)
Friedrich, Otto / Bolcom, W.
Furie, Kenneth / Walker (*Concerto* for Trombone and Orchestra)
Gagne, Cole / Finney (*Landscapes Remembered*), Glass, P.
Galkin, Elliott W. / Walker (*Address* for Orchestra)
Gann, Kyle / Johnston (*Journeys, Quartets 2-4, Sonnets of Desolation*), Perle (*Quintets 1-4* for Winds), Walker (*Lyric for Strings, Prelude and Caprice, Spatials*)
Garvey, Evelyn / Persichetti (*Reflective Keyboard Studies, Sonatas 1-2, 12, Three Toccatinas*), Welcher (*Sonatina*)
Gideon, Miriam / Gideon (*Creature to Creature, Sonnets from Shakespeare, Wing'd Hour*)
Glanville-Hicks, Peggy / Hovhaness, A.
Glass, Philip / Glass, P.
Glickman, Ken / Husa (*Apotheosis of This Earth*)
Good, Emily / Gideon (*Sonnets from Shakespeare, Wing'd Hour*)
Goode, Richard / Perle (*Ballade, Concertino* for Piano, Winds and Timpani)
Grant, Mark / Crumb, G., Grant (*Echoes of a Lost Serenade, Epiphanies, Overture to "Chautauqua"*), Kubik, G., Rieti, V.
Grigoriev, S. L. / Rieti (*Barabau*)
Gronquist, Robert / Madden (*The Chime Child*)
Hardish, Patrick / Saeverud (*Symphony 5*)
Harman, Carter / Gideon (*Sonnets from Shakespeare*)
Haskell, Harry / Paulus (*The Postman Always Rings Twice*)
Hauptman, Fred / Paulus (*The Postman Always Rings Twice*), Zwilich (*Symphony 1*)
Hegberg, Susan / Finney (*Two Studies* for Saxophone and Piano)
Henahan, Donal / Zwilich (*Double Quartet* for Strings)
Henry, Derrick / Paulus (*Concerto* for Violin and Orchestra)
Hinson, Maurice / Ince (*My Friend Mozart* for Piano), Schwantner (*Veiled Autumn (Kindertodeslied)* for Piano)
Hovhaness, Alan / Hovhaness (*Magnificat, Symphony 25*)
Hume, Paul / Perle (*Six Etudes*)
Hummel, David / Sondheim (Bibl. data for musical shows)
Husa, Karel / Husa (*Apotheosis of This Earth, Concerto for Wind Ensemble*)
Hutchings, Arthur / Rubbra, E.
Ince, Kamran / Ince, K., Ince (*Cross Scintillations, Ebullient Shadows, Infrared, Waves of Talya*)
Jacobson, Robert / Mayer (*A Death in the Family*)
Jezic, Diane Peacock / Schonthal (*Quartet 1* for Strings)
Johnson, Bret / Josephs (*Requiem*)

INDEX OF ANNOTATORS

Jones, Harold / Briccetti (*Sonata* for Flute and Piano)
Jones, Nick / Paulus (*Concerto* for Violin and Orchestra)
Kandell, Leslie / Schuman (*The Mighty Casey, A Question of Taste*)
Kastendieck, Miles / Hovhaness (*Magnificat*)
Kerner, Leighton / Bolcom (*Songs of Innocence and of Experience*), Reise (*Rasputin*)
Kiraly, Philippa / Schwantner (*Toward Light*)
Knussen, Oliver / Panufnik (*Symphony 5*), Perle (*Concertino* for Piano, Winds and Timpani, *A Short Symphony*)
Kolodin, Irving / Walker (*Concerto* for Trombone and Orchestra)
Kozinn, Allan / Bolcom (*Twelve New Etudes*), Corigliano (*Concerto* for Clarinet and Orchestra, *Pied Piper Fantasy*), Schnittke, A.
Kroeger, Karl / Perle (*A Short Symphony*)
Lansky, Paul / Perle, G., Perle (*Six New Etudes*)
Larson, Steve / Albright (*Five Chromatic Dances*)
Laufe, Abe / Sondheim (*Company, A Little Night Music*)
Layton, Robert / Bax (*Symphony 5*), Rubbra (*Symphonies 6, 8*)
Lerdahl, Fred / Lerdahl (*Fantasy Etudes, Quartet 2* for Strings)
Lessard, Suzannah / Rieti (*Ballets*)
Lewis, Geraint / Menotti (*The Marriage*)
Lowens, Irving / Husa (*Apotheosis of This Earth*), Moross (*Concerto* for Flute with String Quartet, *Sonata* for Piano Duet with String Quartet) Walker (*Lyric for Strings*)
Lucha-Burns, Carol / Sondheim (Musical shows)
Lynch, Richard Chigley / Sondheim (Musical shows)
MacDonald, Malcolm / Panufnik (*Symphonies 1-4*)
Machover, Tod / Machover (*Bug-Mudra*)
Magrath, Jane / Rieti (*Dodici Preludi*)
Malitz, Nancy / Bolcom (*Songs of Innocence and of Experience*)
Malloch, William / Revueltas (*La noche de los mayas*)
Martorella, Philip P. / Martorella, P.P.
Mason, Francis / Rieti (*La Sonnambula*)
Mayer, Martin / Bolcom (*Songs of Innocence and of Experience*)
Mayer, William / Mayer (*Enter Ariel, Octagon* for Piano and Orchestra, *Passage*)
McLean, Joseph / Thomas (*echos*)
McLellan, Joseph / Corigliano (*Pied Piper Fantasy*), Schonthal (*Totengesänge*)
Milkowski, Bill / Corea (*Inside Out*)
Miller, Dennis / Perle, G.
Mills, Margaret / Schonthal (*The Canticles of Hieronymus*)
Monson, Karen / Eaton (*Danton and Robespierre*)
Mordden, Ethan / Hovhaness (*Symphonies 2, 4 & 7*)
Morgan, Robert P. / Schnittke (*Concerto Grosso*)
Noon, David / Schnittke (*In Memoriam...*)
O'Reilly, F. Warren / Husa (*Apotheosis of This Earth*)
Orland, Henry / Mayer (*A Death in the Family*)
Page, Tim / Walker (*Sonata 4* for Piano), Zwilich, E. T.

INDEX OF ANNOTATORS

Panufnik, Andrzej / Panufnik (*Autumn Music*)
Parker, Craig B. / Schuman (*Three Colloquies*)
Parsons, Arrand / Lutoslawski (*Symphony 3*)
Paulus, Stephen / Paulus, S.
Pavlakis, Christopher / Becker (*Symphony 3*)
Perle, George / Perle, G.
Perlis, Vivian / Husa (*Music for Prague, 1968*), Schuman (*The Mighty Casey, A Question of Taste*)
Perna, Dana / Josephs (*Concerto* for Brass, *Concerto 1* for Piano and Orchestra, *Doubles* for Two Pianos, *Requiem*), Moross (*Frankie and Johnny*), Perna, D., Rieti, V.
Pernick, Benjamin / Blomdahl (*Symphony 3*), Eaton (*Danton and Robespierre*), Penderecki (*Concerto* for Violin and Orchestra)
Persichetti, Vincent / Persichetti (*Serenade 7, Sonatas 10-11*), Schuman (*Quartet 4* for Strings, *Symphony 3*)
Petersen, Catherine L. / Persichetti (*Serenade 4*)
Pike, Lionel / Simpson (*Quartets 7-8* for Strings)
Pincus, Andrew L. / Henze, H.W., Thomas (*echos*), Zwilich (*Symphony 1*)
Pirie, Peter J. / Bax (*Symphony 6*)
Point, Michael / Welcher (*Prairie Light*)
Porter, Andrew / Eaton (*Danton and Robespierre*), Glass (*Einstein on the Beach*), Ince (*Infrared*), Lerdahl (*Quartet 1*), Perle (*Songs of Praise and Lamentation*), Picker (*Octet, Rhapsody* for Violin and Piano), Paulus (*The Village Singer*), Tippett (*Quartets 1-3*)
Rabinowitz, Peter J. / Reise (*Symphony 2*), Zwilich (*Double Quartet* for Strings)
Rapaport, Paul / Panufnik (*Symphony 7*), Simpson (*Quartets 7-9* for Strings)
Reed, Alfred / Reed, A.
Reilly, Robert R. / Saeverud (*Symphony 9*)
Reinthaler, Joan / Bassett (*Sextet*)
Rich, Alan / Bolcom (*Songs of Innocence and of Experience*)
Rich, Frank / Sondheim (*Sunday in the Park with George*)
Roca, Octavio / Reise (*Rasputin*)
Rockwell, John / Bolcom (*Songs of Innocence and of Experience*), Panufnik, A.
Rorem, Ned / Rorem (*Eagles, String Symphony, Sunday Morning*)
Rosen, Jerome / Wilder (*Sonata for Clarinet and Piano*)
Rosner, Arnold / Rosner, A.
Rouse, Christopher / Rouse, C., Rouse (*Gorgon, Phantasmata, Symphony 1*), Schuman (*Three Colloquies*)
Roussel, Hubert / Hovhaness (*Symphony 2*)
Roy, James G., Jr. / Husa (*Music for Prague, Quartet 3* for Strings, *Two Sonnets from Michelangelo*)
Rubin, David M. / Persichetti, V.
Sachs, David / Gideon (*The Resounding Lyre, Spirit Above the Dust*)
Samuel, Rhian / Zwilich (*Symphony 2*)

Schmalz, Peter / Persichetti (*Parable* for Solo Trombone), Schuman (*Three Colloquies*)
Schnittke, Alfred / Schnittke, A.
Schreiber, Flora Rheta / Schuman (*Symphony 3*)
Schuman, William / Schuman, W., Schuman (*Symphonies*)
Schwartz, Elliott / Reynolds (*Quick Are the Mouths of Earth*), Schwantner (*New Morning for the World*)
Schwarz, Boris / Rieti, V.
Schwarz, K. Robert / Adams (*Nixon in China*), Machover (*VALIS*), Panufnik (*Symphony 3*), Rorem (*Eagles, String Symphony, Sunday Morning*), Schuman (*Concerto for Violin and Orchestra*)
Seay, Albert / Rieti, V.
Shackelford, Rudy / Persichetti, V.
Shuler, David / Persichetti (*Dryden Liturgical Suite*)
Shupp, Enos F., Jr. / Hovhaness (*Symphony 9*)
Simmons, Walter G. / Bloch (*Quartet 2*), Corigliano (*Concerto for Clarinet and Orchestra*), Flagello (*Symphony 2, Te Deum*), Hovhaness (*Alleluia and Fugue, Anahid, And God Created Great Whales, Concertos 1 & 8, Elibris, Lousadzak, Symphony 2, Talin*), Lerdahl (*Quartet 2 for Strings*), Panufnik (*Autumn Music, Symphonies 1 & 3*), Persichetti (*Concerto* for Piano, Four Hands, *Sonatas 3, 9-11* for Piano), Reed (*Symphonies 1-2*), Rosner (*The Chronicle of Nine, Quartet 4, Sonata 2* for Cello and Piano, *Sonata* for Horn and Piano, *Symphony 5*), Rubbra (*Symphonies 2, 5-6, 8, 10*), Schwantner, J.
Sluder, Claude K. / Schonthal (*Music for Horn and Chamber Orchestra*)
Smith, Patrick J. / Bolcom (*Songs of Innocence and of Experience*)
Snook, Paul / Blomdahl (*Symphony 3*), Josephs (*Doubles for Two Pianos*), Kubik, G., Moross (*Concerto for Flute with String Quartet*), Rorem (*Serenade on Five English Poems*), Saeverud (*Symphonies 6-7*), Tippett (*Concerto* for Double String Orchestra), Tubin (*Symphonies 2, 4 & 6*)
Steinberg, Michael / Adams, J.
Stevenson, Ronald / Simpson, R.
Stiller, Andrew / Machover (*VALIS*), Skrowaczewski (*Trio* for Clarinet, Bassoon and Piano)
Strickland, Edward / Glass (*Einstein on the Beach*)
Stucky, Steven / Lutoslawski (*Symphony 3*)
Sturm, George / Gideon, M.
Svard, Lois / Bolcom (*Twelve New Etudes*), Welcher (*Dance Variations*)
Swansbourne, Clive / Tippett (*Sonata 4* for Piano)
Swed, Mark / Perle, G.
Swift, Richard G. / Perle (*Quintets* for Winds)
Terry, Walter / Rieti (*Native Dancers*)
Thomas, Augusta Read / Thomas (*Black Moon, Haiku, Two Pieces for Orchestra, Requiem, Vigil, Wind Dance*)
Thomson, Virgil / Hovhaness, A., Revueltas, S.
Tiedman, Richard E. / Brian (*Symphony 3*)
Timbrell, Charles / Bolcom (*Twelve New Etudes*)
Tippett, Michael / Tippett (*Quartets 1-3*)

INDEX OF ANNOTATORS

Trotter, Herman / Argento (*Te Deum*)
Truscott, Harold / Rubbra (*Symphony* 2)
Tucker, Marilyn / Walker (*Address for Orchestra*)
Turok, Paul / Hovhaness (*Fra Angelico*)
Ulrich, Allan / Welcher (*Quartet 1* for Strings)
Von Rhein, John / Corigliano (*Pied Piper Fantasy*)
Wait, Mark / Bolcom, W., Persichetti (*Sonatas* for Piano), Walker (*Sonata 4* for Piano)
Waleson, Heidi / Reise (*Rasputin*), Zwilich, E.T.
Wallner, Bo / Blomdahl, K-B.
Warburton, Thomas / Albright (*Five Chromatic Dances* for Piano)
Webster, Daniel / Bassett (*Echoes from an Invisible World, Variations* for Orchestra), Reise (*Symphony* 2)
Weirich, Robert / Albright (*Five Chromatic Dances*)
Welcher, Dan / Welcher (*Concerto* for Flute and Orchestra)
Wells, William B. / Henze (*Orpheus Behind the Wire*)
Wentworth, Jean & Wentworth, Kenneth / Persichetti (*Concerto* for Piano, Four Hands)
Wierzbicki, James / Paulus (*The Postman Always Rings Twice*), Rózsa (*Quartets 1-2* for Strings, *Rhapsody* for Cello and Piano), Simpson (*Quartets 10-11* for Strings)
Wigler, Stephen / Rouse (*Symphony 1*)
Wiser, John D. / Schnittke (*Concerto 3* for Violin and Chamber Orchestra, *Quartet 2* for Strings)
Zwilich, Ellen Taaffe / Zwilich, E.T.

Other Music Titles Available from Pro/Am Music Resources, Inc.

BIOGRAPHIES & COMPOSER STUDIES

ALKAN, REISSUE *by Ronald Smith. Vol. 1: The Enigma. Vol. 2: The Music.*
BEETHOVEN'S EMPIRE OF THE MIND *by John Crabbe.*
BÉLA BARTÓK: His Life in Pictures and Documents *ed. by Ferenc Bónis.*
BERNARD STEVENS AND HIS MUSIC: A Symposium *compiled and edited by Bertha Stevens.*
JANÁCEK: Leaves from His Life *by Leos Janácek. Edited & transl. by Vilem & Margaret Tausky.*
JOHN FOULDS AND HIS MUSIC: An Introduction *by Malcolm MacDonald.*
LIPATTI *(Tanasescu & Bargauanu):* see PIANO, below.
LISZT AND HIS COUNTRY, 1869-1873 *by Deszo Legány.*
MASCAGNI: An Autobiography Compiled, Edited and Translated from Original Sources *by David Stivender.*
MAX REGER *by Gerhard Wuensch.*
MICHAEL TIPPETT, O.M.: A Celebration *edited by Geraint Lewis. Fwd. by Peter Maxwell Davies.*
THE MUSIC OF SYZMANOWSKI *by Jim Samson.*
MY LIFE WITH BOHUSLAV MARTINU *by Charlotte Martinu.*
THE OPRICHNIK: An Opera in Four Acts by Peter Il'ich Tchaikvoksy. *Transl. & notes by Philip Taylor.*
PERCY GRAINGER: The Man Behind the Music *by Eileen Dorum.*
PERCY GRAINGER: The Pictorial Biography *by Robert Simon. Fwd. by Frederick Fennell.*
RAVEL ACCORDING TO RAVEL *(Perlemuter & Jourdan-Morhange):* see PIANO, below.
RONALD STEVENSON: A Musical Biography *by Malcolm MacDonald.*
SCHUBERT'S MUSIC FOR PIANO FOUR-HANDS *(Weekley & Arganbright):* see PIANO, below.
SOMETHING ABOUT THE MUSIC 1: Interviews with 17 American Experimental Composers *by Geoff Smith & Nicola Walker.*
SOMETHING ABOUT THE MUSIC 2: Anthology of Critical Opinions *edited by Thomas P. Lewis.*
SOMETHING ABOUT THE MUSIC 3: Landmarks of Twentieth-Century Music *by Nick Rossi.*
SORABJI: A Critical Celebration *edited by Paul Rapoport.*
A SOURCE GUIDE TO THE MUSIC OF PERCY GRAINGER *edited by Thomas P. Lewis.*
THE SYMPHONIES OF HAVERGAL BRIAN: Symphonies 30-32, Survey, and Summing-Up *by Malcolm MacDonald.*
VERDI AND WAGNER *by Ernö Lendvai.*
THE WORKS OF ALAN HOVHANESS: A Catalog, Opus 1 – Opus 360 *by Richard Howard.*
ZOLTAN KODALY: His Life in Pictures and Documents *by László Eosze.*

Other Music Titles Available from Pro/Am Music Resources, Inc. (continued)

GENERAL SUBJECTS

ACOUSTICS AND THE PERFORMANCE OF MUSIC *by Jürgen Meyer.*
AMERICAN MINIMAL MUSIC, REISSUE *by Wim Mertens. Transl. by J. Hautekiet.*
A CONCISE HISTORY OF HUNGARIAN MUSIC, 2ND ENL. ED. *by Bence Szabolozi.*
THE FOLK MUSIC REVIVAL IN SCOTLAND, REISSUE *by Ailie Munro.*
GOGOLIAN INTERLUDES: Gogol's Story "Christmas Eve" as the Subject of the Operas by Tchaikovsky and Rimsky-Korsakov *by Philip Taylor.*
THE MUSICAL INSTRUMENT COLLECTOR, REVISED EDITION *by J. Robert Willcutt & Kenneth R. Ball.*
A MUSICIAN'S GUIDE TO COPYRIGHT AND PUBLISHING, ENLARGED EDITION *by Willis Wager.*
MUSICOLOGY IN PRACTICE: Collected Essays by Denis Stevens *edited by Thomas P. Lewis.* Vol. 1: 1948-1970. Vol. 2: 1971-1988.
THE PRO/AM BOOK OF MUSIC AND MYTHOLOGY *compiled, edited & with commentaries by Thomas P. Lewis.*
THE PRO/AM GUIDE TO U.S. BOOKS ABOUT MUSIC: Annotated Guide to Current & Backlist Titles *edited by Thomas P. Lewis.* 2 vols.
SKETCHES FROM MY LIFE *by Natalia Sats.*

GUITAR

THE AMP BOOK: A Guitarist's Introductory Guide to Tube Amplifiers *by Donald Brosnac.*
ANIMAL MAGNETISM FOR MUSICIANS: Making a Bass Guitar and Pickup from Scratch *by Erno Zwaan.*
ANTONIO DE TORRES: Guitar Maker—His Life and Work *by José L. Romanillos. Fwd. by Julian Bream.*
THE ART OF FLAMENCO *by D. E. Pohren.*
THE ART OF PRACTICING *by Alice Artzt.*
CLASSIC GUITAR CONSTRUCTION *by Irving Sloane.*
THE FENDER GUITAR *by Ken Achard.*
THE FLAMENCO GUITAR, REISSUE *by David George.*
THE GIBSON GUITAR *by Ian C. Bishop.* 2 vols.
GUITAR HISTORY: Volume 1—Guitars Made by the Fender Company *by Donald Brosnac.*
GUITAR HISTORY: Volume 2—Gibson SGs *by John Bulli.*
GUITAR HISTORY: Volume 3—Gibson Catalogs of the Sixties *edited by Richard Hetrick.*

Other Music Titles Available from Pro/Am Music Resources, Inc. (continued)

GUITAR REPAIR: A Manual of Repair for Guitars and Fretted Instruments *by Irving Sloane.*
THE HISTORY AND DEVELOPMENT OF THE AMERICAN GUITAR *by Ken Achard.*
AN INTRODUCTION TO SCIENTIFIC GUITAR DESIGN *by Donald Brosnac.*
LEFT HANDED GUITAR *by Nicholas Clarke.*
LIVES AND LEGENDS OF FLAMENCO, 2ND EDITION *by D. E. Pohren.*
MANUAL OF GUITAR TECHNOLOGY: The History and Technology of Plucked String Instruments *by Franz Jahnel. English vers. by Dr. J.C. Harvey.*
THE NATURAL CLASSICAL GUITAR, REISSUE *by Lee F. Ryan.*
THE SEGOVIA TECHNIQUE, REISSUE *by Vladimir Bobri.*
THE SOUND OF ROCK: A History of Marshall Valve Guitar Amplifiers *by Mike Doyle.*
THE STEEL STRING GUITAR: Construction and Repair, UPDATED EDITION *by David Russell Young.*
STEEL STRING GUITAR CONSTRUCTION *by Irving Sloane.*
A WAY OF LIFE, REISSUE *by D. E. Pohren.*

PIANO / HARPSICHORD

THE ANATOMY OF A NEW YORK DEBUT RECITAL *by Carol Montparker.*
AT THE PIANO WITH FAURÉ, REISSUE *by Marguerite Long.*
EUROPEAN PIANO ATLAS *by H. K. Herzog.*
GLOSSARY OF HARPSICHORD TERMS *by Susanne Costa.*
KENTNER: A Symposium *edited by Harold Taylor. Fwd. by Yehudi Menuhin.*
LIPATTI *by Dragos Tanasescu & Grigore Bargauanu.*
THE PIANIST'S TALENT *by Harold Taylor. Fwd. by John Ogdon.*
THE PIANO AND HOW TO CARE FOR IT *by Otto Funke.*
THE PIANO HAMMER *by Walter Pfeifer.*
PIANO NOMENCLATURE, 2ND EDITION *by Nikolaus Schimmel & H. K. Herzog.*
RAVEL ACCORDING TO RAVEL *by Vlado Perlemuter & Hélène Jourdan-Morhange.*
SCHUBERT'S MUSIC FOR PIANO FOUR-HANDS *by Dallas Weekley & Nancy Arganbright.*
TECHNIQUE OF PIANO PLAYING, 5TH EDITION *by József Gát.*
THE TUNING OF MY HARPSICHORD *by Herbert Anton Kellner.*

See also:
ALKAN (2 volumes) *(Smith).*
LISZT AND HIS COUNTRY, 1869-1873 *(Legány).*
PERCY GRAINGER: The Man Behind the Music *(Dorum).*
PERCY GRAINGER: The Pictorial Biography *(Simon)..*

Other Music Titles Available from Pro/Am Music Resources, Inc. (continued)

RONALD STEVENSON: A Musical Biography *(MacDonald)*.
SORABJI: A Critical Celebration *(Rapoport)*.
A SOURCE GUIDE TO THE MUSIC OF PERCY GRAINGER *(Lewis)*.
TENSIONS IN THE PERFORMANCE OF MUSIC: A Symposium, REVISED & EXTENDED EDITION *(Grindea)*.

PERFORMANCE PRACTICE / "HOW-TO" INSTRUCTIONAL

GUIDE TO THE PRACTICAL STUDY OF HARMONY *by Peter Il'ich Tchaikovsky*.
HOW TO SELECT A BOW FOR VIOLIN FAMILY INSTRUMENTS *by Balthasar Planta*.
THE JOY OF ORNAMENTATION: Being Giovanni Luca Conforto's *Treatise on Ornamentation* (Rome, 1593) *with a Preface by Sir Yehudi Menuhin and an Introduction by Denis Stevens*.
THE MUSICIANS' THEORY BOOK: Reference to Fundamentals, Harmony, Counterpoint, Fugue and Form *by Asger Hamerik*.
THE STUDENT'S DICTIONARY OF MUSICAL TERMS.
TENSIONS IN THE PERFORMANCE OF MUSIC: A Symposium, REVISED & EXTENDED EDITION *edited by Carola Grindea. Fwd. by Yehudi Menuhin*.
THE VIOLIN: Precepts and Observations *by Sourene Arakelian*.